The Shakespeare Companion

The
Shakespeare
Companion

Gareth and Barbara Lloyd Evans

Charles Scribner's Sons
New York

1 3 5 7 9 11 13 15 17 19   I/C   20 18 16 14 12 10 8 6 4 2

Printed in Great Britain
Library of Congress Catalog Card Number 78-54611
ISBN 0-684-15870-1

CONTENTS

III *The Works*

IV *Stratford upon Avon and Shakespeare*

LIST OF ILLUSTRATIONS

For

Jacquetta and Jack Priestley

With love

'We have heard the chimes at midnight.'

TO THE READER

The impact of Shakespeare is universal — on young and old, native and foreigner, specialist and layman, professional and amateur, in the past, the present and, who can doubt it, the future. He is read at some time by the whining schoolboy, the exam-plagued student, the people of the theatre, the man in his study and the man by his fire. His words and phrases have rooted themselves inextricably in the language, his themes and attitudes become a sounding-board for the political man, the thoughtful man and the man of action — even the after-dinner speaker — of succeeding centuries.

To us, the authors, he has become also a presence. Living in Stratford upon Avon we are daily made aware of his connections with the town, and nightly half expect to meet his ghost stalking round some dark corner of the Guild Chapel or the Grammar School. In this book we have tried to catch up the threads of his universal appeal and his spirit and to provide material that a multiplicity of readers of Shakespeare will find both useful and engaging. So much of his life and career has the quality of a 'who-dunnit' mystery about it — so much explained and yet so much tantalizingly unknown, and we have sought to present a reflection of the kind of intrepid curiosity not unknown to Sherlock Holmes and Dr Watson.

The book consists of four main sections: The Man and His Times; Shakespeare in Performance; The Works; Stratford upon Avon and Shakespeare. In the first section, **The Man and His Times,** we seek to give a sense of the man himself, what he may have looked like, who his friends and contemporaries were both in Stratford and London, the plays that attempted to rival his, the men of fame who shared his horizons, and the myths, legends and mysteries that have grown, moss-like, around him as subsequent generations have grown more and more aware of his worth. To see him plain, as clearly as our knowledge allows, is the motivation of this section, and for this purpose the Calendar of Events is crucial to the reader who wishes to do the same. The Calendar is the key to all the items that appear in this section. Names, references, events, that are listed in the Calendar are amplified or explained in what follows. For example, the bare announcement in the Calendar of the name, date of birth and death, of Ben Jonson — the bare bones, so to speak — is given flesh and, we hope, something of spirit in the comment on Jonson which can be found under

'Playwrights of Shakespeare's Time'. Again, any reader, curious to learn more about what seem to have been Shakespeare's tax problems, announced under certain dates in the Calendar, may look up 'Tax' under 'Terms of Reference' and may perhaps gain comfort from discovering that even the world's greatest dramatist occasionally fell foul of the revenue men. The whole of this first section, then, is a new form of biography which does not rely on discursive possibilities and assumptions (however reasonable) into which the facts are sown, but provides all the known facts about the man, places him firmly in his historical and geographical environment, and discusses the implications of these facts.

It is frequently stated, but not always remembered, that a play remains a kind of skeleton until performance gives it a living shape and robust form. In the second section, **Shakespeare in Performance,** the production of Shakespeare's plays over the centuries from his time to our own is commented upon as a continuing narrative which attempts to show something of the astonishing variety of the way Shakespeare's plays have been presented. All aspects are discussed — theatres, acting, interpretation, staging, sets, costumes, audiences. The narrative contains a great deal of contemporary comment so that we see famous players, like Garrick, through the eyes of those who actually saw him perform. The intention, therefore, is to sandwich the informative with the intriguing, the soberly factual with the entertaining; and, for ease of reference, the discussion is divided up into time-areas. Attention is paid to Shakespeare in North America, with particular treatment of Shakespeare and the history of production in the United States and Canada.

Further details of the actors and actresses who have made Shakespeare their particular forte, the parts they played, and any idiosyncrasies they may have shown are given in 'Principal Shakespearean Actors and Actresses', where they are listed alphabetically and their individual contributions to the presentation of Shakespeare are commented on.

The twentieth century created for itself a new art-form — the film. Film-makers were not slow to see the advantages to be gained from the filming of Shakespeare's plays. A brief account is given of some of the outstanding films made in England, the USA, the Soviet Union and elsewhere. To the account is appended (alphabetically, by the name of the play) a list of the films made and their producers.

Finally in this section we consider Shakespeare and music. From the time of their first production many of the plays called for music, particularly, of course, those with songs in them. Shakespeare makes frequent references to music throughout his work — so many that one is bound to reflect that this implies his deep personal commitment to it. Since his time many composers have been stimulated by a character, a mood or a play and sought to express their reaction in music — be it opera based on one of the plays, incidental music, or a symphonic poem based on a play or a character. We describe the varying uses and effects of music in the plays themselves, with reference to contemporary or near-contemporary musicians whose settings for the songs are still popular and widely known even after the lapse of three or four centuries. We include a selection of musical pieces, listed by century, that have been occasioned by Shakespeare's writings and which can often reveal new aspects, new approaches to a play or character, or perhaps provide suggestions for music or a production set in a period other than Shakespeare's own.

The third section, **The Works,** may perhaps be described as the nitty-gritty of this book and is intended to be both informative and, to a lesser extent, critical. First, brief plot summaries are provided, on an act-by-act, scene-by-scene basis, so that what the audience sees on the stage should (unless the director has cut or transposed areas of the text) follow the lines of the plot-summary. In fact, the very way in which the summaries leap from point A to point B and then back to point A again demonstrates Shakespeare's art as a weaver of stories, how his plots interlock, catch up on themselves and never leave the viewer at a loss. There follows a list of Dramatis Personae. From this one can trace the character to the play source, and then, through the plot summary, find greater detail about the character's place in the play itself.

In this section, under 'Shakespeare's Infinite Variety', we have tried briefly to vivify the plain statements of plot and character and to bring to the forefront the reality of the plays themselves by examples of Shakespeare's rich variety as a writer, both as dramatist and poet. The choice of extracts is, of course, personal. One could make many such selections, all quite different. This is only one possibility and as representative as space allowed.

Since such a large proportion of Shakespeare's history plays concerns a sequence of Kings of England, whether by right of birth or by act of usurpation, and deals with those citizens, both high and low, whose lives are affected by royal decisions, we have provided a simplified genealogical tree. The kings themselves are clearly designated by bold type, so that at a reasonable glance the reader can become aware of a pattern of relationships which will visually implement the aural realities of the text.

The section includes a brief critical discussion of the poems, information about their publication and, as far as the sonnets are concerned, brief speculation on their contents. Where biographical mysteries in the sonnets are concerned, our intention has been to reflect the different theories that have been suggested by others over the years but not to offer any personal conclusions. Our emphasis has been on assessing the achievement of the poems as poetry. The sonnets are listed alphabetically by the first word of the first line and the reference number given is that of the 1609 Thomas Thorpe arrangement which is the order followed by most publishers of the sequence.

'The Book of the Play' is concerned with the text itself — how it came about, the different sources for it, and the printing and publishing activities which were involved in both the individual plays and the great collected First Folio edition of 1623. This is done in the form of concise terms of reference, alphabetically by subject.

Following this we have a feature which is rare if not unique in a compilation of this kind. It is that most necessary material and basis for all understanding of Shakespeare's plays — a Glossary of the words and phrases whose meaning is not obvious to a non-specialist reader. The words are set out alphabetically in the form in which they are found in Shakespeare's writing and are not rationalized into new forms. This means that the words that the reader or speaker meets on the page will appear in the same form in the Glossary, and any variations in meaning in the use of that word are listed. Often the meanings of whole passages that seem obscure can be clarified if the modern counterpart of only one or two focal words is known. We believe that this Glossary will not only allow the reader to cope with single words, but will help unravel phrases that might otherwise prove stumbling blocks to the overall enjoyment of play or poem.

The last section, **Stratford upon Avon and Shakespeare,** is for the visitor or would-be visitor to Stratford. It gives an account of the buildings that may be seen and explored, a map to show the way to them, and one to illustrate how the town looked in the eighteenth century when what is sometimes referred to as the 'Shakespeare Industry' began. All the properties which are under the supervision of the Shakespeare Birthplace Trust that are either directly or indirectly associated with him are listed and described. All of them except, possibly, his mother's home (Mary Arden's House), which is some three miles out of Stratford, are within easy walking distance. This section is intended to reflect something of our personal joy at living where people, once, *did* see Shakespeare plain, and to add to the historical and aesthetic dimensions with which this Companion is largely concerned, that other, essential, geographical dimension. Our hope is that with this book to hand the reader's quest for Shakespeare's times, his imagination and the places where he walked and dwelt will be made easier and not without pleasure.

Stratford upon Avon, 1978   Barbara Lloyd Evans
                                                             Gareth Lloyd Evans

I The Man and His Times

There's no art
To find the mind's construction in the face.
(*Macbeth*)

CALENDAR OF EVENTS

Shakespeare's Family and Relatives

FATHER	**John Shakespeare**
MOTHER	**Mary Arden**
WIFE	**Anne Hathaway**
SISTERS	**Joan (1)** died in infancy
	Margaret
	Joan (2) married William Hart
	Anne
BROTHERS	**Gilbert**
	Richard
	Edmund
SON	**Hamnet** (twin)
DAUGHTERS	**Susanna** married Dr John Hall
	Judith (twin of Hamnet)
NEPHEWS AND NIECES	**William Hart**
	Thomas Hart
	Michael Hart
	Mary Hart
GRANDCHILDREN	**Shakespeare Quiney**
	Richard Quiney
	Thomas Quiney
	Elizabeth Nash née Hall, became Lady Bernard on second marriage
GRAND-NEPHEWS	**Thomas Hart**
	George Hart

The Hart family line survives both in England and in Australia. The direct Shakespeare line died out with the death of Elizabeth, Lady Bernard, in 1670.

SHAKESPEARE'S LIFE, WORK AND FAMILY	OTHER EVENTS IN SHAKE-SPEARE'S AGE
1556 Oct. 2 John Shakespeare buys house in Greenhill and Henley streets.	
Nov. 24 Mary Arden is left 60 acres of land in Wilmcote, and 10 marks.	
1557 J. Shakespeare and M. Arden married at Aston Cantlow(?)	Thomas Lodge b. (d. 1625). George Peele b. (d. 1596).
1558 Sept. 15 Joan Shakespeare (1) christened.	Queen Elizabeth succeeds to throne. Robert Greene b. (d. 1592). Thomas Kyd b. (d. 1594).
1560	George Chapman b. (d. 1634). Henry Chettle b. (d. 1594).
1561	Francis Bacon b. (d. 1626). Mary Herbert b. (d. 1621).
1562 Dec. 2 Margaret Shakespeare christened.	Arthur Brooke's *Romeus and Juliet* published.
1563 Apr. 30 Margaret Shakespeare buried.	Cecil, Earl of Salisbury b. (d. 1612). Samuel Daniel b. (d. 1619). Michael Drayton b. (d. 1631).
1564 Apr. 26 **Entry of baptism of Wm Shakespeare in Holy Trinity Church, Stratford.**	Christopher Marlowe b. (d. 1593). Michelangelo d. (b. 1475). Galileo b. (d. 1642). John Hawkins begins 2nd voyage to New World.
1565	Francis Meres b. (d. 1647). Mary, Queen of Scots marries Darnley. Hawkins introduces sweet potatoes and tobacco to England.
1566 July 4 John Shakespeare elected Alderman.	Robert Devereux, Earl of Essex b. (d. 1601). James, future King of England and Scotland, b. (d. 1625).
1567 Oct. 13 Gilbert Shakespeare christened.	Thomas Campion b. (d. 1620). Thomas Nashe b. (d. 1601). Darnley murdered (by Bothwell?). Mary, Queen of Scots marries Bothwell and is forced to abdicate. Richard Burbage b. (d. 1619). Hawkins and Francis Drake voyage to West Indies.
1568 Sept. 4 John Shakespeare becomes High Bailiff (i.e. Mayor).	Mary, Queen of Scots takes refuge in England. Bishops' Bible published.
1569 Apr. 15 Joan Shakespeare (2) christened.	Cosimo di Medici made Grand Duke of Tuscany.

1570			Mercator's map of world made. Thomas Middleton b. (d. 1627). Thomas Dekker b. (d. 1632). Thomas Heywood b. (d. 1641). Nicholas Hilliard's portrait of Queen Elizabeth. Guy Fawkes b. (executed 1605).
1571	Sept. 5	John Shakespeare made Chief Alderman. Warrant for his arrest issued for non-payment of debt of £30.	Benvenuto Cellini d. (b. 1500). Johann Kepler b. (d. 1630).
1572	Sept. 28	Anne Shakespeare christened.	Ben Jonson b. (d. 1637). Thomas Dekker b. (?) (d. 1632). John Donne b. (d. 1631). Massacre of St Bartholomew's Day. Drake attacks Spanish harbours in America.
1573			Caravaggio b. (d. 1610). Inigo Jones b. (d. 1652). Drake sees Pacific Ocean for the first time.
1574	Mar. 11	Richard Shakespeare christened.	Burbage gets license to open London theatre.
1575		John Shakespeare buys 2 houses in Henley Street for £40.	Queen Elizabeth on progress visits Kenilworth. John Marston b. (d. 1634).
1576		John Shakespeare applies for coat-of-arms.	The Theatre opens in London. Titian d. (b. 1477). Martin Frobisher discovers Frobisher Bay, Canada.
1577		John Shakespeare ceases to attend Council meetings.	Robert Burton b. (d. 1640). The Curtain Theatre opens in London. Holinshed's *Chronicle* published. Rubens b. (d. 1640). Drake starts circumnavigation of world.
1578	Nov. 14	John Shakespeare mortgages wife's property to raise loan of £40 from Edmund Lambert. Excused from payment of levy in Stratford for poor relief.	James VI (later James I of England) becomes King of Scotland. Lyly's *Euphues* published. Mary Fitton b. (d. 1647).
1579	Apr. 4	Anne Shakespeare buried.	John Fletcher b. (d. 1625). Stephen Gosson's *Schoole of Abuse* published. Drake 'annexes' New Albion, California, for England. Edmund Spenser's *The Shephearde's Calendar* published.
1580		John Shakespeare fined £40	Richard Farrant d. (b. 1530).

		for failure to attend Queen's Bench Court to provide security against breach of the peace.	Thomas Middleton b. (d. 1627). John Webster b. (d. 1625). Frans Hals b. (d. 1666). Palladio d. (b. 1508).
	May 3	Edmund Shakespeare christened.	Drake returns from circumnavigation of world. Earthquake in London recorded.
1581			Elizabeth knights Francis Drake.
1582	Nov. 27	Special license issued by Bishop of Worcester for marriage of Shakespeare and Anne Whateley of Temple Grafton, near Stratford.	First English colony in Newfoundland. Hakluyt's *Divers Voyages Touching the Discovery of America* published.
	Nov. 28	Fulke Sandells and John Richardson of Stratford provide bond of £40 to indemnify Bishop of Worcester's permission for marriage of Shakespeare and Anne Hathaway.	
1583	May 26	Susanna Shakespeare christened.	Queen's Company of Players founded. Orlando Gibbons b. (d. 1625).
1584			Ivan the Terrible d. (b. 1530). Francis Beaumont b. (d. 1616). Walter Raleigh annexes Virginia.
1585	Feb. 2	Hamnet and Judith Shakespeare (twins) christened.	Thomas Tallis d. (b. 1505).
1586			John Ford b. (d. *c.* 1639). Sir Philip Sidney d. (b. 1554).
1587		John Lambert inherits from his father the mortgaged property (see entry for 1578) forfeited by John Shakespeare for failure to repay £40 loan.	Mary, Queen of Scots executed. Rose Theatre built in London. Nathan Field b. (d. ?). Thomas Nashe b. (d. *c.* 1601). Companies of Earls of Essex and Leicester act at Stratford. Marlowe's *Tamburlaine* written.
1588			Defeat of Spanish Armada. Earl of Leicester d. (b. 1532). Robert Armin b. (d. 1610). Richard Tarlton d. (b. ?). Marlowe's *Dr Faustus* performed for first time. Montaigne's *Essays* (Vol. 3) published. Veronese d. (b. 1528).
1590			Thomas Lodge's *Rosalynde: Euphues Golden Legacy* published. Marlowe's *The Jew of Malta* first performed.

1591

1592 Mar. 3   *Harey the Vj* (probably first part of Shakespeare's *Henry VI*) performed and recorded in Henslowe's Diary.

Sept. 25   John Shakespeare named as recusant — one who, against the law, did not go at least once a month to church.

1593 Apr. 18   First publication of Shakespeare's *Venus and Adonis* recorded in Stationer's Register.

1594 Jan. 24   Possible first performance of *Titus Andronicus* recorded in Henslowe's Diary.

Feb. 6   First publication of *Titus Andronicus* recorded in Stationer's Register.

May 2   Performance of *The Taming of a Shrew* recorded by Henslowe.

May 9   *The Ravyshement of Lucrece* recorded in Stationer's Register — better known as Shakespeare's *The Rape of Lucrece.*

June 5   *Titus Andronicus* performed at Newington Butts.

June 12   *Titus Andronicus* performed at Newington Butts.

Dec. 28   Shakespeare's *The Comedy of Errors* performed at Gray's Inn.

Spenser's *The Faerie Queene* (Bks 1–3) published. Robert Herrick b. (d. 1674). Sidney's *Astrophel and Stella* published. Christopher Wren b. (d. 1658)

Robert Greene d. (b. 1558). Henslowe begins his Diary. Kyd's *The Spanish Tragedy* published. 15,000 die of plague in London. *Groatsworth of Wit*, pamphlet by Robert Greene, entered in Stationer's Register. Contains slurring reference to Shakespeare as an upstart young dramatist. *Kind-Harts Dreame*, pamphlet by Henry Chettle, contains reply and apology for Greene's references to Shakespeare.

May 30, Christopher Marlowe d. (b. 1564). The play of *Sir Thomas More* written (?) with contributions from Munday, Chettle, Heywood, Dekker, Shakespeare. George Herbert b. (d. 1633). Isaac Walton b. (d. 1683). Poussin b. (d. 1665).

Thomas Kyd d. (b. 1557). Greene's *Friar Bacon and Friar Bungay* published. Marlowe's *Edward II* published. Tintoretto d. (b. 1518).

Titus Andronicus anonymously published. Second publication of *Venus and Adonis*.

1595 Mar. 15 Shakespeare mentioned among players paid £20 in all for plays presented previous December before Queen Elizabeth.

Sidney's *Defence of Poesie* published. Spenser's *Amoretti* published. Walter Raleigh explores Orinoco.

1596 Aug. 11 Hamnet buried at Stratford.
Oct. 20 Application for grant of arms by John Shakespeare (in 1576) successful.
Nov. 29 Writ of Attachment issued to Sheriff of Surrey to enforce Shakespeare and three others to keep the peace.

Swan Theatre built on Bankside. Spenser's *Faerie Queene* (Bks 4–6) published. Opening of Blackfriars Theatre. Descartes b. (d. 1650). Sir Francis Drake d. (b. 1546). Galileo invents thermometer.

1597 Apr. 22 Garter ceremonies at Windsor include probable first performance of *The Merry Wives of Windsor*.
May 4 Shakespeare buys New Place, two cottages and two barns in Stratford.
Aug. 29 *Richard II* entered in Stationer's Register.
Oct. 20 *Richard III* entered in Stationer's Register.
Nov. 15 Tax Collector of St Helen's, Bishopsgate, reports non-payment of 5 shillings tax by Shakespeare.
Romeo and Juliet entered in Stationer's Register. *Richard II* published. *Richard III* published.

Bacon's *Essays* (version 1) published. Second Spanish Armada scattered by storm. James VI's *Daemonologie* published. Dowland's *Songes* published.

1598 Jan. 24 Abraham Sturley writes to Richard Quiney about contacting Shakespeare concerning land in Shottery and helping to get Stratford's taxes reduced.
Feb. 4 Town record of Chapel Street, Stratford, shows Shakespeare as holding 10 quarters (80 bushels) of 'corne and malte'.
Feb. 25 *Henry IV* (*1*) entered in Stationer's Register and printed later in year.
July 22 *The Merchant of Venice* entered in Stationer's Register.
Oct. 1 Shakespeare listed as defaulter for non-payment of taxes in St Helen's Parish, London.

Rebellion in Ireland. Marlowe's *Hero and Leander* published. Thomas Carew b. (d. 1639). George Peele d. (b. 1558). Thomas Bodley begins rebuilding of Oxford Library. Bernini b. (d. 1680). Shakespeare referred to in *Palladis Tamia* by Francis Meres. The 'Theatre' demolished.

Oct. 25   Richard Quiney, again in
          London, writes to Shake-
          speare as 'my Loveing good
          ffrend and contreymann'
          asking for loan to pay debts.
          Letter apparently undelivered.

?Oct. 30 Adrian Quiney writes to son,
          Richard, at the Bell, Carter
          Lane, London, urging him to
          bring home any money he
          borrows from Shakespeare.

Nov. 4   Abraham Sturley writes to
          Richard Quiney implying that
          he expects Shakespeare to
          provide a loan.

Dec.   *Love's Labour's Lost* published.
          Richard III (Q2) published.
          Richard II (Q2 and Q3)
          published. *The Rape of
          Lucrece* (Q2) published.

1599 Feb. 21   Shakespeare named with   Edmund Spenser d.
               others as lessee/shareholder in   (b. 1552). Chamberlain's Men
               land for Globe Theatre.   occupy Globe Theatre. Thomas

Oct. 6   Shakespeare recorded as   Platter of Basle sees *Julius
          owing taxes in St Helen's   Caesar* at Globe. Arrest of
          Parish, Bishopsgate.   Earl of Essex. Oliver Crom-
          Romeo and Juliet (Q2) pub-   well b. (d. 1658). *Venus
          lished. *Henry IV (1)* (Q2) pub-   and Adonis* praised by John
          lished. *Venus and Adonis* (Q3)   Weever in his poem *Ad
          published. *The Passionate   Gulielmum Shakespeare.*
          Pilgrim* published by William
          Jaggard.

1600 Aug. 4   *Henry V, As You Like It, Much*   Fortune Theatre built by
               Ado About Nothing entered in   Alleyn. Charles — future king
               Stationer's Register.   of England — b. (executed

Aug. 23   *Much Ado About Nothing,*   1649). Dekker's *The Shoe-
          Henry IV (2) entered in   maker's Holiday* published.
          Stationer's Register, as 'by'   Thomas Morley's *Ayres* (Bk 1)
          Shakespeare — first mention   published. Population of
          of his name in Register.   England and Ireland
                                             estimated at 5½ million.
Aug. 28   Christening of William,
          Shakespeare's nephew by his
          sister, Joan Hart.

Oct. 6   Shakespeare recorded as
          owing 13s. 4d. in tax in
          Sussex (which included
          Surrey for tax purposes).

Oct. 8   *A Midsummer Night's Dream*
          entered in Stationer's
          Register.

Oct. 28   *Much Ado About Nothing* (Q1)
          published.
          A Midsummer Night's Dream

(Q1) published. *Henry V*
(Q1) published. *Henry IV (2)*
(Q1) published. *The Merchant
of Venice* (Q1) published.
Titus Andronicus (Q2) pub-
lished. *The Rape of Lucrece*
(Q2, Q3) published.

1601 Mar. 25 Thomas Whittington, a shepherd for Joan Hathaway,
bequeaths 40 shillings to the
poor of Stratford, owed to
him by Shakespeare's wife.

Sept. 8 John Shakespeare buried,
Holy Trinity, Stratford.

Earl of Essex leads revolt
against Queen Elizabeth.
Essex and the Earl of
Southampton tried — Essex
executed, Southampton
reprieved. Thomas Nashe d.
(b. 1567). References to
Shakespeare in anonymous
play, *The Returne from Parnassus* (Pt 1).

1602 Jan. 18 *The Merry Wives of Windsor*
entered in Stationer's
Register.

May 1 Shakespeare buys 107 acres of
farm-land in Old Stratford
from William and John
Combe for £320.

July 26 *Hamlet* entered in Stationer's
Register.

Sept. 28 Shakespeare acquires from
Walter Getley ¼ acre of land
and cottage in Chapel Lane.
The Merry Wives of Windsor
(Q1) published. *Henry V* (Q2)
published. *Richard III* (Q3)
published.

Ben Jonson *The Poetaster*
published. Thomas Dekker's
Satiromastix published. Bodleian Library, Oxford, opened.
Part 2 of anonymous play,
The Returne from Parnassus,
contains references to Shakespeare and Richard Burbage.

1603 Jan. 1 *A Midsummer Night's Dream*
performed at Hampton Court.

Feb. 7 *Troilus and Cressida* entered in
Stationer's Register.

May 19 Shakespeare's name included
in patent granted to Lord
Chamberlain's Men renaming
them the 'King's Men'.

May *Hamlet* (Q1) published.

June 5 Mary Hart christened at
Stratford.

Walter Raleigh imprisoned.
Queen Elizabeth d. James I
arrives in London. Henslowe
ends his Diary. Monteverdi's
Madrigals, Bk 4, published.
William Gilbert (scientist) d.
(b. 1540). Shakespeare
exhorted to write honouring
the memory of Queen
Elizabeth by Henry Chettle
in his poem *Englandes Mourning
Garment.*

1604 Mar. 15 Shakespeare mentioned in
accounts by Master of the
Great Wardrobe as receiving
4½ yards of cloth for
appearing at James I's coronation with the King's
Men.

Apr. Privy Council warrant for a

Earl of Oxford d. (b. 1550).
25 volumes of Lope da Vega's
plays published. James I's
Counterblast to Tobacco
published.

		play names Shakespeare as one of King's Men.	
	July	Phillip Rogers sued for 3s. 1od. for malt supplied by Shakespeare.	
	Nov. 1	*Othello* performed at Whitehall.	
	Nov. 4	*The Merry Wives of Windsor* performed at Court.	
	Dec. 26	*Measure for Measure* performed at Court. *Hamlet* (Q2) published. *Henry IV* (*1*) (Q3) published.	
1605	Jan.	*Love's Labour's Lost* performed at Court.	The Gunpowder Plot. Bacon's *The Advancement of Learning* published. Guy Fawkes arrested. Cervantes' *Don Quixote* (Pt 1) published. Monteverdi's *Madrigals* (Bk 5) published. Shakespeare's name appears on title-page of *The London Prodigal.*
	Jan. 7	*Henry V* performed at Court.	
	Feb. 10	*The Merchant of Venice* performed at Court.	
	Feb. 12	*The Merchant of Venice* performed at Court.	
	May 4	Shakespeare left 30 shillings in gold by fellow-actor, Augustine Phillips.	
	July 24	Thomas Hart christened at Stratford. Shakespeare pays £440 for ¼ of Bishopton tithes lease. *Richard III* (Q4) published.	
1606	May 5	Susanna Shakespeare named as recusant for failing to receive Easter Sunday communion. *King Lear* performed at Whitehall by King's Men.	John Lyly d. (b. 1554). Guy Fawkes sentenced to death. Corneille b. (d. 1684). William Davenant b. (d. 1688). Rembrandt b. (d. 1669).
1607	June 5	Susanna Shakespeare marries Dr John Hall at Holy Trinity, Stratford.	Colonization of Virginia. The Great Frost. Thomas Deloney d. (b. 1543). Cyril Tourneur's *The Revenger's Tragedy* published. Founding of Jamestown, Virginia.
	Aug. 12	An Edward Shakespeare, son of Edmund Shakespeare, player, recorded as buried at St Giles, Cripplegate, London.	
	Sept. 5	*Hamlet* performed aboard 'Dragon' — English ship in Sierra Leone.	
	Nov. 26	*King Lear* entered in Stationer's Register.	
	Dec. 17	Burial of Mary Hart at Stratford.	
	Dec. 31	Edmund Shakespeare, player, recorded as buried at St Saviour's, Southwark, London.	

1608	Feb. 21	Elizabeth Hall christened at Stratford.	John Milton b. (d. 1674). Galileo constructs astro-
	May 20	*Antony and Cleopatra* entered in Stationer's Register.	nomical telescope.
	Aug. 9	Shakespeare and 6 colleagues lease Blackfriars Theatre for 21 years.	
	Sept. 9	Shakespeare's mother buried at Stratford.	
	Sept. 23	Michael Hart christened.	
	Oct. 16	Shakespeare becomes god-father to William Walker of Stratford.	
	Dec. 17	John Addenbrooke arrested for non-payment of debt to Shakespeare.	
1609	May 20	Shakespeare's sonnets entered in Stationer's Register. *Pericles* (Q1, Q2) pub-lished. *Troilus and Cressida* published.	Henry Hudson explores Delaware and Hudson rivers.
1610		Shakespeare completes con-veyance of land amounting to 127 acres begun in 1602.	Ben Jonson's *The Alchemist* published. Caravaggio d. (b. 1579). Thomas Herriott discovers sunspots. Galileo observes Jupiter's satellites. Hudson discovers Hudson's Bay.
1611	Apr.	Simon Forman sees *Cymbeline* and records it in his *Booke of Plaies*.	Chapman's translation of *The Iliad* completed. Authorized version of Bible published. Henry Hudson dies.
	May 15	Forman records performance of *The Winter's Tale* at the Globe Theatre. *Pericles* (Q3) published. *Hamlet* (Q3) published. *Titus Andronicus* (Q3) pub-lished.	
1612	Jan. 28	Gilbert Shakespeare buried at Stratford.	Fulke Greville's *Life of the Renowned Sir Philip Sidney* published. John Webster's *The White Devil* published. Tobacco planted in Virginia.
	May 11	Shakespeare and John Wilkins witnesses in Belott-Mountjoy suit. His place of residence given as Stratford in his deposition.	
	Nov. 1	*The Tempest* performed by King's Men.	
	Nov. 5	*The Winter's Tale* performed by King's Men. *Richard III* (Q5) published.	
1613	Jan. 28	John Combe bequeaths Shakespeare £5.	Webster's *The Duchess of Malfi* first performed. Francis
	Feb. 14	Richard Shakespeare buried.	Bacon is Attorney-General.

Mar. 10 Shakespeare buys Blackfriars Gate-house in London.

Mar. 31 Shakespeare and Richard Burbage each receive 44 shillings for an impresa for Earl of Rutland's shield.

May 20 Payments to King's Men for performance of *Much Ado About Nothing, The Tempest, The Winter's Tale, Henry IV (1 and 2), Othello* and *Julius Caesar.*

July 15 Susanna Hall sues John Lane, for defamation of her character, in Consistory court.

1614 Sept. 5 Thomas Greene prepares document showing that Shakespeare owns approximately 127 acres in Stratford.

Nov. 17 Thomas Greene records that Shakespeare and Dr John Hall (Shakespeare's son-in-law) are in London on business concerning Stratford tithes.

1615 Apr. 26 Shakespeare involved in law suit with Mathew Bacon concerning Blackfriars property.

Sept. Thomas Greene refers to Shakespeare and possible land enclosures.

1616 ?Jan. 25 Shakespeare's will drawn up.

Feb. 10 Judith Shakespeare marries Thomas Quiney.

Mar. 12 Thomas and Judith Quiney excommunicated.

Mar. 25 Shakespeare revises will.

Apr. 17 William Hart buried.

Apr. 25 **William Shakespeare's burial recorded in Register of Holy Trinity, Stratford.**

1617 Feb. 9 Richard Quiney christened.

May 8 Shakespeare Quiney buried.

Dec. Ben Jonson in conversations with William Drummond makes references to Shakespeare.

Dr Hall and Susanna occupy New Place. *Venus and Adonis* (Q9) published.

1619 May 20 *Pericles* performed.

Dec. *The Winter's Tale, Hamlet,* and

Richard Crashaw b. (d. 1650). Globe Theatre burns down, during performance of *Henry VIII.* Champlain explores part of Ottawa River. Thomas Bodley d. (b. 1545).

Thomas Overbury's *Characters* published. Webster's *The Duchess of Malfi* published. Raleigh's *History of the World* published. Jonson's *Bartholomew Fair* published. El Greco d. (b. 1541). Block explores Long Island Sound. Pocahontas marries John Rolfe.

Cervantes' *Don Quixote* (Pt 2) published. Chapman completes translation of the *Odyssey.* Galileo faces Inquisition.

Raleigh goes in search of El Dorado. Collected Folio edition of Jonson's works published. William Baffin discovers Baffin Bay.

Ben Jonson is Poet Laureate. Murillo b. (d. 1682). Raleigh reaches Orinoco River mouth. Walter Raleigh d. (b. 1552). Pocahontas d. (b. 1595).

First negro slaves arrive in Virginia.

		Henry IV (2) performed at Court.	
1620	Jan. 23	Thomas Quiney (Jnr) christened.	Pilgrim Fathers land at New Plymouth, Massachusetts. Bacon's *Novum Organum* published.
1621	Oct. 6	*Othello* entered in Stationer's Register.	Burton's *Anatomy of Melancholy* published.
1622	Apr. 22	Elizabeth Hall marries Thomas Nashe. *Othello* published. *Henry IV* (1) (Q6) published. *Richard III* (Q6) published.	
1623	Feb. 2	*Twelfth Night* performed at Court.	William Byrd d. (b. 1543). First English settlement in New Hampshire.
	Aug. 8	Burial of Shakespeare's wife, Anne, at Stratford.	
	Nov. 8	Publication of First Folio.	

SHAKESPEARE THE MAN

Shakespeare's Appearance

The two authentic portraits of Shakespeare are the Martin Droeshout engraving, printed as frontispiece to the First Folio edition of the plays (1623), and the bust in Holy Trinity Church, Stratford upon Avon (*see* Stratford upon Avon and Shakespeare). Although these were commissioned and completed some years after Shakespeare's death, there were sufficient people who had known him during his lifetime still alive (his wife, his two daughters, Susanna and Judith, his sons-in-law, Dr John Hall, Thomas Quiney, many of his Stratford acquaintances, and his fellow players in London) to disown a poor likeness.

1. The Bust. In the commendatory verses printed in the First Folio, Leonard Digges writes that Shakespeare's plays will keep his name alive, for

> . . . when that stone is rent
> And Time dissolves thy Stratford Moniment,
> Here [i.e. in this volume of plays] we alive shall view thee still.

From this reference to the bust, it seems it must have been in place by 1623, when the First Folio was printed, and that Anne, Shakespeare's widow, although she died in the August of 1623, would in all probability have seen and accepted it as satisfactory. Indeed, although legend has it that it was Dr John Hall who commissioned the bust, Anne may well have had some part in the setting up of a memorial. It has been suggested that the bust was made from a death mask of Shakespeare himself, the face, as we have it, reflecting a certain puffy smoothness as a result.

There have been various drawings and engravings of the bust over the years. One of the most puzzling, and the earliest we have, is that of Sir William Dugdale in his account of Warwickshire, 1656. It differs radically from the present monument, and has given rise to speculation — either, that Dugdale or his amanuensis nodded, providing a totally inaccurate illustration, or that, in 1748, when repair work was carried out, alterations were made to both the bust and its surround. It may be said, although of course no final conclusive decision can be made at present, that many of Dugdale's illustrations are inaccurate as far as a general drawing of a monument is concerned, and that John Hall, who carried out the restoration work, was given very strict orders to restore it to as near the original as possible. He made a painting of it (now with the Birthplace Trust) before he started work, which in shape tallies with the present memorial. One cannot, however, say how genuine the colours are. In 1790 the first finger and part of the thumb had to be replaced, and a quill was inserted to represent the pen, and then, in 1793, Malone had the bust brought 'back to its original state by painting it in good stone colours'. Colours were restored to the figure in 1861, and these — auburn hair and beard, scarlet doublet, black gown, a band of white, green and crimson cushion, with black tassels and cords — are the colours, somewhat faded, of today.

2. The Droeshout Engraving. As for the Droeshout engraving, Ben Jonson, Shakespeare's contemporary, friend and rival playwright, bears witness (and one need not decry these lines as unreliable merely because they perform a conventional function) to it as a true likeness in his commendatory lines prefacing the First Folio. He writes that he wishes the engraver could

> . . . have drawn his wit
> As well in brasse, as he hath hit
> His face . . .

There are in fact several versions of the Droeshout portrait, from the various stages of printing. Of the first 'proof' version, four impressions are extant — one in the British Museum, one in the Bodleian Library, Oxford and two in the Folger Library, Washington, USA. This is a lighter, less intense version that was obviously darkened in and accentuated, and was the one used for the First Folio. The third version, used in the Second and Third Folios (1632, 1633–4), has small retouchings only. The fourth version, for the Fourth Folio (1685), has heavy reworking, necessary for an engraving whose lines have become somewhat blurred through use, before being used again.

These two depictions, then, and perhaps the one slight delineation we have of him in words — Aubrey, a none-too-reliable gossip, says that he 'was a handsome well-shap't man' — must set the seal as far as metal, stone or words allow on Shakespeare's appearance. Though even here error can creep in — in the Folio engraving, for example, the shoulders are out of proportion with the head, making the whole somewhat top-heavy.

3. Portraits. However, other portraits do exist, all claiming to be of Shakespeare, all having their supporters, with their pedigrees in varying degrees vouched-for. Some resemble the bust, some the Droeshout, some neither. None, at present, can be traced back decisively to Shakespeare himself, though many are 17th-century paintings. Two of the most interesting are the 'Flower' and the 'Chandos' portraits. For a long time the Flower was thought to be the original from which the Droeshout was engraved. It is inscribed 'William Shakespeare. 1609' but this inscription is suspect, as it is written in a cursive hand, unknown at that time. As it resembles more closely the final version of the engraving, the one that was actually used in the printing of the First Folio, rather than the 'proof' version, it has been concluded that the painting was done from the engraving rather than the other way round, so that what we have is not a picture from life, but a portrait based on an engraving. The painting, donated to the Royal Shakespeare Theatre Museum by Mrs Flower, is in the picture gallery there. A famous copy of it by William Blake is in the Manchester Corporation Art Gallery.

At present, the original painting (if painting it was — *see* Death Mask *below*) from which Droeshout took his engraving is not known. There have been many claimants — for example the Ely portrait, discovered in 1845, bought by the Bishop of Ely, now in the Birthplace, Stratford upon Avon; and the Felton, which appeared in 1792, bought by one Samuel Felton of Shropshire from a salesroom for £5, dismissed by David Piper as not only a fake but a deliberate joke.

The Chandos painting is very different from any of these. It attracts, by comparison with others, because of the romantic informality of the subject. While the head still has its large bald dome, the hair is somewhat long and wild, the moustache more pronounced, and the chin set off by a thin, straggly beard; the eyes still stare hauntingly out, but, and it is this that catches the eye, the left ear flaunts a gold earring. (It is interesting that in the Hall portrait also Shakespeare sports an earring — but on the right ear.) By repute, the Chandos portrait was left to Sir William Davenant (*see* Commonwealth and Restoration) by Joseph Taylor, an actor in the King's Men's Company. It was amongst items sold from the estate of the Duke of Buckingham and Chandos in 1848, which is when the factual record of the picture begins. It is now in the National Gallery, London.

Of the many others, the Ashbourne and the 'Janssen' are possibly worth mentioning for their quality as paintings. The Ashbourne, inscribed Aet 47. 1611, owned at one time by the Duke of Somerset, is a fine full-length portrait of a man of Shakespeare's appearance, with a sword-belt, a thumb-ring, holding a gauntleted glove and his elbow resting on a skull. It is now in the Folger Library, Washington, USA. The Janssen (ascribed to this Dutch painter, but not conclusively so), inscribed Aet 46. 1610 (although it seems that the 6 has been tampered with), portrays an elegant face and shoulders set off by elegant dress, with particularly fine detail in the painting of the collar. It also is now in the Folger Library. (For further information about the portraits of Shakespeare, *see* M. H. Spielmann, 'Shakespeare's Portraits' in the *Encyclopaedia Britannica*; for the Droeshout, M. H. Spielmann, *The Title Page of the First Folio*, 1924.)

The following portraits are in the possession of the Birthplace Trust and are on display in their properties: the Stratford (or Hunt), Wright, Soest (or Zoust), Chesterfield and Ely portraits. Some or all of these may be authentic. There is no conclusive proof.

4. Miniatures. There have been two unauthenticated claimants, and recently a third has been added. The Auriol, inscribed Aet 33, with the forehead and hair of the Chandos portrait, and a very ornate collar, now in America, is particularly lifeless and unattractive. The other two are by Hilliard, one of a fair-haired young man with sharp, currant-like eyes; the second, claimed to be of Shakespeare (*see* Leslie Hotson, *Shakespeare by Hilliard*, 1977), is of a young man with light auburn hair, beard and moustache, the longer ends of which droop over the corners of his mouth. Unfortunately any of the 'give-away' baldness there might be is hidden under a flamboyant feathered hat. The man's right hand holds another hand, adorned at the wrist by an ornate cuff and stretched out from the clouds above. (The portrait has hitherto been known as 'Unknown Man Clasping a Hand Issuing from a Cloud' by Nicholas Hilliard.) It is inscribed 'Attici amoris ergo' on the one side of the head, and 'Ano. Dm. 1588', on the other. The arrogance of the gaze suggests a young man, not only sure of himself, but of his good fortune. Could this be the Shakespeare who four years later was denounced as 'an upstart crow, beautified with our feathers'?

5. Kesselstadt Death Mask. There is a death mask dated 1616, now in the Grand Ducal Museum at Darmstadt, claimed to be the death mask of Shakespeare himself, the one from which the bust was sculptured by Gheerart Janssen. (For further information *see* J. P. Norris, *Portraits of Shakespeare*; M. H. Spielmann, 'Shakespeare's Portraits' in the *Encyclopaedia Britannica*.)

6. The Westminster Abbey Memorial. This was designed by W. Hunt, and erected in 1741. The funds for it were raised by two theatre performances. The sculpture used the Chandos-type head.

Myths, Legends and Mysteries of Shakespeare's Life

MYTHS AND LEGENDS

1. Little is Known of Shakespeare's Life
One of the most common pleas of the sceptical is that what is known about Shakespeare's life could easily be written on one side of a small postcard, with room to spare. Invariably, those who urge this have no knowledge of the extent, nature or whereabouts of documentary material relating to his life. If they did they would find it necessary to purchase an extra consignment of postcards. The following points are crucial: (a) We know more about the life of Shakespeare, both in terms of facts and of rational conclusions that they suggest, than of any other Elizabethan dramatist. (b) The Calendar of Events indicates how much factual material (baptismal records, death and burial records, buying and selling of commodities and properties, dates of publications and productions) relating to him and his family, actually exists. How many sceptics could assemble as much evidence about a member of their own family even in our age where documentation has become common? (c) Documents relating to Shakespeare's activities, including letters to him and material relating to his family, are extant in quantity in the Shakespeare Centre records office at Stratford upon Avon. Few could reasonably remain sceptical if they examined these.

2. The Plays Were Written by Someone Else
To suggest that Francis Bacon wrote the plays but, not wishing his name to be associated with a lowly profession, paid a willing Stratford yokel for the use of his name, is a commonplace of popular response. Bacon's name began seriously to be advanced in 1769 and he has led the field in an astonishing collection of claimants for the authorship of the plays. The following points should be noted: (a) There is absolutely no observable connection between the known facts of his life and those of Shakespeare. (b) There is nothing in the known works of Bacon to suggest any connection with the plays of William Shakespeare. The fact that they both have a large vocabulary means no more and no less than that verbal genius has a habit of exhibiting amplitude. (c) Bacon wrote a great deal in Latin and, though he also wrote in English, regarded the classical language as superior. It is difficult to believe that in addition to his huge output and

his busy political life, he would have chosen to spend so much time writing in a language he considered of secondary importance in a form hardly regarded as respectable. (d) Bacon's work in English exhibits little of the enormous imaginative, metaphorical and symbolical activity or of the dramatic potency of Shakespeare's plays. A Baconian may argue that one would hardly expect to find such qualities in non-dramatic works like Bacon's essays. This is true, yet the basic cast of an artist's creative imagination will always be, to a degree, revealed in his work — for instance, Shakespeare's sonnets contain, in little, many of the qualities of his plays, including dramatic tension and a degree of characterization. (e) It is difficult to believe that Bacon, a man of affairs, could have long kept the secret. In any case to assume that he secretly wrote plays and remained undiscovered implies a gross ignorance of the status and practice of play-writing. A dramatist worked with and in the passionate chaos of theatre. To keep identity secret in such circumstances would be beyond possibility.

But Bacon is only at the forefront of the band of Pretenders. Others include — Cecil, Earl of Salisbury; the Earl of Essex; John Donne; Ben Jonson; Walter Raleigh; the Earl of Southampton (a very persistent claimant); Cardinal Wolsey. These are mind-boggling enough, but the list is given a trace of the utterly ludicrous by the inclusion of Mary, Queen of Scots, Queen Elizabeth, a group of Jesuits, and an Irish nun. Those with a penchant for an account of grotesque fiction should read the excellently compiled *The Shakespeare Claimants*, H. N. Gibson, 1962.

The claims have one common denominator which is best put in question form — how could a country lad acquire the wisdom, experience, vocabulary to create such masterpieces? This is a serious question and an approach to answering it involves a number of disparate considerations (*see* Mysteries, 4, *below*).

3. There Is No Record of Shakespeare's Ever Having Gone to School

Again, this is used as a weapon to attack the authenticity of his existence. The simple answer is that there is no record of the vast majority of Elizabethans who went to school. Either records were not kept methodically, or they were not kept long, or they were lost. It is salutary to reflect how often in reading the autobiographies and biographies of even 20th-century men of letters gaps of this kind are found.

But evidence of schooling does not rest alone in school registers and reports. The most vivid evidence lies in how what is taught at school reveals itself in later life. In Shakespeare's case not only is his knowledge of history, and particularly the classics, absolutely compatible with the text books common to an Elizabethan grammar school, but with that and that alone. If he had proceeded to university his classical allusions would have been wider and expressed differently. Rational deduction makes the following probable to the point of being inevitable: (a) He went, first, to a 'Pettie's' school, either one attached as a junior annexe to the grammar school, or a separate one run by a 'dame' (they are sometimes called 'dames' schools'). In the latter case, the dame would almost certainly be a widow who, to eke out a living, taught youngsters the alphabet, numbers, the catechism, meal-graces, and recitation of psalms. More advanced dames' schools taught elementary reading and writing. (b) At seven years he went to the King Edward VI Grammar School for boys (*see* Mysteries, 4 and 6, *below*) and stayed there until the age of about fourteen. The evidence is strong. His father was a prominent town official — it is likely that he would have sent his eldest son to a grammar school specifically created for burgesses of the town. Moreover, John Shakespeare took a particular interest in the grammar school, being one of a committee responsible for major renovations and for appointing the headmaster. It is inconceivable in these circumstances that the eldest son did not attend the school. Circumstantial evidence lies in the superb parody of a typical Latin lesson to a junior class in Shakespeare's *The Merry Wives of Windsor*, but the strongest evidence is the nature and scope of his knowledge as revealed in the plays.

4. Shakespeare Poached Deer at Charlecote Park

Charlecote Park, three miles outside Stratford, was the site of the great house of the Lucy family. The parkland was, and still is, beautiful and extensive. In the late 17th century it was put about that Shakespeare, as a wayward youth, poached Sir Thomas Lucy's deer, and made a frequent practice of it. The earliest editor of Shakespeare's plays, Nicholas Rowe, says he was arrested and severely punished, subsequently leaving for London to escape further persecution from an incensed and vindictive land-owner (which Sir Thomas probably was). Archdeacon Davies of Gloucestershire reported in the 18th century that William Shakespeare 'was much given in stealing venison and rabbits' for which he was 'oft whipped, and sometimes imprisoned'.

There is no evidence whatsoever for this story. What must be weighed before accepting or rejecting it is that there were probably no deer in Charlecote Park at the end of the 16th century, though there was a 'statutable' (i.e. recognized) rabbit-warren. Lucy, however, was interested in game-preserving and, while there was almost certainly not a statutable deer-enclosure at Charlecote, some probably roamed in woods outside the Park. If Shakespeare had poached and been indicted the punishment would have been three months' imprisonment and the payment of three times the damage and costs. But the case against him is not proven.

However, little love seems to have been lost between Shakespeare and the Lucy family. It is likely that Justice Shallow in *Henry IV, Part 2* is a portrait of Sir Thomas. More probably, the pun on the word 'luces' and 'louses' in the first scene of *The Merry Wives of Windsor*, is a scarcely-veiled thumbing of the nose to the family. The whole scene can easily, if wished, be read as an ironic remembrancer of old adventures.

5. Shakespeare Was a Page-Boy after Leaving School

There is no evidence for this. It is a somewhat romantic notion uncertainly founded on: (a) The need to discover a reason for Shakespeare's leaving Stratford for London. As a page-boy to a household like the Lucy's, or even grander, it is assumed he would have access to visiting notabilities and, having gained favour, gone with them to the metropolis. (b) A curiously snobbish notion that the high positions his father held for a time in civic government in Stratford prompted him to hob-nob with the elevated. What better way in than by using a talented son as a foot in the door!

6. Shakespeare Was a Lawyer's Clerk after Leaving School

This, as a tenable possibility, is not to be lightly put aside. There is no factual evidence, but the circumstantial evidence is formidable: (a) Throughout his younger days he would have become well-acquainted with local Stratford lawyers because of his father's professional affairs both commercial and in town-business, and indeed in the more severely litigious matters with which the volatile John Shakespeare was involved — like violating the peace. (b) Throughout his life, Shakespeare was concerned, like many of his class and economic status, with legal matters — particularly the buying, selling and renting of land. He seems to have been both assiduous and knowledgeable in attending to his affairs, and he became prosperous. (c) His plays are full of legal phrases and lawyers and evidences of a good acquaintance with the law. What is significant, however, is that his obvious knowledge is not of 'Inns of Court' law, but of 'country law', that is, he is at ease with matters he is likely to have been close to as a youth and, later, in his dealings with Stratford and, although to a lesser extent, London lawyers. In particular see the 'local' interpretations of 'crowner's' (i.e. coroner's) quest law, in the gravedigging scene of *Hamlet*.

7. Shakespeare Was a Schoolmaster in the Country after Leaving School

John Aubrey, in *Brief Lives*, written during the 17th century, but published in 1813, began this story, and another one (*see 8, below*). He writes — 'He understood Latine pretty well: for he had been in his younger yeares a School-master in the Countrey.' Aubrey is deliciously unreliable but, in the margin of *Brief Lives* is written — 'from Mr — Beeston'. Beeston was a reliable chronicler, the son of a member of the King's Company, to which Shakespeare also belonged. So perhaps, indeed, he did for a while indulge in what many writers have done — teaching before creating.

8. Shakespeare Followed His Father's Profession as Butcher after Leaving School

Another story from Aubrey (*see* 7, *above*), and related with dramatic relish — 'I have been told heretofore by some of the neighbours, that when he was a boy he exercised his father's Trade, but when he kill'd a Calfe, he would doe it in a *high style*, & make a Speech.' It's a stirring thought and who knows whether Aubrey might not have hit upon something near the truth. Boys have been known to follow in their father's footsteps, and then to kick over the traces and depart.

9. Shakespeare Became a Soldier of Fortune after Leaving School

His plays show a good acquaintance with soldiering and weaponry, so there seems no reason why someone should not have advanced the idea that between leaving school and going to London (about 1578–88) he was a soldier of fortune. There was no lack of opportunity. He could have chosen, for example, to join Robert Dudley's expeditionary force campaigning in the Netherlands. The difficulty is that not only is there no evidence but we have, somehow, to fit in foreign military service with marriage and the fathering of children. But *see* Duff Cooper's book, *Sergeant Shakespeare*, 1949.

10. His First London Job Was Tending to the Horses of Patrons of the Globe Theatre

There are two objections to this hardy, ubiquitous story. The first is that there is no evidence whatsoever, and the second is that the Globe Theatre was not built until 1599 — ten years at least after Shakespeare arrived in London. It seems treacherous even to suggest that a story given to us all in childhood is an absolute myth. One may avoid treachery by reflecting on the possibility that he looked after horses at some other theatre and that, after all, the early attachments of many of our eminent dramatists to their chosen profession have been no less menial.

11. 'Shakespeare's' Plays Were Created by a Committee

So incredulous are some people that one man could be capable of writing the plays, that it has been seriously put forward that all thirty-seven were written by a 'committee' of brilliant authors who agreed to use the pseudonym 'Shakespeare'. Yet the sceptics will cheerfully and completely accept the individual and profound genius of Leonardo, Michelangelo and Beethoven. The notion of committee authorship is quite different from the fact of shared authorship. It was common in Elizabethan times for more than one writer to be involved in a single play. The hand of Shakespeare may well be in the extant manuscript play of *Sir Thomas More*. Conversely, in *Henry VI, Henry VIII* and *Pericles* it is more than likely that others shared the authorship with Shakespeare. (*See* Collaborator.)

12. There are Hidden Messages in Cryptograms in Shakespeare's Plays

This is not far removed from the world of James Bond. The theory that there are cryptograms in the plays is mainly associated with the Baconians. Baulked by any evidence to satisfy their faith in his authorship of the plays, some have claimed that he left clear evidence — clear, that is, to anyone who can break the code. A leading Baconian — Ignatius Donnelly — published *The Great Cryptogram* in 1888. This was a massive explanation of Bacon's hidden messages in the First Folio which proved not only his authorship of 'Shakespeare's' plays but also of other Elizabethan works, including Marlowe's. Bacon, too, apparently wrote 'Montaigne's' essays and 'Burton's' *Anatomy of Melancholy*. It should be observed that Shakespeare's plays contain so many words *in toto* that cryptograms can, without doubt, be very easily 'erected' from them. The elbow-room for inventiveness, as James Bond discovered in his activities, is vast.

13. Shakespeare Died after a Drunken Orgy

John Ward, Vicar of Stratford from 1662 to 1681, wrote in his diary that, 'Shakespeare, Drayton and Ben Jonson had a merry meeting, and it seems drank too hard, for Shakespeare died of a fever there contracted . . .' A slightly more colourful version was current in 1762 which changes the story to encompass a drinking competition Shakespeare is supposed to have engaged in with some men of Bidford (eight miles from Stratford) — a village noted then for its excessive drinking habits. 'He inquired of a shepherd for the Bidford drinkers; who replied they were absent; but the Bidford suppers were at home; and I suppose, continued the sheep keeper, they will be sufficient for you: and so, indeed, they were. He was forced to take up his lodging under that tree for some hours.' 'Drayton', referred to in the Ward version, was a well-known Warwickshire poet.

It is not known if these stories are true — many people cling to them to enhance a romantic notion in the absence of evidence.

MYSTERIES

1. How Is It We Know Little about His Youth?

Why should we? No one knew he was to become famous and there was no tradition of biography. The documentation of evidence was haphazard. For respectable Elizabethans the better part of Shakespeare's achievement was that he made money, bought property and died respectable. The art of play-writing was not regarded as either important or respectable.

2. Who Was Anne Whateley?

This is one of the most intriguing of the Shakespeare 'mysteries'. It can easily be given a romantic aura — indeed it can be made to yield a salacious strain. This girl's name appears on Shakespeare's marriage licence as being of Temple Grafton. Some people believe the marriage clerk mistook 'Hathaway' for 'Whateley'. Others insist that such a mistake, even in the haphazard traditions of Elizabethan documentation, is beyond credence. They therefore believe that Shakespeare became betrothed to Anne Whateley, that relatives and friends of the pregnant Anne Hathaway got wind of it, that they prevented the marriage to Anne Whateley, but that her name, oddly, remained on a licence. Some say it was a different William Shakespeare whose name appears on the licence — Shakespeare was a common enough name in Warwickshire. But was she, on the other hand, Shakespeare's 'other Anne'? Whateleys still live in Stratford and district, but neither they nor the scholars can tell what the answer is. (*See* Marriage.)

3. Who Was the Dark Lady of the Sonnets?

Was it Anne Whateley? Shakespeare's sonnets, numbers 126–52, seem to refer to a 'dark lady' (*see* The Poems). But did she exist in fact, or in his imagination? Lack of knowledge has not deterred the most astonishing scholarly and not-so-scholarly activity to fix her identity. Some have claimed her to be Queen Elizabeth, some believe her to be Elizabeth Vernon, mistress, later wife, of the Earl of Southampton. One believes her to be, literally, a dark lady — a negress. Perhaps the most persistent claims have been made for Mary Fitton, a maid of honour at the Queen's Court. The latest theory, expounded with his usual infective enthusiasm, is A. L. Rowse's. He puts forward the name of a lady of Italian extraction — Emilia Bassana — but this is as much conjectural, and fanciful, as most theories about the strange lady.

4. How Could a Country Lad Have Written Such Immortal Masterpieces?

The main reason for this incredulity lies in the simple mistaking of what constitutes Shakespeare's dramatic genius. It does not have that quality by which most people judge human extraordinariness — factual knowledge, complex theories, organized ideas, deep and wide philosophical patterns. These qualities, admirable in themselves, can be nurtured immensely by formal education. But, on the contrary, Shakespeare's genius is an immense and superbly articulated exaggeration of common sense. We do not find original thought in his plays, but we find immensely perceptive intuitions which are a true reading of what existence is, or seems to be, to all men. We search in vain for philosophical patterns, but we cannot escape a vision of 'the way the world wags'. Those who fear the deeps and eddies of his language believe it to be esoteric, abstruse, difficult, yet some gentle effort would astound them into a recognition that he never loses touch or sight or smell or hearing of the language that his contemporaries spoke; he glorified the common language, making the ordinary sound new, fresh and important. Above all, his genius depended on memory — not of learning tracts, treatises, sermons, but of committing to his imagination what he heard and saw about him. He was the most natural dramatist who ever lived in the sense that he metamorphosed what he heard and saw about him. The dusty traveller sitting in the Mermaid Tavern in London, just arrived from wars on the Continent, never realized what was to happen to his replies when the quiet stranger sipping his beer turned and asked him — 'How is it with you, cos?'

5. How Could an Unknown Country Boy Get to London and Become a Dramatist?

The sceptics ask this question but, curiously, never inquire how a butcher's boy became Cardinal Wolsey, or, indeed, a country lawyer became President Lincoln. Of all the so-called 'mysteries' this one is most easily dismissed. Stratford was on the main line of communication between London and the north. Famous London acting companies regularly played there during Shakespeare's youth. He must have (without reasonable doubt) got to know them well in the days when his father, as chamberlain, was official host to such visitors. He had an 'entrée' and no doubt took advantage of it. What mystery is there in that a young man who subsequently proved his worth a thousand times should find a chance to attach himself, in some menial task even, to one of the London companies which visited Stratford? It is quite natural. The record of 'stage-struck' youngsters in subsequent centuries, including our own, only goes to suggest what happened. He left with the players and wrote to tell his family where he was. This probably happened in 1587.

6. How Could One Man Acquire So Much Knowledge?

A common but misleading criterion of artistic genius and talent is the actual amount of factual knowledge revealed in an artist's work. If we apply this test to Shakespeare we find that he falls far short of both the amount and quality revealed, for example, in the works of Ben Jonson, Francis Bacon, John Milton — the last two, in particular, who, however, often used their erudition to a degree to create original thought.

To apply the test, then, rigidly, cannot but lead to the conclusion that Shakespeare's was decidedly the lesser genius. This, however, is palpably ridiculous. The truth is that it is neither quantity nor the ability to create original thought which characterizes Shakespeare's genius, but the nature of his factual knowledge and the uses to which he puts it.

Bacon could classify natural objects, but Shakespeare can tell you what herbs are poisonous and what are not. Milton could bring forth all the hosts of hell for your examination, but Shakespeare's Macbeth can tell you what it is like to contemplate the horrors of eternal damnation. Ben Jonson can use a Latin tag to give his wit the subtle sauce of classical erudition, but only Shakespeare can capture the authentic speech of his contemporaries and make it reverberate in his Justice Shallow, Silence, Bottom the Weaver, Bardolph and a host of others.

Shakespeare gives little evidence of having much knowledge of geography outside England, but the Italy of his *Romeo and Juliet*, the France of his *Henry V* have an extraordinary atmosphere of authenticity. He is either careless or frankly ignorant about many things — Ben Jonson would never have introduced clocks into a play about the ancient Rome of Julius Caesar — but we forget these as we are completely convinced of the truth of his vision of his world and of human nature. The trifles which many far more erudite artists would leave contemptuously unconsidered, were things which he heard and saw about him. The difference between his genius and that of most others is that he recognized and respected the trivia of his contemporaries as the truest source to feed his poetic imagination.

7. Did He Leave His 'Second Best Bed' to His Wife Because He Disliked Her?

Shakespeare's will was drawn up in January 1616, and revised in March 1616, about a month before his death. The only reference to his wife is as follows: '. . . I gyve unto my wief my second best bed with the furniture.' When we compare this with, for example, the large bequests to his daughter, Susanna, it reads even more like a calculated insult. Yet the affair of the second best bed must take its place with deer-poaching, holding horses' heads and other matters.

This bequest is far more likely to indicate love than hate, and the absence of any other more substantial gift is explicable by the same token. Anne Shakespeare would be comfortably installed in the care of her daughter Susanna for the rest of her life, at the family house in New Place, so no special bequest for this was required. She would, by law, be entitled during her lifetime to the income from one-third of all of Shakespeare's estates; in this case not only was she automatically very well provided for, but Shakespeare was avoiding her being involved in worrying litigation which might have occurred had he made special dispensations for her on top of legal requirements. Finally, if he had left her the first or best bed this would indeed have been insulting, for that bed was, in a household of such standing, reserved for guests. It would have implied that she had been but a guest in the house. The second best bed was the marriage-bed and it was being specially remembered by Shakespeare in his will.

This kind of will, as it applies to the wife, was quite common in Elizabethan times in families of similar standing to that of Shakespeare.

8. Who Wrote the Curse on Shakespeare's Tomb?

Mankind is fascinated and terrified by curses — the compulsive attraction of Tutankhamun is evidence enough. On Shakespeare's grave the following curse is carved into the stonework:

> Good frend for Jesus' sake forbeare
> To digg the dust encloased heare!
> Bleste be yᵉ man yᵗ spares these stones,
> And curst be he yᵗ moves my bones.

Frankly, as a curse it lacks what we might call punch while, as a piece of verse, it is vile. Did Shakespeare write it? According to William Hall, who visited Stratford in 1694, he did it to suit 'the capacity of clerks and sextons, for the most part a very ignorant set of people'. But why should he be so assiduous to address his words to clerks and sextons? Hall explains this, too, and from what is known of Elizabethan and later practice, his explanation is very feasible. There was a grim tradition by which, after the lapse of some years, bones were removed from graves and thrown into the charnel-house, to make way for new burials. Needless to say the clerks and sextons benefited financially from the transaction — whoever made the highest bid for grave-room got the wormy prize. Shakespeare's grave was vulnerable, being in a prominent place below the altar. It is said that to ensure eternal peace the threat of the curse was reinforced by the eminently practical course of burying him seventeen feet deep.

As to the authorship of the doggerel curse, there is no proof that it was by Shakespeare. Indeed, it may have been placed there by his relatives.

People of Shakespeare's Stratford

Addenbrooke, John (*fl.* 1607–10). One of several Stratford men involved in litigation with Shakespeare's family. In 1608 William Shakespeare sued him for £6 debt. Shakespeare won but Addenbrooke absconded and eventually the money was paid by Addenbrooke's guarantor, Thomas Hornbey.

Arden Family. Shakespeare's mother's family probably originally came from near Birmingham, but became associated with the Stratford area in the 15th century. Robert Arden (Shakespeare's father-in-law) was a prosperous farmer with two freeholds in Snitterfield and one (now called Mary Arden's house) in Wilmcote. He left Mary, his youngest daughter (and Shakespeare's mother) a substantial legacy of all his Wilmcote property.

Clopton Family. Notable family of Stratford from the 15th century. Sir Hugh Clopton (d. *c.* 1496) built the bridge that bears his name, over the Avon, and also New Place which Shakespeare eventually bought. The family occupied Clopton Manor, on the outskirts of Stratford, during the 16th century. In 1605 the manor was used (without Clopton's consent) for meetings of the Gunpowder conspirators.

Combe Family. Neighbours of Shakespeare's family at Stratford. (1) William Combe (1551–1610), MP. Sold land to Shakespeare, 1602. (2) John (*c.* 1560–1614), William's nephew. Wealthy moneylender — left Shakespeare £5 in his will. (3) Thomas (d. 1609), John's brother. Landowner — held half of sublease of Stratford tithes; Shakespeare held other half. (4) William (1586–1667), son of Thomas. Shakespeare, Thomas Greene, Richard Lane entered legal complaint in 1611 against him for failure to pay rent on Stratford tithes. (5) Thomas (1589–1657), his brother. Received sword in Shakespeare's will.

Field, Richard (1561–1624). Stratford man, son of Henry Field, a tanner whose stocks were evaluated by John Shakespeare, 1592. Settled in London, 1579, and became printer (of *Venus and Adonis*, 1593 and *The Rape of Lucrece*, 1594). Prominent member of Stationer's Company.

Getley, Walter (?). He was in the household administration of the dowager Countess of Warwick, conducted negotiations for the sale of property to Shakespeare in 1602. This property was on land held by the Countess and it faced New Place Gardens.

Greene, Thomas (d. 1640). The most prominent of an important Stratford family. In 1601 he represented Stratford as a solicitor in London. From 1603–17, town clerk of Stratford. He had six children, one of whom, William, may have been Shakespeare's godson. In 1609 he and his family lived in New Place while waiting to move into a new house. He refers to Shakespeare, in his Diary, as his 'cosen'. His brother, John, was, in 1618, a trustee of the Blackfriars Gate-house bought by Shakespeare acting on behalf of Susanna.

Hall, Dr John (1575–1635). Shakespeare's son-in-law, husband of Susanna. Graduate of Cambridge who studied also in France. Very prominent physician — his *Select Observations on English Bodies* was published in 1657. Some suggestion that Hall was a Puritan. His house, Hall's Croft, is one of the properties at Stratford upon Avon administered by the Shakespeare Birthplace Trust.

Hart, William (d. 1616). A hatter of Stratford who married Shakespeare's younger sister, Joan. Little else is known of him except that he seems to have had a habit of getting into debt, and that he died within a few days of his eminent coz — Shakespeare.

Hathaway Family. They were landowners in Shottery, near Stratford. Their house was called 'Hewlands' (now known as Anne Hathaway's cottage). Anne's father, Richard (d. 1581) had seven children and seems to have been a prosperous small farmer. His will (which leaves bequests to all his children) is still extant. (*See* Calendar of Events.)

Lambert Family. Edmund Lambert married Joan Arden, Shakespeare's aunt. John and Mary Shakespeare borrowed £40 from Edmund in 1578, giving Mary's inherited house and land at Wilmcote as security. The loan remained unpaid and Edmund's son, John, inherited the property. He was promptly sued by John Shakespeare for not paying an additional £20 for completing the ownership. Prolonged litigation followed, the outcome of which is unknown, for the property passed to an entirely different family (Edkins) in the 17th century.

Lane, John (b. 1562). As member of a family who were neighbours to the Shakespeares, Lane may have been a schoolfellow of the dramatist. His father sued Shakespeare's uncle, Henry, for repayment of a loan of £20 in 1586. John's son (also John) was sued in 1613 for defamation of Susanna Shakespeare's character. In 1619 he libelled and attacked the vicar of Stratford. Neighbourliness could hardly have existed between the two families.

Nash, Thomas (d. 1587). A neighbour of Shakespeare's. His two sons, Anthony and John, were left 26s. 8d. to buy memorial rings in Shakespeare's will. Anthony became a wealthy Stratfordian and his son, Thomas (1593–1647) married Elizabeth Hall — Shakespeare's granddaughter. He was buried immediately to the right of Shakespeare in the chancel of Holy Trinity Church.

Quiney Family. Both friends and relatives of Shakespeare. (1) Adrian Quiney, alderman, bailiff of High Street, Stratford, died 1607. (2) Richard Quiney, died 1602, was his son, who wrote to Shakespeare asking for a loan of £30. It was sent from London in October 1598. There is no record of a reply. He was also involved in negotiations for buying land from Shakespeare (*see* Abraham Sturley). (3) Thomas Quiney (*c.* 1580–1662) married Judith, Shakespeare's younger daughter. The marriage (celebrated at a time of the year normally forbidden by the Church) resulted in their excommunication. In 1616 Quiney was tried for having 'carnal intercourse' with Margaret Wheeler. In the same year Shakespeare changed his will — which suggests his suspicion of Quiney.

Richardson, John (*fl.* 1582). He, with Fulke Sandells, travelled to Worcester in 1582 to stand surety to the Bishop of Worcester for £40 if, after he had issued a licence for the marriage of Shakespeare and Anne Hathaway, anything was discovered which would make the marriage invalid. They presumably undertook this task on behalf of the Hathaway family.

Rogers, Phillip (*fl.* 1604). A Stratford apothecary against whom Shakespeare brought an action for the non-payment of a small bill for malt (1604). This is yet one more example of Shakespeare's almost pernickety attention to business detail.

Sandells, Fulke (b. 1551). Involved in obtaining a licence for Shakespeare's marriage (*see* John Richardson). He was involved in the will-making of Richard Hathaway (Anne's father).

Sturley, Abraham (d. 1614). Acquaintance and fellow Stratfordian of Shakespeare. Between 1599 and 1601 wrote letters to Richard Quiney containing material relating to the dramatist. One letter concerned tithes at Stratford, the other expresses a hope that Shakespeare can lend money. Both he and Quiney were in debt, but subsequently appear to have recovered fortune.

Underhill, William (1555–97). Owner of New Place before selling it to Shakespeare, 1597. Once imprisoned as a Catholic recusant.

Whateley, Anne. Her name appears on Shakespeare's marriage licence (*see* Myths, Legends and Mysteries; Marriage). Virtually nothing is known of the family, but the name strongly remains in Stratford today.

Whittington, Thomas (d. 1601). A shepherd employed by Richard Hathaway (Anne's father). In 1601 his will contained the item — 'I geve and bequeth unto the poore people of Stratford 40s. that is in the hand of Anne Shaxspere, wyf unto Mr Wyllyam Shaxspere, and is due debt unto me, beyng payd to myne Executor by the said Wyllyam Shaxspere or his assigns, according to the true meanyng of this my wyll.'

Playwrights of Shakespeare's Time

Beaumont, Francis (*c.* 1584–1616). Prolific dramatist, associated eternally with John Fletcher. Plays he wholly or partly wrote include *The Knight of the Burning Pestle, Philaster, A Maid's Tragedy*. Some plays acted by the King's Men.

Chapman, George (1559–1634). Poet and playwright, praised by Meres. Author of *Bussy D'Ambois*. Wrote much for the Children's Companies. Collaborated with Ben Jonson. Some critics find influence of Chapman in *All's Well That Ends Well, Troilus and Cressida* and *Measure for Measure*. A superb poet but unsteady dramatist.

Chettle, Henry (*c.* 1560–*c.* 1607). One of Henslowe's 'victims'. Prolific collaborator and dramatist (at least 48 plays). Meres considers him best comic dramatist of the time. Chettle later apologized for his part in Greene's attack on Shakespeare — '. . . divers of worship have reported his uprightness of dealing, which argues his honesty . . .' (See *Sir Thomas More.*)

Davenant, Sir William (1606–68). Playwright, theatre manager and poet. With Killigrew licensed to perform Shakespeare's plays after the Restoration. Notorious for his adaptations, and for his claim to be Shakespeare's illegitimate son. (*See* Commonwealth and Restoration.)

Dekker, Thomas (1572–*c.* 1632). Possibly one of Henslowe's 'victims'. Dramatic author and collaborator in about 44 plays. Had notorious literary quarrel with Ben Jonson, and replied to Jonson's ridicule in *The Poetaster* with his own *Satiromastix* (1601). Superb pamphleteer. See *The Wonderful Years*, 1603, concerning the plague in London; also *The Gull's Hornbook* (1609) which purports to advise gallants on how to behave in a theatre: 'Present not yourselves on the stage (especially at a new play) until the quaking Prologue hath (by rubbing) got colour into his cheeks.' Best known for *The Shoemaker's Holiday* (1599) — delightful comedy of London life.

Drayton, Michael (*c.* 1563–1631). Born Warwickshire, frequent visitor to Clifford Chambers near Stratford upon Avon. Author of *Poly-Olbion* (1613–22) — a rhyming survey of England. Collaborator in about 20 plays, including *Sir John Oldcastle* (1599), an apparent attempt to refurbish the image of the historical source of Falstaff recently tarnished in Shakespeare's *Henry IV* — 'It is no pampered glutton we present.'

Probably knew Shakespeare but no confirmation exists of the tradition that 'Shakespeare, Drayton and Ben Jonson had a merry meeting, and it seems drank too hard, for Shakespeare died of a fever there contracted'. Some believe Drayton to be the rival poet mentioned in the sonnets.

Farrant, Richard (d. 1580). Master of the Children of Windsor, Deputy Master of the Children of the Chapel, founder of the first Blackfriars Theatre. Most famous presenter of children's performances and entertainments.

Field, Nathan (b. 1587). Actor/dramatist, formerly one of the Chapel Children. Friend and colleague of Ben Jonson. May have replaced Shakespeare in the King's Company in 1616. One of the principal actors mentioned in the First Folio. A man of wild habits.

Fletcher, John (1579–1625). Beaumont's collaborator. Member of the King's Company (to which Shakespeare belonged). Almost certainly part-author of *Henry VIII*. Wrote a number of plays alone, mainly romances and melodramas. Very popular in Restoration period.

Ford, John (1586–1639). One of so-called 'decadent' playwrights at the end of the Elizabethan/Jacobean period, so described for frequent sensationalism of plots, eccentricity of characters, devious morality of themes, and unevenness of style. However, this did not prevent Ford from writing powerful dramas (*'Tis a Pity She's a Whore*, c. 1626; *The Broken Heart*, c. 1629).

Gosson, Stephen (1554–1624). Playwright, poet, polemicist. Wrote one of the most scathing attacks on the stage of the age — *The Schoole of Abuse*, 1579. He called actors 'uncircumcised philistines', though he did not condemn all of them. In 1600 became Rector of St Botolph's, Bishopsgate.

Greene, Robert (1558–92). Talented, dissolute, contentious pamphleteer and playwright. Having deserted his wife he took a mistress, the sister of Cutting Ball, a violent thief. He died after a 'surfeit of pickle herringe and Rennish wine'. His plays include *Friar Bacon and Friar Bungay*, c. 1589, and *Orlando Furioso*, c. 1591. Greene best remembered for his attack on Shakespeare in *Greenes Groatsworth of Wit bought with a Million of Repentance*, 1592. Shakespeare 'is an upstart crow, beautified with our feathers, that with his *Tygers hart wrapt in a Players hyde*, supposes he is as well able to bombast out a blanke verse as the best of you: and being an absolute *Johannes factotum*, is in his own conceit the onely Shakescene in a countrey'. The 'Tyger' reference is a parody of a line in *Henry VI, Part 3*.

Heywood, Thomas (1573–1641). Actor/dramatist. Possibly one of Henslowe's 'victims'. 'Thomas Hawoode came and hiered hime seallfe with me . . .' (Henslowe's Diary). Heywood claims a hand in 220 plays, which makes him probably the chief collaborator of the age.

One only is remembered — *A Woman Killed with Kindness*, 1603. He wrote a touching reference to Shakespeare in *Hierarchie of the Blessed Angels*, 1635: 'Mellifluous Shake-speare, whose inchanting Quill/ Commanded Mirth or Passion, was but *Will*.'

Jonson, Benjamin (1572–1637). Arguably the second greatest dramatist of the age. In turn, bricklayer, soldier, actor/playwright. A contentious, probably cynical perfectionist, he admired Shakespeare, but deplored his 'facile' working methods — '. . . he flow'd with that facility, that sometime it was necessary he should be stopp'd'. Heavily involved in bitter quarrels (1599–1601) involving several dramatists, apparently concerning contrary opinions on relative stylistic merits. Quarrels took the form of satirical plays, e.g. *Histriomastix* by John Marston, countered by Jonson's *Every Man in His Humour*. His best plays — *Volpone*, *Epicoene*, *The Alchemist*, notable for biting satire, powerful intellectual grasp of theme, social comment, wit, allegorically-inclined characterization, moral strictness and superb control of both dramatic and descriptive language. Jonson is no less accomplished as writer of masques (in brilliant but quarrelsome collaboration with Inigo Jones). By receiving royal pension of 100 marks became the first (unofficial) poet laureate. Unlike Shakespeare he carefully supervised his works for publication. Jonson wrote of Shakespeare on his death: 'He was not of an age, but for all time.' Ironically, if Shakespeare had never lived, we might have said the same of Jonson. A head and shoulders oil portrait (18th century) is in the Royal Shakespeare Theatre's picture gallery.

Kyd, Thomas (1558–94). Jonson calls him 'Sporting Kyd' in unflattering comparison with Shakespeare. He wrote a far from 'sporting' play — *The Spanish Tragedy* (1589), arguably the most popular tragedy of the 16th century — full of blood, ghosts, revenge and recrimination. The play, to a degree, is the pattern for later 'revenge' plays such as *Hamlet* and *Titus Andronicus*. Kyd died in poverty.

Lodge, Thomas (*c.* 1557–1625). Poet, playwright, novelist. Famous for his prose-romance (written in a form which justifies the term 'novel'), *Rosalynde*, 1590. This became a source for *As You Like It*. He defended his profession against Gosson's attacks.

Lyly, John (*c.* 1554–1606). Noted for his prose-romances *Euphues* — *The Anatomy of Wit*, 1579 and *Euphues and his England*, 1580. Written in highly sophisticated flowery style whose eccentricities gave rise to the adjective 'euphuistic'. Shakespeare parodied it in *Love's Labour's Lost*.

Marlowe, Christopher (1564–93). The best-known Elizabethan playwright after Shakespeare, his career stopped short with his murder in a Deptford pub. He was probably involved in what the world now counts as espionage, and was a known atheist. Has been widely regarded as Shakespeare's equal and potentially his superior. This view rests on *Tamburlaine*, *c.* 1587; *Dr Faustus*, *c.* 1588; *The Jew of Malta*, *c.* 1589;

Edward II, c. 1592; *The Massacre at Paris, c.* 1593; *Dido Queen of Carthage,* 1593. A minority opinion judges Marlowe's structural immaturity, underdeveloped characterization and a superb lyrical gift which often subsumes dramatic force, to debar him from equality with Shakespeare. It is possible that *Richard II* owes something to Shakespeare's reading of *Edward II.*

Marston, John (*c.* 1575-1634). Jonson's great rival whom he satirized in *Histriomastix,* but to whom he dedicated *The Malcontent,* 1604. Like Shakespeare, a Warwickshire man.

Massinger, Philip (1583-1640). Dramatist and collaborator of Fletcher, possibly one of Henslowe's 'victims'. Regarded as one of the 'decadent' Jacobeans (*see* John Ford). Nevertheless his *A New Way to Pay Old Debts,* 1626, is satirically powerful and has one memorable character — Sir Giles Overreach.

Middleton, Thomas (*c.* 1570-1627). Sometimes regarded with Ford and Massinger as a 'decadent' dramatist. His plays *The Changeling,* 1622, and *Women Beware Women,* rank high as Jacobean tragedies. Lines from *The Witch, c.* 1610-16, appear in Shakespeare's *Macbeth* (*see* Interpolations).

Munday, Anthony (*c.* 1553-1633). Actor/dramatist, employed by Henslowe. Described by Meres as 'our best plotter'. The play, of which he was part author, *Sir John Oldcastle,* 1599, was attributed to Shakespeare by Jaggard the publisher. Munday's handwriting has been identified, together with apparent examples of Shakespeare's, Heywood's, Chettle's and Dekker's in an incomplete play MS, *Sir Thomas More.*

Nashe, Thomas (1567-*c.* 1601). Novelist, dramatist, pamphleteer, polemicist. In an epistle attached to *The Anatomie of Absurditie,* he acidly criticizes some actors as parasites and some dramatists, including Kyd, as illiterates. He praises Peele and other 'University' dramatists known as 'the University Wits' — ie. Greene, Marlowe, Lyly, Peele, Lodge and himself. Nashe was a great quarreller, a mediocre dramatist, but an important early figure in the history of the novel (see his *The Unfortunate Traveller, or the Life of Jack Wilton,* 1594). His satire, *Pierce Peniless — His Supplication to the Divell,* 1592, praises the actors he had hitherto attacked, and he has a flattering direct reference to Shakespeare's(?) *Henry VI* performed in the same year.

Peele, George (*c.* 1557-96). Notable for revitalizing the old chronicle/historical play by firm characterization, dramatic incident and lyrical but firm language, see his *Edward I, c.* 1593. Attacked by Greene, he seems to have led a blameless life, although he died, apparently, of the pox.

Rowley, William (*c.* 1585-1642). Actor and dramatist and, in 1625, listed as a member of the King's Company. At one time credited with part-authorship of *Pericles*, but this not upheld by modern scholarship. In 1662 a play, *The Birth of Merlin*, was attributed to him and Shakespeare.

Shirley, James (1596–1666). One of Shakespeare's notable successors. A prolific writer of plays, he became leading writer for the King's Company in 1640. The influence of Shakespeare strongly beats in a number of his plays, see *The Triumph of Beautie*, 1646, with its possible echoes of *A Midsummer Night's Dream*.

Tarlton, Richard (d. 1588). Popular clown and unconventional individual who was a favourite of Queen Elizabeth. No details are known of his roles, but he was probably an ad-libber rather than one who stuck to the lines written for him. His comedy was broad and possibly vulgar. He wrote a collection of jokes — *Tarlton's Jests*, and may have been a model for Hamlet's description of Yorick.

Tourneur, Cyril (d. 1626). Soldier, satirist, dramatist and involved in government service. Author of *The Atheist's Tragedy*, c. 1607 and *The Revenger's Tragedy*, 1606 (with collaborator?). The Royal Shakespeare Theatre's production of the latter in 1966 revealed that the melodramatic and sensational plot, equivocal moral stances, fantastic characterization and craggy language has astonishing dramatic force and theatrical coherence.

Webster, John (d. 1634). Little known of this prestigious but perhaps somewhat overrated dramatist, who was also a collaborator (notably, perhaps, with Tourneur in *The Revenger's Tragedy*). His most famous plays — *The White Devil*, c. 1609 and *The Duchess of Malfi*, c. 1613 — contain dramatic poetry of the highest order, but lack, for some tastes, the economy of construction and the psychological realism of characterization which is typical of Shakespeare's tragedies. Some regard him as second only to Shakespeare as a tragic dramatist.

Wilkins, George (*fl.* 1603–8). A mystery man. He was a hack writer, but the actual extent of his hand in any work attributed to him is problematical. Author of *The Painfull Adventures of Pericles, Prince of Tyre*, 1608, a novel which bears strong resemblances to Shakespeare's *Pericles*. Some scholars believe Wilkins had a hand in writing the play — the inferior first two acts have been attributed to him. Probable fellow-witness with Shakespeare in Belott-Mountjoy suit.

Bacon, Francis (1561–1626). Essayist, politician, philosopher, statesman. The connection made between his name and Shakespeare's plays is not only a fruitless and pointless exercise but detracts from Bacon's own greatness as a man of letters. From 1584, when he became an MP, to his death, he was a man of affairs. He was instrumental in the arraignment of Essex, he was Lord Chancellor, he became Baron Verulam, he became Viscount St Albans, he was convicted of bribery and shorn of his high status and office. His most notable work is in his *Essays*, 1597, revised 1625, in *Novum Organum*, 1620 and *The Advancement of Learning*, 1605.

Bacon, Mathew (*fl.* 1590–1613). London born, a scrivener by trade, Bacon was defendant in an action (involving legal technicality rather than civil or criminal offence). It concerned Bacon's former ownership of the Blackfriars Gate-house purchased by Shakespeare in 1613. The action, brought by Shakespeare and his neighbours, is important in establishing Shakespeare's London residence.

Bernini, Gianlorenzo (1598–1680). Italian architect, painter, sculptor. Much of his work is found in St Peter's, Rome. He also wrote comedies, and was a renowned conversationalist.

Bodley, Thomas (1545–1613). Scholar, diplomat, founder of Bodleian Library, Oxford. Born Exeter.

Bothwell, James Hepburn, Earl of (*c.* 1536–78). *See* Mary, Queen of Scots.

Brooke, Arthur (d. 1563). Translator and poet. He would be forgotten were it not that his interminable, dull, undramatic and virtually unreadable poem, *The Tragicall Historye of Romeus and Juliet*, 1562 — a metrical version of a story in Boaistuau's *Histoires Tragiques*, 1559 — was the main source for Shakespeare's *Romeo and Juliet*.

Burton, Richard (1577–1640). Author of *The Anatomy of Melancholy*, 1621, perhaps best described as a handbook of psychological disorders as interpreted by an Elizabethan with an astonishing rag-bag of ideas about religion, superstition, astrology, mediaeval notions of the workings of the mind and body, and a typically late 16th-century enthusiasm for discovery, description and explanation. Burton wrote a Latin comedy, but his disposition was gloomy — 'In an interval of vapours he would be extremely cheerful, and then he would fall into such a state of despondency that he could only get relief by going to the Bridge-foot at Oxford and hear the bargemen swear at one another.'

Byrd, William (*c.* 1543–1623). The first and greatest of English madrigal composers and of polyphonic music.

Campion, Thomas (1567–1620). Poet, superb song-writer — may have written for the stage. See his four books of airs published between 1601 and 1617.

Caravaggio, Michelangelo Merisi da (1573–1610). Italian painter of both secular and religious subjects.

Carew, Thomas (*c.* 1598–*c.* 1639). Poet and roué, confidante of Charles I. Intimate friend of Davenant (who claimed to be Shakespeare's illegitimate son).

Cecil, Robert, Earl of Salisbury (1563–1612). Secretary of State to Queen Elizabeth. The Cecils were and are a great political and artistic family. Robert Cecil and his father William, Lord Burghley, presented expensive theatrical entertainments. *Love's Labour's Lost* possibly performed at Robert Cecil's house.

Cellini, Benvenuto (1500–71). Florentine artist in precious metal. His *Autobiography* gives a vivid, racy account of the day-to-day life of a high Renaissance artist/craftsman.

Cervantes Saavedra, Miguel de (1547–1616). Spanish novelist, poet and playwright who died in the same year as Shakespeare. Author of *Don Quixote*. Wrote a great deal for the stage, but without distinction.

Champlain, Samuel de (1567–1635). French explorer, first governor of French Canada.

Charles I, King (1600–49). King of Great Britain and Ireland, second son of James I and Anne of Denmark. His political recklessness led to an unbreachable rift with the House of Commons, and his trial was quickly followed by execution.

Corneille, Pierre (1606–84). French dramatist and poet of uneven quality, ranging from middling to superb.

Crashaw, Richard (1613–50). English poet of great classical learning and felicity of expression.

Cromwell, Oliver (1599–1658). Lord Protector, 1653–8 — Cromwell had a profound influence on the fate of Shakespeare's plays in particular and theatre in general by his repressive measures. (*See* Commonwealth and Restoration.)

Daniel, Samuel (*c.* 1563–1619). Tutor to William Herbert. Superb sonneteer (see his sequence, *Delia*). Author of *The Complaint of Rosamond* which compares with Shakespeare's *Lover's Complaint*. His plays include masques and pastoral tragi-comedies. Believed by some the rival poet apparently described in Shakespeare's sonnets.

Darnley, Henry Stuart, Lord (1545–67). Husband of Mary, Queen of Scots, father of James I, murdered, some think by the connivance of Mary and her lover, Bothwell.

Deloney, Thomas (1543–1607). English pamphleteer and ballad-monger, some of whose works were scoffed at by Will Kempe, Shakespeare's actor/associate. Also wrote novels and stories: *Jack of Newberie*, 1697, *The Gentle Craft*, 1597 and *c.* 1598 — a collection of anecdotes about shoemakers.

Descartes, René (1596–1650). French philosopher/scientist. Author of *Discourse on Method* — a seminal book from which future logicians, metaphysicians and physicists gained much intellectual nourishment.

Donne, John (1573–1631). English poet and sermon-writer. Dean of St Paul's. Born only nine years after Shakespeare, his poetry seems in its style, imagery and reference to be of a totally different era. The scientific spirit, and indeed something of its verbal resource gives Donne's religious and love-lyrics an unexpectedness of tone and phrase, and sometimes a dissonance which some find disturbing.

Dowland, John (*c.* 1563–*c.* 1626). Composer, lutenist. Continental traveller (particularly Italy). His *First Booke of Songes or Ayres of Foure Partes, with Tableture for the Lute*, 1597 was immensely popular, and was followed by three others. Dowland is notable for his melodic perfection and the ability of his settings to accommodate words with a delightful naturalness. His '. . . heavenly touch/Upon the Lute, doth ravish humaine sense' (Barnfield).

Drake, Sir Francis (*c.* 1545–95). English admiral. The scourge of the Spanish by his officially-sanctioned privateering on the Spanish Main and in the West Indies. He penetrated the Panama isthmus and later reached the Brazilian coast and the estuary of the River Plate. He reached Java, the Cape of Good Hope and Guinea in his circumnavigation of the world. He died in the West Indies.

Drummond, William, of Hawthornden (1585–1649). Scottish man of letters. Memorable for his conversations with Ben Jonson (published 1842) containing references to Shakespeare.

Dryden, John (1631–1700). Critic, poet, playwright. Author of *All for Love* — his version of the Antony and Cleopatra story — it falls far short of Shakespeare's. Dryden, while respecting Shakespeare's genius, lamented his lapses from 'good taste' and from strict neo-classical rules of composition and decorum. Dryden was heavily involved in adaptations of Shakespeare's plays. (*See* Commonwealth and Restoration.)

El Greco (1541–1614). Religious sculptor and painter, architect, born in Crete but associated with Toledo, Spain.

Elizabeth I, Queen (1533–1603). Daughter of Anne Boleyn and Henry VIII, the shrewdest, most self-willed, unpredictable and stylish monarch in the history of the English throne. The times were ripe for her and she was right for the times. England was flexing its muscles preparatory to its emergence as a major European (and later, world) power. Fortunately, she was a lover of music, poetry and theatre, otherwise the pressures of Puritan constriction and official censorship might well have stunted the growth of what turned out to be the most prolific of ages in the history of culture. Shakespeare refers to her, but only obliquely — it was never wise to be too explicit, and he was a master of the sidelong glance. The nearest to a direct reference is in *Henry VIII*, and there is a possible reference in *A Midsummer Night's Dream* ('. . . the imperial votaress'). Sonnet 107 may also be an indirect comment on her.

Essex, Robert Devereux, Earl of (1566–1601). 2nd Earl, became Queen Elizabeth's favourite and, some thought and think, her lover. Eventually his marriage and political and military indiscretions alienated them and, following a disastrous military adventure in Ireland, he was banished her presence. In February 1601 he led a band of disaffected men (including the Earl of Southampton) in a hopeless attempt to seize the crown. Essex was executed, Southampton spared. Shakespeare probably knew him (some believe Hamlet is based upon his character). A more specific connection was that the day before his abortive attempt on the crown his supporters paid the Lord Chamberlain's Men specially to perform Shakespeare's *Richard II* with its vivid scene depicting usurpation. The Queen apparently took no action against the players or Shakespeare.

Fawkes, Guy (1570–1605). Eternalized by his participation in Gunpowder Plot. A fanatic in religion, his courage and coolness fated him to be chosen for the actual deed. Shakespeare was at the height of his fame, and writing tragedies at the time. He may well have known about the plot (Catesby, a conspirator, owned Bishopton Manor, near Stratford, and land at Lapworth, ten miles away) but, displaying typical caution, he avoided it in his plays.

Fitton, Mary (*c.* 1578–1647). From a Cheshire family, immortalized by an untenable theory that she was Shakespeare's 'Dark Lady' of the sonnets. Two portraits of her show her as a fair lady.

Forman, Simon (1552–1611). Astrologer — a respected profession in Elizabethan England, though sometimes officially disapproved of. Gained court favour by prescribing love-potions. Memorable for notebook containing accounts of performances of *Macbeth*, *The Winter's Tale*, *Cymbeline*.

Frobisher, Martin (1535–94). English navigator who voyaged to Guinea, Africa, etc. In 1576 he searched for the elusive north-west passage. He discovered Frobisher's Bay and Jackman's Sound while looking for gold in the area. His patron was the Earl of Warwick.

Galileo Galilei (1564–1642). Astronomer/philosopher of Pisa, born in same year as Shakespeare. His discoveries were prodigious and their implications are in stark contrast to the 'mediaeval' notion of the universe which dominates Shakespeare's plays.

Gibbons, Orlando (1583–1625). Great organist of the Chapel Royal and then of Westminster Abbey. Shakespeare probably knew his church music, madrigals and other work for viols and virginals, and may have known him.

Gilbert, William (1540–1603). Virtual discoverer of the science of magnetism, and physician-in-ordinary to Queen Elizabeth. Both Galileo and Erasmus respected him. He used the word 'electric'. Shakespeare may well at least have heard of him, but he displays virtually no contact whatsoever with scientific ideas or inventions.

Greville, Sir Fulke, Lord Brooke (1554–1628). English poet born in Warwickshire and buried in St Mary's Church, Warwick. Friend of Sir Philip Sidney, and possibly of Shakespeare. Chancellor of the Exchequer for seven years — this, however, did not prevent his being killed by his servant.

Hakluyt, Richard (*c.* 1552–1616). Geographer, clergyman, writer. Collected accounts of English voyages which he published in 1589 in what became known as Hakluyt's *Voyages*. The opening scene of *The Tempest* has been attributed to Shakespeare's reading of an account of a shipwreck in Bermuda published by Samuel Purchas who inherited Hakluyt's collection and added to it.

Hall(e), Edward (*c.* 1498–1547). Lawyer and political servant of Henry VIII. Wrote *The Union of the Two Noble and Illustre Famelies of Lancastre and York*, completed and published posthumously by Richard Grafton, 1548. Major source for Shakespeare's English history plays, particularly *Henry VI*. In 1944 claims were made that handwritten notes in the margins of the 1550 edition are in Shakespeare's hand.

Hals, Frans (*c.* 1580–1666). Flemish painter of exquisite portraits, including 'The Laughing Cavalier'.

Hawkins, Sir John (1532–95). English naval commander. First Englishman to enter the slave-trade. Captain of a ship in defeat of Spanish Armada.

Henslowe, Philip (d. 1616). *See* Henslowe's Diary; Elizabethan Theatre.

Herbert, George (1593–1633). Poet and divine, born in Wales. His religious poetry is characterized by an easiness of movement and sound and for its use of day-to-day language — giving his intense faith a powerful immediacy.

Herbert, Henry, 2nd Earl of Pembroke (*c.* 1534–1601). His third wife was Mary Herbert. Patron of Pembroke's Men, to which company Shakespeare may have belonged before joining Lord Chamberlain's.

Herbert, Mary, Countess of Pembroke (1561–1621). Remarkable testimony to female ability to resist male monopoly of artistic (and other) pursuits in 16th century. Sister of Philip Sidney, married Henry

Herbert, Earl of Pembroke. Spenser dedicated his *Ruines of Time*, and Sidney wrote *The Countess of Pembroke's Arcadia*, for her; she was Samuel Daniel's patron. She was a great entertainer and confidante of poets, playwrights and royalty.

Herbert, William, 3rd Earl of Pembroke (1580–1630). Son of Henry and Mary Herbert. Believed by some to be the 'Mr. W.H.' of Shakespeare's sonnets. The First Folio is dedicated to him and his brother Philip. His mistress, Mary Fitton, put forward as the 'Dark Lady' of the sonnets.

Herrick, Robert (1591–1674). English poet, author of 'Gather ye Rosebuds . . .' Man of fashion who frequented the Mermaid Tavern two decades after Shakespeare had been a drinker there.

Hilliard, Nicholas (1537–1619). Superb miniature painter, who became portrait-painter to Queen Elizabeth. A miniature attributed to him called 'The Somerville' is supposedly a portrait of Shakespeare. It is remarkably unlike either Shakespeare's bust at Stratford Church or the Droeshout engraving in the First Folio (*see* Shakespeare's Appearance). Elizabeth, Sidney, Raleigh, Drake, among others, sat for him.

Holinshed, Raphael (d. *c.* 1580). Compiled and edited proposed history of world from the Flood to reign of Elizabeth. The only portion published — *The first volume of the chronicles of England, Scotlande and Irelande . . . conteyning the description and chronicles of England from the first inhabiting unto the conquest*, 1577, 1578 — was a major source for Shakespeare's history plays of England.

Hudson, Henry (d. 1611). English navigator employed by Muscovy Company, and, eventually, Dutch East India Company. Explored Hudson River, 1607, and Hudson Bay, 1610.

Ivan the Terrible (1530–84). Tsar of Russia, Grand Duke of Moscow, he conquered Kazan, Astrakhan and Siberia. He was a good ruler but ruthless and peremptory about human life. Shakespeare, who does not mention places and peoples much nearer home, surprisingly refers, in *Love's Labour's Lost*, both to 'Muscovy' and 'Muscovite'.

Jaggard Family. *See* Printing and Publishing.

James VI (and I) (1566–1625). King James VI of Scotland (1567–1625), King James I of England (1603–25). Son of Mary, Queen of Scots and assiduous patron of theatre (*see* Chamberlain's/King's Men) and of dramatists. Shakespeare's writing of *Macbeth* may well have been partly motivated by a desire to flatter him.

Jones, Inigo (1573–1651). England's greatest scenic designer and painter and architect (he designed the piazza in old Covent Garden). Collaborator with Ben Jonson in staging of masques. No evidence exists that Shakespeare ever employed him, but he must surely have known him — if only through Jonson.

Kepler, Johann (1571–1630). Astronomer, born Württemberg. His first work followed traditional (mediaeval) astrological lines but his later work was more certainly in astronomy. His laws of 'equal areas' and 'elliptical orbits' are part of the foundation of modern astronomical studies. Shakespeare, of whom Kepler was a near-contemporary, either did not know, or chose to avoid, the new study of the heavens and his plays are replete with references to, thematic uses of, the old astrological ways.

Leicester, Robert Dudley, Earl of (*c.* 1532–88). Favourite of Queen Elizabeth. In 1560 his wife, Amy Robsart, died mysteriously and it was believed that he or Elizabeth had planned it. Commanded expedition to Netherlands, 1585, and became its inefficient Governor.

Mary, Queen of England (1516–58). Elder daughter of Henry VIII by Catherine of Aragon. Distinguished linguist, indefatigably Catholic and half-sister of Elizabeth. In 1553 she succeeded her brother, Edward VI. In attempting to restore status of Catholicism in England, recklessly married Philip II of Spain. Much bloodshed and burning of heretics characterized her reign, giving her the name 'Bloody Mary'.

Mary, Queen of Scots (1542–87). Daughter of James V of Scotland by Mary of Guise. Became Queen when a week old. Married the Dauphin of France, but lost her influence there on his death. Married Darnley, her cousin, who became titular King of Scotland. Their son became James I of England. After Darnley's murder, Mary became wife of Bothwell, but rebellion in Scotland caused her to fly to England. Elizabeth imprisoned Mary, fearing her as a rival for the English throne (Mary had a right of succession). Eventually she was executed, becoming something of a Catholic martyr. Her body lies in Westminster Abbey.

Medici, Cosimo di (1519–74). Duke of Florence, Grand Duke of Tuscany. One of the extraordinary Medici family whose political and military deviousness and power, both in Florence and Rome, from the mid-14th to the end of the 16th century was equalled only by its astonishing patronage of Brunelleschi, Michelozzo, Donatello, Gozzoli, Michelangelo, Botticelli, Raphael. Began the famous Uffizi collection of paintings in Florence.

Mercator, Gerhard (1512–94). Mathematician of German origin. He projected meridians on maps as equidistant parallel lines, and latitudes as parallel straight lines at right angles to them. Shakespeare seems not to have been aware of his map.

Meres, Francis (1565–1647). Rector and schoolmaster. Invaluable source of evidence about reputations of Elizabethan dramatists — see his *Palladis Tamia, Wit's Treasury*, 1598. He wrote of Shakespeare that he was 'mellifluous and honey-tongued', had a 'sweete wittie soule', was 'the most excellent' in comedy and tragedy. If, he writes, the

Muses spoke English they 'would speak with *Shakespeares* fine, filed phrase'. Meres informs us that Shakespeare's sonnets were circulating among his friends in 1598.

Michelangelo (1475–1564). He died the year Shakespeare was born, and we can only speculate whether the world's greatest dramatist heard of or saw the work of the world's greatest sculptor.

Milton, John (1608–74). Great English poet, dramatist and pampleteer. One of his first published poems, entitled *An Epitaph on the Admirable Dramatick Poet, W. Shakespeare*, which appeared anonymously contains the famous words — '. . . sweetest Shakespeare, Fancy's child,/Warble his native wood-notes wild.'

Montaigne, Michel Eyquem de (1533–92). French essayist who broke a long period of retirement and intellectual reflection to become Mayor of Bordeaux. His *Essais* (a word which he coined for a form he virtually invented) appeared in 1580 (Book 1) and 1588 (Books 2 and 3). Translated into English by John Florio, 1603. Verbal echoes of Montaigne have been claimed as present in *Hamlet, King Lear* and *The Tempest*.

Monteverde(i), Claudio (1568–1643). Originator of modern style of musical composition. Born Mantua.

Morley, Thomas (1557–1602). English musician. Organist at St Paul's. Composed madrigals and church music.

Murillo, Bartolome Esteban (1617–82). Spanish painter, born Seville.

Neville, Alexander (1544–1614). Classicist and translator of Seneca's plays. His version of Seneca's *Oedipus* appeared in a translation in *Seneca his Tenne Tragedies*, 1581, a volume which may have influenced Shakespeare in his writing of *Titus Andronicus*.

Overbury, Thomas (1581–1613). His delightful collection of *Characters* (types and professions) immortalizes his name. He was poisoned very slowly to death in the Tower of London for his opposition to the marriage of the divorced Countess of Essex to Robert Carr (later Earl of Somerset).

Oxford, Edward de Vere, 17th Earl of (1550–1604). One of the men claimed to be the author of Shakespeare's plays. He was a favoured courtier, a delightful poet and, it was said, wrote plays. None of the plays has survived and, like the Baconian theory, the Oxford theory of authorship of Shakespeare has no basis; it was propounded in 1920 by a gentleman with the not-inappropriate name of J. T. Looney.

Palladio, Andrea (1518–80). Architect, born Padua. Designed, for example, San Georgio Maggiore in Venice. His book, *I Quattro Libri dell'Architettura*, 1570, influenced Inigo Jones and, therefore, early 17th-century theatre/stage design.

Platter, Thomas (*fl.* 1599). Swiss doctor who, on his travels in England, September/October 1599, recorded his experience of a performance of *Julius Caesar* — 'I went with my companions over the water, and in the strewn roof-house saw the tragedy of the first Emperor Julius with at least fifteen characters very well acted. At the end of the comedy [play] they danced according to their custom with extreme elegance.' Gives invaluable information about the stage, galleries and prices of admission.

Pocahontas (1595–1617). Indian princess, daughter of Virginian chief. Married John Rolfe, one of original Jamestown settlers. Came to England in year of Shakespeare's death. Buried Gravesend, London.

Poussin, Claude (1593–1665). Worked mostly in Rome; of French origin and regarded as first French classical painter. He illustrated a 1623 edition of Ovid's *Metamorphoses* (which had earlier been used as a source by Shakespeare).

Raleigh, Sir Walter (*c.* 1552–1618). A delightful lyric poet, a not very successful politician, a brave soldier and adventurer, a tactless but probably honest courtier (he married one of the Queen's maids of honour, much to Elizabeth's wrath) and an atheist. His last letter to his wife and children, written while awaiting execution, is a touching indication that he was also probably a dutiful husband and father.

Rembrandt van Rijn (1606–69). One of the world's greatest painters. Born Leiden, Holland. Famous particularly for astonishing series, over a period of years, of self-portraits.

Rubens, Sir Peter Paul (1577–1640). Great Flemish artist, especially painter. Spent much time in Rome.

Rutland, Francis Manners, 6th Earl of (1578–1632). *See* Impresa.

Sidney, Sir Philip (1554–86). Poet, critic, courtier. Most glamorous, popular and, seemingly, attractive courtier/scholar of the 16th century. His many qualities were utilized as poet, diplomat and soldier. Killed at Zutphen during one of the politico/religious battles fought in the Low Countries during the century. His *Apologie for Poetrie*, a graceful, wise and important critical essay on the art, revealing the kind of classical learning ideally regarded as necessary by a cultivated gentleman of the time, reflects a civilized and imaginative mind. *Arcadia* (a pastoral novel) was published in 1590 and his sonnet sequence *Astrophel and Stella* — inspired by his frustrated love of Penelope Devereux — in 1591 in an unauthorized edition.

Southampton, Henry Wriothesley, 3rd Earl of (1573–1624). Well-known patron of the arts — particularly literature. Favourite of Queen Elizabeth and friend of Essex, whose rebellion he joined. His death sentence was commuted to life imprisonment. He was released on accession of Jame I. *Venus and Adonis* is dedicated to him, as is *Lucrece*. Some believe that the 'Mr. W.H.' of the sonnets is a disguise for Henry Wriothesley. Others believe a very strong relationship existed between him and Shakespeare.

Spenser, Edmund (1552–99). One of England's greatest poets — *The Faerie Queene*, 1590–6 and *The Shepherd's Calendar*, 1579, entitle him to the accolade apart from his sonnets and *Epithalamion*, 1595. Shakespeare's early plays strongly influenced by Spenser's language — lyrical, highly wrought, elaborately imaged.

Tallis, Thomas (1515–85). English composer and teacher (*see* William Byrd). Specialized in church music.

Tate, Nahum (1652–1715). Dramatist and adaptor—e.g. of *King Lear*, *Richard II* and *Coriolanus*. (*See* Commonwealth and Restoration.)

Tintoretto, Jacopo Robusi (1518–94). Venetian painter. Before beginning a picture he experimented with wax models of his intended figures arranged on a miniature stage and lit from different angles — the same technique employed by stage-directors for 'blocking' (i.e. visually preparing) their productions.

Titian (Tiziano Vecellio) (*c.* 1487–1576). Italian painter of Venetian school. His influence, particularly in the handling of colour in oils, has been immense.

Vega Carpio, Lope Felix de (1562–1635). Spanish dramatist and poet who dominated the Spanish literary scene as Dr Johnson did in England. He wrote probably about 560 plays of all kinds. Two years older than Shakespeare, there seems to have been no contact between them.

Veronese, Paolo Caliare (*c.* 1528–88). Painter, born Verona.

Walton, Isaac (1593–1683). Famous for his book, *The Compleat Angler*, 1653, an exquisite view of the art and craft of fishing. His *Lives* — consisting of biographies, with critical comments — is an underrated wealth of information on, and reflection about, contemporary writers.

Weever, John (1576–1632). Poet who, in *Epigrammes in the oldest Cut, and newest Fashion*, pub. 1599, included a poem on Shakespeare which refers to him as 'honie-tong'd'. In *The mirror of Martyrs or the life and death of Sir John Oldcastle* he involved himself in the row which resulted because of the resentment of the Oldcastles at Shakespeare's version of one of their ancestors in the character of Falstaff.

Worcester, Bishop of. The incumbent Bishop of Worcester had ecclesiastical control of church affairs in Shakespeare's town (Worcester is approximately thirty miles from Stratford). For example, marriage licences (*see* Licence) had to be obtained from him.

Wren, Sir Christopher (1632–1723). Architect and scientist. Builder of St Paul's and fifty-two other London churches, but not all survive. His work was not confined to London, as commonly believed — he was involved in building the libraries of Lincoln Cathedral, Trinity College, Cambridge, and repairing Salisbury Cathedral, among many other works.

America. Name derived from Amerigo Vespucci. Land discovered by
Columbus, 1492, is now debated by claims involving Norse seamen.
Successive European attempts at colonization dominated by Spain and
England, with both in fierce contention during the Elizabethan period.
Shakespeare uses the word in *The Comedy of Errors* but associates it with
'Indies' — presumably the West Indies. (*See* Drake, Raleigh, Hawkins,
California, Virginia.)

Aston Cantlow. Village eight miles north-west of Stratford. Probable
marriage-place of John Shakespeare and Mary Arden.

Baffin Bay. The name given to the sea-area between Baffinland (a large
island off the north-east coast of Canada) and Greenland.

Bankside. One of Elizabethan London's least salubrious areas; part of
Southwark and extending half a mile west of London Bridge, south
side. Site of swamp, the Clink prison, brothels, bear and bull baiting.
Shakespeare probably lived there 1596–9 — it was also site of Swan,
Hope, Rose, Globe theatres.

Bell, The (Carter Lane). London inn from which Richard Quiney wrote
to Shakespeare as his 'Loveing good ffrend and contreymann' in 1598,
asking for a loan. The Bell Inn was near St Paul's.

Bermudas (Bermoothes). *See* Glossary. Shakespeare calls them 'Bermoothes' — 'to fetch dew from the still vexed Bermoothes' (*The
Tempest*, I.ii.229). 'Vexed' refers to their reputation for stormy weather
and the large incidence of shipwrecks. This is a rare example (given
piquancy by its appearance in *The Tempest*, with its shipwreck) of Shakespeare's direct reference to a place discovered during his own century,
or immediately before it. In 1609 Sir George Somers's ship was wrecked
off Bermuda, which was still uninhabited. *The Tempest* was written *c*. 1611.

Bishopsgate (St Helen's). St Helen's, parish in ward of Bishopsgate.
Shakespeare lived there 1596, and defaulted in tax payment.

Bishopton. A hamlet one mile north of Stratford (though in Victorian
times it had pretensions as a spa) in which were located tithes bought by
Shakespeare in 1605.

Blackfriars. The area abutting St Paul's cathedral. The Blackfriars
Theatre, which Shakespeare's company, the King's Men, leased in 1609
was about 100 yards south-west of the cathedral.

California (New Albion). In 1579 Sir Francis Drake repaired his ships on the Californian coast and called the country New Albion. This is the first known English contact. Shakespeare does not mention it by name, but his plays are full of references to discovery, strange islands, adventurers.

Chapel Lane. Runs east-west from Chapel Street to the river at Stratford. Shakespeare bought copyhold of cottage there from W. Getley, 1602. Its proximity to New Place suggests purchase for servant or gardener. In 1638 the property was in the possession of Susanna and Dr John Hall.

Chapel Street. Chapel Street is the mid-portion of the long main street of Stratford, of which the north section is High Street, and the south, Church Street. The Chapel referred to is the Guild Chapel. Shakespeare's house, New Place, stood where Chapel Lane joins Chapel Street.

Cripplegate (St Giles). One of the seven gates (the others are Bishopsgate, Moorgate, Aldersgate, Aldgate, Newgate, Ludgate) in the ancient walls of London which gave entrance and exit to principal thoroughfares. Cripplegate was on the north side, not far from St Paul's. Shakespeare lodged there for a time.

Gray's Inn. *See* Inns of Court.

Greenhill Street. Sometimes known as More Towns End, in Stratford. Shakespeare's father bought a freehold estate with croft and garden from George Turner in 1556.

Hampton Court. One of Queen Elizabeth's palaces. (*See* Courts.)

Henley Street. Site of house now designated as Shakespeare's birthplace. By 1552 Shakespeare's father was either a tenant or householder in Henley Street — probably in the western end of a large double-house which later became known as Shakespeare's Birthplace. In modern Stratford the headquarters of the Shakespeare Birthplace Trust, with its records office containing books and manuscripts and a fine library, is situated in Henley Street. (*See* Stratford upon Avon and Shakespeare.)

Holy Trinity Church. The parish church of Stratford, with portions dating from the 13th century. Shakespeare and members of his family were buried there. (*See* Myths, Legends and Mysteries; Stratford upon Avon and Shakespeare.)

Ireland. The persistence of Ireland in the British consciousness, and of its problem in British political history, is exemplified by events in Shakespeare's lifetime. Fierce rebellions, incited by religious fanaticism and/or claims for territory, raged. Both the Spanish and the British took sides. In 1595 Elizabeth sent the Earl of Essex to quell Tyrone's rebellion. Essex made peace and returned home in disgrace. Underlying the violence of the time was the Irish resistance to the Reformation, and the important role it played in the Spanish/English power game. Shakespeare, in *Henry V*, perhaps judiciously makes his Irish captain a wild, reckless quarreller.

Jamestown. First permanent English settlement founded there, 13 May 1607. Shakespeare does not mention it, but in his plays — *see* e.g. *Pericles, The Tempest* — the sense of voyaging and exploration is very strong.

Kenilworth. Town fourteen miles north-east of Stratford. Site of Earl of Leicester's castle which Queen Elizabeth granted him and visited (*see* Progress) 1566, 1572, 1575. The ruins of the castle still stand and are a fascinating tourist attraction.

London. In Elizabethan times, as now, the mecca for those in England seeking excitement, bustle, variety of entertainment, possible commercial, social and political advancement. Its area was well defined — southern boundary, the Thames; northern boundary created by line running from Fleet River (west) to Tower (east) in semicircle. City was surrounded by walls with gates (e.g. Aldgate, Billingsgate). By 1600 approximately 200,000 population in the whole complex. This cosmopolitan centre, which traded with many European countries, was the centre, in almost a monopolistic sense, of the country's trading and cultural activities and, in Elizabeth's time, exercised powerful political control over the rest of the country. Except for oases of gardens behind the walls of noble houses, the city was an untidy, filthy place with open sewers. The Thames, which abounded with fish, was a busy thoroughfare, crossed by the famous London Bridge — the only one. St Paul's was the focal point for social and commercial activities — lawyers met their clients in the main aisle, and advertisements (some for play performances) adorned the walls. The inns were numerous and were the centres of gossip. The theatres were notorious.

Newfoundland. Large island at mouth of St Lawrence River, Canada, discovered by John Cabot, 1497.

New Hampshire. North-eastern state of USA. Part of New England.

New Place. Shakespeare's purchase, on 4 May 1597, of this, the second largest house in Stratford, signalled his restoration of the family's prestige after his father's disgrace and the assertion of his own affluence. He paid £60 to Wm Underhill. The house was built *c.* 1490 by Sir Hugh Clopton and stood at the corner of Chapel Street and Chapel Lane. It was, according to Leland, an antiquary, 'a praty [pretty] house of bricke and tymbre'. After Shakespeare's death its history is indistinct, but in 1759 its owner, Rev. Francis Gastrell, destroyed it in pique at the intrusion of his privacy by inquisitive visitors. The beautiful garden remains.

Newington Butts. Village of Newington, one mile from London Bridge, in Surrey. Theatre called N. Butts ('butts' are archery targets) built possibly *c.* 1576, and managed by Henslowe. Shakespeare's company performed there for ten days in 1594 playing, among other things, *Titus Andronicus, Hamlet* and possibly *The Merchant of Venice*.

Old Stratford. Often called Old Town, it consists of the area around Holy Trinity Church and, presumably, is the site of the mediaeval Stratford. It consists now of a number of streets (e.g. West Street, Bull Street, Broad Street) and is largely a residential area of small terrace houses, though there is also some small industry. The Shakespeare family did not live in Old Town.

Orinoco. River of northern S. America, flowing north and east through Venezuela to Atlantic.

Ottawa River. Tributary of St Lawrence River, Canada, on which capital city is situated.

St Helen's Parish. In Bishopsgate, north London. On 15 November 1597 the 'Petty Collectors' (tax men) made a list of people who had not paid their taxes, through death, or deliberate avoidance, or absence. Shakespeare is assessed at 5 shillings on goods valued at £5.

Shoreditch. North, outside London city limits; site of The Theatre and the Curtain. Dangerous area of prostitutes, pickpockets, muggers.

Shottery. One and a half miles from Stratford, village famous as home of Anne Hathaway. In the marriage bond she is referred to as 'of Stratford'. Her home is a mecca for tourists and is a well-preserved example of a reasonably affluent Elizabethan farming family.

Southwark. District (now borough) of Surrey on south side of Thames. In Shakespeare's time London Bridge led directly into it. Bankside was part of Southwark. Site of church of St Mary Overies (now Southwark Cathedral). Shakespeare's brother, Edmund, described in the burial register as 'a Player base borne', was buried at St Saviour's Cathedral in Southwark on New Year's Eve, 1607, with a 'forenoone knell of ye great bell'. The cost of this peal with the funeral was 20 shillings — a considerable sum. Perhaps it was paid for this failed actor by his illustrious brother.

Stratford upon Avon. In 1570s a busy agricultural centre of 2,000 population. Received charter of civic independence in 1553 and subsequently governed by corporation. (*See* Stratford upon Avon and Shakespeare.)

Surrey. Southern English county in which part of the vast conurbation of London is now situated.

Sussex. One of England's southern counties. In the 16th century the Earl of Sussex's company of players was well known in the provinces for its touring.

Temple Grafton. Six miles west of Stratford, centre of mystery concerning Shakespeare's marriage (*see* Myths, Legends and Mysteries; Marriage). Possible site of Shakespeare's wedding. The vicar at the time was John Frith, described in a Puritan survey as 'an old priest and unsound in religion, he can neither preach nor read well, his chiefest trade is to cure hawks that are hurt or diseased, for which purpose many do usually repair to him'. *See* Oliver Martext in *As You Like It* for a possible fictional version of old Frith.

Virginia. First permanent English settlement in N. America. Walter Raleigh is persistently associated with it but he did not colonize it, though he named the land he explored 'Virginia' — after Queen Elizabeth's vaunted maidenhead. The period 1583–8 was active with landings on the coast, and Shakespeare must have known of Raleigh's exploits. (*See* Jamestown.)

Whitehall. One of Elizabeth's royal palaces. (*See* Courts.)

Wilmcote. Three and a half miles north-west of Stratford, small village, home of Shakespeare's mother, Mary Arden. House, superbly preserved, still remains.

Worcester. City, thirty miles west of Stratford and, in the 16th century, centre of religious diocese including Stratford. Register of Shakespeare's marriage preserved there.

TERMS OF REFERENCE

Acting Companies. *See* Elizabethan Theatre.

Actresses. *See* Principal Shakespearean Actors and Actresses; Shakespeare on the Stage.

Aldermen. Senior (i.e. 'elder' men) members of a local council, elected for their status, experience and sometimes for their financial reliability or affluence.

Allusions. Shakespeare's plays, in common with his contemporaries', contain allusions of many kinds — literary, historical, geographical, topical, etc. These constitute not only a fascinating record of what his mind and imagination retained but a valuable help to dating the plays, e.g. a reference in *Henry V* to Essex's Irish Expedition makes its date of composition certain, between March and September 1599.

Anachronisms. Shakespeare, not uniquely in his age, was obviously careless or inattentive about details. For example clocks are mentioned in *Julius Caesar*, his Romans wear hats and gloves, and Caesar a doublet (doubtless Shakespeare saw his Romans in Elizabethan actors' costume). He also 'mixes' genres — in *The Winter's Tale*, a pagan Delphic oracle, a Christian interment and an Emperor of Russia all rub shoulders.

Anonymous (Publications). Elizabethan publishing is replete with anonymous authors. The widespread practice of multiple authorship of plays makes it certain that the part-authors of many are unknown to us, since only the name of the major or best-known participant appears on the title-page. 'Anon' may disguise well-known writers. The dangers of falling foul of censorship or official disapproval made anonymity sometimes a necessity.

Apocrypha. Thirty-seven plays are attributed to Shakespeare, but, particularly in the 19th century, many others were claimed for him, including *The Two Noble Kinsmen* and a fragment — *Sir Thomas More*. The First Folio of 1623 is regarded by most as containing all of Shakespeare's work, but apocryphal works (e.g. *Locrine, A Yorkshire Tragedy*) appear in the Third Folio, 1663.

Arms (Coat-of-). In mediaeval times the display of horse-trappings, shields, coats and helmets decorated with distinctive symbols (the 'arms') was essentially connected with military prowess. By Shakespeare's time the possession of a coat-of-arms was a mark of gentlemanly distinction. They had to be applied for to the College of Heralds who decided the merits of the application and the nature of the heraldic devices to be issued. John Shakespeare applied for a coat-of-arms in 1568/9, but it was not granted till later (perhaps 1599). Its description is 'in a field of gold upon a bend sable a spear of the first, the point upward headed argent, with a crest of a falcon with his wings displayed, standing on a wreath of his colours, supporting a spear, armed, headed, and steeled silver'. Reproductions of the arms include the motto 'Non Sans Droict'. The Shakespeare family, however, never used this motto.

Audience. *See* Shakespeare on the Stage.

Authenticity. Who Shakespeare was and who wrote Shakespeare's plays are the two more extreme questions asked by sceptics. On a more serious level the authenticity of some or part of some plays in the First Folio has been and is seriously debated. For example, *Henry VIII* is almost certainly largely by Fletcher and various other hands have been mooted for sections of the three parts of *Henry VI*. *The Taming of a Shrew*, an anonymous play with strong resemblances to Shakespeare's *The Shrew*, is believed by some to be an earlier version of Shakespeare. (*See* Myths, Legends and Mysteries.)

Baconian Theory. Notion begun by American, Delia Bacon, 1857, claiming Bacon's authorship of Shakespeare's plays on grounds that only Bacon had intellectual equipment sufficient. Subsequent Baconians perpetuated the theory and 'supported' it by, for example, alleged discovery of a cypher in the plays proving Bacon's authorship, and parallel expressions in his works and the plays. Baconian Society formed 1886. Eccentric notion persists — without any rational basis.

Bailiff. In England, a Sheriff's or county court's delegate who served writs, warrants, processes of all kinds, but especially for debt or non-payment of rent. They were especially active in Elizabethan England. Shakespeare refers to a 'Bum-bailiff'.

Baptism. Children were baptized as soon as possible (usually within three days) in Elizabethan England because of the very high infant mortality rate. Shakespeare's baptism and that of members of his family is recorded in Holy Trinity Church, Stratford.

Bear-Baiting. A popular spectacle legitimized by Henry VIII and, in London, practised in Southwark. Henslowe was as notorious a presenter of bear-baiting as of plays. There were two versions: (1) a chained bear was attacked by six mastiffs; (2) a blinded bear was attacked by dogs. The bear usually survived.

Belott-Mountjoy. Name given to a legal dispute involving: (1) Christopher Mountjoy, a tiara-maker; (2) Mary Mountjoy, his daughter; (3) his son-in-law and apprentice, Stephen Belott. Belott affirmed in court that on his marriage to Mary (19 November 1604) he was promised £60 (dowry) and £200 eventually (in Mountjoy's will). By 1612 neither promise was fulfilled and Belott sued. Shakespeare, who lodged at Mountjoy's in 1604, was witness to the original terms, and made deposition which included that he knew Mountjoy and Belott 'as he now remembrethe for the space of tenne yeres or thereaboutes', that Belott 'did well and honestly behave himselfe', that Mountjoy 'did all the tyme of the said complainantes service with him beare and shew great good will and affeccion towardes the said complainant', that 'he knoweth not what implementes and necessaries of household stuffe the defendant gave the plaintiff in marriadge with his daughter Marye'. Belott won the suit.

Bibles. Shakespeare mentions the Bible directly only once (*The Merry Wives of Windsor*) and one of its books (Numbers) only (*Henry V*). His references to personages, and his allusions, quotations, paraphrases are not profuse but frequent, and used naturally as if he were well-acquainted with the Bible and expected his audience to be. Typical examples of usage are: in *Richard II* (Judas), *The Merchant of Venice* ('The quality of mercy') and in the quotations in *Henry VI*. Bibles available to Shakespeare were: (1) two Wycliffite translations; (2) Tyndale's New Testament; (3) Coverdale's Bible; (4) Thomas Matthew's Bible; (5) the Great Bible — an official version with a preface by Cranmer (2nd edition); (6) the Genevan Bible (sometimes called 'Breeches Bible'); (7) the Bishop's Bible — another official version. Shakespeare seems to have used (6) and (7) mostly, together with the *Book of Common Prayer*.

Blackfriars Theatre. *See* Elizabethan Theatre.

Blank Verse. Commonly used to describe Shakespeare's poetic structure, and introduced into England early in the 16th century. The first blank verse play was *Gorboduc* by Sackville and Norton (*c.* 1560). The characteristics of Shakespeare's blank verse are: (1) it is unrhymed; (2) it is usually found with five beats of emphasis in a ten-syllabled line — e.g. 'Oh whát a rógue and péasant sláve am Í'; (3) in its mature state it is very flexible in rhythm and in its ability to run on from one line to another, avoiding an impression of mechanical movement — e.g. 'Whether 'tis nobler in the mind to suffer/The slings and arrows of outrageous fortune'.

Bond. On 28 November 1582 two Stratford citizens (Fulke Sandells and John Richardson) took out a bond indemnifying the Bishop of Worcester if anything should occur to prevent the marriage of 'William Shagspere and Anne Hathwey of Stratford'. The bond strengthens the case of those who believe that Shakespeare intended to marry Anne Whateley, not Hathaway. (*See* Licence; Marriage; Myths, Legends and Mysteries.)

Book. In the Elizabethan theatre the 'book' was what we would call a prompt copy. This was the acting version of the author's text, after cutting, modification and preparation for performance. This was prepared by the Book-keeper whose duties included submitting it to the Master of the Revels for censoring. (*See* The Text.)

Boy Actors. It is generally accepted that no women appeared in public theatres before 1660. Well-trained boys played the female parts, progressing to the most exacting through a two or three years' apprenticeship to established actors. (*See* Children's Companies; Elizabethan Theatre.)

Breach (of the Peace). An offence against public order, or a disturbance of public peace, or any act likely to create or incite disorder. Shakespeare's father was bound over for breaches of the peace during Shakespeare's youth in Stratford.

Bull-Baiting. Much the same as bear-baiting, with the occasional frisson of observing a monkey mounted on the bull's back while dogs attacked.

Burial. Legend has attached itself to Shakespeare's burial-place; one, in particular, has attachment to both fact and respectability. Washington Irving, visiting Holy Trinity Church in the 19th century, claims he looked into Shakespeare's grave when earth gave in from an adjoining grave. He saw nothing, according to one report; he saw a skull according to another. In the 20th century strenuous attempts have been made to obtain permission to open the grave. They have received dusty answers. The following considerations must be reflected on by anyone planning to open the grave with the hope of finding 'lost' documents, or even bones: (1) Flesh, bone and vellum would have a chance of survival only if buried in a lead coffin. The chances of Shakespeare's being so casketed are infinitesimal — lead was expensive. (2) It could well be that he was buried very deep (it was a frequent custom in the 16th century) and below river flood-level. As the gravedigger in *Hamlet* says: '. . . your water is a sore decayer of your whoreson dead body' (V. i). (3) It was not the custom to put documents in coffins. (*See* Myths, Legends and Mysteries.)

Bust, Shakespeare's. *See* Shakespeare's Appearance.

Chamberlain's/King's Men. The company of actors to which Shakespeare was attached for the greater part of his working life. The Chamberlain was a royal official responsible for the sovereign's entertainment, wardrobe, travel, among other duties. In Elizabeth's time the Chamberlains kept a close and influential relationship with theatre in London and Shakespeare was fortunate to be a member of the Lord Chamberlain's men; it gave him access to the Court. They became the King's Men on the accession of James I.

Children's Companies. Companies of boy actors, some of great distinction and constituting great opposition to adult companies. Shakespeare has Hamlet make an unflattering reference to them as 'little eyasses' (young hawks) who are usurping the popularity of the adult players.

Chronology. The passage of time and the loss of evidence makes the actual dating of composition, first performance and publication of Shakespeare's work very difficult in a number of specific cases. The problems are compounded by the following: (1) Shakespeare, like most of his colleagues, seems to have had no interest in keeping data about the when's and wherefore's of his writing career. (2) Plays were not generally considered to be of more than transitory importance and how and when this or that version was written never bothered the heads of their creators. (3) Elizabethan publishing methods did not encourage accuracy of dating. (4) The first collected edition of Shakespeare's plays — the First Folio — gives no precise indication as to the dating of each work.

Collaborator. Collaboration in authorship was, arguably, the rule rather than the exception in Elizabethan dramatic writing (e.g. Beaumont and Fletcher). Some Elizabethan plays were constructed by as many as five or six different playwrights. The organization of the theatres, the chaotic nature of commissioning, the insatiable demand for new plays, all made collaboration a necessity. Shakespeare may well have begun his career as collaborator.

Constable. Shakespeare has two usages of this word: (1) In *Much Ado About Nothing* Dogberry is Constable of the Watch — i.e. officially appointed to be in charge of law and order in a locality. (2) In *Henry V* the Constable of France, where the word implies very high rank in the royal household.

Conveyance. A legal document or deed by which property or tithe is 'conveyed'. Shakespeare was much involved with such documents as his affluence grew.

Council. *See* Privy Council.

Courts (of Law). The two most likely best known to Shakespeare are: (1) Queen's Bench: a division of the High Court of England. It is concerned with civil matters — contract, recovery of land, etc.; also with the criminal aspect of assizes. This court can issue orders to supervise lesser courts and officials. (2) Consistory: a church court with the vicar as judge. It met every month dealing with all manner of offences and misdemeanours — including adultery, prostitution, incest, blasphemy, usury, drunkenness, absence from church, bigamy, etc. Punishment included public penance involving detailed description of the offence committed. The serious offenders wore a white sheet, carried a white rod (or wand) and were bareheaded or barefooted (cf. Coriolanus's penance in Act II, Sc. iii). The penance could be either in front of a church congregation or in the market place. Excommunication was the punishment for refusal to carry out religious duties, pay church dues, etc. (*See* Excommunication.)

Courts (Royal). The court was where Elizabeth happened to be, but she had several palaces, chiefly Whitehall in central London, used generally in winter. Nearby were St James's, Somerset House and Durham Place, housing distinguished visitors. The Tower was used only on the night before a coronation. It normally housed prisoners of note plus a lion called Edward VI, a tiger, lynx, wolf, porcupine and eagle. Greenwich Palace was downstream on the Thames, Richmond and Hampton Court upstream. Windsor was one of the oldest and largest.

Curtain, The. *See* Elizabethan Theatre.

Debt. The Shakespeare family was, apparently, immune neither from occasional slackness in paying debts nor rigorousness in collecting them. For example, in 1597 William Shakespeare owed 5 shillings tax in Bishopsgate Ward, London, but defaulted. His father was in severe financial difficulties in 1577 and in 1578 mortgaged part of his wife's inheritance to meet debts. In 1600 William owed 13s. 4d. in tax for the County of Sussex.

Demonology. James I was a writer of some enthusiasm. His *Daemonologie*, 1597 is a study of witchcraft expressed with all the fervour and extreme conviction of a Scotsman who hated, feared and persecuted those unfortunates he deemed to be witches. The book may be a minor source for *Macbeth*.

Deposition. *See* Belott-Mountjoy.

Diary. *See* Henslowe's Diary.

'Dragon'. An East India Company ship commanded by Wm Keeling who, in the journal of a voyage to the East Indies, recorded performances on board of *Hamlet* and *Richard II*, while anchored off Sierra Leone (September 1607). On 31 March 1608, on the same voyage, performance of *Hamlet* was repeated.

Droeshout Engraving. One of very few portraits of Shakespeare which merit being seriously considered as authentic likenesses. Engraved by Martin Droeshout (1601–*c*. 1650), son of a Flemish engraver. His portrait is prefixed to the First Folio, but can hardly be drawn from life (Droeshout was fifteen when Shakespeare died). He may have worked on a portrait by another, older, man. Ben Jonson evidently thought it a good likeness — in the preface to the First Folio he writes that Droeshout '. . . had a strife/with Nature, to out-do the life'. (*See* Shakespeare's Appearance.)

Enclosures. Throughout the period 15th–17th century a slow revolution in farming methods had profound social and economic results and gradually changed vast portions of the English landscape. The mediaeval system involved ownership of non-adjacent strips of land by individual peasants. In the 15th century powerful landowners enclosed (by hedges and ditches) large areas containing many strips. This benefited sheep-farming by creating large areas of pastureland, but deprived peasants of their strips for cultivation. Intermittent riots against enclosures occurred during the period. Shakespeare was heavily involved in attempts to enclose land in Stratford (*see* Tithes) which he owned or rented. Riots in Stratford took place in 1615 and 1616. It is not possible to decide if Shakespeare agreed with enclosures.

Excommunication. A form of punishment widely threatened and used in Shakespeare's time. By it, anyone committing a misdemeanour deemed to be an offence against the code and practices of the established church could be either temporarily or permanently excluded from the membership, fellowship and communion of the church. There were two forms: (a) minor — deprivation of the right to participate in the sacrament; (b) major — total excommunication. The results could be very serious, since the complete integration of religious and secular activity meant that excommunication implied a cutting off of intercourse (e.g. business, professional) from the community at large. Penalties were exacted from those who consorted with excommunicants. Susanna Shakespeare was excommunicated with her husband for marrying at a time forbidden by the church.

Folio. A size of paper (11 to 16 in. long and 8 to 11 in. wide) used in book publication, particularly for extensive work in the 16th century. Most famous is the so-called First Folio of Shakespeare's plays — the earliest collected edition, published 1623.

> DESIGNATION: *Mr. William Shakespeares Comedies, Histories, & Tragedies. Published according to the True Originale Copies.*
>
> PRINTER: Wm Jaggard and Edward Blount.
>
> PUBLISHERS: 'W. Jaggard, Ed. Blount, I. Smethweeke, and W. Aspley.'
>
> CONTENTS: 36 plays, 18 never before published.
>
> PRELIMINARY MATTER: Verse by Ben Jonson; portrait of Wm Shakespeare; dedication to Earls of Pembroke and Montgomery; epistle by editors (Heminges and Condell); two commendatory poems by Jonson and Hugh Holland; list of contents (omitting *Troilus and Cressida*); two additional commendatory poems by Leonard Digges and 'I.M.'; a list of principal actors who appeared in the plays; the plays.
>
> PRINTING: 1,000 copies (approx.). 238 still remain. 907 pages.
>
> PRICE: £1 — roughly equivalent to £25 plus today.
>
> METHOD: Five compositors of varying ability working on copy derived from various sources — e.g. author's MS, theatre prompt-text, printed quarto text.
>
> SECOND FOLIO: 1632, carefully edited version of F1.
>
> THIRD FOLIO: 1663, reprint 1664. Seven plays added to 36 of F1. Of these only *Pericles* accepted as Shakespeare's.
>
> FOURTH FOLIO: 1685. A reprint of Third Folio with much correction and modernization.

(*See* The Text; Printing and Publishing.)

Fortune Theatre. *See* Elizabethan Theatre.

Garter Ceremony. Edward III instituted the order of the Garter *c.* 1348. The emblem is blue and the motto is the famous 'Honi soi qui mal y pense'. Its patron (by association) is St George. The ceremony of induction of new additions to the twenty-six (excluding the monarch) permitted members of the order is held in St George's Chapel, Windsor, each St George's Day. Shakespeare's *The Merry Wives of Windsor* is said to have been written specially for the celebrations attending on the induction ceremony on 24 May 1597, when the patron of the Lord Chamberlain's Company was admitted to the order. Each knight has a stall in the choir of St George's Chapel and his coat-of-arms and garter-plate are placed at his stall permanently.

Garter King-of-Arms. One of the officers of the Order of the Garter. Head of the College of Heralds — royal appointees who control the granting of arms and the establishment of pedigrees.

Ghosts. The Elizabethans believed in many forms of the supernatural. Half at least of Shakespeare's plays contain some reference to spirits, goblins, demons, devils, witches, fancies, apparitions, ghosts, etc. Some of his most powerful dramatic effects are gained by the return to earth of a ghost (e.g. Hamlet's father and Julius Caesar). One of the most thrilling scenes in the history of drama is centred on Macbeth's seeing of a spectral dagger. Shakespeare's experience and imagination were rooted in the common beliefs and folklore of his time.

Globe Theatre. *See* Elizabethan Theatre.

Great Frost, The. In 1607 the River Thames froze over solidly for a considerable time, and carnivals and markets were held on the stretch nearest the City of London. There are no direct references to it in Shakespeare, but he is very sensitive to climate and weather (*see* his references to floods in *A Midsummer Night's Dream*).

Gunpowder Plot. Abortive Roman Catholic plot to blow up Parliament building, led by Robert Catesby (a Warwickshire man distantly related to Shakespeare). Guy Fawkes also played a leading part in planting thirty-six barrels of gunpowder on 5 November 1605 under the House of Lords. The plot was discovered, the conspirators executed. A number of them came from near Stratford, and Clopton House was the scene of conspiratorial meetings, as was the Mermaid Tavern in London. (*See* Guy Fawkes.)

Henslowe's Diary. Of inestimable value to historians of Elizabethan theatre, the work of a probably justifiably maligned theatre tycoon, manipulator and entrepreneur, Philip Henslowe (d. 1616). (*See* Elizabethan Theatre.)

Impresa. A fragile (paper or pasteboard) shield decorated with a knight's coat-of-arms for use on ceremonial occasions. Shakespeare seemingly collaborated with Burbage in making an impresa for the 6th

Earl of Rutland in 1613; he received 44 shillings in gold. Perhaps this curious happening is explained by their access to theatre props.

Inns of Court. Lincoln's, Gray's, Middle Temple, Inner Temple. These were a mixture of élite professional club, academic institution and finishing school (teaching dancing, singing and instrument playing) — for gentlemen training for the law. Their social activities involved dramatic performances — *The Comedy of Errors* (Gray's Inn), *Twelfth Night* (Middle Temple). (1) '... a Comedy of Errors ... was played by the Players. So the Night was begun, and continued to the end, in nothing but Confusion and Errors; whereupon, it was ever afterwards called, *The Night of Errors*.' (From the records of Gray's Inn.) (2) 'At our feast wee had a play called "Twelve Night, or What you Will".' (Diary of John Manningham.)

Interpolations. Additions made to the text of a play from sources other than the author himself. In Shakespeare's case interpolations are found, for example, in *Macbeth*, where the Hecate speeches found in the Folio are almost certainly by Middleton. (*See* The Text.)

Lessee. Either a tenant or one to whom a lease of land or property is granted. Shakespeare was considerably involved in property law. He himself leased property and was the lessee of land on the Welcombe enclosure.

Licence. On 27 November 1582 an entry was made in the Bishop of Worcester's Register recording the issue of a licence for marriage between 'Willelmum Shaxpere', and 'Annam Whateley' of Temple Grafton. The bride-to-be's name has occasioned much speculation. It may be a mistake for 'Hathaway', it may not be Shakespeare the dramatist who was referred to, it may be that Shakespeare had promised himself to Anne Whateley before discovering that Anne Hathaway was pregnant by him. (*See* Bond; Marriage; Myths, Legends and Mysteries.)

Loan. There is no record of Shakespeare's borrowing a loan but there is evidence of his being asked to lend money. (*See* Quiney Family.)

'London Prodigal, The'. The title-page of this play (pub. 1605) reads: '... as it was plaide by the Kings Majesties servants. By William Shakespeare.' It is, almost without doubt, *not* by him. It may be read (with five other apocryphal plays) in *The Shakespeare Apocrypha*, Oxford, 1908.

Marriage. A deal of mystery surrounds Shakespeare's marriage (*see* Bond; Licence; Myths, Legends and Mysteries). There is no record of where it took place or who solemnized it. The village church of Temple Grafton (a few miles from Stratford) is suggested by those who believe he married Anne Whateley. Holy Trinity, Stratford, would be likely if, as is almost certain, he married Anne Hathaway. If, however, a Catholic ceremony (which was officially suppressed) was asked for, the marriage could have taken place clandestinely almost anywhere in the Stratford area.

Master of the Great Wardrobe. One of the officers of the Queen's household, under the direction of the Lord Chamberlain. His function was to supervise the Queen's wardrobe of state. His duties probably included the provision of gifts of cloth or clothing to acting companies.

Master of the Revels. Elizabeth's court entertainments were organized by the Office of the Revels with a Master and several assistants. Ben Jonson died before taking up the Mastership. The office liaised with acting companies, watched rehearsals, supplied props, costumes from its own wardrobe, and paid actors.

Pamphlets. A favourite literary occupation in the late 16th and early 17th centuries. They were short pieces of writing either proselytizing for some cause or beginning or continuing an argument. The main areas of contention were religious and literary. Personal abuse was often involved. (*See* Robert Greene.)

Patent. A document authorizing the granting of a right or privilege or office. One of James I's first acts on accession was to issue a royal patent making the former Lord Chamberlain's Company into the King's Company. James became its patron and its members, including Shakespeare, became, in effect, employees of the crown.

Patron. In 16th-century England rich members of the nobility hoped to flatter their own images by patronizing writers. A few may have genuinely been motivated by a desire to advance the cause of Art. Whatever the motivation, many writers benefited from this fickle system, not least Shakespeare. His company was patronized, first by the Lord Chamberlain, then by King James. His poetry was patronized by the Earl of Southampton (see *Venus and Adonis* and *The Rape of Lucrece*). Patronage involved money, gifts and, from the patronized, a flattering dedication.

Payment. Certain documents indicating payment to and by Shakespeare for goods and services give us a picture of the extent to which this great artist was also a man of business shrewdness, intent upon raising the fortunes of his family and attaining affluence. His detailed concern with buying malt in advance of a probable famine in that commodity, as shown in a tiny entry like — Shakespeare 'told me that they assured him they meant to inclose noe further than to gospell bush . . .' (1614, from the Diary of Thomas Greene) — indicates his interest and concern in the affairs of his own town and the land about it.

Performances. *See* Shakespeare on the Stage.

Plague. Most people have heard of the many outbreaks of plague in Western Europe during the mediaeval and Elizabethan periods; few know what it was or what its symptoms and effects were. It was probably the bubonic type characterized by gland-swellings, carbuncles, fever, suppurating sores. Examples of its devastation are (1) 1466, 40,000 die in Paris; (2) 200,000 die in Moscow; (3) 1563-4, 1,000 per week, (10 weeks), die in London. London had a huge epidemic in 1593. Inadequate hygiene was a major cause, but there was no cure, although many were urged — 'apply a live pigeon cut in two parts, or else a plaster made of the yolk of an egg, honey, herb of grace, chopped exceeding small, and wheat flour . . .' During several plagues (e.g. 1592–4) severe restrictions were put on theatres, and acting companies often went on tour from the stricken city.

Privy Council. Formed in the late 14th century as a powerful advisory body to the monarch. By the 16th century the supreme judicial and executive agent of the state. Privy Councillors, as the name suggests, had direct access to the monarch. In 1600 there were eleven councillors, held firmly in check by Elizabeth, but still powerful. The Star Chamber was, in fact, the Privy Council sitting as a court. Through the council and Lord Chamberlain the theatres were constantly under surveillance. They censored plays for treason and heresy, and could close playhouses. On the whole, however, and perhaps due to the Queen's influence, the theatres benefited more than suffered from the Privy Council during her reign.

Probate. Simply, an act by which something is proved. When a will receives probate it means that it has been examined and its provisions accepted legally.

Progress. A progress was a procession and Queen Elizabeth specialized in them in a spectacular way. She used them as a means of making herself known to her subjects, keeping an eye on her most powerful ones and flattering them, and as an instrument of fiscal policy. She would regularly go in 'progress' to stay at some nobleman's great house for an indefinite period. Scores of baggage carts, many members of her household, carts with royal furnishings, and ancillaries, would precede her, say, to the seat of the Earl of Leicester, or to Warwick or Kenilworth. She stayed with the Lucy Family at Charlecote in 1566. The inhabitants of Banbury, Oxford, would have cheered her on her way, the Lucys would have been flattered by her presence; for a knighthood conferred on the head of the family, she received free, opulent, board and lodging. With the really mighty lords she was in a bargaining position. They vied with each other in giving expensive gifts, vouchsafing confidences, and political manoeuvring. She watched, heard, took, and, by so doing, saved household expenses, acquired rich gifts and kept her fingers on the pulse of her nation. Elizabeth's progresses were the calculated acts of a political genius.

Publication. *See* Printing and Publishing.

Purchases. The bare information that, for example, Shakespeare bought New Place in 1597 or the Blackfriars Gatehouse in 1613 or held tithes in Stratford is only the tip of an iceberg. Knowledge involves knowing what New Place consisted of, where the Blackfriars Gatehouse was situated, why tithes existed and where, in Stratford, Shakespeare's were located. The answers to such questions and many others connected with Shakespeare's purchases give us the contours of the map of his industry and interest and intention. For example, by the time he died his land-holdings and purchases in Stratford utterly dominated the town and its environs — was this the son's answer to the collapse of his father's fortunes and the blemish on the Shakespeare name? (*See* Calendar of Events.)

Quarto. A paper size (several varieties — Crown, 10 by 7½ in.; Royal, 12¼ by 10 in.; Foolscap, 8½ by 6¾ in.). A single sheet is folded twice producing four leaves (eight page sides). (*See* Printing and Publishing.)

Recusant. One who refused to attend the services of the newly established Church of England in the 16th century. Usually applied to Roman Catholics, but not exclusively, for extreme Puritan belief might lead to a conscientious and firm refusal to take part in Anglican services. After an absence of one month the church authorities 'posted' the names of alleged recusants on the church-door. John Shakespeare's name was listed in 1592, though fear of being arrested, on the instructions of bailiffs, for non-payment of debts may have prompted his absence, rather than religious conviction. Included in the same list are George Bardolfe and William Fluellen — two Stratfordians about whom we know nothing, but they are immortalized in Shakespeare's use of their surnames in *Henry IV* and *Henry V*.

'Return from Parnassus, The'. Between 1598 and 1602 three plays were written and performed at St John's College, Cambridge. They are — *The Pilgrimage to Parnassus*; *The First Part of the Returne from Parnassus*; *The Seconde Part of the Returne from Parnassus*. These anonymous plays are crammed with allusions to university life and theatre. For example, in the third play, two students are auditioned by Will Kempe and Richard Burbage. Shakespeare's name is mentioned in the dialogue more than once.

'Rose' Theatre. *See* Elizabethan Theatre.

St Bartholomew's Day Massacre. A notorious massacre incited by religious passion, faith and bigotry which took place in Paris in 1572. It forms the basis for Marlowe's *The Massacre at Paris* — 1593. Marlowe also involves the murder of the Duke of Guise in 1588. There is an interesting echo in Marlowe's play of lines from Shakespeare's *Henry VI, Part 3*. Marlowe wrote: 'Sweet Duke of Guise, our prop to lean upon/ Now thou art dead, here is no stay for us.' Shakespeare wrote: 'Sweet Duke of York, our prop to lean upon/Now thou art gone, we have no staff, no stay.'

Shareholder. *See* Elizabethan Theatre.

Sheriff. An officer of the law, but not by any means always possessing the dramatic ambience Hollywood so successfully manufactures. In

England, a sheriff in the 16th century was responsible for keeping prisoners under lock and key, executing writs, preparing a jury, and overseeing the death sentence. In 20th-century England to be sheriff is largely an honorary post.

'Sir Thomas More'. An intriguing manuscript of an incomplete play first printed 1844 but possibly dating from 1593. Thirty-two badly preserved pages contain five different hands — identified as Anthony Munday, Henry Chettle, Thomas Heywood: Anon, Shakespeare, Thomas Dekker. *See* A. W. Pollard and others, *Shakespeare's Hand in the Play of Sir Thomas More*, 1923.

Spanish Armada. Most of Shakespeare's life was spent in the shadow of political tension and military skirmishing with Spain. The defeat of the Spanish Armada in 1588 effectively established English domination, but Shakespeare neither expressly nor by implication mentions it.

Stationer's Register. The Stationer's Company had a monopoly (except for Oxford and Cambridge University presses) for the printing of books in England. All booksellers and printers were Freemen of the Company and ensured copyright by registering their work with the Company at a fee. The system was far from foolproof. Many plays were printed and not registered, many texts registered were dubiously acquired. (*See also* Printing and Publishing.)

Suit (at Law). *See* Belott-Mountjoy.

Swan Theatre. *See* Elizabethan Theatre.

Taxes. Shakespeare was niggardly in his payment of taxes in London. (*See* Debt.)

'The Theatre'. *See* Elizabethan Theatre.

Tithes. Literally 'a tenth part'. It usually refers to a portion of expected or assumed yearly profit from stock or land. Shakespeare held tithes on land in Stratford upon Avon from which he derived income. (*See* Enclosures.)

Writ (of Attachment). On 29 November 1596, William Wayte took out a writ to ensure that Shakespeare and three others were bound to keep the peace — 'for fear of death, and so forth'. Wayte himself had previously had a similar writ served on him by Francis Langley, owner of the Swan Theatre. The writ was issued by the Sheriff of Surrey, and is, therefore, an indication that by 1596 Shakespeare had moved to the south (Surrey) side of the River Thames. Nothing further is known of this affair.

II Shakespeare in Performance

Nor do not saw the air too much with your hand, thus; but use all gently
Hamlet

SHAKESPEARE ON THE STAGE, 1590–1978

Elizabethan Theatre

One of the most beguiling and dangerous images which haunts the imagination of Shakespeare lovers is the Globe Theatre. For many it is an emblem of the greatness of Shakespeare, the magic of theatre and the happy rumbustiousness of the Elizabethan age. It is a romantic image, harmless if kept in its place, but perilous to anyone seeking the truth about Shakespeare and his world of theatre. The Globe was the centre of his working life, but did not monopolize him.

We must distinguish between several kinds of theatre, though Shakespeare himself spent most of his working life associated with two main types — the so-called public (of which the Globe was one) and private theatres. But he had doubtless learned much about stages, about the fickleness of audiences and the temperaments of players, from a type of theatre which had its origin in the inns of the late mediaeval period.

INN YARD THEATRE

The association of plays and the inn atmosphere seems natural. It is possible to warm the imagination by drink while enjoying a fiction; for the players, the effects of alcohol on a well-disposed audience are not without advantages; the association of players with vagabondage and of vagabondage with truculent fellowship would have made the inn seem the inevitable home for the displaying of histrionic arts. A landlord who knew his company would encourage its presence for reasons of profit. There are both tangible and intangible reasons for associating plays with pubs, both now and in the Elizabethan period. But not the least tangible is that pubs, like churches, are ubiquitous.

The Elizabethan inns had a special suitability for plays and players. Many were built on a pattern, derived from mediaeval times, dictated by the necessity to stable horses and accommodate people. We have to imagine a main building with two projecting annexes at each of two corners and at right angles to it — or we have to visit, for example, the New Inn at Gloucester, England, which still preserves this pattern. For the purpose of playing, a trestle stage was erected giving access to the main building and flanked by the annexes; it thus projected into the inn yard and was uncovered. Regulars and guests had the privilege of watching the play under shelter from the windows of the annexes or, if they didn't mind hindquarters sight of the actors, they watched the action from the main building of the inn looking down upon the projecting stage. Strangers and personae non gratae or incontinent drinkers stood in the inn yard sharing it with the stage, the actors and British weather.

By the 1550s in London, shrewd landlords had made their yards into permanent or semi-permanent theatres. The earliest recorded performances were at the Saracen's Head in Islington and the Boar's Head in Aldgate, in 1557. But there were other famous venues — the Bull at Bishopsgate, the Bel Savage on Ludgate Hill. In *Henry IV, Part 1* Falstaff's home-from-home is assumed to be the Boar's Head tavern, although the name is not used in the text, only broadly hinted at — 'Doth the old boar feed in the old frank?' — but it could refer to any of six Boar's Head Inns in London in the 1570s and 1580s.

We have little inkling of what inn yard performances were like, but we know what the authorities in London thought of the audiences. In 1574 they made regulations to control performances because of 'ffrayes and quarrelles, eavell practizes of incontinency in great Innes, havinge chambres and secrete places adjoyninge to their open stagies and gally-ries'.

The London inn theatres were lively places, the plays performed — mainly interludes — necessarily broad and obvious in appeal, the actors, well-used to contending with the alternative to their skills — drink and conviviality. In country towns, like Stratford, the curiosity value of inter-mittent visits concentrated more attention upon the plays than upon the sack and sherris. Shakespeare knew both versions — that is unquestionable.

PRIVATE HOUSE THEATRE

In one sense this form of theatre could not be more different from that of the inn yards. No great nobleman actually converted any part of his great house into a theatre, but nevertheless, the mobility of London acting companies made it inevitable that those country lords disposed to plays had many opportunities to employ professionals. The usual design of an Oxford or Cambridge college refectory dating from the 16th century or before is the best remembrancer now of how the private house performances were presented.

With certain differences, the refectory reflects the inn yard theatre. The wall behind the high table represents the main building of the inn yard and the stage projecting from it provides access. The audience's accommodation in the refectory was, however, comprehensively more comfortable. All were seated; there was a roof; the actors were, like the audience, protected. But despite the similar spatial relationship of stage to audience, the 'theatre' we are now considering was enclosed and, therefore, unlike the inn yard, dependent upon artificial lighting — in Elizabethan times a matter of unpredictable torches and acrid candles.

PUBLIC HALL THEATRE

This third type shared the ad hoc status of the private house type. There were three main kinds: (1) Large halls in buildings owned by municipal authorities, like the council chamber of the Stratford corporation. (2) Grand halls or areas of ceremonial appearance, easily convertible into temporary places for all kinds of theatrical entertainment, like the various courts of Queen Elizabeth at Whitehall, Richmond, Hampton or Greenwich. In 1561 an old barnstormer of a play, *Gorboduc*, was performed at Whitehall Court and the chamber was 'to be furnished with scaffolds to sit upon'. It is worth realizing that these scaffolds held seats on both side walls. With variations, therefore, the basic pattern of the inn yard theatre was maintained. (3) The great hall of some institution, like that of one or other of the Inns of Court. These Inns were really residential colleges to accommodate law students. By all accounts they lived up to the livelier associations of the word 'inn'. They became famous and notorious, for entertainments, which included dances, masques and plays.

PUBLIC THEATRES

The type of theatre which most stirs the imagination was the custom-built public theatre of which the Globe is, and perhaps was at the time, the most famous. The generic name encompasses two important facts — (1) that such theatres were the first specifically built for dramatic performances, not adapted, (2) that their audiences were drawn from all classes of society and not sectional, as in the case of the other types except the inn yards. During the astonishing cultural flowering of the last twenty years of the 16th century, public and private theatres were built in some profusion — if we measure their number in proportion to the population of London (approximately 200,000).

Between 1576 when The Theatre (the first public theatre) was built, and 1614 when the second Globe Theatre opened, sixteen public and private theatres were available for this small number of people. Of these at least six were large public ones. The full list represents the greatest period of theatrical achievement in the history of Western civilization.

The Theatre	1576, pulled down 1598	Shoreditch
Curtain	1576, ceased? 1660	Bishopsgate
(1) Blackfriars	1576, lease closed 1584	Nr Ludgate Hill
(2) Blackfriars	1600, dismantled 1655	Nr Ludgate Hill
(1) Fortune	1600, destroyed by fire 1621	Finsbury
(2) Fortune	1623, wrecked 1649	Finsbury
Red Bull	c. 1605, last mentioned 1663	Clerkenwell
Whitefriars	1608, last known 1629	Nr Fleet Street
Phoenix (or Cockpit)	1616, ceased? 1665	Drury Lane
Salisbury Court	1629, destroyed 1666	Nr Fleet Street
Newington Butts	c. 1580, ceased? c. 1596	1 mile south-west of London Bridge
Rose	c. 1587, last mentioned 1622	South bank of River Thames
Swan	c. 1595, last mentioned 1632	South bank (west)
(1) Globe	1599, burnt down 1613	South bank (east)
(2) Globe	1614, pulled down 1644	South bank (east)
Hope	1614, pulled down 1656	South bank

The Social Background

No clear picture of what the public theatres looked like and how they worked is possible without first realizing that whereas the Queen favoured dramatic performances and was easily inclined to encourage patronage of actors and dramatists, the city authorities who, during the 1580s and 1590s, became increasingly dominated by grim-lipped Puritans, looked with disfavour on the growing popularity of drama and theatres. From the 20th century it looks like a wild game of pig-in-the-middle being played by these two forces, with beleaguered but sometimes cunning theatre administrators doing their best to avoid the consequences. Where they were built, how long they were allowed to remain open, how actors and dramatists were regarded, how audiences reacted — all these were affected by the interaction of official disapproval and royal favour.

In May 1574, James Burbage was given the right, as a servant of the Earl of Leicester, to perform 'Comedies, Tragedies, Enterludes and Stage playes' in the City of London and elsewhere. The only condition was that the censorship regulations should not be contravened and that no performances should be given during times of worship or of an outbreak of plague. This right was by royal warrant and intended to cover performances in inn yard theatres.

On 6 December 1574 the City corporation, stung by what it considered to be unwarrantable royal interference in the City of London, announced what it would and would not tolerate from the theatrical profession — and the penalties involved. Hurt pride and moral outrage is indicated by the preamble which talks about 'inordinate haunting of great multitude of people' in the inn theatres, about the frequent outbreak of 'frayes and quarrels', about 'evil practises of incontinency' and 'allewring [enticing] of maids, especially orphans'. It is a horrifying picture. This is an official document and its strength of feeling is a mild sample of the vitriolic attacks which, in pamphlets and sermons, were made on the theatrical profession. One pamphleteer claimed that plays were used to teach 'craft, mischief, deceit, filthiness', in addition to giving examples of betrayal, flattery, lying, blaspheming, swearing, filthy love songs and pride. Meanwhile, royal patronage continued. Throughout Elizabeth's and James I's reigns there were many invited performances at Court. One of James's first acts on succession was to issue a royal patent establishing himself as patron of the most famous of the Elizabethan companies — the Lord Chamberlain's. Its name was changed to the King's Men, its members were designated as 'grooms of the chamber' and wore the king's livery on notable occasions. Its most important member was William Shakespeare.

So, the battle lines were clear, the skirmishes were stern, and sometimes, despite personal royal regard, the bureaucracy of disapproving city councils was supported by officialdom nearer the throne. In 1596 the Corporation gained the support of the Privy Council to prohibit plays within the City of London. This was a victory. But with that characteristic British ability to sail close to the legal wind without foundering, it was claimed and tacitly upheld that public performances anywhere were really rehearsals only for Court performances!

The inn yard theatres within the jurisdiction of the City authorities bore the brunt of the skirmishing, and the prospective builders of new public theatres decided that it was politic to avoid the battle if possible, and so the public theatre buildings were built outside the City limits, with the main ones on the south bank of the Thames.

The Structure of the Public Theatres

A good deal of guesswork is involved in imagining what an Elizabethan public theatre looked like — it is an assumption that there was a standard pattern. We do not have detailed plans, but nevertheless a consensus picture of a large public theatre, like the Globe or the Fortune or the Rose suggests a kind of amphitheatre. The Colisseum in Rome, much reduced in size, gives us the shape — but it may have varied from round to octagonal to near rectangular. The inside walls consisted of three galleries starting at ground level which arched round until they were stopped by the intervention of the stage. There was no seating on the ground floor, except in the surrounding gallery, and the two upper galleries had benches or stools. It is apparent that those standing on the ground floor were unprotected from the weather. The stage stuck out towards the centre of the ground floor. We must now revert to our image of an inn yard theatre. The stage is observed from three sides, the back of the stage has access to rooms behind, you stood if you paid least, you were protected if you paid more.

The picture we have is given some credibility by the precious existence of the contract for the Fortune Theatre which was modelled on that of the Globe. The irony is that it was so similar that many details which would have been invaluable to history are merely indicated as 'like unto the Globe'. What we learn of importance is: (1) The foundations to be of piles, brick, lime and sand; (2) three storeys ascending in heights (a) 12 ft, (b) 11 ft, (c) 9 ft — these are the galleries; (3) the stage and tiring house (i.e. the accommodation back-stage) to have a canopy (called 'a shade') to protect the players; (4) the stage 43 ft wide (this is considerable — for comparison the Royal Shakespeare stage is approximately 59 ft); (5) the depth of the stage 27 ft 6 in. and to extend exactly half way into the 'yard' or ground floor: the interior diameter of the theatre is therefore 55 ft. It is estimated that the Globe and Fortune theatres could accommodate 2,000 people (Royal Shakespeare Theatre, 1,353).

The sum of our exact knowledge of one perhaps typical Elizabethan public theatre is in the above figures. Conjecture now begins to play an increasing role. There is, however, an orthodox view which, though it poses problems and has its critics, seems, in essentials, to fit the available evidence better than any alternative.

Let us imagine that, as affluent Elizabethans, we have decided to go to a performance at the Globe Theatre. Our affluence is a blessing, since it means that we can afford to go to the top gallery, and escape the extreme rowdiness of the 'groundlings' standing in the pit on the ground floor. Performance-time (usually two o'clock in the afternoon) has been announced on play posters, a flag unfurled from a small tower (the 'hut') over the tiring house area confirms that the theatre is open, and warning trumpets sound at intervals from half-an-hour before the performance. We pay our admission to the 'gatherer' at the door, one penny to stand with the groundlings, an extra sixpence for a 'box' in the second gallery and an extra twelve pence for a 'private room' in the upper gallery. We see the projecting stage, about five feet high, and above it the stage roof (shadow) held up by two pillars, above that the tiring house roof with its hut. At the back wall, on stage level, we notice a curtained alcove flanked by two doors leading back stage to the tiring house. Above this alcove and doors, and forming a continuation of the second-storey gallery of the auditorium, is what can be used as a musician's gallery, or for certain scenes in the play. If we examine the stage-area more closely, we see a trap door centre-stage, and we cannot miss the 'cloth' — painted material, like canvas — which hangs down from the pillared roof of the stage. This has two uses — the first, decorative (the Lord Admiral's company had 'a clothe of the Sone and Mone'; the Globe may, indeed, have had a depiction of 'the great Globe itself', the earth), the second functional — the hanging cloth hides, until the time is right for revelation, any 'miracle' of Elizabethan theatrical technology. In the roof above the stage is a good deal of stage machinery, useful for example for a god or goddess to descend in a chariot (as in *The Tempest*, Act V) or for other spectacular effects. The back-stage staff of the theatre is resourceful — it can render a highly effective thunderstorm by rolling cannon balls across the oak-floor of the area above the stage.

At two o'clock, the Prologue introduces the play in ringing tones to grasp the audience's attention and command their silence. One of his problems is to soften the relationship between the groundlings and those young gallants who have frequently paid sixpence for a stool to sit on the stage, and who refuse to budge whoever's light they are in: 'neither are you to be hunted from thence, though the Scarecrows in the yard hoot at you, hiss at you, spit at you, yea, throw durt even in your teeth.' Speed of performance is essential for the only source of light of any strength is daylight. The problem of illumination, which in the 20th century is solved, is fundamental for the Elizabethans. We have to remember that, quite apart from the skittish English climate, the theatres' season was a very short one. No performances could take place in Lent (the short winter months precluded them anyway), and the bright summer months bred the plague and the theatres were forced to close. Early autumn and spring, notorious for capricious weather, were the high days of theatre-going.

The Stage
Inside the public theatre we see the potential of what we now call a 'thrust' or 'apron' stage — that main area reaching into the heart of the auditorium — and speculate on the problematical uses of the alcove at the back wall of the stage and the 'musician's gallery' above it.

Given the very large dimensions of the main stage area, it is easy to see how it could accommodate the actions of Shakespeare's plays. Shakespeare, however, was very conscious of the naturalistic limitations even of the Globe Theatre stage. In *Henry V* his opening chorus apologizes because the battle of Agincourt cannot be satisfactorily demonstrated on its 'unworthy scaffold' — it is too small to impersonate 'the vasty fields of

France'. He is equally apologetic about the size of his armies and asks his audience to divide each actor into a 'thousand parts' so that at least some imaginary relationship to the military hordes may be achieved. Indeed, throughout Shakespeare's plays, especially those involving battles, there is evidence of an attempt to make what is too small or inadequate in actuality into a 'cypher' for the real thing. In fact, most of his great battle scenes are skirmishes between a few people, not great set-pieces, and have directions like 'alarum', 'excursion', indicating that he wants his few actors, aided by noises off, to bustle about giving the effect of large activity. Shakespeare countered his own awareness of the naturalistic deficiencies of even the great Globe's stage by this method and also by adopting the artistic principle, which is illustrated in the opening chorus of *Henry V*, of 'Think, when we talk of horses, that you see them . . .' In short, he compensated for natural deficiencies by high dramatic and poetic art — that which gives illusion the face of truth. But the Globe Theatre stage did not encourage naturalistic drama, because, though it thrust out to meet the audience and to involve it, it certainly nurtured any dramatist who was able to lure the audience into believing that what 'seems' to be and what 'is' can be made, by the magic of art, into one and the same thing.

We are certain about the possibilities of the main stage — and even those pillars which held up the stage-roof could well have aided rather than obstructed the dramatist's art. It is amazing what effects of intimacy, secretiveness, dramatic tension an actor can achieve with a good script and an inanimate object like a pillar. Imagine what a Burbage or Alleyn or, indeed, an Olivier or Gielgud, could do in that first scene in *Hamlet* where, on the great open stage, the court of Denmark is assembled and Hamlet has to convey to us his lack of trust in them. On the Globe stage the actor could move to one of those pillars and, using it like a defensive wall to isolate himself, tell us about his anguish. So, it was possible, on reasonable conjecture, for that open stage to accommodate the 'private' scene, the soliloquy, the lovers' meeting as effectively as the great battles, the conferences, the quarrels. It was a question of making the forces of illusion work for you.

But the problematical recess back-stage and the equally problematical musicians' gallery above it are accepted by some as important additional acting areas, particularly for the presentation of 'inner' scenes, as, for example, Juliet's tomb (the recess), Juliet's bedroom (musicians' gallery), the monument in *Antony and Cleopatra* (musicians' gallery), Desdemona's bedchamber (the recess). Scepticism about this is based on one perennial crux of stage-design — sight lines. One glance at a conjectural drawing of the orthodox view of a typical Elizabethan public stage will confirm that sight-line problems existed. The pillars and stage-roof mean that the recess and the musicians' gallery can only be seen completely by those on the ground-floor — by those who have paid least! This does not make commercial sense, and the Elizabethan theatre-managers were commercially very sensitive. Apart from this, what dramatist is going to write an important scene — as, for example, the superbly lyrical parting of Romeo and Juliet in her bedroom — which at least a third of its audience is not able to see? Audiences demand the ocular proof as well as the verbal splendour.

The circumstantial evidence is too strong, however, to reject the existence of the recess. Moreover the logistics of architecture make the 'musicians' gallery' as a continuation of the auditorium's second-storey gallery, very feasible. What, then, is the answer? There are two probabilities. First, that the 'musicians' gallery' really did house music-makers — there was a good deal of music played in Elizabethan theatres — and that occasionally an action would begin up there (as sometimes today, often in pantomime or farce, action begins in unusual parts of the theatre like the dress circle, the stalls) but went on to have its significant life on the main stage. We accept many conventions in the modern theatre without any question. We must allow the Elizabethans, who produced the greatest body of drama of Western civilization, their ability both to create and use their own conventions.

As to the recess, its curtain seems to be the significant feature. Again, we should appeal to the elasticity of convention. There is no reason why (as, for example, for Juliet's or Desdemona's bedchamber) the scene should not begin in the recess and flow out, so to speak, on to the main stage, carrying the audience's conviction of a confined space with it. But what if we have a scene, a confined place, where movement is not possible — as in Juliet's tomb? We have to emphasize the force of convention here, and it does not seem beyond the bounds of feasibility to postulate that such a scene would begin as a tableau within the recess, perhaps lit by torches, but that the vital action upon Romeo's arrival happened on the main stage. So the tableau was there for those who could see it — perhaps in the form of a prop bier which was ritually pushed forward into full view. We have grown so accustomed to modern stage conventions that we forget the extent to which stage furniture is brought on, pushed about, rearranged, taken off by stage-hands while the action proceeds — and no one complains that realistic effect has been destroyed! If it is argued that this explanation of the recess is dangerously near giving it the status of an expendable luxury — after all there would be no need to postulate a tableau if the recess did not exist — then it must be remembered first, that (apart from the possibility of tableaux) the recess could be used as an extra exit and entrance to back stage and, second, that there is nothing more dramatic than an actor who appears suddenly from (even if you could see the recess) behind a curtain or (if you could not see it) apparently from nowhere into full visibility on the main stage.

Scenery, Props and Costume

The way the Elizabethans used these three components of theatrical presentation suggests that despite convention they still had an urge for verisimilitude — it's all right to imagine Agincourt but it's much more sensational if you can impersonate it! Sir Philip Sidney in his *Defence of Poesie*, 1583, succinctly reveals the mixture of acceptance and aspiration in Elizabethan theatre. First, he describes convention — 'you shall have *Asia* of the one side, and *Affrick* of the other, and so many other under-kingdoms, that the Player, when he commeth in, must ever begin with telling where he is . . . By and by, we heare newes of shipwracke in the same place, and then wee are to blame if we accept it not for a Rock.' Then he gives a graphic example of what, to the Elizabethans, would have been a very realistic appearance — 'a hideous monster, with fire and smoke'.

But, in their pursuit of verisimilitude, they could go much further than this. The theatre-manager, Henslowe, kept a list of the scenery and props of his company in 1598. It included two steeples, one chime of bells, one old Mahomet's head, one wooden hatchet, a cupid's bow and quiver, a lion-skin, a ghost's crown, a chain of dragons, and so forth.

Henslowe also kept a list of costumes, but here we have to be cautious about accepting the evidence as proof of a quest for verisimilitude in the same sense that applies to stage furniture. In his list we find a black velvet cloak, a damask cloth decorated with velvet, a cardinal's gown, a woman's gown, a red silk gown and so forth. But where are the mediaeval costumes for the Histories, the ancient Britons' dress for *King Lear*, the Scots tartans for *Macbeth*? The truth is that the Elizabethans did not go in for historical veracity. Their Shakespeare was modern-dress Shakespeare, although occasionally they may have made a gesture to the past by wearing a toga over their Elizabethan dress to conjure up Imperial Rome. It appears, on the evidence, that Elizabethan actors dressed not so much to realize character as to cut a dash — 'it is the English usage for eminent lords or knights at their decease to bequeath and leave almost the best of their clothes to their serving men, which it is unseemly for the latter to wear, so that they offer them for sale for a small sum to the actors' (Platter, 1599). In fact, the actors of a successful company were the 'glass of fashion'.

PRIVATE THEATRES

These were second in importance only to the public theatres. The most obvious difference between them is quickly stated. The public type were unroofed, apart from the shade over the main stage, the private ones were completely roofed over and enclosed. The effects were profound; artificial sources of light were necessary and made a difference in atmosphere, visual effect, even acting style. In Shakespeare's lifetime the following private theatres existed in London:

(1) Blackfriars	1576, closed 1584	Nr Ludgate Hill
(2) Blackfriars	1600, demolished 1655	Nr Ludgate Hill
Whitefriars	*c.* 1608, closed 1629	Adjacent to the river at Fleet Street
Salisbury Court	1629, closed 1671	Adjacent to the river at Fleet Street
Phoenix	*c.* 1616, closed 1663?	Drury Lane
Porter's Hall	1616, closed 1617	Nr Ludgate Hill?

Another distinctive feature of private theatres was the use of boys' companies. The first Blackfriars Theatre was in the City limits but escaped the harrassment of officialdom because it was converted from part of a group of monastic buildings. It was constructed by a Richard Farrant for performances by what became a famous boys' acting company — the Children of the Chapel Royal at Windsor, of which he was Master and organist. The association of private theatres with such companies is important. In contradistinction to the public theatres where the boy actors took their place with, and were trained by, adults, the boys' companies of the private theatres performed only with their own contemporaries, and were trained by such men as Farrant, as their coach/managers. Technically, such companies as the Choristers of St Paul's, Westminster, Eton College, the Chapel Royal, were exclusively singers but soon astute people like Farrant saw the commercial possibilities of presenting them in dramatic spectacles in which music and singing did not always have a major say. Thus they became associated with private theatres.

Structure of Private Theatres

It would be unwise to take the evidence of the structure of the first known private theatre (the Blackfriars) as an absolute pattern for them all, yet, apart from possible difference in size, it seems that the pattern it displayed remained generally true for the others. It was 66 ft from north to south, and 46 ft east to west (Fortune 80 ft). The stage, in this apparent rectangle, was at the south end, with a great staircase at the opposite end. The stage width was approximately 39 ft (Fortune 43 ft). There were possibly two galleries.

The admission prices differed from those of the public theatres. Sixpence gained a standing place in a side gallery. If you wished to sit in the pit you paid an extra shilling. For two shillings and sixpence you could sit, like a gallant, on the stage itself. Lighting, boys' companies, pit-seats, prices — these imply a different kind of performance from that at the Globe and the other public theatres.

Conjecture, based on teasingly incomplete evidence, suggests that the stage area was similar to that of the public theatres, but without the protective roof and, therefore, pillars. Reason demands that the galleries (probably two tiers) ran across each side wall and the wall facing the stage. It is probable that the audience was all seated. In fact they were 'private' more certainly in the sense that they were closed to the skies, than that they were socially exclusive.

Elizabethan Acting

What is most lacking in our knowledge is not what we might see of the theatre itself or of what the actors wore, but how they moved and spoke. How they acted is perhaps the greatest mystery of the Elizabethan theatre.

Much ink has flowed over much paper in voyages of speculation to describe and understand the principles and practice of Elizabethan acting. One conclusion is that it would have seemed to us expansive, melodramatic, oratorical, 'hammy'. It is claimed that when Hamlet complains that he deplores actors who 'saw the air' with their hands he refers to a common exaggerated style, whereas when he asks that players should not 'o'erstep the modesty of nature' he is appealing for a quieter, natural way. So another school of thought has claimed that there were two basic styles — one exaggerated, the other natural. We can never be sure, but we must remember the following: (1) Ever since sufficient records of acting have been preserved (i.e. from the end of the 18th century) each age has exhibited one or more basic styles of acting to one of which the run-of-the-mill players subscribe, but (2) The great actor always makes his own rules, avoids the fashionable and, indeed, sets a fashion for the next generation. By all accounts Burbage, Alleyn, Armin were great actors. There is no reason to believe that they were less individualistic, less able to avoid the acting clichés of the time than their successors — Garrick, Kean, Irving. (3) The effect, so rarely considered, of the absence of actresses and the consequent use of boys and men to play women's parts on 'style' of acting. When boys play female roles they tend, as a kind of protection, to 'distance' their interpretation by a sort of ritual; they tend to adopt certain conventional images of feminine movement and do not aim, normally, at complete naturalism. (4) The strong possibility that the training of an Elizabethan actor involved a good deal of ritual in movement and gesture and probably in speech. (5) The comprehensive and rigorous training — the Elizabethan actor had to be an accomplished swordsman, singer, dancer, to an extent few modern actors either achieve or are given the opportunity to achieve.

These considerations should govern any study of the process by which a boy became a full-fledged member of an acting company. All the circumstantial evidence available points to Elizabethan grammar schools as

the main recruiting source for actors. There was a well-organized apprenticeship system. Each boy entered the profession (took 'indentures', that
is) at any age between ten and thirteen (they needed to be captured early
to take advantage of unbroken voices). Each boy was attached to and
trained by an established player, and could expect, all being well, to
proceed through the tiring thickets of odd-job work to specialized parts
and perhaps, eventually, to the élite position of shareholder. Some
reliance on the grammar schools is of importance, since the kind of
education (particularly in verbal understanding and communication)
seems to have influenced the basic 'style' of Elizabethan acting. (*See*
Bertram Joseph's book, *Elizabethan Acting*, 1951, and its considerably
revised edition, 1964.)

Our knowledge is insufficient to warrant firm conclusions about the
most common style or styles of Elizabethan acting. We can make guesses
about some matters however: (1) The size of the Globe/Fortune stage
must have tended to influence the actor towards 'broad' acting. (2) The
fact that the stage was both flanked and faced by the audience probably
encouraged 'dimensional' acting — where the actor is bound to direct his
power not in one direction (as in the proscenium theatre) but in several.
(3) The flanking galleries increased the need for 'dimensional' acting in a
vertical direction. It was said of Burbage, '... I have seen the knave paint
grief in such a lively colour, that for false and acted passion he has drawne
true teares from the spectators. Ladies in the boxes kept time with sighs, and
teares to his sad accents ...' (4) The proximity of the groundlings possibly
put a brake on over-expansiveness of communication. Perhaps, indeed, one
style of Elizabethan acting consisted of a rhythm between expansive and
intimate, broad and restricted, extrovert and introvert. Such a 'rhythm'
has some confirmation in the organization of a number of Shakespeare's
plays — where the self-examining soliloquy, or the self-revealing speech,
spoken, we may imagine, with conspiratorial frankness to the closest part
of the audience, seems in sharp contrast to the well-populated scenes of
great action and debate. (5) The fact that boys played women's parts must
have influenced the general acting style. In plays like *Love's Labour's Lost,
Twelfth Night, As You Like It*, with very strong female roles, the overall
acting style cannot but have been edged into a certain condition by the
boys. That condition was probably formalistic, and would seem artificial
and contrived to us.

The Audiences

From the 1560s to the 1640s the population of London was about 200,000.
The estimated maximum capacity of the Globe, the Fortune and the Swan
theatres was about 2000. Henslowe's Diary makes it apparent that, apart
from the drawing-power of new plays, and on public holidays, the average
attendance at a large public theatre was half its capacity. The estimated

maximum capacity of private theatres was about 1000. Such figures can lure the unwary into reckless assumptions. The only reasonable conclusion is that (remembering the number of public and private theatres, the huge number of plays written from *c.* 1580–1620) London audiences were very well catered for. What is uncertain, however, is the percentage of the population attending at any given period, or at any given performance or any documented theatre.

What we can be more certain about is that one section of the population thought of plays, players and theatres as agents of the devil, and that another welcomed them heartily, if noisily. These sections very roughly approximated to Puritan and official and non-Puritan and unofficial. The attitude of the one (in an extreme form) is well reflected here — 'the cause of plagues is sin . . . and the cause of sin are plays, therefore the cause of plagues are plays'. The attitude of the other is clearly if vigorously expressed here: 'I will defend it [theatre] against any cullion or club-footed usurer of them all, there is no immortality can be given a man on earth like unto plays.'

Prices support the conclusion that there was a greater percentage of the less well-off in the big public theatres than in the private; it is wrong to assume, however, that only the affluent 'went private'. Generally, however, we can agree with an antiquary who wrote in 1699, that in the Blackfriars (private) were to be found 'men of grave and sober Behaviour' but that the Red Bull (public) was 'mostly frequented by Citizens, and the meaner sort of People'.

Many apocryphal stories have clotted around Shakespeare and the Elizabethans, and some true ones — not the least being those about the nature and behaviour of audiences in the public theatres. Orange-wenches (who sold more than fruit), pickpockets (or cutpurses), hissing, booing, rioting, whoring, wife-stealing, were rife and vicious; hissing and booing were common rather than exceptional; rioting and brawling, normally a possibility, became a probability on the feast-days when apprentices, rendered permissive by freedom, exercised their mindless muscularity; elegant seduction and expensive prostitution took place in the upper galleries where the drama of real life often rivalled the fiction taking place below.

The disposition of the audiences in the private theatres was less sensational, but only to a degree. We must remember that there was no complete distinction between the two kinds of theatre so far as acting companies were concerned. Although the boys' companies were especially associated with private theatres, Shakespeare's company, the King's Men acted both at the Globe (public) and the Blackfriars (private), and at least two of his plays, *The Tempest* and *The Winter's Tale*, may well have been written for a private theatre.

The private theatres were élitist not in the sense that they rigorously catered for the affluent but that prices tended to dictate the social composition of the audience:

> I will hasten to the money Box, [i.e. the box-office]
> And take my shilling out again, for now
> I have considered that it is too much,
> I'll go to th'Bull or Fortune, and there see
> A Play for two pense, with a Jig to boot.

Elizabethan Acting Companies

THE BOYS' COMPANIES

Children of Paul's
Children of the Chapel and
  Queen's Revels
Children of Windsor
Children of the King's Revels
Children of Bristol
Westminster School
Eton College
Merchant Taylors' School
Earl of Leicester's Boys
Earl of Oxford's Boys
Mr Stanley's Boys

THE ADULT COMPANIES

Court Interluders
Earl of Leicester's Men
Lord Rich's Men
Lord Abergavenny's Men
Earl of Sussex's Men
Sir Robert Lane's Men
Earl of Lincoln's (Lord Clinton's) Men
Earl of Warwick's Men
Earl of Oxford's Men
Earl of Essex's Men
Lord Vaux's Men
Lord Berkeley's Men
Queen Elizabeth's Men
Earl of Arundel's Men
Earl of Hertford's Men
Mr Evelyn's Men
Earl of Derby's (Lord Strange's) Men
Earl of Pembroke's Men
Lord Admiral's (became successively Lord Howard's, Earl of Nottingham's, Prince Henry's and Elector Palatine's Men)
Lord Chamberlain's (Lord Hunsdon's) and King's Men
Earl of Worcester's and Queen Anne's Men
Duke of Lennox's Men
Duke of York's (Prince Charles's) Men
Lady Elizabeth's Men

Henry Irving, in the 19th century, was the first actor to be knighted — the accolade was withheld from such eminent predecessors as David Garrick, Edmund Kean, William Macready. This was because the profession was regarded as suspect. Acting was, for many people, the equivalent of vagabondage. Henry Irving's knighthood conferred official respectability, but even today mention of the word 'actor' or 'theatre' is likely to raise, from someone, an eyebrow slightly bristling with mistrust. Noël Coward enjoined Mrs Worthington, in his famous song, not to put her daughter on the stage. Many people believe his instinct was right.

There is logic in the distrust. The troupes of players which wandered about the country in the 15th and 16th centuries, stopping at fairs, doing their turns and painting the town red, were a reckless, feckless, sometimes dangerous lot. They were, so to speak, mercenary entertainers, without any scruples about local mores. Women accompanied them like camp-followers in an army — indeed the absence of the female sex from the Elizabethan professional acting companies has been attributed to the infamous reputation of the troupes.

In 1572 an 'Acte for the punishment of Vacabondes' attempted to control the strollers. It bundled together 'Fencers', 'Bearewardes' (those involved in the spectacle of bear-baiting), 'Comon players', 'Minstrels', 'Juglers', 'Pedlars', 'Tynkers' and others, and ordained that they had to be authorized either by two justices or one noble lord.

By 1598, a further act stated that authorization could be made only by a noble lord. These enactments had two effects: firstly to isolate those strolling entertainers who had no sponsor, secondly to attract a kind of status to those players who were authorized. This was dignification by association. But it was a two-way process. The conceit of designation — the Lord Leicester's, the Lord Worcester's, the Earl of Pembroke's — gave the sponsor the thrill of possession and the frisson of public recognition.

Nevertheless, the umbrella of noble patronage had to be supplemented by practical safeguards. Elizabethan acting companies were, in fact, limited companies. The actors invested their money in the property — consisting of all the paraphernalia of costumes, sets and play-scripts (you could buy a play from an author outright for about £7). The actors took on the responsibility and shared the profits. Most companies had senior participants called 'sharers' (Shakespeare was one). One acted as business manager. He supervised the hiring of actors and apprentices, and controlled the work of the gatherers (box-office personnel), the tire-men (props men), stage-keepers (stage-hands), musicians and the book-keeper — the last being of great importance. He was the prompter, but also prepared the book — that is the text — for performance. He had the crucial task of submitting his 'book' to the Master of the Revels for censorship. He needed strong nerves to deal with temperamental actors and the vagaries of censorship. Small wonder that a hint of frenzy is indicated in the antics of a book-keeper depicted in *The Maid in the Mill* (Anon. 1623). A woman's screams are heard from the tiring-house, and a character explains them — 'they are out of their parts sure: it may be 'tis the Book-holder's fault . . .' A farcical version of a book-keeper is Peter Quince in *A Midsummer Night's Dream*.

Some theatres were run by powerful and even ruthless tycoons — Philip Henslowe (the Rose), Francis Langley (the Swan). Some companies rented theatres. Other houses, like the Globe and the Blackfriars and the Red Bull, were owned by companies — the first two by the Lord Chamberlain's Men, the third by the Lord Worcester's. They were fortunate, for Henslowe in particular drove hard bargains. He took half the money from the galleries, kept the theatre in repair and paid the licence to the Master of the Revels. This apparently innocent procedure hides somewhat murky complexities. In 1615 the Lady Elizabeth's company drew up a document called *Articles of Grievance and of Oppression against Phillip Henslowe*. It makes grim reading, and its findings are supported by the best possible supporting evidence — Philip Henslowe's own Diary. It was Henslowe's practice simply to keep the companies in his debt — on the principle that overdrafts create money and power. He acted as a banker, advancing capital for purchase of costumes, plays, scenery (his Diary itemizes this). Actors, rarely noted for monetary caution, borrowed money only to find themselves 'bound' to him. He instituted a system of fines, and even extended his tentacles to control a dramatist — Henry Chettle. He was, briefly, a shark, and members of the profession were his 'victims'.

The affairs of the Chamberlain's Men were under the control of the company of actors itself. Two brothers, Cuthbert and Richard Burbage, built the Globe. They held one half of the shares, the other half being divided between five senior members — including Shakespeare. The sharers or 'housekeepers' took profits from the yard and half of the galleries.

The most famous company when Shakespeare was in his late teens was the Queen Elizabeth's Men. On the afternoon of 15 June 1583 they played at the Red Lion, Norwich. In that summer they played at Bristol, Cambridge, Leicester, Gloucester, Aldeburgh, Nottingham and Shrewsbury. In 1585–6 they were at Coventry and elsewhere, and in 1586–7 at Bath, Worcester, Canterbury and Stratford upon Avon. In that year Shakespeare was twenty-three. The Queen's Men lacked two players — one had killed the other in self-defence! Could it be that a stage-struck young man whose father, as Mayor in the old days, had entertained visiting companies, joined them and, eventually, returned to London with them?

Conjecture aside, the peregrinations of the Queen's Men typify one important feature of Elizabethan companies — they travelled for a substantial portion of most years. The London season was short, rendered so by the ravages of the plague and persistent closures of theatres by the authorities. London audiences, therefore, had no monopoly on the most famous companies, but it is doubtful whether the provinces saw the same repertoire as did the capital. Interludes probably formed the main item on the list of plays to travel. Moreover, for economy's sake the companies probably travelled light — in both materials and men. Nevertheless, towns like Stratford, Bath, Leicester, Shrewsbury and others — but particularly Stratford, being at a crucial geographical point — saw, and doubtless rejoiced in, the famous.

All the major characteristics of theatre appeared in a unique, at times sensational, form in Shakespeare's time: failure, success, heartache, inefficiency, proficiency, mediocrity, superbity, insecurity, art compromised by grasping lucre, careful economics devastated by undisciplined aspirations. Yet it seems to have had a special panache—perhaps because the country was acquiring a sense of power and a braggadocio talent for expressing it. Shakespeare was in the middle of it — shrewd in monetary calculation, lucky in circumstance and sublime in artistic vision, he both served it and glorified it.

Commonwealth and Restoration (1642–1690)

Kinds and Conditions of Theatre

Oliver Cromwell achieved by Act of Parliament what officialdom and moral pressure failed to do in the reigns of Elizabeth, James and Charles — he closed the London theatres. This was done by an ordinance of 2 September 1642. To all intents and purposes no stage-play could be performed, but repression encourages violation of its very authority and incites curiosity about that which is repressed. Although the great London theatres were closed down — all of them for ever as it turned out — Cromwell could not quell the intense interest in dramatic entertainment. All kinds of subterfuges were used to circumvent the law — one of the most successful was to present dramatic entertainments with music, whose addition apparently lent respectability and thus gave immunity from Cromwell. Countless plays were performed during the Commonwealth, in inns, noble households, and college halls, disguised as what came to be known as 'operas' to designate a sophisticated genre, and 'drolls' which employed words and music in a cruder form, and mixed them with dancing, fooling and acrobatics. Indeed, Cromwell's repression, while it stopped the public performance of 'straight' plays (including Shakespeare's), paradoxically encouraged several developments — first, of English opera (the first being *The Siege of Rhodes* by Davenant in 1656), second, of 'drolls' and solo entertainments in inns which, in time, led to the development of music hall and vaudeville and, third, the adaptation of Shakespeare's plays to accommodate enough music to keep them within the law — but this had deleterious results which became obvious later.

Other results Cromwell could not have foreseen. Actors were, on the whole, staunchly Royalist during the Civil War. As the King's defeat became inevitable, many escaped to the Continent and formed or joined émigré companies. They experienced the theatre worlds of France, Italy and elsewhere. On their return at the Restoration, they brought new ideas and practices (the use of actresses for example). Charles II, too, returned from exile with French notions which, with his love of theatrical entertainment, he could command to be made flesh.

Cromwell, by repression, probably hastened fundamental changes in English theatre, but if we scoff at his attempts to destroy it we must be cautious about assuming that the restored Charles II immediately gave the order for a theatrical free-for-all. He proceeded with caution, even severity, and, in fact, created a pattern in London theatre which persisted until the 19th century: '. . . And in regard of the extraordinary licentiousness that hath been lately used in things of this nature, our pleasure is that there shall be noe more places of representations, nor companies of actors of playes . . . in our citties of London and Westminster, or in the liberties of them, than the two to be now erected by vertue of this authority.'

In August 1660 a grant incorporating those words was issued to Thomas Killigrew and Sir William Davenant — this amounted to a monopoly. They were 'to erect two companies of players . . . and to purchase, builde, and erect, on hire at their charge, as they shall think fitt, two houses or theatres'. In other words two theatres only could legally perform 'straight' plays. Needless to say, ways around this were as assiduously sought as in the time of Cromwell's repression. Shakespeare's plays were divided up between the two men. Killigrew was not hypnotized by the Bard and was as much drawn to Jonson and Fletcher. In ten years he presented only *Othello, Henry IV, Julius Caesar*, and a few comedies, among them *A Midsummer Night's Dream* and *The Merry Wives of Windsor*. Davenant was obsessed with Shakespeare — he believed himself (or claimed) to be his illegitimate son. Indeed, in December 1660 a patent was issued which 'reserved' certain plays for him. They included *The Tempest, Hamlet, Macbeth* and *King Lear*. Moreover, the words of the regulation seem to accept Davenant's (spurious) special relationship with Shakespeare — it says that he was given the plays '. . . in order to reform and make [them] fitt for the company of actors appointed under his direction and command'. These words are important in any attempt to understand the characteristic Restoration attitude to Shakespeare's plays.

The Duke of York's Company (Davenant's) had several homes — Salisbury Court, then Lincoln's Inn Fields, then Dorset Gardens: built in 1670, possibly from a design of Christopher Wren's, it was 140 ft long, 57 ft wide. It had apartments for actors (Betterton had one), seven lower boxes — each seating twenty people — and seven on the upper level. The King's Company (Killigrew's) eventually found a home at a newly-built theatre — Theatre Royal, Drury Lane: erected in 1674, its dimensions were 140 by 58 ft. Its pit benches had no backboards but became famous for their green cloth coverings. There were significant differences in practice from the Elizabethan public theatres. In 1660 performances began at 3.00 or 3.30 pm; by 1695 this was 4.00 pm; by 1700 6.00 or 6.30 pm. At Killigrew's and Davenant's theatres boxes cost 4s. 6d., the pit 2s. 6d., the gallery 1s. 6d. and 1s.

The Stage
The typical design of a Restoration stage and auditorium seems a revolutionary departure from the Elizabethan public playhouse, like the Globe.

In fact it was evolution, shouldered along by the Continental experience of returned émigrés.

The 'look' of a Restoration theatre is best realized by visualizing the type of theatre still predominant in the 20th century despite the advent of modern structures. In Europe and the United States 19th-century proscenium stages and auditoriums are still in the majority. These relate naturally to Restoration stages. We see, in both, a stage like a box, with actors playing inside it. It is flanked and backed by scenery consisting of painted canvas cloths and 'flats'. It has a front curtain — something the Globe Theatre never had. There are, too, side boxes seating the affluent — and those nearest the stage are within touching distance of the actors.

In front of this, projecting towards the audience, was the forestage. Victorian theatres still show remnants of this. The typical Restoration stage then, had a large box, a curtain and a projecting platform (in one theatre it was curved and projected 17 ft into the audience). What happened was that the small recess, together with its curtain, at the back of the Elizabethan public stage grew into a full size proscenium stage (that is, it became the box) and that the Elizabethan apron remained (and became the projecting platform). The connection between Restoration and Elizabethan is seen even more strongly in that most of the acting in both eras took place on the apron/forestage. Here the comparison ends and the results of Continental experience appear.

The proscenium box was virtually a display and entrance/exit area. The display consisted of scenery made of painted wings and shutters movable in grooves. In each of the side walls were two or three doors (topped by windows) allowing multiple entrances/exits. One of the 'marvels' for the audience was that the scenes could be changed before their very eyes, as different decorated shutters replaced others in their grooves. The visual emphasis in Restoration productions was intensified by the use of 'devices' (Davenant was very ingenious with them) producing sensational effects — people and objects could be made to fly, disappear, reappear and (a triumph of technology) property ships could be made to sink into a cruel scenic sea! Most people revelled in these ocular feasts, others had a jaundiced if involuntarily admiring eye:

> Damn'd Plays shall be adorn'd with mighty Scenes,
> And Fustian shall be spoke in huge Machines.
> And we will purling streams and Fireworks show,
> And you may live to see it Rain and Snow.

Lighting was hardly less basic than that of the Elizabethan theatres; it consisted of wax candles, lanterns and daylight through a skylight in the auditorium.

The Audience

The hoi-polloi were catered for in the rapidly-developing 'music hall' pubs — makeshift houses. Killigrew and Davenant catered mainly but not exclusively for high society and the Court. There was much competition for prominent boxes — 'Leaning over other ladies awhile to whisper with the King, she rose out of the box and went into the King's right hand . . . She did it only to show the world that she is not out of favour yet, as was believed.' There was still apprehension about Ladies of Quality attending performances — 'venturing bare-faced' is Pepys's description — so for many years the wearing of masks (vizards) was commonplace until abolished by Queen Anne in 1714.

Although theatre managers and dramatists largely catered for upper-class tastes, there was social stratification of a kind which was significant for the future. A French visitor in 1698 described what he saw at the second Theatre Royal: 'The Pit is an Amphitheater, fill'd with Benches without Backboards . . . men of Quality, particularly the younger sort, some Ladies of Reputation and Vertue, and abundance of Damsels that haunt for Prey, sit all together in this Place, higgledy-piggledy . . . Farther up, against the Wall, under the first Gallery, and just opposite to the Stage, rises another Amphitheatre, which is taken up by Persons of the best Quality, among whom are generally very few Men. The Galleries, whereof there are only two Rows, are fill'd with none but ordinary People, particularly the upper one.' It strikes us at once — the social geography of the Elizabethan theatre has been reversed. The cheapest seats and the lesser people (the 'ordinary' ones) are up in the galleries, the dearest and greater further down. In the heyday of Victorian theatre 'up in the gallery' was strictly reserved for the impecunious and the rowdy, the middle dress-circle for their masters; the old pit, now the stalls, for the affluent, and the boxes for the socially important. Everyone was seated, but not many could get in — the earliest Restoration theatres (such as the Theatre Royal) held no more than five hundred people.

It was a volatile audience, permissive, noisy, extrovert, even dangerous. 'Sept. 2, 1675. Last Saturday at ye Dukes play-house ther happened a quarrel between Mr. Scroppe, who was in drinke, and Sir Tho. Armstronge. Mr. Scroope [sic] gave Sir Tho. very ill language and, at last, drew upon him: whereupon Sir Tho. drew, and ye first passe ran Mr. Scroope through ye heart, who fell dead upon ye place without speaking a word.' Orange wenches, prostitutes, cads and pickpockets still abounded. Yet, for all this similarity to the Elizabethan audience, there is something foreign about Restoration theatre — a kind of mannered flamboyance and extravagance that seems a long way from the rich English mixture of velvet and fustian of Shakespeare's time. This foreign-ness is reflected almost grotesquely in the fate that befell Shakespeare's plays during the period. Indeed, many of the versions performed are mere ghosts of the original and the acting and costumes used increase the sense that we are in an alien country of theatrical experience.

The Restoration had an ambivalent attitude towards Shakespeare. It admired him as a genius, but deplored the fact that, having lived in what they considered a barbaric age, his plays had so many faults of construction, language and taste. How unfortunate for him not to have been born into their age which had achieved the ultimate in artistic expression! The ambivalence is characteristically expressed here — 'Shakespeare, tho rude, yet his immortal wit/Shall never to the stroke of time submit' — but they were often less gentle when it came to individual plays. *Hamlet* is an 'indifferent play' with 'an indifferent good part for a madman'. Samuel Pepys thought *A Midsummer Night's Dream* '. . . the most insipid ridiculous play that ever I saw in my life'.

Where had Shakespeare gone wrong? A consensus of informed Restoration opinion shows the following: (1) Shakespeare, unlike Ben Jonson, lacked the discipline of classical drama, particularly noticeable in his ignoring of the unity of Time (i.e. the duration of the action should be as near as possible to the duration of the performance), unity of Place (i.e. the location of the action should so far as possible remain the same), unity of Action (i.e. the circumstances of the events should so far as possible be concerned with no more than one plot). (2) Some of his plays are theatrically unattractive — in the sense that they are unpleasant (e.g. *Measure for Measure*) or far-fetched (e.g. *A Midsummer Night's Dream*). (3) Shakespeare's language is generally defective; he uses too much 'figurative language' (e.g. 'No, this my hand will rather the multitudinous seas incarnadine, making the green one red') which is extravagant and unnatural. (4) He lacks decorum (e.g. violent deaths are depicted — these are offensive to refined tastes). (5) He is dangerously prone to give too much dramatic prominence to the lower orders, giving them dominant roles in high serious action (e.g. in the English History plays). (6) He 'mixes' his styles and genres, introducing comic characters into tragedies (e.g. the drunken porter in *Macbeth*, the Fool in *King Lear*). (7) He is sometimes guilty of 'moral' imbalance — for example not always showing evil in the descendant, but often in the ascendant, as in *Macbeth*, and in a lack of moral taste in some of his endings, e.g. Lear and Cordelia should not die; he, because he has repented, she, because she is virtuous. (8) Women are gentle creatures and not to suffer cruelties from men, neither should they unnaturally inflict cruelty (but see his Queen Margaret and Lady Macbeth).

The regulation which enjoined Davenant to 'reform and make fitt' Shakespeare's plays for the stage is a most infamous piece of legislation. The phrase became a sort of motto for managers, directors, actors and playwrights in their astounding cooking sprees to make Shakespeare palatable. Of all the perpetrations mere cutting is the least crime.

Davenant greatly reduced the player-scenes in *Hamlet*; the Prince's
famous advice to the players is missing; twenty-seven lines are cut from
the famous soliloquy — 'O what a rogue and peasant slave'; a good deal
of Act I, Scene i has disappeared.

Ferocious cutting was commonplace and the reasons for it explain other
kind of interference with Shakespeare's plays. Cutting is based on the
principle of purification of Shakespeare by curtailment.

The second form of purification was full-scale adaptation. Samuel
Pepys records seeing *The Law against Lovers* in 1661. Lo and behold it is
Measure for Measure shrived (by Restoration standards)! The Mariana story
is omitted, as are the comic characters. Juliet has become a major character. Angelo turns out a hero in Act IV, declaring he loved Isabella all the
time and was only testing her out! He is given a mild punishment, but he
and the ex-nun-novitiate live happily ever after; and Claudio too. This is
manipulation enough, but it's not all. A sub-plot has a character
called Benedick (Angelo's brother) and another, Beatrice (Angelo's
ward) who are in love. Thus *Much Ado About Nothing* is brought to the
bedside of *Measure for Measure* to propagate a bastard! Needless to
say this Davenant version leaves little of Shakespeare's language un-
touched.

The third form of purification was to retain the skeleton and some of the
flesh of a play, but change its spirit. For example, apart from cuts and
ministrations to characters in *Macbeth* (Lady Macduff's role is considerably expanded and, true to Restoration sensibilities, we do not witness her
death), the play is riddled with dancing, singing and contortionist acts.
The terrible malpractice it suffered is summed up in what Davenant
wrote as Macbeth's dying line — 'Farewell vain World, and what's most
vain in it, Ambition.'

The greatest poet and critic of the age, Dryden, was a notable adaptor
who keyed his changes to the spirit of his own age. His *Truth Found Too
Late*, 1679, was a mechanized, unsubtle, dead version of *Troilus and
Cressida* in which Cressida is faithful! In other hands *A Midsummer Night's
Dream* became *The Fairy Queen*, 1692, *Measure for Measure* became *Beauty
the Best Advocate*, 1700 and *Twelfth Night* lay buried deep inside *Love
Betray'd; or the Agreeable Disappointment*, 1703. The incredible failure of
dramatic taste in an age so discriminating in other respects is entirely
represented in Nahum Tate's version of *King Lear* — its last few lines
tell all:

> Lear: Why I have news that will recall thy youth;
>   Ha! did'st thou hear't, or did the inspiring Gods
>   Whisper to me alone? Old Lear shall be a King again.
> Kent: The Prince that like a God has Pow'r, has said it.

Cordelia: *Cordelia* then shall be a Queen, mark that;
          Cordelia shall be a Queen; winds catch the sound;
          And bear it on your rosie wings to Heav'n
          Cordelia is a Queen.

Shakespearean Acting in the Restoration

The fundamental difference between the constituents of Elizabethan and Restoration acting is represented by the fact that actresses were introduced into the professional theatre for the first time, in 1666 (*see* Margaret Hughes). They were allowed with some official piety — a royal patent granted to Killigrew in 1662 stated that 'all the woemen's part ... may be performed by woemen soe long as their recreacones (recreations) ... may ... be esteemed not onely harmless delight but useful and instructive.' If trepidation hid behind this, it was well justified — the coming of actresses did little to encourage harmless delight!

Restoration acting was 'personality' acting — the actor or actress attempted to cast a spell over the audience rather than embody in detail the character they were playing. In other words psychological realism was secondary to sensational histrionics. Even the great Betterton who attempted some degree of realism often seems to have been concerned with cutting a dash rather than creating a character '. . . upon his Entrance into every scene, he seem'd to seize upon the Eyes and Ears of the Giddy and Inadvertent!' He was praised for delineating each character differently, but he still seized the imagination as Betterton rather than as the character — 'There cannot be a stronger Proof of the Charms of harmonious Elocution, than the many, even unnatural Scenes and Flights of the false sublime it has lifted into Applause' — in other words he could turn good and bad into account by his personality. This was no less true of the actresses — Mrs Barry (Betterton's partner) '. . . had a Presence of elevated Dignity, her Mien and Motion superb, and gracefully majestick; her Voice full, clear, and strong, so that no Violence or Passion could be too much for her'. Mrs Bracegirdle whatever part she played never made 'an *Exit*, but that she left the Audience in an Imitation of her pleasant Countenance'.

Costume

The ritualistic nature of the acting was partly dictated by costume. Players were generally personally responsible for obtaining hats, feathers, gloves, sword belts, stockings and shoes. But the theatre usually provided perukes, lace, shoes, hats, plumes of feathers and, sometimes, lengths of fine cloth. Items in this list immediately suggest (1) a certain finery and (2) a certain bizarrerie. In fact Restoration costume was, basically, opulent modern dress topped with excess in perukes, feathers, etc. This lent an entirely unreal aspect to what was worn. Such costume airily defied historical accuracy. The combination of Restoration dress, plumed feathers and a fake mediaeval breastplate must have taxed the credibility of any performance. Nevertheless, some descriptions of acting of the time do make us remember that individual genius or talent can, on occasion, transcend the usual way of the world — '. . . sudden Emotions of Amazement and Horror, turn instantly on the Sight of his Father's Spirit, as pale as his Neckcloth, when every Article of his Body seem'd to be affected with a Tremor inexpressible; so that, had his Father's Ghost actually risen before him, he could not have been seized with more real Agonies; and this was felt so strongly by the Audience, that the Blood seemed to shudder in their Veins likewise, and they in some Measure partook of the Astonishment and Horror, with which they saw this excellent Actor affected' (a contemporary account of Betterton as Hamlet).

Late 17th and Early 18th Century (1690–1740)

The Restoration period from 1660 to the end of the century also generated a tremendous activity in dramatic representation. Significantly the first thing the word 'Restoration' implies has nothing to do with politics or religion, but with art. Restoration comedy has become an emblem for the whole of what we take to be the social reality of the period; our sense of the period is nourished less by the historian than by the dramatists. The century was replete with dramatists and impressarios and actors and actresses, good, bad and indifferent. It bequeathed to the 18th century beliefs and practices about drama and theatre which were still apparent at the end of that century. It had many colourful figures, like Colley Cibber, whose pugilistic-sounding name disguised a man of enormously atheltic imagination and energy. It had, too, its paradoxes despite its reputation for an unremitting permissiveness and moral turpitude. Collier, for example, was an inveterate enemy of the 'evils' of theatre, and wrote the most strongly-worded condemnation in the history of theatre polemics. These two men represented extremes of attitude.

In the first two decades of the 18th century there was a broadening out of theatre activity to include a greater diversity of class and taste. Queen Anne stimulated interest, and liked to have entertainments brought to her at Court. If she had gone out she would have had sufficient evidence of the colourful life of theatre to send her packing home — '. . . going through the *Play-House Yard* . . . one Saucy Impudent Slut or another would, in a manner, be forcing their *Oranges* on us . . . no Place could more represent the Pit of Hell than that . . . Looking upwards, I saw the upper galleries was taken up by such Rubbish as *Butlars* [sic], *Chamber-Maids*, quacking *Apothecaries*, and *Apprentices* . . . In the Middle Gallery sat the Middling sort of People, such as Merchants wives . . . among whom creep Ladies Waiting-Women, *Lawyers Clerks*, and *Valet de Chambres* . . . In the side Boxes . . . were got upstart Officers . . . and other pragmatical Beaux, Complimenting and Courting a parcel of Strumpets . . . In the front Boxes sat Persons of Quality . . . Some of Scolasticks were got on the stage.'

The production of Shakespeare's plays legitimately was still, of course, confined to the two patent theatres, Covent Garden and Drury Lane. At one time a notable impressario, John Rich, held the patent for both theatres and therefore the monopoly of legitimate Shakespeare, but Colley Cibber eventually took over at Drury Lane and the virtual monopoly was bequeathed to him. Devious attempts were made by others to circumvent the monopoly — at Goodman's Fields Theatre, for example, a concert had a very long intermission indeed in which a performance of a version of *The Winter's Tale* took place 'gratis' — the word 'gratis' removed performances from condemnation as a violation of the patent.

During the first two decades of the 18th century, Shakespeare's tragedies and histories (but not his comedies) were frequently performed. *Hamlet* and *Macbeth* were pre-eminently popular, followed by *Othello* and *King Lear* in that order. *The Tempest* was performed regularly and, curiously, three plays which even today do not have an altogether prominent place in Shakespearean repertory — *Timon of Athens*, *Henry VIII* and *All's Well That Ends Well*. The immense popularity of Restoration comedy accounts for the relative unpopularity of Shakespeare's romantic comedies, but these three Cinderellas of the canon caught the imagination.

Interpretation of Shakespeare's Plays

Little had changed since the high if not holy days of Restoration adaptation. In fact, they still used the basic acting texts of the inveterate meddlers of the Restoration — Davenant, Dryden, Tate and Betterton. In other words, versions of Shakespeare, rather than Shakespeare plain were paramount. Some typical examples were:

(1) *The Cobler of Preston* which disguised the Christopher Sly scenes from *The Merry Wives of Windsor*. Sly was changed to Toby Guzzle, his wife to Dame Hackett. There was also a Sir Jasper Manley and a miller called Grist. A specimen of dialogue shows the contemporary or near-contemporary slant taken: 'Dub-Rub, Dub a Dub! Rumps and Round-heads, Rumps and Round-Heads! I'll be a Rebel, down with the Rump, down with the Rump; and yet I do not rebell, look 'ee because I hate the Government, but because there should be no Government at all . . .' Its character-names with their fearsome puns and the heavy-handed political jokes remind one of pantomime. The comparison is apt. The effects of the highly popular art of pantomime on theatre is a marked characteristic of the time.

(2) *Jane Shore* by Rowe (one of the earliest editors of Shakespeare). This was a plodding piece deriving from the Hastings scenes in *Richard III*. Rowe had the grace to state that it was 'in imitation of Shakespeare's style' — but that didn't help very much!

(3) *The Invader of his Country or the Fatal Resentment*. This was by John Dennis, a literary rag-bag of the times. It is an example of the worst kind of sententiousness. Unbelievably, it was a version of *Coriolanus*. The play was withdrawn after three performances — an example of the best kind of criticism. The prologue to this terrible assault on a great Shakespeare

play serves admirably to justify Pope's castigation of Dennis as pompous, and to exhibit the tone of its author's rendition of the original. The prologue speaks of Shakespeare:

> In whose Original we may descry
> Where Master-strokes in wild Confusion lye,
> Here brought to as much Order as we can
> Reduce those Beauties upon Shakespear's plan.

The most durable and, in many ways, the most theatrically effective of all the adaptations was Colley Cibber's *Richard III*, first performed at Drury Lane in 1700 but which remained a standard acting text until well into the 19th century. Indeed, remnants of Cibberism have appeared in 20th-century productions — notably in Laurence Olivier's film version in 1955. Cibber's version is a piebald affair. Much of Shakespeare has disappeared, including Margaret's famous curse and Clarence's moving account of his dream. Speeches from *Henry IV*, *Henry V* and *Richard II* appear, but perhaps the most famous (and, indeed, most effective) transposition is the superb declaration of intent to get the crown by Duke Richard of Gloucester from *Henry VI, Part 3* which Cibber used to open his version of *Richard III*. Cibberisms are rife, the most spectacular being the line he wrote for Richard to express his feelings about Buckingham — 'Off with his head: so much for Buckingham.' Even the most fervent purist might find it difficult to sneer at this. It has that peremptory vicious playfulness so typical of Richard.

Staging of Shakespeare's Plays

There was, it seems, no profound change in staging throughout the period. Stage architecture remained basically the same — apron, rear stage, proscenium doors. There was apparently greater sophistication in the use of painted flats which were common throughout the period: for example, at the end of a scene, instead of the players leaving by the proscenium doors, they remained on stage while flats behind them were replaced. After the change, the players moved into the new locale.

There seems to have been, too, some variation in the use of the front curtain between acts. Sometimes two side flats at mid-stage were brought together, so that only the apron was visible to the audience. The first scene of the next act was then prepared behind the closed flats. Addison, in the *Tatler* magazine, wrote an amusing account of what awaited behind the flats. It is a send-up, but we can discern what the late 17th- and early 18th-century audiences were subjected to. 'One shower of Snow in the Whitest *French* Paper', 'A Rainbow, a little faded', 'A Sea, consisting of a Dozen large Waves', 'A Serpent to sting *Cleopatra*', 'A new Moon, something decay'd'.

The late 17th- and early 18th-century stage was cluttered with stage

objects backed by flats with conventional scenes painted upon them —
these flats can be regarded as much as painter's canvasses as stage-scenery.
There probably was, too, some influence from the elaborate sets used for
the rapidly developing art of opera at the Haymarket Theatre. To us they
would have seemed unnatural and 'cut-out', but to the time they were
very acceptable and, in any case, the other senses were satisfied. One contemporary account refers to the pity and terror incited in audiences in
productions of tragedy. It is 'due to Thunder and Lightning, which are
often made use of at the descending of a God, or the Rising of a Ghost . . .
I have known a Bell introduced into several Tragedies with good Effect;
and have seen the whole Assembly in a very great Alarm all the while it
has been ringing. But there is nothing which delights and terrifies our
English Theatre so much as a Ghost, especially when he appears in a
bloody Shirt.'

In some theatres the prompter wore a whistle round his neck and blew
it as a signal for a scene change. At a single blow of the whistle 'I have
seen', said a contemporary commentator, 'Cities turned into Forests, and
dreary Desarts converted into superb Palaces . . . I have seen Heaven and
Earth pass away, and Chaos ensue . . .' To us, perhaps, these audiences
were gullible, but who can doubt that the theatres were fulfilling the first
duty of the theatrical art — to employ illusion.

Lighting

Stages were lit by suspended hoops of candles (an innovation of Cibber's).
Little variety of effect was possible, players were in danger from hot wax,
but the light given was pleasing and mellow. The hoops could be retracted
into the flies producing effects of varying intensity, but the imagination
boggles at the fire hazard. Candles were also used as footlights, at least by
1735.

Costume

Whatever visual excesses were indulged in immediately after the Restoration they were outdone both in scenery and in costume in the latter
decades of the 17th century and the first three or four of the 18th. The
attitude to costume was completely laissez-faire and the result invariably
bizarre and, above all, unsuited to the character being depicted. This was
particularly true of tragedy. Heroines always had large hooped skirts with
a train and, however inappropriate to the situation, the train was borne by
a small page. Heroes and heroines wore enormous wigs or head-furniture
sometimes of frizzled 'Afro-Asian' hair. Jewellery, objets d'art, plumes,
made the player's head look like an eastern bazaar. Addison commented
— 'The ordinary Method of making an Hero, is to clap a Plume of
Feathers upon his Head, which rises so very high, that there is often a
greater length from his Chin to the Top of his Head, than to the Sole of his

Foot.' As to the ladies' trains, he comments — 'I am not so attentive to any thing she speaks, as to the right adjusting of her Train lest it should chance to trip up her Heels, or incommode her. . . .'

Such bizarrerie reflects, yet again, the influence of Pantomime; moreover, such paraphernalia inevitably drew attention to the player rather than to the character being depicted. Truly, these were the heydays of personality acting — it was 'behaviourism' of a most advanced kind. Rarely, again, was Shakespeare production, visually, to be so utterly permissive; even at the time voices were heard condemning it, and attempts were made to replace it with something more rational. Aaron Hill, a dramatist, adaptor and stage-theoretician, wrote, in 1735 — 'I have been greatly offended at the ridiculous Dresses, in which our inferior sons of the Buskin make their appearance . . . I am sensible, it would be more Expensive, to cloath Every Actor with Propriety . . . so it would, to qualify Managers with Judgement. Yet, Both the one, and the Other, are what the Publick have a right to expect.' Whatever the public expected, the players had to wear what they found in their musty dressing rooms. It was first come, first served. The anarchy of the situation is pitifully (and perhaps a little comically) represented by the action of the famous actor, Charles Macklin, who killed a fellow-actor by poking him in the eye with an instrument because he wore a wig that Macklin wanted!

Acting

Bizarrerie also characterized the dominant acting style of the late Restoration period. Until the advent of Macklin, then Garrick, the style was dominated by one man, James Quin — the idol of the theatres, particularly Drury Lane. The novelist, Smollett, described his acting thus: 'His utterance is a continual sing-song, like the chanting of vespers; and his action resembles that of heaving ballast into the hold of a ship.' But convention breeds reaction and by 1741, when Macklin played Shylock, a quite new style of acting was not only in being but had been accepted. A commentator wrote of Macklin — 'We are at present getting more into nature in playing; and if the violence of gesture be not quite suppressed, we have nothing of the recitative of the old tragedy.'

One significant characteristic is the amount of theorizing about the art and nature of acting. This contributed to the emergence of a more naturalistic style of acting which David Garrick brought to perfection. Cibber, Anthony Aston, Aaron Hill, John Hill and Macklin all wrote with intensity and intelligence and all, to a degree, proselytized on behalf of naturalism. Cibber praised Edward Kynaston for playing 'as if he had lost the player and were the real king he personated', and Aaron Hill said that in order to 'act a passion well, the actor must never attempt its imitation, until his fancy has conceived so strong an image, or idea of it, as to move the same impressive springs within his mind, which form that passion, when it is undesigned, and natural'. Macklin wrote that the actor 'must suit his looks, tones, gesture, and manners to the character: *the suiting the character to the powers of the actor, is imposture*' (our italics).

A description of Macklin's Shylock clearly exemplifies what this meant in practice: 'He wears a long black gown, long wide trousers, and a red tricorne, after the fashion of Italian Jews, I suppose.' He spoke the words 'three thousand ducats' slowly and impressively, 'The double "th" and the two sibilants, especially the second after the "t", which Macklin lisps as lickerishly as if he were savouring the ducats . . . make so deep an impression in the man's favour that nothing can destroy it. Three such words uttered thus at the outset give the keynote of his whole character.' Naturalism, to Macklin, involved detailed study of the role and emphasized truth to human nature, not exploitation of grandiose effect.

Audiences

The most obvious characteristics were their predisposition to riot, their permissiveness about where they sat, and the sharp social distinctions which were observed.

Riots had a variety of causes — the price of seats, some unformed hatred, the weather, political confrontation, private rancour turning into public militancy. So prevalent was the threat that it became the custom to place armed guards (sometimes grenadiers) at each proscenium door — this often had an unplanned visual impact on productions — throughout performances. King Charles originally ordered this after a performance at Drury Lane when considerable damage was done to the auditorium when an Earl, said to have been drunk for six years, crossed front-stage to greet a friend and incensed the audience.

The haphazardness of seating and general behaviour is indicated in an announcement of the Drury Lane management in 1738 which reads — 'To prevent any Interruption in the Musick, Dancing, Machinery, or other Parts of the Performance, 'tis hoped no Gentleman will take it ill, that he cannot be admitted behind the scenes, or into the orchestra.' Notable persons were allowed to sit in the orchestra pit, and spectators were frequently invited by the players to sit on the stage. Attempts to avoid possible rioting implicit in this included building side-boxes on the stage. But this frequently led to dissension among the well-to-do members of the audience who sometimes arrived to find all places occupied. At Drury Lane in 1738 it cost exactly five times as much (five shillings) to sit in a side-box, as in the upper gallery. The pit was three shillings and the first gallery (in modern terms, the dress circle) was two shillings. Considering the evidence of an extraordinary ability by some to occupy any part of the theatre that took their fancy, one wonders how many actually paid to get in.

1. The Swan Theatre from a drawing of 1596 by Johannes de Witt. The only known picture of an Elizabethan playhouse stage.

2. Reproduction of the interior of the Globe Theatre, built for a British television series on the life of Shakespeare.

3. Title-page from *A Tragedy in Latin called Roxana*, 1632, showing apron stage and curtained alcove with spectators above.

4. Frontispiece, depicting a 17th-century performance from *The Wits: or Sport upon Sport*. A rare depiction of an actual performance.

The Fifteenth Day.

By HIS MAJESTY's Company of Comedians,
AT THE
THEATRE ROYAL in Drury-Lane,
This present FRIDAY, being the Ninth of JANUARY, 1741.
Will be Presented a COMEDY call'd

AS YOU LIKE IT.

Written by SHAKESPEAR.
Duke, sen. by Mr. MILLS,
Duke Frederick by Mr. WRIGHT,
Jaques by Mr. QUIN,
Orlando by Mr. MILWARD,
Amiens by Mr. LOWE,
Touchstone by Mr. CHAPMAN,

Oliver by Mr. Cashell,	Silvius by Mr. Woodward,	
Adam by Mr. Berry	Phœbe by Miss Bennet,	

Le Beu ⎱ ⎰ Mr. Ridout, ⎪ Charles ⎰ Mr. Winstone,
Jaques de Boys ⎬ by ⎨ Mr. Turbutt, ⎪ William, ⎬ by ⎨ Mr. Ray,
Corin ⎰ ⎱ Mr. Taswell, ⎪ Audry ⎱ Mrs. Egerton,

Cælia by Mrs. CLIVE,
Rosalind by Mrs. PRITCHARD,
The Songs new Set by Mr. ARNE.

With Entertainments of DANCING, Particularly,
End of Act I. a Comic Dance, call'd The French Peasants, by
Mons. NIVELON and Madem. DUVAL, &c.
End of Act III. La Prov.ncalle, by
Mademoiselle CHATEAUNEUF.
End of Act IV. a Dance call'd La Tamborein Matelote, by
Monsieur and Madam MALTERE, &c.

To which will be added, a Pantomime Entertainment, call'd

ROBIN GOODFELLOW;
Or, The RIVAL SISTERS.

HARLEQUIN to be Perform'd by Mr. WOODWARD,
First Colombine, Miss. MANN, Second Colombine, Mrs. WALTER,
And the Part of Slouch, by Mr. MACKLIN,
Concluding with a Grand Serious Ballet, by
Monsieur and Madam MALTERE, &c.

The DANCES depending greatly on the Music, 'tis humbly hop'd no Persons
will take it ill, that they can't be admitted into the Music room.
Boxes 5 s. Pit 3 s. First Gallery 2 s. Upper Gallery 1 s.
To begin exactly at Six o'Clock   VIVAT REX.

PROGRAMME OF THE REVIVAL OF AS YOU LIKE IT, AT DRURY LANE
THEATRE, 1741

From the Harvard Theatre collection

5. Programme for *As You Like It*, 1741. Note the items of pantomime, ballet and comic dancing.

6. Drury Lane Theatre, London, 1773, from an engraving by Benedetto Pastorini. Note the size, and the pit bench-seating. Crown Copyright. Victoria and Albert Museum.

7. Royalty Theatre, London, 1787, clearly showing dramatic backdrop, orchestra pit, boxes and galleries. From a contemporary print.

8. Interior of Sadlers Wells Theatre, London, 1809. From an engraving by Pugin and Rowlandson. Crown Copyright. Victoria and Albert Museum.

9. Scene from Macready's revival of *Henry V*, 1839. From *Scharf's Recollections of Scenic Effects at Covent Garden*, 1838–9.

10. The banquet scene in *Macbeth*, at the Lyceum Theatre, London, 1888, showing massive, elaborately detailed set. Crown Copyright. Victoria and Albert Museum.

11. Interior of the Olivier Theatre at the new National Theatre on the South Bank, London.

12. Interior of the Festival Theatre, Stratford, Ontario. A remarkable modern version of an Elizabethan stage.

The Age of David Garrick (1741–1779)

Richard Cumberland described his first experience of Garrick's acting — '... it seemed as if a whole century had been stept over in the transition of a single scene; old things were done away, and a new order at once brought forward, bright and luminous, and clearly destined to dispel the barbarisms and bigotry of a tasteless age.' The 'barbarisms and bigotry' were represented in the acting of James Quin, long the darling of the English stage, whose style and mode were made redundant by the astonishing début of Garrick on 19 October 1741. Quin himself is alleged to have commented, after seeing this performance of *Richard III*, that if Garrick was right then they had all previously been wrong. He dominated the English stage as actor, manager, director, and he was not an inconsiderable dramatist. Few in the history of English theatre have equalled his dominance in so many aspects of his art, and hardly anybody has equalled his influence on future generations. His life is very fully documented and it gives a strange impression of predestination — early struggles, sudden fame, adulation by the unknown, friendship and admiration from the famous. He was the intimate of Dr Johnson, Goldsmith, Burke, Diderot and many others and when, finally, the lights dimmed and went out for him, there was universal grief. The history of almost forty years of theatre is, in effect, the history of David Garrick's career.

Garrick as Manager

The greatest actors almost always display a marked commitment to other aspects of their art. Betterton, Garrick, Macready, Irving, Gielgud, Olivier, all have made their marks as managers, directors, impressarios. Garrick not only impressed his contemporaries as manager of Drury Lane, but initiated basic reforms in organization and convention. He was an authoritarian and brooked little argument — he had a violent temper when roused. He demanded punctuality at rehearsals — a reform not altogether approved, especially by the more senior members of his company. Their habit was to arrive at rehearsal when convenient to them, and this depended on their mood or digestive state. 'On 12th October, 1769 a rehearsal of *As You Like It* was call'd by Mrs. Barry's desire at ten. She sent word to have the Rehearsal put off for half an hour.' Many, emboldened a little by tradition, spoke their parts as if no one else existed and, having spoken, took up languid postures until their next cue. Garrick insisted on unity of production and demanded full participation. He incensed many but mollified them by introducing an insurance scheme for players which became a model for the future. Perhaps his most sensational work as a manager was to abolish the tradition of allowing spectators on the stage. Not all the players approved of his ban — they often benefited by gifts from ardent admirers. Nevertheless Garrick persisted. Who can blame him in the light of such evidence as this? — 'The first time Holland acted Hamlet . . . on seeing the Ghost he was much frightened . . . and his hat flew *à-la-mode* off his head. An unoffensive woman in a red cloak (a friend of Holland's) hearing Hamlet complain the air bit shrewdly . . . with infinite composure crossed the stage, took up the hat, and with the greatest care placed it fast on Hamlet's head . . . But the audience burst out into such incessant peals of laughter, that the Ghost moved off without any ceremony, and Hamlet, scorning to be outdone in courtesy, immediately followed with roars of applause.' With typical shrewdness Garrick had the Drury Lane auditorium enlarged so that, on players' benefit nights, increased revenue would compensate for what they may have lost from the fickle patronage of stage-audiences.

Garrick as Director
His most important directorial quality was his ability to exercise discipline on his company. It is now fashionable to laud ensemble playing — but very often those who praise loudest are least able to achieve it in practice. Garrick's achievement at Drury Lane was remarkable in creating a unified company, dedicated to the creation of wholeness of impression in its stage-presentations. It would be wrong to harbour the illusion that Garrick introduced selflessness and abolished the exploding of individual temperament — neither the psychology of the actor nor the conditions of the time would allow that. But he tempered the exercise of individual talent and personality. He achieved this partly by a process which, today, would not seem exceptional, but in his day had a quite revolutionary colouring to it. He chose the best actor and actress for the part as opposed to the traditional practice by which the best parts were seized by the best known — '. . . in general the characters were very well suited to those who represented them'.

He was exhaustive and inspiring as a teacher both by precept and example. 'Kitty' Clive was a superb comedienne in Garrick's company — Dr Johnson said of her, 'What Clive did best she did better than Garrick, but could not do half so many things well.' Yet Kitty would have achieved little without Garrick's teaching and encouragement — and she knew it. She wrote to him in 1774 — 'Wonderful Sir. — Who have been for thirty years contradicting an old established proverb, "you cannot make bricks without straw"; but you have done what is infinitely more difficult, for you have made actors and actresses without genius, that is you have made them pass for such, though it has given you infinite trouble.' All accounts of Garrick's work stress his care and patience for detail and his in-built discipline — but he was not a solemn mentor: 'He generally seasoned the dry part of the lecture [in his rehearsals] with acute remarks, shrewd applications to the company present, or some gay jokes, which the comedians of the theatre, who survive their old master, will recollect with pleasure.'

One of the great tests of both actor and director is how they cope with Shakespeare. As an actor, Garrick triumphed, but, alas, as a director he never allowed his unquenchable reverence for the Bard to persuade him that the best way to love Shakespeare is to allow *his* text to guide the actor and director. Garrick fell in line with his contemporaries and indulged in wholesale adaptation and alteration. Boswell complained that Dr Johnson had not mentioned Garrick in his preface to his edition of Shakespeare's plays. Johnson replied — 'My dear Sir, had I mentioned him, I must have mentioned many more; Mrs. Pritchard, Mrs. Cibber, — nay, and Mr. Cibber too; he too altered Shakespeare.' Garrick's most extraordinary venture was his butchered version of *Hamlet* — ironically, a play which, hitherto, had escaped the worst 'restorative' ministrations. Garrick, who was susceptible to the words of the great, seems to have been emboldened to attack *Hamlet* because Voltaire thought the play barbarous. We should also notice that the actor in Garrick no doubt, if unconsciously, sought opportunities to display solo performance — for instance, the meeting of the ghost with Hamlet was extended through Shakespeare's Act II, which became Act III in Garrick's version, and each subsequent act was thereby shunted forward. Young Fortinbras, who appears, in Shakespeare's play, only at the end of Act V, appears much earlier in Garrick. The superb Grave-diggers were cut, Gertrude is not killed on stage, Ophelia has no funeral! Garrick did, however, restore Polonius's advice to Laertes which was traditionally cut, and the account of Fortinbras's army. Yet in this excoriated adaptation Garrick triumphed.

Garrick's announcement that he was going to produce *Macbeth* stated, 'as written by Shakespeare'. The traditional version used by the 18th century was Davenant's. There was an immediate outcry from many people who were satisfied with this version — many fondly believing it to be Shakespeare's. Garrick changed his mind, although to be fair to him he restored Shakespeare's words in many scenes. Davenant's version of Macbeth's famous soliloquy before the murder of Duncan begins:

If it were well when done; then it were well
It were done quickly; if his Death might be
Without the Death of nature in my self
And killing my own rest; it wou'd suffice.

Garrick's 'restored' version, which is almost exactly that of the First
Folio, begins:

> If it were done, when 'tis done, then 'twere well
> It were done quickly; if that but this blow
> Might be the be-all and the end-all . . . Here.
> But here, upon this bank and shoal of time,
> We'd jump the life to come . . .

But his *Macbeth* is still an adaptation. The Lady Macduff scenes are
omitted. The Porter has gone. Malcolm's self-deprecation in the England
scene is severely cut. The Witches indulge in some singing and dancing.
The most astonishing perpetration is a death-speech for Macbeth written
by Garrick himself. It is worth recording as an example of unbelievably
bad taste:

> 'Tis done! The scene of life will quickly close.
> Ambition's vain, delusive dreams are fled,
> . . .
> I cannot rise! I dare not ask for mercy —
> It is too late, hell drags me down. I sink,
> I sink — Oh! — my soul is lost for ever!
> Oh!

Boswell, commenting to Dr Johnson with admiration at some thought that
Garrick had uttered, said '. . . he seemed to dip deep into his mind for the
reflection'. After reading Macbeth's last speech à la Garrick we might be
inclined to agree with Dr Johnson's reply — 'He had not far to dip,
sir . . .' Perhaps the lesson is that, whether in the 18th or 20th century, it is
not wise to leave Shakespeare entirely in the hands of theatre-men.

Garrick, then, displayed an astounding mixture of respect and chaotic
ill-taste. In this he did not, as in so many other respects, transcend his age.
Yet, in other directorial respects he displayed sensitivity, and was not
afraid to experiment, sometimes in a fashion which influenced theatre for
generations. Although in the matter of scenery he effected little change, he
began an important development in the use of lighting. Since the beginning of the 18th century candles had supplied the illumination, and were
used to create three light sources — in hoops of chandeliers which could
be raised or lowered, in enclosed 'lamps' in the wings, and in footlights.
Accounts from 1700 to 1750 show increasing ingenuity in attempts to
increase the flexibility of these three light-sources. Footlights at Covent
Garden, for example, could be raised or lowered from and into a trough
below the stage, by a system of counterweights. But Garrick was even
bolder. In 1765 at Drury Lane he introduced a completely different form
of illumination after a tour of the Continent. It sounds conspicuously
dangerous and inefficient, but it worked sufficiently well to become

standard for some time. He banished the hoops, lit his stage largely from the wings, and apparently used a combination of candlelight and oil lamps sometimes shining through coloured transparencies. There is some doubt as to how the latter worked, particularly their function as footlights, but there was much commendation of the brightness that was created.

Garrick as Actor

One of the greatest shocks which Garrick delivered at his triumphant performance of Richard III in 1741 was his style, described, with amazement, by one critic as 'easy and familiar, yet forcible'. The first three words represented the shock. His first performance of a major role gave a final stunning blow to the old style which Quin had so grandiloquently embodied — 'He rolled out his heroics with an air of dignified indifference that seemed to disdain the plaudits that were bestowed upon him.' Garrick was, conversely — 'Young and light and alive in every muscle and every feature', and 'came bounding on the stage'. We are fortunate in having a vivid description of what this meant in detail — indeed we are made to feel very close to him:

'His stature is rather low than of middle height, and his body thickset. His limbs are in the most pleasing proportion, and the whole man is put together most charmingly. Even the eye of the connoisseur cannot remark any defect either in his limbs, in the manner they are knit, or in his movements. In the latter one is enchanted to observe the fullness of his strength, which, when shown to advantage, is more pleasing than extravagant gestures. With him there is no rampaging, gliding, or slouching, and where other players in the movements of their arms and legs allow themselves six inches or more scope in every direction farther than the canons of beauty would permit, he hits the mark with admirable certainty and firmness. It is therefore refreshing to see his manner of walking, shrugging his shoulders, putting his hands in his pockets, putting on his hat, now pulling it down over his eyes and then pushing it sideways off his forehead, all this with so slight a movement of his limbs as though each were his right hand. It gives one a sense of freedom and well-being to observe the strength, and certainty of his movements and what complete command he has over the muscles of his body. I am convinced that his thickset form does much towards producing this effect. His shapely legs become gradually thinner from the powerful thighs downwards, until they end in the neatest foot you can imagine; in the same way his large arms taper into a little hand. How imposing the effect of this must be you can well imagine.'

This is a portrait of a man not handsome but powerfully compact. Garrick did not rely on natural grace or beauty of countenance to mesmerize his audience. His body was a finely-tuned instrument, upon which an intelligent and intuitive mind played. Garrick was physically strong and kept himself fit, trimming his body to cope with the demands of his mental processes. A comparison with Laurence Olivier is inevitable. He, too, is a finely tuned instrument, aware of the necessity of physical power and fitness. Like Garrick his body is trained to adapt itself to his intuitions, perceptions and intelligence. They both exemplify the professionalism in the manipulation of acquired skills, as opposed to the more common exploitation of personality. Both brought to acting a kind of naturalism — the former having learnt much from Macklin, the latter from Garrick. Naturalism basically means a style which does not involve an exploitation of the actor's personality but suits words to action, action to words, in a manner which convinces the audience that they are experiencing human actuality. Naturalism is the opposite of a style which concentrates on a series of postures, both in action and speech, sometimes beautiful and graceful and bewitching to the beholder, but often bearing little relevance to interpretation. Garrick's Hamlet exemplified the extent of his committal to naturalism:

'Hamlet has folded his arms under his cloak and pulled his hat down over his eyes; it is a cold night and just twelve o'clock: the theatre is darkened, and the whole audience of some thousands are as quiet, and their faces as motionless, as though they were painted on the walls of the theatre: even from the farthest end of the playhouse one could hear a pin drop. Suddenly, as Hamlet moves towards the back of the stage slightly to the left and turns his back on the audience, Horatio starts, and says, "Look, my lord, it comes", points to the right, where the ghost has already appeared and stands motionless, before any one is aware of him. At these words Garrick turns sharply and at the same moment staggers back two or three paces with his knees giving way under him; his hat falls to the ground and both his arms, especially the left, are stretched out nearly to their full length, with the hands as high as his head, the right arm more bent and the hands lower, and the fingers apart; his mouth is open: thus he stands rooted to the spot, with legs apart, but no loss of dignity, supported by his friends, who are better acquainted with the apparition and fear lest he should collapse. His whole demeanour is so expressive of terror that it made my flesh creep even before he began to speak. The almost terror-struck silence of the audience, which preceded this appearance and filled one with a sense of insecurity, probably did much to enhance this effect. At last he speaks, not at the beginning, but at the end of a breath, with a trembling voice: "Angels and ministers of grace defend us!" words which supply anything this scene may lack and make it one of the greatest and most terrible which will ever be played on any stage. The ghost beckons to him; I wish you could see him, with eyes fixed on the ghost, though he is speaking to his companions, freeing himself from their restraining hands, as they warn him not to follow and hold him back. But at length, when they have tried his patience too far, he turns his face towards them, tears himself with great violence from their grasp, and draws his sword on them with a swiftness that makes one shudder, saying: "By heaven! I'll make a ghost of him that lets me!"'

Garrick's acting was intelligent in that it gave, as Olivier's does, an impression of deep study of character and of words. A contemporary referred to his voice which was 'distinct, articulate, sensible', and to its 'tone', which 'sounds as if it were influenced by a thinking mind'. He added that, 'Mr. Garrick is, by study and observation continually adding to his stock of science.'

But we must not assume that the naturalistic actor presents such a 'life-like' image that his acting is scaled down to lifesize. On the contrary, actors, by definition, have to be larger than life. They are bound to be big, tending to exaggeration, and they would not be actors if they did not exploit the magic of their own naked personalities. It is, however, a matter of degree. The differences between Garrick and Quin were a matter of degree. In the former the magic of individual personality showed as an expression on his face, in the latter the personality was all. Garrick, it is true, was accused of hogging the stage, of milking applause, but evidences of egocentricity were mere details in an acting style which always put truth to nature before personal display.

But no actor can work in a vacuum, and Garrick was fortunate in his contemporaries. They were all, to a degree, influenced by his style, not the least of them Hannah Pritchard, who took over the role of Lady Macbeth from Peg Woffington (Garrick's mistress) in 1748. Peg was a superb comedienne with a 'deplorable tragedy voice' but Hannah was second only to Sarah Siddons in her mastery of the part. Garrick's intelligence seems implicit in her interpretation. In the banquet scene '. . . she practised every possible artifice to hide the transaction that passed between her husband and the vision his disturbed imagination had raised'. The 18th century was rich in actresses who seemed particularly keen to vie with one another in the role of Lady Macbeth (sometimes off-stage as much as on-stage!) — Mrs Barry, Mrs Cibber, Mrs Yates were formidable talents. One of Garrick's greatest male rivals was the Irish actor, Spranger Barry. He tended to the old school, and was guilty, to use the word of the times, of 'impropriety', especially in speaking. He had a certain habit — 'His pauses . . . of which he was extremely enamoured . . . were at times too unartificially repeated.' But he was a dignified and magnetic actor, exerting his influence with great speed on his audience, though he never approached Garrick in popular esteem.

Costume in the Age of Garrick

One phrase in a review of Garrick's Hotspur is a clue to the almost unbelievable chaos which engulfed costuming for the stage: 'His dress in Hotspur was objected to: a laced frock and a Ramille wig were thought too insignificant for the character.' The evidence to support what we might call the 'alienation effect' of the dressing of the fiery Northumberland militant, comes thick and fast. When Spranger Barry played Macbeth in 1752 he wore a full-bottomed peruke — a wig with a full flow of hair spreading over the wearer's neck and back. In the death scene, a conscientious thespian named Ryan, playing Macduff, initiated the following catastrophe — 'Ryan being eager to despatch him, entangled his hand in the vast profusion of Macbeth's hair; and by jerking back his sword after the concluding stab, away came poor perriwig along with it . . .' Garrick wore contemporary dress for Macbeth, Mrs Yates wore several large 18th-century skirts as Lady Macbeth. The ridiculous habits already noted continued, but the frequent contemporary comments suggest that a movement for reform had begun. Behind all the excesses — all militating against truth to character — lay one cold fact: theatre managements (including Garrick's) were notoriously parsimonious in allocating money both for sets and costumes. Either players provided their own or used what they found lying dusty in green rooms and store cupboards. But the naturalism Garrick brought to acting inevitably produced pressure to see naturalism in costume. The comments of Mrs Bellamy, herself an actress, in *An Apology for the Life of George Anne Bellamy*, 1783, and the fervent theories of Aaron Hill in *The Prompter*, Jan. 1735, indicate that the theatre would not much longer have to tolerate quite so much niggardliness or quite so much of laissez-faire.

Late 18th to Late 19th Century (1780–1880)

As we look back, the 19th century seems not only a huge expanse of time, but a self-contained unit. The length of the reign (1837–1901) of one monarch, Victoria, is responsible. Yet this is too simple a view. One of the century's greatest poets, Wordsworth, was born only 154 years after Shakespeare's death, and died only 127 years before Elizabeth II's jubilee. The world of Jane Austen seems very 18th century in pattern, yet all her novels were published in the 19th century. Tennyson, counted as one of its most 'typical' poets, nevertheless looks ahead with trepidation at a world of flying machines and technology. One of its finest actors, Henry Irving, was born one year only after Victoria's accession, but there are people still alive who saw him act.

The 19th century was, then, like other centuries, an amalgam of realities, some replete with the past, some pregnant with the future, and all generalizations must take account of this. Those applicable are: (1) A continuous growth of interest in drama and theatre, evidenced by the printed word — i.e. commentaries and critiques by some of the century's most perceptive minds, like Coleridge, Lamb, Hazlitt, and in attendances at theatres — particularly in the last two decades. (2) The confirming evidence of a proliferation of theatre-building not only in London, but in the provinces. (3) A huge development of touring companies to satisfy the appetites of provincial audiences. This had begun in the 18th century, but the 19th century saw its peak of activity. Many of the great Shakespearean players from Garrick to Irving cut their teeth on the hard experience of provincial touring. (4) The increase in power and presence of the actor-manager. This was simply a system of organization in which the star actor had fiscal and artistic control of a company — sometimes the former grasp was much firmer than the latter. The effects were both good and bad — it depended on the personality of the star. The overriding effect, however, was the extent to which the star's name attracted audiences in London and the provinces. (5) In 1843 the patent which for 183 years gave Drury Lane and Covent Garden a monopoly in presentation of 'legitimate' drama ended. The result was an eventual boom in theatre-building and a great revival of serious drama by the end of the century. (6) The 19th century was quick in applying such new discoveries as gas and electricity in theatres — this had a profound effect not only on the audience's visual experience but on acting techniques. It is astonishing now to realize that one of the greatest revolutions in the history of stage presentation was the opportunity given to audiences to see actors' faces clearly and in detail. (7) The growth of theatres and of interest was paralleled by the acceptance of the 'reviewer' as a natural element in popular journalism. Growing literacy and the coming of the mass/popular press meant that comment on productions was both speedily and widely disseminated. (8) The building of large auditoriums encouraged opulent and intricate set-designs in which, as the century proceeded, naturalistic effect predominated — '. . . the crowning picture is the naval battle between the Romans and the Egyptians . . . The appearance of two contending galleys and the heartiness with which their respective crews showered arrows on each other raised the audience . . . to a state of excitement which would not be calmed . . .' (On *Antony and Cleopatra* at Drury Lane, 1873.) (9) In Shakespearean production there was a steady pursuit by the major actor-managers of authenticity in costuming — 'When the curtain rose, and discovered King John dressed as his effigy appears in Worcester Cathedral, surrounded by his barons sheathed in mail, with cylindrical helmets and correct armorial shields . . . there was a roar of approbation . . .' (On *King John* at Covent Garden, 1823–4 season.) (10) There was a continual improvement in the texts used for Shakespeare productions in which Kean, Phelps, Macready and Irving played, in various degrees, an honourable part, not uninfluenced by the work of scholars, particularly in the latter part of the century. (11) The Shakespeare 'industry' begun, albeit unwittingly, by Garrick's Jubilee festivities of 1769, thrived and grew. The foundations of Bardolatry at Stratford upon Avon and elsewhere were laid, some of them sound — like the first Stratford drama festival of 1879 and the eventual control of the buildings associated with Shakespeare by the Birthplace Trust; some shifty — like the spawning of bogus relics; some excessive, but relatively harmless — like the gushing forth of a tourist industry; but, in this, Stratford shows less cupidity and somewhat more care than many other literary meccas in Europe and the New World.

THE THEATRES c. 1790–1817

The two 'patent' theatres — Covent Garden and Drury Lane — have a bewildering record of demolition and resurrection, and, in the 19th century the first such events of importance were the fires that destroyed the former in September 1808 and the latter in February 1809 — there seems no sinister consanguinity in the proximity of dates. Drury Lane did not reappear until 1812, but by September 1809 a new Covent Garden was built. From the outside it was an imitation of the Temple of Minerva on the Acropolis, and its interior amplitude well reflects the new spirit of visual splendour which was to dominate stage-production. Stage-width was 42 ft 6 in., depth 68 ft, height to top of proscenium arch, 36 ft 9 in. (considerably bigger than the New Amsterdam Theatre's stage in New York). The three tiers of boxes, topped by a gallery, encircled the house, and the royal boxes flanked the projecting stage, as in the Restoration and 18th-century theatres. In fact, apart from size, no significant change in auditorium architecture had taken place. The new Drury Lane still stands today, a splendid monument to an age when grace had not yet quite been made obese by affluence. Its stage area is less than Covent Garden but it holds more — i.e. 3,600 as against 3,044.

From 1788 to 1789 John Kemble was acting manager of Drury Lane and was associated with it until he took over control of Covent Garden in 1803. He, therefore, was predominant in Shakespeare production and set its style for a period of about twenty years. He was directly responsible for preparing versions of twenty-seven of Shakespeare's plays. Characteristics of production at both theatres followed similar lines.

Sets
Largeness and splendour of visual effect. Kemble and his admirers sincerely thought that his painstaking attention to detail and apparent authenticity of stage-sets was natural — but this is relative. For example, for *Richard III* at Drury Lane in 1794 Kemble had actually gone to the trouble of depicting the Tower of London not as 19th-century Londoners knew it, but as it would have been in Richard's time. Moreover he had the Palace of Westminster 'as it was' in the 15th century. Unfortunately, in both cases, the quest for naturalism was abortive — first, because an audience's sense of naturalism is related to what they know, and a 15th-century depiction of their Tower landmark in painted canvas and wood would have seemed unnatural because of unfamiliarity; second, because the Palace of Westminster is not, as it had to be on Drury Lane's stage, 42 ft wide and 32 ft high. The very attempt to be lifelike defeats itself since theatre is the art of illusion. This may be arguable but, conclusively, Kemble's concern for naturalism was not aided by such extravagances as a bed for Imogen in *Cymbeline* which was so high that a tall actor almost required a ladder to look at the sleeping lady. But Kemble's intent was serious and diligent. His *King Lear* of 1809 (a play tacitly banned from the stage for a time because of George III's mental disorders) was studiously 'Saxon' in dress and set — in an attempt to make it pre-Christian. This seems to have satisfied audiences, who did not know that Lear is Celtic!

Texts
'Carefully' prepared acting texts existed, but with dubious results. In 1815 Kemble published twenty-six of his acting texts — evidence of his

(perhaps conceited) concern for Shakespeare's words. By comparison
with some Restoration versions, some of Kemble's are acceptable, but
when we read of his principle of preparation we can see how far he is from
being exemplary. He examined the plays to see 'what corrections could
be properly admitted into his text' — i.e. a purely subjective decision.
He cut 'not as disputing the judgment of the author, but as suiting the
time of representation to the habits of his audience' — his author was not,
of course, in a position to dispute what Kemble judged to be what his
18th-century audience wanted! He also cut 'a little favouring the powers
of his actors' — i.e. if x can't do it, cut it! What was the result? Kemble
retained many interpolations from versions made by Dryden, Davenant,
Tate, Cibber, etc. He gave names to many characters — servants for
example — unnamed by Shakespeare, e.g. the Captain in *Twelfth Night*
is called Roberto! He introduced fragments of dialogue by the 18th-
century poet Thomson (author of *The Seasons*), who never wrote a play,
into *Coriolanus*. He gave Ferdinand and Miranda much to sing in one
version of *The Tempest* as he did for Lorenzo and Jessica in *The Merchant
of Venice*, in which the latter is called 'Jessy'. He introduced a funeral
procession for *Antony and Cleopatra* in which Dolabella speaks the following
garble of Cleopatra's lines:

> His legs bestrid the ocean; — his rear'd arm
> Crested the world — his voice was propertied
> As all the tuned spheres, unto his friends;
> But when he meant to quail, and strike the orb,
> He was a rattling thunder.

Costume

Kemble was less precise with costume than with setting. His 1783 Hamlet
was in contemporary court dress — including the British (not Danish!)
Order of the Garter. He seems generally to have used the most eye-
catching he could find except for certain excursions (as with his Saxon
King Lear) into historical atmosphere. His undisciplined approach was,
for actresses, bridled by the insistence and example of Sarah Siddons. She
effected the disappearance of the traditional huge head-dresses and
extravagantly billowing dresses for tragic female parts — '. . . she now saw
that tragedy was debased by the flutter of light materials, and that the
head, and all its powerful action from the shoulder, should never be
encumbered by the monstrous inventions of the hair-dresser and the
milliner.' She substituted a Grecian simplicity of line and texture which
eventually came to be taken as a sort of uniform for female tragic acting.
Sir Joshua Reynolds, the painter, encouraged Sarah Siddons in her
attempts to rid the stage of the old ludicrous 'tragic' costume. He referred,
approvingly according to her, to the new look she gave to her head, as 'the

round apple form'. Mrs Siddons was pleased and flattered — 'He approved very much of my costumes, and of my hair without powder, which at that time was used in great profusion, with a reddish-brown tint, and a great quantity of pomatum, which, well kneaded together, modelled the fair ladies' tresses into large curls like demi-cannon . . . My short waist, too, was to him a pleasing contrast to the long stiff stays and hoop petticoats, which were then the fashion, even on the stage, and it obtained his unqualified approbation.'

Acting

Both Kemble's and Mrs Siddons's acting seems to have been dominated by a certain gravity of both voice and mien. He was described as being of 'a solemn and deliberate temperament — his walk was always slow, and his expression of countenance contemplative'. The dignity of his speaking seems to have emanated more from an artificial than a natural source — he was always articulate but it 'seemed to proceed rather from organization than voice . . .' Mrs Siddons queened it on the English stage, there is no doubt. Writers refer to her self-possession, her 'weightiness', in the sense that every movement and sentence seemed considered upon before it was allowed to be employed. She was remarkable for her quite uncommon practice at that time of actually seeming to be part of the action of the play even when she was not speaking — 'never did I see her eye wander from the business of the scene' — most other players tended to lose interest when, so to speak, it wasn't their turn. Even Kemble carried on 'eye-conversations' with friends in the audience while he was on stage. Mrs Siddons steadfastly remained in character. The dignified gravity of her acting seems to have been, to an extent, inspired by her love of sculpture which 'made a remarkable impression upon her, as to simplicity of attire and severity of attitude'.

It cannot too often be stressed that although the acting style of great individuals undoubtedly influences the general style of their contemporaries, other forces are also at work. We must not assume that the gravity of Kemble and Siddons was everywhere to be seen. Indeed, the very fact that the hunger of theatregoers for a type of drama very different from Shakespeare and the classics increased, itself encouraged a very different acting style. Early 19th-century melodrama was hardly Shakespearean, and many of Kemble's and Siddons's contemporaries were hardly classical in their approach to acting — 'among performers, who are favourites with the public in particular, it is far from uncommon to see them so totally forget decency, the respect due to an audience, and the contempt which they bring upon themselves, as to look about them, into the boxes and the pit, in order either to discover who they know, or even, at some times, impudently to make slight nodds, signs, or grins . . . Performers are not infrequently seen to read a letter on the stage . . .' Among the amazing antics frequently observed by commentators of early 19th-century acting are: an actor cooling himself by flapping his hat, dropping it and leaving it for a stage-hand to pick up for him; leaving the stage by the wrong door or by any convenient aperture; coming on stage out of character and only assuming it *after* the player is assured that the audience knows who he is! Among specific faults and general habits of acting, the following are emphasized: '. . . performers who, at the first sentence with their right hand, and the second with their left, continue an alternate through each speech'; 'there are others who continually shake a little finger . . .'; 'a frequent clenching of the fist . . . to make the audience believe how much they are in earnest'; 'the arms akimbo is also often thought the attitude of grandeur'; '. . . many performers who will continue, through a whole scene, with the profile, a little more or a little less, toward the audience'.

We may find such a catalogue quaint, amusing, incredible and we may smile indulgently or even scoff. But can we lay hands upon hearts and declare that we have never, even in this so-called advanced 20th century, witnessed one or all of those thespian foibles? There are some things in life and theatre which never change.

SHAKESPEARE PRODUCTION c. 1817–1840

Kemble may have seemed eccentric to some moderns, but his policy was definite and he was the arbiter of taste. When he departed in 1817 there was, as all-round theatre-man, no one of his stature to take the leadership. Strange things happened: from 1833–5, for example, Alfred Bunn managed both Drury Lane and Covent Garden, with this as one bizarre result — '. . . at certain periods of the evening it is quite common to see the actors and actresses running . . . from one house to the other — the Drury Lane Romeo rushing . . . in his black puffs and bugles, to act Sir Christopher Curvy at Covent Garden bumping himself full butt at the corner, against [a Covent Garden actor] scudding before the breeze . . . [to] . . . Drury Lane . . . and then the ladies, slip-slops, spangles and sandals, rain or blow, hail or snow, away they go, Peruvian Virgins, with suns at their bosoms, at full tilt, to become Witches, on Macbeth's Heath.' The amount of Shakespeare performed declined in this period, though there were many operatic versions and in spite of the electric presence of Edmund Kean. The staple diet is well represented by a *Comedy of Errors* of 1819 which included music by Mozart and Arne. It had a hunting scene with quartet and horns, the words deriving from *Love's Labour's Lost*. Certain lines from *Antony and Cleopatra* had been made into a song and transplanted. 'Blow, blow, thou winter's wind', and 'It was a lover', from *As You Like It* also manifested themselves, as did Desdemona's Willow Song, a sonnet set to music, a song made up from lines from a version of *King Lear* and *The Tempest*. No one claims *A Comedy of Errors* to deserve sacrosanct respect, but this treatment makes Restoration Shakespeare seem positively decent. But, beneath such activity, attempts to restore Shakespeare's texts were going forward, a little tentatively, perhaps nervously but, like the drip of water on rock, with relentless effect. Robert W. Elliston managed Drury Lane 1819–26 and, in that time, although he turned *Macbeth* into an opera, he did some meritorious restoration of Shakespeare's text.

Shakespeare's Text

For Kean's *Coriolanus* in 1820 Elliston wrote in the playbill his intention 'to restore the text of Shakespeare, with omissions only'. Although Kean was a relative failure, some critics were agreeably surprised with what the restored text revealed, and Elliston was encouraged to do something about the encrustations *King Lear* had collected about it over a century or more. In 1820 he still used Tate's version, which was a comprehensive re-vamping of the play, but made two important changes — (1) He gave the play back Shakespeare's language for the opening of the Heath scene — 'Blow winds . . .' etc. (2) More of Shakespeare's language was now to be found in the scene where Cordelia is restored to Lear, though Tate's tasteless ending (*see* Commonwealth and Restoration) was not touched. In 1823, Elliston burned his boats and restored Shakespeare's tragic ending to the play. It was a triumph — crowned by Kean's acting — but some found it difficult to swallow — '. . . at times the audience were almost in a titter, and more especially where he repeated . . . the word "Never — never — never — never — never" . . . and very nearly produced that most disagreeable sound to a tragedian's ear — *a horse-laugh*.' The restorations to *King Lear* were the most important in eventual result — since others were emboldened by what could be achieved with a great play to work to find the true texts of lesser plays. But Elliston's *Richard III* was the most comprehensive example of restoration. Colley Cibber's version of the play had triumphed for over a hundred years. This was cobbled from *Henry VI, Part 3, Richard II, Richard III, Henry IV, Part 2* and *Henry V*, and Cibber himself. In 1821 Elliston and Kean swept most of Cibber's changes away and, among other things, reintroduced Queen Margaret, Clarence and Hastings. This new version came as a terrible shock to many people, not least to the critic of *The Times* who believed it to be only a new arrangement not a return to Shakespeare, and concluded it to be 'inferior in dramatic effect' to Cibber's. Certainly it was less *grand guignol* than Cibber's and certainly it cannot claim to have returned completely to the original text, but the spirit is there and much of the original substance. It is a testimony to the growing sensitivity about returning to Shakespeare's own lines which is characteristic of the whole of the century.

Shakespearean Productions

We may best visualize what typical productions were like in the period by allowing our imaginations to put into pictures the vivid descriptions of eye-witnesses of actual performances of the time — of a comedy, a tragedy, and a history. On 29 November 1821 a version of *The Two Gentlemen of Verona* was performed at Covent Garden. The critic of *European Magazine* reported — 'The opening of the scene displayed the Ducal Palace and great square of Milan illuminated, golden gondolas on the river, and all the usual appendages of a foreign gala, masquers, dancing girls and mountebanks.' He continues: 'Spring came enthroned on a pile of unblown flowers, which the nymph touched with her wand, and the buds turned into blossoms.' This bit of stage trickery (however it was achieved) continued for autumn and winter with seasonal changes in flowers taking place at a stroke or touch. The first act ended with 'a view of Lapland'. Subsequent visual splendours in the production included, 'Earth . . . in majesty, seated in a car drawn by lions over clouds . . . Vulcan in his forge . . . a portrait of Juno, attended by her peacocks.' But this was scanty hors d'oeuvre, for, 'The stage was then suddenly invaded by water, and on its bosom rolled Cleopatra's galley . . . and an artificial mountain reaching to the clouds, the explosion of which discovered a gorgeous Temple of Apollo.' Needless to say the applause 'rose to enthusiasm at this spectacle', but perhaps the reader ought to be reminded that the play which this spectacle so effectively garnished was *The Two Gentlemen of Verona*!

In June 1821 in the same magazine, possibly the same critic commented on *Henry IV, Part 2*. He noted that the grand attraction of the evening was the introduction into the last part of the production of three scenes from *Henry V*. '. . . First, the processional platform with its splendid retinue; next, the magnificent inauguration in Westminster Abbey; and last, and best, the gorgeous banquet in the Hall, with the introduction of the mailed champion, and the ceremony of the challenge . . . all was light and blazonry, and gold and glory . . .' It needs no academic perspicacity to perceive that these scenes are no more part of *Henry V* than they are of *Henry IV, Part 2*! But the critic is not so much revealed as an ignoramus as a chronicler typifying a prevailing attitude. When he refers to scenes from *Henry V* he means from a production of that play in which the scenes had been received with such approbation that they had been used again. This is revealing, but even more important is the tacit allowance that what the theatre presented is what Shakespeare wrote. We are still a long way from an acceptance of the text as the received truth of the play.

Edmund Kean's famous portrayal of Lear was reviewed by *The Times* critic on 25 April 1820. There is little reference to the visual aspects of the production, but one remark is of great significance — 'The scene of the storm was less effective than many others, because the manager, by a strange error, had caused the tempest to be exhibited with so much accuracy that the performer could scarcely be heard amidst the confusion ... The machinery may be transferred to the next new pantomime.' The last sentence is not merely tart but emphasizes the extent to which (as was noted in the case of *Henry IV, Part 2*) scenery was used again and again. But the salient point is the fact that even a star like Kean seems to have had to fight at times a losing battle against production practice which overwhelmed both play, stage and actor with visual splendour which involved both a mania for excess and a penchant for accuracy.

Lighting

The second decade of the 19th century saw the introduction of the use of gas for illumination in both Covent Garden and Drury Lane — an event whose implications were immense. We can more easily understand (even if we cannot fully appreciate) the extraordinary visual excesses noted in the last section if we realize that all those pageants and banquets and gondolas, etc., could be fully illuminated. The principle behind the policy is neither new nor has it been abandoned in the 20th century — if you have it, by heavens use it! The announcement of the arrival of gas at Covent Garden is worthy of note for its pride and excitement apart from its historical importance. The theatre-bill for the season 1815 says that the new lighting '. . . has been effected by a MAGNIFICENT CHANDELIER, which from the Centre of the Ceiling diffuses a soft and brilliant Light around, without obstructing the View of a single Spectator. In its effect, the Body of Light is equal to 300 ARGAND LAMPS'. (Aimé Argand, 1755–1803, invented a burner admitting air within a cylindrical flame.) It may be thought that the Covent Garden management were wise to announce in the same bill that it also had a new system of ventilation 'by which the theatre can be either cooled or warmed, and the Atmosphere of the different Parts of the House can be kept to one pleasant Temperature throughout the different Seasons of the year'. The chandelier was augmented by 'Grecian lights' around the back of the Dress Circle (a few old theatres still have them, if only as ornaments) which 'shed a soft medium Light'.

Drury Lane followed in 1817 and a reporter in the *Examiner* gives us the most vivid account of the effect of this new system of illumination — 'Their effect, as they appear suddenly from the gloom, is like the striking of daylight . . . white, regular and pervading'; he is referring to different light-sources at stage-front and side. It perhaps strikes us as strange to read his joy that the lighting 'will enable the spectator to see every part of the stage with equal clearness', but in that joy lies the affirmation of a tremendous revolution in the art and craft of production and, more important, acting. Never again would an actor be in shadow — unless it were contrived for him. In the storm scene of Kean's *King Lear* referred to in the preceding section, not only was Kean's performance drowned by noise effects but, on the first night at least, all sorts of combinations of colours rotated on his face and on the stage. The fact that Kean appears to have condoned all the technical paraphernalia only reinforces the extent to which Shakespeare's plays were at the mercy of so many new toys and fads and fancies.

Costume

John Philip Kemble had been severe about the incongruities in costume which were commonplace in Shakespeare productions, but his own versions of authenticity had about them a certain self-indulgence and romanticism. Charles Kemble, however, firmly nailed his colours to the mast of accuracy and in 1823 produced a *King John* memorable for the painstaking attention to historical correctness, even to illuminated manuscripts, tombstone figures, stained-glass windows. Kemble was influenced by J. R. Planché who was a founder of the British Archaeological Association and a member of the College of Heralds. Planché was a pioneer in historically accurate costuming and setting and, though a little precious in his quest for exactness, he should be honoured for his efforts to rid Shakespeare production of clutter and rubbish. Planché had complained to Kemble that Shakespeare was staged with make-shift scenery and, at best, a new dress or two for the main players. Kemble commissioned him to 'dress' *King John* in the authentic manner we have noted.

No one else quite matched Planché's meticulousness but there was, throughout the period, a sensitivity about costuming that indicated a decided move away from traditional ad-hocery. Managements went out of the way in their advertisements to announce that the production had 'New Scenes, Dresses, and Decorations', critics were on the qui-vive for errors, less of taste, than of accuracy — 'The introduction of the yeomen of the guard in the service of Henry IV, when it is remembered that the corps was not established till the reign of Henry VII will startle not only the venerable antiquary, but the little school-boy, who will think it a pity that some of his play-fellows had not been consulted, during their holidays, upon this point' — a prissy piece of pedantry, topped with messianic conviction — 'A more glaring anachronism never slipped upon the stage.' Even plays, like *Cymbeline*, vague in historical context, were subject to pertinacious but somewhat reckless attention — 'With NEW SCENERY, DRESSES and DECORATIONS, executed from the Best Authorities . . . displaying . . . the Habits, Weapons, and Buildings of the Gaulish and Belgic Colonists of the Southern Counties . . .' But the age was fickle. We may applaud its anxious urge to be right but we must smile at its disposition to be crazily wrong — 'We went a short time since to Covent Garden, to witness . . . *The Merry Wives of Windsor*, and oh! what a medley of costume was there! *Justice Shallow, Bardolph*, and 'mine ancient', were each in dresses of different periods, and *Sir John*, himself had on the jerkin, slops, hat, boots, and Scottish broadsword, which has been long since immortalized by the Staffordshire potteries as a chimney ornament ... and *Doctor Caius* looked like one of the portraits of *Kneller*, with a *black-wig, court-sword*, and ruffles!' — we have to turn to some of the absurdities of our own age to find such matter as will make us smile again.

Acting

The theatrical appetites of the first two or three decades were sensationally if fitfully satisfied by the acting genius of Edmund Kean. His wild, unpredictable temperament, his love for wine and women and, possibly, a fear of failing, ensured that his life would be short and his contribution to the history of Shakespearean acting incandescent. He made his début on 26 January 1814 as Shylock at Drury Lane. Nothing could have been less propitious for what happened. He had few friends, no one at Drury Lane seemed to care for him, fierce snowstorms blocked many of the capital's streets, the theatre was half-empty. But the following morning the great dramatic critic William Hazlitt wrote that in this performance he saw '... the first gleam of genius breaking athwart the gloom of the stage'. His triumph was no less complete than Garrick's début had been, and achieved with an equal, but quite dissimilar, display of genius which was contrary to accepted custom. For one thing, his Shylock, unlike the traditional, half-comic pantomime villain with a red beard and wig, which had held sway since the days of Sam Dogget a century or so earlier, was a dark-skinned villain, intent on murder and frightening to see and hear. For another, his acting was conceived in, and expressed with, human passion. Garrick was a master of naturalistic detail and communicated it with a fine precision which included emotion but did not completely rely on it. Kean was possessed by an instinctive ability to feel and present with almost uncanny realism the depths and varieties of man's passions. 'In giving effect to the conflict of passion arising out of the contrast of situation, in varied vehemence of declaration, in keenness of sarcasm, in the rapidity of his transitions from one tone or feeling to another, in propriety and novelty of action, presenting a succession of striking pictures, and giving perpetually fresh shocks of delight and surprise, it would be difficult to single out a competitor.' In short this was 'romantic' acting in an age now dubbed 'the romantic period'. Like the poetry of Keats and Shelley it sought to express the truth of the artist's apprehension of reality with lyric force and imaginative power.

Kean triumphed in Shakespeare's tragic parts, but was deficient in comedy. His Richard III, Hamlet, Iago and Macbeth reinforced the significance of the advent of romantic realism in acting and, in an era not otherwise greatly distinguished in the theatre, were eagerly applauded, both in London and in Philadelphia, Boston and Baltimore, though his 1820 tour in the United States ended in hostility: Kean insisted on acting a season in May despite objections that Bostonians didn't attend the theatre out of season! A later visit to Boston in 1825 did nothing to unfreeze the local inhabitants, but New Yorkers, after some initial coldness, warmed towards him. He left New York with his pride intact; he had left Boston disguised to avoid an ugly mobbing. Subsequently Montreal and Quebec went out of their way to welcome him! The manner of his death seems, ironically, so apt to the nature of his life. He played Othello to his son's Iago on 25 March 1833. By Act III he was exhausted. He broke down after gasping the words, 'Farewell! Othello's occupation's gone.' Iago reached for him and as Kean collapsed on his son's shoulder he shouted, 'Oh God! I'm dying.' In fact, unexpectedly, he lingered on until the month of May.

The only actress to rival Kean in his hold on public attention was Fanny Kemble, one of the amazing theatrical family. She seems neither to have been thoroughly committed to acting nor to have developed a distinctive style. Leigh Hunt, writing of her Juliet, said that her tones were something between those of her great kinswoman, Mrs Siddons (her aunt, in fact), and the 'mellow monotony of the late Mrs Powell'. She seems indeed to have been very studied in both voice and movement — Macready, in his Diary, said he had never seen any one 'so bad, so unnatural, so affected, so conceited' — but she still held her public by sheer force of personality. In fairness to her it should be recorded that she wrote of Macready (soon to be Kean's successor) that 'he growls and prowls and roams and foams around the stage, in every direction, like a tiger in his cage ...' and that in her *On the Stage*, 1863, she wrote some very perspicacious reflections on the art of acting.

One development in these early 19th-century decades should, in what it portended, be applauded on both sides of the Atlantic. It was the beginning of internationalism in the acting profession. Kean acted in the United States, Fanny Kemble became popular there, and Edwin Forrest, Junius Brutus Booth and James William Wallack (the last with particular applause) appeared in England. Individual experiences were not always happy — we have noted Kean's brush with Boston, and Booth found Drury Lane not to his taste — but to-ing and fro-ing by the acting professions across the Atlantic came to be regarded as both natural, necessary and, usually, desirable.

SHAKESPEARE PRODUCTION c. 1840–1880

The heart of the 19th century was a great age for Shakespearean production, although quality was uneven and achievement often slight. The greatness was in the effort expended, in some of the innovations made, the possibilities created for the future, and the intermittent examples of fine and careful work in acting, costume, set and Shakespeare's text. The first part of the period was dominated by the actor-manager, William Charles Macready, and the second by Samuel Phelps — both of them brilliant, wayward, awkward geniuses, possessed of much foolhardiness and a great deal of perception, imagination and intellectual balance. Macready, no less than many of his predecessors and successors, seems to have considered it axiomatic to manage both Drury Lane and Covent Garden at some point. His work in both theatres represents the most typical features of the fate of Shakespeare's works in the 19th century.

Interpretation — Macready

Macready was a tragic actor and his ministrations to Shakespeare are weighted towards the tragedies, though he was a notable Leontes and Hotspur, and was much praised for his production of *As You Like It*. Perhaps, indeed, something of his physical make-up and uneasily controlled temperament conditioned him to the darker hues. He had to master (*see* Acting) some physical eccentricities and God-given foibles of the body, and he seems never to have been a completely relaxed man. But whatever the source of his attitude towards Shakespeare's plays one quality stands out — his almost fierce determination to explore every possible detail of text and scenery and costume until he was satisfied — or relatively so. He did not stint to produce not only the most meticulously prepared but also the most magnificently presented realizations of Shakespeare's plays.

When he first went to Covent Garden it was not as a novice — he had acted with many of the great names, including Sarah Siddons. He knew what he was about. In addition to meticulous preparation he wanted to rehabilitate Shakespeare's text. In this his wishes were sometimes at variance with his resolution, but in the case of *King Lear* his will triumphed. In 1838 a critic reported on his *King Lear* that, 'On Thursday evening — and the date will be marked in the annals of the stage — [King Lear] was freed from the interpolations which have disgraced it for nearly two centuries.' In Macready's Diary for the night before the opening is the remark, 'My opinion of the introduction of the Fool is that . . . it will either weary and annoy or distract the spectator . . . and think that at last we shall be obliged to dispense with it.' Macready had been very daring — reintroducing the Fool after decades of absence from the play — and giving the part to a woman! There are cuts to the play, but none of the frills and furbelows of earlier days. He cleaned up *Coriolanus* without completely ridding it of accretions by other hands, and although, like so many directors before and after him, he cut the words of Act I, Scene i of *The Tempest* and relied on visual effect, he restored the Masque at the end and gave back to Ariel many of that spirit's words. The play which has been most victimized by despoiling hands in its theatrical history — *A Midsummer Night's Dream* — was, during the same period, presented in a version nearer to the original than had been allowed for over a hundred years. This was done by Madame de Vestris at Covent Garden. In fact, what Macready was largely achieving in the more serious plays she, with Charles Mathews, was attempting with the comedies — a Shakespearean restoration.

Interpretation is governed by a director's attitude to the text and to the visual presentation of the plays. In this respect Macready showed himself to be a true child of the romantic spirit. The great romantic poets and critics had shown a reverence for Shakespeare coupled with a sensitive awareness that the 'truth' of his plays could only be achieved by a meticulous study of what he actually wrote. But, parallel with this, was that aspect of romanticism which looked at experience more with the wondering gaze of the imagination than with the cool stare of the intellect. Thus, to find Shakespeare's 'truth' demanded a commitment to his text — this Macready attempted. Equally, however, to keep faith with the romantic spirit demanded a certain kind of vision of his work — this Macready had. His interpretations of Shakespeare combined what could easily court disaster. He never totally failed, but he trod the boundaries both of catastrophe and complete success.

The characteristics of Macready's interpretative imagination were: (1) A 'filling-out' visually of Shakespeare's text to underline the meaning — his 'Birnam Wood' scene in *Macbeth* had each soldier carrying a large bough and, in company with his comrades, creating what was called a 'dioramic' effect as the line, so menacing to Macbeth, stretched into the distance. (2) A richness of dimension, quite apart from a sense of dimension, by the use of colour and design. In his *King Lear*, 'Lear's knights are distinguished from the other retainers of the court' by 'ingenious difference of costume' which 'is introduced with a painter's eye to effect.' (3) A constant effort to link one part of the play to another to emphasize Shakespeare's meaning. In his production of *Coriolanus*, 'the rude magnificence of the Capitol is ever in contrast with the turbulent commotion of the Forum'. (4) Using detail to reinforce a sense of realism yet with an overriding poetic atmosphere — '. . . the *aula* of *Tullus's* mansion, lit by the glimmering brazier on the hearth, *Coriolanus* sitting, shrouded in his mantle on the sacred spot, which is flanked on one side by a lofty trophy, on the other by the ancestral image; the solemn beauty of the whole picture carrying us back to the most touching of all classical associations — the inviolability of the hearth . . .' (*Coriolanus*, 1835).

Acting — Macready

Macready, like Kean before him, dominated the scene, and doubtless inspired many copiers and repelled others. His success is a very firm example of the triumph of will, technique and art over what might have been natural adversity. His height was acceptable for the stage — 5 ft 10 in., his stance was habitually very erect, at times stiff. His face was not particularly pleasing — a nose of indeterminate destination where shape was concerned, a chin of stubborn aspect, but his eyes were a vivid blue; his voice was more bass than tenor but it could achieve melody. But whether he had a stammer or not cannot be ascertained though the peculiarities of his speaking strongly suggest an attempt to master some kind of affliction. His pauses were sometimes inordinate, often embarrassing. His ability to give words greater weight and length than necessary was legendary, and he did it by adding syllables that were strangers to the words. He seems to have attempted to quieten restive audiences by melodramatic cries. In short, he was known to 'ham it up' at times. This sometimes extended to his use of gesture and movement, so perhaps that which gave his speaking such eccentricity was not an affliction of the flesh but a foible of the personality. He was, as was his acting, a strange mixture of unrestrained flamboyance and quiet ordinariness. So individualistic was his acting that it would be hazardous to infer that it was equally influential on others. Nevertheless, the cumulative combination of the romantic flair and force of both Macready and his predecessor, Kean, must have helped to produce a general style which erred more on the expressive and poetic than on the reticent and plain.

Costumes, Scenery and Lighting — Macready

No reader of contemporary accounts of Shakespeare production in this age of Macready can fail to be impressed by the consensus of agreement that, in costume and setting there was an opulence, attention to detail and a prevailing attempt to make what was seen not only seem real but, in some way, to have atmosphere. Critic after critic refers to the 'beauty' of something that is meticulously detailed, and there are numerous references to the various 'atmospheres' that the best Shakespeare productions of the time (and these were usually Macready's) were able to create — 'misty', 'gloomy', 'picturesque', 'tempestuous', 'fiery', are adjectives constantly in use to indicate the effects achieved by the skill of the designers and, increasingly, of the lighting engineers, and the stage-crews. A production of *The Tempest* referred to by the critic of *John Bull*, and apparently not by Macready, but obviously influenced by him, seems to have exemplified the ingenuity of the technicians excellently: 'The first scene discovered a huge vessel, fully rigged and manned, tossed about on a tempestuous ocean. The size of the ship, and the ingenuity with which it was managed, now rising so as to discover the keel, and then dipping to the level of the stage, seeming to sink into the mimic waters, rendered the effect particularly real, to which the ease with which the apparently weighty machinery was worked, and the facility with which it tacked about, helped to contribute.' Whether Macready used limelight or not is disputable, but he certainly had the facility of gas which, by now, was capable of being used with great flexibility of effect — 'The moonlit garden in the fifth act is particularly beautiful, sparkling with soft light, and melting away into a poetic indistinctness at the back' (Macready's *The Merchant of Venice*, 1841).

The Theatres in the Mid-Century

In 1843 Parliament withdrew Drury Lane's and Covent Garden's monopoly for the presentation of Shakespeare and so-called 'legitimate' plays — a monopoly dating back to the Restoration. Macready had advised the government to do this, and his counsel coincided with his giving up of the managership of Drury Lane. The result was that no longer were 'non-patent' theatres obliged to disguise Shakespeare and other drama with songs, dances, entertainments to avoid the embargo on their presenting them straight. Moreover it was a shot in the arm for other large London theatres, some of which immediately began an era of distinguished contribution to the production of legitimate drama. In 1847 Covent Garden became, and remained, a theatre devoted to opera, and Drury Lane, while maintaining a close relationship to drama proper, gradually associated itself with other forms of entertainment — including opera. To us it seems curious that a theatre, i.e. Sadlers Wells, which, today, has special associations with opera and ballet, should have taken over the function of Covent Garden and Drury Lane in the 1840s as the showpiece of Shakespeare production. There, Samuel Phelps, the second great name of the middle part of the 19th-century theatre, had eighteen years of management. His only rival was Charles Kean (son of Edmund) at the Princess theatre.

With the revoking of the patent monopoly a new theatregoing pattern developed which is reflected in British subsidized provincial theatres today. It was hardly to be thought that the major theatres of the West End and Central London would be allowed to have a tacit exclusiveness to present Shakespeare. In London suburbs smaller theatres were built or converted and a new audience — mainly lower-middle class, had the opportunity to see both Shakespeare and other legitimate drama. For this audience the Theatre Royal, Marylebone, held as much glamour for suburbanites as did Sadlers Wells for the sophisticated afficionados of central London. Outlying theatres, whether in London, or elsewhere in England, did not, of course, habitually present star actors. They had resident companies, or relied on travelling companies but, occasionally, a London star would brave the sticks and chance his arm and his voice — Macready played at Marylebone in 1848 for a fortnight's season. Actors and actresses well known in American theatre history also ventured into these off-central theatres — Laura Keene, Helen Faucit and J. W. Wallack Jnr. In one such suburban theatre, called the Surrey, on Shakespeare's birthday, 1864, the second part of *Henry VI* was played; it is unlikely that it had ever been played anywhere since the Elizabethan period.

In mid-19th-century England, following the Act of 1843, there was a boom in theatre-building and conversion. The Industrial Revolution with its spirit of experiment and its inventive practice was in full spate and, when new theatres were mooted, or old ones scheduled for face-lifting, the very latest in technology was involved in the fabric. Gas-lighting improved — and, blessedly, so did ventilation; seating was less ergonomically disastrous, sight-lines were improved in some theatres by the banishment of stage-aprons. But money also changed the social pattern of the theatres. We have seen how the class pattern of the Elizabethan period — with the cheapest area in the yard — had begun to change in the 18th century so that the galleries upstairs (formerly the haunt of the affluent) became the domain of the less well-off. In 1843 the Haymarket Theatre was renovated and all traces of the apron-stage went, the orchestra was given a sunken area extending to beneath the stage, and the space originally occupied by the residual apron was filled with seats called orchestra stalls — 'which can be retained for the parties taking them the whole of the evening'. Here was the assertion by the middle and upper-middle class of a place in the limelight. The Industrial Revolution and the wealth of mid-19th-century England had its main impetus from middle-class ingenuity, even if lower-class blood and sweat and upper-class finance and exploitation maintained the momentum. The orchestra stalls from this time onward became demonstrably to the middle class what boxes were to the upper, and the gallery to the lower. The Haymarket was the place to go and be seen in mid-century. It had glamour and confidence and a galaxy of splendid Shakespearean players, particularly women, some of whom had or were to have transatlantic connections — Julia Bennett Barrow, William Farren, Charles Kean, Mrs Nisbett, Helen Faucit, Charlotte and Susan Cushman (who played Romeo and Juliet), J. W. Wallack and Barry Sullivan.

Interpretation of Shakespeare's Plays — Phelps and Kean

If the Haymarket was the glass of fashion so far as Shakespeare's plays were concerned, Sadlers Wells was the mould of form, with Samuel Phelps as the busy tailor. He now occupies an eminent position in the estimation of many theatre historians. They conclude him to be a major figure in the restoration of Shakespeare's text. But we must not overstress Phelps's role in this process. Phelps was important, his inclination was strongly in the direction of giving back to Shakespeare what belonged to him. But 'restoration' is a comparative word — some of Phelps's texts look very un-Shakespearean to us and, in some respects, were no advance on earlier versions. His importance, too, was one of degree. Indeed, one of his contemporaries (far less honoured than Phelps) — Ben Webster —

made, perhaps, one of the most crucial obeisances to the future, not only by presenting *The Taming of the Shrew* in a very full text (including the induction scene with Christopher Sly, which was traditionally cut), but by using screens and curtains. By the early years of the 20th century curtains were accepted as commonplace — they were a daring innovation in 1844. In 1856 Phelps emulated Webster by playing a virtually full text. In assessing Phelps's interpretations the fact that he was an actor must be taken into account. He eventually took over from Macready as the leading tragedian and, though never in the main line of the history of acting, he was skilful and impressive enough for Macready to prevent him for a time from playing major roles under his management — that difficult man was jealous.

But a director who is also an actor will always bring to the interpretation of Shakespeare a complex set of attitudes. Any directorial urge to restore the full text may well be swamped by a thespian desire to cut it to suit acting talent; any sense that a particular play should, directorially, be presented one way can easily be forgotten in the actor's lust to present it in another. This dichotomy can be seen in Phelps. As a director his work was scrupulous — in detail, in attempts to render Shakespeare faithfully, in an avoidance of flowery additions either to set or text: '. . . so much splendour of decoration is rarely governed by so pure a taste . . .' As an actor (and under the influence of Macready) he had a tendency to over-emotionalizing, to bending character too much in the direction of his own personality. In short, as a director, he was 'safe' to the point of being pedestrian, as an actor he was derivative.

Phelps's interpretation of Shakespeare set the pace for his era and is well expressed in two contemporary accounts — one which celebrates his directorial qualities, the other his acting style. The dichotomy is obvious. 'The scenery is always beautiful, but it is not allowed to draw attention from the poet, with whose whole conception it is made to blend in the most perfect harmony . . . Shakespeare appears in his integrity.' His Othello was a careful and intelligent reading of the part but in a detailed eyewitness account we catch glimpses of how Phelps could not resist an emotional surge which drew Othello near the bosky frontiers of sentimentality — 'When he hangs groaning over his dead wife he does not accept as a cue to his behaviour Emilia's counsel, 'Nay, lay thee down and roar', but follows, here and throughout the scene, Othello's own description of himself, as

> One whose subdued eyes,
> Albeit unused to the melting mood,
> Drop tears as fast as the Arabian trees
> Their medicinal gum.

The sensitive point of these lines is the pathetic irony implied in a man of steel who has never cried before and his sudden vulnerability to tears. That is not sentimental. But this is how Phelps played it — 'With a cry of tenderness he dies upon his way to Desdemona's couch, and falls with his arms strained towards her.' Significantly the curtain fell on his death — in Shakespeare's play it does not.

One particular feature of Phelps's interpretation is important because it is an emblem of something we tend automatically to associate with 'Victorianism'. Sentimentality was a pervading characteristic, and the words 'tenderness', 'pity', 'sweetness', 'pathos' fall in tearful showers from the pens of eyewitnesses of performances in mid-century. But, more than that, the word 'moral' is also a frequent visitor to the critic's page. Phelps's Macbeth seems to have been a powerful theatrical lesson in the dangers of evil. He and his contemporaries in 'Victorian' fashion drove home the moral lessons they discovered in Shakespeare.

Another example of Victorianism — a progeny of affluent national expansion — was also a dominant feature of the mid-century. In 1859 Charles, Edmund Kean's son, stepped forward on to the stage of the Princess's Theatre and delivered his farewell managerial speech. It amounted to an *apologia pro vita sua* — a justification of his principles of Shakespearean production. It is a remarkable document. Three short excerpts starkly emphasize the earnestness of the speaker, the nature of his principles, and the differences between one important movement in Shakespeare production (Phelps's) and another — for Kean became as famous as Phelps: (1) He says he has never 'permitted historical truth to be sacrificed to theatrical effect' and instances the Siege of Harfleur in his production of *Henry V*. '. . . it was no ideal battle, no imaginary fight; it was a correct representation of what actually had taken place . . . all taken from the account left to us by a priest who accompanied the army.' (2) He says — 'I have always entertained the conviction that . . . historical accuracy might be so blended with pictorial effect, that instruction and amusement would go hand in hand.' (3) He says, with some acidity — 'If, as is sometimes affirmed, my system is injurious to the poet, it must be equally so to the actor; and surely my most determined opponents will admit that at least I have pursued a very disinterested policy in thus incurring for many years so much labour and expense for the purpose of professional suicide.'

The Victorian urge for amplitude and the growing determination to be historically accurate joined with a passion to do good by education. Entertainment was not enough — a play should teach while it delights. This commendable principle was not unique to the Victorians, the Elizabethans shared it. But the third of Kean's statements is less a justification than a kind of self-condemnation. His productions were incredibly historically and naturalistically correct, but the more pictorially loaded they were, the less of Shakespeare's poetry was heard. One critic said, 'I do not wish the splendour less, or its attraction less, but only ask for more heed to the securing of a perfect harmony between the conceptions of the decorator and those of the poet.' *King John* was cut to ribbons, *Macbeth* was given back its Restoration ballet/opera scenes, the drunken Porter disappeared, and Lady Macbeth and Donalbain (one a participant, the other a suspect) do not appear in the scene after Duncan's murder! Kean, with magnificent bad taste and ill judgment but often impeccable and totally misdirected scholarship, would have put the clock back two hundred years — but the efforts of the plodding but sensitive Phelps were, fortunately, too strong and too much part of a tide that was to leave poor Kean behind.

Both Phelps and Kean frequently drew attention in their play-bills to the fact that the scenery for a production was 'new'. To us this seems an unnecessary claim but, in both the 18th and 19th centuries sets were frequently used more than once for different productions of the same play, and it was not unknown for them to appear for a play for which they were not originally designed. But the mid-century marked the beginning of a long era when no expense was spared in buying the best material and the best artists and designers. The art of scene painting was very much nearer the art of landscape painting than it later became and certainly than it is now. A boxed set with a real ceiling was first used in 1832 but, in the forties, fifties and sixties, the 18th-century system of flats in grooves and back-drop curtains was still the common form of presentation — and each flat was either a 'picture' in itself or part of a larger picture.

Both Phelps and Kean used this common form of presentation, but used it in combination with what, in a sense, is a very non-theatrical form of setting — i.e. architectural representation — as if the stage were a large space upon which actual (or seemingly actual) buildings were to be built. It is in the use made of flats, grooves and architecture that the difference between Phelps and Kean is found, for neither of them experimented with new forms of set-design in any significant way.

Their notions of how this space was to be filled were basically poles apart. A graphic illustration is in the relative complement of their productions of *Henry V*. Phelps had forty players, Kean had five hundred and fifty! These astonishing figures (for even Phelps's is large by today's standards) can help us to establish a clear basic distinction between them. For all his careful attention to detail Phelps was, essentially, an impressionist; the man had poetic sensibility even if his judgment was faulty. He recognized that true theatrical effect comes from the way you deploy your forces not from the number you employ. He did not, like Kean, believe that 'biggest is bestest'. There was always in a Phelps production a unity of poetic effect — e.g. in *Richard III*, 'The dawn of morning is accompanied with the distant hum of preparation, then the faint roll of drums is heard mingling with the bugle call.'

In his pursuit of the 'poetic' Phelps was much given to a (sometimes excessive) use of gauze — 'The first scene was very skilfully managed' with 'the stage . . . darkened to a much greater degree than usual, so much so that but the imperfect outlines of the weird sisters were visible. In front only a dim, lurid light played, and as the hags stepped backwards, the darkness, aided by a combination of gauze screens, procured one of the most perfect effects of vanishing we ever saw.' Modern theatregoers might well reflect that directors today, for all their technical resources, attain no better poetic effect than did Phelps, with far less mechanical aid. One such aid he used frequently; this was a diorama — a moving-scene. He employed it in *A Midsummer Night's Dream* with splendid success, so that, as one scene (behind green gauze) was replaced by another (sliding along its groove or dropping from the flies) and as the lights were deployed, a sense of 'dissolve' was achieved. This technique, a commonplace of 20th-century filmic practice, was also employed by Kean, notably in his production of *The Winter's Tale*. Other managers used gauze and dissolve effects, and diorama with a self-consciousness that suggests recognition of a debt to these two theatrical pacemakers. Sometimes Phelps's ingenuity, could be cumbersome — perhaps, indeed, Kean's extravagant largesse of numbers for *Henry V* was preferable to Phelps's strained attempt to impersonate the hosts of Agincourt — 'Madame Tussaud modelled eight wax heads — these were fitted on dummy figures of wicker work, clad in the costume and armour of the period. Every man of the gallant forty carried two of these figures, one on either side, attached to a sort of framework, which was lashed to his waist; hence it seemed as if they were marching three abreast.' This was impressionism with gammy legs, so to speak.

But Kean was architectural and archaeological — 'poetry' was, to him, secondary to accuracy — 'As the curtain rose, we saw before us Syracuse at the epoch of her greatest prosperity, about 300 BC, and gazed on the fountains of Arethusa and the Temple of Minerva . . .' (*The Winter's Tale*, 1856). Ellen Terry played Mamillius in this production, and she also played Puck in Kean's *A Midsummer Night's Dream*. The often absurd results of Kean's attempts to be accurate (but with Puck how does one know whether one is accurate?) is ruthlessly exposed in Ellen Terry's account of an on-stage incident. 'I had to fly off the stage as swiftly as I could, and a dummy Puck was whisked through the air from the point where I disappeared.' At one performance the dummy dropped to the stage and Miss Terry (the real Puck) rushed back on stage to pick it up. Kean specialized in stage-machinery, especially in the tricky business of causing characters to appear, disappear and reappear as if by magic.

Shakespeare survived Kean and thrived on Phelps's treatment of him. The most fortunate people were the paying customers — they had the best of two very different products of mens' imaginations.

Costume in the Mid-Century
In the mid-19th century we are a long way from the ad-hocery of previous
centuries, though the oddity in costume was still frequent. It is impressive
to read of Kean's amazing fidelity to historical costume in *Richard III* and
in *Henry VIII*, and Phelps was no slouch in attempts to make garments
seem real and natural. Nevertheless, anomalies appeared and these are
demonstrable by reference to the growing habit of illustrated texts of
Shakespeare showing actors and actresses as they appeared in specific
productions. In Phelps's 1849 production of *Antony and Cleopatra* an
illustration in *The Illustrated London News* of Elinor Glyn as Cleopatra
shows us a very British-Empire-like Egyptian background in front of
which the fatal Queen stands — but she looks like the young Victoria —
not so much fatal as Windsor imperial! In Kean's *The Winter's Tale* his
wife, as Hermione, wore a Victorian contemporary hair-do and a number
of starched petticoats — so like the home life of our dear Queen! The urge
to be 'real', the desire to impress and the buoyant sense of the time con-
spired to produce costuming whose only consistency was magnificence of
effect — verisimilitude, in the long run, took second place to effect.

Acting in the Mid-Century
The allurements of sentimentality and effectiveness of appearance
dominated acting. Phelps pursued restraint and ease but was an easy prey
to his own disposition to cut a melodramatic dash, to rouse emotion
without specific reason — which is one aspect of sentimentality. Mid-
Victorian acting as exemplified by one of its leading players was peculiarly
self-indulgent emotionally and devoted to making emotionally-inspired
points. Actresses were no less given to the same practice. Note the use of
the word 'sublime' in the description of this Cleopatra — 'She combined
grace and dignity . . . Gorgeous in person, in costume and in action . . .
Withal she was classical, and her poses severely statuesque. Her death was
sublime.' It must have been very moving but — is it Shakespeare's
Cleopatra? Again, Mrs Charles Kean's Queen Katharine in *Henry VIII*
raises doubts — 'The attitude in which, half-rising from her couch, she
followed with her eyes the departing forms, might serve as a study for
some picture of a saint's "ecstasy".' Very touching — but not Shakespeare's Queen. As certainly as in interpretation and in setting, acting
emphasized the 'Victorianization' of Shakespeare — but then as now, the
century was seeing Shakespeare in its own image.

Shakespeare's Text — Phelps
The last performance by Phelps was of Brutus and in his farewell speech
he rightly and proudly spoke of his achievements. He had wanted to
present all Shakespeare's plays — he had, in fact, produced thirty-four of
them. This was and still is a remarkable achievement in itself, but it

must also be examined to see what kind of texts were used in this long caravanserai.

Without doubt Phelps and Webster put paid to the tradition of nearly two centuries whereby Shakespeare's texts were considered to be fair game for anybody's militant imaginative whims. Phelps's most lauded achievement was to diminish to the point virtually of disappearance the dominance of Colley Cibber's version of *Richard III*. The murder of Clarence was restored, the long-drawn-out wailing of the grieving mothers was back, the council meeting and the denunciation of Hastings was returned from limbo. But, yet again, caution is necessary. In some cases Phelps indulged in exactly the same practice that had made Cibber's version such a notorious success — that is, grafting pieces of one scene on to another, compressing two characters into one, and some rearranging of single lines.

But Phelps's greatest achievement was to give his contemporaries a *Macbeth* without the traditional singing witches and without a lot of verbal paraphernalia written by Davenant. He restored Lady Macduff (a fine candidate for Victorian sentimental treatment) and her little boy (perhaps one of the few candidates in Shakespeare's plays for justifiable homicide both in textual and realistic terms). His greatest omission was the doctor.

Relentlessly, but perhaps without the panache of genius, Phelps moved nearer to presenting his public with true Shakespeare. But Webster was the more adventurous man. He risked financial ruin by presenting Shakespeare plays which were very rarely, if ever, performed, notably *The Two Gentlemen of Verona* (a box-office failure). Phelps again emulated him and produced a notable *Timon of Athens*, to great critical acclaim, and *Pericles*, with cautious critical acceptance.

Late Victorian and Edwardian

Irving, the Actor-Manager

From about 1880 to the beginning of World War I the English theatre was dominated by one of the most brilliant collections of actor-managers in the history of theatre. England reached the apogee of its imperial power, and national power (as in Elizabeth I's time) breeds strong and often inventive individuals quite apart from cultivating an affluence (at least for a minority) which enables that power to be disseminated and displayed and for the inventiveness to have access. In this period English theatre flourished mightily, not only in London but in most parts of the country. Every town of even modest size had, it seemed, its own theatre or theatres, many of them of an opulence and decoration befitting imperial status. Touring companies travelled far and wide often taking with them West End stars anxious to display their talents widely or to have a busman's holiday. Seats were cheap, conditions were more comfortable, technological advances in gas and, later, electricity, made spectacle into a wondrous affair. Theatre was big business, whatever it was artistically, and while most of the theatre-managers are to be honoured for their artistic contributions, it cannot be doubted that the hope of financial gain was a strong reason for the extraordinary proliferation of men anxious not only to direct and act but also to manage.

The greatest was Henry Irving, though arguably his acting talent, so far at least as Shakespeare was concerned, fell far short of his abilities as a theatre-manager. With him the profession of acting was given, at last, the official seal of respectability, when he was knighted. With him the developing acceptance that theatre is an international medium became final. He toured three times in the United States and what he did was emulated and surpassed by his colleagues on both sides of the Atlantic. Moreover France, Germany and, to an extent, Italy became represented in productions of Shakespeare. Irving was at the centre of this booming industry and Shakespeare, he very well knew, was central to any attempt to maintain the boom — though what he knew and what he was capable of did not always correspond. But he made the Lyceum Theatre, with which he was associated from 1871 to 1902, immortal for the quality of production in general and, although Shakespeare and he were not on the very finest of artistic terms, he succeeded in breaking the grip that Phelps's Sadlers Wells and Drury Lane had had on the work of the Bard.

At the basis of Irving's approach were two principles — the first, undoubtedly influenced by Phelps and Kean, was that all of Shakespeare's plays require very strong, vivid and exciting visual presentation; the second was that the acting must be realistic — in tragedy and comedy. His two principles which he studiously attempted to put into practice greatly influenced the work of other actor-managers. Indeed, the production of Shakespeare's plays by most of the actor-managers of the period was dominated by two concepts, deriving from Irving but, eventually, from Phelps, Kean, and others — 'pictorial' and 'realistic'.

Pictorial Shakespeare

Irving, speaking to the Garrick Club, said that if Shakespeare were alive he would 'try it with scenery'. What Irving meant can be quickly realized by reflecting on the visual aspects of some of his own productions:

(1) *Hamlet*, 1879. (The first Ghost scene) : 'Standing among a number of massive rocks, the Ghost proceeds with the supernatural impartment. The soft light of the moon falls upon the spectral figure; not a sound from below can be heard; the faint flashes of the dawn are stealing over the immense expanse of water before us . . .' (The Ophelia burial): 'The churchyard is on a hill near the palace, and, as night comes on, the funeral procession winds slowly up the ascent.'

(2) *Much Ado About Nothing*, 1882. 'They [modern designers] are able to model as well as to paint their scenes, to introduce really cylindrical columns and really plastic bas-reliefs, and in rural tableaux to simulate trees and plants, the leaves of which are corporeally agitated by the air . . . and a vast number of new fabric . . . offering as they do, evidence of the study now of Japanese and now of mediaeval art, have effected a complete revolution in the embellishment of a play.'

(3) *Twelfth Night*, 1884. '. . . although there is a slight suggestion of Orientalism in the garb of the minstrels . . . and there is an element of Sclavonic [sic] wildness and uncouthness in the array of guards, the costumes and the architecture belong essentially to the period of the Venetian domination.'

Whatever else Irving had learnt from Kean it was not archaeological or architectural exactitude. He had, in fact, compounded Kean's *embarrass de richesse* with gay abandon — in *Twelfth Night* and *Much Ado* alone the accounts take our imagination into Japan, the mediaeval period, the Orient, the 'Sclavonic' countries and Venice. Further, Irving's imagination was intensely romantically poetic. Visually, he saw Shakespeare as through a beautiful glass — rather darkly however. There is something Wagnerian about the *Hamlet* description, and something quaintly fey-

pastoral about the trembling leaves of *Much Ado*. But whatever Irving lost
of Kean's almost manic pursuit of exactitude he matched with something
that neither Kean nor anyone before him had been able to achieve. The
reference in the *Much Ado* review to the use of modelling to impersonate
stone or wood suggests a different kind of exactitude from Kean's. Irving
did not baulk if, in *Romeo and Juliet*, the architecture was Florentine when
it should be Veronese, so long as it looked and maybe even felt like
architecture.

Yet, most reports of Irving's productions, except Bernard Shaw's,
declare that they always had good taste and harmony. Indeed, to move to
yet another aspect of Irving's visual interpretations, the word 'harmony'
constantly occurs both in reviews and in Irving's own writing. He said in
his *Art of Acting* (1885) — 'It is most important that an actor should learn
that he is a figure in a picture, and that the least exaggeration destroys the
harmony of the composition.' Irving learnt, for example, how to handle
crowd-scenes — he was a glutton for multiplicity, so long as his own
singularity of presence could be seen to emerge from it — from the
Meininger company. This had been formed by the Duke of Saxe-
Meiningen and his wife, a former actress. It had close affiliations with
London and performed at Drury Lane in 1881. The company was a model
of discipline, and worked by dividing itself into small groups, each with a
mature actor in charge. Each group was intensely rehearsed and taught to
develop a relationship with the other groups. The company's famed
depictions of crowd scenes were masterpieces of co-ordinated realism.
Photographs of Shakespeare performances of the period frequently show
large crowd scenes in which every individual is characterized. This,
certainly, was the result of the Meiningers' influence.

There were some distinguished dissidents from Irving's conception.
Wilson Barrett (a rival of Irving's) presented a *Hamlet* in 1884 which
attempted a kind of early Danish naturalism and succeeded in being
merely ugly! The *Illustrated London News*'s critic, with unexpected transatlantic finality, averred that, 'I have seldom looked upon such a set of
guys as those whom historical accuracy has placed upon the stage of the
Princess's.' But there is, indeed, nothing to set in decided and combative
contrast to the genius of Henry Irving and the spirit of the age that
fostered the kind of product he fashioned for the delight of the public. He
had one great high-priest who bid fair to outdo his master — Beerbohm
Tree — but his astonishing visual treatment of Shakespeare came later.

Shakespeare's Text

The steady scrubbing away of verbal barnacles on Shakespeare's text
continued — everyone, even Charles Kean, seemed agreed that whatever
the audience heard had to be Shakespeare. However, there was a let-out
clause — it was still the prerogative of the director or actor-manager to

decide not only how much of Shakespeare was to be included, but also where it was to be put. The history of the steady improvement of texts is besmirched by cuts and often bizarre resiting of speeches and scenes. No one ever considered, even as a remote possibility, the idea that perhaps Shakespeare *did* know what he was doing. There is a curious irony in the fact that the use of cumbersome scenery and slots and flats in 18th- and 19th-century productions added a great deal of time to the duration of a full Shakespeare text — but it was not Shakespeare who was responsible for what were often said to be his 'long' plays, but the very methods employed to realize them on stage.

Shakespeare's text, in the late 19th century was still, then, at the mercy of the manager, even if it was now reprieved, in most theatres, from the indignity of additional or replacement dialogue by other hands. It must be remembered, too, that Victorian susceptibilities could be particularly hard on Shakespeare's alleged bawdy or true bawdy — when, that is, the genuine article could be recognized. The Victorian age was no more innocent than any other, but there is a certain disarming naiveté to be observed in the relentless way so many acting texts of Shakespeare omitted obvious and presumed bawdy while missing some of the best bits — as our vulgar century would say. Veritable wastelands in the text were perpetrated by thin-lipped moralists, with only one feature left in the desolate verbal landscape — and that was the one that got away. 'Hey nonny-no', for instance, seemed so relaxedly rural it was always kept. A quick glance at a modern edition will reveal that it may be rural and relaxed — but innocent? No!

Victorian acting-texts were at the mercy of many things: the star-system, for the actor-manager, was, both administratively and artistically, in the spotlight; Victorian sensibilities — especially in matters salacious; Victorian counterpointing of healthy entertainment with mental 'improvement'; Victorian sentimentality which, to a degree, was a product of material success. Irving seems to have been peculiarly suited to meet these comprehensive conditions. His acting-text of *Hamlet* cunningly keeps the sweet Prince (even in that menacingly cynical early scene with Ophelia), so that Irving's determination to present an interpretation which shows how much Hamlet loved Ophelia despite everything is also kept — despite Hamlet's desire (melodramatic, but at least, expressed) to 'drink hot blood', and despite the last speech of Fortinbras which implies a public inquiry. The play ended with this sweet lover's death! One is inclined to say — 'Hey, nonny, no'.

There is only one way to understand the implications of the comparative when one says that late 19th-century texts were 'nearer' to Shakespeare than early 19th-century texts, and that is to examine them. Henry Irving co-edited a handsome multi-volumed edition of the plays with introductions and notes by eminent critics. It is salutary to note what Irving cut —

he has obliged posterity by indicating his acting cuts with a wavy margin line. In *Macbeth*, for example, Malcolm and Donalbain's determination to fly is cut thus leaving them much more capable of being thought guilty than the original text allows. The murder of Banquo and Fleance is cut (though Irving's printed edition has a melodramatic illustration of it). Lady Macduff and her death scene is cut. The so-called 'England' scene (IV. iii) between Malcolm and Macduff is mauled. The death of young Siward is cut. The play ends with the words 'And damn'd be him that first cries "Hold, enough".' What Irving was prepared to do, others emulated. The mercy is that deep inside the Victorian mind was a balancing effect which prevented wholesale slaughter.

Sometimes, admittedly, it is difficult to understand how the Victorians prevented themselves from indulging in excesses which would make Restoration malpractice look respectable! The whims of the actor-manager and manageress were extraordinary, where the text was concerned. In 1885 William Kendal so manipulated *As You Like It* that Jaques, the melancholy and cantankerous man, 'became more reasonable'! Mary Anderson grossly cut *The Winter's Tale*, ending the Shepherd's celebration with a speech by Florizel which, in the original text, comes at the beginning. She concluded the play with a couplet taken from *All's Well That Ends Well* — but, at least, it was Shakespeare she used and not latter-day Colley Cibber. Richard Mansfield omitted one of Shakespeare's most melodramatic female characters, Queen Margaret, from *Richard III*, together with the death of Clarence, which contains one of Shakespeare's finest elegiac dramatic speeches. Shakespeare's texts were deployed, in this astonishing century, not only to suit Victorian tastes, but to accommodate the tremendous paraphernalia of scenery. If it were more convenient to do a play in three acts rather than the customary five, then it was so done. A notorious (in terms of potential audience-discomfort) production of *Julius Caesar* (Beerbohm Tree, 1895) had a first act of two hours which ended with Antony's speech over Caesar's bleeding cadaver. But, if we are disposed to scoff, we should perhaps consider how future generations may regard some of our 20th-century efforts.

Shakespearean Acting

The invention of photography conditions the way we form judgments about the actors and actresses of the late 19th century. One inescapable fact emerges as we gaze on their (usually) posed images. They look 'larger-than-life'. The exigencies of a relatively primitive film-developing process cannot entirely be responsible for those eyes that seem to flash, the male hair that falls so insouciantly, the female hair that sits with such grandeur. Tricks of light cannot account for so many faces that have such beautiful haughtiness or symmetrical contempt, so many noses that seem Grecian, and lips that one can imagine curling with spleen or softening into controlled passion. On the evidence of photography Victorian players had style which made them 'bigger', or seem to be; the aura of mystery, perhaps with a rakish tinge to it, made them 'more interesting'. When the star Victorian players stepped on to the stage, by and large, any role he or she was to perform had to conform itself in great measure to the performer, not vice versa — it was, so to speak, Hamlet's Irving one went to see, not Irving's Hamlet. Beerbohm Tree's Malvolio was described as 'himself being amusing' and his Benedick as 'himself not being at all amusing'. Bernard Shaw said the only thing that would ensure Tree's being a good Falstaff was if he were born again as unlike himself as possible. Sir George Alexander, whatever part he played, always made sure that what he wore on stage was as impeccable as what he wore off it. Sir Frank Benson, a matinée idol, always ranted when he spoke verse (whoever's it was) and rattled when he spoke prose — as Hesketh Pearson remarked — 'it all sounded magnificent when one was fourteen years old'.

But there is a paradox here. Although Victorian acting was 'personality' acting and, on the evidence (which must always be taken with great caution) of a number of surviving recordings on most inadequate equipment, was, as is commonly said, 'hamming' (overemphatic, that is, in every respect) — the quest of almost every notable Victorian player was for what they called 'realism'. By this they meant 'truth to human nature'. However larger-than-life it all seems to us, and perhaps seemed then, the urge was to create a characterization which would move the audience to recognize truth to human nature in what they saw and heard. One of the most intriguing characteristics of a surprisingly large number of Victorian actors — though actresses seem to have been immune — was a marked eccentricity of voice or delivery or movement — or all three. In some cases this eccentricity was a natural result of some physical condition, in others it was acquired or invented. In both cases it became accepted as a 'natural' feature and was used as an aid to 'realistic' interpretation — so that, for example, any role played by Irving became very characteristically Irvingesque, because of his marked limp and his unmistakable manner of delivery. He had a slightly 'dragging' leg which (to his credit) he tried not to exploit. Indeed, Ellen Terry claims that he spent years attempting to overcome it. His voice, then, rasping, and his pronunciation — over emphatic — were blights of nature he could do nothing to conquer. But there was, in Irving's personality a quality which, in our cliché-caught age, would be described as 'magnetic'. For once distinguished evidence gives the cliché some validity. Ellen Terry, describing a train journey with Irving relates how she watched him; his face held her eyes for it seemed to her to change its appearance several times a minute. Beneath this changing atmosphere she detected, however, a facial landscape that seemed to her 'half puzzled, half despairing'. She asked him what he was thinking about and he answered that he found it strange that he should have made such a reputation with nothing to help him — that his legs and voice had been against him. When Ellen Terry observed his 'splendid head', 'wonderful hands' and 'the whole strange beauty of him' — she was, in fact, thinking of his 'magnetism', and when he'd finished his sad little catechism she murmured to herself — 'Ah, you little know.'

Johnston Forbes-Robertson. He was the reluctant star who, when he retired from the stage, did so with a great relief. He began training as an artist but, expecting that the stage might make more money than art to help support a large family of brothers and sisters, he went to the Royal Academy. He was encouraged by Phelps who prided himself on being a stylistic descendant of Garrick's naturalism. Forbes-Robertson was a model of the Victorian ideal of the actor — handsome, regular features, charm of manner, melodiously elegant of speech, lithe and graceful of movement. Many contemporary critics considered him the finest Hamlet of his generation and he played it in a way which appealed to the Victorian notion of the part — noble in every aspect, superbly spoken, and with a vulnerable charm. He does not, however, appear to have fallen into the trap of sentimentality. Shaw, who could smell it out, testifies to this — he refers to most Hamlets who die 'to slow music, like Little Nell', but Forbes-Robertson 'bowled them all out by being clever enough to be simple'. He played Romeo to Modjeska's Juliet, Claudio for Irving at the Lyceum, Leontes in Mary Anderson's production of *The Winter's Tale*, and Henry VIII. He was associated with the fiery Mrs Patrick Campbell in productions of *Romeo and Juliet* and *Macbeth* and he played, without much energy, Othello and Shylock. Many of those who saw these two roles found him wanting in interpretation, but his speaking was superb.

Herbert Tree. Although a popular actor, he was not in the first rank. W. S. Gilbert referred to his Hamlet as being funny without being vulgar. Discerning critics thought his Macbeth curiously unmilitary and his Othello flatly un-jealous. He often relied on intuition, guesswork and fertile inventiveness when it came to remembering Shakespeare's lines. He was unheroic in appearance, hoarse in delivery and slightly grotesque in movement. He was a 'personality' actor who exploited every trick. As Richard II he entered with a dog, and when the animal (superbly trained) licked Bolingbroke's hand, Tree broke his heart with a sob and left the stage. As Malvolio he came majestically down a flight of stairs and, in a contrived, well-rehearsed way, crashed to a sitting position. He put on his eyeglass, looked at the surroundings with disdain as if his fall were part of a divine plan. But, as Shaw says, 'When he came to speak those lines . . .

Tree made nothing of them, not knowing a game which he had never studied.'

But Tree was a very great manager and performed inestimable services both for his profession and for the public. His productions were always magnificent, if gaudy. *The Tempest* had a ship tossing about on real water to the discomfiture of the orchestra stalls. In *A Midsummer Night's Dream* real rabbits inhabited the wood. *Twelfth Night* had real grass and flowers, and in *Richard II* Tree himself appeared on a real horse, much to the apprehension of the orchestra stalls. He was criticized for lavish vulgarity, but he said, 'I prefer a spectacle on stage to spectacles in the audience.' Vulgar or not, he persuaded countless hundreds to come to see Shakespeare. They came, not just for what might have been vulgar spectacle, but to experience fine acting. Tree enhanced his profession by a kind of generosity in the sense that he never submerged the actors and actresses who played with him by cutting their lines — as Irving did. He found, like Garrick, the best actors for the parts. His record of 'discoveries' is prodigious: Lewis Waller, Oscar Asche, Henry Ainley, Owen Nares, Lyn Harding, Matheson Lang. He incited superb performances from Ellen Terry in *The Winter's Tale* and Madge Kendal in *The Merry Wives of Windsor*. He was a genuine eccentric, with a touch of erratic genius.

Frank Benson. This knighted, tireless actor-manager is still revered by many at Stratford upon Avon. He was probably the most experienced, most travelled actor of all time, who took his touring company all over the United Kingdom. Like Tree he was a far greater manager than an actor and, like him, he relied upon personal magnetism rather than histrionic prowess. He ranted, intoned, mumbled, groaned as he gripped Shakespeare's lines in a half-nelson. Restless in movement, he attitudinized and up-staged, but almost everyone loved him, perhaps because he seemed so healthily English. He was generally believed to be related to the Archbishop of Canterbury, played cricket, football, hockey, ran and swam and rowed. It is little to be wondered at that the fight and battle scenes of his productions were enormously realistic — indeed in some plays he introduced fights that are not called for! As Petruchio he jumped over tables and descended swiftly from ropes fifty years before Douglas Fairbanks and nearly a hundred before Errol Flynn. His Macbeth was beyond criticism — it was appalling. His Dr Caius in *The Merry Wives of Windsor* was exquisitely funny. His Richard III was a disaster and his Antony merely quaint.

Yet, like Tree, his memory must be crowned with laurels. He was generous to a fault, kindly without thought of recompense — although his company once accepted half-salary to keep him in business. He always put art before box-office. He ran, at one time, three touring companies and, between them, they performed thirty-five out of Shakespeare's thirty-seven plays. He was the first man to perform the complete text of *Hamlet*, in two parts. From 1891 to 1919 he was in charge of the Shakespeare Festivals at Stratford upon Avon. He did much there to establish its now international status. The town rewarded him by making him a Freeman, the theatre-committee thanked him by forcing his retirement, without a pension. Countless thousands who were schoolchildren in the Benson era at Stratford, learned to love Shakespeare from his astonishing seven or eight different productions per week. He was tireless in rehearsing himself and his company, and he laid down the basis for Equity, the actors' association. His profession adored him — he was a most gentle knight.

Lewis Waller. He was a matinée idol from the 1890s to his death in 1915. He was in the grand manner, the heroic mould, with a superb, thrilling voice and a large presence. His Henry V can still be heard, in excerpt, on a commercial recording. The exigencies of primitive technology don't do justice to the voice, but the passion and something of the melody is still to be heard. Women adored him — a K.O.W. club was formed by females maddened by adoration who went to performance after performance to show they were 'Keen On Waller'. Waller's reaction was a little sardonic — 'Will no one rid me of these turbulent priestesses?' He preferred lighter roles — musical comedy might well have been his true forte — Shaw described his Brutus as a watercolour sketch without weight or depth. His Hotspur was an outrageous but effective display of braggadocio acting, sometimes without, as Shaw said, 'a pretence of any dramatic motive'. But he was representative of his time, highly-skilled in giving the public what they wanted — magic.

John Martin-Harvey. He lived from 1863 to 1944, the last relic of the actor-manager era. He was all actor, and revered and copied Henry Irving. He seems never to have stopped acting; he cut a theatrical dash wherever he went — on and off-stage. He was not primarily a Shakespearean, but his Hamlet, Henry V, Petruchio and Richard III were highly regarded by the public and by some critics. These four parts were well chosen, for each of them has a degree of flamboyance and theatricality which is what Martin-Harvey could best achieve. It was said he could not impersonate an ordinary human being, and there is nothing ordinary about that particular quartet. His voice was flexible, his gestures and general visual appearance had astonishing effect. He was able to communicate mood, atmosphere, with the slightest of movements — a glance, a lifted finger. There was always a slight edge of menace or the sardonic about his performances.

Ellen Terry. On the occasion of her jubilee, Bernard Shaw (not noticeably gifted as a lyrical versifier) sent her a letter containing four stanzas one of which goes:

> . . . change plays its part
> In every known direction
> Save your imperishable art
> And our unchanged affection.

'Imperishable art' and 'unchanged affection' sum up the feelings of her contemporaries about and for Ellen Terry. Many thought her superior to Sarah Siddons, but at the standard at which both performed comparison seems pointless. At the age of nine she appeared as Mamillius in *The Winter's Tale*, but the glorious period of her Shakespearean acting began in 1878 when she became Henry Irving's leading lady at the Lyceum, and triumphed as Beatrice, Cordelia, Desdemona, Olivia, Viola and Lady Macbeth. Strangely, she never played Rosalind.

She was an actress of remarkable intelligence which she applied both to specific interpretations and to her critical studying of roles. Her memoirs contain much of value to students of theatre, and her comments, like her acting, were always vital, fresh, unexpected: of Juliet she wrote, 'could a girl of fourteen play such a part? Yes, if she were not youthful, only young with the youth of the poet, tragically old as some youth is.' In thinking of Ophelia, she wrote, 'It is not [sic] good observing life and bringing the result to the stage without selection, without a definite idea. The idea must come first, the realism afterwards.' Her Beatrice revealed her intelligence in action. 'Laughter and tears are only divided by the narrowest channel, and the art with which Miss Ellen Terry expresses this in the scene after the cruel condemnation of her cousin is quite admirable.' She was not afraid of unconventional readings of text. Her 'O! God, that I were a man! I would eat his heart in the market-place' (Beatrice) was not 'the scornful rage of a vixen, or the scream of a vulgar shrew, but a sudden, passionate sob of suppressed emotion . . . when we object to unconventional readings we must remember the kind of woman presented to us'. Her Lady Macbeth shocked many people by its unconventionality. It was domestic, practical, calculating and yet at the same time it initiated a tradition of dressing the character in exotic costume — she wore a glittering gold embroidered skirt, blouse and cap. In another scene she wore a gown of peacock green, with a mantle of claret; the gown was decorated with beetle's wings. Her performance had a 'bright, prompt, fascinating impulse with an audacity of realism'. When she returned from Duncan's body after placing the daggers there, she made a gesture that curdled the audience's blood — she delicately lifted a robe, which had fallen to the ground, by the very tips of her fingers, to avoid its becoming bloodstained.

Her Portia was famous, and excerpts from a reading by her are still available, but they do scant justice. *The Times* of 3 November 1879 described it as 'perfect charm throughout'. The critic of *Blackwood's* magazine interpreted this charm as mere prettiness, but this was a minority opinion. Nevertheless, it serves to indicate the basic nature of Ellen Terry's acting, which seems to have trodden a knife-edge between bright, witty intelligent appeal and a tendency to slightly mawkish sentimentality. It is a testimony to her self-critical ability and to her intelligence that she rarely fell off it. Her technique, beauty, strong will, above all, enabled her to maintain, for most of her professional life, a superb balance.

Janet Achurch. She was something of a rival to Ellen Terry and merits notice not only for her innate qualities but because she was one of the first English actresses to appear in Ibsen's plays. Shaw reserved for her an admiration and affection second only to that he expended on Ellen Terry, though he chided her for abandoning naturalism for what he called the rhetorical style when she played Cleopatra in 1897.

Mrs Patrick Campbell. A dragon, a bitch, a witch, an enchantress, a *belle dame sans merci*. Any of these epithets could at some time have been used to describe one mood or aspect or other of this woman who lived from 1865 to 1940, and spent much of that time demolishing her intellectual inferiors with her wit or entrapping unwary males with her solid femininity. Yeats described her acting as having simplicity, precision and delicacy and, indeed, she was, when she decided not to be eccentric, an actress of great technical skill and emotional sensitivity. Her Ophelia was praised for its astonishing commitment to the depiction of madness — Victorian performances had customarily concentrated on a kind of zany, fey charm. Her Lady Macbeth was said by Shaw in a letter to her to be 'too ladylike'; her Juliet showed more temper than passion — but there were moments in both roles when she seemed incomparable. Indeed, Mrs Campbell was, perhaps, a tragic personality, not able to maintain a consistency of mood or technique or emotional rapport with any character. The significance of her triumph in depicting Ophelia's madness may indicate a personality more consistently in tune with distress than anything else. There is a wry story of her, which perhaps testifies as much to the dark colouring of her mind as it does to the mordancy of her wit. A boy of sixteen met Mrs Campbell in Montreal. She said, 'Oh, my dear boy, why do you take dope?' He replied that he did not take dope. In her dark velvet voice she said, 'Then what tragedy you must have known to have eyes like that.'

The 19th century is replete with the names of actors and actresses who helped to make the Shakespearean theatre of the last half of the century one of the most exciting in the world. One quality is common to them all

— they had astonishing 'character'. They stood out in crowds, they were 'cap-à-pie' people of the theatre. In many this quality came out as eccentricity, in most it emerged as a magic of presence. Barry Sullivan who bent every part to his own person, Lillie Langtry (called the Jersey Lily), who was as intimate as possible with Edward VII, who organized her own company, merely passed muster as an actress, but whose Rosalind was loved for its sweetness; Lillah McCarthy who, late-ish in life, played Hermione and Viola and triumphed; Ada Rehan, an American, who made the part of Katherine the Shrew very much her own, and whose acting was distinguished by an astonishing ability to catch the music of Shakespeare's lines; Ben Greet, who specialized in open-air productions, was a brilliant teacher of acting, and helped to found the Old Vic; the Bancrofts (Sir Squire and his wife Marie) who paid higher salaries than anyone else, paid for actresses' costumes and established the box-set; Granville-Barker (a playwright and critic of near genius) who was an associate of William Poel and his Elizabethan Stage Society. Barker was one of the first to champion subsidized theatre and a great proselytizer of the need for directors to respect the texts of Shakespeare's plays. The line stretches forth and it is impossible not to reflect on what a variety of choice the Victorian audiences had, not only in London but in the provinces. So far as the latter half of the 19th century was concerned, Shakespearean theatre was, in a very real sense, total theatre.

Sets and Scenery

Given the immense variety and versatility of theatre talent in the latter half of the 19th century it is not surprising to find a reflection of it in the setting and costuming of Shakespeare's plays. It seems to be a law of theatrical history that general trend is always in a state of tension with individual taste or style. The theatre of the late 19th century had been bequeathed, by Phelps, Charles Kean, Macready and others, strongly based principles and practices which constituted, eventually, a convention that most theatre-managers and actors adopted as received and accepted truth. But, with so much thoroughbred individual talent abroad, the bequeathed convention was always in a state of siege.

The bequest of Charles Kean, Phelps and Macready was realism in sets, costumes and acting. The quest for accuracy which characterized, in varying degrees, their work, was continued by their successors, and there are many examples of Shakespeare productions in the 1870s and 1880s where the painstaking attention to detail so manifest in Kean's work was emulated — sometimes in a finicky way. Clement Scott wrote in 1884 — 'We are gradually overdoing spectacle so much that poetry must suffer in the long run . . . the form of a lamp, the topography of a street are preferred to the interpretation of any one given part.' How far Scott is right in his estimate of the unfortunate effects is a matter for debate, but there

is no doubt about the accuracy of his estimate of the importance given to
the visually correct and detailed. In *As You Like It* in 1885, a Mr Lewis
Wingfield (the designer) had guards who were attired with 'perfect
accuracy' (who they were guarding is not known), and, 'He has for the
first time put on the stage what looks like grass.' One wonders whether it
required mowing. In Irving's *Much Ado About Nothing*, 1882, plants and
trees had leaves which 'are corporeally agitated by the air'. In his *Romeo
and Juliet*, 1882, the balcony 'is solidly built up with marble pillars,
shaded in front with quivering foliage'. Only if visual effect is in total
harmony with acting and speaking is there no danger of such detail
seeming obtrusive and ridiculous. Sometimes it was both vulgar and silly,
but, often, given the spirit of harmony, it worked. One critic commenting
on Irving's *The Merchant of Venice*, 1879, said that he retained memories of
a real Venice, real palaces, real canals, real gondolas, but above all the
real bridge over the canal. After Jessica's elopement, 'the return of
Shylock over the bridge, across the silent stage, and his knock at the door
of the deserted home!', Ellen Terry said, 'For absolute pathos, achieved
by absolute simplicity of means, I never saw anything in the theatre to
compare with it.'

So, the bequest of the past was the basis of late 19th-century setting.
But added to it was an element peculiarly belonging to the period. There
was a huge emphasis on the pictorial, the picturesque, the decorative.
Never could scene-painters have had such opportunities. The reasons are
not difficult to find. The activities of the Pre-Raphaelite movement, and
particularly of painters and designers like William Morris, pushed the
visual arts to the very forefront of public attention. Morris, in particular,
showed that art need not be an esoteric monopoly of the leisured, nor
unrelated to everyday living. By the end of the century his designs were
to be found on the fabrics and wallpaper even in households who, otherwise, would have no truck with 'bohemian artists'. Moreover, the emphasis on beauty of line and colour was strongly appealing. The theatre,
like society at large, was beguiled by the pictorial, the decorative, the
beautiful. Sets were large, often monumental (as befitted an imperial
nation), and theatres were built large both to cope with them and to
emphasize the imperial posture. The results, in practice, were often
startling. 'Act IV is the sensation act so far as spectacle is concerned. The
first scene gives us a genuine reproduction of old London, "A street in
Westminster", with its three-storied wooden-beamed houses, at every
casement of which are citizens and their wives and daughters... Preceded
by a gorgeous procession, which includes every dignitary in church and
state, with her bridesmaids and girls strewing flowers immediately in
advance of her, seated in a gorgeous palanquin, and borne aloft on her
retainers' shoulders, passes by lovely Anne Boleyn . . . The last act is
occupied entirely by a reproduction of the Church of Grey Friars at

Greenwich . . . with its ancient stained glass windows and time-worn stones.' (Irving's *Henry VIII*, 1892.)

The amount of colour and detail possible was enormously increased by the advances in lighting. Gas was now generally used and capable of great flexibility of effect — particularly of moonlight and sunset. The shadows it created were darkly mellow and rich. In consort with the development of limelight (first used in 1816), greatly enhanced lighting effects were possible, some having a distinct influence on acting technique. Limelight was a calcium flare producing an intensely white light, and was used for 'beam' (moon, sun, lamp) or 'spot' effects. The latter gave rise to the phrase 'in the limelight', and it literally meant that an actor or actress (almost invariably the star) was 'spotlit' and his movements followed across the stage. The isolating of the player inevitably increased the gap between star and supernumerary; moreover, the brilliance of the lime-light enabled the audience to see more clearly the details of facial changes of expression. The more extrovert players only further exaggerated their contortions, the judicious modified their expressions for fear of derision. The combination of gas and limelight 'beam' is neatly exemplified in a description of the first ghost scene in Irving's *Hamlet*, 1878: 'The soft light of the moon falls upon the spectral figure; not a sound from below can be heard; the faint flashes of the dawn are stealing over the immense expanse of water before us.' The attention to detail is indicated in the observation of the same critic — '. . . the star alluded to by Bernardo, glistening in the northern sky, is also very satisfactory'.

The sets used in the second half of the century were a combination of flats that dropped or slid into grooves, of three-dimensional objects like a rostrum, or a staircase, or a large platform — which gave a sense of archi-tectural largeness — and of painted cloths which could be dropped into place. What seems to us the excessive length of Victorian performances is attributable to the influence of Henry Irving. He stopped the convention by which scene-changing was visible and brought down the front curtain whenever a scene-change was called for; and since visual variety was the spice of theatrical life, an inordinate number of scene-changes were called for on the Victorian stage.

One of the most notable innovations of the latter part of the century was the box-set; its introduction is usually credited to Squire and Marie Bancroft but as is customary in theatre history what seems to be totally innovatory can be usually found to have a precursor. The box-set was destined to play a significant part in the development of naturalistic 'domestic' melodramatic plays and in the staging of the more substantial 'socially realistic' drama of Shaw, Ibsen, Granville-Barker and others. Its effect was, categorically, to 'domesticate' any play that was presented in it. The box imitated a room, and a room was an emblem of domesticated mankind. Major Shakespeare productions in the large theatres were not greatly affected; they still largely clung to their effective use of a relatively more open kind of stage. But outside London and especially in the small theatres the box-set became standard and had a cramping effect on stage-presentation — *King Lear* may well be termed a 'domestic' tragedy, but it also demands heath, storm and a visual impression of cataclysmic events. Boxed in, even Shakespeare's most geographically restricted plays like *The Merry Wives of Windsor* seem choked.

The apotheosis of 'realism' in set design and general presentation was reached by Herbert Beerbohm Tree who took over Her Majesty's Theatre in 1898. He effectively took over the leadership of Shakespearean production from Henry Irving and excelled even him in the attention to opulent detail. Tree, in a collection of talks and ruminative essays, is very revealing about the principles and motivations which addicted him and his generation to what they called realism. His remarks are worth considering, first, because he was the High Priest of the style and, second, because he was the last major producer to employ it before the bewildering activities of the 20th century put so much of what had become conventional in Shakespeare production into a melting pot with quantities of 'new' ingredients.

Tree relates the growth of realistic presentation to a trend of taste generally in the public which made it demand that Shakespeare should be presented 'as worthily and as munificently as the manager can afford'. To do this the cutting of plays is essential to 'bring most . . . within the three hours' limit which he himself has described as the proper traffic of the stage'. What Tree does not say is that the proliferation of realistic sets, with the constant need to drop the front curtain to change them, was itself the main contributor to the violation of Shakespeare's three-hour rule.

Tree is fervent in declaring that 'scenic embellishments should not overwhelm the dramatic interest, or the balance is upset — the illusion is gone! This nice balance depends upon the tact of the presiding artist.' But, in the late 19th century that tact was under severe strain when, as often happened, the 'presiding artist' was also the star actor. Tree claims that the realistic method 'departs in no way from the manner in which [Shakespeare] himself indicated that his works should be presented'. As proof of this he points to the 'apology' by the Chorus in *Henry V* concerning the Globe Theatre's inability to accommodate 'the vasty fields of France'. Tree declares that Shakespeare 'regretted the deficiencies of the stage of his day'. He may have done, but it is hardly strong evidence to use the words of a fictional character in a play to support the contention. Shakespeare may have deplored the constricting results of the use of boys to play female parts — but that did not prevent him creating an immortal gallery of fictional women.

Tree's enthusiasm and sincerity is everywhere apparent — but so is his special pleading. That we can recognize this with hindsight should not prevent us from marvelling at the copious audacity and imaginative agility which, for example, created this for his production of *A Midsummer Night's Dream* in 1900: '[Mr Tree] has reached what may, until science brings about new possibilities, be regarded as the limits of the conceivable . . . The glades near Athens in which the action passes are the perfection of Sylvan loveliness.' This 'sylvan loveliness' consisted of 'a carpet of thyme and wild-flowers, brakes and thickets full of blossom, and a background seen through the tall trees, of the pearly dawn or the deep hues of the night sky.' To add the cream to this gateaux 'the rendering of *the whole* [our italics] of Mendelssohn's charming music added to the grace of the play' — what price the three-hour traffic that Shakespeare required! Tree's fervent proselytization of realism is seen to have its Achilles' heel when we read that, for his *Twelfth Night*, 1901, the garden of Olivia extended terrace by terrace to the extreme back of the stage, with very real grass, real fountains, paths and descending steps — 'The actors were literally in an Italian garden.' The catch however is this — 'Of course the disadvantage lay in the fact that, once put up, this scene could not easily be removed, and it was perforce used for many of the Shakespearean episodes for which it was absurdly inappropriate.'

Costume

What applies to sets and scenery applies to the costuming of Shakespeare. The quest for realism went along with the principle and practice of opulent appearance to present Shakespeare 'worthily'. But there was an extra factor involved — personal vanity. This was as apparent in male as in female costume, often with bizarre results. The theory was splendid, the resources huge — as *The Illustrated London News* excitedly announced in 1882 — 'Draperies again, are much more freely used on the modern stage . . . with a vast number of new fabrics of practically novel colours; and the designs of these fabrics, offering as they do, evidence of the study of Japanese and now of mediaeval art, have effected a complete revolution in the embellishment of a play . . . the old barbarous style of bedizening the subordinate characters . . . the coarse tinselling of breastplates and shields, the smearing with yellow ochre of the gauntlets and russet boots of the 'supers', and the substitution of glazed calico for real satin . . . have been wholly banished. All is handsome, appropriate and honest.' Well, yes, unless Beauty was offended or personal whim wanted something else!

There is a telling indication of how appropriateness and honesty could be sacrificed on the altar of handsomeness. In Irving's *Hamlet*, 1879, 'The Danish costume of the dark ages was far from picturesque, and the adoption for this revival of dresses of a sixteenth-century character was the wiser of two courses. These costumes, it need hardly be said, were in good taste and agreeable contrast.' The imposition also of personal whim is graphically proven by the extant photographs of the time of many of the performers in their great roles. Lady Macbeth was particularly sartorially victimized by the parade of actresses, each with one eye on fashion and the other on some extraordinarily bizarre visual image of the part — however intelligent the interpretation might have been. Ellen Terry's dresses, which have been noted, set the pace. It is perhaps significant to recount that when Bernard Shaw criticized her sleep-walking scene (dove-grey on pure-white clinging gown) because neither in dress nor appearance did she look as if she had got out of bed, she replied that Sargent's painting of her as Lady Macbeth embodied all that she intended to do in the part. This painting shows her in a spectral green/blue gown, with long red hair, a pale face, and she holds a crown with both hands above her head. It is, in every sense, a Pre-Raphaelite portrait in which the sitter has been given the characteristics of the typical Pre-Raphaelite woman — mysterious, vulnerable, haunted, pale-faced and red-haired, with a sentimental aura. This is no more a convincing image of Shakespeare's Lady Macbeth than if Othello was portrayed as a white man — but Pre-Raphaelitism *was* the height of fashion when Ellen Terry performed the part.

Mrs Patrick Campbell's Lady Macbeth wardrobe included a dress which looked as if it had been torn off a barbarian. Its bodice resembled a coat of mail but covered with blue, gold and green sequins. Violet Vanbrugh, in a Beerbohm Tree production in 1911, wore soft fabrics of blues and purples draped over one another, slightly Grecian, utterly beautiful! Irving, in 1875, looked positively Scandinavian as Macbeth, with a winged helmet, a thin moustache which actually blew about in the breeze, chain-mail and a broad-sword of immense proportions. Forbes-Robertson looked like 'an uncouth Scottish Thane' but he spoke beautifully, like a philosopher. Benson's Macbeth was kilted, long-haired, long-sworded and decidedly Scottish in a somewhat theatrical way, but photographs show what looks like a huge eagle's feather sticking from the side of his crown. His Antony (1894) in one scene obviously intended to reveal his more permissive and lustful side shows him, if a photograph can be trusted, looking like a Victorian Bacchus. He wears what look like thigh-length running shorts and a short-sleeved version of a T-shirt. On his head he wears a crown of leaves with furry material dangling from it. He looks, to us, quite ridiculous. But for every example of the silly and the bizarre one may find three examples which still look impressive. Benson's gaudy Richard II with slightly-tilted crown and dangling mace; Tree's wavy-haired, elegantly bearded, fur-collared and insipidly-coloured gown for the same monarch; Forbes-Robertson's black-gowned Hamlet with dazzling white shirt, collarette of gold and double-waist-belt in the same metal — the very image of Prince and scholar.

Either the photographic material extant does not do them justice or the actresses of the period were more given to personal sartorial excess than the actors, for there seems less evidence on the credit side than for the men. Ellen Terry is particularly disappointing in photographs. The dresses she wears (particularly as Beatrice and Imogen — two of her finest roles) are either curiously Victorian and matronly or (as with Imogen) they look artificial, as if she sat in them uneasily. The best indication of how true the descriptions of her acting are is in a photograph of her Juliet — the costume is cluttered with fabric and too 'bosomy' but her hair, drawn back and tied, is young and a little wild. The face is revealed — urgent, terribly youthful, fresh, intelligent, full of emotional possibility. On the other hand, Mrs Patrick Campbell's bad-tempered Juliet was splendidly served by her costume, which was very Italianate, high-waisted, tunic-necked with flowing lower sleeves and shoulders in a flimsy material which contrasts with the velvet of the middle sleeve and the dress. The head which surmounts this is Pre-Raphaelite — the long hair, long neck and soulful expression looks like an impersonation of Rossetti's painting of Beata Beatrix.

Good or bad, indifferent or exciting, the costumes that Victorian audiences saw were a maelstrom of variety in shape, material and colour. In an affluent age this fully justifies the theatre's constant predilection to be extravagant for it is a part of magic. Whether it is always the right magic is another matter.

The 20th Century

The 19th-Century Heritage

By the 1970s most of the strong conventions of all kinds which had developed during the latter half of the 19th century had disappeared. It is now almost as if that energetic theatre-world of the great actor-managers had never existed. Only fugitively do we catch glimpses of their world. Some may regret, some applaud, the vast changes, but one debt of the 20th century to the 19th must be recorded.

One of the bequests of the Victorian actor-managers to the 20th century was an audience in most parts of the country eager to experience Shakespeare. This was the result of the efforts of the touring companies which flourished up to the beginning of the Great War, and gradually declined in the 1920s and 1930s. If we are romanticly inclined we will see them as in a direct line to the so-called Elizabethan strolling players. Perhaps they saw themselves as such, but, of course, there were two singular motivations — money, and fame. They played in large and small towns, big and little theatres. Their repertoire was carefully 'popular' — *Hamlet* and *Macbeth* as the heavies, *Romeo and Juliet* as the passionately tragic, *The Merchant of Venice* for crafty character-acting, *The Taming of the Shrew* for extrovert acting and romping, *Julius Caesar* for a play of 'significance' politically, *As You Like It* and *Twelfth Night* for sweet comedy and romance.

The repertoire and acting-texts were duplicated for most of the touring companies. All the companies cut the Dumb Show in *Hamlet*, Cinna the Poet in *Julius Caesar*, the Doctor in *Macbeth*, and the induction scene in *The Taming of the Shrew*. Also, one might well be excused for believing they shared their sets and costumes. Macbeth always looked like a late-Victorian portrait of a vicious, greatly-horned highland bull; Hamlet was always Victorian/Viking/Danish; Shylock invariably wore a long tattered gown, a skimpy beard and carried scales; Romeo wore black tights and a black doublet, and the Romans were all heavily toga'd. Often, they would, perforce, use curtains instead of a set. There was a tradition that the gravediggers in *Hamlet* had a 'bath' filled with earth for the grave; the garden in *Twelfth Night* frequently had a painted backcloth showing a formal 18th-century mansion with a painted balustrade and steps — on the stage were imitation hedges in tubs.

Yet the touring companies generated excitement, enjoyed status and gave pleasure. In those rickety contexts of backcloth and cardboard, baths and cut-outs, they strode like giants. The stars would be picked out — if the luxury of limelight were available. If it were not they strode to front-stage and recited, intoned, boomed, would be silent — and you would clap whenever they wished you to. They doubled parts for economy, crammed as many performances of different plays into a week's visit as possible. Their memories were phenomenal and when, like Homer, they nodded, nobody cared — the star could always fill in with something. The most indefatigable (*see* Neo-Romanticism) was Donald Wolfit. He was the last of the great touring managers, responsible for providing thousands with an education in Shakespeare realized with electric vitality and often, as in *King Lear*, deep and penetrating wisdom of interpretation.

The touring companies were eventually replaced by civic theatres, but nothing could replace the curious magic — like the simultaneous arrival of a circus and Wells Fargo — they brought with them. If they had never existed few of Britain's provincial civic theatres would now be in being.

General Tendencies

The most obvious feature is the huge development of what has become known as the Shakespeare Industry. No artist in world history has attracted such incessant and vast attention — some laudable, some ludicrous, some despicable. Theatres everywhere — West End of London, provincial, open-air, touring, state-aided, commercial — are committed to the performance of his plays. The invention of the film and TV camera and the development of their vast and embroiling system of mass-communication has not only increased the exposure of Shakespeare to the public, but introduced two entirely new media exhibiting a product of a kind never before seen. In both the United States and Canada the appetite for Shakespeare is enormous and the methods for satisfying it impressive in quality and variety. Both countries have distinguished Shakespeare Festivals in a number of centres, both have nurtured distinguished Shakespearean players, many of their University Drama Departments reveal an avidity and ingenuity in the study and presentation of the plays which is as important as it is refreshing. (*See* Shakespeare in North America.)

The increased exposure of Shakespeare's plays is not confined to the English-speaking world. His work is now known internationally, and is translated into very many languages. Its influence is widespread — but, in many countries, it comes from reading rather than from experiencing a production. The development of theatre has, in fact, not kept pace with the spread of Shakespeare's works, though the ability of technology to increase the speed by which bodies can be transported has meant that far more people have seen a Shakespeare play in this century than in the whole space of time from the 17th to the 20th century.

There is, too, a significant amount of 'cross-fertilization' of acting and directing in different countries. Paul Robeson electrified English audiences with his Othello. Gielgud and Olivier, alas almost entirely on film, have given American audiences an insight into what is really meant by 'English acting' — i.e. it is rather more than a polite accent, underpinned by a stiff upper lip. Peter Brook is an 'international' director. Tyrone Guthrie helped to give Canada one of the finest Shakespearean theatres in the world, and Tanya Moiseiwitsch dressed it elegantly. Richard Burton could have given Shakespeare a valuable currency in the United States, but eventually gave the impression of confusing acting with display; this was compensated for by the spurious version of the 'method' school of acting, which was bowdlerized in England.

The United States has had a special role, quite apart from the distinction of its leading Shakespearean players, in the new look that the 20th century has given to the Bard. There has been a sensational development in scientific/technological aids, often originating in the United States, to the presentation of the plays, affecting both visual and aural experiences of audiences. These (like the Eisenhower lighting system) have profoundly influenced every aspect of production and acting. The sophisticated effects of which modern lighting techniques are capable put the actor very much more at the mercy of outside factors than he ever was. A light-switch can change his expression — whether he likes it or not, or even knows it!

Indeed, there has never before been such an expenditure of apparent thought and obvious ink on the actor and actress as such. The old romantic glow which suffused their appearance both on and off stage has gone. The stage-door Johnnies and the dewey-eyed Joans of yore, when their heroes and heroines emerged from the gas-lit stage-door area into the ordinary air, thought Gods and Goddesses had come again — just for an instant. The instincts which prompt us to make myths out of theatre people are not altogether stilled, but now, every jot and tittle (even allowing for rumour) of their lives is known. Mystery cannot easily survive the revelations of the gossip-columnist. Still, there is, presumably, a certain glamour and romance in believing that a well-known personage is different from ourselves, if only because he or she *is* well known.

The actor has been presented to public view by a new process. A virtually new kind of academic study has emerged where the subject is the nature of acting and of the acting 'temperament'. The Stanislavsky mode, the 'Method', the Theatre of Cruelty, have been copiously documented and actors, like Redgrave and Gielgud, have contributed importantly. One cannot read the feature pages of our newspapers without somewhere finding players baring their souls not only about their love lives but about what motivates their acting — the phrases 'charging my batteries' and 'the right to fail' are commonplace clichés of the more banal version of this process which also has, blessedly, its deeper and more thoughtful aspects.

But study does not end with the actor. The industry of academic scholarship and higher journalism has expanded immensely, in variety and in the internationalism of its interest. Twentieth-century scholarship also boasts its stars. Granville-Barker, Allardyce Nicoll, Dover Wilson, Caroline Spurgeon, Jan Kott have, in their different ways, opened the windows to Shakespeare's soul and imagination — or what they believe these to be. The best have expanded our knowledge and our own imaginations; the worst have, at the least, excited us to reaction or provided material for amusement. The United States is in the forefront of Shakespeare scholarship — in particular through the work of Hardin Craig, G. E. Bentley, G. F. Reynolds, Arthur Colby Sprague and Charlton Hinman; the last-named perhaps less well known but greatly to be respected for his work on giving us the best, perhaps the definitive, facsimile of the 1623 Folio. The debit and credit account of scholarship and its associated activities is vast but, in digest form, it looks like this:

CREDIT

(1) Establishment of the Folio text (in particular). Never before have we been so near to 'Shakespeare's text' as it was known to the editors of the Folio, and perhaps even as it was known to his audiences.
(2) A much greater use, particularly since World War II, by theatre directors, of the resources of scholarship.
(3) Painstaking, historically respectable, studies of social, religious, political, artistic, theatrical, dramatic context of Shakespeare's age.
(4) Increased teaching of Shakespeare at pre-university level.
(5) Far greater opportunities (particularly in UK) for the younger generation to amplify and vivify its study of Shakespeare by seeing his plays produced by professional companies, and to deepen its understanding through reading copious commentary and critical appraisal in works of scholarship.

DEBIT

(1) A misapplication of scholarship which attributed Shakespeare's plays or portions of them to others, sometimes judiciously but far too often in a kind of 'disintegrative' spirit and practice.
(2) Mutual suspicion of stage and study. Some directors still believe professors to be interfering fusspots; some professors still believe directors to be ignorant whippersnappers. But the war is abating slowly.
(3) Increasing attempts to ignore, Shakespeare's 'Elizabethanism' and to make his work 'speak' to the 20th century by manipulation of his themes and deliberate 'placing' of the plays anywhere other than the 16th century; i.e. — a new 'Restoration' of Shakespeare.
(4) Teaching often inefficient — good effects of scholarship slow to percolate through to school level. Some 'overloading' of Shakespeare by comment and critique. Some distortion of his plays by 'gimmicky' productions.

20th-Century Interpretation

The most telling difference between the fate of Shakespeare's plays during the 20th century and in preceding centuries is represented by the comprehensiveness of the attention paid to the canon. By the 1970s no theatregoer could complain of his tastes being neglected. With the exception of *Timon of Athens, Pericles* and *The Two Gentlemen of Verona* the vast majority of the plays were regularly performed from the early years of the century onward. This in itself largely accounts for the bewildering variety of interpretation during the seventy years, as director vied with director to present a different vision. Moreover, the influence of scholars (no less keen than theatre-directors to urge their 'unique' views) had a growing effect on the way the plays were imagined and presented. It is impossible to present a generalized statement about interpretation which will not incur vehement contradiction. There has been, simply, so much Shakespeare production, there have been so many brilliant individualists involved in it, that a summary courts peril. Still, all directors, actors, scholars, set designers are subject to those large universal influences and stimuli which all on the planet have experienced — war, social change, political upheaval among them — nothing, including Shakespeare's plays, is immune.

At the beginning of the century, and in one or two cases beyond World War I, the work of the late-Victorian actor-managers was still a dominant element in Shakespeare production — most of it falling into the category of neo-romanticism. But, steadily, the reaction to their conventions and traditions gathered momentum and by the beginning of World War I, 'modernism' was a force to be contended with (*see* Gordon Craig). In interpretation, the influence of psychology — particularly that of Freud — has been dominant. Shakespeare production shares, with the novel and with poetry, the burden or the privilege (it depends on one's viewpoint) of Freud and his colleagues' ubiquitous influence.

The Tragedies. The most telling effects have been on the interpretation of the tragedies where 'psychological realism' began to attack the citadel of romanticism, particularly in the interpretation of the tragic and villainheroes. The great late 19th-century tragic interpretations had, by and large, picked on one or two particular traits or 'lines of development' in, say, *Hamlet*, and based a larger-than-life performance upon them. Tree's Hamlet, in the first decade of the century, concentrated on Hamlet's 'spiritual and physical beauty', H. B. Irving's in 1905 depicted a sweet nature unhappily soured. This was insufficient for a generation learning to understand about 'Oedipus complexes' and 'psychoneurosis'. It was some time before anyone attempted a 'neurotic' Hamlet, but Freud opened the gates for directors and actors to introduce ambiguity into their readings of the parts. Ambiguity in interpretation takes away the clear-cut, conventional, QED ending of a tragedy. In the past theatregoers had known where they were when Macbeth perished. They knew he was a villain, that his end was just, that Macduff was virtuous and, quite often, they were given strong hints that Macbeth repented in his last gasps. But that was that. They also knew that Othello was misled, that he only had himself to blame, that he had a certain nobility, but that (unfortunately) he got his just deserts. But that was that. The productions implied clear-cut judgment in pre-Freudian days; after Freud, more and more productions left the matter less clear, more ambiguous.

The emphasis of tragedy was subtly being redefined to mean not only the terrible results of what a man did, but the terrible results of what a man was — yet the complex implications of what he was tended to remain an open question. Even characters like Shylock which traditionally (and with the notable exception of Macklin) had been either comically mischievous c r naturalistically wicked, got caught in the tragic net as the 20th century wore on. What Shylock *was* in terms of environment, race, temperament and religion, now came to dominate the relatively simple matters of what Shylock *did*. Most Shylocks of the 20th century, and there have been some notable ones (Redgrave, O'Toole, Emlyn Williams, Olivier), have left their audiences disturbed. Few will forget Olivier's off-stage cry of pain after the Jew left for ever. It was an aural symbol of what the 20th century has made of Shylock — a man more sinned against than sinning. All the notable interpretations of Macbeth — Redgrave, Tearle, Clunes, Olivier; of Lear — Randle Ayrton, Wolfit, Gielgud, Scofield; of Hamlet — Forbes-Robertson, Ion Swinley, Redgrave, Gielgud, Olivier; of Othello — Forbes-Robertson, Matheson Lang, Robeson, Olivier, have, to a degree, humanized the characters, introduced ambiguity into their interpretations, and, in their pursuit of psychological realism, pulled theatregoers into that sense of committal to the character which induces the response — 'there but for the grace of God, go I'.

The History Plays. The penetrating influence of psychology has affected both the English and Roman history plays. Prince Hal is no longer simply the spendthrift royal who turns into something like the proverbial Knight on a White Horse. Scholarship, too, has played some part in giving a density to his character — particularly his motives and his relationship with his father. He has sometimes been played as a very young Hamlet (Richard Burton, Stratford, 1951), or as a man resolute in what he wants from kingship, but set on a lonely course which alienates him from his father (Ian Holm, Stratford, 1966). Interpretations of Falstaff have veered between the traditional English Bacchus (superbly memorialized in J. B. Priestley's famous essay in *Shakespeare's Comic Characters*) — which George Robey attempted (almost successfully) in 1934, and a more sinister alter-pater. Ralph Richardson in, arguably, the greatest performance of the role in living memory, succeeded in combining both.

In the Roman plays Brutus, Cassius and Coriolanus have been placed in the labyrinth of psychological realism. Brutus, like Hal, has been made a close relative of Hamlet. There was a magnificent realization of this by John Wood at Stratford, 1972. Cassius has been drawn into the net b cause of his relationship with Brutus. The quarrel scene, with its mixed motivations, is now almost conventionally presented as a display of 'inner tensions' — their angry words camouflaging their love. Coriolanus was traditionally played as a testy, affluent, patrician warrior, totally unpredictable. In Poel's 1930s production this traditional interpretation was very securely embodied — Coriolanus appeared first in a leopard-skin, and later in the full-dress regalia of a Colonel of the Hussars. Olivier's astonishing tour de force (Stratford, 1959) preserved something of the traditional, but the petulance, pride and fiery spirit were presented less as the necessary attributes of a noble, coltish warrior, than as disturbing characteristics of a dangerous personality. By 1967 at Stratford, Ian Richardson had completed the transformation. His Coriolanus, played with restless energy, superb voice and subtle timing was, for all its fire and fury, a suitable case for treatment. When carefully employed, psychological realism has given a depth to characterization in the history plays in sharp contrast to the rather 'shallow' presentations common in the earlier part of the century. Notable performances of Henry V (as, for example, Lewis Waller's in 1900) concentrated on passionate generalizing rather than specific interpretation — Waller has been described as performing in a 'romantic blazon'.

More recently the history plays have been employed also to illustrate some contemporary event and to make an implied comment upon it. *Julius Caesar* has been used as an image of fascism, *Coriolanus* as an emblem of class warfare. *Henry V*, paradoxically (considering its patriotic fervour), has been almost consistently used in the 1960s and 1970s — the decades of Korea, Vietnam, the Bay of Pigs, Crete, Cyprus — to show the folly of war.

The Comedies. This century has witnessed a rescue operation for some of Shakespeare's comedies — particularly the early ones, which had been in a theatrical limbo. In 1904 Granville-Barker enchanted a number of influential critics and most of his audiences by his production of *The Two Gentlemen of Verona*. From 1905 (when Benson produced it) *The Comedy of Errors* appeared regularly in the repertoires of the Old Vic and of Stratford. But apart from a rediscovery of the fresh and sharp delights of these early plays the century is replete with revivals of the major comedies, with all the great and near-great — Gwen Ffrangcon Davies, Edith Evans, Peggy Ashcroft, Dorothy Tutin, Judi Dench, Hay Petrie, George Hayes, Michael Redgrave, Gielgud, Olivier — devoting a high proportion of time and talent to them.

The interpretation of the major comedies has been weighted towards romantic presentation. The advances in lighting and aural background and in materials (man-made) available for costume and stage-furniture have greatly increased opportunities to create that warm magic one automatically associates with *Twelfth Night, As You Like It* and *A Midsummer Night's Dream*. But, in the 1960s and 1970s a shift in interpretative emphasis which had begun earlier became more obvious. Anthony Quayle's 1949 production of *Much Ado About Nothing* with Diana Wynyard best exemplified the shift. The traditional merry banter of Beatrice and Benedick was muted by the introduction of a more serious vein. We could well believe in Diana Wynyard's exquisitely cool performance that 'a star danced' when her Beatrice was born, but, it seemed to be implied, since then the arabesques had become a little less spontaneous. The banter disguised a hurt. Many subsequent productions in the provinces and at Stratford, the Old Vic and elsewhere have presented 'bitter-sweet' versions of the comedies. The sunlight on the garden at Illyria has been shown to be a passing thing, the open-hearted joys of Arden must, like life itself, be seized at the full before the shadows come. Significantly, interpretations of Malvolio, Jaques and Duke Theseus have tended to concentrate less on their functional position in the plot and more on the 'complexities' of their characters. Malvolio is no longer a self-opinionated bumped-up steward, Jaques, now, is not an inconsequential fantastic, Duke Theseus is no longer the rather sententious master-of-ceremonies. All three have moved closer to the centre of interpretation — the play is habitually revealed as if through their eyes. It hardly needs stressing that Shakespeare's bawdy is hardly ever cut in modern productions — whatever else is guillotined. Comic business which formerly went usually on traditional lines has become extraordinarily inventive — sometimes at the expense of the play's meaning.

But these changes are interwoven with other threads and skeins which both complicate the overall pattern and, at the same time, amply illustrate the extraordinary variety of activity in Shakespearean production during the past seven decades.

Kinds of Interpretation

By and large what dominated Shakespearean production before the 20th century was the desire to present his plays in as theatrically vital a form as possible. Different epochs had different ideas of what this meant — and, in some cases, what appeared on the stage had little to do with Shakespeare. No one in the theatre of the past concerned himself overmuch with academic or philosophical justification of character interpretation or presentation. Garrick never 'explained' his Hamlet though he might well have been prepared to expound it as if it were the only Hamlet. No actors, including 20th-century ones, are ever very disposed to explain what they do. But, in the 20th century, with the coming of the all-powerful director, and with the pressure of scholarship and commentary, the poor actor is pressurized so that sometimes (and sometimes ill-advisedly) he will be tempted into public explanation. Canny, defensive actors like Olivier and Scofield avoid this; friendly, well-disposed and eloquent actors, like Gielgud, do not. Some directors, like Brook and Guthrie, Hall and Barton seem at times as much concerned with their 'interpretation' of a play as with the task of embodying it on stage. However much some directors quarrel with or suspect critics and scholars, it is amazing how many try to emulate the academics by weighty declarations about 'meaning' and 'interpretation'. Indeed, a deal of fun can be gained from observing attempts by theatre men to be 'academic' and by academics to be 'theatre men'. The pages of our learned and not-so-learned journals are crammed with the brain-children of directors impersonating professors, and the stages of many of our institutions of learning, both high and low, resound with the progeny of professorial teaching who fancy themselves as the Tyrone Guthries *de nos jours*. All this is in the service of ensuring that you and I, the reader and audience, know what the plays mean — but that is not always what Shakespeare seems to have meant!

The 20th century does not show very clearly defined areas of time in which one type of interpretation predominated. Yet four persistent activities are discernible which, though not mutually exclusive, are individual enough to be definable. The problem is less one of definition than of assessing their relative importance. Two have had their high peaks but we are now living in the ascendancy of the third and fourth. The quest for (1) the so-called 'purity' of the Elizabethan theatre and its apparently natural opposite, (2) the curious romantic/realism bequeathed by the 19th century has been subsumed in (3) the obsessive-seeming attempt to show the relevance of Shakespeare to the 20th century by drastic ministrations to the text and, as a kind of offshoot, (4) the employment of the plays as a sort of peg to hang a thesis on. We may designate these as (1) neo-Elizabethanism, (2) neo-romanticism, (3) neo-Restoration and (4) polemical.

Neo-Elizabethanism. By the end of the 19th century lavishly produced Shakespeare was the rule in the large London theatres whose managements could afford to pay to 'dress' the stage in often quite astonishing visual paraphernalia. The motivations were paradoxical — on the one hand, the urge was to be absolutely authentic in everything the audience saw, so that the appearance of real rabbits and trees that bore real leaves, among other attempts at naturalism, became commonplace. Yet, on the other hand, this was accompanied by a desire to clothe Shakespeare's plays in mystery, elusiveness, romance — for example, the use of gauze in front of real trees was intended to produce a misty effect — whether the play required it or not. Moreover, the greater possibilities for effect from lighting were frequently directed less towards supporting the natural than embellishing it, so that strange lights played with delightful but unnecessary abandon.

In considering this curious paradox we have to remember that the typical 19th-century attitude towards Shakespeare was that he was a man, but that about his head rays of supernatural glory shone. The 18th century had been nothing if not rational in its estimate of Shakespeare — respecting him, even loving him, but aware of what it deemed his human faults. It was left to the 19th century, which displayed an astonishing hard-headedness in its everyday affairs while reserving and displaying its right to be piously other-worldly, to create a hybrid Bard — half child of the Industrial Revolution, half pious spirit. From this came the extraordinary mixture propagated by many 19th-century managers.

Neo-Elizabethanism was a reaction born out of the continuing quest for the true text and an accompanying urge to rediscover the 'purity' of performance on the Elizabethan stage — 'purity' was (perhaps a little illogically) equated with bareness. The assumption was that 19th-century clutter (of both text and stage) obscured Shakespeare's true dramatic genius; at the end of the century, when neo-Elizabethanism was at its height, scholarly research had not yet shown that the traditional view of the Elizabethan stage as bare and sparse was somewhat distorted. The arch-priest of neo-Elizabethanism was William Poel (1852–1934), an experienced actor and director who, in 1894, founded the Elizabethan Stage Society. Poel had assiduously researched and built a stage he believed to be truly Elizabethan. He performed many 16th- and 17th-century plays in halls and courtyards and resuscitated others which had rarely, if ever, been produced for three hundred years and more, including *Arden of Feversham*, sometimes attributed to Shakespeare. Poel made no money, excited not a little scoffing, and an uncharitable view would see his activities as a slightly precious reaction to Victorian lavishness.

But 20th-century Shakespeare theatre owes a great deal to this almost-forgotten man. He did much to cut away the barnacles on set and design and costume. He emphasized the text — not as a convenient version, but as truly as he could find it. He placed great reliance on the actor and far less on effects extraneous to the actor. He encouraged both scholars and directors to look again at many 16th- and 17th-century plays which had long been condemned to dust and cobweb. His neo-Elizabethanism never caught on as an exclusive alternative to 19th-century opulence but his influence was pervasive. The permissiveness of some late 20th-century Shakespeare production would undoubtedly be more extreme than it is if Poel had never existed — his ghost is both a reproach and an example to any director who recklessly throws overboard all the attachments Shakespeare's plays have to their creator and their own time. Shakespeare pro-

duction at Connecticut, Oregon, Ontario, Stratford (England), for all its
experimentation and manipulation, still at least genuflects to the notion
that the text is primary and that to forget it is both dangerous and
arrogant.

In certain contexts Poel's influence has been specific. College and university productions nearly always tend to neo-Elizabethanism rather than
to modernism; major companies like the Royal Shakespeare Company,
though they may interfere to a degree with the text, do it in full and
declared knowledge and give every appearance of using the most authoritative scholarly texts; small companies make sporadic attempts to present
neo-Elizabethan productions and, intermittently, plans are announced for
the building of a replica of the Globe Theatre. Often, they remain plans,
occasionally — as in the sophisticated, careful reconstruction brief for a
British Independent Television series of programmes on the life of Shakespeare — they testify to the fascination of the subject. Poel and neo-
Elizabethanism had, in their time, a touch of cultism, and cultism is a
close neighbour of a bizarre antiquarianism, but there was nothing bizarre
or démodé about Poel's well-informed instinct that the nearer the production is to the text, the more theatrically and dramatically effective the
result. Time has proven Poel to be right, though often by default rather
than affirmation.

Neo-Romanticism. Theatrical romanticism can be defined as that attitude
towards a play which will always see it as larger even than the exaggerated
life which theatre customarily embodies. The romantic director seeks out
actors who by personality, voice, gesture, cut a dash; he searches for a
designer who will, even at the risk of swamping his players, present a visual
spectacle to stir the spirit and imagination; he 'celebrates' the play with
an interpretation which will resonantly present the main themes and issues
without inciting controversy — ambition, evil and blood in *Macbeth*,
jealousy and evil in *Othello*, and so on. The romantic version of Shakespeare's plays is, in its way, a sort of emblem of theatre itself — this is why
it is so widespread geographically and so enduring — for it has all the dash
and magic and wonder and sometimes winsome braggadocio of the world
of illusion. Romanticism is not simply a matter of directorial interpretation, although this is what governs its scope and form, for it shows itself
also where the director has only a partial control over it — in acting, for
example, where the individual player has significant personal control.

The director's grip is also only partial on set-design, for in the 20th
century the designer has achieved an extraordinary power and status —
his individual 'artistic' vision often superimposing itself on or embedding
itself within the director's interpretation. Agreement between director,
actor and set-designer can only be partial. One of the greatest 20th-
century set-designers, Leslie Hurry, brought to his Shakespeare sets a

quality of fantasy, impressionism, often a whirligig of shape and colour, which seemed more suited to romantic ballet than to plays like *King Lear* (Stratford, 1950) and *Henry VI* (Old Vic, 1957). Any production of Shakespeare involving John Gielgud is, *ipso facto*, romantic, in the sense that his own histrionic emphasis will be on vocal and physical grace and an avoidance of any aspect of naturalism likely to produce vulgarity. Gielgud 'celebrates' a role rather than picking and feeling his way until he has unmasked it — warts and all. A remarkable example of neo-romanticism was Michael Benthall's Old Vic production of *All's Well That Ends Well* in 1953. Perhaps a little perturbed by the play's sharp edges and dark corners, Benthall gave it a fairy-tale quality — as if it neither had, nor could have, happened in actuality. It had a Tuscan pastoral background, and from time to time little Gothic structures appeared back stage, looking like toy buildings. Even Peter Brook, now celebrated as among the foremost of avant-garde directors, passed through his own 'romantic' period. His *Love's Labour's Lost* (Stratford, 1946) is just as memorable as his more recent *A Midsummer Night's Dream* but the first was the apotheosis of romanticism while the second was a brilliant attempt to explore the implications of illusion and reality. His *Love's Labour's Lost* was Watteau-esque, but also had a touching fragility from the use of gauze and soft lighting. The clowning was whimsical rather than broad, and the acting highly stylized.

The main ingredients of neo-romanticism, apart from the basic compound of director, players and designer, are lighting and, most importantly, the setting of the play in a historical period which is neither modern nor Elizabethan. As soon as an audience is transported, as in Tyrone Guthrie's *All's Well That Ends Well* (Stratford, 1959) to what seemed to be 19th-century Ruritania, or as in John Barton's *Much Ado About Nothing* (Stratford, 1976) to what was conceivably a hill station near the Khyber Pass, romanticism begins its work. Peter Hall knew, in his days as artistic director at Stratford upon Avon, the effect of lighting. His *A Midsummer Night's Dream* (1962) was, visually, astonishingly 'Victorian'. Oberon approached Titania for their first duel of words from a bosky wood made mysterious by gauze and green lighting — and Oberon's words were uttered by the company's most distinguished romantic actor — Ian Richardson. When he spoke, 'Ill met by moonlight, proud Titania', the moonlight glowed, and his voice sounded like the music of the spheres!

Neo-romanticism is still abroad in the world of Shakespeare production, and these examples are only small wisps of the miasma and mists of its spirit which has beguiled the 20th century. Henry Ainley transfixed both the Roman mob and his audiences as Antony in 1920 — his voice like a ringing bell made Shakespeare's lines into a kind of chanted litany. Sybil Thorndike as Imogen in 1923 was declared by the wickedly accurate critic, James Agate, to have swallowed the part in a gulp and to be still looking round the stage for something to be effective with. In the 1920s Frank Benson, barnstorming with his touring company, turned the most parsimonious settings into romantic affairs by judicious lighting and, particularly, by large, grandiloquent but effective acting.

Of all the few heirs of the great Victorian actor-managers, Donald Wolfit embodied the spirit of romanticism with his touring company that began its operations in 1937 and continued throughout the war years. Quite apart from his acting there was something essentially romantic in the very peripatetics of this extraordinary man. He would have been quite at home as a leading actor in an Elizabethan travelling company. Moreover, the range of his touring itself suggests a man marked out in a romantic way from his fellows — England, Canada, France, Belgium, Cairo, Alexandria, Kenya, Ethiopia, Uganda, Italy, New Zealand, Malaya, Australia, India, Persian Gulf, Lebanon. One would not have been surprised to see him raise his stage in Samarkand and out-do Marco Polo in the telling of tales. All his performances, but particularly his King Lear, were larger than life, gripping in the controlled ferocity of gestures and voice. There was more than a touch of Svengali in Wolfit when he approached his audience with his burning, haunted eyes.

But neo-romanticism has not always looked back. Noguchi produced *King Lear* in 1955 with space-men suits, geometrical shapes, chairs shaped like thick boomerangs. *The Tempest* (Stratford, 1963) had a wall whose lower half was of perspex but whose top half was a screen lit by projectors on small trolleys. The effect was advanced science-fiction — perhaps the most obvious contribution this century has made to the history of romanticism.

Neo-Restoration Shakespeare. Undoubtedly, neo-romanticism shades into neo-Restoration — that is, Shakespeare's plays manipulated to make them speak very directly to (and of) the 20th century. The most convenient way of distinguishing the two genres, though it cannot possibly be definitive, is to examine the extent to which Shakespeare's text has been retained or manipulated by cutting, additions, transpositions. Neo-romantic Shakespeare, for all its grandiloquence, is often true to the text; neo-Restoration Shakespeare, for all its hot intent to speak directly to its modern audience, often betrays the text. There is a certain irony in that many of the proselytizers of making Shakespeare speak to the 20th century have not only had an academic involvement in the studying of the text but avow their commitment to it; but many seem to find it hard to realize that the reality of a work of art has as much to do with the dramatist's structuring as with his themes. Even 'candid' statements by directors about their intentions often hide (unwittingly) an enormous presumption. Joan Littlewood, an artistically agile and experimental director, declared before her *Macbeth* production that she wished to get rid of the interpretations of 19th-century 'sentimentalists'. This is a splendid motive, which many would welcome, but there was a rider to her frankness — she referred to 19th-century 'sentimental' interpretations as 'highly poetical'. But *Macbeth is* a highly poetical play, and you are more guilty than the 'sentimentalists' if you produce it as Miss Littlewood eventually did, with her actors speaking carelessly, and often unintelligibly. The director's abhorrence of the 'sentimental' did not, however, prevent her having a Scottish lament played over the dead Lady Macduff and her chicks! Tyrone Guthrie, a director of insistent virtuosity, wayward inventiveness and brilliant technique, also revealed an astonishing recklessness towards the reality of the text of *Macbeth*. He refused to have the witches open the play lest the audience concluded that they are a powerful governing force in the tragedy. But aren't they?

But attempts to see Shakespeare through different coloured spectacles are a commonplace of theatrical history. Indeed, if all Shakespearean production followed the same severe guide-lines, it would be a dull world, and his plays would soon die. But, latterly, it has often seemed that the alternative to death is a life in which they would exist warped, wounded, wealed and whizz-kidded.

There are a number of variants of neo-Restoration treatment. One of the most prevalent in the 1920s and 1930s was largely visual, and showed itself in a flurry of modern-dress productions. One of the first, and certainly the most talked-of, was Barry Jackson's *Hamlet* (London, 1926). This had been preceded by a modern-dress *Cymbeline* at the Birmingham Repertory Theatre, of which Jackson was the founder and the presiding genius. Hamlet (Colin Keith-Johnston) was slickly modern, Polonius (Bromley Davenport) was slyly political, and the first Gravedigger (Cedric Hardwicke) wore a bowler hat. Jackson's motive was conscious, deliberate and justifiable. He wanted to see how Hamlet would affect audiences without the conditioning effect of the usual black garb with white shirt, ornaments and fragile look. The same motive prompted this extraordinary man to produce a modern-dress *The Taming of the Shrew* and *Macbeth* at the Court Theatre, London, in 1928. The latter began and ended with machine-gun fire, Macbeth was a gruff colonel in tweeds, Lady Macbeth in fashionable modern short skirts. There was a great deal of khaki uniform worn, silk dressing gowns, much whisky was drunk, many cigarettes in long holders were smoked. The lines were spoken with a staccato suddenness.

Audiences were fascinated though, as with Oscar Asche's *The Merry Wives of Windsor*, 1929, they sometimes tacitly rebelled — this version ran for one week only. But the fact that they were fascinated could, paradoxically, be a powerful argument against this kind of neo-Restoration. By presenting the plays uncluttered by conventional visual impressions Barry Jackson hoped to concentrate the audience's mind wonderfully upon the play itself, but *not* to beguile its imagination — but such faith was all against his habitual sensitivity. In these productions, audiences were made to concentrate on the more sensational visual experience — and somewhere inside the khaki, cigarettes, dressing gowns, there was a play struggling to get out.

Throughout the century, modern-dress versions have cropped up from time to time — some obviously responding to near-contemporary situations, like Frank Dunlop's fascist *Julius Caesar* at Nottingham, Barry Jackson's *Timon of Athens* (Birmingham, 1947) — 'it has a good deal in common with contemporary Birmingham'. Michael Benthall's early Victorian *Hamlet* (Stratford, 1948) does not strictly belong to modern-dress neo-Restoration, but it is mentioned here simply because the reasons Benthall gave for doing it neatly sum up the views of many of those who have done modern-dress productions; more importantly, they illustrate the curious abeyance of logic sometimes found in their propositions. Benthall said — 'In Elizabethan costume most of *Hamlet*'s essential modern realism is lost. I have aimed at retaining its romance and present-day truth by presenting it in a mid-nineteenth-century setting.' The imagination may be excused for boggling at Benthall's cross-fertilizations of 'realism', 'romance' and 'present-day truth'. A newspaper review of Jackson's 1928 *Macbeth* is an effective answer — '. . . translating Shakespeare into twentieth-century terms leads to a most misleading equation. Human nature may remain constant, but manners and customs and habits of thought change with history. No modern general believes in witches.' Really, modern-dress Shakespeare should be experienced in a similar frame of mind to that we adopt when seeing versions such as *West Side Story* (*Romeo and Juliet*). They are fascinating arpeggios on a theme — and should be judged as such.

The second main type of 20th-century neo-Restoration employs unusual or experimental visual material which is an emblem of a more profound manipulation of the language, text and main themes of the plays. The appearance of this type, commonly found in the 1960s and 1970s, has much to do with the drastic political and social changes in society. In a sense it is true that the Shakespearean theatre since World War II has truly confirmed the theory that theatre always, to a degree, reflects its society. The motivations expressed by some of the leading directors like Peter Hall, John Barton, Trevor Nunn, Tyrone Guthrie, Peter Brook and others, less distinguished, like Charles Marowicz, reveal passionate and sincere dedication to the proposition that in order that a great dramatist like Shakespeare should have the maximum amount of effect on modern audiences, his plays should not be left to stagnate in old ways of presentation, but should reflect contemporary society in their realization on stage. The inevitable result is that the director chooses how best this can be achieved, and the choice — to a degree — always involves manipulation.

One typical example was Hall's *Henry V* (Stratford, 1966). The patriotic (perhaps jingoistic) glamour of the spirit of Shakespeare's play ill-suited the budding egalitarian notions and practices of the mid 1960s. 'Elitism' was out, 'class' was a dirty word, 'democracy', variously defined, was very much an 'in' word. In Hall's production Henry, at no point, wore anything to suggest either triumphant kingship or the possession of 'a largesse, universal as the sun'. He even wooed in a rough tunic, as if he had just left the trenches on the Somme. Katharine of France was gloriously attired, haughty in mien, so that the impression was given that Henry's 'democratic' Englishness was taming Gallic hauteur. But as the scene progressed, Katharine's speech became more 'demotic' in tone, and her vowels less pure. Clearly the 'democratizing' process was working. No visual distinction was made between monarch and men, no glamour given to war, no vibrancy given to the poetry, no truck with the implications of Renaissance autocracy. The theatrical results were magnificent, the 'new' messages certainly came through — only afterwards did it become clear that half of them were not only not Shakespeare's but that they contradicted the whole unity of Shakespeare's play. In Hall's *Hamlet*, 1966, there was a powerfully presented dramatic sermon on the 'apathy' of contemporary England, its fears, frustrations, despairs. Ophelia, young and vulnerable, was bewildered from the very beginning, Hamlet (a late teenager) gave no sense of a belief in God, and mistrusted everything. So a version of the modern teenager was depicted — poignant, helpless, angry. Polonius was a sniffing, shifty politico, Claudius a megalomaniac man-at-the-top, Gertrude, a scared, stupid, sexual gourmet. The production was extraordinarily popular with young people.

The proponents of this kind of neo-Restoration Shakespeare have much on their side. Audiences often applaud them enthusiastically, young people flock to see them, the plays are often theatrically vivified, and there can be no doubt that, from time to time, trenchant connections are made with (and the most positive comments uttered on) contemporary events and values. Those who express unease are often accused of a kind of neo-Puritanism.

But the case against has equally strong planks. This is best made again by example. In the Royal Shakespeare Theatre's superb seasons of the English history plays in the 1960s, the two parts of *Henry IV* (arguably Shakespeare's most brilliantly sustained imaginative effort) were subjected to a good deal of thematic change to align it to modern conditions. The themes of honour, divine right, the sin of usurpation were either reduced, muted or changed. The reasons, presumably, were that a modern audience is not au fait with Renaissance conceptions of honour (either the commendable or the cynical ones), that it certainly is not interested in the divine right of kings, and that (with the decay of organized religious worship) the notion of sin, let alone the sin of usurpation, is unconsidered. So honour was made totally cynical, divine right was glossed over by a kind of embarrassed jokiness, the sin of usurpation reduced to its modern equivalent — not a guilt-ridden monarch, but a president of a company board who had craftily ousted his predecessor and was plagued by stomach ulcers as a result. This was *not* explicitly portrayed, but the image inexorably raised itself in the mind as the jig-saw of neo-Restoration technique was assembled.

But, however theatrically sensational and brilliantly executed the result, this replacement of Shakespeare had a very temporary hold — other images have quickly replaced it. Moreover, even if the modern audience is not hot for honour, sin, divine right, it might be morally, intellectually and dramatically efficacious if its temperature were raised by seeing them embodied. The danger is that neo-Restoration Shakespeare should become so extensive that no theatre audience (particularly young people) ever has the chance to experience what neo-Restoration is replacing. Mostly, such changes to Shakespeare are done with careful conviction, but at times an arrogance (perhaps unconscious) is apparent, which forgets that to produce such changes in the text requires an artistic/imaginative decision of a kind at least equal to that which Shakespeare exerted on the original.

But the greatest danger in neo-Restoration Shakespeare occurs when the director initiates a process which in its effects is no more and no less than an example of 'improving' Shakespeare — an activity beloved of the 18th century. The dangers of 'improvement' are no less even when the motives seem laudable. A good example is the fate of one scene in *Julius Caesar* which has been frequently cut. Cinna, a very minor poet, ventures out of doors to go to Caesar's funeral. He is surrounded by the mob who are incensed at Caesar's death. He is questioned and all seems well until they learn his name. They butcher him as he cries out that he is Cinna the poet, not Cinna the hated politician. He dies because he bears the wrong name. A recent champion of neo-Restoration Shakespeare explained his reasons for cutting the scene — (1) We already know this mob is in a killing mood. Why hold up the action to show them butchering an unknown poet? (2) Cinna has never been seen in the play before and will never be seen again. He is unnecessary and expendable. (3) The essential aim of the director at this point in the play is to convey to the audience the torrent of mob-action. The arguments sound reasonable, but they hide a huge insensitivity to the impact the scene can make. In William Shirer's *Life and Death of the Third Reich*, he describes how a very minor musician, Willi Schmidt, was, one night in his apartment, having a musical evening with his wife and children. Three of Hitler's thugs banged on the door and demanded of his wife that Willi Schmidt should come to them. He did. The last his wife ever heard or saw of him was as he was being kicked down the stairs shouting — 'I am not Willi Schmidt the politician, I am Willi Schmidt the musician.' As with Rome's mob it made no difference — he bore the wrong name. Truly, the 'modernity' of

Shakespeare is, more often than not, already implicit — it requires no embellishment.

Moreover, Shakespeare's sensitivity to audience-effect was far superior to that of the directors who cut this scene — (1) He knew that one of the first things to suffer from mindless militancy is a society's cultural values — the fact that Schmidt is an unknown musician renders the message even more poignant, just as the fact that many of the books burnt in Hitler's terrible pogrom in the 1930s were written by the unknown. (2) Shakespeare knew (and the deaths of Richard III, Macbeth, Hector, Coriolanus, and others exemplify this) that if a dramatist wishes to burn into our imaginations the naked meaning of violence, it is more effectively done by showing one man (Cinna, for example) being beset by many. The brutal loneliness of death is far more effectively achieved in that way than by the clash of large or equal forces — the armies of Agincourt, for example.

Neo-Restoration Shakespeare has provided much entertainment and enlightenment but, like all movements, it has perils and weaknesses. English practitioners of it in the last twenty-five years have, by and large, shown a sense of responsibility, but not all decades are likely to produce as many good practitioners as have been witnessed in the near past. In the late 20th century the dangers seem likely to increase rather than diminish if only because society seems increasingly to base its values on instant response to experience rather than on reflection and comparison. Nowadays, 'modernity's' life is even shorter than it ever was — today's Top of the Pops is tonight's dead duck. The advantages of neo-Restoration Shakespeare can only be nurtured if directors remember that there is a difference between the impulse which says — 'Here is a 16th-century play, what can *I* do to it?', and that which says — 'Here is a 16th-century play, what can *it* do to me?'

Polemical Shakespeare. All actors, actresses, designers, directors, scholars, theatregoers — all who have anything to do with theatre — see Shakespeare inside an image, or as part of an image that their own imaginations have created. There is nothing new about critical studies of Shakespeare or productions of his plays which urge the truth of this or that image. Up to the middle of the 20th century the image-making was very largely concerned with an imaginative or emotional or intellectual conception of what this or that play meant or represented or was attempting to communicate. In the latter part of this century, however, we have seen a growth of image-making which seems strongly related (maybe is even the progeny of) the increased socio-political awareness and activity of groups and individuals throughout the world. In particular the influence of the various forms of communism (many of them having only the most tenuous connection with this political credo) and of socialism (a word which is defined in so many different ways by different people that it has become almost indefinable in any rational sense) have worked strongly on both theorists and practitioners of Shakespeare's work. Russian and 'Iron Curtain' productions of his plays have, naturally enough, tended to emphasize the extent to which Shakespeare presents the lowly, the humble, the dispossessed and, inevitably, have drawn the conclusion that his political stance was a 'marxist' one. Neither the followers of Marx nor, indeed, of Freud, when they urge the 'marxist' or 'psychological' caste of Shakespeare's plays, seem to worry themselves with what some might consider the crucial fact that he had never heard of either of them! The corollary of the notion that Shakespeare ideologically championed the lowly, is the assumption that he, equally ideologically, abhorred the mighty. Shakespeare's kings and rulers are often presented in 'polemical' productions as murderous, expendable and evil. Curiously, however, the tragedies have undergone far less stringent applications of political dogma (*see* Shakespeare and the Film). The Russians, in particular, are in the forefront of the distinguished interpretations of Shakespeare's tragic heroes on film.

The most publicized polemical agent is Jan Kott whose book *Shakespeare, Our Contemporary*, 1964, has had an influence out of all proportion to its critical worth. Peter Brook was largely responsible for introducing Kott's work to the Western world. Its title tells all — Shakespeare is seen through the eyes of a man who is not only of the 20th century, but of a very distinct political persuasion. In England, the polemicists are best represented in the work of Charles Marowicz, whose versions of Shakespeare use the plays to present, in as stark a fashion as possible, a point of view which has usually only a peripheral relationship to the play as written by Shakespeare. *Othello* and *The Merchant of Venice* are plays of obvious and keen concern to the polemicists who, while they often produce results of ferocious sincerity and theatrical sensationalism, seem to ignore the fact that although, for example, Othello was black, Shakespeare had never heard of what we call the 'colour' problem, and that although Shylock was a Jew, Shakespeare seems as much concerned with Christian perfidy as with Hebrew guile, and with romantic pursuits as with doubtful moral behaviour.

Polemical Shakespeare is obviously related to neo-Restoration Shakespeare, but it is often far more extreme in its ministrations to the text and in its presentation. However intense is the sincerity of its refusal to serve Shakespeare in any other context than that of a particular ideology or issue or -ism, it has an air of expendability, fragility and impermanence — for it has hitched its wagon to something Shakespeare was ignorant of and may, in any case, itself be a fad or mode or foible. This, considering what, in the pursuit of its ends, it omits from Shakespeare's real world, is a kind of poetic justice.

Shakespeare and the Directors, 1920–1978

The century is characterized, in theatre, both by the visionary patronage of private individuals, and by the ideological control of the public will. In England, three individuals in particular stand out — and no account of the nature of Shakespeare production is complete without them — Barry Jackson, Lilian Baylis and Miss A. E. F. Horniman.

Barry Jackson (1879–1961), whose work at the Birmingham Repertory Theatre has already been commented upon, built that theatre upon the basis of an amateur group — The Pilgrim Players — who turned professional in 1913. At Birmingham, Jackson nurtured the talents of an astonishing number of players: Olivier, Madeleine Carroll, Greer Garson, Albert Finney, Richard Pasco, Ian Richardson, Paul Scofield, Margaret Leighton — the list is a mere indication — all played there and have testified to having learned much there. After World War II Jackson became director of the then Shakespeare Memorial Theatre at Stratford. By 1948 he had left, leaving the theatre in the soundest financial position in its history. At Stratford he encouraged the talents of Peter Brook among many others, and even at this late stage in his career never lost his restless experimental urge.

Lilian Baylis (1874–1937) was a woman of outstanding will, imagination and, eventually, power. She founded the Old Vic Theatre (precursor to the National Theatre) and Sadlers Wells, but began her theatrical adventures as manager of a temperance music-hall. Her motivation in creating the Old Vic indicates that, like Barry Jackson, she had a prophetic imagination. Realizing how the century would increasingly be forced to cater in every way for the underprivileged, she insisted that the Old Vic should provide good drama at cheap prices for the masses. Shakespeare figured large in her plans and the theatre became, from 1914 onwards, regarded as the unofficial national theatre and the showpiece for his plays. Many great performances took place there, players longed to act there. Indeed, in the twenties, thirties and forties, the formula for success was simple — Birmingham Rep to Old Vic.

Miss Horniman (1860–1937) as she was always called, was another remarkable woman. She spent much of her wealth in building the Abbey Theatre in Dublin but after a, perhaps inevitable, disagreement with Yeats, she renovated the old Gaiety Theatre in Manchester. It specialized in new plays by local authors, but its importance to Shakespeare production was in its training of young actors, many of whom achieved fame later in Birmingham or at the Old Vic.

Such individuals were powerful and almost entirely beneficial moulders of the history of Shakespearean production, but their power has today been taken over by the directors. Indeed, in the 21st century it may well be that the 20th century will be seen as the age of the director, as the 19th century was the age of the actor-manager. The power of the director has grown until, when one tries to bring to mind, for example, Shakespeare productions of the 1960s and 1970s, almost invariably the name of the director appears before that of the principal players. This is not because the players have become anonymous but, partly, because the directors have, through mass-communication, acquired star-status, and partly because some modern directors seem obsessively given to making statements to the media, and publishing articles and books — in fact it has almost become obligatory for this to happen. Consequently, whereas in the twenties, thirties and fifties it was Gielgud's Hamlet it is now Hall's or Nunn's, or whereas it was Olivier's Macbeth it is now Marowicz's or Papp's.

Directors are thick on the ground — and their power as administrators and initiators of policy is immense — but it is their personal relationship to the plays which seems both crucial and paramount in assessing how Shakespeare has been produced. At times the whole apparatus of rehearsal and stage-realization seems to be a kind of objectivizing not so much of one man's vision, as of one man's prejudice or 'hang-up' or fierce shibboleth or notion or political stance; occasionally one even gets the sense that the play is being used as a kind of therapy, on the modern assumption that the best way to get rid of an inner complex is to face it and express it. One director, indeed, ventured the statement that he would not direct *Antony and Cleopatra* 'until it is ready for me'. One must distinguish between quirkiness of this kind (which is not uncommon) and the eccentricities due to genius. Tyrone Guthrie often got dangerously near what seemed a bizarre, self-regarding quirkery. Yet for all his eccentricity (in his *All's Well That Ends Well* at Stratford in 1959 or in his Napoleonically-dressed *Coriolanus* at Nottingham in 1963) Guthrie looked outwards — vision always does; it is only the pursuit of gimmickry that is self-regarding.

All the many famous directors of the century have been subject to influence both from within and without their own brotherhood. These, in an age of mass-communication and compulsion to write down, have been, of course, various. Appia, Craig, Barker, Poel, Brecht, Jan Kott, Stanislavsky, the Method, symbolism, expressionism, Freud, Marx, Che Guevara, Martin Luther King, Hitler, *et al.*, have, as was said of Falstaff, 'latewalked in the realm'. Guthrie, Peter Brook, Peter Hall have influenced their colleagues — cannibalism as well as flattery is a notorious characteristic of the world of theatre. The present survey is selective and the principle behind the selection is an attempt to indicate the immense variety of the century.

Ben Greet (1857–1936). One of the last actor-managers, Greet played opposite many stars of the early part of the century — Beerbohm Tree and Mary Anderson, in particular. His talent lay less in acting than in his ability to attract audiences by his productions. He wanted to spread the gospel of Shakespeare widely, and particularly among schoolchildren, for whom he organized special performances. Apart from this, Greet had great faith in open-air performances and their ability, perhaps because of novelty, to attract audiences. Despite the British climate, he was successful, as indeed he was in his partnership with Lilian Baylis at the Old Vic. His productions (from 1914 onwards) of Shakespeare set the course for the famous tradition of Shakespearean production which developed at the Vic during the twenties and thirties. He toured the United States accompanied by the young Sybil Thorndike and repeated his amazing success with audiences. He was essentially a producer of relatively plain, direct Shakespeare, but it was all done with huge enthusiasm.

Nugent Monck (1877–1958). Monck was a protégé of William Poel and a studious interpreter of the texts, very much within the context of a deep knowledge and wise love of the 'Elizabethan' theatre. At his Maddermarket Theatre in Norwich he built an Elizabethan stage and presented all of Shakespeare's plays and rarely-performed examples from Shakespeare's contemporaries. His company was entirely amateur, and acted to a very high standard. Monck directed a notable *Pericles* at Stratford in 1947, but it is a measure of how even the most dedicated 'Elizabethan' can be lured into self-indulgence that he cut the whole of Act I — presumably having accepted a widely held theory that Shakespeare did not write it (*see* George Wilkins).

Iden Payne (1881–1976). Like Monck he had much of the scholar in him — he taught drama at Carnegie Institute of Technology for fifteen years. In the United States he directed for the Theatre Guild at New York and the Goodman Repertory Company at Chicago. In 1934 he became director of the then Shakespeare Memorial Theatre at Stratford. He also directed at the Oregon Shakespeare Festival. Payne was a protégé of Benson and had worked with Miss Horniman, and there was more than a touch of 19th-century visual opulence in his imagination. His *Antony and Cleopatra* (Stratford) had a torchlight procession, his *Hamlet* (Stratford) had a huge mullioned window. Payne is important in that he developed (tentatively, for Poel's 'Elizabethanism' also tempted him) the locating of the plays in periods other than either Elizabethan or 20th century. *Cymbeline* was in Jacobean setting, *The Winter's Tale* was Byzantine. He was an uneven director, but his place in theatre history is secure if only because he was responsible for Donald Wolfit's appearance as Hamlet at Stratford in 1936 — a most remarkable and passionate Prince.

Glen Byam Shaw (1904–   ). An underrated actor (he was a notable Laertes, Benvolio and Horatio), Shaw is best regarded through his distinguished directorial work. He directed Gielgud as Richard II in 1935

and in *The Merchant of Venice* in 1938. He was a successful director of the
Old Vic theatre school. His best achievements came as, first, co-director
(with Anthony Quayle) of the then Shakespeare Memorial Theatre
(1952–6) and, second, as director alone (1956–9). There was nothing
spectacular about Shaw's productions but, in an almost covert way, he
was one of the initiators of a change in visual presentation. Representa-
tionalism, despite the experimental work that was seen from time to time,
still dominated sets. But Shaw, in his *King Lear*, 1959, used a farm wagon
to stand for a whole set, in his *Julius Caesar*, 1957, he used a star which
shone and remained from the Forum scene onwards, reminding us that the
spirit of Caesar ('constant as the Northern Star') still existed. His strength
as a director was his ability to speak to actors in their own language, and
his self-discipline which enabled him to both seem and be inventive
without being gimmicky. All Shaw's production effects arose out of the
text and were never imposed upon it.

William Bridges-Adams (1889–1965). Perhaps the most underrated director
of the 20th century. He was, perhaps, too modest to blow, or allow to be
blown, any trumpets on his behalf. He acted with the Oxford University
Dramatic Society and in provincial repertory. In 1919 he was director at
Stratford and also founded the New Shakespeare Company. He toured in
North America and was the author of a number of remarkably sagacious
books on theatre. As a director Bridges-Adams had absorbed the influence
of Poel and Granville-Barker, and added to it his own fine intellectual
balance. He believed in maintaining a full text and in keeping sets and
designs within the control of the play's language. For example, his *Henry V*
at the Strand Theatre in London used panels and curtains; his *Tempest*,
1934, was done as a masque, with costumes by the notable artist Rex
Whistler; *Love's Labour's Lost*, 1934, had a single gigantic oak. No other
director of this century so consistently unified all parts of his productions,
so that the finished effect was not only a complete world in itself, but was
the play's world. In a Bridges-Adams production the audience felt they
had become sharing citizens of a totally credible world with totally
credible people.

Theodore Komisarjevsky (1882–1954). The work of this Russian émigré who
became a British subject demonstrates that 'eccentric' Shakespeare and
'neo-Restoration' Shakespeare is not confined to the 1960s and 1970s. At
Stratford in 1932 his *The Merchant of Venice* was literally shocking. Thick-
skinned critics gasped, and Benson-fans stared with dropping jaws. Portia
wore spectacles that looked like bicycle wheels, the Duke kept falling
asleep, the set slid and rose and dropped with frightening rapidity. In 1935
he set *The Merry Wives of Windsor* in Vienna, in 1950 (at Montreal) the text
of *Cymbeline* was amplified by the lines, 'We're off to see the wizard, the

wonderful wizard of Oz.' His productions were energetic, colourful, play-ful and, occasionally, but only occasionally, bore some relationship to the plays.

Tyrone Guthrie (1900–71). The most intellectually and imaginatively effer-vescent of directors. He worked at the Old Vic; he was artistically instru-mental in the huge success of the opening of the Stratford (Ontario) Festival; he directed on the Continent, in Israel, Ireland, New York, and founded the Tyrone Guthrie Theatre in Minneapolis. Guthrie was an arch-enemy of the academics who (he believed) wish to claim Shakespeare as their property. Unfortunately, he too often gave the impression that the alternative was that Shakespeare should be Guthrie's own exclusive property. His great strength was his ability to persuade his actors to play to the top of their bent, his astonishing visual sense, his knack (once he had decided what direction the play was to go — often *not* Shakespeare's direction) of creating an artistic whole. But this was compounded with certain weaknesses — he regarded the text as expendable and there was an Irish irreverence in his attitude towards the themes of the plays — whether they be tragic or comic. This irreverence usually showed itself in irrelevant business — a sneeze, a scratching finger, a quivering leg, a thumping walk. His *Troilus and Cressida* (Old Vic, 1956) was frivolous. The Trojans wore yellow with blindingly bright breastplates. All the Greeks had the moustaches we associate with Greek bandits, and they sported spiked helmets. Helen played on a grand piano, and Thersites carried a camera. His *All's Well That Ends Well* (Stratford, 1959) was a grossly cut version. Lavache had disappeared and the action seemed disposed variously between Ruritania and the Khyber Pass in 1900. It is difficult to assess Guthrie, since it is difficult to know how seriously he took himself. Yet great players acted for him (Edith Evans as the Countess of Rousillon, for example) and the profession adored him. He was a combination of maverick, leprechaun and Barnum and Bailey.

Peter Hall (1930–   ). The most distinguished and famous of a group of university graduates who, in the 1960s and 1970s, brought youthful ideas and imaginations to Shakespeare production. Their influence and their occupancy of positions of power in theatre is one of the most remarkable phenomena of the century. The majority graduated from Cambridge where they had the inestimable benefit of being taught by one of the most sensitive 'readers' of Shakespeare's text — George Rylands. Others, like Peter Brook, were Oxford-taught — and Oxford's would-be directors were equally well served by the gentle, wise and verbally precise Nevill Coghill. Peter Hall (now knighted and director of the National Theatre) has directed films and opera and came to prominence with his production of *Waiting for Godot*. He will, however, always be associated most with his exciting, fecund and sometimes infuriating directorship of the Royal Shakespeare Theatre (1960–8).

Hall's arrival at Stratford signalled the end of directorial régimes which had been almost always based on long experience and led by men beyond the first flush of manhood. Hall and his associates were regarded by many as upstart whizz-kids, by others as a welcome breath of spring breeze, by even others as an exemplar of a general movement in society which gave youth the helm and age the thumbs down. Hall's policy may be summed up as follows: (1) He did not so much reject the star system as place alongside it a process of training of young players who were given every opportunity to acquire stardom in the Royal Shakespeare Company. Gielgud, Ashcroft (a consultant director), Edith Evans, among other luminaries, appeared at Stratford during Hall's reign, but they contended with the thrusting talents of Diana Rigg, Ian Richardson, Ian Holm, David Warner and others. (2) Hall believed in the efficacy of 'ensemble' playing. In the early part of his directorship, actors were encouraged in mutual criticism, verse-speaking sessions were held and led by the distinguished French director Michel St-Denis and, later, by Hall's Cambridge recruit, John Barton. There was a sense of democratic activity. Productions of the history plays were shared between three directors, actors who played major roles in one play found themselves carrying spears in another. (3) Hall believed in security. Actors were frequently placed on a three-year contract. This was an enormous relief, especially to young unknowns, and a decided aid to the development of ensemble. (4) Hall fervently believed in the principle of making Shakespeare speak to the 20th century. He seems, in the sixties, to have had a missionary zeal in propagating and realizing this (*see* Neo-Restoration). Whatever qualifications there may be about the artistic results, the box-office success was gigantic. (5) Hall not only made the old Memorial Theatre part of the establishment (it became the Royal Shakespeare Theatre under his direction) but made his organization truly international. He acquired the tenancy of the Aldwych Theatre in London as a second home for his company, and embarked on tours to Australia, Japan, Russia and the United States. (6) He initiated the system of associate artists. Designers, directors and actors were nominally (and therefore prestigiously) attached to the company. It gave a sense of depth of artistic talent available and a sense of belonging and cohesiveness to the players concerned.

As a theatre director Hall is efficient and imaginative. Every aspect of the Stratford establishment — design, costume, music, speech-training — was revitalized by his enthusiasm and his expertise. What Hall did cost much money, and he was frequently accused of extravagance. He was adept at fending off such criticism and at persuading the Arts Council to increase its subsidy. When he left the theatre it was an entirely different organization from that which he found in 1960 — even to the extent of considerable alterations to the building's implacable proscenium-stage to open it out towards the audience.

Hall's own productions were characterized by the desire to make them speak to our time, by visual inventiveness (his *Hamlet* had two huge mechanical ghosts and a good deal of his *Troilus and Cressida* was played in a sand-pit) and by a curiously ambivalent attitude towards the text. On the one hand it could be sensed that Hall both understood and respected the meaning of it, on the other he sometimes displayed a kind of irreverence, as if he thought it necessary to echo the flippant attitude towards words and poetic nuance so characteristic of the 1960s. His ability to find the right player for the role was almost unerring, and his urge for ensemble playing ensured that his productions (notably of the English history plays and *A Midsummer Night's Dream*) flowed easily. He encouraged contemporaries like John Barton to develop their special skills — Barton's were clearly revealed as a fine ear for the text and a very agile skill in adaptation. His greatest success (1964) was to reduce the three parts of *Henry VI* into two — to this day there are people who believe Shakespeare wrote two plays, one called *Henry VI*, the other, *Edward IV*. In fact the latter was an amalgam of Shakespeare's *Henry VI, Parts 2 and 3* and Barton himself. In his *Twelfth Night* Barton revealed an amazing sensitivity to the relationship between music, words and visual effects — in many ways, this production was the truest to Shakespeare seen in Stratford since 1960.

Peter Brook (1925–   ). If any single person is entitled to be called a citizen of world theatre, it is Peter Brook. Few would dispute that he is a director of genius, in the sense that his skill is comprehensive — he is innovative in theory and in practice. Brook has directed in England, Europe, Africa and the United States. He has allowed his mind free access to stimuli from many sources — France, Germany, the East, Artaud, Appia, Brecht, Jan Kott, the Theatre of Cruelty, etc. Almost every Shakespearean production he has undertaken has surprised, and some have disturbed. His *Titus Andronicus* at Stratford, with Olivier, in 1964, was so realistic in its depiction of blood and in the horrors of the unwitting cannibalism of the last scene, that special provisions for first aid had to be made in the theatre — which were frequently used. His *King Lear*, 1962, with Paul Scofield, was existentialist in effect, but perhaps his *A Midsummer Night's Dream* (Stratford and London, 1970, New York, 1971) was his most sensational effort. The action took place in a gymnasium-like set with a railed gangway around its three sides at the top, with ladders to it from the stage. The players quite deliberately stepped out of character as they completed each portion of dialogue or action and retreated to the upper gangway where (in their own 'real' personalities, as it were) they watched their colleagues proceed on stage with illusion. Oberon spent much time on a swing, and plates were spun on sticks in the manner of jugglers. It was a brilliant theatrical exercise, and an exploration of illusion and reality and of the relationship of actor to role. Whether it was Shakespeare's play is questionable. Brook sees theatre and its forms as an essential part of humankind's existence, not in the conventional sense that it may be used to mirror or comment on contemporary society, but more as a means of exploring the mystery of personality, of motive, of what is and what seems. It is only because he has also such a sharp sense of the magic of theatre that he can be acquitted of the charge of occasionally 'employing' a play for his own ends rather than embodying it in terms of the playwright's requirements.

Other Directors. The process of selection is invidious, especially in a century rich in directorial talent. A comprehensive study would require much attention to be paid, for example, to the following talents — and many others. Franco Zeffirelli is an Italian who has worked at the Old Vic and at Stratford, notable for his happy-go-lucky excisions of the text while, paradoxically, retaining the essential atmosphere of the play — his *Romeo and Juliet*, 1960, released the play's passion in a manner rarely achieved. Michael Elliott has an elegance in the economy with which he dresses his stage, and a most persuasive way with players. His *As You Like It* (Stratford 1961) was set on a green hillock with a tree growing on it around which the action gyrated superbly; Vanessa Redgrave's Rosalind was a triumphant embodiment of urgent love and fresh beauty. Trevor Nunn, Peter Hall's successor at Stratford, while he has clearly maintained the theatre's international status, has, perhaps understandably, not quite given the impression of the firm on-going policy and purpose of his predecessor; yet, under his régime, Brook, Barton, Clifford Williams and others have flourished, and his own productions — notably of *The Winter's Tale, The Comedy of Errors* and the non-Shakespearean *The Revenger's Tragedy* — amply confirm him as possessing controlled imagination, intellectual discipline and a care for the text. Nunn is at his best when he is artist; as administrator he does not always give the impression of a firm grasp. Nevertheless, he has developed the company's work in London, and, notably, has opened a small studio/experimental theatre (The Other Place) at Stratford whose repertory (for example Nunn's superb production of *Macbeth*, 1976, with Ian McKellen and Judi Dench) rivals, in quality, that of the main theatre. Michael Langham, Michael Benthall and George Devine were instrumental in the success of the attempt, announced by the Old Vic in 1953, to produce all thirty-six plays of the First Folio. Their directorial skills were displayed not least in the way in which thoroughbred players like Claire Bloom, Michael Hordern, Fay Compton, Richard Burton, John Neville and others, were persuaded to perform so efficiently and excitingly in harness. A most underrated director, Douglas Seale, enters theatrical history for his production of the three parts of *Henry VI* at the Birmingham Repertory Theatre, 1951, and subsequently at the Old Vic. He rescued these plays, with brilliant designs by Finlay James, from a long oblivion.

Honour must also be accorded to work in provincial theatres — so often the Cinderellas of the world of theatre, yet so frequently the givers of life to their better-known London cousins. At Birmingham, Nottingham, Leicester, Liverpool, Bristol (whose theatre is another Old Vic), Guildford, Manchester, Croydon and many other places, Shakespeare's plays have often achieved remarkable embodiment in the hands of people few of whose names are known outside the United Kingdom — Richard Eyre, Bernard Hepton, John Neville, Clive Perry, Val May, Robin Midgeley — but whose standards are as stringent as those of the internationally-acclaimed Royal Shakespeare Company and the National Theatre. This last-named has yet to establish itself, having been dogged by ill-fortune, dark economics and bureaucratic effeteness. It must not be overlooked, however, that before it closed, the little theatre in Waterloo Road — the Old Vic — had the honour of housing the first National Theatre company, and, indeed, long before then was regarded as the unofficial 'National'.

Acting in the Twentieth Century

The problems of presenting a complete account of Shakespearean production in the 20th century are only too apparent. The same problems arise with acting. There is an *embarras de richesse* to contend with, and selection is always in danger of distorting the truth. Yet certain generalizations press for attention from the mass of evidence available from film, tape-recording, eye-witness account and memory. These aids make probable that the 20th century will be recorded, so far as theatre is concerned, more nearly accurately than its predecessors. The theory is that film and recording allow actors and actresses to provide their own evidence and they are thus immunized from the iniquities of faulty memory or ineffective account. Nevertheless, such evidence must be treated with care. A film is not a play, a camera *is* an interposition between actor and audience, celluloid is not flesh, neither (if we think of television) is a group of two or three gathered together with coffee, beer, hamburgers or fish and chips in a cosy parlour the same as four or five hundred assembled in rows in the National Theatre, or wherever. The tape-recorder is selective; the actor, used to the envelopment of an audience, may find the silent stick of a microphone as invigorating as a mortuary, and the voice alone is no complete register of the whole performance. Stage-acting is total commitment, camera and microphone acting is partial.

It is clear, however, from all the evidence, that the first three decades of the 20th century saw a continuation of the 'romantic' 19th-century style of acting. This style achieved its prominence through the effect that well-known and famous players had on their lesser brethren — emulation is a perennial characteristic both of the green room and of the stage itself. The romantic style is very much larger-than-life, it stresses vocal beauty and physical elegance, and it can, in excess, exercise the personality of the actor rather than explore the deeps of the role. In romantic acting the great speeches become arias and characterization tends to be reduced to the embodiment of one dominant element. Henry Ainley, Godfrey Tearle, Sybil Thorndike, Ion Swinley are typical and important examples, and perhaps Paul Robeson is the most precise example. His Othello was remarkable in bringing the resources of an operatic mode to a character conceived in a verbal mode and, miraculously, gave it human credibility — though the human that emerged was of gigantic physical presence and vocal power. The 20th century is, in fact, replete with fine exponents of the art of being conspicuously larger than ordinary — Baliol Holloway, Frank Cellier, George Hayes (notable in Shakespearean comedy), Robert Atkins (a coldly fierce Duke Richard of Gloucester), Charles Laughton (an immense Henry VIII), Frederick Valk and others. Apart from Sybil Thorndike and Mrs Patrick Campbell, the romantic mode, in its largest sense, did not sit well, nor indeed was it much worn, by actresses — though Angela Baddeley (a fine Nurse in *Romeo and Juliet*), Dorothy Green (an underrated Cleopatra), Martita Hunt and Catherine Lacey showed, in a variety of roles, that a creeping-under-the-carpet style of performance did not suit their extrovert temperaments.

But during the century, and particularly after World War II, what seemed a new mode pressed for attention. It is too simple to attribute its advent to any one cause, but undoubtedly the phenomenon of Laurence Olivier's genius made a large contribution to what was a complicated process. He, with no acting tradition in his family, no obvious lyricism in his speaking, a face that is more mobile than poetic, and a presence that has a kind of craggy, sometimes untidy, virility rather than elegance, seems to be the apotheosis (for some people) of the new age — 'demo-cratic', naturalistic, strident rather than mellifluous, direct rather than devious. Such generalizations were frequently made in the forties, fifties and sixties (less so now). Their truth remains to be examined but it is clear that Olivier was regarded as a challenge to the old mode of romanticism and that, rightly or wrongly, he helped to weaken its authority and ubiquity. Modern 'naturalism' is now as accepted as romanticism formerly was. But Olivier was not its only (unwitting) proselytizer and demon-strator. The post-1945 social revolution was a powerful factor, with its self-conscious urge for egalitarianism, classlessness, the claims of the common denominator to be heard, the hatred of élitism. The traditional 'special' hero vanished from drama, his place being taken by angry young men.

Olivier's versatility itself encouraged the belief that he was a modern 'naturalistic' actor. He played one of the most typical anti-heroes, Archie Rice (in John Osborne's *The Entertainer*). Of Olivier, the feeling was that however often he appeared in the drawing-room he was always on his way to the kitchen. But John Gielgud, his great contemporary, was said to have no truck with the new dispensation. It was said of him that he would never walk out of the drawing-room into the kitchen. These two men have brought to Shakespeare a sensitivity, imagination and understanding that encourages the belief that no other century has been better served in the depiction of the major Shakespearean male roles.

John Gielgud (1904–   ). Gielgud's voice immediately puts the listener in mind of the old spell-binders. From his Hamlet (as early as 1929) to his King Lear, 1940, and including the exquisite comic playing of Benedick in *Much Ado About Nothing*, 1950, and the icy realization of Angelo in *Measure for Measure*, 1950, Gielgud has seemed a giant — even though the size is more borne in upon us by our ears than our eyes. His voice is immediately recognizable (as those of the old barn-stormers were) and he gives the impression of moulding every character to his own vocal and, to an extent, physical lineaments. He is still, even in this unromantic age, regarded as a marvellous embodiment of the widely held notion that theatre is and must be larger-than-life. When Gielgud performs he seems, in a sense, and more than any other major actor, himself, but he is always larger than himself. His acting is of the heroic age and Gielgud still satisfies the urge of those in the audience who have not abandoned entirely their faiths and myths, and long for a glimpse of Gods striding the earth again.

Gielgud, where Shakespeare is concerned, achieves character through language and not, it would seem, through any preconceived idea or gradual intellectual study. He does not seem to go for 'psychological realism' and he does not flatten out Shakespeare's language to achieve a 20th-century illusion of actuality. What he seems to search for is the emotional flow of a speech or a line and when he has found its essence, its colour, its pace, its rhythm, this is presented to the audience as the state of mind or feelings of the character at the time. He brings to Shakespeare's language his intelligence, sensitivity and his voice, but nothing of the sometimes over-strenuous zeal to express the 'psychological truth' of the character that we find in many modern actors. Indeed, Gielgud incites the audience into an acceptance of 'poetic' truth not unconnected with the effect of great music. When you listen to and watch a Gielgud performance you are not inclined to inquire into the psychological veracity of his inter-pretation, but either accept (which is usual) or reject (which is rare) the total image of the character that unfolds. Gielgud either catches the correct image or he does not. There is nothing in between — compromise on this level of sensibility is impossible.

But it would be wrong to assume that he only indulges in superb vocal generalization. If you examine his interpretations you find a sharp attention to detail — in pause, pace, stress, colouring, even in the kind of silence he creates. His Hamlet is his masterpiece — vulnerable, dignified, passionate and, surprisingly perhaps, angry, especially in the 'Rogue and peasant slave' soliloquy. His Lear is remembered by many as the greatest of the century (though devotees of Wolfit would challenge this). From the very first this ageing monarch was taut in voice and mind with the curse of his own stupidity. But Gielgud took the character step by step in a journey which encompassed unreasonableness, passion, mulishness, near-insanity, pathos, resolution, resignation and acceptance. He explored every facet of the character and, as he did so, Lear grew in stature and changed from suffering man to an almost Olympian hero — shattered but triumphant. His Benedick was an exercise in witty acting, in every sense — in pausing, emphasis, eye-glances, lithe movement. Perhaps the performance was the only 20th-century example of the way a kind of Restoration style of speech and movement (totally formalized and 'artificial') can be adapted to a Shakespearean character.

Laurence Olivier (1907–   ). Olivier 'actualizes' his interpretations in the sense that he seems to give you every conceivable detail of a character in an attempt to convince you that it is a living, breathing person. Consequently Olivier's versions seem much closer to you, more obviously human, than the more poetically-conceived creatures of Gielgud. But Olivier, though more certainly naturalistic than Gielgud, *is* larger-than-life; though he may seem to use life's common materials more consistently than Gielgud, the final product is large — as if you are looking through binoculars at someone only a few yards away. Olivier makes the 'heroic' into something familiar. He, as a contemporary noted of Garrick, achieves his role 'by study and observation constantly adding to his stock of science'. He has a much more complete and reliable equipment than Gielgud — his body seems very much more under deep conscious control, his ability to disguise himself is, unlike Gielgud's, very pronounced, his physical presence is to him what his voice is to Gielgud. He is, significantly, reported to have declared that he would rather lose his voice than his eyes. That voice has been described as a shrill trumpet, whereas Gielgud's is a violin. The distinction is well made, for devotees of that wind instrument will know that it can be sweet as well as harsh, mellow as well as strident, soft as well as triumphantly loud, and that it has a certain slightly choked lyricism. All these qualities Olivier's voice has, and the evidence echoes around the chambers of memory — the almost guttural incantation (done with a shaking head) of the words ''twas a rough night' as his Macbeth waited for Duncan's murder to be discovered, the half-howl of Coriolanus at the line he hurls at the plebs after his banishment — 'there is a world elsewhere', the half-tender, half-wry tone as Hamlet visits his mother in her chamber and inquires — 'How is it with you, Lady?' Olivier has an astonishing ability to pick up such phrases (often treated as unconsidered trifles by lesser actors) and to make them resonate for an instant.

But the vocal range is not confined to such intermittents — no one who heard his speaking of Henry V's 'Crispian' speech can surely have failed to experience a physical frisson at its huge vocal orchestration. He began slowly, then the pace mounted as if in rhythm with unseen horses, then slackened, the tone moving from sharp urgency to melting familiarity as he identified with his 'band of brothers' — the common soldiers to whom he made the word 'Crispian' sound like a benediction. By the end of the speech the pace became faster and faster, yet each word counted, and the voice rose to an unbelievable crescendo with 'God for Harry, England and St George'. The last word was held and the volume slowly decreased — as if a trumpet call faded across a battlefield. The unique quality of Olivier's vocal equipment is that, unlike Gielgud's, it is, in volume and stress, a huge magnification of ordinary speech. He does not attempt a 'poetic' flow with its own rules and regulations, rather he searches for, then vocally celebrates, the specific sense of the line. He does not, like Gielgud, create a unit of music from each speech, but rather, a unit of sense, and the 'music' which his voice gives it aids the sense rather than garnishes it. He will, too, often employ accent or 'special tone' to complete character — a slight Scots accent in *Macbeth*, a completely believable 'mummerset' as Justice Shallow, a thick, deep baritone for Othello.

The dangers of being too explicit in distinguishing romantic and naturalistic acting are demonstrated amply even by a general comparison between Olivier's and Gielgud's style. Nevertheless, if one places Gielgud's famous versions of the great roles alongside Olivier's — particularly Olivier's Macbeth, 1956, Hamlet, 1937, Titus Andronicus — there can be little doubt that the former is a superb creator of wonderfully observed poetic images while the latter seems to have looked at actuality through a microscope, and given us Life. Together, their acting of Shakespeare constitutes probably the most comprehensive realization of the great parts in dramatic history.

Edith Evans (1888–1976). The *grande dame* of the English stage for half a century was certainly one of the most famous actresses of the century — whether she was a great actress is arguable. She gave the impression of versatility by the variety of roles she played — Cressida (for William Poel), Millamant (*The Way of the World*), Portia, Cleopatra, Rosalind, Mistress Page, the Nurse in *Romeo and Juliet* (all at the Old Vic), Lady Bracknell, Lady Fidget, Madame Ranevsky, Countess of Rousillon, Volumnia — but some would say there was a certain sameness in her interpretations. Some found her voice affected with an aristocratic querulousness (well-suited for Restoration comedy) and her demeanour over-stately. Others found her (as in her notable performance of Rosalind) sparkling, so that the regality of her tones and gestures were a natural part of a nature that was under control without losing spontaneity. Indeed, although a consensus would probably declare that she was a tragedienne, Edith Evans was probably at her best in comedy — there her innate impression of breeding often seemed to be self-mocked — this gave a piquancy and sharpness to her performances. Observers of her most famous performance (apart from Wilde's Lady Bracknell) — the Nurse in *Romeo and Juliet* — differ widely in their assessments. Many declare that she completely submerged her powerful self in a characterization which, in movement, gesture, tone, pace, accent, was the apotheosis of a shrewd but vulgar crone. Others recall only that everything seemed studied, and that inside this constructed hag, there lurked what was more natural to Edith Evans — a Roman matron (Volumnia) or a witty, ageing aristocrat (Countess of Rousillon), two of her finest performances.

Peggy Ashcroft (1907–   ). Arguably the actress, after Ellen Terry, most entitled to the accolade of 'great'. The two most significant characteristics of her career are, first, the manner in which (even up to her seventieth year) her acting has consistently matured and her character-range increased, and second, her amazing physical indestructibility: she has that gift, precious to the actor, a blessing to the actress, of youthfulness of appearance. She is a classical actress in the strictest sense — her roles largely come from established dramatic masterpieces — of Ibsen, Chekhov, Sheridan, Webster and Shakespeare. Her Rosalind, Viola, Beatrice, Portia and Margaret of Anjou (in *Henry VI*) have each notably enlarged appreciation of these characters. Every Ashcroft performance breathes of intelligence. She is not outstandingly endowed physically but, even as the romantic heroines, her ability to convey the lines with a clarity that can only come with perfect understanding, and the unique sense of urgent honesty which lights up her face, but particularly her eyes, gives her a radiant presence denied others with far more obvious physical attractions. She has, too, an unusual ability to play a role while simultaneously giving us two kinds of experience. As Beatrice, for example, a secret sorrow was allowed to glance like a cloud across the habitual sharp sunlight of the character — truly conceived in the letter and spirit of Shakespeare's text. One of her most outstanding performances was as Margaret of Anjou in the John Barton adaptation of *Henry VI*. She aged, completely convincingly, from a young girl to a wrinkled, prematurely old, woman; she created a character in whom a kind of wantonness was mixed with a gloating love of cruelty. She comprehensively proved that Shakespeare's Queen Margaret is one of his greatest female creations. She was fifty-six when she created this masterpiece.

The Rich Century. The line dividing the kind of genius represented by
Olivier, Gielgud, Evans and Ashcroft from the greatness, near-greatness
or distinction of many other actors and actresses is very fine and makes the
kind of distinctions demanded by space and implied by selection even
more invidious. Others might find the absence of Michael Redgrave, Paul
Scofield, Diana Wynyard, Gwen Ffrangcon Davies, Irene Worth, Dorothy
Tutin and others, from specific description, an offence. A younger generation might well be affronted at the absence of Ian Richardson, Albert
Finney, Judi Dench, Derek Jacobi, Ian McKellen. A historian's unease at
so many absences is a measure of the amazing richness of English acting.
Most of all, perhaps, Redgrave and Scofield deserve much more than
apology.

   Michael Redgrave (1908–   ) is one of the most sensitive and intellectually virile of 20th-century actors. His books, *Mask or Face* and *The
Actor's Ways and Means*, bring us nearer to the heart of the mystery of
acting than any other ever published. His Hamlet, Shylock, Macbeth,
Hotspur, Lear and Benedick are all memorable for the care paid to detail,
for their emotional force, for the absolute clarity of intention. Yet Redgrave may have been prevented from a completely free soaring into greatness simply by the subtlety of his mental and emotional sensitivity —
there is a point at which an actor has to stop feeling and thinking, and rely
on the X factor — the intuition, the ad hoc decision; Redgrave rarely
seems able to find that point. Paul Scofield (1922–   ) is an actor of
immense attraction, and a product of Barry Jackson's Birmingham
Repertory Theatre. His attractiveness, physically, lies in his face, which in
its crevassed lines and kind eyes suggests suffering and compassion. As
King Lear this gave an added pathos to his interpretation within which
lay a deep intelligence, but gave his Macbeth the image of fallen angel
rather than of self-torturer. It may well be that Scofield's real forte is
comedy. As Don Armado, Aguecheek and Mercutio, the facial characteristics were manoeuvred into marvellously witty, ironic shapes and his
voice — which in tragedy sometimes seems to struggle to find the correct
level — conducted wonderful tonal dialogues with itself. Scofield's voice
is an extraordinary instrument requiring most careful control. It has a
high and very low register which seem divided off very distinctly from one
another, so that instead of tonal modulation we often hear a jump, as it
were, as the actor moves between the two. The dichotomy in the voice is
an emblem, too, of what seems a dichotomy in Scofield's acting process.
As we watch him we seem to observe two functions — one where he
appears to be employed in the final agonized task of wringing the full
meaning from the text, so that his voice and his speaking jerk from one
apprehension to another; the other, in which physical and facial movement seem to be trying to keep in parallel with his intellectual and
emotional discoveries. Scofield is essentially a thinking actor and his

many virtues, as well as his eccentricities, are, surely, never the result of
ad hoc decision.

Of the younger generation the stage is rich in both male and female
players. The National Theatre, the Royal Shakespeare Company, the Old
Vic and a handful or so of provincial repertory theatres have nurtured:
Ian Richardson — in the Gielgud mould, whose very young Hamlet at the
Birmingham theatre was, inexplicably, never given the opportunity to
reach a larger public when he joined the Royal Shakespeare Company at
Stratford. There, his Oberon, Bertram, Malcolm, Richard II and Bolingbroke revealed a subtle lyrical power. Albert Finney, another Birmingham
product, who understudied (and played) Olivier's Coriolanus. His Prince
Hal was a remarkable display of controlled energy. Finney is perhaps the
leading example of a relatively new breed of players who make no pretence
to hide their provincial accents — a kind of pride in down-to-brass-tacks.
Ian McKellen is something of a loner, in the sense that he does not seem
to relish too long a stint with any of the large 'establishment' companies,
though with the Royal Shakespeare Company (1976) he created the finest
Macbeth since Olivier's. McKellen (a romantic actor with a voice that
seduces by stealth and piercing directness) is in the tradition of the old
great actor-managers. His career exemplifies the way in which the so-
called London/national critics are sometimes several steps behind their
provincial colleagues. McKellen's Hamlet and Richard II, hailed in the
early seventies as masterpieces by a young discovery, were only the latest
examples of a distinguished acting career which had proceeded at the
Belgrade Theatre, Coventry, for some time before London 'discovered'
him. The same fate or fortune befell an actor of the older generation,
David Waller, whose work at the same theatre over a considerable period
went frustratingly unheeded by the 'nationals'. Dorothy Tutin is a
versatile and affecting actress whose performances have been somewhat
underestimated. She has played Juliet, Viola, Portia, Ophelia and
Cressida with her characteristic pert winsomeness, allied to a very cool-
seeming intelligence. She has the ability to isolate and 'celebrate' lyrical
moments, and she is able to make silence work for her. Nicoll Williamson
is a compelling actor who gives the impression of revelling in what might
be called 'maverick' interpretations. These usually involve a species of the
unexpected not always compatible with any conceivable requirement of
the role. His Hamlet was angry, explosive, magnetic and often loud, his
Malvolio seemed to oscillate between a Scots and a Welsh accent as it was
by turn lascivious, pathetic and farcical. Williamson enlivens the world of
Shakespeare's plays, but sometimes his keen intelligence seems misapplied.
Richard Pasco — another Birmingham product — has steadily grown in
stature at the Royal Shakespeare Company. His long career has encompassed many of the major and upper-secondary roles. He alternated the
roles of Richard II and Bolingbroke with Ian Richardson. His face is

strikingly handsome. The mouth looks vulnerable but there is a sturdy hardness overall which gives the critic pause from assuming that Pasco is simply a romantic player. In fact, he is as successful with anger, passion and implied cruelty as with the more tender emotions. Judi Dench shares with McKellen the title of loner. Although she, like him, has served time with 'establishment' theatres (she, at the Old Vic and Stratford) she gives the impression that she does not like to be tied. She was an exceptionally touching Juliet in Zeffirelli's Old Vic production. Her Viola and Beatrice were characterized by fun and lyrical gravity. Her voice has been variously described as 'bubble and squeak' and 'huskily sexy'. It is a voice that demands attention — but its chief characteristic, except when Judi Dench has it well under control, is to give the impression that she is about to burst into laughter. In an ill-judged piece of casting (Regan in Nunn's 1976 *King Lear*) the control was incomplete. In Nunn's daring, triumphantly successful casting of her as Lady Macbeth (1976–7) the control and interpretation were magnificent — despite Dench's assertion in a published interview in 1974/5 that she would never again play the part after a disastrous experience in an African tour. John Neville, during the Old Vic seasons of the 1950s, seemed set fair to assume eventually the mantle of Gielgud. His aquiline features, well-shaped brow and compelling eyes, seemed to justify the description — 'the young Gielgud'. He has played many of the major roles and alternated Othello and Iago with Richard Burton at the Old Vic (1955–6). His strength lies in his intelligent and emotionally sensitive reading of the text; he has, too, a penchant for the fantastic. His weakness is hard to distinguish, but something arrested his early promise. Somewhere inside him is a quality which prevents him from seeming to engage totally and forcefully with a role. Eric Porter is a product of Wolfit's touring company, Birmingham and the Old Vic. He has played Henry IV, Banquo, Bolingbroke, Malvolio, Shylock and King Lear, never failing to produce a performance of unremitting intelligence. He is a splendid reader of a text, and his lines of interpretation are invariably clear and unambiguous. He understands but does not seem able to commit himself to the display of passion, and he can 'explain' emotion without embodying it unreservedly.

The roll-call of players whose names should be remembered contains a high number whose contribution to the rich fertility of Shakespearean acting has been underrated to a degree: Harry Andrews, whose versatility is extraordinary; Michael Hordern, whose ability to present rounded characterizations of secondary roles is unequalled; Alan Badel whose Hamlet (Stratford, 1956) dignified and elevated a production that was unworthy of his talent; Alec Clunes, the finest Claudius of his generation; Ernest Milton who, in a career notable for a variety of roles, could give any production a quality of zest and intelligence; Barbara Jefford, an actress of powerful address, whose Cleopatra and Lady Macbeth rank among the finest of the post-war era; Geraldine McEwan, whose Olivia rescued what had been traditionally a thankless part and gave it a cool and witty reality; Eileen Herlie, who unaccountably, faded from public view in the late 1950s but whose dark beauty and imposing presence made her an outstanding tragic actress; Gwen Ffrangcon Davies whose Lady Macbeth to Gielgud's Macbeth, in 1942, was compelling and whose overrall record is distinguished. Some others became, flittingly, household names, sometimes justifiably, sometimes because the media encouraged it — Vivien Leigh, Margaret Leighton, Phyllis Neilson-Terry, Alec Guinness, Maxine Audley, Felix Aylmer — and sometimes because they brought to Shakespeare perhaps not quite the authority they gave to other dramatist's work, but a kind of glamour which pleased and which the world's greatest dramatist can survive. The careers of many such players were spawned and controlled by Hollywood — Rathbone, Brando, Shearer, Howard *et al.* The Royal Shakespeare Company created its own stars — Ian Holm, David Warner, David Waller and, most conspicuously, Donald Sinden — who leapt over the spiked wall that divides film-celebrity from dramatic actor with a sureness and success that was a credit to the faith of the company and to his own will and ability. Janet Suzman, Susan Fleetwood, Francesca Annis and Barbara Leigh-Hunt, but, in particular, Elizabeth Spriggs — whose assumption of major roles has been too long delayed — are among the best examples of the extent to which the richness of Shakespearean acting has been nurtured equally by both sexes.

If we look at playbills of the 18th and 19th centuries we will find the names of many actors and actresses which mean nothing to us — all that is known is that they played certain parts and departed eventually into the receiving darkness. It is an arrogance to try and forecast which of the names from our own century will glow and be recalled decades hence. The fact that so much more of the work of players can now be recorded and passed on to the future can have a double effect — it can both help judgment and, oddly, distort it. Even a bad actor is sometimes capable of one superb performance, and this may be the one that survives. Again, recording, both visual and aural, can either diminish or increase the quality of a performance. If forecasting, then, is arrogant, and if the future will have its own problems of assessment, the historian, trapped in his own time, may avoid the one and shrug away the other as irrelevant to him and fall back on the underrated procedure of an act of faith. This unequi-vocally asserts that never in the history of theatre has there been a time which harboured so much good and great acting. In a century not other-wise notable for the propagation of matters civilized and beneficent, would that the future concurs with this faith — ''Tis a consummation devoutly to be wish'd.'

The following contain many invaluable eye-witness accounts of Shakespearean productions:

G. C. D. ODELL, *Shakespeare from Betterton to Irving*, 2 vols., 1920
C. B. HOGAN, *Shakespeare in the Theatre*, 1952–7
A. C. SPRAGUE, *Shakespearean Players and Performances*, 1954
G. LLOYD EVANS (ed.), *Shakespeare in the Limelight*, 1964
J. C. TREWIN, *Shakespeare on the English Stage, 1900–1964*, 1964
A. C. SPRAGUE and J. C. TREWIN, *Shakespeare's Plays Today: Some Customs and Conventions of the Stage*, 1970

SHAKESPEARE IN NORTH AMERICA

The United States

A characteristically American dramatic literature, in the strict sense of the term, is mainly, if not exclusively, a product of the 20th century. Yet a recognizably American theatre tradition began to show much earlier, even in pre-revolutionary days, and it was, from the beginning, closely identified with Shakespeare. The cross-fertilization of acting styles between the USA and the UK which reached a peak in the latter half of the 19th century, though it showed a very strong English bias, is a testimony to the pertinacity of American actors and actresses. Although the English influence has always been a strong one there is an impressive list of Americans who defied the influence, thrived and asserted their own individuality.

The Shakespeare connection is natural. Apart from his obvious relevance as the greatest dramatist of the Western world, he is a showpiece of the cultural pride of the two English-speaking nations. Moreover, many of the roots and branches of both American and English culture find a common sustenance in the moral values, the customs, the intellectual and emotional realities, and the language of Shakespeare. There is, too, for many Americans, a rich piquancy in the truth that the speech of the Pilgrim Fathers in idiom and, for many, probably in pronunciation, was near to that of Shakespeare and his contemporaries — in this sense Shakespeare's works exemplify the English connection for those (and there are still many of them) who find some pride and even a kind of nostalgia in it.

The earliest Shakespeare theatre in the USA was very English. In 1752 Lewis Hallam took his 'London Company of Comedians' to Virginia, where his repertoire included *The Merchant of Venice, Richard III, Hamlet* and *Othello*. The motherland's influence is confirmed by the texts used — the standard 'restored' and adapted versions typical of English 17th- and 18th-century performances. Hallam was popular in the South, but in Philadelphia he encountered the American equivalent of Elizabethan Puritan opposition — the Quakers.

A Jamaican, David Douglass, took over both his company and his widow on Hallam's death in 1756, and played in New York, Philadelphia, Newport, Rhode Island and elsewhere. The care these pioneers needed to mollify the religious is beguilingly illustrated in the playbill for Douglass's

Othello at the King's Arms Tavern, Newport, 1759 — 'a series of MORAL DIALOGUES in five parts, Depicting the evil effects of Jealousy and other Bad Passions and Proving that Happiness can only Spring from the Pursuit of Virtue.'

Between 1776 and 1783 the effects of war and frequent official and unofficial disapproval caused severe restrictions and, indeed, not until the beginning of the 19th century was there a vital stirring of interest in Shakespeare. But, by 1800, permanent companies were formed — New York, Philadelphia, Charleston, Providence and Boston. Yet, on the whole, energetic eccentricity outmatched artistic distinction. John Hodgkinson, for example, who could learn hundreds of lines at a sitting, was bow-legged, claimed the Prince of Wales as his patron, and played (apparently with enormous vivacity) every Shakespearean part he could lay hands on. The influence of the mother-country still dominated. No American printing of a Shakespeare play appeared before *c.* 1759, and after the revolutionary war actors like George Frederick Cooke, Edmund Kean, and Junius Brutus Booth descended on the American continent in profusion and with considerable effect.

The first American actor convincingly able to compete with, and often to triumph over, the best England could provide was Edwin Forrest (1806–72). He was associated with the famous Walnut Street Theatre, Philadelphia, but appeared elsewhere, and notably in London in 1836. He was to the USA what Kean was to England — a kind of elemental force. Phrases like 'sustained crescendo', 'a cataract of illimitable rage', characterize descriptions of him. Like Garrick he kept his body in splendid tune, but adding flagellation and severe diet to normal exercise. His forte was tragedy, his triumphs were as Othello and Lear. With him American acting became internationally famed and was given a 'classical' exponent. His partner in *Macbeth* and *Othello* was Charlotte Cushman (1816–76), America's greatest 19th-century and tragic actress. In London she stole the honours from him by the strength and intelligence of her performance. She had an ability to change gear, sexually, so to speak, so that her voice, appearance, gestures could at one moment seem mannish, at another feminine. Her transformations as Rosalind astonished audiences, and her Romeo (with her sister playing Juliet) was 'one of the most extraordinary pieces of acting, perhaps, ever exhibited by a woman'. She and Forrest lie at the heart of the USA's emergence into full commitment and distinction in Shakespearean theatre. But this process was aided by the 19th-century growth of American Shakespeare scholarship and literary criticism, and, from the 1790s onwards, the proliferation of theatre-building — Chestnut Street Theatre, Philadelphia, 1794; Federal Street Theatre, Boston, 1794; Park Theatre, New York, 1798; the Broadway, 1847; the Astor Place, 1847; the Washington, 1804. In terms of the equipment and visual presentation of Shakespeare, both in the 18th and 19th centuries, little difference was apparent from English modes — indeed not until Edwin Booth (1833–93) can it be said that a characteristic American ingenuity linked with imagination began to assert itself in presenting Shakespeare. His versatility and controlled passion and keen intellectuality created memorable performances of Shakespeare's tragic heroes — he alternated the parts of Iago and Othello with Irving. As a manager he encouraged 'local' American talent. James Hackett was one of the first on either side of the Atlantic to study his roles by a 'psychological' method.

But perhaps America's greatest contributions to the spread of Shakespeare's works and their appreciation have been: (1) Touring companies which, at the end of the 19th and beginning of the 20th centuries, emulated the original frontiersmen with their brave forages westerly, playing in saloons, bars, one-horse-towns, public halls in aspiring communities, and theatres in cities rapidly acquiring affluence. Both English and American 'stars' were involved. (2) USA university and college drama departments — where theory is related to practice and professional expertise is constantly to hand in both respects. There is a much stronger relationship between academic institution and professional theatre in the USA than in England. (3) The 'Festival' conception and reality, derived from England but highly developed in the USA. In the former, the heart of Shakespeare production is at Stratford upon Avon, but the London West End is important, too. In the latter, Festival Shakespeare predominates and flourishes in many places but Broadway, in this respect, is unimportant.

Among the more important US festivals are: *Ashland, Oregon,* founded, 1935 — university and semi-professional with professional guests; *Hofstra, Long Island,* with a replica of J. C. Adams's Elizabethan theatre, now replaced with a new auditorium which still preserves the style of the original; *Colorado University* — outdoor theatre whose productions emphasize the text; *Phoenix, Arizona* — like Colorado, combines lectures, discussions, etc., with live theatre; *Great Lakes Festival, Lakewood, Ohio* — huge auditorium (2000); the stage has Elizabethan features; *San Diego* has an 'Old Globe Theatre', with Elizabethan staging — it also has a Falstaff Tavern; *Stratford, Connecticut* — prestigious festival whose standards seem to have varied over the years. Among others are those at the Kennedy Centre; New Jersey; Utah; Champlain.

The opportunity for British audiences to see and assess and compare the talents of American actors and directors is strictly limited. The traffic tends to be one-way, partly because of the inhibitions imposed by both countries' conditions of employment for aliens, partly by finance, and, to a degree, by the 'awe', or a residue of it, which Americans have traditionally had for British actors. The British experience of American Shakespeare is very largely through films, an area in which the USA has been indefatigable in bulk, sensation-making and experiment. The best of American filmed Shakespeare (*see* Shakespeare on Film) is dominated by the wayward genius of Orson Welles. But his international fame must not be allowed to overshadow the reputation (even in hearsay) of many other names the UK has heard of but rarely, if ever, seen in their natural habitat — the stage. Massey, Hepburn, Tandy, Cronyn, Maurice Evans, Helen Hayes, Katherine Cornell and many others. If, in the UK, only the names of Joseph Papp and Eric Christmas are well known, this does not mean that there are not many other directors, equally talented, at work in the USA.

Shakespeare in the USA is a vast industry, and its most eminent aspects are the quality of its scholarship, the virile relationship between that scholarship and stage-production, the extraordinary and fruitful proliferation of its festivals and, of course, the unique kind of fresh enthusiasm of its audiences.

Canada

In cultural and many other matters Canada has long lain in the shadow of the USA. Yet, so far as theatre is concerned, in two respects she matches her powerful neighbour, and in one respect, outdoes it. Although the history of Shakespeare production in Canada is, in effect, confined to the 20th century, there is, contrary to a persistent general belief, a well-developed system of theatre organization and centres, particularly in the eastern provinces. The many tensions created by the existence of English-speaking and French-speaking populations have endangered national unity but, paradoxically, have to a degree enabled theatre in Canada to be enriched, especially in its actors and directors, by infusions of two immensely fertile cultures. Moreover, the existence of the Canada Council — a transatlantic equivalent of the British Arts Council — has by its advice, encouragement and money, brought talent of many kinds to the forefront, and helped to form a kind of theatre organization and pattern well-beloved in North America — the Arts Centre and the Festival. Distinguished Shakespearean work has been achieved (with that typically transatlantic close relationship between stage and study) at the Globe, Regina; University of Toronto Drama Centre; Theatre New Brunswick; Edmonton; Manitoba Theatre Centre; Banff Festival; Ottawa's National Arts Centre; Montreal Repertory Theatre; Bastion Theatre, Victoria; Theatre Calgary; St Lawrence Centre; Vancouver Playhouse, etc. There is, too, a National Shakespeare Company. Thus, both in the nature and relative size of organization, and in the relationship between theoretical study and practical realization, Canada has no need to envy the USA. Indeed, pound for pound, so to speak, Canada's Shakespeare scholars (some of them British émigrés) are equal to the best in the world, and the university departments and institutions devoted to Shakespeare study at Toronto, McMasters, Waterloo, Vancouver, Queen's, McGill and elsewhere amply testify to this.

In 1953 an event occurred which was to place Canada in the very forefront of World Shakespearean Theatre — to an extent never achieved by the USA. The Stratford Ontario Shakespeare Festival opened, in a sophisticated tent. A permanent auditorium followed in 1957. The original chief guiding hands were those of a local businessman, Tom Patterson, an Irish Director, Tyrone Guthrie, and the designer, Tanya Moiseiwitsch. Its history since has been one of almost uninterrupted success — in three respects. First, the magical appropriateness of the modern version of an Elizabethan stage for an exciting communication of Shakespeare's plays. Productions at Stratford are characterized by the way they engender a sense of close audience involvement; the architectural relationship between stage and auditorium seems perfect, and the interesting levels and shapes of the stage make elaborate scenery superfluous and close concentration on the acting easy. Acoustics are excellent in a building which is elegant, functional and comfortable. Secondly, the best productions there — notably Guthrie's, Michael Langham's and Jean Gascon's — have been among the best in the world, and have attracted audiences from all over the world. Thirdly, the practice of inviting foreign (mainly British) artists to work with Canadians has resulted in a format which has both maintained standards and encouraged Canadian talent, while challenging the visitors.

There are, unquestionably, more Shakespearean stage-actors in Canada of international status than in the USA, and among them are British actors who, for one reason or another, have found Canadian theatre conducive to the ripening of their talents. In Canada, many of these names are household words, and they are much respected and known elsewhere. Christopher Plummer, William Hutt, William Needles, the late Leo Ciceri, Martha Henry, Pat Galloway, Tony Van Bridge, Douglas Rain, Francis Hyland, John Colicos.

It cannot be said that a 'Canadian style' has developed — perhaps we habitually overemphasize the possibility of a national style — and in any case, Canada is a very young country. But without the existence of Stratford, Ontario, world Shakespeare would be conspicuously poorer.

PRINCIPAL SHAKESPEAREAN ACTORS AND ACTRESSES

Further information about many of the actors and actresses listed below will be found in 'Shakespeare on the Stage'. The portraits, etc., referred to in some entries are on permanent display at the Royal Shakespeare Theatre's Picture Gallery, adjoining the theatre at Stratford upon Avon.

Achurch, Janet (1864–1916). English actress much admired by Shaw. A rival to Ellen Terry in force of personality and technique, though her range of Shakespearean roles was not large.

Aldridge, Ira Frederick (*c.* 1805–67). One of first successful black actors. Born Senegambia, trained as missionary in Glasgow, excelled as Othello and Aaron.

Alexander, George (1858–1918). English actor-manager. Associated with Irving, with whom he toured USA. An actor of fine presence but whose talent missed genius emphatically.

Alleyn, Edward (1566–1626). Vies with Burbage for the accolade as the age's greatest tragic actor. Acted in Marlowe's plays. Helped to found Dulwich College (where his and Henslowe's papers are housed). No evidence of his appearance in any of Shakespeare's plays.

Anderson, Judith (1898–   ). American actress, but born in Australia. Played Gertrude to Gielgud's New York Hamlet, 1936. Her Lady Macbeth (with Olivier in London) accounted one of greatest performances of the part in 20th century. Actress of superb vocal range and brooding power exactly suiting the great tragic heroines.

Anderson, Mary (1859–1940). Born California. Idol of many US cities. Acted frequently in London. Played Rosalind at Stratford upon Avon, 1885. Notable Hermione and Portia. (Marble bust, Anderson as Hermione, *Albert Joy*; oil, three-quarter length portrait (1885), *Johnston Forbes-Robertson*; head, pencil on white paper (1913), *Carl J. Becker.*)

Robert Armin (*c.* 1568–1615). One of most fascinating of Shakespeare's colleagues. He had a varied career as goldsmith's apprentice, potboy, playwright (*see*, for example, his *The Two Maids of More Clacke, with the Life and simple manner of John in the Hospital*, 1609). Armin probably played Feste, Touchstone and Lear's Fool, and his sagacious, ambiguous conception of fooling may well have inspired Shakespeare to turn from relatively simple clown characters in his early plays to the more devious and puzzling Fools of the romantic comedies and *King Lear*.

Asche, Thomas Strange Heiss Oscar (1871–1936). Australian actor-manager who studied acting in Norway but worked in England with Benson. Noted for his Othello and for his productions.

Ashcroft, Dame Peggy (1907–   ). Distinguished English actress, notable for intelligence of interpretations and clarity of performance. Her Beatrice to Gielgud's Benedick one of the great duo-performances of the century. Her Portia, Viola, Cordelia and Queen Margaret (in *Henry VI*) also notable. Associate director, Royal Shakespeare Company. (Oil, Ashcroft as 1957 Imogen, *Anthony Devas*.)

Atkins, Robert (1886–1972). Actor-manager. Toured with Martin-Harvey, Forbes-Robertson and Benson. Founded the Bankside Players who presented 'Elizabethan' performances in Blackfriars, London. Director at Shakespeare Memorial Theatre and hardy advocate of outdoor Shakespeare (in Regent's Park). Notable Belch, Touchstone, Bottom.

Bancroft, Sir Squire (1841–1926). English actor-manager. Associated with successful management of Haymarket Theatre. With his wife an innovator in theory and practice — e.g. acting minor roles themselves; developing a sense of character in relation to environment. They also vastly improved conditions of employment and pay for their companies.

Bancroft, Marie Effie Wilton (1839–1921). Wife of Squire Bancroft.

Barrault, Jean-Louis (1910–   ). French actor-director. Left Comédie-Francaise to form his own company in 1946, opening with *Hamlet*, translated by André Gide. Barrault's acting strongly conditioned by the art of mime — which gave his Hamlet a uniquely sensitive visual reality.

Barrett, Wilson (1846–1904). Introduced Modjeska to England. A middling actor and dramatist, but splendid manager of Princess's Theatre.

Barry, Ann (1734–1801). Wife of Spranger Barry, much admired as Juliet, Cordelia, Rosalind, Imogen, Perdita. Very talented without genius, she excelled in pathos. Noted for depicting madness — e.g. her Isabella betrayed signs of an approaching mental breakdown.

Barry, Elizabeth (1658–1713). First considerable English actress. Alleged to have been trained by the infamous Rochester — she bore him a daughter. Member of Duke's Company, played opposite Betterton. 'Mrs Barry was middle-sized, and had darkish hair, light eyes, dark eyebrows and was indifferently plump. Her face somewhat preceded her action, as the latter did her words, her face ever expressing the passions; not like the actresses of late times, who are afraid of putting their faces out of the form of non-meaning, lest they should crack the serum, white-wash, or other cosmetic, trowled on.' (A. Aston in a supplement to Cibber's work 1747.) Captivated audiences despite an indifferent voice and ordinary appearance. Excelled in tragic and melodramatic roles.

Barry, Spranger (*c.* 1717–77). Born Dublin, famous as Othello, Hamlet, Lear, Romeo. Incurred Garrick's anger, resulting in simultaneous productions of *Romeo and Juliet* at Drury Lane (Garrick) and Covent Garden (Barry) — Garrick drawing the applause but Barry inciting the tears. His death occasioned much sympathetic comment — 'He gave dignity to the hero and passion to the lover . . .'

Barrymore, Ethel (1879–1959). One of famous American Barrymore theatrical family. Played Portia, Ophelia and Juliet.

Barrymore, John (1882–1942). At one time best-known American actor in Europe. A matinée idol he did nothing to destroy the image of the debonair, devil-may-care, handsome, sardonic man-of-the-world. Surprised everyone with his New York Hamlet, 1922 and its repetition in London, 1925. His interpretation emphasized the poetic and grave beauty of a vulnerable Prince, and it was superbly spoken.

Bellamy, George Anne (*c.* 1731–88). Born Ireland. Versatile — Queen (*Richard III*), Cordelia, Constance, Portia, Lady Macbeth. Off/on professional relationship with Garrick, Sheridan and other eminences. Decidedly 'on' relationship with gambling, extravagance, sex. Her Juliet (with Garrick) regarded as inferior to Mrs Cibber's simultaneous performance with Barry. Excelled in pathetic parts, aided by her beauty, slim waist, blue eyes and strong but expressive voice.

Benfield, Robert (d. 1649). One of the principal actors in Shakespeare's company. One of three who petitioned the Lord Chamberlain for right to obtain shares in Blackfriars and Globe theatres.

Bensley, Robert (1742–1817). Leading London actor for three decades. As Malvolio, '. . . He looked, spake, and moved like an old Castilian. He was starch, spruce, opinionated, but his superstructure of pride seemed bottomed upon a sense of worth.' (Charles Lamb, *On Some of the Old Actors.*) Eccentric actor, hollow-voiced, staring-eyed, stiff-gaited, 'cutting the stage at right angles, with the head up, and brows down, a coldly correct enunciation, and a full-flowing wig'. Associated with Garrick who called him 'Roaring Bob'.

Benson, Sir Frank Robert (1858–1939). English actor/manager. Pupil of Irving. Great touring manager and in 1886–8 and 1891 director of Stratford upon Avon Festival. Immensely popular, and subsequent to 1891 directed Stratford Festival for twenty years, creating a still unbroken record and an affection which causes older Stratfordians to regard everything since at their theatre as inferior. (Bronze bust (1932), *Fleming Baxter*; oil, three-quarter length portrait (1910), *Hugh Goldwin Riviere.*)

Bernhardt, Sarah (1854–1923). Played Cordelia in French and Hamlet in version by Alexandre Dumas. '. . . the whole thing was imaginative, electrical, and poetical. I do not think I sat out the play of *Hamlet* with less fatigue. It all passed like a delightful dream.' (Clement Scott, *Some Notable Hamlets.*)

Betterton, Thomas (1635–1710). Second only to Garrick as acting genius. Notable as Falstaff, Hamlet, Mercutio, Othello, Pericles, Toby Belch. Son of Charles I's cook. Member of company managed by Davenant who claimed to be Shakespeare's illegitimate son. Actor of compelling presence. 'Could *how* Betterton spoke be as easily known as *what* he spoke; then might you see the muse of Shakespear in her triumph . . . he made the ghost equally terrible to the spectator as to himself.' (Colley Cibber, *Apology*.)

Betty, William Henry West (1791–1874). Universally known as the young Roscius (after famous Roman actor). Born Shrewsbury, son of affluent doctor. First acted in Belfast at twelve years. Played Romeo, Arthur, Hamlet (which he memorized in three hours). Received fulsome adulation and rivalled Kemble in popularity. Broke box office records at Drury Lane and was responsible for Prime Minister Pitt adjourning House of Commons for members to see his Hamlet. Appeared alternately at Drury Lane and Covent Garden as Richard III and Macbeth. (Oil, Betty as Hamlet (1805), *James Northcote*.)

Booth, Barton (1681–1733). Betterton's successor in public affection, he became a reformed drunk. Notable Lear, Brutus, Hotspur, Timon.

Booth, Edwin Thomas (1833–93). Brother of John Wilks Booth, assassin of Lincoln. Son of J. B. Booth. Most famous 19th-century American player of main Shakespearean roles, especially Hamlet. He said he could not 'paint with big brushes — the fine touches come in spite of me, and it's all folly to say: "Don't elaborate, don't refine it" — I can't help it. I'm too damned genteel and exquisite, I s'pose, and some buster with a big voice and a broadaxe gesticulation will oust me one of these fine days.' In 1869 built theatre in New York and specialized in Shakespeare. In 1874 virtually bankrupt. In 1881–2 played Othello and Iago alternately with Irving. (Oil, Booth as Hamlet (1887), *Oliver Ingraham Lay*.)

Booth, Junius Brutus (1796–1852). Kean's rival, father of Edwin, Junius and John Wilkes Booth. A notable Iago and Richard III.

Bourchier, Arthur (1864–1927). Founder of Oxford University Dramatic Society and actor of many Shakespearean roles. Married to Violet Vanbrugh and became member of Lillie Langtrey's company. Played many Shakespearean roles without much distinction but with huge energy and was known for his aversion to criticism.

Bracegirdle, Ann (*c.* 1670–1748). Frequently played opposite Betterton, but equally famous as Congreve's concubine/wife and for her acting of his finest comic roles. Played Desdamona, Juliet, Portia, Ophelia, Cordelia, Isabella.

Bryan, George (*fl.* 1586–1613). Known as a principal actor in Shakespeare's plays in late 16th century. Member of Lord Chamberlain's Company, 1596. Member of English company visiting Elsinore in 1586.

The Indian Queen

13. Mezzotint, probably of Mrs Bracegirdle, by J. Smith. A fine example of bizarre early 18th-century female costume.

14. Betterton as Hamlet. Note the contemporary 18th-century costume.

15. Quin as Coriolanus, 1749. From a contemporary print.

16. *Above left:* Garrick as Hamlet, by Benjamin Wilson, engraved by J. McArdell.

17. *Above right:* Edmund Kean as Richard III. Oil painting by John James Halls, 1814. Crown Copyright. Victoria and Albert Museum.

18. John Philip Kemble as Hamlet, from an engraving of 1785. Note the Vandyke style of costume.

19. *Above left:* Sarah Siddons as Lady Macbeth.

20. *Above right:* Harriet Faucit as Cleopatra at Covent Garden, 1813–14.

21. Mr and Mrs Charles Kean as the Macbeths, 1858. Note Mrs Kean's Victorian dress. Crown Copyright. Victoria and Albert Museum.

22. Henry Irving as Shylock.

23. Ellen Terry as Beatrice, *c.* 1882. Note the elaborately decorated costume.

24. Johnston Forbes-Robertson as Hamlet. Note the 'classical' costume.

25. John Barrymore as Richard III, New York, 1920.

26. Sybil Thorndike as Lady Macbeth, Prince's Theatre, London, 1926. Note the flamboyant costume.

27. Alfred Lunt and Lynn Fontanne in *The Taming of the Shrew*, New York, 1935.

28. *Above left:* Orson Welles as Falstaff in Welles's *Five Kings*, Mercury Theatre, 1939.

29. *Above right:* Ralph Richardson as Falstaff.

30. John Gielgud and Peggy Ashcroft as Benedick and Beatrice, Stratford upon Avon, 1950.

31. *Above left:* Michael Redgrave as Shylock, Stratford upon Avon, 1953.

32. *Above right:* Laurence Olivier as Macbeth, Stratford upon Avon, 1955.

33. Edith Evans as the Countess of Rousillon, Stratford upon Avon, 1959.

34. Paul Scofield as King Lear, Stratford upon Avon, 1962.

35. Ian Richardson as Coriolanus, Stratford upon Avon, 1967.

36. Ian McKellen and Judi Dench in *Macbeth*, Stratford upon Avon, 1977.

Burbage, James (*c.* 1530–97). Father of Richard Burbage. Minor actor but energetic and possibly shady speculator in theatre building — 'was the first builder of Playhouses' — e.g. The Theatre (opened August, 1577) the first 'custom built' commercial theatre in England.

Burbage, Richard (*c.* 1568–1619). One of twenty-six principal actors of Shakespeare's plays in late 16th, early 17th centuries. Contemporary accounts make clear his greatness. Shakespeare possibly wrote *Hamlet*, *Othello*, *Lear* for him. Obviously close friend of Shakespeare's (*see* Will; Impresa). Leading actor of Chamberlain's/King's Company. 'He had all the parts of an excellent orator (animating his words with speaking, and speech with action) his auditors being never more delighted than when he spoke, nor more sorry than when he held his peace. Yet even then he was an excellent actor still, never falling in his part when he had done speaking; but with his looks and gesture, maintaining it still unto the heighth.' (Richard Flecknoe.)

Calvert, Charles (1828–79). English actor-manager, best known in the provinces for Shakespearean productions — especially Theatre Royal and Prince's, Manchester. Directed *Richard II* in Niblo's Garden, New York, 1871, and *Henry V* in New York, 1875.

Campbell, Mrs Patrick (1865–1940). One of England's most fiery and temperamental actresses ('perilously bewitching' — George Bernard Shaw). She triumphed in many modern plays. Played Juliet and Ophelia with Forbes-Robertson.

Cibber, Colley (1671–1757). Colleague of Betterton at Drury Lane. Versatile actor (Shallow, Wolsey, Jaques, Iago), notorious adaptor of Shakespeare, inconsequential Poet Laureate. Most valuable work — *Apology for the Life of Colley Cibber, Comedian: View of the Stage during his own Time* — contains descriptions of life and work of contemporary actors and actresses.

Cibber, Susannah Maria (1714–66). Sister of Dr Arne, outstanding English composer. Married to Theophilus Cibber. Played alongside Garrick. Regarded as best Ophelia of her time.

Cibber, Theophilus (1703–58). Son of Colley Cibber. Minor actor (e.g. Pistol, Parolles). Memorable only for his recording (in *Life of Shakespeare*) of Shakespeare's holding horses' heads outside theatre in his early career.

Clive, Catherine (Kitty) (1711–85). Worked with Colley Cibber at Drury Lane. Married relative of Clive of India. Played opposite Macklin. Much admired by Dr Johnson. Fell foul of Garrick, who rightly admired her comic genius rather than her tragic aspirations. Played Katharine (*Shrew*), Portia, Celia, Olivia, Ophelia.

Clunes, Alec (1912–70). Actor, manager and director. Versatile and with impressive stage-presence. Played at Old Vic and Stratford, and in many other London and provincial theatres. His Claudius in *Hamlet*, 1955, which toured in the UK and went to the Moscow Art Theatre, was, of its time, one of the most intelligent and thoughtful interpretations of this part. It was characterized by a huge sense of conscience and grief which gave it an unaccustomed sympathy.

Coates, 'Romeo' (1772–1848). West Indian, both wealthy and deluded about his prowess as an actor. As Romeo he died upon a silk handkerchief which he used to clean the stage. '. . . the house vociferously bawled out, "Die again, Romeo!" and, obedient . . . he . . . went through the ceremony again . . . The call was again heard and the well-pleased amateur was evidently prepared to enact a third death; but Juliet now rose up from her tomb, and gracefully put an end to this ludicrous scene by advancing to the front of the stage and aptly applying a quotation from Shakespeare — "Dying is such sweet sorrow,/That he will die again until to-morrow".' (R. H. Gronow, *Reminiscences and Recollections*, 1862.)

Coburn, Charles Douville (1877–1961). American actor-manager. Founded, with his wife, Coburn Shakespearian Players, 1906. Superb Falstaff.

Collier, Constance (1878–1955). English actress who played Peaseblossom when three years old. Well known in USA. Played Gertrude to Barrymore's Hamlet in London.

Compton, Fay (1894–   ). Much-loved English actress of great sweetness of presence and versatility. Played at Old Vic and toured in Shakespeare and Shaw plays. Played Ophelia to Barrymore's Hamlet and to Gielgud's.

Condell, Henry (d. 1627). One of principal actors in Shakespeare's plays in late 16th century, early 17th century. Friend of Shakespeare who named him in his will. Co-collector with Heminges of First Folio. Housekeeper (i.e. owner) of Blackfriars and shareholder in Globe Theatre.

Cooke, Alexander (d. 1614). One of the principal actors in Shakespeare's company. Probably originally apprentice to Heminges — one of Shakespeare's closest colleagues.

Cooke, George Frederick (1756–1811). Played Jaques, Richard III, Othello, Falstaff, Henry VIII, Shylock. Contemporary and contentious colleague of Kemble and Mrs Siddons. Drink ruined career and he died in New York, where he had been well received. 'Kean said, and I believe him, that he had never seen Cooke act; nevertheless many critics declared him to have been a copyist of the great George Frederick.' (Edwin Booth.) (Watercolour on ivory, three-quarter face, *Anon.*)

Cornell, Katharine (1898–   ). Distinguished American actress whose Juliet and Cleopatra were only two of a long line of triumphs.

Cowley, Richard (d. 1619). One of principal actors in Shakespeare's plays in late 16th century. Possibly low comedian. Name appears instead of Verges in Act II, Scene ii of Folio printing of *Much Ado About Nothing*. Senior member of King's Company.

Craig, Edward Henry Gordon (1832–1966). Acted with Irving and performed Hamlet six times, but best known as son of Ellen Terry and seminal designer and theoretician of the art of theatre. Designed many productions; no students of theatre should ignore either the illustrations of his sets or his observations in *The Art of the Theatre*, 1905; *On the Art of the Theatre*, 1911; *Towards a New Theatre*, 1911. Craig had contentious views about status of actor — seeming to reduce him to a marionette moving to the orders of a super-director/designer. He conceived of production very much in visual terms, subsuming the verbal and the theatrical to the aesthetic and the visual.

Crosse, Samuel (d. *c.* 1605). One of twenty-six principal actors of Shakespeare's plays in late 16th century. Said to have played comic female roles — Maria, Mistress Quickly, etc.

Cushman, Charlotte Saunders (1816–76). American actress of great distinction — especially in tragedy. Remarkable Lady Macbeth who earned the praise of the niggardly Macready. Also played Beatrice, Rosalind and Portia and exercised a predisposition to don buskins by playing Oberon and Romeo. Played opposite Edwin Forrest. In 1907 a Charlotte Cushman Club was founded in Philadelphia. It is still in being, and has a fascinating theatre museum.

Daly, John Augustin (1839–99). American dramatist-manager-dramatic critic and actor. Opened 5th Avenue Theatre, New York (1869). Associated with Ada Rehan and William Terriss and spent much time in London and eventually built his own theatre in Leicester Square. Responsible for many Shakespeare revivals — especially fond of *The Taming of the Shrew* — but he was reckless with the texts.

Dickens, Charles (1812–70). Played Shallow (in *The Merry Wives of Windsor*) before Queen Victoria. Wrote many critical and perceptive articles on Shakespeare. Played prominent part in raising money to buy the Birthplace. Spent his last days living at Gad's Hill, the scene of Falstaff's escapades in *Henry IV*.

Dogget, Thomas (d. 1721). Famous for comic interpretation of Shylock in *Jew of Venice*, 1701, an adaptation in which the part of Shakespeare's Jew remains almost intact. 'He was the best face-player and gesticulator, and a thorough master of the several dialects except the Scots . . .' (A. Aston.)

Elliston, Robert (1774–1831). Successful actor especially admired by Byron, and generally praised for his Falstaff, Hamlet, Romeo and Hotspur. 'Wherever Elliston walked, sat, or stood still, there was the theatre.' (Charles Lamb.)

Emery, John (1777–1822). Best known as Barnadine, and Caliban — a remarkable portrait of a suffering monster.

Evans, Dame Edith (1888–1977). Distinguished English actress who toured with Ellen Terry. Notable Rosalind, Portia, Beatrice and Volumnia. Applauded for her Nurse in *Romeo and Juliet*. (Oil, Evans as 1959 Volumnia, *Robert Buhler*.)

Evans, Maurice (1901–   ). British actor, but mainly associated with USA, of which he is a citizen. Outstanding Shakespearean tragedian — particularly Hamlet. Played opposite Helen Hayes and Katharine Cornell.

Faucit, Helena Saville (1817–98). Noted Imogen, Lady Macbeth, Desdemona, Cordelia. Author of *On Some of Shakespeare's Female Characters*, 1885 — dedicated to Queen Victoria. Lauded for her performance of Imogen in 1837. Played opposite Macready and in 1879 played Beatrice in opening performance of new Stratford Shakespeare Memorial Theatre. Marble pulpit with a portrait of her as St Helena in Holy Trinity, Stratford, given by her husband in her memory. (Oil, three-quarter length portrait (1873), *Wilhelm Auguste Rudolf*; marble relief, *John Henry Foley*.)

Fechter, Charles (1824–79). A Frenchman whose Hamlet (in English) was much admired despite his accent and misplaced emphases — 'Yet so great is the power of true emotion, that even *this* is forgotten directly he touches the feelings of the audience . . .' Also a notable Iago.

Field, Nathan (1587–1620). Boy actor at Blackfriars Theatre and associate of Ben Jonson. Possibly replaced the gap left in King's Company by Shakespeare's death.

Finn, Henry James (*c.* 1790–1840). American comedy actor. Notable Aguecheek — but also played Hamlet. Member of Charleston Theatre Company and associated with Thomas Kilner in Boston.

Fletcher, Lawrence (d. 1608). Named in the patent granted to the Lord Chamberlain's Company which designated it henceforth to be called the King's Men when James I ascended the throne. Buried at St Saviour's church, London.

Forbes-Robertson, Sir Johnston (1853–1937). Scots actor, pupil of Phelps. Played opposite Mary Anderson, the Bancrofts, Irving. Notable Romeo and Hamlet. His acting characterized by grave elegance, superbly melodious speaking and clear expression. Honorary graduate of Columbia University. (Oil, three-quarter length portrait (1920), *George Vernon Meredith Frampton*; oil, three-quarter portrait (1894), *Hugh de Twenebrokes Glazebrook*; plaster bust (1913), *L. S. Merrifield*.)

Forrest, Edwin (1806–72). Eminent American tragedian. Early poverty may have conditioned his later selfish egocentricity and acquisitiveness. Played all the major Shakespeare tragic roles with powerful voice, magnetic stage presence but, apparently, little subtlety. Second visit to

London a disaster — which he attributed to the wiles of Macready. New York's revenge on London was the Astor Place riot in which Macready was almost killed, twenty-two died and thirty-six were wounded by gunshot of the militia.

Garrick, David (1717–79). Played Antonio, Benedick, Hamlet, Hotspur, King John, Lear, Macbeth, Richard III, Romeo. Probably the greatest all-round theatre personality ever. Manager (Drury Lane); playwright (he wrote twenty plays and adapted many others); director (pioneer in stage-lighting, effects, realistic sets); theatre editor (restored a great deal of Shakespeare's text to his acting editions); impressario (organized the Shakespeare Jubilee, 1769); actor (developed a natural style of acting in contradistinction to the orotund, larger-than-life mode of his predecessors). 'Mr Garrick is but of middling stature . . . His voice is clear and piercing . . . and gait . . . neither strutting nor mincing, neither stiff nor slouching . . . His action corresponds with his voice, and both with the character he is to play.' Intimate friend of Dr Johnson, close acquaintance of Joshua Reynolds, Goldsmith, Edmund Burke, Gibbon, General Burgoyne. Sensitive to Shakespeare's language and made some progress to restoring the true text after decades of adaptation. Introduced first 'insurance' scheme for actors. An exemplary family man and warm personality, though sensitive and impatient of cant and inefficiency. '. . . never let your Shakespeare be out of your hands, or your pocket; keep him about you as a charm . . .' (Garrick, in letter to William Powell, 1764.) (Portrait, engraved colour, *Anon*; oil painting, 'The Apotheosis of Garrick', *George Carter*; oil, half-length portrait, *Robert Edge Pine*; pencil sketch, half-length portrait, *Thomas Worlidge*; oil, half-length portrait, Garrick and wife playing picquet, *attributed to Johann Zoffany*; watercolour, head and shoulders, *Anon*; watercolour on ivory, 18th-century miniature, *Penelope Coates*.

Gielgud, Sir John (1904–   ). Notable Hamlet, Romeo, Lear, Leontes, Benedick. With Olivier represents the best in English acting of 20th century. His interpretations memorable for vocal range and subtlety. His productions notable for disciplined visual imagination. His acting blood derives from his great-aunt, Ellen Terry. His directing acumen from Edward Gordon Craig (his uncle). 'Of all the arts, I think acting must be the least concrete, the most solitary.' (Gielgud, *Early Stages*.) (Bronze portrait bust (1962), *David Wynne*.)

Gilburne, Samuel (*fl.* 1605). One of the principal actors in Shakespeare's company. Apprentice actor to Augustine Phillips, who left him a bass viol in his will.

Glyn, Isabella (1823–89). Scots actress well known in USA. Famous for Shakespeare readings and for her performance of Cleopatra.

Gough, Robert (d. 1624). One of principal actors in Shakespeare's plays late 16th century.

Greet, Ben (1857–1936). Famous actor-manager who promoted open-air productions under the name of 'pastoral' — an ironic title in view of the English climate. Very well known in USA for his touring companies and for his professional friendship with Mary Anderson. Helped to create Old Vic, and became particularly interested in productions for children. A pioneer in the resuscitation of pre-Shakespearean plays long neglected by directors. An enthusiastic character actor.

Guinness, Sir Alec (1914–   ). One of the most popular actors in England, and world-famous for his film roles in non-Shakespearean parts. He has had a long experience of playing many Shakespearean characters (e.g. Richard III, Hamlet, Lear's Fool) but has never achieved the acceptance in Shakespeare performances which he gained for his film acting. Essentially a personality actor of great charm, grave wit and sharp intelligence and his speaking of verse is so distinguished that it increases regret that his work in Shakespeare has not perhaps fulfilled all expectations.

Hackett, James (1800–71). American actor, and first to be accepted as star in London. Notable Falstaff. (Hackett as Macbeth, *Joseph Watkins*.)

Hardwicke, Sir Cedric (1893–1964). Acted with the Benson company and the Old Vic. Matured into Shakespearean roles at Birmingham Repertory Theatre. A notable gravedigger in *Hamlet* and a rich Toby Belch. Long sojourn in Hollywood, where he became a star of world fame, brought his stage career virtually to a halt, but he played Belch again at the Old Vic in 1948. He had a splendidly rich voice, a commanding presence and a habit of stealing scenes which suggests that his film career did not so much stretch his talents as inhibit them.

Hart, Charles (d. 1683). Leading member of Killigrew's Company. With several others, is said to have been Nell Gwyn's lover. Believed by some to have been illegitimate son of Joan Hart, Shakespeare's sister. Played Hotspur, Brutus, Othello.

Heminges, John (d. 1630). A principal actor of Shakespeare's plays in late 16th and early 17th centuries. A close friend as well as colleague of Shakespeare who appointed him trustee of his Blackfriars property, leaving him a bequest in his will. Achieved immortality as co-collector of Shakespeare's First Folio with Henry Condell.

Hughes, Margaret (d. 1719). First woman recorded as professional actress in England, 1660. Mistress of Prince Rupert. Played Desdemona.

Hughes, William (?). Boy actor, 16th/17th century. Contemporary of Shakespeare. Claimed by some as the 'Mr. W.H.' mentioned in dedication of Shakespeare's sonnets.

Irving, Sir Henry (1838–1905). Famous 19th-century actor/manager, associated with Lyceum Theatre and Ellen Terry. First professional actor to be knighted. Noted for performances (e.g. Benedick, Hamlet, Lear, Macbeth, Shylock) verging on eccentric, productions veering towards sensational (e.g. flying and singing witches in *Macbeth*) and interpretations which sometimes dislocated the text. Probably Bernard Shaw's least favourite actor: 'Would it not be well for Mr Irving to set the example of trying to put a stop to the vulgar and distressing practice of recalling actors at the end of acts, or even scenes?' Others thought differently: 'His gait [as Lear], his looks, his gestures, all reveal the noble, imperious mind already degenerating into senile irritability . . .' (Gordon Crosse, *Shakespearean Playgoing 1890–1952*.) (Oil, Irving as 1892 Lear, *Bernard Partridge*; bronze plaque (1893), *L. E. Blackwell*; death mask, 20 October 1905; terracotta bust (1878), *Percy Fitzgerald*; Irving and Terry, 'Death of Ophelia' (1892), *Bernard Partridge*.)

Jordan, Dorothea (1762–1816). This scandalous woman (whose performances sometimes caused riots) was a brilliant comedienne, praised by Byron, Leigh Hunt, Joshua Reynolds and others. Mistress of William IV. Well-regarded at Drury Lane as comic actress. Notable Olivia, Rosalind, Imogen, Beatrice, Helena.

Kean, Charles (1811–68). Son of Edmund Kean; an actor of great and controlled skill (e.g. King John, Lear, Leontes, Richard II, Richard III, Shylock), he designed visually affluent productions which influenced Irving. Notable Leontes in 1856 with the juvenile Ellen Terry as Mamillius. (Miniature, watercolour on ivory, *Ozias Humphrey*.)

Kean, Mrs C. (1805–80). Irish actress whose early lack of success was redeemed when (as Ellen Tree) she married the eccentric but talented Charles Kean. Played Desdemona, Lady Macbeth, Hermione, Constance, etc. 'She had in youth much beauty and fascination, and in riper age was handsome and intellectual.' (Oil, Mrs Kean as Hermione, *Charles Robert Leslie*.)

Kean, Edmund (1787–1833). Distinguished Coriolanus, Hamlet, Iago, Lear, Macbeth, Othello, Richard II, Richard III, Richard of York, Shylock, Timon. The 'Heathcliff' of Shakespearean acting — wayward, passionate, a deprived child, he was the greatest of 'romantic' actors. His performances often sacrificed the play, other actors and overall interpretation, in their self-indulgence — but Coleridge found him the greatest of his time. '. . . the coming to himself when he sees his hands bloody; the manner in which his voice clung to his throat, and choked his utterance; his agony and tears, the force of nature overcome by passion — beggared description.' (William Hazlitt on Kean's Macbeth in *A View of the English Stage*.)

Kemble, Charles (1775–1854). Son of Roger Kemble. Played Hamlet, Romeo, Macbeth. Excelled as Mercutio. Manager of Covent Garden. Often played opposite his brother and his sister, Sarah Siddons. (Oil, head and shoulders, *Henry Wyatt*.)

Kemble, Fanny (1809–93). Played Juliet, Portia, Beatrice. Daughter of Charles Kemble. Triumphed both in England and USA. Wrote *Notes* *on Some of Shakespeare's Plays*, 1882. 'The combination of the power of representing passion and emotion with that of imagining or conceiving it — that is, of the theatrical talent with the dramatic temperament — is essential to make a good actor.' (Fanny Kemble, *On the Stage*, 1863.) (Oil, composite, including Charles Kemble, Charles Young, *Henry Andrews*; oil, The Kemble Family, *George Henry Marlow*.)

Kemble, J. P. (1757–1823). An enthusiastic, but never a great actor, who played Brutus, Coriolanus, Hamlet, Henry V, Hotspur, King John, King Lear, Leontes, Macbeth, Othello, Posthumous, and was well regarded. One of twelve children, four of whom became theatrically famous. Partnered his sister, Sarah Siddons, in several Shakespeare plays. Manager of Drury Lane, Covent Garden. Pioneered historically 'correct' costume. (Oil, head and shoulders, *Thomas Lawrence*; oil, portrait, *Anon.*)

Kemble, Stephen (1758–1822). One of Kemble family who acted but did not triumph. 'His obesity was so great that he played Falstaff without stuffing . . . the effect was more painful than amusing . . . He used to say to an author, "D——n your dialogue! give me the situations!"' (J. R. Planché, *Recollections and Reflections*.)

Kempe, William (d. 1608). Principal actor in Shakespeare's plays, late 16th century. By tradition and scanty evidence played broad clownish parts in Shakespeare's early plays, and Dogberry. Original Globe Theatre share-holder. Left Lord Chamberlain's company, 1599. Celebrated for dancing from London to Norwich between 11 February and 11 March 1599. His name appears instead of that of the character, Dogberry, at the very end of Act II, Scene iv of *Much Ado About Nothing*.

Kendal, Dame Madge (1848–1935). One of twenty-two children of an actor-manager. Sister of T. W. Robertson, the late 19th-century 'naturalistic' dramatist. Her partnership with William Kendal was, both maritally and professionally, a success. She specialized in comedy and 'gentle' parts.

Kingsley, Mary (1862–1936). Member of Ben Greet's company and Barry Sullivan's leading lady. (Oil, half-length portrait, Kingsley as Joan of Arc (1914), *Gilbert A. Pownall*.)

Kynaston, Edward (*c.* 1645–1706). Specialized in women's parts in Restoration theatre. Played both with Killigrew's company and with Betterton, and was a notable Henry IV and Antony.

Lacy, John (d. 1681). One of the earliest Restoration adaptors of Shakespeare. Converted *The Taming of the Shrew* into *Sauny the Scot*, 1667, in which the main character becomes Grumio — played by Lacy himself. The setting is England, not Italy; and the play is in prose. This version replaced Shakespeare's until Garrick restored the original.

Langtry, Lillie (1853–1929). One of Edward VII's intimates, she was a sensation at her début in 1881 — not for her acting, but for her beauty and her audacity. Her reputation as society beauty probably encouraged her to play Cleopatra — a rare example of this particular conceit. '... to those who are inclined to be disappointed with the play after the First Act is over, I say, "wait for the end ..."' (*Punch*, 6 December 1890).

Leigh, Vivien (1913–67). Wife of Laurence Olivier. Beautiful, expertly spoken but low-keyed Shakespearean actress whose best performances were opposite her husband — i.e. as Lady Macbeth and Lavinia. Her Viola was visually exquisite.

Lowin, John (1576–1653). With the King's Men in 1603. Housekeeper of Globe and/or Blackfriars. A very large man, who probably played Falstaff.

McCarthy, Lillah (1875–1960). Hermione, Viola, Helena, were her best Shakespearean roles. Married to H. Granville-Barker, she created several of Shaw's heroines. Member of Ben Greet's company.

Macklin, Charles (1700–97). Famous, intemperate, Irish actor — rival of Garrick. Memorable Iago but his Shylock more important — played him not in the then customary comic way but as a tragic villain. This performance, by report, reduced George II to frightened insomnia. 'The voice of the actor must alter in its intonations, according to the qualities that the words express: from this idea music seems to have taken its birth. The number seven harmonizes in music, and so it does in acting.' (Macklin, *The Art and Duty of an Actor* 1799.) 'Charles Macklin ... was the only player I ever heard of that made acting a science.' (Thomas Davies.)

Macready, William Charles (1793–1873). One of 19th century's most effective actors (e.g. Benedick, Coriolanus, Hamlet, Henry IV, Henry V, Iachimo, Lear, Macbeth, Othello, Richard III, Romeo), actor-manager, and creator of visually spectacular productions. 'Acted Hamlet really with particular care, energy and discrimination; the audience gave less applause to the first soliloquy than I am in the habit of receiving ...' (Macready's Diaries.) '... the only perfect picture that we have had of Lear since the age of Betterton.' (Charles Dickens in *The Examiner*, 4 February 1838.) (Oil, Macready as Macbeth, *John Jackson*; plaster bust, *Peter Hollins*.)

Mansfield, Richard (1857–1907). American actor, born Berlin. Played Richard III in London and Henry V in New York — riding a real horse at Agincourt. A typically 'romantic' actor.

Marlowe, Julia (1865–1950). Played Viola, Juliet, Rosalind, Ophelia, Lady Macbeth. American actress, born England. Excelled as Cleopatra. 'Great acting then does not depend upon the voice solely ... There is grandeur in stillness, and it is the eye that is the mind's signal ...' (Marlowe on Cibber, Garrick, Kean, Kemble, etc., in *The Eloquence of Silence*, 1913.)

Martin-Harvey, Sir John (1863–1944). Famous actor-manager. Protégé and follower of Irving, at Lyceum Theatre. Outstanding Hamlet, Richard III and proficient all-rounder in Shakespeare's major roles. Tireless tourer in USA and Canada, and provincial theatres, and did much to popularize classical and modern drama. (Oil, Martin-Harvey as Richard III, *Bernard Munns*.)

Modjeska, Helena (1844–1909). Polish actress, emigrated to California, became a leading actress in the USA for nearly thirty years. Noted for performance of Juliet to Forbes-Robertson's Romeo, though some found the experience a strain because of her accent. She was, however, an actress of subtle intelligence and her physical technique was superbly disciplined and modulated to the requirements of character. (Oil, portrait (1880), *Johnston Forbes-Robertson*.)

Neilson, Adelaide (1846–80). English born: huge success in Shakespeare's tragic parts, particularly Juliet, in the USA. Her poverty-stricken upbringing probably intensified her tragic impact. (Oil, portrait, *Thomas Benjamin Kennington*.)

Neilson, Julia (1868–1957). Married Fred, brother of Ellen Terry, and collaborated with him in theatre management. A famous Rosalind.

Olivier, Laurence, Baron (1907–   ). Excelled as Romeo, Mercutio, Hamlet, Belch, Macbeth, Titus, Othello, Coriolanus, Hotspur, Shallow Henry V, Richard III. With John Gielgud represents the highest achievement of 20th century in Shakespearean acting. Artistic director of Chichester and National Theatres; outstanding director of Shakespeare on film. Huge repertoire outside Shakespeare. Acting characterized by meticulous attention to detail, and naturalism of voice and gesture which is, at best, judiciously allowed to soar into lyrical and ritualistic patterns. His *Henry V*, *Richard III* and *Hamlet* most successful of all 20th-century translation of Shakespeare to film. 'If we did not know Olivier to be a great actor by other tests we should know it from the manner of his deaths.' (Redgrave, *The Stanislavsky Myth*, 1946.) (Oil, Olivier as 1955 Macbeth (1956), *Ruskin Spear*.)

O'Neill, Eliza (1791–1872). Irish actress who played Juliet, Isabella. Regarded as Sarah Siddons's successor. 'To her might justly be ascribed the negative praise, in my mind the highest commendation that, as an artist, man or woman can receive, of a total absence of any approach to affectation.' (Charles Macready, *Reminiscences*.)

Ostler, Will(iam) (d. 1614). Member of King's Company by 1610. Began career as a child-actor.

Palmer, John (1744–98). An extravaganza, as man and actor. Succeeded as Shakespeare's less reliable citizens — Toby Belch and Iago. He was, as an actor, a 'gentleman with a slight infusion of the footman'. (Charles Lamb.)

Phelps, Samuel (1804–78). Played Antony, Armado, Bottom, Coriolanus, Lear, Macbeth, Hamlet, Malvolio, Pericles, Shallow (*Henry IV*),
Sly, Timon. Associated with Macready. Manager of Sadlers Wells.
Produced thirty-four of Shakespeare's plays. Careful attitude to texts
and sets. As actor limited in intelligence but assiduous in intention. As
director, visually sensitive and careful in training of young actors and
actresses. (Oil, full-length portrait, Phelps as Hamlet, *Nicholas Joseph
Crowley*.)

Phillips, Augustine (d. 1605). One of the leading actors in Lord
Chamberlain's Company. In his will he left £5 to be distributed among
his fellows — including Shakespeare.

Pope, Thomas (d. *c.* 1603). Founder-member of Chamberlain's Company. Believed to have played sophisticated comic roles in Shakespeare's
plays.

Pritchard, Hannah (1711–68). Second only to Sarah Siddons in the
power of her interpretation of Lady Macbeth. Associate of Quin.

Quayle, Anthony (1913–   ). Arguably one of the most underrated
directors, and possibly actors, of the century. Acted at the Old Vic,
subsequently became artistic director of the then Shakespeare Memorial
Theatre at Stratford (1948–56). Excellent Pandarus, Bottom, Aaron,
Falstaff. His productions marked by rich sense of visual and aural
poetry. He steered the Stratford theatre through a difficult post-war
period and extended its range by tours to Australia and New Zealand.
(Oil, Quayle as 1951 Falstaff, *William Dobell*.)

Quin, James (1693–1766). Played Falstaff, Ghost (*Hamlet*), Othello,
Richard III, Brutus, Coriolanus, Lear, Macbeth. Star of Covent
Garden; Garrick's rival. Old-style actor, much given to 'saw the air'
and 'mouth his words'. Garrick's epitaph adorns his tomb in Bath
Abbey. 'If this young fellow is right, then we have all been wrong.'
(Quin on Garrick's sensational début as Richard III.)

Redgrave, Sir Michael (1908–   ). One of England's most distinguished actors at the Old Vic, Stratford and many provincial theatres.
A notable Hamlet, Benedick, Hotspur, Shylock, and an intellectually
interesting but over-emotive Macbeth. One of the century's finest
theorists of the art of acting. 'There are in England today, roughly
speaking, two styles of acting: the acting in which the effect springs
from the cause, and that which begins with effect and which rarely, and
only in part, seeks the cause. The latter style is very much the pre-
ponderant. It is very seldom we see a production in which more than a
few actors are faithful to the author, the director and their artistic
conscience.' (Redgrave, *The Stanislavsky Myth*, 1946.)

Rehan, Ada (1860–1916). Played Juliet, Rosalind, Katharine (*Shrew*),
Viola. A leading Shakespearean in the USA. Born in Ireland and played
in Newark (N.J.), Philadelphia, Louisville, Baltimore, with Edwin

Booth. Also London, Berlin, Paris, New York, San Francisco. Noted for comic parts. (Oil, three-quarter length portrait, Rehan as Katharine (*Shrew*), *Eliot Gregory*; bronze bust, Rehan as 1887 Katharine, *J. S. Hartley*.)

Rice, John (*fl.* 1607–30). By 1607 was apprentice actor of King's Men. Appears in actor's list appended to First Folio.

Richardson, Sir Ralph (1902–   ). Played Macbeth, Prospero, Caliban, Henry V, Iago, Enobarbus. Memorable as greatest Falstaff of 20th century.

Robinson, Richard (d. 1640). Principal actor in Shakespeare's plays in 17th century. Probably married Richard Burbage's widow.

Sanderson, Mary (d. 1712). Wife and stage-partner of Thomas Betterton. One of the first professional actresses in England; in Davenant's company. Played Ophelia, Lady Macbeth, Juliet and, as Betterton's wife, was first lady of stage. Like her husband's, her acting characterized by strong and controlled sense of reality.

Scofield, Paul (1922–   ). A product of the Birmingham Repertory Theatre, one of the most respected actors of the middle generation in England today. His Armado, Mercutio, Aguecheek and Pericles established his reputation which was enhanced by his Hamlet (in London and Moscow) and his Macbeth and King Lear at Stratford — though in all three cases it is arguable whether the result confirmed the expectations. (Body colour, gouache, Scofield as 1948 Clown (*The Winter's Tale*), *Laura Knight*.)

Shank, John (d. 1636). Principal actor in Shakespeare's plays in 17th century. Possibly replaced Armin as chief comedian of King's Company, 1615.

Siddons, Sarah (1755–1831). Perhaps greatest Shakespearean actress in history. Member of Kemble family. Unsuccessful beginning as touring player. Most famous parts, Desdemona, Ophelia, Volumnia and, above all, Lady Macbeth. Dr Johnson's signature was written on hem of gown she wears in Reynolds's painting of her as the Tragic Muse. 'Mrs Siddons' . . . performances were, in the strict sense of the word, excellent, while the two treatises she has left upon the characters of Queen Constance and Lady Macbeth — two of her finest parts — are feeble . . . The reflective and analytical quality has little to do with the complex process of acting.' (Fanny Kemble, *On the Stage*, 1863.) (Miniature, watercolour on ivory (1784), *Horace Hone*; plaster bust, Siddons as the tragic muse (1812), *Joachim Smith*.)

Sincklo (or Sincler), John (*fl.* 1590–1604). Probably member of Chamberlain's Company. His name appears in a stage direction of *Henry VI, Part 3*, in the Induction to *The Taming of the Shrew* and in the Quarto *Henry IV, Part 2*. Said to have been remarkably thin and played Pinch and Shadow.

Sly, William (d. 1608). Member of Chamberlain's Company, 1594–1605. Versatile actor of plays by Jonson, Marston. Possibly acted Tybalt, Hotspur, Laertes, Macduff and Edmund. Portrait exists at Dulwich College.

Sothern, Edward Hugh (1859–1933). American actor — husband and partner of Julia Marlowe. His Malvolio distinguished by an attempt to make the character sympathetic. Also played Hamlet. He and his wife presented sets, props and costumes for a performance at the then Stratford Memorial Theatre in 1924.

Stirling, Mary Anne (1815–95). English actress. In Drury Lane played Beatrice, Celia, Cordelia (to Macready's Lear). In 1882 the Nurse in Irving's *Romeo and Juliet*. (Oil on canvas, unfinished portrait, *Henry Wyndham Phillips*; oil, Mrs Stirling as Nurse (*Romeo and Juliet*) (1884), *Anna Lea Merritt*.)

Sullivan, Barry (1821–91). Irish actor. Played Hamlet and Benedick to Helen Faucit's Beatrice at opening of Memorial Theatre, Stratford, 1879. A vigorous actor who played more than 300 Shakespeare roles. (Oil, portrait, *Anon.*)

Swinley, Ion (1891–1937). Unfulfilled, because of his untimely death, Shakespearean actor, generally accepted as in first rank. His Hamlet, Henry V and Romeo highly regarded.

Tarlton, Richard (d. 1588). Popular comedian and particular favourite of Queen Elizabeth. Man of many accomplishments — dancer, singer, droll and joke-cracker. Sentiment and tradition sees him as source of Yorick in *Hamlet*.

Terriss, William (1847–97). Sometimes known as William Lewin. Started career as sailor, then tried medicine, then engineering. Took up acting, was engaged by Bancroft, was unsuccessful, then bred sheep and tamed wild horses in Falkland Islands. Returned to England to great success — played opposite Ellen Terry and Adelaide Neilson, and joined Irving's company. An actor of great charm with a racy technique. Killed by a lunatic outside Adelphi Theatre, to the general grief.

Terry, Ellen (1847–1928). Notable Beatrice, Imogen, Juliet, Portia, Puck, Viola, Arthur (*King John*), Ophelia, Cordelia, Lady Macbeth, Volumnia. Vies with Sarah Siddons for accolade as greatest Shake-spearean actress. Well known in the USA. Mother of Gordon Craig, the stage-designer. 'Imagination! Imagination! I put it first years ago when I was asked what qualities I thought necessary for success upon the stage. And I am still of the same opinion. Imagination, industry, and intelligence — "the three I's" — are all indispensable to the actress, but of these three the greatest is, without any doubt, imagination.' (Oil, profile head, *James Ware*; miniature watercolour on ivory, Terry as Cordelia, *Mrs Norman Grosvenor*; marble bust (1879), *William Brodie*; watercolour sketch, Terry and Irving, 'Death of Ophelia' (1892), *Bernard Partridge*.)

Thorndike, Dame Sybil (1882–1976). Played many of Shakespeare's heroines, including Lady Macbeth, and (during wartime) a number of his male roles — Fool (*Lear*), Gobbo, Ferdinand, Popular, mannered, elocutionary. The last female example of the old barnstorming school, but rightly honoured for her dedication to bringing Shakespeare to a wide audience.

Tooley, Nicholas (*c.* 1575–1623). Principal actor in Shakespeare's plays late 16th century, early 17th century. Witness of Burbage's will.

Tree, Beerbohm (1853–1917). Played Falstaff, Benedick, Prospero, Malvolio, Macbeth, Othello. Popular actor-manager at Haymarket and Her Majesty's theatres. Noted for opulent productions, mauled texts and 'personality' acting. 'Take the famous "For God's sake let us sit upon the ground, and tell sad stories of the death of kings". My sole recollection . . . is that . . . sitting in the stalls . . . a paper was passed to me. I opened it and read: "If you will rise and move a resolution, I will second it."' (Bernard Shaw plus friend on a performance of Tree.)

Underwood, John (d. 1624). One of principal actors of Shakespeare's plays late 16th, early 17th centuries. Had shares in Globe and Black-friars theatres.

Vanbrugh, Violet (1867–1942). Played Portia, Lady Macbeth. Played opposite Irving, and also Bourchier whom she married. The Vanbrugh Theatre at the Royal Academy of Dramatic Art is named for her and her sister. (Oil, portrait as Lady Macbeth sleepwalking (1906), *Charles A. Buchel*.)

Verbruggen, Susanna (d. 1703). Played opposite Betterton. Married to the actor, John Verbruggen.

Vestris, Lucia Elizabeth (1797–1856). Born London, of Italian extraction. Operatic star who played Ariel to Macready's Prospero. (Oil, full-front, *Alfred Edward Chanon*; miniature, watercolour on ivory, *Alfred Edward Chalon*.)

Waller, Lewis (1860–1915). English actor, associated with Beerbohm Tree. Matinée idol for his good looks and 'heroic' aspect and voice. Both his production of the play and his performance of Henry V memorable. Recordings of some of his speeches are still commercially available. (Oil, Waller as Henry V (1900), *Arthur Hacker*; sculpture, Waller as Brutus.)

Ward, Genevieve (1837–1922). Born New York. Both opera singer and tragedienne. Sang at La Scala and, after straining her voice by over-exposure of it in Paris, London and New York, turned actress. Played opposite Irving and Benson. (Oil, three-quarter length portrait (1906), *Hugh Goldwin Rivière*.)

Welles, Orson (1915–   ). Energetic, unpredictable, sincere and generally 'way-out' director and actor of the plays, mostly on film. *Macbeth*, *Othello* and *King Lear* are his best-known versions of Shakespeare. His films are characterized by heavy cutting, visual extravagance, sometimes eccentric characterization and occasional flashes of insight and poetry.

Wilks, Robert (1665–1732). Popular and very talented actor both in tragedy and comedy who triumphed as Hamlet, Othello and Macduff. Instrumental in reviving the fortunes of Drury Lane at the beginning of the 18th century.

Woffington, Margaret (Peg) (*c.* 1714–60). Restoration actress whose contemporary fame shaded into notoriety. Garrick's mistress and a warm-hearted general benefactress. Played Portia, Rosalind, Viola, Helena, Constance.

Wolfit, Sir Donald (1902–68). Last great actor-manager. A passionate 'loner' and dedicated 'personality' actor. Toured England and abroad with own company. Memorable as disseminator of Shakespeare's plays to wide audience and for his emotional and exhausting Lear. Also a notable Hamlet, Cassius, Claudius.

Young, Charles Mayne (1777–1856). Cassius, Prospero, were his main triumphs. Succeeded Kemble as the leading tragic actor of the time. His Cassius was played to Kemble's Brutus and he later played King John in the extraordinary 'naturalistic' version of the play (by Charles Kemble) in 1823.

SHAKESPEARE ON FILM

The filming of Shakespeare's plays has been a mixed blessing. The advantages and disadvantages, as far as both intention and methods are concerned, weigh so evenly, that they can neither be wholeheartedly dismissed nor wholeheartedly approved.

In intention, film directors veer between two extremes. On the one hand are those who seek to make a studied record of a particular production or actor. In this category is, amongst others, Forbes-Robertson's playing of Hamlet, filmed just before his retirement in 1913, a good example in silent film of an older more flamboyant style of acting, each movement and gesture heavy with meaning and implication. In 1965 the National Theatre's production of *Othello*, with Laurence Olivier's interpretation of Othello as a negro, was filmed, which set out deliberately to 'preserve and enhance' the *Othello* that one might have seen any night at the National. Peter Brook's filming of *King Lear* in 1968/9 was also based on a stage production he had given at Stratford upon Avon for the Royal Shakespeare Company in 1962. Both stage and film productions had Paul Scofield in the lead, Irene Worth as Goneril and Alan Webb as Kent, but the film itself was taken out of the theatre and its confines, to a rough castle on location in Denmark. The producer was Michael Birkett, who also produced Peter Hall's *A Midsummer Night's Dream* (see below), and he built on what he had learned from filming that play, particularly as far as linking Shakespeare's speeches with screen pictures is concerned. However, as with Hall's *Dream*, the advantages of using actors who already know the play and a particular interpretation of it, and who had recently played together in it, are perceptible. There is a kind of easy familiarity with the text and the aims of the production, that give the film power and drive.

At the other extreme are cinematic versions that completely reinterpret the play. The best of the earliest examples of this is Max Reinhardt's *A Midsummer Night's Dream*, 1935, where a pretty fairy world is expressed in Isadora Duncan-type dancing, all to Mendelssohn's music, with a few grotesque Disney effects thrown in — to modern taste oversweet and sentimental. More recently (1965) there is Orson Welles's *Chimes at Midnight* the 'story of a betrayal of friendship', in which Welles, taking extracts from all the plays in which Falstaff appears, explores Falstaff's relationship with Prince Hal. The result is both moving and more to modern taste.

Each of these extremes can be equally, if differently, bizarre. The first can produce a stiff, stifled version, that seems cramped on the screen. The National Theatre *Othello* suffers in this way, as well as from the over-large performance of Olivier, perfectly suited to a stage and auditorium, but overbearing on the screen. The second can be so free-ranging that the original text is lost sight of altogether and the name of Shakespeare becomes a mere courtesy title. Much depends on the integrity and knowledge of the film director involved.

As far as methods are concerned, again, filming has great advantages as well as disadvantages. Vast panoramas, large armies confronting each other, are impossible on the stage — even a mob may seem less menacing because of the smallness of its numbers. The sense of awe and dread, occasioned by state ritual (visualized in banners, flags or other heraldic devices), by large opposing armies (whether in civil strife or invading forces), when presented on screen, have an effect that is merciless, because it seems so totally inevitable. This can offset, with biting irony, the smaller confrontations — of, for example, king with noble, father with son. So the relationship, implicit in Shakespeare's plays, between the general and the particular, the group and the individual, the great and the small, can be more forcefully and obviously, even if less subtly, depicted on the screen.

Where, however, words are involved, problems arise. Long speeches sit ill with mobile screen effects, and the very density of Shakespeare's language, rich with the imagery and the evocations of poetry, is alien to film techniques and to a lot of cinema-goers alike. The easiest and most obvious way of dealing with it is, of course, to cut, leaving the visual to replace the verbal. This is seldom wholly satisfying. One of the happiest marriages of meaning with visual expression is Olivier's *Henry V*, 1944. Here the film starts boldly, recording a presentation of the play as it might have been acted in Shakespeare's day at the Globe Theatre. Gradually, almost imperceptibly, the imperfect Elizabethan actors fade into 'real' people and the play takes wing with a kind of flourish and immediacy that is most compelling. In the presentation of the Battle of Agincourt, with the charge of the French knights and the onslaught of the English bowmen, backed superbly by William Walton's music, Olivier provides the exciting visual highpoint of the film. On stage the full battle has of necessity to be omitted — only the preparations for battle, a brief suggestion of the battle itself and the aftermath can be offered to the audience. Olivier's filmed battle sequence richly realizes this turning point in the play.

In his three films, *Henry V*, *Hamlet*, 1948 and *Richard III*, 1955, Olivier, bringing with him his own actor's intimate knowledge of the plays and their effects, explores various methods of filming Shakespeare. Each style is suited to the demands of the play chosen — wide, panoramic, heroic, colourful, for *Henry V*; intense, claustrophobic, precise for *Hamlet* (in black

and white); and hypnotic, confidential for *Richard III*. In his filming
Olivier shows a sensitivity in dealing with the text, and a subtlety of
acting (he himself plays Henry, Hamlet and Richard), which catches the
audience's imagination, and, as a result, has made these films deservedly
popular.

Orson Welles is another actor who has directed Shakespeare on film and
played the title roles — *Macbeth*, 1948, *Othello*, 1952 and *Chimes at Midnight*, 1965. Each bears the stamp of his personality, with the text cut and
rearranged to subserve the meaning Welles wished to extract from the
play. *Othello*, for example, opens with a sequence showing the funeral
cortège of the dead Othello and his bride, watched over by a caged Iago.
Macbeth, on the other hand, was a kind of essay in filming Shakespeare,
completed in twenty-three days, and the vivid wayward adaptation gives
the play a unique quality making it seem timeless, belonging to no particular place or period.

On the other hand, films like Franco Zeffirelli's *The Taming of the Shrew*,
1966 and his *Romeo and Juliet*, 1968, and Peter Hall's *A Midsummer Night's
Dream* seem to emanate from the location chosen. An opulent sense of
Renaissance Italy enriches Zeffirelli's films, with the décor and the
players chosen for their likeness to 16th-century Italian places and people.
Sadly, in choosing to emphasize action and appearance, Zeffirelli left
what remained of the poetry to look after itself. Hall's *A Midsummer Night's
Dream* is set in a wet, windy, autumnal wood in Warwickshire and acted
by a company which had already presented it on stage; it chills and
amuses rather than charms. Its 'erotic, physical, down-to-earth flavour'
contrasts sharply with the earlier, cleaner, Reinhardt sweetness. However
the text is complete, and all the players good in their roles. Only the
camera, at times, betrays a restless fussiness. This style of emphasized
naturalism seems as fitting for the *Dream* as Welles's poetic limbo is for
Macbeth, and since the canon of Shakespeare's plays is so large and varied,
it may well be possible for any director to choose the play he feels at home
with, whose idiom his style of directing may best convey.

The text problems are even greater, of course, when filming Shakespeare's plays in a foreign language. However meticulously translated, the
play loses some of its original strength, so that (as in the Russian films,
where Pasternak is often the translator) the heightened prose that takes
over from the poetry can only be an approximation, and the new text lacks
the unifying effect that Shakespeare's own language has on his plays. Very
often, to replace this, to give the play a unified coherence, the director
interprets the play in terms of his own country's cultural attitudes and
filming techniques. Of *Hamlet*, for example, the Russian director Kozintsev
states, '. . . the general theme of Shakespeare is the fate of humanity in the
condition of society based on inhuman conditions', and he saw his task as
changing 'the poetical imagery of the work into the visual' with that

belief in mind. Similarly, of Kozintsev's interpretation of *Lear*, made in 1970, Roger Manvell writes, it 'is concerned with a civilization which is crumbling through the evils of inequality and injustice . . . As he [Lear] draws nearer to the poorest of his subjects, his wisdom develops, and he learns the true nature of society.'

The Japanese director, Kurosawa, in his film based on *Macbeth*, called *Kumonosu-Djo* ('the castle of the spider's web') — subtitled in English *The Throne of Blood* — reveals a similar approach. The film takes over much of the story of *Macbeth*, but places it in 16th-century Japan using older Japanese dramatic forms and myths, familiar to a Japanese audience. He then expresses the whole in peculiarly Japanese film terms, with slow-moving close-ups, exaggerated gestures, deliberate facial movements, and a mannered way of moving (Macbeth), contrasted with a suppression of reaction and facial expression, making both face and body like masks hiding unfathomable thoughts (Lady Macbeth). In fact, he transmutes *Macbeth* into a new experience, often to Western eyes odd and alien, but quite as hypnotic, quite as frightening, as the original.

This variety in the filming of Shakespeare bodes well for the future, both for the cinema, and for the more recent new medium, television, and of course, not only in English-speaking countries, but throughout the world. For, as Roger Manvell writes in his excellent book, *Shakespeare and the Film*, 1971:

> By these means new significance can be found in familiar words and another dimension of thought and feeling be added to our cumulative interpretation of the plays. If the film as a virtually new medium for their presentation, can in any way help expand the recognition of what still lies to be discovered in Shakespeare's writing, it will have made its contribution.

Films of Shakespeare's Plays

TITLE	LOCATION	COMPANY	DIRECTOR
As You Like It (1936)	Great Britain	Inter-Allied Film	Paul Czinner
Hamlet (1948)	Great Britain	Two Cities Films	Laurence Olivier
Hamlet (1964)	USSR	Lenfilm	Grigori Kozintsev
Hamlet (1969)	Great Britain	Woodfall	Tony Richardson
Henry V (1944)	Great Britain	Two Cities Films	Laurence Olivier
Julius Caesar (1953)	USA	MGM	Joseph L. Mankiewicz
Julius Caesar (1969)	Great Britain	Commonwealth United	Stuart Burge
King Lear (1970)	USSR	Lenfilm	Grigori Kozintsev
King Lear (1969/70)	Denmark	Athena-Laterna Films	Peter Brook

TITLE	LOCATION	COMPANY	DIRECTOR
Macbeth (1948)	USA	Republic Pictures and Mercury Films	Orson Welles
Macbeth (1960)	Great Britain	Grand Prize Films	George Schaefer
A Midsummer Night's Dream (1935)	USA	Warner Brothers	Max Reinhardt, William Dieterle
A Midsummer Night's Dream (1969)	Great Britain	Royal Shakespeare Theatre and Alan Clore	Peter Hall
Othello (1952)	Morocco	Mogador-Films (Mercury)	Orson Welles
Othello (1955)	USSR	Mosfilm	Sergei Yutkevitch
Othello (1965)	Great Britain	BHE	Stuart Burge
Richard III (1955)	Great Britain	London Films	Laurence Olivier
Romeo and Juliet (1936)	USA	MGM	George Cukor
Romeo and Juliet (1954)	Great Britain	Verona Productions	Renato Castellani
Romeo and Juliet (1968)	Great Britain/ Italy	BHE (London) Verona Productions	Franco Zeffirelli
The Taming of the Shrew (1929)	USA	Pickford Corporation	Sam Taylor
The Taming of the Shrew (1966)	USA/Italy	——	Production: Richard Burton, Elizabeth Taylor, Franco Zeffirelli
The Winter's Tale (1966)	Great Britain	Cressida/Hurst Park	Frank Dunlop

Films Based on Plays of Shakespeare

Chimes at Midnight (1965)	Spain/ Switzerland	International Films Espagnol	Orson Welles
Kumonosu-Djo: The Throne of Blood (1957)	Japan	Toho	Akira Kurosawa

SHAKESPEARE AND MUSIC

There is no doubt that music affected Shakespeare. His constant, always commendatory, references to it, and its effects, are present throughout his plays and poems. 'If music be the food of love', cries Orsino in *Twelfth Night*, obviously believing that it is the chief nourisher in life's feast; the 'man that hath no music in himself/Nor it not moved by the concord of sweet sounds' is, according to Lorenzo in *The Merchant of Venice*, only 'fit for treasons, strategems and spoils'; in *The Tempest*, Prospero's island is alive with 'sounds and sweet airs', that pacify the monster, Caliban, and it is the unseen Ariel's songs, pipe and tabor, that entice the newcomers about the island. Shakespeare, also, frequently uses music as a basis of comparison. Hamlet, for example, accuses Guildenstern of trying to play upon him as he would on the stops of a musical instrument; and the most famous of all images that condenses into a phrase the message of the whole range of his history plays — be they Roman or English — is contained in a metaphor from music: 'Untune that string and hark what discord follows.'

Considering then the constant references to music, it is not surprising that Shakespeare often gave occasion for the actual use of music. Sometimes it is merely briefly indicated by a line or refrain — Ophelia's mad songs in *Hamlet* illustrate this; sometimes he calls for songs that were popular in his own day — Autolycus' songs belong here (*The Winter's Tale*). Others, however, are not only given occasion, but Shakespeare himself provides the words. Often these have come to us as poems complete in themselves — 'Where the bee sucks' (*The Tempest*), 'Blow, blow, thou winter wind' (*As You Like It*). Some are ornaments to the text, perhaps bringing the play to a fitting conclusion as in the nostalgic 'When that I was but a little tiny boy', sung as a finale to *Twelfth Night* by the Fool, Feste, or the two extremes of Spring and Winter, the cuckoo's and the owl's songs, at the end of *Love's Labour's Lost*. Some, however, are an integral part of the play itself, reflecting the action or implementing the mood at a particular point. The songs 'Blow, blow, thou winter wind' and 'Under the greenwood tree' catch the atmosphere and mood of winter and summer in a pastoral world. Similarly, Pandarus' 'Love, love, nothing but love' arises naturally at that point in the play and reflects both Pandarus' sycophantic nature, and the cynical attitude towards love that suffuses *Troilus and Cressida*. Even the song that accompanies Bassanio's choice of casket in *The Merchant of Venice* may be purposeful, for all its rhymes, 'bred', 'head', 'nourishèd', hint fairly forcibly to Bassanio — choose the *lead* casket.

The kinds of songs that were undoubtedly popular in the 16th and 17th centuries are frequent — for example, the songs brought by ballad mongers and pedlars to be sold at fairs (Autolycus in *The Winter's Tale*); songs for convivial occasions — Iago's drinking song (*Othello*) or the rowdy round perpetrated by Sir Toby Belch and his companions (*Twelfth Night*); songs to arouse love — the serenade to a 'mistress's eyebrows' — used in *The Two Gentlemen of Verona* ('Who is Sylvia?'); or to evoke sleep — the lullaby, 'Ye spotted snakes' in *A Midsummer Night's Dream*. In both *As You Like It* and *The Tempest* there are masques in the play itself, which give suitable occasion for music and elaborate décor, the pattern of verse here being particularly suited for use with music, or even to being sung.

For some of these songs there are still in existence settings contemporary, or nearly contemporary, with Shakespeare. The following composers wrote settings for various songs which are still extant:

Thomas Ford (1580–1648)	'Sigh no more, ladies'	*Much Ado About Nothing*
John Hilton (1599–1657)	'What shall he have . . .'	*As You Like It*
Robert Johnson (*c.* 1583/5– *c.* 1633/4)	'Where the bee sucks' 'Full fathom five'	*The Tempest* *The Tempest*
Robert Jones (*c.* 1575–1615)	'Farewell, dear heart'	*Twelfth Night*
Thomas Morley (b. 1557)	'It was a lover and his lass' 'O Mistress mine'	*As You Like It* *Twelfth Night*
John Wilson (1595–1674) (poss. Jack Wilson, the actor)	'Lawn white as driven snow' 'Take, O take those lips away'	*The Winter's Tale* *Measure for Measure*

In the 17th century music was often added to the plays, sometimes taking over the original and wholly destroying it. Davenant's production of *Macbeth*, which began with the mere addition of music in 1663, later developed into an 'opera', with a complete musical score. Similarly *The Tempest* was produced in 'operatic' form, arranged by Thomas Shadwell, with music by John Banister and Pelham Humfrey. Henry Purcell himself provided the music for a masque that Thomas Shadwell added to a production of *Timon of Athens* in 1678, and also for *The Fairy Queen*, a version of *A Midsummer Night's Dream*, produced in 1692. There is even a recitative setting by a musician, Morelli, employed by Pepys as a music master, with a guitar accompaniment, for Hamlet's soliloquy, 'To be or not to be'.

Finally, of course, a great many composers have been stimulated by Shakespeare's plays, either making new works out of them (operas, for example), or expressing characters or areas of a play in musical terms, or writing incidental music for a particular play or performance. The following is a list (by century and alphabetically by the composer's name) of the most famous who have written music for, or about some aspect of, a play:

18th Century

ARNE, DR THOMAS   Settings for many songs; incidental music for the masque in *The Tempest* (1746).

SCARLATTI, DOMENICO   Opera based on *Hamlet* (1715).

19th Century

BEETHOVEN, LUDVIG VON   Overture — *Coriolan* (1807).

BELLINI, VINCENZO   Opera based on *Romeo and Juliet* (1830).

BERLIOZ, HECTOR   Dramatic Fantasia on *The Tempest* (1830); overture to *King Lear* (1831); symphony — *Romeo and Juliet* (1839); Ballade sur la mort d'Ophélie et marche funèbre pour la dernière scene d'*Hamlet* (1848); opera — *Béatrice et Bénédict*, based on *Much Ado About Nothing* (1862).

BRAHMS, JOHANNES   Song — 'Come away, Death' (*Twelfth Night*); five of Ophelia's songs (*Hamlet*).

DVOŘÁK, ANTON   Overture — *Othello* (1891).

GERMAN, EDWARD   Symphonic poem — *Hamlet* (1897); dances for *Henry VIII* (1889–98); incidental music for *Richard III*, *Romeo and Juliet*, *As You Like It* and *Much Ado About Nothing*.

LISZT, FRANZ   Symphonic poem — *Hamlet* (1861).

MENDELSSOHN, FELIX   Music for *A Midsummer Night's Dream* (1826–43).

ROSSINI, GIOACCHINO   Opera — *Othello* (1816).

SCHUBERT, FRANZ   Setting of 'When that I was and a little tiny boy'; 'Who is Sylvia?'; 'Hark, hark the lark' (*Twelfth Night*).

SMETANA, BEDRICH   Opera — *Viola* — based on *Twelfth Night* (1884); symphonic poem — *Richard III* (1862).

STRAUSS, RICHARD   Tone poem — *Macbeth* (1890).

SULLIVAN, ARTHUR   Incidental music — *The Tempest* (1872); scores for *The Merchant of Venice*, *The Merry Wives of Windsor*, *Henry VIII*, *Timon of Athens*, *Macbeth*.

TCHAIKOVSKY, PETER ILYICH   Fantasy — *The Tempest* (1873); overture — fantasy — *Romeo and Juliet* (1880); music for *Hamlet* (1891).

VERDI, GUISEPPE   Operas — *Macbetto* (1847); *Otello* (1887); *Falstaff* (1893).

WAGNER, RICHARD   *Das Liebesverbot*, after *Measure for Measure* (1835/6).

WEBER, CARL MARIA VON   'Tell me where is fancy bred' (*The Merchant of Venice*), a setting for voices and guitar (1821); opera — *Oberon* — based on *A Midsummer Night's Dream* (1826).

20th Century

BRITTEN, BENJAMIN   *Rape of Lucretia* — based loosely on *Lucrece* (1946); opera — *A Midsummer Night's Dream* (1960).

COPLAND, AARON   Music for Orson Welles's production *Five Kings* (1939).

DEBUSSY, CLAUDE   Music for *King Lear* (1904).

DELIUS, FREDERICK   *A Village Romeo and Juliet*, based on *Romeo and Juliet* (1907).

ELGAR, SIR EDWARD   Symphonic study — *Falstaff* (1913).

HENGGER, ARTHUR   Overture, prelude and songs for *The Tempest* (1923).

HUMPERDINCK, ENGELBERT   Music for *The Merchant of Venice, Romeo and Juliet, The Tempest, Twelfth Night, The Winter's Tale, As You Like It* (1905–7).

IRELAND, JOHN   Setting for 'When daffodils begin to peer' (*The Winter's Tale*); incidental music for *Julius Caesar* (1942).

KHACHATURIAN, ARAM   Music for *Macbeth*.

ORFF, CARL   Various sets of incidental music for *A Midsummer Night's Dream* (1939).

PROKOFIEFF, SERGEI   Ballet — *Romeo and Juliet* (1934).

SHOSTAKOVICH, DMITRI   Songs and incidental music for *Hamlet* (1931/2).

SIBELIUS, JEAN   Songs and incidental music for *Twelfth Night* (1909).

VAUGHAN WILLIAMS, RALPH   *Sir John in Love* (*The Merry Wives of Windsor*) (1929); many settings for the songs; Serenade to Music (Act V, *The Merchant of Venice*) (1938).

WALTON, WILLIAM   Scores for Laurence Olivier's films of *Henry V* (1944); and *Hamlet* (1947).

Also

COLE PORTER   *Kiss Me Kate*, based on *The Taming of the Shrew*.

RODGERS (RICHARD) AND HART (THOMAS)   *The Boys from Syracuse*, based on *The Comedy of Errors*.

III The Works

His beauty shall in these black lines be seen
And they shall live, and he, in them, still green.
(Sonnet 63)

THE PLAYS

Plot Summaries

Plot: The outline of the play is given by act, and the synopsis follows as closely as possible the unfolding of the play itself. What the audience sees on the stage should, if the producer is true to his text, follow the lines of the synopsis.

Text: The text reference given is to the earliest known extant publication of each particular play (Q1). Where more than one quarto is listed the reason is given — e.g. Q1 may be a 'bad' quarto, i.e. unreliable. If there is no quarto publication, the play will be found printed for the first time in the First Folio (F1), 1623.

Sources: As opinions about the sources for the plots of Shakespeare's plays, or elements in them, are constantly being revised, the references given here are the most likely, important or interesting. No attempt is made to give an exhaustive list. Those curious about such matters are directed to *The Narrative and Dramatic Sources of Shakespeare*, Geoffrey Bullough, 1957–   , and *The Sources of Shakespeare's Plays*, Kenneth Muir, 1977.

In the synopses, details of the sources most common to the plays are:

1. *Holinshed.* Raphael Holinshed (c. 1529–80), *The Histories of England*, 1577. The enlarged edition, 1587, is the one probably used by Shakespeare for his English history plays.

2. *Plutarch.* Plutarch (c. AD 50–130), *Parallel Lives*, biographies of the Greeks and Romans, translated from the French version of Jacques Amyot by Sir Thomas North as *The Lives of the Noble Grecians and Romans*, 1579. Source for Shakespeare's Roman plays.

3. *Decameron.* Boccaccio's *Decameron*, collection of tales written as though told by a group taking refuge outside Florence from the plague. Used by Shakespeare for his romantic comedies. (Roman numeral = day number; Arabic numeral = story number.)

ALL'S WELL THAT ENDS WELL

Text: F1.
Source: Decameron, III, 9 or the English translation by William Painter: *The Palace of Pleasure,* 1566-7

Act I   Helena, orphaned daughter of a celebrated physician, loves Bertram, son of the Countess of Rousillon, in whose household she has been brought up. Bertram leaves to join the court of the ailing King of France, with Parolles, a worthless coward, and Lafeu, a faithful old lord. Helena follows hoping to cure the King, and so better herself.

Act II   Helena cures the King; as reward, is allowed to choose a husband from court. She chooses Bertram, who objects to such a mean alliance. The King insists. Bertram agrees to marry her, but after the ceremony, aided and abetted by Parolles, runs away to Florence.

Act III   Helena returns to Rousillon. Bertram writes that he will accept her as wife when she gets the ring, a treasured heirloom, from his finger, and bears his child. Helena, disguised as a pilgrim, sets out for Florence. There, Bertram has attempted to seduce Diana, a widow's daughter. Helena persuades her to agree to Bertram's demands, to ask for his ring and an assignation, when Helena will take her place.

Act IV   Parolles' fellow officers trick him into revealing his arrogance and cowardice. Diana gets the ring, arranges a midnight meeting. In the dark, Helena takes her place, giving Bertram a ring as a keepsake. Bertram, hearing his wife is dead, returns home.

Act V   As the Countess and Lafeu also believe Helena to be dead, Lafeu arranges a match between his daughter and Bertram. Bertram gives her the ring Helena had given him. The King, recognizing it as the one he gave Helena as a token of his protection, orders Bertram's arrest. Diana arrives in Paris, accuses Bertram of seducing her and not marrying her. Bertram seeks to disclaim her, and the King, impatient with riddles she speaks, orders her also to prison. Her mother produces 'bail' for her. The 'bail' is Helena, pregnant with Bertram's child. Bertram having had his conditions fulfilled, acquiesces happily in his marital reunion with Helena.

ANTONY AND CLEOPATRA

Text: F1.
Main Source: Plutarch.

Act I   Mark Antony, besotted with Cleopatra, Queen of Egypt, lingers in Alexandria. Learning of his wife, Fulvia's, death and of the uprising of Sextus Pompeius (great Pompey's son) against Octavius Caesar, rejecting Cleopatra's pleas, he, with Enobarbus, leaves for Rome.

Act II   Antony agrees to patch up his differences with (Octavius) Caesar by marrying Octavia, Caesar's sister. Enobarbus describes Cleopatra and life in Egypt, refusing to believe Antony will desert Cleopatra. Antony and Caesar meet with Pompey (Pompeius), settle quarrels, feasting on board Pompey's ship, where Pompey refuses the opportunity to become the master of the world by murdering his guests. Cleopatra, informed of Antony's marriage, beats the messenger.

Act III   Cleopatra, asking about Octavia, realizes she offers no competition. Antony and Octavia reach Athens, to learn that Caesar has mocked Antony and sent troops to attack Pompey. Octavia returns to Rome to heal the breach with Caesar. Antony sets off for Egypt, where he divides the Eastern provinces between Cleopatra and her children. Caesar persuades Octavia of Antony's treachery, and moves in battle-array to Actium. Antony decides, against advice, to fight Caesar at sea, where Cleopatra's ships turn tail, and Antony, following, is defeated.

Act IV   Enobarbus dejectedly goes over to Caesar who decides to meet Antony in battle. Antony at first wins, but again the Egyptians desert. Afraid, Cleopatra, with her maids, hides in her Monument, sending a message to Antony that she is dead. Antony resolves to end his life; having fallen on his sword, is taken into the Monument. There, in Cleopatra's arms, he dies.

Act V   Cleopatra, fearing to become part of a Roman triumph, receives Caesar, who leaves, thinking her safe. Cleopatra, however, arranges for asps to be brought, and attired in her royal robes, applying the asps to her breast and arm, she dies, her maids following her example. Caesar finds her, and orders that she be buried with Antony.

AS YOU LIKE IT

Text: F1.
Main source: Thomas Lodge's novel, *Rosalynde*, pub. 1590.

Act I   Orlando, deprived of his proper place by his older brother, Oliver, demands his birthright. Oliver decides to get rid of him by matching him against the killer wrestler, Charles. The match is at Duke Frederick's court, before his daughter, Celia, and niece, Rosalind. Rosalind's father is the rightful Duke, whom Frederick has banished to the Forest of Arden. Orlando wins, and is given a chain by Rosalind. They fall in love. Orlando, fearful for his life, flees for Arden. Frederick, jealous of Rosalind's growing popularity, banishes her. She leaves, disguised as a boy (Ganymede) with Celia (Aliena) as her sister, for the Forest of Arden. Touchstone, the court fool, goes with them.

Act II   In Arden. Rosalind and Celia arrive, overhearing Silvius, a young shepherd, declare to Corin, an old shepherd, his love for the disdainful Phebe. Orlando arrives in the forest, and is accepted into the banished Duke's company. He tells the Duke his story, prompting Jacques' declaration that 'all the world's a stage'.

Act III   Orlando bedecks the trees with love poems to Rosalind. Ganymede (Rosalind) promises to cure him of his lovesickness; he is to woo Ganymede as if (s)he were Rosalind. Touchstone falls for Audrey, an ill-favoured wench. Phebe falls in love with Ganymede.

Act IV   Orlando woos Ganymede, as agreed, and Rosalind (Ganymede) confesses to Celia her love for Orlando. Oliver, ordered by Frederick to find Orlando, meets Ganymede and Aliena. He describes how Orlando saved his life, showing them a bloody napkin. Ganymede faints.

Act V   Oliver falls in love with, and proposes to Aliena. Ganymede promises that, at the same time, Orlando shall marry Rosalind, and Silvius and Phebe be satisfied. On the marriage day, Rosalind reveals herself, taking Orlando in marriage, and persuading Phebe to accept Silvius. Touchstone marries Audrey. Duke Frederick decides to restore his banished brother, and retire from the world. Jacques, a perpetual student of human nature, follows the repentant Frederick.

THE COMEDY OF ERRORS

Text: F1.

Main source: Adaptation of Plautus, *Menaechmi*, with additions from his *Amphitruo*. Poss. Gower, *Confessio Amantis*, 1390.

[Antipholus (1) and Dromio (1) = of Syracuse
Antipholus (2) and Dromio (2) = of Ephesus]

Act I   Aegeon of Syracuse, under penalty of death, explains to the Duke of Ephesus that he is there searching for his son, Antipholus (1), and servant, Dromio (1), who had left Syracuse to seek their twin brothers separated from them in a storm, when their mother, Aegeon's wife, was also lost. Aegeon is given twenty-four hours to raise a ransom. Meanwhile, already at Ephesus, Antipholus (1) sends Dromio (1) to the Centaur Inn with money for safe-keeping. Dromio (2) mistaking Antipholus (1) for his master, Antipholus (2), who lives in Ephesus, calls him home to dinner, and, denying all knowledge of money, is beaten.

Act II   Adriana, wife of Antipholus (2) discusses men with Luciana, her sister. Dromio (2), smarting from the beating, reports to Adriana his master's odd behaviour. Dromio (1) coming from the inn, denying all knowledge of dinner arrangements, is beaten by Antipholus (2). Adriana meets Antipholus (1) and thinking him to be her husband, takes him in to dinner.

Act III   Antipholus (2), Dromio (2) arrive home with Angelo, a goldsmith, who is making a chain for Adriana. Refused entrance by Dromio (1), Antipholus (2) leaves angrily to dine at the Porpentine with the Hostess there, to whom he promises a chain in exchange for a ring. At home, after dinner, Luciana urges Antipholus (1) to treat Adriana better. He responds by declaring his love for Luciana. Dromio (1) is claimed by a greasy kitchen wench. Antipholus (1) bewildered, decides to leave town; sends Dromio (1) to find out a ship. As he is going, mistaken for Antipholus (2), he is given the chain by Angelo.

Act IV   Antipholus (2), sending Dromio (2) for a rope to beat his wife, meets Angelo and demands his chain. Angelo insists he has had it already. Angelo's creditors seek Antipholus (2)'s arrest. Dromio (1) returning with news of the ship, and no rope, is beaten by Antipholus (2), and sent to Adriana for bail money. Adriana gives him the money, which he, meeting Antipholus (1), hands over. The Hostess demands the chain from the totally confused Antipholus (1). Antipholus (2), asking Dromio (2) for the bail money, is offered only a rope. Adriana calls in Dr Pinch, a quack, to restore her husband's sanity.

Act V Antipholus (1) seeks refuge in a Priory. The Abbess, questioning Adriana, refuses to give him up. Adriana appeals to the Duke to restore her husband. Finally all is revealed, twins meeting with twins. The Abbess is Aegeon's lost wife. Aegeon is reprieved. All are reunited — and parents, twin sons and servants, husbands and wives, live happily ever after.

CORIOLANUS

Text: F1.
Sources include: Plutarch. Livy, *Annales*, Book 32. W. Camden, *Remaines of a Greater Worke concerning Britaine*, 1605. W. Averell, *Meruailous Combat of Contrarieties*. Sir Philip Sidney, *Apologie for Poetrie*, 1595.

Act I The hungry plebians of Rome are on the point of rebellion against their patrician rulers. Menenius Agrippa persuades them that they should combine for the common good. Caius Martius, a young arrogant patrician, despises their stupidity and inconstancy. The Senate appoints five Tribunes of the People to protect them. Martius is sent to quell a Volscian uprising led by Tullus Aufidius. He captures Corioli almost singlehanded, and is named Coriolanus after the victory. Aufidius vows to destroy him.

Act II Coriolanus wins the Senate's approval as a candidate for consulship. He resents, however, the necessary display of public humility. The Tribunes refuse to support him, suspecting his insincerity and pride.

Act III Aufidius, at Antium, again prepares to attack Rome. The Tribunes accuse Coriolanus of refusing free grain to the starving people, whom he declares are not worth feeding. The citizens demand his death. Protected by the Senators, he is finally persuaded by his mother to face the people and ask their support. In the Forum, losing his temper, pouring scorn on them, he is sent into exile.

Act IV He goes to Antium, offers himself to Aufidius, as victim or friend. Aufidius agrees to his joining the attack on Rome. Rumours of this reach Rome, where the citizens regret their hasty action. Aufidius grows jealous of Coriolanus' increasing popularity, and distrusts Coriolanus' relationship with Rome.

Act V Despite the Senators' pleas to spare Rome, Coriolanus remains unmoved. The visit and pleading of his mother, Volumnia, Virgilia (his wife) and his son, however, persuade him to a peace treaty. Aufidius bitterly accuses him of betrayal. Coriolanus taunts Aufidius with his defeat at Corioli. Enraged, Aufidius, with his men, kills Coriolanus. His anger spent, he orders the corpse a true warrior's burial.

CYMBELINE

Text: F1.

Sources include: Holished. *Decameron*, II, 9. *The Mirrour for Magistrates*, 1587 edn. Anon, *Frederyke of Jennen*, 1560. *The Rare Triumphs of Love and Fortune*, a romantic play presented at court, printed 1589.

Act I Posthumus Leonatus marries Imogen, daughter of Cymbeline, King of England, against Cymbeline's wishes. Banished, he gives Imogen a bracelet, she gives him a ring, as parting tokens. The queen, Cymbeline's second wife, plotting to set her own son, Cloten, an oaf, on the throne, persuades Pisanio (Posthumus' servant) to take a 'restorative' drug to his master. She believes it to be poison, but her physician, suspicious of her motives, substitutes a sleeping draught. In Rome, Posthumus meets Iachimo, who, decrying all women, boasts he will seduce Imogen. Seeking her in England, Iachimo tells Imogen Posthumus is unfaithful, but she refuses him as a lover. Iachimo apologizes, arranging to leave a trunk of valuables in her bedchamber.

Act II Imogen asleep, Iachimo creeps from the trunk, takes her bracelet, notes the room furnishings, and the mole on Imogen's breast. Later Cloten, wooing her with music, is rejected scornfully. Imogen finds her bracelet missing. In Rome, Posthumus, presented with Iachimo's 'proof', vows vengeance on Imogen.

Act III Rome, represented by General Lucius, demands tribute from Britain. Cymbeline refuses; he, his Queen and Cloten determine to break free from Rome's yoke. Posthumus sends Pisanio with a letter arranging to meet Imogen at Milford Haven. On the way, Pisanio, instead of killing her as Posthumus had ordered, shows her Posthumus' letter, giving her the Queen's potion should she need a restorative. Imogen, dressing as a boy (Fidele), and in order to get to Rome to confront Posthumus, seeks service with Lucius. Lost in Wales, she is sheltered by Belarius (a general unjustly dismissed by Cymbeline and exiled to Wales) and Guiderius and Aviragus (sons, seemingly, of Belarius; really of the King). The boys come to love Fidele dearly.

Act IV Imogen, ill, her hosts away hunting, takes the potion. Meanwhile Cloten, dressed as Posthumus, follows Imogen, intending to kill Posthumus and ravish her. He meets, is killed and beheaded by Guiderius. Imogen's hosts return to find her 'dead'. The boys 'bury' her, with Cloten's decapitated body by her. Imogen, recovering, believes it to be Posthumus. She seeks out Lucius, who is about to attack Cymbeline. Guiderius and Aviragus decide to fight on Cymbeline's side.

Act V Posthumus, now in England, unwilling to fight against his own country, disguising himself as a peasant, seeks death from the Romans. The battle is saved for Britain by Belarius and his 'sons'. Posthumus is taken prisoner. The vision Posthumus sees of future happiness comes true when all is revealed — the Queen's death and treachery; Iachimo's guilt and treachery; Fidele's true identity and constancy; Belarius' and the boys' identity. Posthumus is freed and reunited with Imogen. Cymbeline acknowledges Rome, and all ends in peace and happiness.

HAMLET

Text: Q1 (poor), 1603; Q2, 1604; F1, including 85 lines not in Q2.

Sources include: An earlier version of the story — *Ur-Hamlet* — now lost, acted 1594. Saxo Grammaticus, *Historia Danica, c.* 1200. François de Belleforest, *Histoires Tragiques, Extraicts des Oeuvres Italiennes de Bandel*, 1559–82. Timothy Bright, *Treatise of Melancholy*, 1586.

Act I   Night at Elsinore Castle. The ghost of Hamlet, former King of Denmark, appears to the guards and Horatio, a student friend of Prince Hamlet (the dead King's son), who informs the Prince. Claudius, now King and married to Gertrude, the dead King's widow, sends emissaries to Fortinbras's uncle, King of Norway, asking him to restrain his nephew who plans to attack Denmark. Claudius and Gertrude reprimand Hamlet for his odd dress and behaviour. Alone, Hamlet speaks bitterly of their untimely marriage. He arranges to watch for the Ghost. Laertes (son of the elderly statesman, Polonius), about to leave for France, warns his sister, Ophelia, against Hamlet's courtship. At night the Ghost confirms to Hamlet that he was poisoned by Claudius, his wife's lover. Hamlet swears to avenge him.

Act II   Unsure of the Ghost's honesty, Hamlet prevaricates, feigning madness, frightening Ophelia, who has rejected his advances. Polonius assures Claudius Hamlet is mad for love, but Claudius, uncertain, sends two friends of Hamlet's, Rosencrantz and Guildenstern, to probe further. Players come to the castle. Hamlet arranges with them a performance of a play resembling his father's murder, to test Claudius' reactions.

Act III   Hamlet, with Claudius and Polonius eavesdropping, treats Ophelia as a whore. Claudius decides to send him away. Polonius arranges for Gertrude to talk to him in her bedchamber, with himself behind the arras. At the play, Claudius reacts violently, ordering Rosencrantz and Guildenstern to take Hamlet immediately to England. Alone, Claudius prays, admitting his guilt. Hamlet, finding him praying, refuses to kill him, lest his soul go to heaven. Hamlet visits his mother, berates her viciously, and hearing a noise behind the arras, stabs Polonius to death.

Act IV   Gertrude, certain now of Hamlet's madness, agrees he be sent to England. Rosencrantz and Guildenstern accompany him, with sealed letters from Claudius, demanding Hamlet's death on arrival. Enraged at his father's murder, Laertes, returning to Elsinore, finding his sister mad, vows to destroy Hamlet. Sailors bring letters from Hamlet announcing his return to Denmark. Claudius plots with Laertes to kill Hamlet in a duelling accident, with poison-tipped foil, and poisoned drink for good measure. The Queen relates Ophelia's drowning.

Act V   The burial of Ophelia, where Hamlet and Laertes meet, fight, and are parted. Hamlet tells how he was saved by pirates and has disposed of Rosencrantz and Guildenstern. Osric presents the challenge for the duel between Hamlet and Laertes. During the fight, by mistake, Gertrude drinks the poisoned wine, and the foils are switched so that both contestants are wounded by the poisoned foil. As Gertrude, dying, warns Hamlet, Laertes collapses and dies. After stabbing Claudius, and forcing him to drink the remaining wine, Hamlet also dies, naming Fortinbras his successor. Fortinbras, proclaimed King, orders a state military funeral for Hamlet.

HENRY IV, Part 1

Text: Q1, 1598.
Main sources: Holinshed. Also *The Mirrour for Magistrates,* 1559. Samuel Daniel, *Civil Wars,* 1595. John Stow, *Chronicles of England,* 1580.

Act I   King Henry IV, faced by an uprising under Owen Glendower in Wales, and the refusal of Harry Percy (Hotspur) to surrender prisoners to the King after defeating the Scots, is unable to lead a crusade, as a penance for the murder of Richard II, to the Holy Land. Prince Hal, his eldest son — companion to Sir John Falstaff, a fat rogue, Poins, Bardolph and Peto — plans a robbery at Gadshill to reveal Falstaff's cowardice. Hotspur is angry when Henry still refuses to ransom Hotspur's brother-in-law, Mortimer, recently married to the daughter of his captor, Glendower. Joined by Northumberland and Worcester, and expecting support from Glendower, Douglas and the Archbishop of York, he decides to rebel against the King.

Act II   After the robbery at Gadshill, Hal and Poins reappear, disguised, chasing off the frightened Falstaff and Bardolph. Hotspur bids farewell to his wife and sets off for Wales. At the Boar's Head Tavern when Falstaff boasts of the robbery, Hal calls his bluff. The King sends for Hal. When Falstaff, impersonating the King, acts out what the King will say to Hal, Hal, in turn pretending to be King, upbraids Falstaff ruthlessly.

Act III   The rebel leaders gather. Hotspur quarrels over the proposed division of the Kingdom after victory. The King berates Hal for his behaviour, contrasting him with the honour-seeking Hotspur. Hal promises to outdo Hotspur or die. The King initiates plans to fight the rebels. Hal informs Falstaff that he is reconciled with his father, and is now off to fight at his father's side. He offers Falstaff a command.

Act IV   When the rebels learn that Northumberland is ill, Glendower delayed, and the royal forces on their way, Hotspur urges immediate battle. Falstaff collecting a ragged army, sets out for Shrewsbury. When Blunt is sent from the King to learn of the rebels' grievances, Hotspur relates all the King's ingratitude to his family (the Percys).

Act V   The King offers, through Worcester and Vernon, pardon to the rebels if they disband. Hal offers to fight Hotspur in single combat. Falstaff cynically considers martial honour. Worcester, not trusting the King's offer, keeps it from Hotspur. In the subsequent battle of Shrewsbury, Hal saves his father, kills Hotspur. The King's side wins. Falstaff claims to have killed Hotspur. Worcester and Vernon are executed, Douglas for his valour, freed. Prince John, Hal's brother, and Westmoreland are sent to fight off Northumberland and Scroop; the King and Hal set out to suppress Glendower.

HENRY IV, Part 2

Text: Q1, 1600.
Main sources: Holinshed. Anon, *The Famous Victories of Henry Vth,* pub. 1598. Also Samuel Daniel, *Civil Wars,* 1595.

Act I   After Rumour's warning (as Chorus) that he has spread false news that Hotspur has won the battle of Shrewsbury, Northumberland learns that his son, Hotspur, is dead, the battle lost, and the King's troops are approaching under Prince John and Westmoreland. He decides to rally his supporters. The Chief Justice, impatient at Falstaff's braggadocio manner, warns him to behave, reminding him that he is to accompany Prince John to fight Northumberland. The Archbishop of York decides to continue supporting Northumberland.

Act II   Mistress Quickly, hostess of the Boar's Head Tavern, demands Falstaff's arrest for debt, but he wheedles her into withdrawing her summons, lending him more money and giving him supper. Hal and Poins returning from battle, wishing to trick Falstaff, disguise themselves as potmen. Northumberland decides to leave for Scotland, until he sees how the rebellion fares. Falstaff joins Doll Tearsheet and Mistress Quickly for supper and music, with Bardolph and Pistol. Hal and Poins, having overheard Falstaff's comments on the Prince, reveal themselves. Hal leaves to rejoin the King, Falstaff to his command.

Act III   The King, disheartened about the rebellion, is comforted by news of Glendower's death. Falstaff, recruiting troops in the Cotswolds, is welcomed by Justices Shallow (a friend from youth) and Silence.

Act IV   York learns that Northumberland has left. Westmoreland urges York and his confederates, Mowbray and Hastings, to make peace with Prince John. York agrees, and, despite Mowbray's misgivings, orders the rebels to disperse. Immediately Prince John and Westmoreland arrest the rebel leaders for high treason. Falstaff, arriving with a prisoner, asks leave to return to Gloucestershire, while Prince John, learning that his father is ill, hurries to Westminster. The sick King, hearing of the rebels' defeat, falls asleep, the crown beside him. Hal, believing his father dead, takes up the crown, when Henry, awaking, accuses him of wishing him dead. Hal refutes this, speaking warmly to the King, who advises him to secure his position as king by the distraction of an expedition abroad.

Act V   Falstaff and Bardolph settle in with the goodhearted Shallow. The King dies. Falstaff, hearing of Hal's succession, sets out, sure of his promotion, for London. On the coronation route, Falstaff calls out familiarly to Hal, who rejects him. As a bewildered Falstaff claims he will be sent for privately, he and his cronies are ordered to the Fleet prison. Prince John comments that all will be well — for them, when they have learnt their lesson, for the realm, as a result of Hal's honesty and justice, and for the future, with the expedition to France.

HENRY V

Text: Q1 (poor), 1600; Q2, 1602.
Main sources: Holinshed. Anon, *The Famous Victories of Henry Vth*, pub. 1598. Edward Halle, *The Union of the Two Noble and Illustre Famelies of Lancastre and York*, 1548.

Prologue   The Chorus presents the scene, apologizing for the theatre's inadequacies.

Act I   The Archbishop of Canterbury, commenting on the change in Hal from frivolous prince to wise king, tells the Bishop of Ely of his offer of money to Henry, should he decide to claim the throne and lands in France. The Sallic Law, justifying Henry's claim, is expounded to the King. He receives the French Ambassadors and angered by the Dauphin's gift — tennis balls — replies that he will fight for his rights in France.

The Chorus, relating that Cambridge, Scroop and Grey are traitors, sets the embarkation scene at Southampton.

Act II   Two of the expedition — Corporal Nym and Lieutenant Bardolph — meet Pistol, now married to Mistress Quickly (once betrothed to Nym). As Pistol and Nym fight, Mistress Quickly is fetched to the ailing Falstaff. At Southampton the King, after ordering the traitors' arrest, sails for France. Bardolph, Nym and Pistol hear Mistress Quickly's account of Falstaff's death, then leave for France. The French King, Charles, organizes his defences; the Dauphin is warned by the Constable of France not to underestimate Henry. Exeter brings letters to Charles, demanding Henry be given the French crown and lands, or he will take them by force.

The Chorus presents the siege of Harfleur.

Act III   Henry, helped by English (Gower), Welsh (Fluellen), Irish (Macmorris) and Scottish (Jamy) officers, and, in the ranks, Nym, Bardolph and Pistol, wins the day. Because of sickness in his army and the advent of winter, Henry plans returning to England. The French Princess, Katharine, has her first lesson in speaking English. Charles sends Mountjoy to warn Henry against war. Fluellen refuses Pistol help for Bardolph, about to be hanged for stealing from a church. Henry informs Mountjoy that he is going to Calais, but will fight, if necessary, despite the weakness of his army. The night before Agincourt. The French confidently prepare.

Act IV   The scene visualized by the Chorus, as Henry, disguised in a cloak, wanders amongst his troops. He challenges, by an exchange of gloves, a soldier, Williams, who declares the King answerable for the sins of all those killed. Henry prays for success in the ensuing battle. Sunrise. Henry rouses the spirits of his army, picturing their unique achievement on this, St Crispin's Day. After a final visit by Mountjoy, the battle is fought. Henry wins. Afterwards, meeting Williams, and recalling the challenge, Henry gives 'his' glove to Fluellen as a favour, whom Williams meets and challenges. The King explains and Williams is given back his glove filled with money. Exeter lists the prisoners taken, and the dead.

The Chorus tells of Henry's triumphant homecoming, and his return to France to complete peace terms.

Act V   Fluellen, meeting Pistol, makes him eat a leek for mocking it and the

Welsh. Pistol, learning of his wife's death, decides to return to England, to live by begging and thieving. Henry meets Charles, arranges final terms, proposes to Kate (Katharine), sealing the whole bargain with a kiss.

HENRY VI, Part 1

Text: F1.
Main sources: Holinshed. Edward Halle, *The Union of the Two Noble and Illustre Famelies of Lancastre and York,* 1548.

Act I The funeral of Henry V. News arrives from France that the English have been beaten back, Talbot taken prisoner, and the Dauphin crowned King; rivalry breaks out amongst the nobles for control of the young Henry VI. At Orleans, the French, unable to raise the siege, send for Joan La Pucelle. Her strange powers tested, she agrees to lead the French. In London, Gloucester and his men, attempting to take the Tower of London, are prevented by the Cardinal of Winchester's men. The Mayor of London berates both groups, who leave, threatening each other's destruction. Talbot, released, returning to the Orleans siege, fights La Pucelle. The French take Orleans.

Act II Talbot, assisted by the Duke of Burgundy, regains Orleans. Although the Countess of Auvergne imprisons Talbot in her castle, he is immediately released by troops secretly accompanying him. In Temple Garden, London, in an argument between Somerset and Richard Plantagenet, Plantagenet and his followers choose the white rose as their emblem, Somerset, the red. Plantagenet, taunted about his father's death for treason, swears to disprove this. Old Mortimer, a prisoner in the Tower, tells Plantagenet that he, through his mother, Mortimer's sister, is the rightful heir to Richard II.

Act III Gloucester and Winchester continue their quarrel. Their men enter fighting. King Henry, warning of the dangers of civil strife, with the help of Warwick, enforces a truce, restoring Richard Plantagenet to favour as Duke of York. On Gloucester's advice Henry sets out for France to be crowned King there. At Rouen, La Pucelle wins the city, but is chased out by Talbot and Burgundy. Seeking to split their combined powers, she wins Burgundy over to the French. Meanwhile in Paris, Talbot pays his respects to King Henry, and is made Earl of Shrewsbury.

Act IV At the King's coronation Fastolfe (Falstaff) delivers a letter — it is from Burgundy saying he has joined the French. A quarrel breaks out between Vernon (for York) and Basset (for Somerset) over the roses they wear. The King trying to settle the dispute picks, arbitrarily, a rose (a red one), urging them to conserve their energy to fight France. Talbot, refused entry at Bordeaux, sends to York for reinforcements. York refuses to help. Somerset blames York for egging Talbot on and not keeping him properly supplied. Talbot, after failing to persuade his son to leave before the battle begins, at first saves him, but later himself dies with his son's body in his arms.

Act V Gloucester tells the King that the Pope, the Emperor and others, suggest he make terms with the French and marry the daughter of the Earl of Armagnac, the Dauphin's kinsman, to ensure peace. Henry agrees, sending Winchester, now Cardinal Beaufort, to make arrangements. At Angiers, La Pucelle, rejected by the fiends she calls up to help her, is taken prisoner by York. Suffolk takes prisoner Margaret, daughter of the Duke of Anjou, and attracted to her, decides to keep her near him by marrying her to the King. La Pucelle, condemned to death by burning, declares she is with child, the father uncertain. The ribald comments this rouses lead her to curse York and Warwick and England. The Cardinal arrives to make terms. The King, enraptured by Suffolk's description of Margaret, and ignoring his existing engagement, sends for Margaret to be his Queen.

HENRY VI, Part 2

Text: Q1, 1594, and Q2, 1600 present difficulties, being similar to F1, but with alterations and omissions, and are possibly reconstructions of the play made by players who appeared in an abridged version; F1.

Main sources: Edward Halle, *The Union of the Two Noble and Illustre Famelies of Lancastre and York*, 1548. Also Foxe, *Book of Martyrs*, 1563.

Act I   Suffolk delivers Margaret, the Duke of Anjou's daughter, to the King, who is to marry her, but Gloucester, the Lord Protector, is angry with the terms (the surrender of Maine and Anjou to Margaret's father) arranged. Buckingham, Somerset and Cardinal Beaufort (Winchester) decide to join Suffolk to oust Gloucester, while Salisbury, Warwick and York join together against Beaufort. York intends to get the crown for himself. The Duchess of Gloucester goads her husband to be more ambitious. She consults Hume, a priest in league with a witch and a conjuror of spirits, about the future. Hume, in the Cardinal's pay, encourages her ambitions. The Queen, learning (particularly from one Peter, who accuses his master, Horner, of treason) of Gloucester's popularity and power, resents it. Suffolk informs her of the faction to oust Gloucester. The nobles squabble about who should be regent in France — Somerset or York; the Queen insults Gloucester and his wife; Peter, revealing that his master had declared Richard of York the true heir to the throne, throws suspicion on York's loyalty. Peter and his master are ordered to fight it out and Somerset is chosen Regent of France. The Duchess of Gloucester is shown spirits who declare the King will be deposed by a Duke, Suffolk will die by water, and Somerset should fear castles. York and Buckingham arrest her for treason.

Act II   Gloucester arranges to settle his quarrel with the Cardinal by combat. He reveals the King's gullibility, and when Buckingham brings the news of the Duchess's arrest, Gloucester protests his innocence. York persuades Salisbury and Warwick that his right to the crown is legitimate. The Duchess is tried, and, after doing penance, banished to the Isle of Man, and her husband relieved of his Protectorship. Horner fights Peter and is killed. Gloucester's wife warns him of a faction out to destroy him.

Act III   Parliament is called. The Queen, supported by Suffolk, the Cardinal, Buckingham and York, urges Henry to be wary of Gloucester, but Henry believes him innocent. However when Gloucester arrives, Suffolk arrests him for treason. Henry leaves, grief-stricken, and Queen and nobles decide on Gloucester's death. When a message brings news of a rebellion in Ireland, York agrees to lead an expedition there (giving him the men he needs to get the crown). He leaves Jack Cade to stir up trouble in England. Henry learns Gloucester has been murdered, and angry commoners accuse Suffolk and Beaufort. Despite the Queen's pleas, Suffolk is banished. The King, visiting the dying Cardinal, learns of his complicity in the murder.

Act IV Suffolk is killed by pirates at sea, as prophesied. Jack Cade raises his rebellion, pretending to be John Mortimer, heir to Richard II. The King leaves as Cade's followers, promised cheap bread and wine, rampage through London. In Southwark the rebels, meeting Buckingham and Old Clifford, are offered a free pardon to forsake Cade. As the King learns that the rebellion is ended, news comes of York's advent with a large army. Cade, hiding in a garden in Kent, is killed by the owner, Iden.

Act V The two armies assemble. York, stating that he has come merely to ensure the removal of Somerset and to fight Cade, is assured that Somerset is in the Tower and Iden brings in the head of Cade. However as York is about to disband his army, Somerset arrives with the Queen. York, furious, demands the crown. In the ensuing Battle of St Albans York kills old Clifford, whose son swears vengeance; Somerset is killed under an alehouse sign, The Castle, by Richard Plantagenet, York's deformed son. The King and Margaret flee to London.

HENRY VI, Part 3

Text: Q1 (unreliable), 1598 (*see* Part 2); F1.
Main sources: Holinshed. Edward Halle, *The Union of the Two Noble and Illustre Famelies of Lancastre and York*, 1548. Also Foxe, *Book of Martyrs*, 1563.

Act I York, with his sons, Edward and Richard, and Warwick, all bearing white roses, having defeated Henry, follow him to London, where York seats himself on the throne. Henry and his followers, with red roses, find him. Henry, admitting the weakness of his own claim, makes York his heir, provided he himself can reign in peace. The Queen, angry at this, decides to fight on for their son, Edward's, sake. As Richard persuades his father to assume kingship, news come that the Queen's army is approaching. In the ensuing battle, Clifford avenges his father's death by killing Rutland, York's youngest son. York, taken prisoner by the Queen, is mocked at, and stabbed to death.

Act II Edward and Richard, York's sons, take the sight of three suns uniting into one great light as a good omen, and despite the news of the deaths of York and Rutland, and of Warwick's defeat in battle, renew their pledge to dethrone Henry. They meet Henry and the Queen at York, where Henry refuses to yield. Battle ensues, with Richard determined to avenge his brother's (Rutland's) death. The King retires from the battle, and contemplates the peace of country life. He sees, sadly, the effects of civil war as a son enters carrying his dead father, whom he has slain, and a father with his dead son. The Queen and Prince urge Henry to flee to Scotland. Edward, victorious, agreeing that Warwick arrange a marriage for him with Lady Bona, King Lewis of France's sister-in-law, honours his brothers, making Richard Duke of Gloucester, and George, Duke of Clarence, and sets off for London to be crowned.

Act III   Henry leaves Scotland in disguise to see his beloved England, and is captured by two huntsmen. Lady Grey, suing King Edward for the return of her confiscated lands, attracts the King, but rejects his blunt proposals. News comes that Henry is prisoner. Left alone, Richard reveals his determination to get the crown despite his deformities. Queen Margaret and Prince Edward seek help in France, where Warwick arrives, asking for Lady Bona's hand for King Edward. King Lewis agrees, then learns that Edward has married Lady Grey. Lewis angry, promises support to Margaret. Warwick, insulted, renounces King Edward and joins Margaret, pledging his own daughter in marriage to Prince Edward.

Act IV   Clarence, offended by King Edward's marriage, and discontented, as is Richard, with the King's other arranged marriages, decides to seek Warwick's other daughter in marriage. He joins Warwick, now landed in England with French forces. Together they take Edward prisoner. Edward's wife, Elizabeth (Lady Grey) seeks sanctuary. Edward, with the help of Richard, escapes. Henry, freed from prison, but wishing to live in quiet privacy, entrusts the government to Warwick and Clarence. Edward goes to Burgundy for aid, and returning, takes the city of York, sending Henry back to the Tower.

Act V   Edward offers Warwick a pardon if he yields. Warwick refuses. Clarence, deciding he cannot fight against his own brother, throws down his red rose and takes up the white. In the ensuing battle Warwick is killed, and Edward, winning, sets off to face Margaret and her forces at Tewkesbury. Again Edward triumphs, and captures Margaret and the Prince. The Prince is stabbed to death by Edward, Richard and Clarence. Queen Margaret's pleas for death are rejected. Richard seeks out Henry and kills him, determined to become King. Meanwhile Edward and his Queen, oblivious of Richard's intentions, send Margaret away to France, preparing to enjoy their reign.

HENRY VIII

Text: F1. In collaboration with (v. poss.) John Fletcher.
Sources include: Holinshed. Foxe, *Book of Martyrs* (the Cranmer story), 1563. Speed, *History of Great Britaine*, 1611.

Act I   Norfolk describes the meeting of Henry VIII and Francis I of France at the Field of the Cloth of Gold. Buckingham and Abergavenny voice their concern about the greedy, ambitious Cardinal Wolsey. As Norfolk warns them to be cautious, Wolsey passes, marking down Buckingham for future examination. Buckingham intends to denounce Wolsey to the King, but is arrested as a traitor before he can do so. The King, considering Buckingham's treachery, is entreated by Queen Katharine to reduce taxes imposed by Wolsey in the King's name. The King agrees. Wolsey, however, ensures that the people think he has himself interceded with the King on their behalf. The Surveyor presents Buckingham's indictment. Despite the revelation that the Surveyor himself has a grudge against Buckingham, Henry accepts the allegations, ordering Buckingham's trial. Sir Thomas Lovell bringing news that the new affectations from France are to be banned, sets out with the Lord Chamberlain and Lord Sands for supper at Wolsey's house. There, the King, masqued as a shepherd, encounters and dances with Anne Bullen.

Act II   Buckingham is condemned. Gossip is afoot that the King has separated from Queen Katharine because of some illegality in their marriage (a man should not marry his dead brother's wife), pointed out to him by Wolsey, to revenge himself against the Emperor Charles (who arranged the original match) for not giving him the Archbishopric of Toledo. Cardinal Campeius comes from the Pope to adjudge the case. Resentment grows against Wolsey. Anne, sorry for Katharine, declares she would never want to be a Queen, but accepts from Henry the title of Marchioness of Pembroke and £1000 a year. At the inquiry into Henry's marriage, Katharine, recognizing she is no match for Wolsey's cunning, withdraws to appeal to the Pope. The King, believing his childlessness a divine rebuke for his illegal marriage, grows angry when the inquiry is adjourned. He seeks Cranmer's help.

Act III   Katharine refuses Wolsey's request to put herself under the King's protection thus avoiding a legal battle. Suffolk tells how Wolsey's letters to the Pope, asking him to delay a divorce until Wolsey can get rid of Anne Bullen (whom he is against the King marrying), have fallen into the King's hands. Henry, discovering that Wolsey has been lining his own pockets, orders Norfolk to take the Great Seal of State from him, and Surrey, Buckinghams's son-in-law, informs Wolsey that the King will also take all his possessions. Cromwell informs Wolsey that the King has appointed Sir Thomas More in his place, made Cranmer Archbishop of Canterbury and secretly married Anne.

Act IV   Anne is crowned Queen. Katharine, now sick, learns of Wolsey's death. Sensing death near, she leaves letters asking the King to look after their daughter, Mary.

Act V   Lovell informs Gardiner, Bishop of Winchester, that the Queen is in labour. Gardiner discloses his efforts to get rid of Cranmer, accusing him of heresy. The King tells Cranmer he must be examined before the Council, giving him a ring so that he may appeal to the King if necessary. The King leaves to visit his wife, delivered of a girl, Elizabeth. Cranmer is accused of heresy and ordered to the Tower. As he produces the ring, the King, entering the Council chamber, upbraids the nobles for their despicable treatment of an honest man, asking Cranmer to be godfather to his daughter. At the christening, Cranmer welcomes the infant Elizabeth, who, a wise pattern to all, will bring a thousand, thousand blessings on the land.

The Chorus hopes the play has pleased the audience.

JULIUS CAESAR

Text: F1.
Main source: Plutarch.

Act I Rome's celebrations for Lupercal, and Caesar's victory over Pompey,
  are viewed sourly by the tribunes of the people, Marullus and Flavius,
  supporters of Pompey. Caesar, going to the festival games, is warned to
  beware the Ides of March. Shouts are heard from the games. Cassius probes
  Brutus' fear of Caesar's growing power. Casca informs them that Caesar has
  refused thrice to be crowned King. Cassius plans that Cinna shall throw
  letters, expressing fear of Caesar's ambitions, in at Brutus' window, to incite
  him to act. A night of strange disturbances erupts, as Cassius and Casca set
  out to visit Brutus.
Act II Brutus, in his garden, considering how dangerous Caesar's growing
  power is to the state, receives the letters. The conspirators (Cassius, Casca,
  Decius, Cinna, Metellus Cimber and Trebonius) arrive to persuade him to
  join them to destroy Caesar (but not, Brutus insists, Mark Antony), for the
  common good, at the Capitol next day. Portia, Brutus' wife, remarks on his
  agitation and grief. Ligarius visits Brutus and is persuaded to join the conspiracy. The night's unnatural disturbances upset Calpurnia, Caesar's wife,
  who tries unsuccessfully to prevent Caesar going to the Capitol that day, the
  Ides of March. Escorted by Antony and other Senators (including the conspirators) he sets off. Portia questions a Soothsayer, waiting to warn Caesar,
  about what is happening.
Act III Caesar brushes aside the Soothsayer, and, as Metellus pleads for his
  banished brother, the conspirators gather together, and each in turn stabs
  Caesar, Brutus last. Brutus arranges to speak first at Caesar's funeral,
  explaining Caesar's treachery to the State, and the need for his death.
  Antony, however, in a speech of great irony, inflames the mob against the
  conspirators, who, rampaging through Rome, kill Cinna, the poet, in mistake
  for Cinna, the conspirator. Cassius and Brutus flee.
Act IV Antony finding allies in Octavius (Caesar's great-nephew) and
  Lepidus, forms a triumvirate to take control. In the ensuing power-struggle,
  Antony is as scornful of Lepidus' ability as Brutus is angry at Cassius' selfish
  hotheadedness. Brutus and Cassius quarrel bitterly, until Cassius offers his
  dagger to Brutus, to kill him as they killed Caesar. Brutus' anger subsiding,
  they reaffirm their friendship. Brutus informs Cassius that Portia has com-
  mitted suicide. Despite Cassius' strong objections, Brutus decides that they
  will fight the triumvirate at Philippi. That night Caesar's ghost appears to
  Brutus, threatening he, too, will be at Philippi.
Act V The battle. Pindarus, Cassius' slave, reports, mistakenly, that the
  battle is lost. Cassius, despairing, seeks his own death at Pindarus' hands.
  Brutus seeing Cassius dead, and knowing all is lost, runs on his own sword.
  Antony and Octavius, victorious, recognizing Brutus' honourable altruism,
  order his martial funeral.

KING JOHN

Text: F1.

Main sources: Anon, *The Troublesome Raigne of John, King of England*, published in two quartos in 1591, and reprinted in 1611 and 1622 as by Shakespeare. It is not known precisely the relationship of this play to *King John* — whether it provided source material, or whether it was an earlier version of Shakespeare's own play.

Act I   King John, requested by Philip, King of France, to give up his crown to Arthur, son of John's elder brother, Geoffrey, refuses, declaring war. Robert Faulconbridge asks for the King's ruling over his inheritance, his elder brother, Philip, being a bastard. When Lady Faulconbridge reveals that Philip's father is really Richard I, Philip gladly forgoes his inheritance to follow the King, being dubbed Sir Richard Plantagenet.

Act II   Before Angiers. Philip receives John's reply, followed immediately by John and his army. Queen Elinor (John's mother) and Constance (Arthur's mother) quarrel over the crown, while the Bastard threatens the Duke of Austria, Philip's ally, who caused his father, Richard I's, death. As Angiers declares it will accept only the rightful King of England, the two claimants agree to unite temporarily to take the city. The fearful citizenry suggest peace is brought about by Lewis, the French Dauphin, marrying Blanch of Spain, John's niece. Philip and John agree. John also agrees, much to the Bastard's scorn, to make Arthur Duke of Britaine, Earl of Richmond and Lord of Angiers.

Act III   Constance curses Philip and Austria for the bargain they have made. Pandulph, the Papal legate, arrives to chide John for not accepting Stephen Langton as Archbishop of Canterbury. John rejects Langton, whereupon Pandulph excommunicates John, threatening Philip with a similar fate unless he relinquishes his pact with John immediately. The pact is broken, and battle stations are taken up, with Lewis, the new bridegroom, on one side and Blanch, the new bride, on the other. The English are victorious, the Bastard killing the Duke of Austria, John taking prisoner Arthur, whom he secretly orders Hubert de Burgh to liquidate. Constance bewails the loss of her son. Pandulph suggests that with Arthur removed, Lewis can invade England and, through Blanch, claim the crown himself.

Act IV   Hubert, ordered to blind Arthur, relents and decides to keep him a secret prisoner, pretending he is dead. John, secure on the throne, receives news of Arthur's 'death', but realizes that by it he has alienated the loyalty of Salisbury and Pembroke. News arrives that France is about to invade England, and that both Elinor and Constance are dead. Salisbury, Pembroke and others leave, to mourn at Arthur's grave. As Hubert informs the King that Arthur is still alive, Arthur, attempting to escape by jumping from the castle walls, dies. The Bastard, Salisbury and Pembroke, finding him, do not believe Hubert's protestations of innocence.

Act V   John, yielding to the Pope, asks that the French be disbanded and sent home. The Bastard, announcing that the French, supported by Salisbury and Pembroke, have already landed, urges John prepare for battle. Lewis rejects Pandulph's order to return to France. In the ensuing battle, John, losing,

retires to Swinstead Abbey. As Melun, a French lord, dies, he reveals to
Salisbury and Pembroke that after the battle Lewis intends to kill them.
They return to John. Learning this and that his supplies have been lost,
Lewis prepares to fight. At Swinstead the King is dying, poisoned, it is
believed, by a monk. As he dies, he learns of Lewis's preparations and of the
loss of supporting troops in the Wash. As arrangements are made for John's
burial at Worcester, news comes that Lewis has returned to France, leaving
Pandulph to negotiate peace terms. The Bastard, welcoming the new King
Henry III, reflects that England, if only it remain true to itself, never will 'lie
at the proud foot of a conqueror'.

KING LEAR

Text: Q1 (corrupt), 1608; F1 (possibly edited and corrected edition of Q1).
Sources include: Holinshed. Edmund Spenser, *The Faerie Queene,* II. 10, 1590. John Higgins,
Mirrour for Magistrates, 1574 edn. Sir Philip Sidney, *The Countess of Pembroke's Arcadia,*
1590. Anon, *The True Chronicle History of King Leir,* registered 1594, published 1605.

Act I   King Lear divides his kingdom between Goneril and Regan, his older
daughters, who publicly declare their love for their father, and disinherits
Cordelia, the youngest, for refusing to speak so fulsomely. He decides he will
live in turn with Goneril and Regan. Kent, trying to stand by Cordelia, is
banished. The King of France still wishes to marry Cordelia, despite her
disinheritance, and they leave for France. Edmund, Gloucester's bastard son,
resentful of his position, determines to supplant Edgar, his legitimate brother,
by persuading Gloucester and Edgar that each is plotting against the other.
Lear, with his Fool, sets off for the castle of Goneril and her husband
(Albany). Kent returns, disguised, to follow him. Goneril and her servant
Oswald receive Lear contemptuously, insisting he dismiss fifty of his followers.
Angry, Lear leaves for Regan's castle.
Act II   Regan and Cornwall (her husband) arrive at Gloucester's castle.
Edmund incites Edgar to flee his father's wrath, telling Gloucester that he
has foiled Edgar's attempted patricide. Kent, carrying letters from Lear to
Gloucester, fights Oswald, for which Cornwall orders Kent be put in the
stocks. Lear (enraged at this) reaching Gloucester's castle, complains to
Regan of Goneril. Goneril arrives. The sisters insist Lear control his followers,
and dismiss his unnecessary retinue. Lear, enraged, rushes out into the
stormy night. Gloucester is ordered by Regan to keep his doors locked against
the King.
Act III   On the heath, in a storm, Lear and his ailing Fool, under Kent's
guidance, seek a hovel, where Edgar is hiding, disguised as a Tom a'Bedlam
(a begging halfwit). Gloucester, disobeying orders, takes them all to shelter,
where Lear, now mad, 'tries' his cruel daughters. Gloucester advises Kent to
take Lear to Dover as his life is in danger. Cornwall, learning from Edmund
of Gloucester's action, arrests him, and, to render him helpless, gouges out his
eyes, for which he is wounded by Gloucester's servant. Gloucester, put in the
Bedlam's hands, sets out for Dover.

Act IV   Gloucester asks the Bedlam to lead him to a high cliff. As Goneril sends messages by Edmund, now her lover, to Regan and Cornwall to muster an army against the King, she learns that Cornwall is dead of his wounds. Her actions horrify Albany, who prepares to help the King. Cordelia and France arrive in Dover. The King of France has to return home but Cordelia remains, learning of recent events and that Lear, now mad, is nearby. Regan gets Oswald to inform Goneril that she intends to marry Edmund. Near Dover, Gloucester, led to the edge of an imaginary cliff, 'leaps' over the edge, and is found by a 'countryman' (Edgar in a new guise). Lear arrives, and, although mad, recognizes Gloucester, as Gloucester, despite his blindness, recognizes Lear. Oswald, carrying Goneril's love-letter to Edmund, tries to take Gloucester prisoner, but the 'countryman' interferes, kills Oswald, taking the letter. Cordelia takes the exhausted Lear into her care.

Act V   Goneril and Albany join Regan to resist France's 'invasion' of England. The 'countryman' gives Albany Goneril's letter. In the battle, France's forces losing, Cordelia and Lear are captured. Albany arrests Edmund for treachery, accusing Goneril and Regan of complicity. A challenge is sounded for single combat with Edmund, which the 'countryman' answers, mortally wounding Edmund. Then revealing himself, he tells of Gloucester's death of a broken heart. A message comes that Goneril has poisoned Regan and then killed herself. Edmund, dying, urges immediate reprieve be sent for Lear and Cordelia. They arrive, too late for Cordelia. Lear carries her in, dead, in his arms, and then he too dies. Albany entrusts the state to Edgar, who accepts, and to Kent, who refuses, preferring, for a last time, to follow his master.

LOVE'S LABOUR'S LOST

Text: Q1, 1598.
Source: None definite. Topical allusions — Ducs de Biron and de Longueville were the supporters, de Mayenne, the opponent, of Henry of Navarre in his fight for the French crown, 1589–93.

Act I   Ferdinand, King of Navarre, and three Lords, Dumaine, Longaville and Berowne, swear to dedicate themselves to study for three years, during which no woman shall come within a mile of their 'academe', amusement to be provided by Armado, a fantastical Spaniard, and Costard, a country swain. Armado informs the King that Costard is to be arrested for wooing Jaquenetta, a country girl, within the forbidden area. Armado, who confesses to his page, Moth, that he is in love with Jaquenetta himself, is given charge of Costard.

Act II   The Princess of France, attended by Lord Boyet and Katharine, Maria and Rosaline, arriving to discuss her father's debts to Ferdinand, are lodged beyond the mile limit. When Ferdinand, with his Lords, visits her, Maria recognizes Longaville, a former acquaintance, and Berowne, the mocking Rosaline; Dumaine makes inquiries about Katharine.

Act III   Armado discusses his love for Jaquenetta with Moth. Costard is given two letters, one from Armado to Jaquenetta, one from Berowne, horrified to find himself in love, to the black-eyed Rosaline.

Act IV   Costard misdelivers the letters. When Boyet reads Armado's aloud to the Princess and her ladies, Costard sees Armado for the fool he is. Jaquenetta takes Berowne's letter — a sonnet — to Nathaniel, the curate, to read for her. He is talking 'learnedly' with Holofernes, the schoolmaster, and Dull, the constable. Holofernes, realizing the mistake, suggests she show the letter to the King. Berowne, bemoaning his own lovesickness, spies on the King (declaiming love sonnets written to the Princess), who spies on Longaville (declaiming sonnets written to Maria), who spies on Dumaine (declaiming love-poetry written to Katharine). Berowne mocks them all for their weaknesses, but with Jaquenetta's delivery of his sonnet/letter to Rosaline, he is found equally culpable. Satisfied by Berowne's argument that love is a lawful part of all study, King and Lords pursue their plans to court the ladies by masque and revels.

Act V   Armado and Holofernes plan a masque of The Nine Worthies to entertain the King and the ladies. Discussing favours sent by their lords, and, hearing that these lords are near, disguised as Russians, the ladies exchange favours, and mask themselves. As a result, King and Lords woo the wrong ladies. The trickery is revealed, and as the group watches the masque, the Princess learns of her father's sudden death. She and her escort must leave for France. The Lords and Ferdinand are left to perform tasks that, in time, will win them their ladies. The play ends with the recitation of Holofernes' and Nathaniel's songs of the Cuckoo (Spring) and the Owl (Winter).

MACBETH

Text: F1.
Main source: Holinshed. Also poss. King James I, *Daemonologie*, 1597. Reginald Scott, *Discoverie of Witchcraft*, 1584.

Act I   Macbeth and Banquo, returning to Duncan, King of Scotland, after a strenuous victory over rebels, are confronted by three witches, who promise Macbeth that he will become Thane of Cawdor and King of Scotland, Banquo that his sons will be kings. Made Thane of Cawdor (a reward for his victory) Macbeth considers the possibility of fulfilling the rest of the prophecy. Lady Macbeth (his wife) receiving his letter, telling her of his thoughts and that Duncan is to spend a night at their castle, determines that the King shall be murdered. Duncan arrives, is welcomed, and retires; fearful of the future, but goaded on by Lady Macbeth, Macbeth kills him, using the grooms' daggers.

Act II   Macbeth, unnerved, the daggers still in his hands, returns to Lady Macbeth. Scornful of his inefficiency, as a loud knocking at the gate is heard, she replaces the daggers herself. The Porter lets in Macduff and Lennox, noblemen, attendants on the King, who discover the murder. In the turmoil Malcolm (Duncan's elder son) flees for England, and Donalbain (his younger son) for Ireland. They are believed guilty of the murder. Macbeth becomes King.

Act III   Macbeth, fearful of the Witches' prophecy, decides to get rid of both Banquo and his son, Fleance. He orders two assassins to kill them. Three murderers attack, killing Banquo, but Fleance escapes. That evening, at the state banquet, Macbeth, distraught, sees Banquo's ghost. Lennox, expressing his growing suspicions concerning Macbeth, discloses that Macduff, Thane of Fife, has refused all invitations to court.

Act IV   Macbeth returns to the Witches, who warn him to beware Macduff, and, assuring him that he cannot be killed by any man born of woman, nor until Birnam Wood comes to Dunsinane, they conjure up apparitions of the line of Scottish kings with Banquo's ghost at the end. When Lennox informs him Macduff is fled to England to join Malcolm, Macbeth orders the death of Macduff's wife and children. In England, Malcolm, after questioning Macduff's loyalty, accepts him, and hearing of the massacre of Macduff's family, they make plans to raise an army, to regain the crown.

Act V   Lady Macbeth, distraught with fear and guilt, walks and talks in her sleep, disclosing to the Doctor what has happened. Macbeth, learning of Malcolm's advent, prepares for battle, finding security in the Witches' promises. Meanwhile at Birnam Wood, Malcolm orders his army to camouflage their approach with tree boughs. Macbeth learns of Lady Macbeth's suicide, and of the 'coming' of Birnam Wood, but still trusts the Witches' promise that he has a charmed life. Meeting Macduff in battle, however, he discovers that Macduff was not 'born' but 'untimely ripped' from his mother's womb. With the Witches' prophecy fulfilled, Macduff kills Macbeth, presenting his head to the victorious Malcolm, now acclaimed King of Scotland.

MEASURE FOR MEASURE

Text: F1.
Main source: George Whetstone's *Promos and Cassandra*, 1578 (based on a story from Cinthio, *Hecatommithi*, 1565).

Act I   Duke Vincentio, announcing his departure from Vienna, installs Angelo, an upright man, with Escalus, his adviser, to govern in his absence. Angelo reinstates laws against brothels and lechery, ordering Mistress Overdone's brothels to be pulled down, and Claudio, a young man, to be imprisoned for getting Juliet, his betrothed, with child, although the marriage is merely delayed by dowry complications. Claudio asks Lucio, his friend, to get his sister, Isabella (a novice), to plead with Angelo for him. The Duke, telling Friar Thomas that he has deliberately installed Angelo to get Vienna's long-ignored laws enforced, says that he, disguised as a Friar, will stay around to watch what happens. Isabella agrees to seek a pardon for Claudio.

Act II   Escalus begs Angelo to spare Claudio. Angelo adamantly refuses. Elbow, a constable whose constant malapropisms confuse the issue, brings, before Angelo and Escalus, Pompey (a bawd, tapster to Mistress Overdone) and Froth (a gullible gentleman). Angelo, impatient with their behaviour, leaves Escalus to deal with them. The Provost, governor of the prison, brings Isabella and Lucio to Angelo. Her passionate pleas for mercy for Claudio move Angelo strangely. He orders her to return the next day, recognizing in himself a weakness — a desire for Isabella. The 'Friar' (the disguised Duke) visiting the prison, hears Juliet's account of her and Claudio's misbehaviour. Isabella, returning to Angelo, is told he will pardon Claudio, if she will give herself to him. Angrily, she refuses, sure Claudio will die willingly to protect her chastity.

Act III In prison, the 'Friar' comforts Claudio. Isabella arrives to see her brother, who begs her to agree to Angelo's request. Isabella, upset, is leaving, when the 'Friar', having overheard all, offers help. Angelo, he says, once betrothed to a lady, Mariana, on the loss of her dowry, rejected her. He suggests Isabella accepts Angelo's proposal, but Mariana should take her place. Outside prison, Pompey, again in custody, asks Lucio for help. Lucio refuses, making innuendos to the 'Friar' about the characters of both Angelo and the absent Duke. Mistress Overdone, also arrested, denounces Lucio for his affair with a whore.

Act IV At Mariana's retreat. Isabella, with the 'Friar', gets Mariana to agree to take her place. In prison, Abhorson, the executioner, with his new assistant, Pompey, prepares for the hangings. The Provost receives a message, in the 'Friar's' presence, to hang first Claudio and send his head to Angelo, then Barnardine, a drunken reprobate. The 'Friar' suggests substituting Barnardine for Claudio, but Barnardine, unprepared, refuses to be hanged, and is saved by the opportune death in prison of a pirate, whose head is sent (as Claudio's) to Angelo. The 'Friar' writes to Angelo announcing his return to Vienna. Isabella is told by the 'Friar' that Claudio is dead, and advised to complain to the returning Duke. Angelo fears the Duke's return. The 'Friar' discarding his disguise, sets out for the city where Isabella and Mariana await him.

Act V Isabella accuses Angelo, supported by Mariana, who reveals her relationship with Angelo. Angelo denies both accusations. The Duke, leaving Angelo and Escalus to deal with the two women, returns as the 'Friar', only to be accused himself of supporting the two women's false charges. Lucio pulls off the 'Friar's' hood, revealing the Duke, who orders Angelo to marry Mariana immediately, and then be put to death. Isabella and Mariana plead for him, and when the Provost brings in the still-living Claudio, Juliet and Barnardine, the Duke pardons Angelo. He orders Claudio to marry Juliet, and Lucio, the whore (by whom he had a child), making plans to marry Isabella himself.

THE MERCHANT OF VENICE

Text: Q1, 1600.
Sources: Possibilities include: Ser Giovanni Fiorentino, *Il Pecorone*, 1558. *Gesta Romanorum*, in Richard Robinson's revised edition, 1595. Christopher Marlowe, *The Jew of Malta*, 1589. Alexander Sylvain, *The Orator*, a collection of orations, one entitled 'Of a Jew, who would for his debt, have a pound of the flesh of a Christian', 1596. Anthony Munday, *Zelauto*, 1580. Poss. a lost play, *The Jew*, referred to by Stephen Gosson in his *School of Abuse*, 1579. Poss. *The Ballad of the Crueltie of Gernutus*.

Also, in 1586, Roderigo Lopez, a Jewish-Portuguese doctor, became Queen Elizabeth's physician, and in 1594 was hanged, drawn and quartered for suspected poisoning of the Queen. Marlowe's play was revived to cash in on the public hostility of the time towards the Jews.

Act I   Antonio, a merchant of Venice, despondent despite his friend, Gratiano's, efforts to amuse him, is asked by Bassanio to lend him money to go to Belmont to woo the wealthy Portia, whose father has recently died. Antonio lacks the immediate resources, his argosies being at sea, but offers to borrow money himself to lend Bassanio. In Belmont, Portia discusses with Nerissa, her maid, the terms of her father's will, under which she may only marry he who chooses from three caskets of gold, silver and lead, the one containing her portrait; the unsuccessful suitors are sworn never to consider marriage again. The latest suitor, the Prince of Morocco, awaits his chance. Portia remembers wistfully the Venetian scholar and soldier, Bassanio, who once visited her. Bassanio finds Shylock, a Jewish moneylender, who hates the Christian Antonio for his rejection of usury, prepared to lend money, to be repaid within three months. Should Antonio fail, Shylock demands a pound of his flesh as payment. Antonio agrees to the bond.

Act II   The Prince of Morocco arrives to make his choice. Launcelot Gobbo, Shylock's servant, unhappy in Shylock's service, persuades his near-blind father, Old Gobbo, to ask Bassanio to employ him. Bassanio agrees and plans with Gratiano to sail to Belmont. Meanwhile, Jessica, Shylock's daughter, gives Launcelot a letter for Lorenzo containing their plans to elope. Jessica, disguised as a boy, escapes with Lorenzo, taking with them rings and money. At Belmont, the Prince of Morocco chooses wrongly, the golden casket. Salarino and Salanio describe Shylock's fury at the discovery of his loss, relating rumours that Antonio's argosies have foundered. The Prince of Aragon, the latest suitor, leaves Belmont having chosen wrongly the silver casket. Portia learns of Bassanio's coming.

Act III   Salarino and Salanio bate Shylock about his losses. Bassanio, arriving in Belmont, happily chooses the right casket — the lead one. Gratiano informs Bassanio that he, too, is to wed — Nerissa. Celebrations are called for when Salanio, Lorenzo and Jessica, bring information that Antonio's argosies have failed, and his life is forfeit to Shylock. Bassanio and Gratiano leave immediately for Venice, where Antonio is taken to prison, to await a court hearing. Portia determines to attend the court as Balthazar, a young Doctor of Law, with Nerissa as her clerk.

Act IV   In court, Shylock savours his approaching triumph. Balthazar (Portia), assisting in the case, agrees that Shylock's bond is valid, and, on

Shylock's rejection of money offered in repayment, appeals to him for mercy. Shylock, refusing, is about to cut his pound of flesh, when he is reminded that, according to the bond, he must take flesh only — no blood. Defeated, Shylock is condemned for seeking a Christian's life, then pardoned, provided he become a Christian. He is ordered to give half his wealth to Antonio, who promises to keep it in trust for Lorenzo and Jessica. Shylock withdraws in despair. Bassanio and Gratiano reward the young Doctor and 'his' clerk with rings given them by their wives.

Act V   In Belmont, at night. Portia and Nerissa arrive followed by Bassanio, Gratiano and Antonio. The wives upbraid their husbands for losing their rings. Portia offers Bassanio a replacement ring — the same ring. With the disguise uncovered, and the news that Antonio's argosies are safe, the play ends happily.

THE MERRY WIVES OF WINDSOR

Text: Q1 (poor), 1602; F1.
Source: None known. John Dennis, in his 'Epistle Dedicatory' to *The Comical Gallant*, 1702, writes: 'This comedy ... hath pleased one of the greatest Queens that ever was in the world — this comedy was written at her command [see below], and by her direction, and she was so eager to see it acted, that she commanded it to be finished in fourteen days and was afterwards, as Tradition tells us, very well pleased At the Representation.' In Nicholas Rowe's *Life of Shakespeare*, prefixed to his edition of the *Plays*, 1709, it states, 'Queen Elizabeth was so well pleased with that admirable character of Falstaff in the two parts of Henry IV, that she commanded him [Shakespeare] to continue it for one more play, and shew him in love.'

Act I   Justice Shallow, with his cousin Slender, claims Sir John Falstaff has treated them and their property disparagingly. Sir Hugh Evans, parson and schoolmaster, offers to referee the dispute. At Master Page's house, Sir John, accompanied by Bardolph, Nym and Pistol, denies the accusations. Slender admits his desire to marry Anne, Page's daughter. Falstaff, lacking money, decides to seduce both Mistress Page and Mistress Ford, and then live off them. He writes identical loveletters to them, which Nym and Pistol refuse to deliver. Being dismissed, they decide to revenge themselves by informing the husbands about Falstaff's intentions. Simple (Slender's servant), sent by Sir Hugh to ask Mistress Quickly (Dr Caius' housekeeper) to help Slender win Anne, is discovered by Caius. Caius, in love with Anne himself, challenges Sir Hugh to a duel. Fenton, a young gentleman, gives Mistress Quickly money to help win Anne for himself.

Act II   The wives compare loveletters and decide to teach Falstaff a lesson. Pistol and Nym tell Ford and Page of Falstaff's plans. Page trusts his wife, but Ford decides to test his wife's fidelity by questioning Falstaff. The wives ask Mistress Quickly to get Falstaff to visit Mistress Ford when Ford is out. Master Brook (Ford in disguise) goes to Falstaff, declares his great love for Mistress Ford, asking Falstaff to woo her on his behalf. Falstaff agrees, disclosing his assignation with Mistress Ford. Ford, certain of his wife's disloyalty, determines to prevent this. Shallow, his followers, and the Host of the

Garter, gathering in a field near Windsor to see the Caius–Sir Hugh duel, find Caius ready, but no sign of Sir Hugh.

Act III Sir Hugh, in a field near Frogmore, is also alone. The Host, revealing he had deliberately confused the meeting place, reconciles the antagonists. Mistress Page, going to Mistress Ford, meeting Ford himself, hurries ahead to warn Mistress Ford of his coming. The wives prepare a laundry basket. Hardly has Falstaff arrived, than he has to be hidden from Ford, in the basket with the dirty linen. Page rejects Fenton as suitor to Anne, because of his wild past. The wives decide to repeat their treatment of Falstaff. Mistress Ford, through Mistress Quickly, invites Falstaff to visit her again. 'Brook' (Ford), visiting Falstaff, learns of the escape, and the new assignation, and he determines this time to catch Falstaff.

Act IV While Sir Hugh tests William, Page's son, on his school learning, Falstaff sets off to Mistress Ford's. Mistress Page again brings the warning of Ford's approach. Falstaff this time has to escape dressed as the maid's Aunt from Brainford, a witch, whom Ford hates. Ford unsuccessfully searches the laundry basket, and beats the 'Witch of Brainford' out of the house. The wives, feeling they have achieved their end, reveal the hoax. Page suggests they make a public fool of Falstaff. He is asked to meet Mistress Ford in Windsor Forest, disguised as the ghost of Herne, the hunter, believed to haunt there by night. Anne, William and some other children, disguised as fairies and hobgoblins, will terrorize him. Fenton tells the Host of his and Anne's love, revealing that although her mother has made secret plans for Anne to elope that night in her fairy guise with Caius, and her father made similar plans for her to elope with Slender, she will actually elope with Fenton.

Act V Falstaff tells 'Brook' that he is to meet Mistress Ford in the Forest. Slender and Caius both prepare secretly for their elopment. In Windsor Forest, all goes as planned, Falstaff pinched, burned and upbraided for his lechery, Slender and Caius slinking away with two 'fairies' and Fenton with a third (Anne). Page and Ford reveal to Falstaff their hoax, Slender and Caius discover their 'fairies' are boys disguised, Anne and Fenton return married. Falstaff accepts his 'punishment', as Page accepts the lovers' *fait accompli*. All retire to 'laugh this sport over by a country fire'.

A MIDSUMMER NIGHT'S DREAM

Text: Q1, 1600.
Source: Possibilities include: Theseus/Hippolyta story — Chaucer, *The Knight's Tale*; Plutarch, *Life of Theseus*. Pyramus and Thisbe story — Ovid, *Metamorphoses*, poss. in Golding's translation, 1567. Oberon — Robert Greene, *James IV, c.* 1591; *Huon of Bordeaux*, trans. Lord Berners, 1533. Puck/Robin Goodfellow — Reginald Scott, *Discoverie of Witchcraft*, 1584. The Ass's Head — Apuleius, *The Golden Ass*, trans. William Aldington, 1566.

Act I Theseus, Duke of Athens, arranging to celebrate his marriage with Hippolyta, Queen of the Amazons, whom he has recently defeated in battle, is interrupted by Egeus, who complains that Lysander has bewitched into love his daughter, Hermia, when Egeus wishes her to marry Demetrius. Theseus warns Hermia that unless she complies with her father's wishes, she must die or become a nun. Hermia agrees to elope with Lysander, meeting the next night in a nearby wood. They disclose their plans to Helena (Hermia's childhood friend), who is herself in love with Demetrius. To win his favour, Helena tells him of the lovers' plans. Elsewhere a group of workmen, Quince (carpenter), Nick Bottom (weaver), Flute (bellows mender), and Robin Starveling (tailor), gather to prepare a play to present at Theseus' wedding feast.

Act II   In the wood, Puck (Oberon's right-hand sprite) and a fairy describe the quarrel (which has upset the weather) between Oberon, the King of the Fairies, and his Queen, Titania, over a changeling boy. When Titania leaves Oberon, still refusing to give him the boy, Oberon orders Puck to fetch a flower, the juice of which, squeezed on a sleeping person's eyelids, makes him (her), on waking, fall in love with the first creature he (she) sees. While waiting for Puck, Oberon watches Demetrius (who has followed Hermia to the wood) with Helena (who has followed him) and is pleading with him to love her. Puck, returning with the flower, is told by Oberon to squeeze it on the lids of the Athenian youth (Demetrius), so he will love Helena. Oberon himself will anoint Titania's eyelids. Puck anoints in error the eyes of Lysander whom he finds with Hermia. Helena and Demetrius arrive, wake Lysander, who falls in love with Helena.

Act III   The workmen rehearse their play near where Titania sleeps. When Bottom is 'off-stage', Puck adorns him with an ass's head. Bottom's companions, terrified, run away believing him bewitched. As he sits, puzzled, Titania, waking, falls in love with him, ordering her fairies to attend him. Oberon is overjoyed at this, but, furious at Puck's mistake over Demetrius, tries to remedy it by anointing Demetrius' eyes, who then sees, and loves, Helena. Demetrius and Lysander plan to fight over Helena, while Hermia, confused, quarrels with her. Oberon orders Puck to tire the four lovers out, bring them all together, and as they sleep, he will restore Lysander's true sight, and make all well.

Act IV   While Titania and Bottom sleep, Oberon, the changeling boy now his attendant, releases Titania from the spell, telling Puck to remove Bottom's ass's head. The fairy quarrel ended, harmony is restored and all set off to bless, in dance and song, Theseus' marriage. Theseus and Hippolyta, out early hunting, rouse the lovers, who, on waking, find that for them, too, harmony is restored. Theseus declares they shall all be married that day. Bottom wakes, and still puzzled by his 'dream', seeks out his fellow actors.

Act V   After the wedding ceremony Quince and his group perform their play, simply and somewhat awkwardly, to the general amusement. All retire, and the fairies dance through the house to bless the bride-beds. Puck, as epilogue, commends to his onlookers this 'midsummer night's dream'.

MUCH ADO ABOUT NOTHING

Text: Q1, 1600.
Sources: Claudio/Hero story — possibilities include: Ariosto's *Orlando Furioso*, 1516, trans. Sir John Harington, 1591. François de Belleforest, *Histoires Tragiques, Extraicts des Oeuvres Italiennes de Bandel*, 1559–82. Edmund Spenser, *Faerie Queene*, II. 4, 1590.

Act I Leonato, governor of Messina, welcomes Don Pedro, Prince of Aragon, and Don John, the Prince's bastard brother, with whom the Prince is now reconciled. With them are Claudio, a young Florentine, honoured by the Prince, and Benedick, a Lord from Padua. Beatrice, Leonato's niece, exchanges banter with Benedick, while Claudio falls in love with Hero, Leonato's daughter. The Prince agrees to help him win her. Don John, discontented by Claudio's preferment, on hearing of this plan, swears, with Conrade and Borachio, his followers, to upset it.

Act II At a masqued ball the Prince meets and talks with Hero, while his servant, Balthazar, follows his example with Ursula, Hero's maid; Beatrice discusses Benedick with the masqued and unrecognized Benedick; Don John persuades Claudio that the Prince is wooing Hero for himself, but, when the Prince and Benedick have reassured Claudio, arrangements are made for Claudio to marry Hero. The Prince then arranges with Hero to inveigle Beatrice and Benedick into marriage. Borachio tells Don John that, to deceive Claudio into believing Hero unfaithful to him, he will ask Margaret (Hero's maid who loves him) to come that night to Hero's window in Hero's clothes, where, with the Prince and Claudio listening nearby, they will exchange declarations of love. Meanwhile, the Prince, Claudio and Leonato, with the hidden Benedick listening, discuss Beatrice's 'mad love' for Benedick. Convinced, Benedick tests Beatrice by looking for signs of love in her behaviour.

Act III Hero and Ursula achieve the same end with Beatrice, who cogitates on Benedick's love. The day before the wedding. Don John informs the Prince and Claudio that Hero is unfaithful, promising them proof if they will come to Hero's house that night. Later, the watch overhearing Borachio tell Conrade how he and Don John have deceived the Prince and Claudio, arrest the troublemongers, and take them off to Dogberry, their chief constable, and Verges, the headborough. The next morning Dogberry and Verges bring their prisoners to Leonato, but he is too busy with the wedding arrangements to deal with them.

Act IV In the church, Claudio rejects Hero. Hero appeals to the Prince who declares her a liar. As Hero faints, Claudio, the Prince and Don John leave. When Hero revives, the Friar believing her innocent, suggests they give out she is dead, and keep her hidden until Claudio changes his mind or the truth be known. Beatrice, testing Benedick's love, goads him to 'kill Claudio'. When the Sexton hears of Borachio and Conrade's conversation, he orders they be taken to Leonato immediately.

Act V Leonato, grief-stricken at Hero's death, challenges Claudio to a duel, but is refused. Benedick, himself about to challenge Claudio, is interrupted by Dogberry and Verges with their prisoners, who reveal the truth. After penance at Hero's tomb, Claudio agrees to marry Antonio's (Leonato's brother's) daughter. At the wedding, when the bride's face is unveiled to reveal Hero, when Beatrice and Benedick admit their love for each other, and when it is learned that Don John has been made prisoner, all ends happily.

OTHELLO

Text: Q1, 1622.
Main source: Cinthio, *Hecatommithi*, III. 7, 1595.

Act I   Venice. Iago, Othello's ensign, discontented at Cassio's preferment as Othello's lieutenant, decides upon revenge. With Roderigo, a rich dupe in love with Desdemona, he rouses Brabantio, Desdemona's father, saying that Othello has stolen and ravished his daughter. Brabantio calls the watch. As they reach Othello's lodging, Othello is summoned to the Venice council chamber to discuss the Turkish attack on Cyprus. There Brabantio accuses Othello of bewitching Desdemona. While Othello tells the story of his wooing, she is sent for, and declares her love for him. On the council's decision to send Othello to save Cyprus, she insists on accompanying him. Othello, with Cassio, goes ahead, leaving Desdemona to follow, with Iago and his wife, Emilia.

Act II   Cyprus. A storm disperses the Turkish fleet. Cassio, then Desdemona and Iago, arrive safely, and await Othello. Cassio's courtier-like adulation of Desdemona suggests to Iago a basis for arousing Othello's jealousy. Othello arrives, and celebrations are announced. Plied with drink by Iago, Cassio occasions a brawl. Othello stops it, and, learning the cause, dismisses Cassio from his service.

Act III   Iago suggests Cassio gets Desdemona to plead for him with Othello. Othello, his belief in Cassio's honesty shaken by Iago's hints, finds her constant requests suspicious, and resolves to oversee his wife, and, if she prove false, to discard her. Desdemona accidentally drops a handkerchief given her by Othello, which Emilia finds and gives to Iago. Iago claims that Cassio has Desdemona's handkerchief, and often dreams lasciviously of her. When Othello asks Desdemona for the handkerchief, she replies over-casually that she has it somewhere. Cassio, finding the handkerchief, deliberately left in his room by Iago, all unknowingly, gives it to his whore, Bianca, to copy for him.

Act IV   Othello, increasingly jealous, has a fit, and, on reviving, is taken by Iago to observe him talk with Cassio, supposedly about Desdemona. With coarse laughter, they actually talk about Bianca, who later returns the handkerchief to Cassio. Convinced, Othello vows to kill Desdemona, arranging for Iago to dispose of Cassio. Visitors, with letters recalling Othello, and handing over charge of Cyprus to Cassio, come from Venice. They are shocked when, enraged further by Desdemona's pleading, Othello strikes her. After dinner, Othello bids her retire to bed.

Act V   Roderigo, goaded by Iago to kill Cassio, but instead merely wounding him, is killed by Iago himself. Othello, rousing Desdemona, urges her to pray, and then smothers her. Emilia arrives. Desdemona, momentarily conscious, but dying, declares herself alone responsible. Emilia raises the alarm, telling Othello the truth about the handkerchief. Iago arrives, kills Emilia. Othello attacks him. Learning finally of Iago's total treachery, Othello stabs himself and dies at Desdemona's side. As Iago is ordered to prison and torture, Cassio takes over command.

PERICLES, PRINCE OF TYRE

Text: Q1, 1609. It was not included in F1 or F2, only in the second edition of F3, 1664. Few scholars believe the text is wholly Shakespeare's; he is believed to have written most of Acts III, IV, V.

Main sources: The story of Apollonius of Tyre, retold in John Gower, *Confessio Amantis*, 1390. Laurence Twine, *The Patterne of Paynfull Adventures, c.* 1576.

Act I   The story is presented by John Gower, the poet. He tells of the incestuous relationship of the King of Antioch, Antiochus, with his daughter, on which a riddle is based, to be unravelled by any suitor for the daughter. Pericles, Prince of Tyre, determining to win the Princess, guesses the riddle's meaning. Realizing this, the King urges Pericles to stay for further tests of prowess, but Pericles, suspicious of his motives, leaves Antioch immediately, to escape death at the hands of the King's assassin, Thaliard. At Tyre, fearing Thaliard may find him there, he entrusts the state to his deputy, Helicanus, and leaves for Tarsus. There he helps the Governor, Cleon, and his wife, Dionyza, to relieve a famine.

Act II   Gower, in a dumb show warning of the advent of Thaliard, tells how Pericles, leaving Tarsus by boat, is shipwrecked on the shores of Pentapolis, where fishermen find him, salvaging his armour from the sea.

Pericles takes part in the tournament held by the King, Simonides, to celebrate his daughter's, Thaisa's, birthday. Despite his poor appearance, Pericles wins. At the later feast, Thaisa and her father learn the strange knight is a gentleman of Tyre. She and Pericles dance together. At Tyre, Helicanus, informing the court that Antiochus and his daughter are dead, agrees to take over the rule of Tyre unless Pericles returns within a year. Thaisa informs her father that she wishes to marry Pericles. Simonides agrees.

Act III   Gower, in dumb show, tells how Pericles, learning of Antiochus' death and the imminent crowning of Helicanus, decides to return to Tyre, with Thaisa, now expecting a child; describes their danger in a sea storm.

In the storm, Thaisa dies, giving birth to a daughter. The sailors, to placate the storm, throw the body overboard, coffined in a waterproof chest, with spices and a letter of explanation. It is washed ashore at Ephesus, where Lord Cerimon, a skilled physician, rekindles life in Thaisa. Meanwhile Pericles puts his daughter, Marina, into the care of Cleon and Dionyza. Thaisa, believing her husband and child lost, becomes a priestess at Diana's temple at Ephesus.

Act IV   Gower tells how Pericles lives in Tyre, while Marina grows up in Tarsus, overshadowing Philoten, Cleon and Dionyza's own child; how Dionyza, becoming very jealous of Marina, sends Leonine to kill her.

As he is about to do so, Marina is kidnapped by pirates, who sell her to a brothel in Mytilene, but she vows to remain a virgin. Dionyza tells Cleon what she has done, saying that they will build a memorial to Marina and tell Pericles that she is dead.

Gower, in dumb show, tells of Pericles' visit to the memorial and his grief; of his vow never to wash his face or cut his hair again.

In Mytilene, Lysimachus, the governor, visiting the brothel, is given Marina, but, moved by her pleading, offers instead to protect her. She leaves to teach needlework and music.

Act V   Gower tells of Marina's new position, and how Pericles, in deep despair, unwashed and long-haired, arriving at Mytilene, is visited by Lysimachus.

Hearing of Pericles' state, Lysimachus sends for Marina. She sings, and tells of her own griefs. Gradually Pericles realizes her true identity. In his sleep, Diana urges him to go to her temple at Ephesus.

Gower tells of feasting in Mytilene, how Lysimachus is to marry Marina, after Pericles has visited Ephesus.

At the temple of Diana, Pericles tells his story to the Priestess — Thaisa. There is a joyful reunion. Pericles declares that Marina and Lysimachus shall rule in Tyre, while he and Thaisa, Simonides being dead, will spend the rest of their days in Pentapolis.

RICHARD II

Text: Q1, 1597; Q4, 1608, 'with new additions of the Parliament Sceane, and the deposing of King Richard'. This deposition scene seems to have been part of the original text, but cut when Q1 was printed.

Main source: Holinshed. Also Anon, *Thomas of Woodstock*. Samuel Daniel, *Civil Wars.* Poss. Berner's translation of Froissart.

Act I   Before King Richard, Henry Bolingbroke (John of Gaunt's son) challenges Thomas Mowbray, Duke of Norfolk, to combat, accusing him of misusing royal funds and plotting Gloucester's death, accusations Mowbray denies. No settlement being found, trial by combat is arranged. Gaunt refuses the Duchess of Gloucester's appeals to avenge her husband's death. As the combat begins, Richard chooses to banish both men, Mowbray for life, Bolingbroke for six years. Richard remarks on Bolingbroke's popularity with the people, and is about to set off for Ireland, to quell a rebellion, when he is called to the dying Gaunt's bedside.

Act II   Richard petulantly rejects Gaunt's advice on how to maintain 'this royal throne of kings', and, as soon as Gaunt dies, seizes all his properties, despite York's protests that they are rightfully Bolingbroke's. Northumberland, Ross and Willoughby discuss Richard's misrule, revealing that Bolingbroke with a large following has set sail for England. The Queen, sad for Richard away in Ireland, receives news that Bolingbroke has arrived, being joined by Northumberland and his son, Henry Percy, and Ross and Willoughby. Upset by this, York, left as regent, leaves for Berkeley Castle in Gloucestershire. The King's favourites, Green and Bushy, leave for the safety of Bristol Castle, Bagot for Ireland. At Berkeley, Bolingbroke explains to York, who has insufficient power to withstand him, that he comes to claim his inheritance. Richard's Welsh troops, fearing the King dead in Ireland, and disliking the omens, disband themselves.

Act III   At Bristol, Bolingbroke takes Bushy and Green prisoner, condemning them to death. Richard, landing in Wales, sure that the upstart Bolingbroke will be suppressed, learns from Salisbury and Scroop that he has been deserted. Even the common people are arming against him. In despair, he seeks refuge in Flint Castle. Bolingbroke arrives, promising to disperse his men if his banishment is revoked and his property restored. Richard, lamenting his loss of royal authority, agrees. The Queen, overhearing the gardeners talking of England, learns that Richard has been brought to London by Bolingbroke.

Act IV   In parliament, Gloucester's death is discussed, Bagot accusing Aumerle of complicity. Bolingbroke says that Mowbray can settle the matter, then learns he is dead. Bolingbroke, despite the Cardinal's protests that no mere man can judge a King, insists on ascending the throne and summoning Richard. Richard gives the insignia of state to Bolingbroke, but cannot bring himself to read out the list of his crimes. Distraught, he is taken away to the Tower. The Bishop of Carlisle, the Abbot of Westminster, and Aumerle plot to kill Bolingbroke.

Act V   When the Queen chides Richard for his weakness, he tells her to forget him. Northumberland informs him he is to go to Pomfret and the Queen to be sent to France. Richard warns Northumberland that trouble will break out between him and Bolingbroke. The Duke of York, discovering his son Aumerle is involved in the plot, leaves for Windsor to warn Bolingbroke. However Aumerle arrives first, asking for pardon, closely followed by York himself and then the Duchess. Aumerle is pardoned, but not the Bishop and the Abbot. Exton, believing Bolingbroke wishes Richard dead, finding him imprisoned at Pomfret, murders him. At Windsor, Bolingbroke, now Henry IV, rewards the executioners of his opponents. Only Exton is repudiated by Henry, who realizes that although he wished Richard dead, he cannot love or reward his murderer. To expiate this regicide, he determines to make a pilgrimage to the Holy Land.

RICHARD III

Text: Q1, 1597.
Main sources: Holinshed. Edward Halle, *The Union of the Noble and Illustre Famelies of Lancastre and York,* 1548.

Act I   Yorkist, Edward IV, having triumphed over the Lancastrians, is secure on the throne. Discontented, his brother, Richard of Gloucester, seeks to get the crown for himself. He makes the King so fear Clarence, their brother, that he is sent to the Tower. Learning the King is ill, Richard realizes he must dispose of Clarence before the King dies, to ensure his own succession. Meeting Lady Anne (wife to Prince Edward, Henry VI's son, killed by

Richard and his brother at Tewkesbury) following the coffin of Henry VI (murdered by Richard), Richard mischievously woos and wins her. He accuses Queen Elizabeth of causing trouble for Clarence and Hastings. Queen Margaret, Henry VI's widow, watching the quarrel, curses both Richard and Elizabeth. The King sends for Elizabeth. Richard instructs two murderers how to kill Clarence. At the Tower, they stab him to death and throw his body into a butt of malmsey wine.

Act II   The sick King persuades Elizabeth to make friends with Hastings and Buckingham. Richard does so too, and then announces Clarence's death. The King collapses, believing himself to blame, since it was by his order that Clarence died — for although he had revoked the order, Richard had delayed the pardon until Clarence was dead. As Clarence's children learn of their father's death, the Queen arrives lamenting the King's death. Rivers, Grey and Vaughan are sent to fetch the Prince of Wales from Ludlow. Citizens, afraid, discuss what may happen. When the Duchess of York, and the Queen and the young Duke of York, hear that Rivers and Grey and Vaughan have been imprisoned by Richard and Buckingham, they decide to seek sanctuary.

Act III   The Prince arrives, escorted by Richard and Buckingham. His younger brother, the Duke of York, is fetched from sanctuary. At Richard's suggestion, the brothers are lodged in the Tower until the coronation. Hastings rejects Catesby's request for support for Richard as King. At Pomfret, Rivers, Grey and Vaughan are to be put to death. Richard swears that the Queen and Jane Shore (the dead King's mistress) have bewitched him, and, as Hastings is protecting them, orders Hastings' death. Richard gets Buckingham to tell the citizens of London that Edward and his children are really illegitimate, reminding them how Edward had lusted after their womenfolk. He announces that Richard is seeking their support to get the throne, but gets no response from the crowd. Richard, suitably praying, at first refuses the Lord Mayor's request that he take over the realm, but eventually, seemingly reluctantly, accepts, arranging to be crowned next day.

Act IV   At the Tower, Queen Elizabeth and Anne (now Richard's wife), with Clarence's young daughter, seeking to visit the two Princes, are refused permission by 'King Richard'. Anne is summoned to the coronation. Queen Elizabeth leaves hastily for sanctuary again. Richard now crowned King, hires Tyrell to kill the Princes, who threaten his position. Richard, determined to secure his position by marrying his niece, Elizabeth (Edward IV's daughter), and marrying off Clarence's daughter to a pauper, tells Stanley to give out that his wife is ill. Buckingham asks for the Earldom of Hereford promised him by Richard, but Richard, distracted by a prophesy that the Earl of Richmond (Stanley's stepson and a Lancastrian) will some day be King, dismisses him contemptuously. Later, as Tyrrell comes to tell the King the Princes are dead, news arrives that Buckingham is raising an army. Queen Margaret gloats over Queen Elizabeth and the Duchess of York as they mourn for the dead Princes. Despite his treatment of her, Queen Elizabeth is persuaded to let her daughter know of Richard's wish to marry her. News arrives that Richmond has landed in England and other areas of the country are in arms. Richard, uncertain of Stanley's loyalty, takes his son as hostage.

Act V   While Richmond approaches London, Buckingham is taken prisoner. At Bosworth Field, near Tewkesbury, the two forces line up. Richard, restless, has visions of his defeat, while Richmond sleeps with sweet dreams of victory. Next morning Richard learns Stanley has defected to Richmond. During the battle Richard, unhorsed, fights desperately, but Richmond wins. Stanley, taking the crown from Richard's corpse, gives it to Richmond, who, as Henry VII, plans to marry Elizabeth, Edward IV's daughter, and so bring peace, by linking the white rose and the red.

ROMEO AND JULIET

Text: Q1 (poor); Q2, 1599. Q1 was a 'bad' quarto, possibly a reconstruction from memory, with many inaccuracies and abridged speeches.
Main source: Arthur Brooke's poem, *The Tragicall Historye of Romeus and Juliet*, 1562. This was a very popular story, included also in William Painter, *The Palace of Pleasure*, 1566–7.

A Chorus tells (in sonnet form) of the antagonism between the two houses, Montague (Romeo) and Capulet (Juliet), in Verona, and that the play concerns two 'star-crossed' lovers from these families.

Act I   Capulet's servants quarrel with Montague's servants. A brawl ensues, drawing in Juliet's cousin, Tybalt, a haughty impetuous Capulet, and Benvolio, Romeo's friend. The Prince orders the two families, on pain of death, to stop fighting. Capulet, arranging that Paris may marry Juliet, if she agrees, sends out invitations to a masqued ball. Romeo, learning that Rosalind, his beloved who spurns him, will be there, decides to attend, although it is a Capulet affair.   Lady Capulet informs Juliet and her Nurse of the arrangements with Paris. After listening to Mercutio, Romeo's word-spinning friend, describe Queen Mab, the fairies' midwife, Romeo and his friends, masqued, arrive at the ball. Tybalt, recognizing Romeo, is restrained from challenging him to fight by his uncle. Romeo and Juliet meet and fall in love, only to learn later that each is of the opposing family.

The Chorus tells of Romeo's and Juliet's impetuous and passionate love for each other.

Act II   Romeo, leaving his friends, finds his way into Capulet's orchard. Juliet appears on the balcony above, musing on Romeo. They declare their love. Juliet arranges to send to Romeo at nine next morning to learn how and when they may marry. Romeo, arranging that when Juliet comes to confession to Friar Lawrence's cell, he shall marry them, sends word to Juliet by her Nurse. Juliet, impatient to hear from Romeo, is chided by the Nurse, who, finally, gives her Romeo's message. She and Romeo meet and are married by Friar Lawrence.

Act III   Mercutio, and his friends, encounter Tybalt, and his. They fight and Mercutio is, almost accidentally, killed. Romeo, in anger, kills Tybalt, and then flees from the townspeople who come to take him to the Prince. The Prince banishes Romeo, and fines both families heavily. Meanwhile Juliet, awaiting Romeo, is told by the Nurse what has happened. Romeo seeks safety in Friar Lawrence's cell, where the Nurse brings news of Juliet's distress. Friar Lawrence tells Romeo to go to Juliet but to leave Verona by daybreak. Capulet arranges that Paris shall marry Juliet three days hence, quietly, because of Tybalt's death. Romeo reluctantly leaves Juliet at dawn. Lady Capulet tells her of her imminent marriage to Paris. Juliet, refusing, angers her father who is adamant. She decides to go to Friar Lawrence for counsel.

Act IV   Friar Lawrence, learning from Paris of the intended wedding, suggests to Juliet that she acquiesces, and on the eve of her wedding, takes a draught which will make her appear dead. She will be taken to the family vault. After forty-two hours, she will recover. Meanwhile he will inform Romeo, and together they will take her secretly to Mantua. Juliet does this, and, apparently dead, her body is laid in the vault.

Act V   In Mantua, Romeo, hearing of Juliet's death, buys poison, and sets out for Verona. Meanwhile Friar Lawrence, discovering that his message to Romeo is undelivered, hastens to the vault. Paris bringing flowers to Juliet's tomb, finds Romeo there. Believing he is about to desecrate the tomb, he fights Romeo and is killed. Romeo kisses the 'dead' Juliet, and taking the poison, dies. Friar Lawrence reaches the tomb to find Romeo and Paris dead. Juliet, waking, refuses to leave Romeo. As Friar Lawrence goes she, kissing Romeo, stabs herself to death. They are found by the Prince, the Capulets and the Montagues. Friar Lawrence reveals the whole story. Realizing their own responsibility for the tragedy, the families belatedly make peace.

THE TAMING OF THE SHREW

Text: F1.

Source: There is a play, *The Taming of a Shrew*, published 1594, reprinted 1596, 1607. The relationship of this play to Shakespeare's has been a matter of much speculation whether it is (a) a play by another author, (b) a source for Shakespeare's *The Taming of the Shrew*, (c) a bad quarto version of 'the Shrew', or (d) a bad quarto version of an earlier play from which both 'a Shrew' and 'the Shrew' derive; no decisive conclusions have been reached. The Sly story — ultimately, *The Arabian Nights*. The Bianca story — George Gascoigne, *Supposes*, an adaptation of Ariosto's *I Suppositi*, performed 1566, pub. 1573.

Induction   Christopher Sly, a drunken tinker, found by a group of noblemen out hunting, is taken in and treated as a Lord. Players, arriving, are warned not to mock this 'Lord' when they present their play. Sly, waking, is told that he has been dreaming for fifteen years, is now recovered, and that his lady-wife (a page disguised) and the players await his attendance at a 'pleasant comedy'.

Act I   Lucentio, the wealthy merchant Vincentio's son, arriving in Padua to study, overhears Baptista announce that, until Kate (Katharina), his wild elder daughter, is married, Bianca, his younger, gentler daughter, is to remain at home. Old Gremio and Hortensio, suitors for Bianca's hand, plan to get Kate married off. Lucentio, falling in love with Bianca, decides to woo her, becoming her Latin tutor. His servant, Tranio, covers his absence by pretending to be Lucentio. Petruchio, from Verona, visits his friend Hortensio in Padua, telling him he is seeking a rich wife. Told of the shrewish Kate, Petruchio decides to woo her, with Gremio and Hortensio sharing his expenses. He agrees to introduce Hortensio (as a musician) into the Baptista household. Gremio hires Lucentio (as a Latin tutor) to woo Bianca on his behalf. Lucentio tells Tranio (dressed as Lucentio) to ask for Bianca's hand in marriage.

Act II Kate and Bianca are quarrelling. Gremio presents Lucentio (disguised) as a tutor for Bianca. Petruchio, asking to be allowed to woo Kate, presents Hortensio (disguised) to Baptista as a music tutor for Bianca, while Tranio (disguised as Lucentio) presents himself as a suitor for Bianca. Petruchio, wishing to hasten his wooing, parries words with Kate, and eventually carries her off, despite her protests, to prepare her for the wedding. Baptista, relieved, considers the suitors for Bianca, inclining to Gremio because he is safe, old and rich, but Tranio (as Lucentio) outbids him, and obtains Baptista's consent, provided he can make good his dowry offer.

Act III Meanwhile, disguised, Lucentio and Hortensio vie for Bianca's favours as they teach her. On the day of her marriage, Kate sets off irritably for the church, sure that 'mad' Petruchio will not come. He arrives in tattered clothes on an old nag. Tranio tells Lucentio someone must pretend to be his father, to 'confirm' the dowry promised to Baptista. Petruchio, refusing to stay for the wedding feast, leaves for Verona with Kate.

Act IV Grumio, Petruchio's servant, announces the advent of the newlyweds. They arrive, hungry. Petruchio finds fault with and rejects all the food, seeking to curb Kate as a falconer trains a falcon. In Padua, Hortensio and Tranio, watching Bianca's warm reception of the disguised Lucentio, withdraw their suits. A man is found willing to act as Lucentio's father. Meanwhile Kate, starved of food and sleep for days, is visited by a tailor who shows her new dresses for a visit to her father. Petruchio, disliking all he sees, declares they will return home in their 'honest' old clothes. Tranio presents Lucentio's 'father' to Baptista. Petruchio has so 'trained' Kate that she is prepared to agree to absolutely anything he says. En route to Padua Kate and Petruchio meet Vincentio, travelling to visit his son Lucentio, whom Petruchio addresses first as a maid, then as an old man. Kate meekly accepts Petruchio's contradictory behaviour.

Act V Vincentio, with Petruchio and Kate, arriving at Lucentio's lodgings, finding the pretended father there and Tranio disguised as Lucentio, believes Lucentio has been murdered. All is explained when Lucentio and Bianca appear, having been secretly married. At the wedding feast, to prove which is the most obedient, Petruchio, Hortensio and Lucentio summon their wives. Only Kate comes, and on Petruchio's orders, lectures the other two on a wife's duty to her husband.

Usually stage productions of the play end with an extract from 'A Shrew', showing the players leaving the nobleman's house, and Sly, with a new courage learnt of Petruchio to face women in the future, returned, again totally drunk, to where he was picked up when the play began.

THE TEMPEST

Text: F1, 1623. The masque was possibly added for the wedding of Lady Elizabeth, February 1613.

Sources include: Montaigne's essays, 'Of Cannibals', 'Of Cruelty', translated into English, 1603. William Strachey, *A True Reportory of the Wracke and Redemption of Sir Thomas Gates, A Knight,* 15 July 1610. Sylvester Jourdain, *A Discovery of the Bermudas,* 1610. *The True Declaration of the Estate of Virginia,* from the Virginia Company's official report, 1610. Ovid, *Metamorphoses,* trans. Golding, 1567.

Act I   A severe storm. King Alonso of Naples, his brother Sebastian, son Ferdinand, and Antonio, the usurping Duke of Milan, with various Lords, are shipwrecked on an island, inhabited by Miranda and her father, Prospero, a magician, the true Duke of Milan. Prospero relates to Miranda how Antonio, aided by Alonso, usurped his Dukedom, put Prospero and Miranda to sea, with his books of magic and supplies furnished by a kindly retainer, Gonzalo; how they landed on this island belonging to the dead witch Sycorax; how Prospero found Ariel, an aery spirit, pinioned in a pine, whom he released to assist him, and Caliban, Sycorax's deformed son, whom he tried to educate; how Caliban rejected Prospero's efforts, and after trying to rape Miranda, is now a menial slave. Ariel, impatient to earn his total freedom, serves Prospero by implementing the storm, and, invisible, leading the survivors to the island. He brings Ferdinand to Prospero's cell, where, as Prospero had anticipated, he and Miranda fall in love. Prospero, feigning mistrust of Ferdinand, sets him to work as a slave.

Act II   Those attending the King fear that Ferdinand is drowned. Gonzalo tries to distract Alonso, discussing colonization. Ariel, with music, puts them all to sleep, except Antonio and Sebastian. Antonio encourages Sebastian to murder the sleeping Alonso and take his kingdom. Ariel wakens Gonzalo in time to foil the plot. Elsewhere, Caliban is hiding from Prospero. Trinculo, the King's jester, finding him, shares his cloak as shelter from the storm. Stephano, the King's butler, mistaking them for a two-headed monster, is recognized by Trinculo, and drunkenly declares himself king of the island.

Act III   Prospero watches as Ferdinand and Miranda exchange vows of love. Ariel watches while Caliban suggests Stephano and Trinculo kill Prospero and take the island and Miranda. He causes them to quarrel. Prospero watches over Alonso, offering, then whisking away, a banquet. Ariel dressed as a harpy, reminds Alonso, Antonio and Sebastian of their crimes. Alonso desperate, runs off, followed by the others.

Act IV   Prospero, accepting Ferdinand, arranges a magic betrothal masque for him and Miranda, but, remembering Caliban's conspiracy, abruptly ends it. Ariel tells that the drunken trio are now at Prospero's cell. As they try on his clothes, dog-like spirits chase them off.

Act V   Ariel describes the sorry state of the King's group; Prospero decides to forgo revenge, to forgive, and burn his books of magic and break his staff. Dressed once more in his original Milan attire, Prospero reveals himself to Alonso, welcomes the good Gonzalo, offers to forget Sebastian's plotting, and requires his dukedom of Antonio. He discloses Ferdinand safe with Miranda, and orders Ariel to fetch Caliban, Stephano and Trinculo, and prepare the ship for all to return to Italy. To Ariel he gives his freedom. As epilogue, Prospero asks the audience to waft the travellers safely home with their appreciative applause.

TIMON OF ATHENS

Text: F1.
Sources include: Plutarch. Poss. Lucian, *Timon Misanthropus*. Poss. a lost play, *Timon*, written 1581–90.

Act I   Timon, a popular, wealthy patron of arts, gives money to his 'friend' Ventidius, imprisoned for debt, to his servant Lucilius to marry, and promises money to many others. Only Apemachus is cynical about the 'friendship' of those Timon patronizes. At a banquet, Timon bestows more gifts to the dismay of Flavius, his steward, who realizes that his master's resources are almost depleted.

Act II   Timon's creditors decide to press for payment, but there is no money left. Timon, sure of his friends, is planning to send to Lucullus, Lucius, Sempronius and the Senators for loans, when Flavius tells him he has already been refused money by the Senators. Timon appeals to Ventidius, who has recently inherited a fortune.

Act III   Lucullus refuses Timon; Lucius regrets he cannot help just now; Sempronius refuses, slighted because Timon did not ask him first. Timon's house is besieged by creditors. Timon invites his 'friends' to a feast. At the Senate House, Captain Alcibiades' pleas for the life of a soldier, who has killed a man in a drunken brawl, are rejected, and he himself is banished from Athens. At Timon's house, the company assembles. An embittered Timon reveals that the covered dishes contain only water, which he throws in their faces.

Act IV   Timon leaves Athens, cursing its inhabitants. Flavius follows his master. Timon sets up house in a cave near the sea-shore, and digging for roots to eat, finds gold. Alcibiades, en route to take his revenge on Athens, accompanied by his mistresses, Phrynia and Timandra, comes across the ageing Timon, who gives him gold to pay his soldiers. Apemachus arrives to taunt Timon about his present condition. Thieves arrive to rob him, but Timon, recognizing there is honesty in their purpose, gives them gold. Flavius arrives, and Timon recognizing that here, at least, is one honest man, gives him the rest of his treasure.

Act V   A poet and a painter seek out the by now old, wild, Timon, hoping he will give them gold. All he gives them is a beating. Athenian senators, coming to ask his help against Alcibiades, are spurned. Later, one of Alcibiades' soldiers finds Timon's tomb in the woods. At Athens, Alcibiades, taking the city, agrees that he will destroy only those who are his or Timon's enemies. The soldier brings the news of Timon's death and an imprint of the writing on his tomb, that he 'alive, all living man did hate'. Alcibiades declares he will establish peace with mercy in Athens.

TITUS ANDRONICUS

Text: Q1, 1594; F1 with addition of Act III, Sc. ii.
Source: Uncertain. An 18th-century chapbook, *The History of Titus Andronicus*, which included also a ballad, may be a version of a book entitled *A Noble History of Tytus Andronicus . . . also a ballad thereof . . .*, listed in the Stationer's Register in 1594, may be either a source for the play or based on the play.

Act I   Saturninus and Bassianus, sons of the late Emperor of Rome, seek election to his place, but the people of Rome choose Titus Andronicus, the general who has fought the Goths long and successfully. Titus returns to Rome with Tamora, Queen of the Goths, her sons, Alarbus, Demetrius and Chiron, and her Moorish lover, Aaron, as prisoners, and, despite Tamora's pleading, orders Alarbus to be sacrificed to appease the shades of his own dead sons. As Titus and Lavinia, his daughter, bury their dead, Marcus, Titus' brother, urges Titus to become Emperor. Titus refuses, advising they crown Saturninus instead. As Emperor, Saturninus asks to marry Lavinia. Titus agrees, giving his prisoners to Saturninus, who treats Tamora very courteously. Bassianus, secretly affianced to Lavinia, kidnaps her, and, in the resulting uproar, Titus kills one of his own sons, Mutius. Saturninus, seeking to undermine Titus' influence, rejects Titus and his whole family, deciding to marry Tamora. Titus' own sons turn on him when he refuses to allow Mutius honourable burial in the family tomb. Irritably, Titus gives in. Saturninus accuses Bassianus of raping Lavinia, but Tamora advises Saturninus to appear friendly while she devises a plan for revenge.

Act II   Aaron, overhearing Tamora's sons, Demetrius and Chiron, express their desire for Lavinia, suggests they kidnap and rape her when she is out hunting. Meanwhile Aaron, meeting his paramour Tamora, tells her of the rape plot. They are discovered by Bassianus and Lavinia, whom Tamora, when her sons appear, accuses of torturing her. Demetrius and Chiron kill Bassianus, throwing his body in a pit, and drag Lavinia off. Aaron lures Titus' sons, Quintus and Martius, to the same pit, where Martius falls in. Aaron fetches Saturninus. Tamora gives Saturninus a letter from Aaron implicating Titus' sons in Bassianus' murder. Demetrius and Chiron leave the raped Lavinia, with her hands and tongue cut off lest she disclose her attackers. Found by Marcus, she is taken to Titus.

Act III   Despite Titus' pleas, Quintus and Martius are condemned to death, and Lucius, a third son, is banished. Marcus gives Lavinia to Titus. Titus is ordered by Saturninus to send the hands of Marcus or Lucius, and his own to him, when Quintus and Martius will be safely released. Titus sends his own hand. A messenger returns the hand with the heads of his two sons. Titus vows vengeance, sending Lucius to the Goths to raise an army.

Act IV   Lavinia manages to disclose her rape, and by whom it was done. Titus sends gifts to Tamora's sons, with a cryptic message, which Aaron realizes means he knows the truth. Tamora has given birth to a blackamoor child, fathered by Aaron. Her sons insist the bastard be killed, but Aaron determines to keep it, substituting a fair child, and taking the blackamoor to the Goths. Titus, apparently mad, sends letters to the gods and supplicates

Saturninus. News come that the Goths, led by Lucius, are about to attack Rome.

Act V Aaron, captured with his child, to save the child, reveals all. Tamora, disguised as Revenge, with her two sons dressed as Rape and Murder, try to make Titus recall Lucius. He agrees to invite Lucius with Saturninus and Tamora to a feast, persuading Tamora to leave her sons to help him prepare. As soon as she leaves, he kills them both, using their blood to make a pastry covering for pies containing their heads. At the feast, Titus and Lavinia (veiled) serve the pies. Titus himself kills Lavinia to end her dishonour. He informs Saturninus that those who dishonoured her were in the pies eaten by Tamora, whom he kills. As Saturninus, in turn, kills Titus, he is killed by Lucius. The people of Rome choose Lucius as their next ruler. He orders that Aaron be starved to death, Saturninus, Titus and Lavinia given honourable burial, and Tamora's body be thrown to the birds and beasts of prey.

TROILUS AND CRESSIDA

Text: Q1, 1609. This has two different title pages, Q1B omitting the reference to 'As it was acted by the King's Majesties servants at the Globe', and having, in addition, an epistle to the reader. F1 is from Q1 text, with evidence of some use of Shakespeare's own manuscript.

Sources include: William Caxton, *Recuyell of the Historyes of Troye*, 1475. George Chapman, translation of *The Iliad*, 1598–1611. John Lydgate, *The Sege of Troy*, 1412–20. Chaucer, *Troilus and Criseyde*, c. 1385. Robert Henryson, *Testament of Cressid*, 1593.

Act I The Prologue sets the scene at Troy several years after the beginning of the Greek siege occasioned by the theft of Helen, Menelaus' wife, by Paris, son of King Priam. Troilus, a Trojan, tired of fighting, declares his love for Cressida (daughter of the Trojan, Calchas, who has gone over to the Greeks) to Pandarus, her uncle. Aeneas brings news that Paris has been wounded by Menelaus. As Cressida watches the Greek heroes returning from battle, Pandarus points out Troilus, but Cressida resolves to keep her love for him secret. In the Greek camp Agamemnon grumbles about the war. Ulysses blames Achilles, whose irresponsible, effeminate behaviour has undermined morale. Aeneas brings a challenge from Hector (Priam's son) to any Greek to single combat. Ulysses, realizing it is aimed at Achilles, suggests they fix a lottery so that Ajax, a blockhead, will answer the challenge, thereby goading Achilles to rouse himself.

Act II Ajax, mocked by a scurrilous Greek, Thersites, learns of the challenge. Priam and his son discuss the latest offer of terms from the Greeks — that Helen be returned. Hector urges they accept. Cassandra prophesies Troy's destruction if they refuse, but Paris and Troilus persuade Hector to fight on. Achilles, railed at by Thersites, retires to his tent, refusing to speak with Agamemnon. Ulysses, visiting him, reports that Achilles will neither fight tomorrow nor say why. Agamemnon asks Ajax to rouse Achilles, but, arrogant with Ulysses' and Nestor's praise, Ajax refuses.

Act III Pandarus brings a message from Troilus asking Paris to excuse his absence at supper, for he means to spend the night with Cressida. Cressida confesses her love, swearing to remain true. Calchas asks the Greeks to exchange Antenor, a captured Trojan general, for Cressida. Diomedes is sent to expedite this. Ulysses persuades Agamemnon and Nestor to ignore Achilles as they pass by his tent. Achilles realizes that his reputation is at stake and his love for one of Priam's daughters is known. He sends Thersites to get Ajax to invite Hector to come unarmed, safe conduct guaranteed, to his tent.

Act IV As Diomedes goes to fetch Cressida, Paris sends Aeneas ahead to warn Troilus. Troilus and Cressida part sadly, exchanging gifts. Diomedes, full of Cressida's praise, takes her to the Greek camp, where she happily returns their warm greetings. Hector and Ajax fight, but Hector withdraws, refusing to fight anyone related to Priam's family. He is feasted by all the Greeks, except Achilles, who boasts he will kill him when fighting resumes next day. Troilus learns of Diomedes' wooing of Cressida.

Act V Achilles houses Hector for the night, while Troilus follows Diomedes to Calchas' house, where Diomedes is treated lovingly by Cressida and given Troilus' love token. Embittered, Troilus vows to kill Diomedes. Next day, despite Cassandra's warnings, Hector goes to fight. Now ruthless, Troilus fights first Diomedes, then Ajax and Diomedes, neither winning; Achilles, roused at last by Hector's killing of Patroclus, seeks Hector out, whom he finds unarmed. He and his Myrmidon followers kill Hector. Troilus brings news to the Trojans that Achilles is dragging Hector's body, tied to his horse's tail, around the battle field. As the Trojans fight desperately on, Pandarus, scornfully rejected by Troilus, leaves, since traitors and pandars are so poorly rewarded.

TWELFTH NIGHT

Text: F1.

Sources include: Barnabe Riche, 'Of Apolonius and Silla', in *Farewell to Militarie Profession* 1581. Poss. Anon, *Gl' Ingannati — The Deceived*, publ. 1537.

Act I Orsino, Duke of Illyria, is refused admittance to Olivia, whom he loves, as she still mourns for her dead brother. Viola, wrecked by a storm (in which she believes she has lost her twin brother, Sebastian) on the coast of Illyria, seeks employment, disguised as a young man (Cesario), with Orsino. Maria, Olivia's maid, warns Sir Toby Belch, Olivia's uncle, to behave less riotously. Sir Toby persuades Sir Andrew Aguecheek, a gullible knight, to stay longer with the prospect of marrying his niece. Orsino sends Cesario to woo Olivia on his behalf. As Feste, the fool, chides Olivia for mourning so long, Cesario arrives. Olivia sends her puritanical steward, Malvolio, to dismiss him, but Cesario is insistent. Olivia rejects Orsino's messages, but attracted by Cesario, sends Malvolio after 'him' with a ring she claims 'he' has left.

Act II Sebastian, safe ashore in Illyria, believing his twin sister, Viola, dead, parts from Antonio, his friend, the sea captain, to seek his fortune. Malvolio delivers the ring to a bewildered Cesario. Sir Toby, Aguecheek and Feste carousing late at night, joined by Maria, are threatened with eviction by Malvolio. Maria says she will make a fool of Malvolio by persuading him Olivia is in love with him. Orsino persuades Cesario to visit Olivia again with a gift, a ring. Sir Toby, Aguecheek and Maria watch as Malvolio, considering the possibility of marrying Olivia himself, finds a letter, written by Maria as if from Olivia. It requests he appear smiling and with yellow stockings crossgartered.

Act III   Cesario meets Feste, and then Sir Toby, and Aguecheek, who grows angry at Olivia's warm reception of Cesario, and again says he will leave. Sir Toby persuades him instead to challenge Cesario to a duel. Maria warns them Malvolio is coming. Antonio, following Sebastian, offers him his purse, leaving to arrange lodgings for them both. Malvolio appears, smiling and crossgartered, before Olivia, quoting from her letter. She, believing him mad, puts him into Maria's hands, as she leaves to receive Cesario. Sir Toby has Malvolio put away in a dark room, then writes and delivers a challenge from Aguecheek to Cesario. As Cesario and Aguecheek begin reluctantly to fight, Antonio appears, and defends Cesario (whom he believes to be Sebastian), only to be arrested himself for a former offence committed in Illyria. He asks Cesario for help, calling him Sebastian, which puzzles Cesario for that was 'his' brother's name.

Act IV   Meanwhile Sebastian is mistaken for Cesario in a series of encounters — brawling with Sir Toby and Aguecheek, being taken home by Olivia, and, finally, persuaded to marry her. Sir Toby and his companions, with Feste dressed as a priest, torment Malvolio, who, assuring them he is not mad, asks Feste to bring him pen and paper to write to Olivia.

Act V   Cesario, mistaken for Sebastian, is accused by Antonio of deserting him when he needed help, of behaving oddly to Olivia, his wife. Finally, utterly bewildered, 'he' is assured by the priest that 'he' really has married Olivia. Sir Toby and Aguecheek arrive, bloody after the fighting. Sebastian arrives to apologize to Olivia for fighting. As he greets Antonio, the rest become aware of two Sebastians/Cesarios. All is revealed. Olivia receives Malvolio's note and sends for him. The jest is discovered. Feste owns up. Malvolio leaves, vowing revenge. The Duke welcomes Olivia and her Sebastian, proposing that when Cesario is again dressed as Viola, they also will be married.

THE TWO GENTLEMEN OF VERONA

Text: F1.

Main source: Jorge de Montemayor's story of Felix and Felismena in his *Diana Enamorada*, 1542, trans. into French by Nicolas Collin, and into English by Bartholomew Yonge, completed 1582, pub. 1598. Also poss. a lost play, *The History of Felix and Philiomena*, acted at Court, 1585.

Act I   Leaving Verona to seek his fortune in Milan, Valentine says farewell to his home-loving friend Proteus. Speed, Valentine's servant, who has been delivering a love letter from Proteus to Julia, accompanies him. Julia, discussing marriage with her maid, Lucetta, is given the letter, which she first rejects, then tears up, then, finally, when alone, puts lovingly together again. As Proteus receives her loving reply, his father, Antonio, informs him he, Proteus, is to leave for Milan.

Act II   In Milan, Valentine has fallen in love with Sylvia, the Duke's daughter. He supplies her with love poetry, to give to the one she loves. She returns it to him. Only Speed realizes her meaning. In Verona, Proteus and Julia, parting, exchange rings. Accompanied by Launce, his servant, and the dog, Crab, Proteus leaves. In Milan Valentine learns of Proteus' advent. Valentine and Sylvia welcome him, telling Proteus of their love, but that, since the Duke prefers a richer suitor, Thurio, they plan to elope. Proteus, infatuated by Sylvia's beauty, tells the Duke of the intended elopement, seeking to win Sylvia for himself. Julia, disguised as a boy, sets out from Verona to follow Proteus.

Act III   The Duke awaits Valentine's arrival, and discovering the rope ladder hidden under Valentine's cloak, banishes him. Proteus, told of the banishment, sees Valentine on his way. Thurio complains that Sylvia still does not love him. Proteus offers help. He will extol Thurio's virtues, and slander Valentine's.

Act IV   Valentine and Speed are set upon by a band of outlaws, who, impressed by Valentine's bearing, decide to make him their leader. Valentine agrees, provided they molest neither women nor the poor. Julia, in her boy's garb, overhears Thurio, accompanied by Proteus and musicians, serenading Sylvia. Thurio leaves. Sylvia appears and Proteus declares his love for her, which she scornfully rejects. Sylvia, learning that her father is to force her to marry Thurio, asks Sir Eglamour, a noble old knight, to escort her to Valentine. Launce tells the story of his delivery of a dog as a gift to Sylvia, and of Crab's appalling behaviour. Proteus engages Julia as his page (Sebastian) and sends 'him' with a ring (that was Julia's gift) and a letter to Sylvia. Sylvia again rejects him, expressing to 'Sebastian' her sympathy for Julia.

Act V   Sylvia and Sir Eglamour escape. The Duke pursues them, followed by Thurio, Proteus and 'Sebastian'. The outlaws capture Sylvia, who is then rescued by Proteus and Sebastian. As Proteus is about to take his reward, Valentine, having overseen all, berates him for his treachery. Proteus, utterly ashamed, asks Valentine's forgiveness. 'Sebastian' faints, and inadvertently discloses the ring Proteus gave her. She then reveals who she is. The outlaws bring in the Duke and Thurio, who withdraws his claim to Sylvia when Valentine challenges him to fight. The Duke pardons the outlaws, and all return to Milan for a double wedding and mutual happiness.

THE WINTER'S TALE

Text: F1.
Main source: Robert Greene, *Pandosto or The Triumph of Time*, 1598, reprinted as *Dorastus and Favinia*, 1607. Also Ovid, *Metamorphoses* (the statue story). Robert Greene, *Coney-catching Pamphlets*, 1592.

Act I   Camillo and Archidamus, two lords, discuss the warm reception by Leontes, King of Sicilia, of his childhood friend, Polixenes, King of Bohemia. Polixenes rejects Leontes' request to prolong his visit, until persuaded by the pregnant Hermione, Leontes' wife. This arouses Leontes' jealousy, so that he believes Hermione's unborn child is not his. He finally confides in Camillo, who, apparently persuaded, agrees to poison Polixenes, provided that Leontes take his wife back. Instead, Camillo warns Polixenes, and the two leave immediately for Bohemia.

Act II   Leontes accuses his wife of infidelity, ordering that their son, Mamillius, be taken from her, and she be imprisoned. Meanwhile, he sends Cleomenes and Dion to the oracle at Delphi for confirmation of his accusation. In prison, Hermione gives birth to a daughter. Paulina, Hermione's lady-in-waiting, confronts Leontes with the baby, to soothe his jealousy, but Leontes grows increasingly angry, ordering Antigonus, Paulina's husband, to leave the child in a deserted place, or both Antigonus and his wife will be put to death. News comes that Cleomenes and Dion have returned with a sealed message. Leontes gives orders for the public trial of Hermione.

Act III   At the trial, Hermione, accused of adultery with Polixenes and plotting with Camillo to kill Leontes, declares her innocence. The oracle declares that 'Hermione is chaste . . . Leontes a jealous tyrant . . . and the King shall live without an heir if that which is lost be not found.' Leontes, refusing to accept the oracle's judgment, is informed of his son's death. Hermione swoons and is given into Paulina's care. Accepting this as the gods' punishment, Leontes seeks reconciliation with Polixenes and Hermione. Paulina brings news that the Queen is dead, telling Leontes he is responsible. Leontes vows to mourn away the rest of his life as penance. On the Bohemian seashore, Antigonus leaves the baby, with a christening gown, gold, and her 'character' (naming her Perdita), tied in a bundle, and runs off, pursued by a bear. A shepherd finds the child, and he and his son decide from the garments in the bundle that the baby will bring good luck.

Act IV   Time, the Chorus, informs the audience of the passage of sixteen years; how Leontes still grieves; that Polixenes' son is grown up, and Perdita, believing herself the Shepherd's daughter, become a graceful young girl.

In Bohemia, Polixenes, refusing Camillo permission to visit Sicilia, describes the frequent absences of his son, Florizel, visiting the house of an old shepherd. Polixenes and Camillo, disguised, investigate. Autolycus, a pedlar, a 'snapper up of unconsidered trifles', who once served Prince Florizel, meets the Clown (the Shepherd's son), out buying foodstuffs for their shearing feast. Autolycus picks the Clown's pockets, and, learning about the feast, aims to get more spoils there. At the cottage, Perdita welcomes Doricles (Florizel in country disguise) and other country friends. The disguised

Polixenes and Camillo join in the festivities, finding Perdita attractive, but too low-born for a Prince. After dancing and singing, the Shepherd is about to betroth Perdita to Doricles, when Polixenes reveals himself, forbidding the match. He threatens to disinherit Florizel and have Perdita put to death if they disobey. Florizel plans to elope with Perdita. Camillo suggests they go to Sicilia to Leontes. He makes the passing Autolycus change clothes with Florizel, telling Perdita to muffle herself up, to avoid recognition. Secretly, he tells Polixenes what has happened, hoping that Polixenes will follow them to Sicilia and there be reconciled with both Florizel, Perdita and Leontes. The Shepherd leaves to tell the King that Perdita is not his daughter, and show him the bundle. Meeting Autolycus in his prince's gear, the Shepherd and his son ask him to get them access to the King. Autolycus takes them to his erstwhile master, Florizel.

Act V   In Sicilia Leontes is still mourning, for Paulina has made him promise not to re-marry until she finds him a twin soul to Hermione. Florizel and Perdita arrive. Leontes greets them warmly. News comes that Polixenes, in hot pursuit, having taken prisoner the old Shepherd and his son, has arrived. Autolycus is told how the Shepherd opened the bundle before the two kings; how Leontes realized that Perdita was his lost daughter. Leontes and Polixenes and the young couple, all reconciled, visit a chapel in Paulina's house, to see the 'statue' of Hermione she has had made. As Leontes kisses it, it comes to life, for his wife has spent the intervening years secretly with Paulina. All greet each other in amazement. Paulina is given a new husband, Camillo, and the winter's tale ends happily.

Dramatis Personae

Alphabetical list of the main characters in Shakespeare's works.

ABBREVIATIONS USED

A&C	Antony and Cleopatra	*MM*	Measure for Measure
AW	All's Well That Ends Well	*MND*	A Midsummer Night's Dream
AYLI	As You Like it	*MV*	The Merchant of Venice
CE	The Comedy of Errors	*MWW*	The Merry Wives of Windsor
Cor.	Coriolanus	*Oth.*	Othello
Cym.	Cymbeline	*P&T*	The Phoenix and the Turtle
1H4	Henry IV, Part 1	*Per.*	Pericles
2H4	Henry IV, Part 2	*R2*	Richard II
H5	Henry V	*R3*	Richard III
1H6	Henry VI, Part 1	*R&J*	Romeo and Juliet
2H6	Henry VI, Part 2	*Son.*	Sonnets
3H6	Henry VI, Part 3	*T&C*	Troilus and Cressida
H8	Henry VIII	*T of A*	Timon of Athens
Ham.	Hamlet	*TA*	Titus Andronicus
JC	Julius Caesar	*Tem.*	The Tempest
KJ	King John	*TGV*	The Two Gentlemen of Verona
KL	King Lear	*TN*	Twelfth Night
LLL	Love's Labour's Lost	*TS*	The Taming of the Shrew
Luc.	The Rape of Lucrece	*V&A*	Venus and Adonis
MA	Much Ado About Nothing	*WT*	A Winter's Tale
Mac.	Macbeth		

AARON A Moor. Lover of Queen Tamora *TA*

ABERGAVENNY Lord *H8*

ABHORSON Executioner *MM*

ABRAHAM Servant to Montague *R&J*

ACHILLES Greek commander *T&C*

ADAM Old servant *AYLI*

ADONIS Beloved of Venus *V&A*

ADRIAN A lord, attending King Alonso *Tem.*

ADRIAN A Volscian *Cor.*

ADRIANA Wife of Antipholus of Ephesus *CE*

AEGEON Merchant of Syracuse, father of the twins, Antipholus *CE*

AEMILIA Wife of Aegeon *CE*

AEMILIUS Roman nobleman *TA*

AENEAS Trojan commander *T&C*

AGAMEMNON Greek commander *T&C*

AGRIPPA Friend of Octavius Caesar *A&C*

AGUECHEEK Sir Andrew, a foolish knight *TN*

AJAX Greek commander *T&C*

ALARBUS Eldest son of Queen Tamora *TA*

ALBANY Duke of, Goneril's husband *KL*

ALCIBIADES Athenian general *T of A*

ALENÇON Duke of, French nobleman *1H6*

ALEXANDER Cressida's servant *T&C*

ALEXAS Cleopatra's attendant *A&C*

ALICE Katharine's attendant *H5*

ALIENA Assumed name of Celia *AYLI*

ALONSO King of Naples *Tem.*

AMIENS A lord, attending the banished Duke *AYLI*

ANDROMACHE Hector's wife *T&C*

ANDRONICUS Marcus and Titus — *see* Marcus Andronicus, Titus Andronicus

ANGELICA Juliet's nurse *R&J*

ANGELO Deputy governor of Vienna, who seeks to make Isabella his mistress *MM*

ANGELO Goldsmith *CE*

ANGUS Scottish nobleman *Mac.*

ANJOU Duke of, French nobleman *1H6*

ANJOU Margaret of — *see* Margaret
ANNE Lady, Richard III's wife *R3*
ANTENOR Trojan leader *T&C*
ANTIGONUS Lord in Sicily, married to Paulina *WT*
ANTIOCHUS King of Antioch *Per.*
ANTIPHOLUS of Ephesus, twin son of Aegeon *CE*
ANTIPHOLUS of Syracuse, twin son of Aegeon *CE*
ANTONIO Merchant of Venice, Bassanio's friend *MV*
ANTONIO Prospero's brother, who usurped his Dukedom *Tem.*
ANTONIO Leonato's brother, Hero's uncle *MA*
ANTONIO Proteus' father *TGV*
ANTONY Mark, Roman triumvir, Caesar's friend, Cleopatra's lover *JC*, *A&C*
APEMANTUS Philosopher *TofA*
APOTHECARY *R&J*
ARCHIDAMUS Bohemian lord *WT*
ARIEL Airy spirit, who serves Prospero *Tem.*
ARMADO Don Adriano de, Spanish nobleman *LLL*
ARRAGON Prince of, suitor of Portia *MV*
ARTEMIDORUS Teacher of rhetoric *JC*
ARTHUR Duke of Bretagne *KJ*
ARVIRAGUS Cymbeline's son *Cym.*
AUDREY A country wench, marries Touchstone *AYLI*
AUFIDIUS Tullus, Volscian general *Cor.*
AUMERLE Duke of, later 2nd Duke of York *R2*, *H5*
AUSTRIA Duke of *KJ*
AUTOLYCUS An engaging pedlar and thief *WT*
AUVERGNE Countess of *1H6*

BAGOT Sir William, servant to Richard II *R2*
BALTHASAR A merchant *CE*
BALTHASAR Don Pedro's servant *MA*
BALTHASAR Portia's servant *MV*
BALTHASAR Romeo's servant *R&J*
BALTHASAR Assumed name of Portia *MV*
BANQUO Scottish nobleman, murdered by Macbeth *Mac.*
BAPTISTA Gentleman of Padua, father of Katharina and Bianca *TS*
BAPTISTA Wife to the player king, Gonzago *Ham.*
BARDOLPH Falstaff's crony *1H4, 2H4, H5 MWW*
BARDOLPH Lord *2H4*
BARNARDINE Condemned murderer *MM*
BARTHOLOMEW Boy, acts as Sly's wife in the Induction *TS*

BASSANIO Suitor, later husband, of Portia *MV*
BASSET A Lancastrian *1H6*
BASSIANUS Saturninus' brother *TA*
BATES John, a soldier *H5*
BAWD Wife of Pandar, brothel-keeper *Per.*
BEATRICE Leonato's daughter, Hero's cousin *MA*
BEAUCHAMP *See* Warwick
BEAUFORT *See* Somerset
BEDFORD Prince John, Duke of, 3rd son of Henry IV *2H4, H5, 1H6*
BELARIUS Banished lord, assumed name Morgan *Cym.*
BELCH Sir Toby, uncle of Olivia *TN*
BENEDICK A lord of Padua, in love with Beatrice *MA*
BENVOLIO Romeo's cousin and friend *R&J*
BERKELEY Lord *R2*
BERKELEY Attendant on Lady Anne *R3*
BERNARDO An officer *Ham.*
BEROWNE (BIRON) A nobleman, in love with Rosaline *LLL*
BERTRAM Count of Rousillon, marries Helena *AW*
BEVIS George, follower of Jack Cade *2H6*
BIANCA Younger sister of Katharina, marries Lucentio *TS*
BIANCA Mistress of Cassio *Oth.*
BIGOT Lord *KJ*
BIONDELLO Lucentio's servant *TS*
BIRON *See* Berowne
BLANCH of Spain, niece of King John *KJ*
BL(O)UNT Sir James, great-grandson of Sir Walter *R3*
BL(O)UNT Sir John, son of Sir Walter *2H4*
BL(O)UNT Sir Walter *1H4*
BOATSWAIN *Tem.*
BOHUN Eleanor de, Duchess of Gloucester *R2*
BOLEYN *See* Bullen
BOLINGBROKE *See* Henry IV
BOLINGBROKE Roger, necromancer *2H6*
BONA Sister of the French Queen *3H6*
BORACHIO Follower of Don John *MA*
BOTTOM Nick, a weaver of Athens *MND*
BOULT Servant of Pandar *Per.*
BOURBON John, Duke of, French nobleman, uncle of Charles VI *H5*
BOURBON Lewis, bastard son of the Duke of Bourbon *3H6*
BOURCHIER Cardinal *R3*
BOY Page to Falstaff *2H4, H5*. See Robin
BOY Macduff's son *Mac.*
BOYET A lord attending the Princess of France *LLL*
BRABANTIO Desdemona's father *Oth.*

BRACKENBURY Sir Robert, constable of the Tower of London *R3*

BRANDON Charles, Duke of Suffolk *H8*

BRANDON Sir William, father of above *R3*

BROOK Name assumed by Ford *MWW*

BRUTUS Decius, a conspirator in Caesar's murder *JC*

BRUTUS Junius, a tribune of the people *Cor.*

BRUTUS Marcus, a conspirator in Caesar's murder *JC*

BUCKINGHAM Edward Stafford, 3rd Duke of *H8*

BUCKINGHAM Henry Stafford, 2nd Duke of *R3*

BUCKINGHAM Humphrey Stafford, 1st Duke of *2H6*

BULLCALF Peter, a Cotswold man *2H4*

BULLEN Anne, Henry VIII's second wife *H8*

BURGUNDY John, 3rd Duke of *H5*

BURGUNDY Philip, 4th Duke of *H5, 1H6*

BURGUNDY Duke of (fictitious) *KL*

BUSHY Sir John, favourite of Richard II *R2*

BUTTS Sir William, King's physician *H8*

CADE Jack, rebel leader *2H6*

CADWAL Assumed name of Arviragus, son of Cymbeline *Cym.*

CAESAR Caius Julius, Roman triumvir *JC*

CAESAR Octavius Caius, great-nephew of Julius, Roman triumvir *JC, A&C*

CAITHNESS Thane of, Scottish nobleman *Mac.*

CAIUS Titus' kinsman *TA*

CAIUS Name assumed by Kent *KL*

CAIUS French doctor *MWW*

CAIUS Lucius, ambassador from Rome *Cym.*

CAIUS Marcius, *see* Coriolanus

CALCHAS Trojan priest *T&C*

CALIBAN Deformed offspring of the witch, Sycorax *Tem.*

CALPURNIA Julius Caesar's wife *JC*

CAMBIO Lucentio's assumed name *TS*

CAMBRIDGE Richard, Earl of, *see* York

CAMILLO A lord of Sicilia *WT*

CAMPEIUS Cardinal *H8*

CANIDIUS Antony's officer *A&C*

CANTERBURY Archbishops of, *see* Chichele(y), Cranmer

CAPHIS A servant *TofA*

CAPUCIUS Chapuys, French ambassador *H8*

CAPULET Juliet's father, head of Capulet family *R&J*

CAPULET Lady, Juliet's mother *R&J*

CARLISLE Merke Thomas, Bishop of *R2*

CASCA A tribune and conspirator in Caesar's murder *JC*

CASSANDRA King Priam's daughter, gifted with prophetic powers *T&C*

CASSIO Othello's lieutenant *Oth.*

CASSIUS A conspirator in Caesar's death *JC*

CATESBY Sir William, favourite of Richard III *R3*

CATO The young friend of Brutus *JC*

CAWDOR Thane of, title given to Macbeth *Mac.*

CELIA Duke Frederick's daughter, Rosalind's cousin *AYLI*

CERES Goddess represented in masque *Tem.*

CERIMON A lord of Ephesus *Per.*

CESARIO Viola's assumed name *TN*

CHAMBERLAIN Lord Chamberlain *H8*

CHANCELLOR Lord Chancellor *H8*

CHARLES A wrestler *AYLI*

CHARLES VI *See* France

CHARLES VII *See* France

CHARMIAN Attendant on Cleopatra *A&C*

CHATILLON French ambassador *KJ*

CHICHELE(Y) Archbishop of Canterbury *H5*

CHIRON Tamora's son *TA*

CHORUS Most famous chorus *H5*; also *RJ*; as Prologue *H8*; as Epilogue *H8*; as Rumour *2H4*; as Time *WT*; *see also* Gower

CICERO Roman senator, and orator *JC*

CIMBER Metellus, a conspirator in Caesar's murder *JC*

CINNA A conspirator in Caesar's murder *JC*

CINNA The poet, friend of Caesar *JC*

CLARENCE George, Duke of, brother of Edward IV *3H6, R3*

CLARENCE Thomas, Duke of, 2nd son of Henry IV *2H4* (*H5*, addressed only)

CLAUDIO Brother of Isabella *MM*

CLAUDIO A lord of Florence *MA*

CLAUDIUS King of Denmark, married to King Hamlet's widow, Gertrude; uncle to Prince Hamlet *Ham.*

CLAUDIUS Brutus' servant *JC*

CLEOMENES A lord of Sicilia *WT*

CLEON Governor of Tarsus *Per.*

CLEOPATRA Queen of Egypt, Antony's mistress *A&C*

CLIFFORD Thomas, Lord, 'Old' Clifford *2H6*

CLIFFORD John de, Lord, son of above, 'Young' Clifford *2H6, 3H6*

CLITUS Brutus' servant *JC*

CLOTEN Cymbeline's oafish stepson *Cym.*

CLOWN Brings asp to Cleopatra *A&C*;
servant of Countess of Rousillon *AW*;
servant of Othello *Oth.*; servant of
Mistress Overdone *MM*; brings
pigeons to Titus *TA*; son of Old
Shepherd *WT*; *see also* Costard, Feste,
Fool, Lavache, Touchstone

COBWEB Fairy *MND*

COLEVILE Sir John *2H4*

COLLATINE Lucrece's husband *Luc.*

COMINIUS Roman consul and commander
Cor.

CONRADE Follower of Don John *MA*

CONSTABLE of France *H5*

CONSTANCE Duchess of Brittany, mother
of Arthur *KJ*

CORDELIA King Lear's youngest daughter
KL

CORIN An old shepherd *WT*

CORIOLANUS Marcius Caius, Roman
general *Cor.*

CORNELIUS A doctor *Cym.*

CORNELIUS A courtier *Ham.*

CORNWALL Duke of, Regan's husband
KL

COSTARD A clown *LLL*

COURT Alexander, a soldier *H5*

CRAB Launce's dog *TGV*

CRANMER Thomas, Archbishop of
Canterbury *H8*

CRESSID *See* Cressida

CRESSIDA Calchas' daughter, beloved by
Troilus *T&C*

CROMWELL Thomas, servant of Wolsey,
later Master of the Rolls and King's
secretary *H8*

CUPID God of love, in masque of Amazons
TofA

CURAN A courtier *KL*

CURIO Attendant on Duke Orsino *TN*

CURTIS Petruchio's servant *TS*

CYMBELINE King of Britain, father of
Imogen, d. *c.* AD 2. *Cym.*

DARDANIUS Brutus' servant *JC*

DAUGHTER of the King of Antiochus *Per.*

DAUPHIN Charles, later Charles VII of
France *1H6*

DAUPHIN Lewis, son of Charles VI of
France *H5*

DAUPHIN Lewis, son of Philip II of France
KJ

DAVY Shallow's servant *2H4*

DECIUS BRUTUS *See* Brutus

DEIPHOBUS King Priam's son *T&C*

DEMETRIUS Follower of Antony *A&C*

DEMETRIUS In love with Hermia *MND*

DEMETRIUS Tamora's son *TA*

DENNIS Oliver's servant *AYLI*

DENNY Sir Antony, Privy Councillor *H8*

DERBY Lord Thomas, Earl of *R3*

DERCETAS Friend of Antony *A&C*

DESDEMONA Othello's wife *Oth.*

DIANA The Widow's daughter *AW*

DICK A butcher *2H6*

DIOMEDES Greek leader, who seduces
Cressida *T&C*

DIOMEDES Cleopatra's servant *A&C*

DION A lord of Sicilia *WT*

DIONYZA Cleon's wife *Per.*

DOGBERRY A constable *MA*

DOLABELLA Friend of Octavius Caesar
A&C

DONALBAIN King Duncan's younger son
Mac.

DORCAS A shepherdess *WT*

DORICLES Prince Florizel's assumed name
WT

DORSET Marquis of, Thomas Grey *R3*

DOUGLAS Archibald, 4th Earl of *1H4*

DROMIO of Ephesus, servant of Antipholus
of Ephesus *CE*

DROMIO of Syracuse, servant of Antipholus
of Syracuse *CE*

DUKE Senior, Rosalind's father, the
deposed Duke *AYLI*

DUKE Frederick, the usurping Duke
AYLI

DULL A constable *LLL*

DUMAIN Lord attending the King of
Navarre *LLL*

DUNCAN King of Scotland, murdered by
Macbeth *Mac.*

DUNOIS John, Count of, Bastard of
Orleans *1H6*

EDGAR Duke of Gloucester's legitimate
son *KL*

EDMUND Duke of Gloucester's bastard son
KL

EDWARD IV King of England, 1442–83
2H6, 3H6, R3

EDWARD V Son of above, King of England,
1470–83 *R3*

EDWARD Prince of Wales, only son of
Henry VI, 1453–71 *3H6*

EGEUS Hermia's father *MND*

EGLAMOUR Sir, a chivalrous knight *TGV*

ELBOW A constable *MM*

ELINOR Henry II's widow, mother of
King John *KJ*

ELIZABETH Lady Grey ,Edward IV's wife
3H6, R3

ELIZABETH Henry VII's wife, daughter of
Edward IV *3H6, R3*

ELIZABETH Mortimer, Hotspur's wife
1H4, 2H4

ELIZABETH Queen, as a baby *H8*

ELY Bishop of, John Fordham *H5*
ELY Bishop of, John Morton *R3*
EMILIA Iago's wife, attends Desdemona *Oth.*
EMILIA Attendant of Hermione *WT*
ENOBARBUS Antony's friend and companion *A&C*
EPHESUS Duke of, *see* Solinus
EROS Antony's servant *A&C*
ERPINGHAM Sir Thomas, officer of Henry V *H5*
ESCALUS Angelo's deputy *MM*
ESCALUS Prince of Verona *R&J*
ESCANES A lord of Tyre *Per.*
ESSEX Geoffrey Fitzpeter, Earl of *KJ*
EUPHRONIUS Schoolmaster *A&C*
EVANS Sir Hugh, Welsh clergyman *MWW*
EXETER Thomas Beaufort, Duke of *H5, 1H6*
EXETER Henry Holland, Duke of *3H6*
EXTON Sir Piers, murderer of Richard II *R2*

FABIAN Olivia's servant *TN*
FALSTAFF Sir John, Prince Hal's companion *1H4, 2H4, MWW*
FANG Sheriff's officer *2H6*
FASTOLFE Sir John *1H6*
FAULCONBRIDGE Lady, mother of Robert and Philip *KJ*
FAULCONBRIDGE Philip, bastard son of Richard I *KJ*
FAULCONBRIDGE Robert, legitimate son of Sir Robert Faulconbridge *KJ*
FEEBLE Francis, a recruit *2H4*
FENTON Suitor of Anne Page *MWW*
FERDINAND King of Navarre *LLL*
FERDINAND Son of King of Naples, in love with Miranda *Tem.*
FESTE Olivia's fool *TN*
FIDELE Imogen's assumed name *Cym.*
FIFE Earl of, *see* Macduff
FITZWALTER Lord *R2*
FLAMINIUS Timon's servant *TofA*
FLAVIUS Timon's steward *TofA*
FLAVIUS A tribune *JC*
FLEANCE Banquo's son *Mac.*
FLORENCE Duke of *AW*
FLORIZEL Son of King Polixenes, in love with Perdita *WT*
FLUELLEN A Welsh officer of Henry V *H5*
FLUTE Francis, a bellows mender of Athens *MND*
FOOL A court jester, constant companion of King Lear *KL*
FOOL A court jester *TofA*
FORD Master Frank, gentleman of Windsor *MWW*

FORD Mistress Alice, Ford's wife *MWW*
FORTINBRAS Prince of Norway, nephew of old Fortinbras *Ham.*
FRANCE King of, cured by Helena *AW*
FRANCE King of, marries Cordelia *KL*
FRANCE King of, Charles VI, 1368–1422 *H5*
FRANCE King of, Charles VII, first Dauphin, then King. Son of above *1H6*
FRANCE King of, Lewis XI, son of above, 1423–83 *3H6*
FRANCE King of, Philip II, 1165–1223 *KJ*
FRANCE King of, Lewis VIII, 1187–1226, son of above. As Dauphin *KJ*
FRANCE King of, Lewis, eldest son of Charles VI, as Dauphin *H5*
FRANCE Princess of, wooed by Ferdinand, King of Navarre *LLL*
FRANCIS Friar *MA*
FRANCIS A tapster *1H4*
FRANCISCA A nun *MM*
FRANCISCO Lord attending King Alonso *Tem.*
FRANCISCO A soldier *Ham.*
FREDERICK Duke, usurper of Duke Senior's dukedom *AYLI*
FRIAR Francis, *see above*
FRIAR John *R&J*
FRIAR Laurence *R&J*
FRIAR Lodowick, name assumed by the Duke *MM*
FRIAR Peter *MM*
FRIAR Thomas *MM*
FROTH A foolish gentleman *MM*
FULVIA Wife of Antony *A&C*

GADSHILL Associate of Falstaff *1H4*
GALLUS Friend of Octavius Caesar *A&C*
GANYMEDE Name assumed by Rosalind *AYLI*
GARDENER A gardener *R2*
GARDINER Stephen, Bishop of Winchester *H8*
GARGRAVE Sir Thomas *1H6*
GAUNT John of, Duke of Lancaster *R2*
GENERAL of the French forces *1H6*
GEORGE *See* Bevis
GERTRUDE Widow of the old King Hamlet, mother of Prince Hamlet, wife to Claudius *Ham.*
GHOST of Hamlet's father *Ham.*
GHOST of Richard III's victims *R3*
GHOST of Julius Caesar *JC*
GHOST of the murdered Banquo *Mac.*
GHOST of his family, appearing to Posthumus *Cym.*
GHOST Fiends, appearing to Joan of Arc *1H6*

MAB Fairy's midwife, referred to by Mercutio *R&J*

MACBETH Scottish nobleman, later King of Scotland *Mac.*

MACBETH Lady, wife of the above *Mac.*

MACDUFF Earl of Fife *Mac.*

MACDUFF Lady, wife of the above *Mac.*

MACDUFF Young, son of the Earl *Mac.*

MACMORRIS Irish captain of Henry V *H5*

MALCOLM Eldest son of Duncan, King of Scotland *Mac.*

MALVOLIO Steward to Olivia *TN*

MAMILLIUS Young son of Leontes and Hermione *WT*

MARCELLUS An officer *Ham.*

MARCH Earl of, *see* Mortimer

MARCIUS Coriolanus' son *Cor.*

MARCUS ANDRONICUS Titus' brother *TA*

MARDIAN Eunuch attending Cleopatra *A&C*

MARGARELON Bastard son of Priam *T&C*

MARGARET of Anjou, Queen of Henry VI *1H6, 2H6, 3H6, R3*

MARGARET Attendant on Hero *MA*

MARIA Olivia's gentlewoman *TN*

MARIA Lady attending the Princess of France *LLL*

MARIANA Angelo's betrothed *MM*

MARIANA Friend of the Widow, Diana's mother *AW*

MARINA Pericles' daughter *Per.*

MARTEXT Sir Oliver, a vicar *AYLI*

MARTIUS Titus' son *TA*

MARULLUS A tribune of the people *JC*

MASTER of the ship *Tem.*

MASTER and his mate, pirates *2H6*

MASTER GUNNER of Orleans *1H6*

MAYOR of Saint Albans *2H6*

MAYOR of York *3H6*

MECAENAS Octavius Caesar's friend *A&C*

MELUN A French lord *KJ*

MENAS Pompey's friend, a pirate *A&C*

MENECRATES Pompey's friend, a pirate *A&C*

MENELAUS Greek leader *T&C*

MENENIUS AGRIPPA Coriolanus' friend, a senator *Cor.*

MENTEITH Scottish nobleman *Mac.*

MERCADE A lord attending the Princess of France *LLL*

MERCUTIO Romeo's friend, killed by Tybalt *R&J*

MESSALA Brutus' friend *JC*

METELLUS Cimber, *see* Cimber

MICHAEL One of Cade's rebels *2H6*

MICHAEL Sir, friend of the Archbishop of York *1H6*

MILAN Duke of, *see* Prospero

MILAN Duke of *TGV*

MIRANDA Prospero's daughter, in love with Ferdinand *Tem.*

MONTAGUE Romeo's father, head of Montague household *R&J*

MONTAGUE Lady, Romeo's mother *R&J*

MONTAGUE Marquis of, a Yorkist *3H6*

MONTANO Governor of Cyprus before Othello *Oth.*

MONTGOMERY Sir John, a Yorkist *3H6*

MOPSA A shepherdess *WT*

MORGAN Belarius' assumed name *Cym.*

MOROCCO Prince of, suitor of Portia *MV*

MORTIMER Elizabeth, married to Hotspur *1H4, 2H4*

MORTIMER Edmund, 5th Earl of March *1H6*

MORTIMER Edmund, Sir (confused with above) *1H4*

MORTIMER Lady, wife of the above, Owen Glendower's daughter *1H4*

MORTIMER Sir John and Sir Hugh, supporters of York *3H6*

MORTON Northumberland's retainer *2H4*

MOTH Page to Armado *LLL*

MOTH One of Titania's fairies *MND*

MOULDY Ralph, pressed for service with Falstaff, but released *2H4*

MOUNTJOY A French herald *H5*

MOWBRAY Thomas, Duke of Norfolk *R2*

MOWBRAY Lord, son of the above *2H4*

MUSTARD-SEED One of Titania's fairies *MND*

MUTIUS Titus' son *TA*

NATHANIEL Sir, a curate *LLL*

NATHANIEL Petruchio's servant *TS*

NERISSA Portia's maid *MV*

NESTOR Aged Greek commander *T&C*

NEVILLE Anne, wife to Richard III *R3*

NEVILLE Cicely, wife to Richard, 3rd Duke of York *R3*

NEVILLE John, Marquis of Montague *3H6*

NEVILLE Ralph, *see* Westmoreland

NEVILLE Richard, *see* Salisbury, Warwick

NICANOR A Roman *Cor.*

NORFOLK John Howard, 1st Duke of (in Howard family) *R3*

NORFOLK John Mowbray, 3rd Duke of *3H6*

NORFOLK Thomas Howard, 2nd Duke of, *R3*

NORFOLK Thomas Howard, 3rd Duke of, Earl of Surrey (*see* Surrey, Thomas)

NORFOLK Thomas Mowbray, 1st Duke of *R2*

NORTHUMBERLAND Henry Percy, Earl of *R2, 1H4, 2H4*

NORTHUMBERLAND Lady, wife of the above
2H6
NURSE Juliet's nurse *R&J*
NYM Corporal, companion of Falstaff
MWW, H5

OBERON King of the fairies *MND*
OCTAVIA Antony's wife, after the death of
Fulvia *A&C*
OCTAVIUS *See* Caesar, Octavius
OLIVER Orlando's brother *AYLI*
OLIVIA A rich young lady of Illyria,
marries Sebastian *TN*
OPHELIA Polonius' daughter, in love with
Hamlet *Ham.*
ORLANDO Sir Rowland de Boys' youngest
son *AYLI*
ORLEANS Bastard of *1H6*
ORLEANS Charles, Duke of *H5*
ORSINO Duke of Illyria, loved by Viola
TN
OSRIC A courtier *Ham.*
OSWALD Goneril's servant *KL*
OTHELLO A noble Moor, married to
Desdemona *Oth.*
OVERDONE Mistress, a bawd *TGV*
OXFORD John de, 12th Earl, Lancastrian
3H6, R3

PAGE Boy player in the Induction *TS*
PAGE A gentleman of Windsor *MWW*
PAGE Mistress, wife of the above *MWW*
PAGE Anne, daughter of the above *MWW*
PAGE William, son of the above *MWW*
PAGE Given to Falstaff by Prince Hal
2H4, H5
PANDAR Brothel owner *Per.*
PANDARUS Cressida's uncle *T&C*
PANDULPH Cardinal and Papal legate *KJ*
PANTHINO Antonio's servant *TGV*
PARIS Priam's son, who abducted Helen
T&C
PARIS A young nobleman, affianced to
Juliet *R&J*
PAROLLES Unpleasant companion of
Bertram *AW*
PATIENCE Queen Katharine's attendant
H8
PATROCLUS Greek commander *T&C*
PAULINA Antigonus' wife, attending
Hermione *WT*
PEASEBLOSSOM One of Titania's fairies
MND
PEDANT Pretends to be Lucentio's father
TS
PEDRO Don, Prince of Aragon *MA*
PEMBROKE William Herbert, Earl of, a
Yorkist *3H6*
PEMBROKE William Marshall, Earl of *KJ*

PERCY Henry, 1st Earl of Northumberland
R2, 1H4, 2H4
PERCY Henry (Hotspur), son of the above
R2, 1H4
PERCY Henry, 3rd Earl of Northumberland
3H6
PERCY Lady, wife of Hotspur, eldest
daughter of Edmund Mortimer, 3rd
Earl of March *1H4, 2H4*
PERCY Thomas, Earl of Worcester *1H4*
PERDITA Leontes' daughter, in love with
Florizel *WT*
PERICLES Prince of Tyre *Per.*
PETER Nurse's attendant *R&J*
PETER Thump, apprentice to Horner
2H6
PETER Friar *MM*
PETER Petruchio's servant *TS*
PETER of Pomfret, a prophet *KJ*
See also Bullcalf, Quince, Simple
PETO Falstaff's companion *1H4, 2H4*
PETRUCHIO Gentleman of Verona, woos
Katharina, the shrew *TS*
PHEBE A shepherdess, loved by Silvius
AYLI
PHILARIO Posthumus' friend *Cym.*
PHILEMON Cerimon's servant *Per.*
PHILIP King of France *KJ*
PHILIP The bastard, *see* Faulconbridge
PHILO Antony's friend *A&C*
PHILOSTRATE Master of Revels to Theseus
MND
PHILOTUS Servant of one of Timon's
creditors *TofA*
PHOEBE *See* Phebe
PHRYNIA One of Alcibiades' mistresses
TofA
PINCH A schoolmaster *CE*
PINDARUS Cassius' servant *JC*
PISANIO Posthumus' servant *Cym.*
PISTOL Falstaff's companion and ensign
2H4, H5, MWW
PLANTAGENET Richard, created 3rd Duke
of York by Henry VI. *See* York
POET *JC*
POET *TofA*
POINS Prince Hal's companion *1H4, 2H4*
POLIXENES King of Bohemia, friend of
Leontes *WT*
POLONIUS Lord Chamberlain *Ham.*
POLYDORE Guiderius' assumed name
Cym.
POMPEY Pompeius Sextus, son of Pompey
the Great *A&C*
POMPEY A clown *MM*
PORTER At Macbeth's castle *Mac.*
PORTIA A rich heiress, marries Bassanio
MV
PORTIA Brutus' wife *JC*

POSTHUMUS Leonatus, husband of Imogen *Cym.*

PRIAM King of Troy, father of Troilus *T&C*

PROCULEIUS Octavius Caesar's friend *A&C*

PROSPERO Duke of Milan, father of Miranda *Tem.*

PROTEUS Gentleman of Verona *TGV*

PROVOST Governor of jail in Vienna *MM*

PUBLIUS A senator *JC*

PUBLIUS Marcus Andronicus' son *TA*

PUCELLE La, *see* Joan of Arc

PUCK A mischievous sprite who serves Oberon *MND*

PYRAMUS Bottom's part in the play presented to Theseus *MND*

QUEEN Cymbeline's wife, mother of Cloten *Cym.*

QUEEN Richard II's wife *R2*

QUICKLY Mistress, hostess of the Boar's Head Tavern *1H4, 2H4, MWW, H5*

QUINCE Peter, a carpenter *MND*

QUINTUS Titus' son *TA*

RAGOZINE A dead murderer *MM*

RAMBURES A French lord *H5*

RATCLIFF Sir Richard, supporter of Richard III *R3*

REBECK Musician *R&J*

REGAN King Lear's daughter, Duke of Cornwall's wife *KL*

REIGNIER Duke of Anjou *1H6*

REYNALDO Polonius' servant *Ham.*

RICHARD II King of England, 1367–1400 *R2*

RICHARD III King of England, 1452–85, formerly Duke of Gloucester *2H6, 3H6, R3*

RICHMOND *See* Henry VII

RINALDO Countess of Rousillon's steward *AW*

RIVERS Lord, brother of Elizabeth, Edward IV's wife *3H6, R3*

ROBIN Falstaff's page *MWW*

ROBIN Goodfellow, *see* Puck

RODERIGO A Venetian gentleman *Oth.*

ROGERO A Sicilian gentleman *WT*

ROMEO Montague's son, loved by Juliet *R&J*

ROSALIND Banished Duke's daughter, in love with Orlando *AYLI*

ROSALINE Lady-in-waiting to the Princess of France *LLL*

ROSALINE Niece of Capulet *R&J*

ROSENCRANTZ Childhood friend of Hamlet *Ham.*

ROSS A Scottish lord *Mac.*

ROSS Lord, supporter of Bolingbroke *R2*

ROUSILLON Countess of, mother of Bertram *AW*

RUGBY John, Dr Caius' servant *MWW*

RUMOUR as Prologue *2H4*

RUTLAND Earl of, son of Richard, 3rd Duke of York *3H6*

SALANIO Antonio's friend *MV*

SALARINO Antonio's friend *MV*

SALERIO Poss. misprint, not in all editions. Antonio's friend *MV*

SALISBURY Earl of, defects to the French, later supports Prince Henry, King John's son *KJ*

SALISBURY 3rd Earl of, supporter of Richard II *R2*

SALISBURY 4th Earl of, son of above, killed at Orleans *H5, 1H6*

SALISBURY 1st Earl of, title revived for Richard Neville, supporter of Duke of Gloucester (Richard III) *2H6*

SAMPSON Capulet's servant *R&J*

SANDS Lord *H8*

SATURNINUS Becomes emperor, and marries Tamora *TA*

SAY Lord, Lord Treasurer *2H6*

SCALES Lord *2H6*

SCARUS Antony's friend *A&C*

SCROOP (SCROPE) Sir Stephen, supporter of the King *R2*

SCROOP (SCROPE) Lord, son of Sir Stephen *H5*

SCROOP (SCROPE) Richard, Archbishop of York, brother of Sir Stephen *1H4, 2H4*

SEACOLE (SEACOAL) George, a watchman *MA*

SEBASTIAN Brother of Alonso; plots with Antonio to murder Alonso *Tem.*

SEBASTIAN Twin brother of Viola *TN*

SEBASTIAN Name assumed by Julia *TGV*

SELEUCUS Cleopatra's treasurer *A&C*

SEMPRONIUS A flattering lord *TofA*

SEMPRONIUS A kinsman of Titus *TA*

SERVILIUS Timon's servant *TofA*

SEYTON Macbeth's officer *Mac.*

SHADOW Simon, a conscript of Falstaff *2H4*

SHALLOW Robert, a country Justice *2H4, MWW*

SHEPHERD Old, father of Joan of Arc *1H6*

SHEPHERD Finds and brings up Perdita *WT*

SHREWSBURY Earl of, *see* Talbot

SHYLOCK Jewish money-lender, Jessica's father *MV*

SICINIUS Velutus, a tribune of the people *Cor.*

SILENCE A country Justice, cousin of Shallow *2H4*

SILIUS Ventidius' officer *A&C*

SILVIA Loves and is loved by Valentine *TGV*

SILVIUS A shepherd, in love with Phebe *AYLI*

SIMONIDES King of Pentapolis, father of Thaisa *Per.*

SIMCOX Saunder, an impostor *2H6*

SIMPLE Peter, Slender's servant *MWW*

SIWARD Earl of Northumberland, supporter of Malcolm *Mac.*

SIWARD Young, son of the above *Mac.*

SLENDER Shallow's cousin *MWW*

SLY Christopher, a tinker *TW*

SMITH A weaver, supporter of Cade *2H6*

SNARE Sheriff's officer *2H4*

SNOUT Tom, a tinker in Athens *MND*

SNUG A joiner in Athens *MND*

SOLINUS Duke of Ephesus *CE*

SOMERSET Beaufort, Henry, illegitimate son of John of Gaunt. Bishop of Winchester *1H6, 2H6*

SOMERSET Thomas, 3rd son of John of Gaunt. Duke of Exeter *H5, 1H6*

SOMERSET Beaufort, John, 1st Duke of Somerset *1H6*

SOMERSET Beaufort, Edmund, 2nd Duke of, younger brother of John, above *2H6*

SOMERSET Edmund, 4th Duke of, brother of, and confused with, Henry, 3rd Duke of (his older brother) *3H6*

SOMERVILLE Sir John, a Lancastrian *3H6*

SOOTHSAYER *JC*

SOOTHSAYER *A&C*

SOOTHSAYER *Cym.*

SOUTHAMPTON Earl of, V&A dedicated to him *V&A*

SOUTHWELL John, a priest, and sorcerer *2H6*

SPEED Valentine's servant *TGV*

STAFFORD Humphrey, 1st Duke of Buckingham *2H6*

STAFFORD Sir Humphrey *2H6*

STAFFORD William, brother of the above *2H6*

STAFFORD Lord, a Yorkist *3H6*

STANLEY Sir John *2H4*

STANLEY Sir John, brother of Thomas, Lord Stanley *2H6*

STANLEY Thomas, Lord Stanley, created 1st Earl of Derby by Henry VII *R3*

STANLEY Sir William, brother of Thomas, Lord Stanley *3H6*

STARVELING Robin, a tailor of Athens *MND*

STEPHANO A butler to Alonso *Tem.*

STEPHANO Servant of Portia *MV*

STRATO Brutus' friend *JC*

SUFFOLK William de la Pole, Earl of, then, 1st Duke of *1H6, 2H6*

SUFFOLK Charles Brandon, Duke of *H8*

SURREY Thomas Fitz-Alan, Earl of *2H4*

SURREY Thomas Howard, Earl of, 3rd Duke of Norfolk *H8*

SURREY Thomas Holland, Duke of, 3rd Earl of Kent *R2*

TAILOR Makes Katharina's gown *TS*

TALBOT Lord, later Earl of Shrewsbury *1H6*

TALBOT John, young son of the above *1H6*

TAMORA Queen of Goths, marries Emperor Saturninus *TA*

TARQUIN Sextus, rapes Lucrece *Luc.*

TAURUS Octavius Caesar's commander *A&C*

TEARSHEET Doll, Falstaff's mistress *2H4*

THAISA King Simonides' daughter, marries Pericles *Per.*

THALIARD A lord of Antioch *Per.*

THERSITES A scurrilous Greek *T&C*

THESEUS Duke of Athens *MND*

THISBE Heroine of the play acted before Theseus *MND*

THOMAS A friar *MM*

THUMP Peter, apprentice to Horner *2H6*

THURIO Rich man, rival of Valentine *TGV*

THYREUS Octavius Caesar's friend *A&C*

TIMANDRA Alcibiades' mistress *TofA*

TIME as Chorus *WT*

TIMON A noble Athenian *TofA*

TITANIA Queen of the fairies *MND*

TITINIUS Friend of Brutus and Cassius *JC*

TITUS Andronicus, Roman general *TA*

TITUS Servant *TofA*

TOBY *See* Belch

TOM-A-BEDLAM Name assumed by Edgar *KL*

TOPAS Sir, name assumed by Feste *TN*

TOUCHSTONE The fool of Frederick's court *AYLI*

TRANIO Lucentio's servant *TS*

TRAVERS Northumberland's retainer *2H4*

TREBONIUS A conspirator in the murder of Caesar *JC*

TRESSEL Attendant of Lady Anne *R3*

TRINCULO A jester *Tem.*

TROILUS Son of Priam, in love with Cressida *T&C*

TUBAL Shylock's friend *MV*

TYBALT Juliet's cousin, killed by Romeo *R&J*

TYRREL Sir James, supporter of Richard III *R3*

ULYSSES A Greek commander *T&C*
URSULA Silvia's attendant *TGV*
URSULA Hero's attendant *MA*
URSWICK Sir Chrisopher *R3*

VALENTINE One of the two gentlemen of Verona *TGV*
VALENTINE Orsino's attendant *TN*
VALENTINE Titus' kinsman *TA*
VALERIA Virgilia's friend *Cor.*
VARRIUS Pompey's friend *A&C*
VARRIUS Duke's (silent) friend *MM*
VARRO Brutus' servant *JC*
VARRO Creditor of Timon *TofA*
VAUGHAN Sir Thomas *R3*
VAUX Sir Nicholas *H8*
VAUX Sir William *2H6*
VENICE Duke of, judge *MV*
VENICE Duke of *Oth.*
VENICE Merchant of, *see* Antonio
VENTIDIUS Antony's general *A&C*
VENTIDIUS False friend of Timon *TofA*
VENUS Goddess of Love *V&A*
VERE John de, *see* Oxford
VERGES A petty constable *MA*
VERNON Sir Richard, supports Hotspur *1H4*
VERNON A Yorkist *1H6*
VINCENTIO Duke of Vienna *MM*
VINCENTIO Lucentio's father *TS*
VIOLA Sebastian's twin sister, in love with Orsino *TN*
VIOLENTA Friend (silent) of Diana's mother *AW*
VIRGILIA Coriolanus' wife *Cor.*
VOLTIMAND A courtier *Ham.*
VOLUMNIA Coriolanus' mother *Cor.*
VOLUMNIUS Brutus' friend *JC*

WART One of Falstaff's conscripts *2H4*
WARWICK Richard Neville, Earl of, and of Salisbury *2H6, 3H6*
WESTMINSTER Abbot of *R2*
WESTMORELAND Ralph Neville, 1st Earl of *1H4, 2H4, H5*

WESTMORELAND 2nd Earl of, grandson of the above *3H6*
WHITEMORE Walter, a pirate *2H6*
WIDOW of Florence, Diana's mother *AW*
WILLIAM Country bumpkin *AYLI*
WILLIAMS Michael, a soldier *H5*
WILLOUGHBY Lord *R2*
WINCHESTER Bishop of, *see* Beaufort, Henry
WINCHESTER Bishop of, *see* Gardiner
WITCHES The three *Mac.*
WOLSEY Thomas, cardinal *H8*
WOODSTOCK Thomas of, son of Edward III *R2*
WOODVILLE Elizabeth, wife to Edward IV *R3*
WOODVILLE Richard, Lieutenant of the Tower *1H6*
WORCESTER *See* Percy, Thomas
WRIOTHESLEY *See* Southampton

YORICK Skull of, jester of King Hamlet *Ham.*
YORK Archbishop of, *see* Scroop
YORK Archbishop of, Thomas Rotherham *R3*
YORK Duchess of, wife to Edmund Langley *R2*
YORK Duchess of, *see* Neville, Cicely
YORK Edmund Langley, 1st Duke of *R2*
YORK Edmund, Earl of Rutland *3H6*
YORK Edward, Duke of Aumerle, later 2nd Duke of *R2, H5*
YORK *See* Edward IV, Edward V
YORK George, Duke of Clarence *3H6, R3*
YORK Margaret Plantagenet, daughter of Clarence *R3*
YORK Richard, Earl of Cambridge *H5*
YORK Richard, 3rd Duke of *1H6, 2H6, 3H6*
YORK Richard III, King of England, formerly Duke of Gloucester, 1452–85 *2H6, 3H6, R3*
YORK Richard, Duke of, 2nd son of Edward IV *R3*

THE POEMS

Commentary on the Poems

VENUS AND ADONIS

Text: Published in 1593. Richard Field, a Stratford upon Avon tanner, who also published *The Rape of Lucrece*, printed and published this poem, which was dedicated by its author (as was *The Rape of Lucrece*) to the 'Right Honourable Henrie Wriothesley, Earl of Southampton and Baron of Titchfield'. Shakespeare calls it the 'first heire of my invention'. It was extremely well received, being reprinted in 1595, 1596, 1599, 1602, 1610, 1617 and 1620. This very large number of reprints reflects its popularity, as do the many contemporary references to it, including Gabriel Harvey's margin note, 'The younger sort takes much delight in Shakespeare's Venus, and Adonis: but his Lucrece, and his tragedie of Hamlet, Prince of Denmark, have it in them, to please the wiser sort.' It seems possible it was written during August 1592–April 1593 when the theatres were shut because of the plague.

Source: Ovid's *Metamorphoses*, in the original and Arthur Golding's translation, published 1567.

It is the story of the wooing of a reluctant young man, Adonis, by Venus, the demanding goddess of love, who uses all means at her disposal, from sexual seduction and aggression, to plausible arguments, to win his love. Unfortunately, despite Venus' pleas, Adonis leaves her to go out hunting, is gored to death by a vicious boar. Where his blood falls, a flower grows to his memory.

The poem combines art and nature, the twin pillars of Elizabethan writing, most successfully, both in matter and style. The presentation of the story is, at times, rich, heavy, almost claustrophobic in its sweetness; at others, it reflects the minutiae of the natural country world that Shakespeare himself must have been well acquainted with — the coursing of the hare, 'Wat', for example.

The style reflects the variety in the content, at times complex, almost overburdened; in areas of dialogue, sometimes rhetorical and florid, at others, natural, swift-moving and seeming to suggest a wry smile on the face of the author, who might well at this point agree with Puck, 'Lord, what fools these mortals be'. The poem is written with a degree of intricacy of rhyming (ababcc) that can allow each stanza to be a complete unit, but each stanza (six lines) is sufficiently brief to keep the poem moving easily forward. This was a popular verse form for narrative poetry at the time, and set against, for example, the jog trot of the couplet, one can see its advantages, in passages of description and dialogue, where there is space enough to pause, as well as in the narration. Within the overall scheme is an infinite variety of poetic ornamentation — contrasts, comparisons, parallels and balanced effects, colour and sound patterns, which suggest that the whole was wrought with infinite care, lively imagination and literary wit.

THE RAPE OF LUCRECE

Text: Published in 1594; originally entitled simply *Lucrece*. Richard Field, the tanner from Stratford, who printed and published *Venus and Adonis*, also printed this poem, which was dedicated by its author (as was *Venus and Adonis*) to the 'Right Honourable Henrie Wriothesley, Earl of Southampton and Baron of Titchfield', a dedication warmly expressed, 'What I have done is yours, what I have to doe is yours, being part in all I have, devoted yours.' Like *Venus and Adonis*, it was very popular, being reprinted seven times before 1640.

Source: The story is found in Ovid, *Fasti*, and Livy; in English, in Chaucer, Gower and William Painter, *The Palace of Pleasure*, 1566.

The poem itself is prefaced by an 'argument', i.e. a summary of the story, which relates in full the circumstances of the tale, from which Shakespeare extracts a dramatic core to present in his poem.

The argument tells how one evening after supper, while a group of soldiers are boasting of the qualities of their wives, one, Collatinus, praises his wife Lucretia (Lucrece), above all for her chastity. When they arrive home, only Collatinus finds his wife, Lucrece, behaving dutifully. Sextus Tarquinius sees her and is overcome with desire for her. Later that night — and it is at this point that the poem itself begins — Tarquin returns secretly to her house. There, as her husband's friend, he is invited to stay, and in the night creeps secretly to Lucrece's room, and despite all her arguments and pleas, rapes her. Lucrece sends urgently next morning, when Tarquin has fled, for her father and husband, and, after extracting from them an oath to revenge her, tells her story, then stabs herself to death. The last stanza sums up briefly the sequent events — the bearing of her body through Rome and the banishment of the Tarquin family. It is from the full argument relating the whole story that Shakespeare extracts the dramatic core for his poem. In fact, he deals with the story source here much as he deals with the story sources for the plays — condensing, sharpening, rearranging, all changes working towards a dramatic effect presented in human terms.

In *The Rape of Lucrece*, however, the drama and poetry sit uneasily together. The characters, Tarquin and Lucrece, have a tragic potentiality that only a play could exploit fully. The first half of the poem explores Tarquin's feelings, reactions, motivations and hesitancies in the way that

Hamlet's are explored in the play. The inevitability of what happens to Tarquin, once ensnared in his own evil conduct, recalls Othello's futile efforts held fast in Iago's web. The second half of the poem concerns Lucrece and her lament for what has happened. This part lacks the drama of action of the first part, where Tarquin is described as creeping secretly and silently through the house, gazing at Lucrece asleep, waking and raping her. Here the long complaint has no dramatic context that might have made it both pitiful and convincing. Too often the poetic conceit outweighs all other considerations, and the poem sinks under rhetoric and forced effect, till one wearies not only of Lucrece's complaining but of her self-pity and wordy reaction to the 'foul insurrection' of her 'consecrated wall'. One grows impatient that the 'lady doth protest too much' and one longs for the dramatic brevity of Cordelia's 'Nothing, my lord'. Even the poetic form, a seven-lined stanza (as opposed to the six-lined one of *Venus and Adonis*), rhyming ababbcc, is heavy-ended, delaying, like a slow march, the forward movement of the poem.

THE PHOENIX AND THE TURTLE

Text: Published as one of a group of commendatory poems — 'poetical essaies' — appended to Robert Chester, *Love's Martyr or Rosalind's Complaint* in honour of Sir John Salisbury. It was also published by John Benson in *Poems: Written by Wil. Shakespeare. Gent.*, 1640.

Chester's poem was subtitled 'Allegorically shadowing the truth of Love, in the constant Fate of the Phoenix and Turtle'. It was to celebrate the love of Sir John Salisbury and his wife, from whose union their daughter Jane was born. It was on the theme of the constant love and faithfulness of the phoenix and turtle that Shakespeare's poem was based. In it, the eagle, the swan and the crow are called together to make an anthem, on the occasion of the death of the phoenix and the turtle, to celebrate the unity and constancy of their love. The poem ends with a threnos — an ode of lament — praising the union of beauty, truth, rarity and grace in the phoenix and turtle, and laments with their death, their surcease.

It is a poem whose very simplicity and directness haunt and mystify. Many prosaic interpretations have been offered — political or contemporary allegory; an expression of theology (the relationships between the Holy Trinity); a poem of metaphysical symbols, or of emblematic puzzles — but, whatever keys have been applied, none of them turns cleanly to open out the meaning. The threnos is particularly powerful in its effect; terse and tantalizing as any riddle or rune, it is written in tetrameters — stanzas of three lines rhyming — which are didactic in content yet evocative in effect. It is the contrast between these that gives this part of the poem its sense of mystery. Abstract nouns, never qualified, their vowel sounds musically inter-related, hypnotize the reader or listener. It is, in fact, not so much a poem as an experience, in the sense that one comes from it as one might from a concert, having experienced something traumatic, but not able to explain or express in words exactly what. Here the playwright has become pure poet.

THE PASSIONATE PILGRIM

In 1599 William Jaggard collected together a group of poems, publishing them as *The Passionate Pilgrim* by W. Shakespeare.
Text: Two sheets only remain of a first edition; 2nd edition, 1599; 3rd edition, 1612.

Of this collection five poems are known to be Shakespeare's — Poems 1 and 2 are versions of sonnets 138 and 144; 3, 5 and 16 are versions of parts of the play, *Love's Labour's Lost* (IV. iii, IV. ii, IV. iii). Of the others, two are by well-known writers of the time. Poem 19 is the first four stanzas of Christopher Marlowe's *The Passionate Shepherd to his Love* — 'Come live with me and be my love' — and the fifth stanza is the first of Sir Walter Raleigh's *Nymph's Reply to the Shepherd*. Poem 11 is a version of a sonnet by Bartholomew Griffin, and with it, possibly, go numbers 4, 6 and 9. Poems 8 and 20 are by Richard Barnfield, appearing in his 'Poems in Divers Humors' 1598. Number 17 appears first in Thomas Weelkes's 'Madrigals to Three, Four, Five and Six Voices', 1597, and number 12 may be by Thomas Deloney. Who wrote the others in this volume is not known, and none of them is particularly outstanding.

It is interesting to note that when, in the 1612 edition, Jaggard included other poems by Thomas Heywood, Heywood objected strongly to him 'printing them . . . under the name of another . . . whom I know much offended with W. Jaggard that altogether unknown to him presumed to make so bold with his name'. Shakespeare's name was removed from the title-page of the 1612 edition.

A LOVER'S COMPLAINT

Text: Published, with the sonnets, 1609, and usually attributed to Shakespeare. Also in John Benson, *Poems: written by Wil. Shake-speare. Gent.*

This poem has been the cause of much speculation as to its authorship. It has a laboured air, alien to the 'honey-tongued' and 'mellifluous' Shakespeare. Its stanza form is that of *The Rape of Lucrece*, a seven-lined stanza, rhyme royal, but the words have an archaic flavour, like that Spenser emulated in *The Shepherd's Calendar*, and the imagery is often strained and bizarre without any of the dramatic aptness of Shakespeare's. However, it was printed in the same volume as the sonnets (which are undoubtedly Shakespeare's), under his name, and, as far as we know, not challenged as being by someone else. Whilst every consideration must be given to these facts, one cannot suppress the strong feeling that it is, none of it, Shakespeare's, merely an inferior, and totally superficial, pastiche.

THE SONNETS

Text: Sonnets 138 and 144 in *The Passionate Pilgrim* (a volume of poetry), 1599; Q1, 1609, for Thomas Thorpe; Q2, 1640, for sale by John Benson. In Q1 the collection falls roughly into two parts; the first 126 sonnets concern a young nobleman and his relationship with the poet; 127–52 concern the poet's relationship with the Dark Lady. The collection ends with 153, 154, to Cupid. In Q2 the collection is rearranged under theme headings, e.g. The Glory of Beauty, Injurious Time, etc.

The sonnet is a short lyric of 14 lines, variously divided into rhyming groups of 8 and 6 lines (the Petrarchan, or Italian mode), or 3 groups of 4 lines each, with a final couplet (the English or Shakespearean mode, developed first in England by Henry Howard, 3rd Earl of Surrey). Usually, in the Italian form, the theme is stated and developed in the first 8 lines, and answered or rebutted in some way in the last 6 lines; in the English form, the one Shakespeare made so very much his own that it has become known by his name, the argument is presented in the first 4 lines, with variations or developments or comments in the next two groups of 4 lines, and clinched or rebutted, with resonance, in the final couplet. Each line has the same basic rhythm that is used in the plays — iambic pentameter (i.e. 10 syllabled, 5 stressed feet). Each line, again as in the plays, has changes of stress and pause, so that its spoken meaning may either slot exactly into the basic rhythm, or it may play a kind of roving descant, sometimes at variance, sometimes in union, with the basic beat. While there is therefore always the continuity of the underlying rhythm, and the constancy of the repeated rhymes, there are many ways of stressing each line, and so, many many more of stressing the complete sonnet. This offers, as does any speech from any of Shakespeare's plays, an infinite variety of interpretation, which 'age cannot wither, nor custom stale'.

Sonnets usually explore personal, or quasi-personal, situations (the line between fiction and fact in Elizabethan poetry is a somewhat wayward one) and several sonnets may be collected together to form a sequence. They are persuasively autobiographical in tone and attitude, but, since it is the aim of all sonneteers to achieve this kind of spontaneity, it is often a case of the better poet being the more persuasive, and, as a result, seeming the more sincerely involved. To accept any sonnet of this period at its face value, as a blueprint for the recording of real events and emotions, can lead one to build up bizarre conclusions, all founded on the proverbial sand. However, in comparison with, say, the epic, or lyric, or narrative poetry of the time, there is an obvious immediacy, and the sense of a real living person just disappearing round the next corner always haunts these poems.

Petrarch (Italian poet, 1304–74) set the seal on the form and content of the sonnet sequence in his *Canzoniere*, a group of some three hundred lyrics, most of them sonnets, addressed to his beloved, Laura. This sequence was extremely popular, and the sonnet form was first introduced into England by Sir Thomas Wyatt and Henry Howard, 3rd Earl of Surrey, in *Tottel's Miscellany* (a much-read volume of Elizabethan lyrics) in 1557. By the 1590s, sonnet sequences were springing up everywhere, the earliest and still one of the most enjoyable being Sir Philip Sidney's *Astrophel and Stella*, 1591, addressed to Stella (Penelope Devereux) by her unsuccessful suitor, Astrophel (Sir Philip). Between 1591 and 1597 some fifteen or more sequences were published; then, as a vogue, it burnt itself out (few have been written since), but not before both Edmund Spenser and William Shakespeare had added their offerings to the pyre.

The first reference we have to Shakespeare penning sonnets is in *Palladis Tamia* where Meres comments on Shakespeare's 'sugared sonnets among his private friends'. The normal way of circulating poems of this nature at that time was to pass them between friends, but which of Shakespeare's particular sonnets or friends this refers to, we do not know. Sonnets 138 and 144 were first published in *The Passionate Pilgrim*, 1599, a volume of poetry attributed to Shakespeare, but not all of it by him. It was not until 1609 that the collection of sonnets, complete as we have them now, was first published by Thomas Thorpe. The text of Thorpe's edition is good, but it seems clear that the publication was not overwatched by the author personally, because, for example, the text of sonnets 138 and 144, which had been previously published in *The Passionate Pilgrim*, differed in Thorpe's edition. In fact, it seems possible that the sonnets could have been obtained surreptitiously, for if the story the contents reveal is at all autobiographical, then it is a story that is not only painful, but involves the treachery and deceit of others.

We do not know when the sonnets were written (although 138 and 144 must have been pre-1599, the date of publication of *The Passionate Pilgrim*) nor the order in which they were written, nor whom they concern, nor finally to whom they were dedicated. In the dedication, only the initials 'Mr. W.H.' are given. The two main claimants (and there have, of course, been others), to that dedication are — Henry Wriothesley, 3rd Earl of Southampton, to whom both *Venus and Adonis* and *The Rape of Lucrece* were dedicated, the initials being cunningly reversed; and William

Herbert, 3rd Earl of Pembroke, whose initials at least are in the right order. Neither is it known whether 'Mr. W.H.' was himself one of the protagonists in the drama the sequence unfolds, or related to one of the protagonists, or, even just a friend of Thorpe himself.

Speculations therefore about (a) the authenticity of the authorship of individual sonnets, (b) the order in which, and when they were composed, (c) to whom they were dedicated, (d) who the personalities referred to in the sonnets are, are many and varied. All one can say for certain is that this collection of sonnets deals with several incidents, many common to any sonneteer of that time worth his salt, others which resolve into a dramatic story of love and treachery concerning the Author-Poet, his Friend and a Black-eyed Lady (cf. the Rosalines in *Love's Labour's Lost* and *Romeo and Juliet*). The collection opens with the Poet's early relationship with the Friend, at first formally persuading him to marry and raise a family (1–17). Later they reflect (18–126) a growing and deepening relationship, sometimes sunny, sometimes sterile, sometimes tempestuous, between the two of them. They tell of the advent of another poet, a rival for the Friend's affections, and reach a climax of pain and bitterness when either the Friend steals the Poet's mistress, the Dark Lady, or the Poet's mistress, the Dark Lady, seduces the Friend, and both deceive the Poet. A final group (127–52) is more nearly concerned with the black-haired, black-eyed Lady and the whole collection ends with two (153, 154) very conventional sonnets to Cupid.

There is, throughout, an element of directness, an unaffected clarity of statement, as well as a rich appreciation of the natural world, and of man as a social animal, involved in commerce, the law, the theatre, travelling and dispute. But, above all, the collection mirrors the timeless areas of love and hatred, honesty and deceit, truth and treachery, that are elsewhere reflected dramatically in the plays. The sonnets themselves vary in tone. Some (e.g. 18, 33, 73) are relaxed, rich in natural description; some are colloquial and personal (40) as though the author is in the same room, speaking directly to you; some are taut with arguments that develop, turn back on themselves, the author playing on words, their sounds and their meanings (42, 87, 127); some are celebratory (116), some bitter and accusatory (129, 144); some are tantalizing in the information they offer about their elusive begetter (20, 144). In all of them, however, their brief spell is contained by the rhyming pattern Shakespeare used, always satisfactorily rounded off by the completing couplet; and their lyricism is highlighted everywhere by a dramatic immediacy, expressed with the same power and sustained appositeness of imagery that enriches Shakespeare's plays.

First Lines of the Sonnets

The numbers refer to the numbers of the sonnets as printed in the Thomas Thorpe edition, 1609.

SHAKESPEARE'S INFINITE VARIETY

One can only wonder at Shakespeare's capacity for varying the mode and mood of his dramatic writing. Outstanding speeches in his plays range from the didactic, where a point of view is argued (*see* selection from *As You Like It, The Merchant of Venice*) to the flamboyance of the high rhetorical or heroic (see *Julius Caesar, Henry V* and *Richard II*); from the rich transformation of his source material (see *Antony and Cleopatra*) to the dramatic musings of a character in an agony of indecision (see *Hamlet, Macbeth*); from the fantastic (see *Romeo and Juliet*) to the warm natural descriptions linked so closely to his Warwickshire homeland (see *A Midsummer Night's Dream*). In this section we seek to offer some samples of that variety.

No record of Shakespeare's variety would, however, be complete without extracts from some of his more formal poetry — the songs that sparkle intermittently in his plays, his sonnets and his two long poems, *Venus and Adonis* and *The Rape of Lucrece*. The pieces offered here fall far short of doing Shakespeare justice. They are the personal choice of the authors, covering as many facets of his writing as possible. Many of them are well-known pieces. This is perhaps natural, since they capture so aptly and express so precisely moods or attitudes of mind that are both particular to their own context, and at the same time universal and timeless in their general appeal.

Famous Speeches

ANTONY AND CLEOPATRA (Act II, Sc. ii)

The barge she sat in, like a burnish'd throne,
Burn'd on the water; the poop was beaten gold,
Purple the sails, and so perfumed, that
The winds were love-sick with them; the oars were silver,
Which to the tune of flutes kept stroke, and made
The water which they beat to follow faster,
As amorous of their strokes. For her own person,
It beggar'd all description; she did lie
In her pavilion, — cloth-of-gold of tissue, —
O'er-picturing that Venus where we see
The fancy outwork nature; on each side of her
Stood pretty-dimpled boys, like smiling Cupids,

With divers-colour'd fans, whose wind did seem
To glow the delicate cheeks which they did cool,
And what they undid did.

(Enobarbus)

AS YOU LIKE IT (Act II, Sc. vii)

   All the world's a stage,
And all the men and women merely players:
They have their exits and their entrances;
And one man in his time plays many parts,
His acts being seven ages. At first the infant,
Mewling and puking in the nurse's arms.
And then the whining school-boy, with his satchel,
And shining morning face, creeping like snail
Unwilling to school. And then the lover,
Sighing like furnace, with a woful ballad
Made to his mistress' eyebrow. Then a soldier,
Full of strange oaths, and bearded like the pard,
Jealous in honour, sudden and quick in quarrel,
Seeking the bubble reputation
Even in the cannon's mouth. And then the justice,
In fair round belly with good capon lin'd,
With eyes severe, and beard of formal cut,
Full of wise saws and modern instances;
And so he plays his part. The sixth age shifts
Into the lean and slipper'd pantaloon,
With spectacles on nose and pouch on side,
His youthful hose well sav'd, a world too wide
For his shrunk shank; and his big manly voice,
Turning again toward childish treble, pipes
And whistles in his sound. Last scene of all,
That ends this strange eventful history,
Is second childishness and mere oblivion,
Sans teeth, sans eyes, sans taste, sans everything.

(Jaques)

HAMLET (Act III, Sc. i)

To be, or not to be: that is the question;
Whether 'tis nobler in the mind to suffer
The slings and arrows of outrageous fortune,
Or to take arms against a sea of troubles,

And by opposing end them? To die: to sleep;
No more; and, by a sleep to say we end
The heart-ache and the thousand natural shocks
That flesh is heir to, 'tis a consummation
Devoutly to be wish'd. To die, to sleep;
To sleep: perchance to dream: ay, there's the rub;
For in that sleep of death what dreams may come
When we have shuffled off this mortal coil,
Must give us pause. There's the respect
That makes calamity of so long life;
For who would bear the whips and scorns of time,
The oppressor's wrong, the proud man's contumely,
The pangs of dispriz'd love, the law's delay,
The insolence of office, and the spurns
That patient merit of the unworthy takes,
When he himself might his quietus make
With a bare bodkin? who would fardels bear,
To grunt and sweat under a weary life,
But that the dread of something after death,
The undiscover'd country from whose bourn
No traveller returns, puzzles the will,
And makes us rather bear those ills we have
Than fly to others that we know not of?
Thus conscience does make cowards of us all;
And thus the native hue of resolution
Is sicklied o'er with the pale cast of thought,
And enterprises of great pith and moment
With this regard their currents turn awry,
And lose the name of action.

                                                                    (Hamlet)

HENRY V (Act III, Sc. i)

Once more unto the breach, dear friends, once more;
Or close the wall up with our English dead!
In peace there's nothing so becomes a man
As modest stillness and humility:
But when the blast of war blows in our ears,
Then imitate the action of the tiger;
Stiffen the sinews, summon up the blood,
Disguise fair nature with hard-favour'd rage;
Then lend the eye a terrible aspect;
Let it pry through the portage of the head
Like the brass cannon; let the brow o'erwhelm it

As fearfully as doth a galled rock
O'erhang and jutty his confounded base,
Swill'd with the wild and wasteful ocean.
Now set the teeth and stretch the nostril wide,
Hold hard the breath, and bend up every spirit
To his full height! On, on, you noblest English!
Whose blood is fet from fathers of war-proof;
Fathers that, like so many Alexanders,
Have in these parts from morn till even fought,
And sheath'd their swords for lack of argument.
Dishonour not your mothers; now attest
That those whom you call'd fathers did beget you.
Be copy now to men of grosser blood,
And teach them how to war. And you, good yeomen,
Whose limbs were made in England, show us here
The mettle of your pasture; let us swear
That you are worth your breeding; which I doubt not;
For there is none of you so mean and base
That hath not noble lustre in your eyes.
I see you stand like greyhounds in the slips,
Straining upon the start. The game's afoot:
Follow your spirit; and, upon this charge
Cry 'God for Harry! England and Saint George!'

(King Henry)

JULIUS CAESAR (Act III, Sc. ii)

Friends, Romans, countrymen, lend me your ears;
I come to bury Caesar, not to praise him.
The evil that men do lives after them,
The good is oft interred with their bones;
So let it be with Caesar. The noble Brutus
Hath told you Caesar was ambitious;
If it were so, it was a grievous fault,
And grievously hath Caesar answer'd it.
Here, under leave of Brutus and the rest, —
For Brutus is an honourable man;
So are they all, all honourable men, —
Come I to speak in Caesar's funeral.
He was my friend, faithful and just to me:
But Brutus says he was ambitious;
And Brutus is an honourable man.
He hath brought many captives home to Rome,

Whose ransoms did the general coffers fill:
Did this in Caesar seem ambitious?
When that the poor have cried, Caesar hath wept;
Ambition should be made of sterner stuff:
Yet Brutus says he was ambitious;
And Brutus is an honourable man.
You all did see that on the Lupercal
I thrice presented him a kingly crown,
Which he did thrice refuse: was this ambition?
Yet Brutus says he was ambitious;
And, sure, he is an honourable man.
I speak not to disprove what Brutus spoke,
But here I am to speak what I do know.
You all did love him once, not without cause:
What cause withholds you then to mourn for him?
O judgement! thou art fled to brutish beasts,
And men have lost their reason.

                                              (Mark Antony)

MACBETH (Act V, Sc. v)

To-morrow, and to-morrow, and to-morrow,
Creeps in this petty pace from day to day,
To the last syllable of recorded time;
And all our yesterdays have lighted fools
The way to dusty death. Out, out, brief candle!
Life's but a walking shadow, a poor player
That struts and frets his hour upon the stage,
And then is heard no more; it is a tale
Told by an idiot, full of sound and fury,
Signifying nothing.

                                              (Macbeth)

(Act II, Sc. i)
Is this a dagger which I see before me,
The handle toward my hand? Come, let me clutch thee:
I have thee not, and yet I see thee still.
Art thou not, fatal vision, sensible
To feeling as to sight? or art thou but
A dagger of the mind, a false creation,
Proceeding from the heat-oppressed brain?
I see thee yet, in form as palpable
As this which now I draw.

37. Shakespeare: the Droeshout portrait from the First Folio, 1623.

38. Shakespeare: the 'Flower' portrait.

39. Shakespeare: the 'Chandos' portrait.

40. Shakespeare: from John Hall's painting of the memorial bust before it was restored.

41. The bust in Holy Trinity Church, Stratford upon Avon.

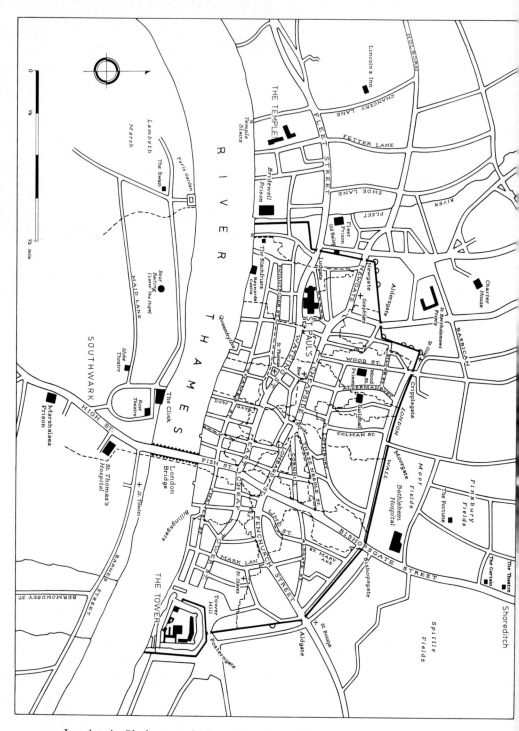

42. London in Shakespeare's time. The sites of the theatres are marked, so far as they can be accurately determined.

43. Mary Arden's House, Wilmcote, near Stratford upon Avon.

44. The Birthplace, Stratford upon Avon.

45. Grammar School and Guild Chapel, Stratford upon Avon.

46. Anne Hathaway's Cottage, Shottery, Stratford upon Avon.

47. Holy Trinity Church, Stratford upon Avon.

48. The Royal Shakespeare Theatre, Stratford upon Avon.

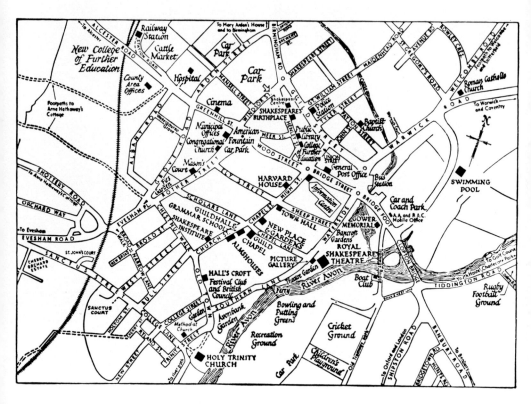

49. Stratford upon Avon today.

Thou marshall'st me the way that I was going;
And such an instrument I was to use.
Mine eyes are made the fools o' the other senses,
Or else worth all the rest: I see thee still;
And on thy blade and dudgeon gouts of blood,
Which was not so before. There's no such thing:
It is the bloody business which informs
Thus to mine eyes. Now o'er the one half-world
Nature seems dead, and wicked dreams abuse
The curtain'd sleep; witchcraft celebrates
Pale Hecate's offerings; and wither'd murder,
Alarum'd by his sentinel, the wolf,
Whose howl's his watch, thus with his stealthy pace,
With Tarquin's ravishing strides, toward his design
Moves like a ghost. Thou sure and firm-set earth,
Hear not my steps, which way they walk, for fear
Thy very stones prate of my whereabout,
And take the present horror from the time,
Which now suits with it. Whiles I threat he lives:
Words to the heat of deeds too cold breath gives.
I go, and it is done; the bell invites me.
Hear it not, Duncan; for it is a knell
That summons thee to heaven or to hell.

(Macbeth)

THE MERCHANT OF VENICE (Act IV, Sc. i)

The quality of mercy is not strain'd,
It droppeth as the gentle rain from heaven
Upon the place beneath: it is twice bless'd;
It blesseth him that gives and him that takes:
'Tis mightiest in the mightiest; it becomes
The throned monarch better than his crown;
His sceptre shows the force of temporal power,
The attribute to awe and majesty,
Wherein doth sit the dread and fear of kings;
But mercy is above this sceptred sway,
It is enthroned in the hearts of kings,
It is an attribute to God himself,
And earthly power doth then show likest God's
When mercy seasons justice.

(Portia)

A MIDSUMMER NIGHT'S DREAM (Act II, Sc. i)

I know a bank whereon the wild thyme blows,
Where oxlips and the nodding violet grows
Quite over-canopied with luscious woodbine,
With sweet musk-roses, and with eglantine:
There sleeps Titania some time of the night,
Lull'd in these flowers with dances and delight;
And there the snake throws her enamell'd skin,
Weed wide enough to wrap a fairy in:
And with the juice of this I'll streak her eyes,
And make her full of hateful fantasies.

(Oberon)

RICHARD II (Act II, Sc. i)

This royal throne of kings, this scepter'd isle,
This earth of majesty, this seat of Mars,
This other Eden, demi-paradise,
This fortress built by Nature for herself
Against infection and the hand of war,
This happy breed of men, this little world,
This precious stone set in the silver sea,
Which serves it in the office of a wall,
Or as a moat defensive to a house,
Against the envy of less happier lands,
This blessed plot, this earth, this realm, this England . . .

(John of Gaunt)

ROMEO AND JULIET (Act I, Sc. iv)

O, then, I see Queen Mab hath been with you.
She is the fairies' midwife, and she comes
In shape no bigger than an agate stone
On the forefinger of an alderman,
Drawn with a team of little atomies
Over men's noses as they lie asleep.
Her wagon-spokes made of long spinners' legs;
The cover, of the wings of grasshoppers;
Her traces, of the smallest spider web;
Her collars, of the moonshine's watery beams;
Her whip, of cricket's bone; the lash of film;
Her wagoner, a small grey-coated gnat,
Not half so big as a round little worm

Pricked from the lazy finger of a maid;
Her chariot is an empty hazelnut,
Made by the joiner squirrel or old grub,
Time out o'mind the fairies' coachmakers.
And in this state she gallops night by night
Through lovers' brains, and then they dream of love;
O'er courtiers' knees, that dream on curtsies straight;
O'er lawyers' fingers, who straight dream on fees;
O'er ladies' lips, who straight on kisses dream,
Which oft the angry Mab with blisters plagues,
Because their breaths with sweetmeats tainted are.
Sometimes she gallops o'er a courtier's nose,
And then he dreams of smelling out a suit.
And sometimes comes she with a tithe-pig's tail
Tickling a parson's nose as 'a lies asleep;
Then he dreams of another benefice.
. . .
This is the hag, when maids lie on their backs
That presses them and learns them first to bear,
Making them women of good carriage.
This is she —

(Mercutio)

Two Songs

CYMBELINE (Act IV, Sc. ii)

Fear no more the heat o' the sun,
  Nor the furious winter's rages;
Thou thy worldly task hast done,
  Home art gone, and ta'en thy wages;
Golden lads and girls all must,
As chimney-sweepers, come to dust.

Fear no more the frown o' the great,
  Thou art past the tyrant's stroke:
Care no more to clothe and eat;
  To thee the reed is as the oak:
The sceptre, learning, physic, must
All follow this, and come to dust.

Fear no more the lightning-flash,
   Nor the all-dreaded thunder-stone;
Fear not slander, censure rash;
   Thou hast finish'd joy and moan:
All lovers young, all lovers must
Consign to thee, and come to dust.

No exorciser harm thee!
   Nor no witchcraft charm thee!
Ghost unlaid forbear thee!
   Nothing ill come near thee!
Quiet consummation have;
And renowned be thy grave!

LOVE'S LABOUR'S LOST (Act V, Sc. ii)

SPRING: When daisies pied and violets blue
   And lady-smocks all silver-white
And cuckoo-buds of yellow hue
   Do paint the meadows with delight,
The cuckoo then, on every tree,
Mocks married men; for thus sings he,
               Cuckoo;
Cuckoo, cuckoo: O, word of fear,
Unpleasing to a married ear!

. . .

WINTER: When icicles hang by the wall,
   And Dick the shepherd blows his nail,
And Tom bears logs into the hall,
   And milk comes frozen home in pail,
When blood is nipp'd, and ways be foul,
Then nightly sings the staring owl,
               Tu-who;
Tu-whit, tu-who — a merry note,
While greasy Joan doth keel the pot.

When all aloud the wind doth blow,
   And coughing drowns the parson's saw,
And birds sit brooding in the snow,
   And Marian's nose looks red and raw,

When roasted crabs hiss in the bowl,
Then nightly sings the staring owl,
                        Tu-who;
Tu-whit, tu-who — a merry note,
While greasy Joan doth keel the pot.

The Sonnets

SONNET 18

Shall I compare thee to a summer's day?
Thou art more lovely and more temperate:
Rough winds do shake the darling buds of May,
And summer's lease hath all too short a date:
Sometime too hot the eye of heaven shines,
And often is his gold complexion dimmed,
And every fair from fair sometime declines,
By chance, or nature's changing course untrimmed;
But thy eternal summer shall not fade,
Nor lose possession of that fair thou ow'st,
Nor shall Death brag thou wand'rest in his shade,
When in eternal lines to Time thou grow'st;
        So long as men can breathe or eyes can see,
        So long lives this, and this gives life to thee.

SONNET 116

Let me not to the marriage of true minds
Admit impediments, love is not love
Which alters when it alteration finds,
Or bends with the remover to remove.
O no, it is an ever-fixed mark
That looks on tempests and is never shaken;
It is the star to every wandering bark,
Whose worth's unknown although his height be taken.
Love's not Time's fool, though rosy lips and cheeks
Within his bending sickle's compass come,
Love alters not with his brief hours and weeks,
But bears it out even to the edge of doom;
        If this be error and upon me proved,
        I never writ, nor no man ever loved.

THE BOOK OF THE PLAY

The Text

Assembled Texts. Some evidence suggests that copy presented for printing was sometimes made up of the various parts allocated to the actors. This might occur if no previous published version existed or if the author's MS were missing. The 'parts' would be strung together on the plot of the play made by the prompter. The *Two Gentlemen of Verona* Folio text, may be an example of this.

Book of the Play. Not a printed version, but the text prepared for performance by the Book-keeper in the theatre who was responsible for cuts, on the qui vive for sensitive allusions, and always taking into account his acting resources.

Deletions. A bracket or vertical line in the left-hand margin of a play MS indicated a deletion of a speech. Sometimes a revised version of the speech was inserted. When such a MS was used by a printer he occasionally made the mistake of ignoring the deletion and printing both it and its revised version — e.g. Berowne's speech on Love and Learning (*Love's Labour's Lost*, IV. iii).

Foul Papers. The dramatist's last complete MS draft. It is generally accepted that many of Shakespeare's plays were printed from his foul papers, or a fair copy of them.

Handwriting. Two basic forms existed in Elizabethan England — the old mediaeval hand, in use since the 11th century, and the new, less angular, Italian hand which gradually supplanted it, not without escaping its influence however. Shakespeare wrote in the old style, if we accept the evidence of six signatures, the words 'by me' on his will, and the problematical evidence that three pages of the MS play *Sir Thomas More* are in his hand. One expert has concluded that Shakespeare 'made no pretence to be an elegant penman'.

Interpolations. We must not think of a play MS's fate in the Elizabethan theatre as being entirely in favour of cuts and alterations. Additions, too, were often made, not always by the original author — e.g. additions to *Macbeth* were made by Middleton. Very probably famous comedians like Kempe added gags in performance which found their way into the printed version.

Manuscript Plays. These are surviving copies in handwriting of plays not always subsequently printed in the Elizabethan period. The most famous is *Sir Thomas More,* the MS of which is said by some to include Shakespeare's hand.

Punctuation. Contrary to some belief there was something approaching an Elizabethan system of punctuation. Commas were used liberally, sometimes with the force of a full stop. Colons were very important, sometimes acting as stops, commas and even exclamation marks. Some critics believe that in printed plays punctuation was governed more by natural speech than scientific rule, though the evidence of the First Folio suggests that the whims of the compositors played a large part.

Spelling. The principles of Elizabethan spelling were arbitrary rather than standard. The same word was frequently spelt in different ways on the same page.

Stage-directions. It is difficult to be sure whether the stage-directions we find in Elizabethan printed play-texts were inserted during rehearsal or were already there in the author's MS. Scholars incline to accept that most in Shakespeare's plays are his own. In *Coriolanus* the nature of the stage-directions (descriptive and imaginative) strongly suggest he wrote them as he envisaged the play in eventual performance — e.g. 'Enter two Officers, to lay cushions, as it were in the Capitol'. Directions added in the theatre would normally be short, relating largely to entrances and exits with no embellishments. Modern readers should beware of stage-directions in the editions they use — many embody the fanciful imaginings of their editors.

Printing and Publishing

Abridgment. A comparison of Quartos and Folios will sometimes show that a play has at some stage been abridged. For example *Hamlet* in the Second Quarto (pub. 1604) is 200 lines shorter than in the Folio and *Othello*'s Quarto is 100 lines shorter than the Folio version. However, no satisfactory general explanation is possible — for example, the Second Quarto of *Romeo and Juliet* is 700 lines longer than the First Quarto.

Acts and Scenes. Modern editions, following the First Folio, indicate act and scene divisions, but the earlier Quarto publications of Shakespeare's plays do not have them. The division derives from a classical convention and is an indication of a growing classical influence in Elizabethan drama. It would be interesting to know if Shakespeare's original MS showed acts and scenes.

Bad Quartos. These are *Romeo and Juliet*, *Henry V*, *The Merry Wives of Windsor* and *Hamlet* (the First Quarto of each). When compared with the Folio or a known good Quarto, they are found to have lapses in meaning, considerable differences in word-order, emasculated or disordered speeches, speeches misplaced and prose masquerading as verse or vice versa. They are often the result of someone (a printer's bad shorthand writer or an actor) attempting to remember a text from a production.

Censorship. Two forms existed in Elizabethan England: (1) concerning performance — by an authorization of 1581 the Master of the Revels was enabled to require all plays to be submitted for examination, mainly for political and religious non-conformity; (2) concerning the printing of plays — in 1607 this authority was extended to the printing of plays. Two examples of censorship in Shakespeare are: (a) in the first three Quartos of *Richard II* the deposition scene is omitted; Elizabeth saw parallels between herself and Richard; (b) the name 'Falstaff' was substituted for 'Oldcastle' in *Henry IV* to avoid offence to the Oldcastle family.

Compositors. We know of no Elizabethan compositors (or typesetters) by name but scholarship (mainly American) has identified a number by intensive study of printed texts. This identification is aided by (1) the fact that type was hand-set, letter by letter; idiosyncratic setting is quickly revealed by this process; (2) general laissez-faire attitudes to spelling conspicuously show individual preferences. An American (Charlton Hinman) brilliantly identified five (A, B, C, D, E) compositors who worked on the great First Folio. One of the five could have been a John Shakespeare of Warwickshire.

Emendation. A correction or change made by either the original printers or a subsequent editor or editors of a Shakespeare play, e.g. (1) the Folio compositor of *Love's Labour's Lost,* working from an earlier Quarto, made 117 corrections, missed 59 errors, compounded 137 of his own; (2) editorial attempts to clarify obscurities, as in *Henry IV, Part 2,* II, iii where the Folio reads 'for his nose was as sharp as a pen, and a Table of greene fields'. The editor Theobald brilliantly emended this to the very moving '. . . and a' babbled of green fields'.

Folios. The name usually given to the four collected editions of Shakespeare's plays which appeared in the 17th century (*see also* Terms of Reference). The dates of publication are — F1: 1623, F2: 1632, F3: 1663, F4: 1685. F2 is virtually a reprint of F1 with modernizations of spelling, corrections of names and stage-directions. F3 contains seven additional plays, including *Pericles* — almost certainly the only one of the seven which was written by Shakespeare. F4 is a reprint of F3 with corrections and also some fresh mistakes of its own. It includes *Pericles* and six apocryphal plays. Of all these editions only the First Folio can be regarded as having received any kind of authoritative supervision by people who knew and worked with Shakespeare.

Forgeries. Shakespeare has attracted both stupid and brilliant forgers, the most adept being J. P. Collier (1798–1883) who claimed, among other things, the possession of a Folio of 1632 with notes and emendations in a 17th-century hand; William Ireland (1777–1835) who forged licences, contracts, receipts, notes to players and a letter to Anne Hathaway.

Galleys. Trays in which a compositor placed lines of type. In the Elizabethan period a galley was used for the printing of a page.

Imprint. In Elizabethan times the publisher's name, place and date of publication (the 'imprint') almost always appeared on the title-page. Often it included the printer's name and the bookseller.

Mislineation. Incorrect printing as, e.g., turning verse into prose and vice-versa.

Misprint. Proof correction by either printer or author of Elizabethan plays was neither habitual nor efficient — except for Ben Jonson. Hinman (*see* Compositors) calculates that only 134 of the 900 pages of the First Folio were proof-corrected. Small wonder that misprints of all kinds abound.

'Originall'. A word frequently found on Elizabethan title-pages — e.g. 'Published according to the True Originall copies' (First Folio). This does not necessarily mean Shakespeare's original MS but an authenticated text that was used in the theatre.

Parallel Texts. The First Folio has 36 plays, of which 18 were never before published, and 4 of those are 'bad' Quartos. Therefore 14 good Quartos remain and were used as the basis for the great collected First Folio edition. The 14 texts are thus called parallel since they are very close in both Quarto and Folio form.

Pirate texts. The illicit obtaining of a play text (*see* Bad Quartos) for printing to make a quick buck.

Printers. Twelve were involved in printing Shakespeare's Quartos between 1594 and 1619. The most famous of these were William and Isaac Jaggard. (*See* Publishers.)

Prompt-book. A transcript of the author's MS made by the Book-keeper which became the received text of the play for performance (after licensing).

Publishers. Not to be confused with printers. Twenty-one were involved in the publication of Shakespeare's plays between 1594 and 1619. They normally employed both printers and booksellers, and a number were disreputable, being involved with 'bad' Quartos. Some, like Cuthbert Burby, were splendid men who issued (as, in his case, with *Romeo and Juliet*) corrected versions of pirated editions. The best-known publishers of Shakespeare's plays were William Jaggard (1569–1623) and his son, Isaac (1595–1627), who were entrusted with the publication of the famous First Folio edition which appeared in 1623, seven years after Shakespeare's death. Direct descendants of the family now live at Stratford.

Shorthand. Numerous manuals were published in the 16th century and it is believed by some that a form was used in the pirating of some of Shakespeare's plays.

Glossary

The Glossary is a rare, if not unique, feature in a book of this kind. It contains words that, for a variety of reasons, are unfamiliar to modern ears. (1) Quite simply, words that have dropped out of circulation since Shakespeare's time and are no longer a part of the 20th-century reader's vocabulary. (2) There are, as happens more frequently, words whose meaning has changed over the centuries, sometimes radically, sometimes only slightly, but always sufficiently to baffle the careful reader or listener. (3) Words from which, in his use of imagery, Shakespeare often wrests a meaning that can only be understood by reference to his other writings, his rural background, or his times. (4) Words Shakespeare often used to elaborate a meaning, but that are normally employed only as technical terms concerned with a particular profession — e.g. the law. (5) Words that are misused, unconsciously by a character, deliberately by Shakespeare (e.g. the malapropisms of Dogberry in *Much Ado About Nothing*), to give an impression of pomposity or muddle-headedness. (6) Words that are misspelt so as to suggest the personality or accent of a particular character (e.g. Fluellen in *Henry V*). (7) Words referring to objects or activities that are peculiar to the British Isles, so much so that they may prove a problem to those unfamiliar with such usage.

The Glossary also includes a translation of the various Latin sentences or phrases Shakespeare introduces into his writing. These are listed by the first letter of the first word in each phrase. Classical names and references are also included, and whatever area of history or myth is pertinent to their presence in the text is briefly referred to. ('DP' refers the reader to the Dramatis Personae.)

The aim in compiling this Glossary has been to offer a clear, brief elucidation of the text and so to further the awareness, understanding and appreciation of both reader and playgoer.

a in; to
abate reduce in esteem
ABC hornbook on which alphabet appears, for teaching a child to read
a-birding bird-shooting
abode delay
abodement omen
abortives unnatural births
abound live in plenty
abra(u)m used to darken mahogany
abroach set in motion
abroad at large
abrook endure
abruption breaking off
absolute intransigent; incomparable; complete
across (ref. to hit in tilting) bad hit, almost a miss
action court action for debt

acture action
adage saying
Adam Adam, first man; Adam Bell, famous archer
adamant very hard magnetic stone
adder snake, believed to be deaf
adder's sense ears
addition title; credit; assessment
addle rotten, stale
address prepare
adhere prove suitable, find congenial
ad Jovem, ad Apollinem, ad Martem to Jove, to Apollo, to Mars
adjunct linked; result of
ad manes fratrum to the shades of our brothers
admire wonder at
admiration amazement
admission approbation

admittance, great admitted into company of great
admonish inform
Adonis youth beloved by Venus
Adonis' garden fertile garden of Adonis
adsum I am here!
advantage, to the in addition
advantages interest, gain
advantaging increase
adventure venture, risk
adversary FOR emissary
advertise inform; instruct
advertising attentive
advise counsel, inform
advised well counselled
advisements SEE avisements
Aeacides SEE Ajax
aediles subordinate officers of the tribunes
Aegle beloved by King Theseus
Aeneas Trojan hero (DP)
aery eagle's brood, eyrie
Aesculapius god of healing and medicine
Aeson father of Jason
afar off indirectly
affability gentle behaviour
affairs business
affairs, mean humble business
affect have liking for; enjoy; desire; aspire to
Affected to, stand have feeling for, be in love with
affection inclination, feeling
affeered sanctioned
affiance trust; loyalty; confidence
affied betrothed; confided
affined bound, controlled by; related
affinity family connection
afford allow, let off
affy trust; betroth
after-eye follow with eye
after-loss later grief
afume full of fumes
against predicting; before, in preparation for; in the face of
Agamemnon Greek leader (DP)
agate precious stone often cut into small human figures, used in ring seals
Agenor King of Tyre, whose daughter, Europa, Jupiter loved
aglet-baby tag of lace, sometimes shaped as small figure
agnize acknowledge
agone ago
agood in earnest
ague fever
aidance assistance
aidant helpful
aim reports approximate reports
aim, cry encourage

aio te, Aeacida, Romanos vincere posse EITHER 'I say that you, Aeacides, will conquer the Romans' OR 'I say that the Romans will conquer you, Aeacides.' Ambiguous prophesy of Oracle to Pyrrhus, son of Achilles
Aire Acre (Arc)
Ajax son of Telamon. When Achilles' arms assigned to Ulysses, Ajax went mad and attacked a herd of sheep he thought were Greeks, killing himself (DP). SEE ALSO Ulysses, Laertes' son
Alcides Hercules
alderliefest dearest of all
ale, sheer ale taken by itself without food
Alecto one of the Furies
Alexander King of Macedon
Aliena the strange one (DP)
alight alight from
alla stoccata thrust in fencing
allayment antidote; easing
alley shady walk
all-hail general recognition, greeting
All Hallowmass All Saints' Day, 1 November
All Hallow's Eve 31 October, day before All Hallowmass
alligant elegant
allow (of) admit, concede
allowance ability, expertise
allowed acknowledged; licensed (e.g. Fool)
allycholly melancholy
Almain German
almanac calendar of heavenly bodies
alms-deed deeds of charity
alms drink drink finished off by another
almshouse refuge or hospital for poor
almsman one who begs alms
along stretched out
Althaea mother of Meleager, Prince of Calydon, who burned brand on which his life depended
Ama(i)mon name of a devil
amain as fast as possible
ambuscadoe ambush
ameers FOR emirs
amend recovery, mend
amending, chime bells in repair
amerce punish with fine
ames-ace two aces (lowest dice throw)
amiable desirable
amort dispirited
Amurath Turkish sultans
an if
an if even if
anatomized taken apart to be studied in detail
anatomy skeleton; corpse
ancient ensign, standard-bearer

ancient of war experienced officer
andirons firedogs
Andromache Hector's wife (DP)
angel coin, originally same as noble, with device of Michael and the dragon on it; (fig.) someone who comes in answer to a need
angle fish-hook
Anna sister to Dido, Queen of Carthage
annexion addition
annoy trouble
annoyance injury
anon immediately
answer retaliation; correspond to
Anthropophagi cannibal tribe
Antiates men of Antium
antic old; clown, buffoon; grotesque masque; grotesque, oddly shaped
anticked make a fool of
Antiochus, the Great Asian Emperor 223–187 BC
Antiopa beloved by King Theseus
Antipodes other side of earth and those who live there
antre cave
apace quickly
ape-bearer travelling showman with performing monkeys
apes: lead apes in hell occupation of old maids to lead apes in hell!
a-pieces in pieces
Apollo god of music, and song
apoplex'd paralysed
apostrophus apostrophe; pause
appaid satisfied
apparent heir (apparent)
appeach inform against
appeal accuse, accusation
appendix appendage
apperil risk
appertinent appertaining to
apple pupil of eye
apple-john apple which keeps well but becomes very wrinkled
appliance expedient
apply well be consistent with
appoint intend
appointment equipment
apprehend imagine; become aware of; seize
apprehension perception, understanding; idea
apprehensive quick to learn
approbation probation, novitiate; proof; put to proof
approbriation peculiarity
approve confirm
approve in prove guilty
approof proof

apron-men workmen
apt natural; willing; plausible
aqua-vitae brandy, spirits
Aquilon north wind
Arabian bird Phoenix
arbitrement combat; judicial inquiry
argal FOR ergo
Argier Algiers
argo FOR ergo
argosy Venetian trading vessel
argue imply
argument theme
Argus the all-seeing god who had a hundred eyes, which, on his death, were transplanted by Hera to the tails of her peacock
Ariachne Arachne, turned into a spider
Ariadne daughter of Minos, king of Crete, who loved Theseus the slayer of the Minotaur
Aries Zodiac sign: ram
Arion Greek musician, saved from sea by dolphin who had heard his music
arithmetician theorist
Armado Armada, fleet (SEE ALSO DP)
arm-gaunt (poss. corrupt) (?) completely armed; martial
armigero (*armiger*) esquire
armipotent mighty in arms
aroint begone
a-row one after another
arraign summon to court of justice
arrant notorious
arras wall tapestry
arras counterpoint tapestry counterpane
arrearages arrears
arrest stop
arrest your words take you at your word
arrogancy arrogance
art learning; ars magica = magic
arter artery
Arthur King of ancient Britain
article clause in contract; condition
article of thy gentry tenor of your rank
articles dilated detailed instructions
articles, of great of great importance
artificial skilful
Ascanius son of Aeneas
a-scorn scorn, despise
asinico little ass
askance turn aside
aslant across
Asmath a demon
aspersion sprinkling
aspic asp
assay test
assigns appendages
assistant helpful
assure guarantee

assured betrothed
assurance confidence
astonished stunned
Astraea goddess of justice
Ate goddess of vengeance, discord and
  strife
at full totally
athwart across
Atlanta renowned as a fast runner
Atlas supported the world on his
  shoulders
atomies specks, little creatures
atone reconcile, become reconciled
Atropos one of the Fates
attach arrest
attached overtaken
attachment arrest, make stop
attainder disgrace; condemnation;
  accusation
attaint stain, disgrace
attainture conviction
attax'd (*attaskt*) blamed
attempt tempt
attemptible assailable
attend wait upon, await
attent attentive
attest bear witness to
attorney substitute
attorneyed performed by an attorney
attorneyship proxy
a-twain in two
auditory audience, listener
augerers (*augurs*) those who predicted the
  future
auger's bore small hole made by carpenter's
  tool
augur prophet, prophesy
Augustus Caesar Augustus, first Roman
  emperor
aunchient FOR ancient
aunt loose woman
Aurora dawn
avaunt dismiss, go away
avaunt, to give her tell her to go
Ave-Marie prayer, 'Hail Mary'
aves salutation
avised aware
avisements, take your consider
avoid leave
avouch justify; testimony
avouchment FOR assure
awful commanding respect
awl cobbler's instrument
ay'll FOR I will

Babylon ancient town, capital of Chaldean
  empire
Babylon, man in who lived there and loved
  one, Susannah

baccare stand back
Bacchanal follower of Bacchus, revels of
  Bacchus
Bacchus god of wine
back returning; mount
back, bow arched back
back, hot strong sexual urge
backed ridden
backfriend false friend
backsword man fencer at single sticks
back-trick backwards leap
backward the past
back-wounding stabbing in the back
badged spotted, marred
badge, housed family emblem
baes baas, bleats
baffle punishment for perjured knight;
  being hung upside down by heels —
  HENCE disgrace
bag money-bag, sack
bail(le) from fetch
bait refresh self; torment; set dogs to
  worry animals; tempt
Bajazeth Turkish emperor
bake make hard, matted
baked about crusted over
baldrick belt
bale evil
bale, have get the worst of
baleful injurious
balk let slip
ball orb of state
ballad songs, often concerned with
  contemporary events
ballad monger seller of ballads
ballow cudgel
balm oil of consecration
balsam (*um*) balm
ban curse
band bond
banditto outlaw
ban-dogs chained dogs
bandy toss to and fro, exchange
bane destruction, destroyer; poison
banket banquet
banks, awful bounds of loyal obedience
banquet feast
banquet, running hasty refreshment; used
  lasciviously — a taster
bar prevent, deny
Barabbas condemned to death, and
  released in exchange for Christ
Barbary on coast of N. Africa, where
  sugar imported from
Barbary hen guinea fowl; prostitute
Barbason name of a fiend
barful full of barriers
Bargulus name of pirate
barked stripped

barm yeast
ba(i)rns children
barricado barrier
Basan hill, cf. Psalms 22 : 12
base-court lower or outer courtyard of castle
basely in a base manner
bases garment worn under armour
Basilico character in old play, 'Solyman and Perseda'
basilisk fabulous serpent which killed with look; large cannon
basis statue base
basket stale juggler practiser of out-dated sword tricks
basket-hilt old-fashioned hilt of sword, with covering like basket-work
bass provide a deep (bass) accompaniment
basta enough
bastard brown and white sweet Spanish wine
baste tack together
bastinado beating with a cudgel
bat staff
batchelor unmarried man or woman
bate abate, weaken; quarrel; rebate; beat wings; refresh; omitted, except
bate-breeding causing strife
bated (of rapiers) blunted, (of breath) withheld
bateless not to be blunted, not to be satisfied
bat-fowling bird-catching, using lights or lanterns to attract the birds
batler (*batlet*) small wooden bat for beating linen in wash
battalia battle array
batten grow fat; fasten
battery attack; cannon noise; knocking
battle troops
battle, maiden bloodless fight
batty bat-like
bauble trinket; jester's stick
baubling worthless
baulked omitted, overlooked
bavin brushwood
bawcock fine fellow
bay herb; barking of hounds
bay, at cornered
bay curtail brown horse with docked tail
bayed cornered
beadle parish constable, who could whip petty offenders
beadsman one who prays, telling rosary beads, for another
beagle small hound
beak prow of ship
beam part of balance from which the scales hang

bear behave; take part; star constellation; bear and ragged staff — badge of Earl of Warwick's family
bear coldly keep cool
bear down is stronger than
bear in hand delude, deceive
bear out survive
bear ward bear-keeper
bearing cloth baptismal shawl
bear't act
beard insult, defy
beastly beast-like
beat centred on; soften
beat on worry about
beaten with brains put down by mockery
beaver lower part of helmet
bechance happen, befall
beck bow, nod; beckoning
become suit well, adorn; honour
becoming make beautiful
bedabbled sprinkled
bedeck deck out
Bedlam lunatic's hospital
bed-swerver adultress
beef-witted stupid, dull-witted
beer, small weak brew, (fig.) trivialities
beetle overhang
beetle-headed thickheaded
befortune befall
begnaw gnaw at
beguile disguise; take attention from; pass pleasantly
behaviour gesture, manner
behest commandment, law
behindhand tardy
beholding perceiving
behoof, for your on your behalf
behove proper for, benefit
being, in here, present
Bel god of the Chaldeans
beldam grandmother; hag or witch
belief conviction
belief, received total conviction
belike perhaps
bellman crier who announces deaths and calls for prayers for the dead
Bellona goddess of war
bellows bag used for blowing fires
bells, shake his falcon's bells attached to its leg
bell-weather leading ram of flock, with bell on neck
belonging ability; endowments
bemadding maddening
bemete measure
bemocked-at foolish
bemoiled dirtied, soiled
ben venuto welcome
bench raise in authority

bencher senator
bench-hole privy hole
bending courteous; submissive
bending to turning on
benefit legal right
benison blessing
bent disposition; effort; full stretch; tendency
berattle fill with noise
berayed (poss.) bedewed, soaked
bergomask a rustic dance of Bergamo, Italy
Bermoothes Bermudas
bescreened hidden
beseeched FOR besieged
beseems befits
beshrew curse
besom broom
besort suit; accompany; retinue
bespeak order
Best, the Christ
bested in a plight
bestow conduct
bestow of bestow on, give
bestowed stowed away
bestraught distraught, distracted
betake take to
beteem allow; give birth to
betid passed
betide happen
betimes at the right moment; early
betumed covered with pitch
between this and his head in these parts, hereabouts
bevel biased, crooked
Bevis name of Saxon knight
bewray disclose
bezonion base fellow
bias natural bent
biddy chickabiddy, chicken
bide endure, bear; delay; insist
big, look big upon threaten
biggen night-cap
bilbo Spanish blade
bilboes shackles used for mutinous sailors
bill pike with curved blade; halberd; list; money order; written notice
bill, brown pike, halberd
billet thick stick
bird, obscure owl
bird-bolt short arrow for bird-shooting
birding piece for shooting birds
birdlime substance spread on bushes to catch birds
Birlady by our Lady
birthdom a birthright, e.g. mother country
biscuit, remainder ship biscuit left over after voyage
black-a-moor negro

blacks colour of print, hence lines
bladder often inflated and used, e.g., in swimming
blains blisters
blank centre of target; blank document; make pale
blast burst; wither up
blaze make known
blazon set out praise of, make known; coat-of-arms; description
blear dim, dull
blench start; swerve
blent blended
blind-worm slow worm
blister slash
Blithild daughter of French King Clothair
bloat bloated
block execution block; blockhead; wood on which hats shaped; for mounting horses
blood passion; rank; kinsman; sexual appetite
blood boltered hair matted with blood
blood, in in vigour of youth
blood, salute my exhilarate
blow blow up; of insects — deposit eggs
blow nails wait patiently
blown swollen, puffed up
blown of the law implementing the law
blowse ruddy, fat-faced wench
blue-caps Scots in 'blue bonnets'
blue eye eye with dark rings round it
boar wild male pig; emblem of Gloucester family
boar, Bartholomew one fattened for Bartholomew Fair, 24 August
boar of Thessaly sent by Artemis to ravage Thessaly
boar-pig young porker
board accost, address; enter by force
board, at at table
bob courtesy, bow; bitter jest
bobbed swindled; hit
bobtail docked tail
bode make ill-omens
bodements prophecies
bodges clumsy phrases
Bodykins God's little body
boggle startle
boggler inconstant person
Bohemian-Tartar wild man
boisterous wild, hurtful
bolds emboldens
bolins bowlines
bollen swollen
bolster share a bolster, i.e. together in bed
bolt thunderbolt; kind of arrow; fetter
bolt, oppose the lock the door

bolter sieve

bolting-hutch wooden receptacle for sifted flour

bombard large leather wine bottle

bombast cotton material used as stuffing — hence padding; (fig.) padded-out language

bona terra, mala gens good land, bad people

bona-rosas good stuff, (fig.) courtesans

bondage being tied up to

bondman slave

bone-ache venereal disease

bones flat bones, rattled together to accompany a song or dance

bones, dry believed sign of veneral disease

bonneted off-cap to, i.e. treat with respect

book learning; agreement; deed

boord peasant, boorish fellow

boot booty, profit; compensate; advantage

boothose over-stocking, legging

bootless useless, pointless

boot, make take advantage, raid

boots: it boots not it's of no avail

bore cheat; calibre of gun; hole

Boreas north wind

borne endured

borne in hand deluded

bor'st carried

bosky wooded

bosom where the heart is — HENCE nearest; dearest; wishes

bossed embossed

botch mend clumsily

botchy ulcerous

bots disease of horses

bottle (of hay) bundle (of hay)

bottom basis; ship; hold of ship; bobbin (SEE ALSO DP)

bottom, to the to the bottom of the cup

bound to keep peace; indebted; boundary

bounded obliged

bounty generosity

bourn boundary, limit

bout, walk a have a dance

bow bend; yoke

bow-boy Cupid

bowels seat of pity, mercy; offspring

bower enclose

bowl wood of game of bowls

boy boy actor

brabble brawl

brace bracelet, arm-covering

braced in readiness, stretched tight

brach hound bitch

brain sickly sick in mind

brainish headstrong

brains, boiled hotheads

brake thicket

bran husks

branch embroider with branches or flowers

branchless mutilated

brand stigma; burning piece of wood

brave provoke, taunt; boast; fine

bravely taken thought well of

bravery finery

braving swaggering

brawled down destroyed

brawn brawny arm, (poss.) form of meat

brazed hardened

breach gap in fortifications; sea-breaker

break the wind become breathless

breast musical voice

breathe accustom

breathed strong winded

breathing take exercise; utterance; delay

breeched covered with breeches; birched

breed raise, bring up

breed thee pay for your upbringing

breed-bate trouble-maker

breeding upbringing, training in social niceties

breff FOR brief

brewer's horse a horse that was renowned for being worn out

Briareus Greek god with a thousand hands

brinded brindled

brinded cat tabby cat

brine salt — HENCE tears

bring bring about

bring out put out

broach begin, bring on; tap; let out; approach

broached speared on a spit

broad unrestrained

broadside discharge of guns from one side of ship

brock badger

brogues rough hide shoe

broil fight battle

broke cut; bargain

broker agent

broking pawn broking

brook tolerate

brow countenance

brow of Egypt gypsy face

brow, strike at the take good aim

Brown religious sect founded by Robert Brown in the reign of Elizabeth

bruit make known; rumour

brunt burden

brush hostile attack; injury

Brutus Lucius Junius, first Consul 509 BC (DP)

bubukles sores

buck clothes for bleaching; male deer; 6th-year buck

buck of first head 5th-year buck

buck-basket laundry basket
bucking washing
buckle join in close fight; fasten
buckle in confine
buckler small shield
Bucklersbury London street where herbs sold
buckram coarse linen stiffened with glue
budge give way
budget bag
buff leather used for sergeant's dress;
    naked
buffet blow, hit
bug bogey, frightening object
bugle glass bead
building in fancy castles in the air
bulk framework (of shop) projecting into
    street; body
bull-beeves beef
bully brave fellow
bully rook fine fellow
bulwark fortification
bum-baily bailiff, who followed debtor to
    arrest him
bunch-backed hunch backed
bung-hole hole in wine or beer barrel
bunting bird (SEE lark)
bur(r) rough head of burdock
burden load, bear down upon; refrain;
    capacity
burgomaster chief magistrate of city
burgonet helmet with visor
burly-bon'd large framed
burnet a plant
burning-glass glass which uses sunrays to
    start fire
burten burden
buskined wearing buskins — hunting boots
buss kiss
butler in charge of cellar
butt archery target; goal
butter-woman woman who carried butter
    to market
buttery bar room in house where milk and
    butter, etc., kept; room in college
    where drink and refreshments kept
buy buy off
buy out redeem
buxom sturdy
buzz rumour
buzzard wild bird of prey; a blundering
    insect; (fig.) a worthless person
by and by soon
by-dependancie accessory circumstances
by-drinking drinking between meals
by'r Lakin by Our Lady

caballeros SEE cavaleros
cable rope or chain on which anchor
    fastened — HENCE scope

cacodemon evil spirit
cade barrel of herring (SEE ALSO DP)
caddises tapes used for garters
caddis-garter worsted tape used for cheap
    garters
cadent falling
Cadmus founder and King of Thebes
caduceus Mercury's serpent-entwined staff
Cadwallader Welsh warrior chief
Caesar Julius Caesar (DP)
cage basket
Cain first son of Adam, murderer of Abel
caitiff poor wretch
cake is dough failed
Calen o costure me (poss.) 'Maiden, my
    treasure', Irish refrain
Calipolis heroine of Peele's *Battle of Alcazar*
calitie FOR qualité
caliver light musket
callet (*callat*) scold, slut
calves-guts used for fiddle strings
cambric fine material
Cambyses king in Thomas Preston's
    tragedy, *Cambyses*
camel blunt heavy person
camel, do act like a camel
Camelot residence of King Arthur
camlet fine cloth
camomile a herb
can understand
Canary sweet white wine from the Canary
    Islands; lively Spanish dance; (fig.)
    dancing about with excitement
Cancer Zodiac sign
candied made of sugar candy, crystallized
candle-cases cases for storing candles
candle-wasters burners of the midnight oil,
    i.e. scholars
Candy Candia (Crete)
canker destructive disease
canker rose dog-rose
canon law, rule; the scriptures
canon, from the out of order
canstick candlestick
cantherizing cauterizing
cantle segment of sphere
canton song
canvas coarse linen
canvas, to toss in a canvas sail, i.e. deal
    with severely
canzonet short song
capable able to inherit; ample; susceptible
    to
capacity receptive faculty, understanding
cap-and-knee sycophantic
cap-à-pie from top to toe
caparison apparel; put trappings on
caper leap about; leap in dancing; bush
    with berries

Capet, Hugh ancestor of French kings
Capitol temple of Jupiter in Rome
capitulate make agreements
capon chicken
capriccio caprice
captivate captured
car chariot
car(r)ack a Spanish or Portuguese treasure ship
caraways sweetmeats made with caraway seeds
carbonadoed meat scored to be grilled
carbuncle red precious stone; skin infection
carcanet jewelled necklace
card, cooling card played by opponent which dashes one's hopes
carded debased, weakened
card-maker maker of combs for combing wool fibres
cards, pack cards arranged for cheating
cardecue quart d'écu, French silver coin of little value
carduus benedictus blessed thistle, medicinal herb
care-crazed crazy with worry
career short gallop at full speed; frisk; course of action
career, in the at full charge, head on
caret (Lat.) it is missing, wanting
care-tuned tuned to sorrow, bearing ill news
carlot peasant
carman carter
carouse a single complete drink
carpet consideration non-military services
carpet-mongers ladies' men
carract carat
carriage conduct; carrying out; load
carrion flesh; feed on decayed meat
carry-tale tale bearer
cart often used for public exposure of prostitutes, or taking felons to gallows
Carthage-queen Dido, Queen of Carthage
carve show courtesy, act in an affable manner
carving designing
case mask; skin, flay
case of matter of
cased put in case, skin
casement window
cashiered dismissed from position or office
casque helmet
cassocks military cloaks
cast dismiss; discard; throw (of dice); examine (of urine); scour (of ponds); cast for statues
Castalion Castilian — King Philip II of Spain
Castiliano name of devil in play *The Devil and his Dame*, 1600

castle, as in a in complete security
cat civet cat
cat, gib castrated male cat
cat, mountain wild cat
cat o' the mountain panther
Cataian inhabitant of Cathay, Chinese (fig.) a scoundrel
cataplasm plaster, poultice
cataract water-spout, great fall of water
catastrophe finale of a play
catch catch at; part song
catch a wrench be diverted
catechism question and answer on religious belief
cater-cousins distant relations
cates delicacies; provisions
catlings catgut
Cato father of Brutus' wife, Portia (SEE ALSO DP)
caudle spicy, warm drink
caudle, hempen hanging halter
caulked seams stopped with tarred ropes
cause motive for action; occasion for a duel
cause of state state affairs
cautel trickery
cautelous crafty
cavaleros (caballeros) good fellows
cavalery cavalier
cavaliero (cavalleria) gallant
caveto beware
caviary caviare, a delicacy
ceinture girdle
censer ornamented pan for burning fumigating perfumes
centaur wild creature, half horse, half man; name of inn
centre centre of the earth
centurion Roman army commander
century hundred soldiers
Cerberus hound, guardian of hell
cerecloth waxed sheet for embalming a body
cerement covering of the dead
ceremony sacred symbol; omen
ceremonious careful about ceremony
Ceres Roman goddess of the harvest and fertility (DP)
certain fixed, determined
certes certainly
cess, out of all excessively
cesse cease
chafed enraged, irritated; of animal, at bay
chaff corn husks
Cham Emperor of China
chamber small piece of ordnance; bedroom
chamber, great hall of great house
chamberer gallant who frequents ladies' chambers

chamber-lye (lie) urine
champai(g)n open, flat country
chance happening; event; misunder-
    standing
chandler maker or seller of candles
change change one's loyalty
changeable varied in colour
changeling fairy child left in exchange for
    a human; fickle
Chanticleer cock in fable of Reynard, the
    Fox
chap crack in skin
chape metal plate on scabbard, to protect
    dagger point
chapless without chaps, i.e. jaws
chapmen salesmen
character write; handwriting; fancy shapes
charactery what is written
characts insignia
chares chores, work
charge fill up; expenditure; burden;
    military command; accusation;
    luggage; assail
chargeful costly
charge-house school or college
charge of foot infantry company
chariest most careful
chariness integrity
Charles the Great Charlemagne
Charles's wain star formation — the
    Plough
charm your tongue i.e. into silence, be quiet
Charneco sweet wine
charnel-house repository for bones of dead
Charon ferryman over Styx
charter a right granted, permission
Chartreux Carthusian order of monks
Charybdis creature who lived under a fig
    tree on a rock (also called Charybdis)
    opposite Scylla, who three times a day
    swallowed the sea there and vomited
    it up again
chase pursuit; sequence in an argument
chases points won or lost in tennis game
chaudron entrails
chawed chewed
che vor' ye I warn you
cheaters escheators, officers of the
    exchequer; one who cheats
check reprimand, rebuke
check at swerve to pounce
cheer face
cheerly cheerfully
cheese, Banbury a cheese which, when
    pared, was very thin
chequins gold coins
cherry-pit child's game with cherry stones
    tossed into a hole
Cheshu FOR Jesu

chevaliers cavalry
cheverel kid skin
chewet pie made of minced meat
chi non ti vede, non ti pretia those who do
    not see, do not praise thee
chide quarrel
child female infant; candidate for
    knighthood
child-changed changed to a child or
    changed by his children
Childeric Merovingian king, deposed by
    King Pepin
childing fruitful
chill faint hearted; for 'I will'
chinks money
chip cut into small pieces
chipochia FOR capocchia, a fool
chirugeonly like a surgeon
choler anger
choleric ill-tempered
chopine shoe with thick sole of cork
chopped marked with cracks
chopping affected
choppy rough, chapped
chops jaws; fat cheeks
chough chough, bird of crow family
Chrish FOR Christ
christendoms Christian (baptized) name
chronicled set down in chronicles, historical
    record
chrysolite topaz, a golden stone
chuck term of endearment
'chud FOR 'If I could'
chuff a dull wealthy man
church-like befitting a clergyman
churl ill-mannered fellow
Chus Jew, friend to Shylock
cicatrice scar
Cimmerian black people
cinquepace (sink-a-pace) a dance based on
    five steps
cinque-spotted with five spots
cipher number o
Circe sorceress, whose cup of poison
    turned men into beasts
circumstance circumlocution; accident;
    ceremony; details
circumstanced give oneself up to
    circumstance
circumstantial with particular details
circumvention know how to circumvent
cite incite; recite; enumerate
citizen city inhabitant; effeminate;
    weakling
cittern wire-stringed musical instrument
city feast formal banquet
civet perfume from civet cat
civil complaisant, not showy: pun for
    Seville

civility good manners

clack-dish begging bowl with hinged lid, clacked to attract attention

clamour sudden stopping of bells

clap, at a at one go

clap into get on with it

clap up do thing quickly

clapper-claw beat; applause; seeking to flatter

claw to scratch for pleasure; flatter

clear spotless

cleaving the pin hit pin in centre of target

Cleitus friend and commander of Alexander the Great, and killed by him in 328 BC

Cleopatra Queen of Egypt (DP)

clepe call

clerestory window high up in wall

clerk scholar

clerkly like a scholar

clew ball of thread

cliff key

climature region

clinquant glittering

clip enclose, embrace

clipped shortened

clipper one who clips bits off coins

clodpole clod-poll, stupid fellow

clog block of wood fastened to legs; encumbrance

cloistress nun of enclosed order

close pent up; secret

close stool privy receptacle

closely secretly

closes, at in conclusion

closet private room

closure end

closure, mutual common end

cloth tapestry; uniform

cloth, painted cheap tapestry

Clothair early French king of Merovingian dynasty

Clotharius SEE Clothair

clothier's yard English arrow was a cloth-yard long

clot-pole thick head

clouded maligned

cloudy scowling, gloomy

clout centre of archery butt; cloth piece

clout, babe of rag doll

clout shoon country bumpkin

clouted hobnailed; patched

clown country bumpkin

cloyed glutted, satiated; claw at

cloyless not glutted

cloyment sickening

clubs the cry for help when attacked by muggers or thieves

clusters mobs

clutch clench, close

clyster-pipes syringe (for a douche)

coals, carry do the dirty work

coast steer by coastline; slink by

coat coat of mail; undercoat, possibly of leather, proof against sword blows

coat, tawny dress of summoners

cock tap of wine cask; trigger on gun; version of 'God' used in oath; ship's small boat

cock-a-hoop abandon all restraint

cock and pie an oath

cockatrice fabulous serpent whose look was fatal (basilisk)

cockered spoiled

cockle mollusc; weed; shell

cockle-hat hat with cockle shell (pilgrim's badge) on it

cockney effeminate person, affected; cook

cockpit round theatre

cockshut twilight

Cock's passion by God's passion

Cocytus river of hell

codling an unripe apple

codpiece a pouch in front of men's breeches ('flies')

coffer strong box, chest; luggage; money

coffin pie-crust

cog cheat; fawn

cognition knowledge

cogscombs FOR coxcomb

cohered agreed with

cohorts band of soldiers

coign corner (-stone)

coil upset; upheaval; hubbub; trouble

coining minting money

coistrel groom, menial servant

Colbrand the Giant Danish giant of popular romances killed by Guy of Warwick

Colchos Colchis where Jason found the Golden Fleece

Colebrook Colnbrook, nr Windsor

collars of esses chains with s-shaped links

colleagued allied

collection inference

collied black, blackened

collop slice (of meat)

coloquintida colocynth (bitter-apple) with purgative qualities

Colossus gigantic statue of Apollo at Rhodes

colour pretext; appearance of right; excuse

colour, hold with suited to, fit in with

colours flags carried in battle

colour, colourable plausible pretext

colt make fool of

colt's tooth youthful wildness

combat fight a duel, single combat

combination treaty
combinate betrothed
come by one's own to get one's own property back
come off get away
come roundly speak plain
com(m)edian actor
comely decent, graceful
coming-in what is to come, the future
comfit sweetmeat
comfit, kissing sweetmeat to sweeten the breath
commerce conference
commission group of persons, jointly responsible; warrant; authority
commission, absolute supreme authority
commit commit adultery
commix mingle with
commodity convenience; advantage; profit; supply; commerce; consignment; merchandise sold
common land used by all
common bosom hearts of common people
commonalty common people
commoner prostitute
common-hackneyed vulgarized, made common and hackneyed
commonwealth body politic
commotion uprising, rebellion
community familiarity
commutual being as one
comonty FOR comedy
compact put together; in league with
comparative in comparison with; abusive person
comparison advantage when compared
compass bring about; achieve; circumference; encircle
compassionate appeal for pity
competence means of subsistence
competency moderation
competent adequate
complain(t) lament
complement affectations of courtesy
complement extern outward show
complete perfectly constituted
complexion appearance; natural disposition; behaviour
complexion, good my spare my blushes
compliment social formalities
complimental courteous
complot conspire, conspiracy
compose come to agreement
composition consistency; truce; agreed amount
compound reach agreement; blend
compound; in compound with mixed in with
comprehend take in, understand
compromise to settle

compt account, score
compt count Judgment day
comptible quick at assessing, sensitive
comptroller steward, with charge of household expenses
compunctious remorseful
computent assessable, able to be reckoned
con by rote learn by heart
conceit idea, image, thought; imagination; an extravagant fancy; opinion; vanity; gift trifles
conceited, well very witty
conceitless witless
concernancy relevance
concolinel poss. scrap of song
concupy lust
concupiscible lustful
condign deserved, merited
condition disposition; rank; pact; habit
condole sympathize
condolement consolation
conduce bring about
conduct leadership
conduit water pipe, channel
coney-catching cheating
conference conversation
confiners inhabitants
confirmed fixed, set
confirmities FOR infirmities
confluence collection
confound spend; confuse; ruin
conger sea-eel
congest gather together
congied with taken leave of
congree agreeing; combining
congreet greet each other
congruent apt, suitable
conies SEE cony
conject conjecture
conjunctive joined together
conjuration warning, entreaty
conjure expel evil spirits
conscience-in truly, really
conscionable honest to one's person or appearance
conserve preserve; candied fruit
conserve of beef salted beef
consist on insist on
consistory college of cardinals
consonancy fellowship; accord; consistency
consort accompany; conspire; group of musicians
conspectuities sight, eye
conspire work
Constantine Emperor, who made Christianity the religion of the Roman Empire
constellation sort of person one is (as decided by the arrangement of the stars)

conster construe, explain
constrain force
constringed compressed
construction interpretation
construction, shrewd malicious interpretation
construe interpret
contagioun catching disease
contagious causing pestilence or disease
contemptible scornful
content acquiesce; disposition; reward
content you don't worry
contention battle
continence self-restraint
continency moderation
continent side, bank; summary; restraining
contract betroth
contraction good faith
contrary opposite; not normal
contrariously separately
contriver intriguer
control thwart
controlment control, check
contumeliously with contumely, with slander
contumely contempt
conveniences suitability, fitness
convent call together, summon; concur
conventicle secret meeting
conversation behaviour, conduct
convertite penitent
convey manage; carry out secretly
conveyance transfer of property; sharp practice
convicted doomed
conviency opportunity
convince overcome
convoy conveyance
cony rabbit
cony-catching cheating, trickery
coops shelters as in a coop (pen)
copatain hat sugar-loaf shaped hat
cope meet, encounter; recompense; sky
copesmate companion
copies, boys' letters to be copied by boys
copious, be make many
copped humped
copy theme, subject
coram Latin preposition; FOR Quorum, number of justices of the peace needed before business could be carried on
coranto lively dance
cordial comfort; reviving medicine
Corinthian drinking companion
Coriolanus Roman general (DP)
corky dried up
Cornelia mother of the Gracchi
corner-cap cap with three-quarter points worn by members of church/university/law or judges

cornet company of cavalry
cornuto horned = cuckold
corollary surplus
Coroners Quest Law (*Crowners*) SEE Myths and Legends
coronet laurel wreath
correction punishment
correspondent agreeable to
corrigible docile
corrival rival
corroborate FOR broken
corse corpse
corslet piece of armour, cuirass
cost expensive article; wealth
costard apple; FOR head (SEE ALSO DP)
costermonger petty dealer
cote cottage
coted outstrip
cot-quean man who busies himself with women's affairs
couch cause to crouch; fix spear at rest
couching (*couchant*) sleeping with; lying down
coulter the blades of the plough
count reckoning; gown
counte (*conte* Ital.) count
countenance authority; good-will; patronage
counter imitation coin
counter-caster one who counts using counters
counter-gate gate of debtors' prison
countermand prohibit; reprieve; repeal law
counterpoised equalled
counter-sealed countersigned or sealed
countervail outweigh
county count
County Palatine count palatine, feudal lord
couples, in leashed together
couplets two young doves
course passage; line of action; hunt after; gist
courser horse
courser's hair horse hair, put in swamp-water attracts small creatures to itself and wriggles like a snake
court of guard guard house
court-cupboard sideboard
court-hand writing used in law courts
courtesy greetings; curtsy; graciousness
cover set the table; cover the head, i.e. put hat on
covert thicket, secret
cower in the hams walks in crouching position
cowish cowardly
cowl-staff pole for carrying basket
cowslip wild spring flower
Cox my passion oath — God's my passion

coxcomb head; professional fool's **cap** — HENCE fool

coy contemptuous; stroke, caress

coyed disdained

coz cousin

cozen cheat, deceive

coziers cobblers

crab crab apple

crabbed sour, bad-tempered

crack burst of sound; boast; young rascal

crack a quart open bottle of wine

crack hemp rogue deserving to be hanged

cracked within the ring a cracked coin — illegal

crafted carried out piece of work; act craftily

cranking winding

cranks winding passages

crasing FOR grazing?; crashing

craven coward(ly)

craze disorder, confuse

creaking making squeak

Crecy Battle of Crecy 1346

credit message; honour; reputation

creeks winding lanes

creep acquaintance get to know

crescive increasing, waxing

Cressida unfaithful Grecian mistress of Troilus (DP)

Cressida's uncle Pandarus (DP)

crest heraldic device on shield or helmet; coat-armour; helmet; plume on helmet; badge; head or neck of animal (e.g. horse)

crest fallen humbled

Cretan of Crete

Crete, hound of species of shaggy dog

crisp wavy, curled

critical censorious

crochets strange idea, fancy

crook bend

crooked malign

crop have children; cut off, down

crop-ear horse with cropped (marked) ears

cross thwart; contradictory; perverse; coin with cross on

crossed debts cancelled

cross-gartered with garters crossed behind the knees

cross-row alphabet

crossways crossroads (where suicides were buried)

crotchet musical note; strange fancies

crow crowbar

crow-flowers crowsfoot (buttercup)

crowkeeper boy who acts as scarecrow

crown coin worth five shillings (25p)

crown imperial plant — fritillaria

crown of the sun French crown (syphilis)

crowner SEE coroner

crudy crude

crupper leather strap securing the saddle

crusadoes Portuguese coins

cry pack of hounds

cry you mercy beg your pardon

cub-drawn sucked dry by cubs

cubiculo apartment

cuckold man with unfaithful wife

cucullus non facit monachum the hood does not make the monk

cudgel beat

cuishes thigh-armour

cullion rascal

culverin smallest cannon

cum privilegio ad imprimendum solum with the sole right to print

cumber trouble

cunning clever; knowledgeable; skill, particularly in magic; discernment

Cupid blind son of Venus

cuppele gorge FOR *couper le gorge*, cut the throat

curd curdle

cure state of health; group of parishioners

curiosity exactness

curious skilful, careful

curious-good over-elaborate

currance flow

current currency; genuine

current, come be acceptable

current, hold still true, still hold

curriers runners

currish like a dog (cur)

cursitory cursory

curst petulant, ill-tempered, shrewish

curtains banners

curtal(l) cut short; dog with docked tail (household dog)

curtle-axe short sword, cutlass

curtsy, make defer to

curvet prance, twist

custalorum FOR *custos rotulorum*, keeper of rolls (records of sessions) in county

custard a clown leaping into large custard

custard-coffin pastry case for baking custard in

customer one who seeks custom — HENCE prostitute

custrel knave

cut a docked (or gelded) horse

cut and long-tail all sorts (used of dogs originally)

cut horse gelding

cutpurse thief who cut off purses

cuttle bully, swaggerer

Cyclops giants, servants of Vulcan

Cydnus river in Cilicia, river in Egypt
Cynthia the moon
cypress a thin material — crape
Cyrus Persian king, SEE Tomyris
Cytherea Venus, goddess of love

dace small fish
Daedalus SEE Icarus
daff take off, doff
Dagonet King Arthur's foolish knight
dainty, makes is over-fastidious
dainty of over-solicitous of
dalliance idle pleasure, talk
Dalmatians tribe from coast of Dalmatia
damask pink and white like a damask rose
Damon from story of the faithful friends,
　　Damon and Pythias
dancing-horse famous performing horse,
　　called Morocco, owned by one, Banks
Daniel a young judge, SEE Ezekiel 28 : 3
Danskers Danes
Daphne wooed by Apollo. To escape from
　　him, changed into a laurel
Dardan(ian) Trojan, Dardaian, Peninsular
dare challenge; make to crouch down in
　　fear
Darius King of Persia, in whose coffer
　　Alexander kept the works of Homer
darkling in the dark
darnel wild rye grass, believed harmful to
　　eyes
darraign prepare
dash stroke, mark
dash, at first from the first
dastard coward
daub dissemble
daubery dabbling, daubing
Daventry town in England
daw jackdaw
de FOR the
dead-killing killing dead
deadly-standing death-bringing stare
deal make use of
deared dearer, more precious
dearn dread
dearth lack of, scarcity; dearness
death's face skull
death's head skull, often engraved or
　　carved
death-practised planned death
deathsman executioner
debile weak
Deborah Judges 4 : 4–6
deboshed debauched
decayed ruined (financially)
deceivable deceptive
deciphered discovered
deck pack of cards
decked covered

decline incline, bend down; recite in order
declined gone down in fortune; grown old
decoct boil, heat
deem thought
deep-mouthed loud and deep bark of
　　hound
defeat destroy; change for worse; disguise
defeature disfigurement
defend forbid
definitive unchangeable
defuse pour
defused indiscernible, shapeless
defy the matter defy the sense, meaning of
degrees social ranks
d'elbow FOR the elbow
delicates delicacies
deliver disclose, make plain
Delphos island, birthplace of Apollo
delve dig; trace
demean behave
demerits sins, offences
demesnes domains
demicannon (lit.) gun with large bore;
　　(fig.) padded and stiffened sleeve
demi-wolf half dog, half wolf
demurring gazing on
denayed denied
denier French coin of little value
denies his person refuses to be present
denote reveal, disclose
denounce declare war
denunciation public announcement
dependency submission, outcome
depender one who defends
depute act on behalf of another
deracinate weed out
derive bring, cause
derived descended
dern dreary
derogate debased
derogation insult
descant treble; comment
descry discover
deserve repay, requite
designment plan; enterprise
desires desirability, charms
despise dishonour
despite scornful hatred; abuse
despite, in in spite of
despiteful malicious
detected for charged with
detection discovery; evidence of infidelity
determinate terminate; resolve
determined particular
detested detestable
Deucalion survivor, in classical mythology,
　　of flood
deuce-ace a throw of a two and a one at
　　dice

devesting undressing

device trick; coat-of-arms; (dramatic) spectacle; manner of thinking; stratagem, plan

dewberries kind of blackberry

dewlap the flesh on the throat

dexteriously dexterously, easily

dey-woman dairy-woman

di faciant laudis summa sit ista tuae may the gods make this the height of your glory

Diablo Devil

dial sundial, clock face

Dian (Diana) goddess of chastity, and of the moon

diapason bass in accord with treble tune

diaper towel

dibble a pointed stick used to make holes in earth for planting

diburse pay out

dich may it do

Dickens poss. Devil

Dickon Dick, King Richard

diction description, expression

Dictynna name for moon

Dido Queen of Carthage, beloved of Aeneas

die one of two dice

diet feed

dieted controlled feeding — HENCE limited

difference distinction; dispute

difference, at in dispute

difference, make discriminate

difference of complexion all kinds and appearances

diffuse pour out; confuse; SEE defused

dignify invest with honour

dignity worthiness

digt has dug

dilate tell at length

dilations expansion of arteries — HENCE heartfelt outbursts

dildos word used in ballad refrains (phallus)

diligence a diligent person

diluculo surgere early to rise

dint blow, dent

Diomede Greek hero

direct session ordinary court sitting

directitude FOR disgrace

direness horror

Dis Roman god of underworld who carried Proserpina (Primavera) away to the underworld

disable belittle; impair

disabling disparagement

disanimates disheartens

disannul cancel out

disaster unfavourable influence of planet/ star — HENCE ill-luck

disbench drive from bench

discandying melting

discase take off robes

discharge perform; pay off

disciplines of the war military science

discommend not commend

discourse of thought process of thinking

discover reveal; betray; recognize; reconnoitre

discretion, do your act as you think fit

disedged take edge off appetite

disfurnish be unprovided; deprive

disgrace contempt; dishonour

disgraced insulted

disgracious disgraceful

dishonest unreliable; unchaste

disjoin separate

disliken make unlike

dislimns breaks up (SEE ALSO limns)

disme tenth

dismission dismissal, refusal of love suit

dismount take out, draw

disnatured unnatural

disparked destroy the park where game kept

dispatch prepare; speed; conclusion of business

dispense pardon; disregard

dispense with condone

dispiteous merciless

displant transport, transplant

disponge drip, rain down

dispose come to terms; manage; direct; stow away

disposition natural temperament; mood; inclination

disprise scorn

dispropertied taken away

disproportion disfigure

dispurse disburse; pay

disquantity reduce size

dis-seat dethrone

dissembling colour, the red, trad. colour of Judas' hair

distaff staff used in spinning

distaste taste ill

distemperature disturbance of humours in body; bad weather

distempered upset, out of temper; diseased

distill diffuse in small drops; extract essence

distinction separating

distract separate; distracted; mentally confused

distraction division; group; madness

distrain seize

ditch-dog dog dead in ditch

dive-dapper dabchick

divers several; various; differing

dives rich man in Bible (Luke 16)
dividant capable of being divided
divulged made public
dizzy-eyed dazed
do de represents shivering
doctor man of learning
doctrine knowledge
doff take off, put aside
dog ape (?) male ape, (?) dog-faced
  baboon
dog at be good at
dog days hottest days of year
dog hole kennel
dog weary dead tired
dogs, ban chained dogs
doit coin of small value; mere trifle
dole lot; share; misery
dolphin symbol of love and lust; poss. for
  Dauphin
dolt stupid person
Dominical red letter used to denote
  Sundays
doom judgment, sentence
doom, great Last Judgment
doo's FOR does
dotage infatuation
dotant old fool; dotard
dote act or speak foolishly; love
  excessively
double repeat oneself
double-dealing cheating
double-fatal doubly fatal
doublet man's jacket
doubt fear; distrust
dough, cake's failure
dout put out, douse
dove bird, sacred to Venus
dovehouse dovecot
dower dowry, marriage-portion
dowlas cheap coarse linen
dowle small feather
down-gyved fallen to the ankle
Downs, the off the coast of Kent
doxy beggar's moll
drab harlot, whore
draff pig-swill
draw pull out; tap ale; levy
drawbridge retractable bridge across a moat
drawn ready; on show; forced from cover;
  involved
dressed (drest) prepared; set up
dressings robes of office
drift meaning; purpose; direction
drive force
drive at rush on; attack
driving drifting
drollery puppet show (poss.)
drollery, living puppet show but with live
  actors

dropping dripping wet
dropsied diseased with dropsy
drossy worthless
drovier drover, cattle-dealer
drug a poisonous mixture
drug-damned hated for its poisons
drumble dawdle
dry-beat severely beat, cudgel
ducat gold piece
dudgeon handle of dagger
due precise; owed as a right
duer more duly
duello code of duelling
dugs nipples; teats
dulcet sweet to hear
dull make insensitive, blunt
dump sorrowful song or dance;
  melancholy
dun game ref. to game involving lifting
  log which represented a horse from
  (imaginary) mire
dungy vile, consisting of dung
dunnest mouse-coloured
dun's the mouse (?) keep quiet
dup to open, do up
durance imprisonment
duty respect

eager wanting greatly; sharp; sour; biting
eale evil
ean drop lambs
ear plough
earn yearn
earnest payment, as a pledge, to secure a
  bargain
ears, by the quarrelling, 'up in arms'
Eastcheap name of street and tavern in
  London
ebon ebony, black
Ebrew Hebrew
ecce signum behold, the sign, the evidence
eche eke out, augment
ecstasy a state of mind anywhere between
  overexcitement and complete madness;
  a fit
edge, give urge on
education upbringing
effect achieve, result
effects, prove be fulfilled
effectual operative; grave
effeminate gentle; capricious; cowardly
effuse pour out
eftest quickest
egal equal
eglantine wild briar
egma enigma
ego et rex meus I and my king
egregious enormous, extraordinary
egregiously in a very shameful manner

Egypt, the firstborn SEE Exodus 11 : 5, 12 : 12 and 29

Egyptian thief Thyamis who tried to kill his captive Chariclea before she was taken by his captors

eisel (eysel) vinegar

Elbe German river

elbow, to rub the joy was believed to make the elbow itch

eld older people, old age

elder, heart of coward (elder = soft wood)

element sphere; sky; constituent part

elements, the four earth, air, fire and water; the weather

elf entangle

elf skin (eel-skin) very thin (poss. FOR elsin — shoemaker's awl)

Elizium (Elysium) resting place of good spirits

ell forty-five inches

Elysium SEE Elizium

emball invest with orb of authority

embarquement embargo, impediment

embassage carrying a message

embassy message

embattle establish in battle order

ember-eves evenings of fasting and prayer before ember-days

emboss ambush, close around

embossed swollen; foaming at the mouth

embowel empty, disembowel

embrace accept

embrasure embrace

embrue (imbrue) shed blood

eminence special honour

Emmanuel used as prefix to letters, public deed, etc. = 'God with us'

empale (impale) surround

emper(i)al FOR emperor

emperic quack

empery supreme dominion, empire

empiricutic like a quack

empleach intertwine

emulation attempt to equal; ambitious rivalry

emulous ambitious

emures walls

enacts workings

enactures action

Enceladus giant, one of Titan's sons, of Typhon

enclave hide

enchantingly by enchantment, witchcraft

enchased ornamented

enclouded enveloped

encompassment talking about, circumvention

encounter meet; oppose

encumbered folded

endamage damage

ender end

endite invite

endues (indues) spreads through; endows

Endymion a beautiful youth, who was kissed by Selene (the moon) as he slept on Mt Latmus

enew in falconry — to drive into water, hence pursue eagerly

enfeoffed become enslaved

enfoldings (infoldings) clothes

enforce stress, emphasize

enforce him ply him

engage pledge, take up challenge

engine war machine; device; plot; instrument

Englished translated into English, ALSO poss. pun, *Inglish* to cuddle

englut engulf

engraff attach firmly

engross make fair copy of; take completely, swallow up

engrossing monopolizing

enguard protect

enjoin bind by oath

enlarge free

enlighten make appear bright

enow enough

enraged passionate; furious

enrank to draw up in battle order

enround surround

ensconce hide behind; protect

enseamed full of grease

ensear dry up

ensign standard bearer; banner, standard

entail hereditary property

enter favourably introduce; engage in conversation

entertain employ; accept; receive kindly; house

entertainment welcome

entertainment, in the in the pay of

entire essential; whole; total

entitule entitle

entranced in a trance

entreat use, treat

entreatment request for company

envenom poison

l'envoy stanza at end of poem summing up the theme

enwheel encircle

Ephesian jolly companion

Epicure lover of a soft life

Epicurean given to luxury

Epicurus Greek philosopher, who believed omens and portents had no meaning

epitheton epithet

equipage that with which one is equipped

equity right; justice

equivalent equal

equivocal ambiguous

equivocate speak ambiguously so as to deceive

equivocator one who swears to a thing, whilst mentally denying it

Ercles Hercules

Erebus region between earth and Hades

ergo therefore

eringo sea-holly, candied root used as sweetmeat, with aphrodisiac qualities

erring wandering

error wandering off course

erst ever

escapend escaped

escot maintain

esperance hope

espial spy

espials spies, eyes

esquire next to knight in rank, entitled to bear heraldic arms

essence existence, being

estate status, position

estate, to bestow

estimation reputation

estridge goshawk

et bonum quo antiquius eo melius the older a thing, the better

et tu Brute you, too, Brutus

eterne eternal

Ethiop(e) Ethiopian of dark complexion

Etna volcano in Sicily

Europa daughter of Agenor, carried off by Jupiter

even exact; equally; level

even pleaches layered evenly

even your content satisfy you

ever-remaining ever-present

evitate avoid

ewer kind of pitcher

examination testimony

exasperate angry

except exclude; object to

exception disapproval

excess usury

exchange alter

exclaim on accuse loudly

exclaims pleas

exclamation noisy reproach

excrement appendage; excrescence; growth on body (hair)

exequies funeral rites

exhalation meteor

exhale draw out

exhibit put up, propose

exhibiter proposer of bill

exhibition financial provision, gift

exigent emergency; end

exion FOR action

exorcis(z)e call up spirits of dead

expect await; expectation

expedience hasty leaving

expedient speedy; fitting

expedition haste; motion

expense expenditure

expiate finish; come

expir'd ended

expostulate discuss

expostulation discourse

expressure impression; expression

exsufflicate inflated, blown up

extemporal extempore

extend stretch, give free scope to; demonstrate; extol

extent assault

extenuate relax

extirp root out

extort to get by torture

extraught derived

extravagancy wandering beyond set limits

extravagant vagrant outside his limits

extremity extreme behaviour

eyas young hawk; (fig.) sprightly child

eye-glass lens of eye

eyes, city's city gates

eyes, good approving looks

eyne eyes

eysell vinegar

fa musical note

face false, deceive

face down maintain to one's face

face-royal face of a king

facinerious criminal, wicked

fact offence; crime

faction, scrupulous small areas of disagreement

factionary active in the party of

fadge turn out, serve, be suitable

fading used in song and dance refrains

fail death; omission

fain wish; gladly; fond

fain to obliged to

fair befall you good luck to you

fair with in wealthy state

fairing gift bought at fair

faith-breach breach of faith

faithed believed

faithless perfidious, treacherous

falchion light curved sword

fall from desert, downfall

fall off withdraw support

falliable fallible

falorous FOR valorous

fame reputation, honour; rumour; make famous

familiar attendant spirit
fan separate grain from chaff by blowing
fancy-monger one who deals in love (fancy)
fancy-sick love sick
fane temple
fang seize with teeth
fantastic strange
fantastical imaginary, capricious
fantasy love; imagination's fancy; whim;
  fancy
fap drunk
farborough FOR thirdborough = constable
farced stuffed
fardel bundle
farrow litter of pigs
farthingale hooped petticoat
farthingale, semi-circle gown with skirt
  sticking out at the front
fartuous FOR virtuous
fashion manner; adapt to a purpose;
  pervert, frame
fashion-monging followers of fashion
fashions skin disease of horses
fast irrevocable
fast and loose a cheating game
fast it out pass time fasting
fasten'd determined
fatal-plotted plotting death
Fates the three Fates of whom one spins,
  one weaves and one cuts the thread of
  man's life
fathom calibre
fatigate tired out
faucet-seller seller of taps
fault break in scent
favour face; appearance; token; present
  (of love); goodwill
favoured, ill-/hard- ugly
favoured, well- good looking, pretty
fawne 1st-year buck
fay faith
fay, by my by my faith
fazed SEE feazed
fealt(h)y loyalty
fearful timid
fears cowards
fears me frightens me
feat dexterous
feated encouraged, spurred on
feathered winged
feazed (fazed) frayed, worn out
fe(o)dary confederate
fee reward
fee, in in absolute possession
fee me an officer engage an officer for me
fee simple full possession of an estate
feeder servant, farm hand, parasite
fee-farm property held in absolute
  possession

fee-grief particular grief
fell skin; deadly, grim; fierce
fellies curved rim of wheel
fellow equal
fellowship alliance, partnership
fence protect
fenny living in a fen
fen-sucked sucked up from fens
fere husband, spouse
fernseed visible only on midsummer eve,
  if gathered gave invisibility to gatherer
festinate hasty, quick
fet fetched
fet, deep- fetched from deep down
fetch make; derive; trick; vetch
fetch of regain
fetch off do away with
fetch him off rescue him
fetch in take in
fettle prepare
fewness in brief
fia away (via)
fico obscene insult
fidiused coined from Aufidius
field battlefield; duelling area
field bed bed on ground
fielded in the battlefield
fife small wind instrument, played with
  the head turned to one side
fig me insult, with gesture of thumb
fights screen used in naval engagement to
  protect crew
figo (fig.) orig. obscene gesture
fig's end expletive (e.g. my arse!)
figure device; true shape; figure of
  speech; idle fancy; depict
figure, by the using diagrams for making
  effigies
filch steal
file army, rank
filed defiled; polished
file our engines sharpen our wits
file with keep pace with
fill shaft
fillet bound up hair
fill-horse cart-horse
fillip flip, toss into the air; lift up; strike
film gossamer
filths harlots
finder of madmen one of jury appointed to
  find out if the accused were sane
fine fee; delicate; forfeit; end; sum of
  money paid by tenant to lord for
  permission to transfer lands to another
fine, in at last, finally
fine-baited very tempting
fines conveyances
fingres FOR fingers
finical finicky in dress

Finsbury Finsbury Fields, outskirts London, place of recreation

firago virago

fire smoke out

fire-drake fiery dragon (man with red nose)

fire-new newly fired

fireworks word poss. used also for whore

firk beat

firstlings first things

fisnomy physiognomy

fistula type of ulcer

fit grimace; extremity of pain; unexpected turn; madness; satisfy; ready; befit, suitable

fitchew polecat noted for smell and lechery; prostitute

fitment what is fit and proper

fives, the swelling of the parotid gland

fixture stability

flag water reed or rush

flag, set up declare war against

flamen priest

flap-dragon a burning raisin floating alight in liquor; swallow down

flaring streaming, flying about

flask container for gunpowder

flat-long the flat side of a sword as opposed to its cutting edge

flats shoals

flaw squall; outburst of feeling; crack

flayed beaten

fleer sneer; grin

fleet while away; fly by quickly; people around

Fleet, the Fleet prison

flesh initiate

fleshed fed with flesh; initiated; made eager for combat; accustomed

fleshment act of fleshing

flewed having large chaps

flexure act of bending

flibbertigibbet fiend of antics and grimaces

fliers those who run away

flighty in the imagination, projected

flinch fail, fall short

fling have a go at

flirt-gill fast girl

flocks wool

flood tide

flood, at the at the peak

Florentius knight in Gower's 'Confessio Amantis', who married an old hag who could answer his riddle

flote sea

flourish plume of helmet; fanfare of trumpets

flout fly in the face of; mock at

flower-de-luce white lily

flowing abundant

flush in prime

flux secretion; ebb and flow

fluxive flooding, tearful

fly at the brook hawking at water-fowl

fly out of itself change its nature

flying off desertion

foil disgrace; rapier, blunted for fencing

foin thrust

foison harvest

folly foolishness; licentious behaviour

fond foolish; infatuated

fool court jester; term of endearment

fool-begged foolish

footboy lackey

foot-cloth horse trappings

footed landed

footing landing; dancing

foot-landrakers footpads

fop fool

foppery deceit; foolish behaviour

for from

forage prey

forbear his presence avoid

forbod forbidden

forced stuffed

fordoes undoes, ruins

fordone destroyed, exhaused

fore-end first part

foregoers forbears

foreign not related; stranger, alien

fore me exclamation — upon my word!

fore-hand leading man

fore-horse leading horse

forepast earlier

fore-rank most important

fore-say foretell

foreskirt that which precedes

forespent expended previously; exhausted; passed, finished with

forespoke gainsaid

fore-spurrer one who spurred his horse ahead; harbinger

fore-stall discredit; spoil beforehand; judge beforehand; deprive

forester guardian of the forest

forfeit loss of life

forfeit in a barber's shop = drawn teeth

forfeiture when bond debt became payable

forfend forbid, prevent

fork leg

fork heads barbed arrows

forked horned — HENCE cuckolded

forks poss. support for hair

form, good well-cut shape

form: to set a form to to give point to

formal normal

forsworn abandoned
forthcoming arrested for trial
forthrights straight paths
forthy by which
fortify uphold
fortuna de la guerre fortunes of war
fortune, at at random
fortune, malevolence of misfortune
forward vanguard; above, beyond;
    promising; eager
forward top forelock
forwardness rashness
fostering cherishing
found find weaknesses
foundations charitable establishments
founded secure, sure
fountain spring
foutra term of contempt
fowler bird-catcher
fox, drawn fox drawn from cover in hunt
fox, hide children's game of hide and seek
foxship cunning
fracted broken
fraction breaking apart
frame structure; order, pattern
frame self conform
frame, out of self out of shape, disordered
frampold disagreeable
franchises liberties
Francisco Frenchman
frank free; swine enclosure
franked shut up in sty
franked in hold shut in custody
franklin landed freeholder
Frateretto name of fiend
fraught freight, burden; laden with
frayed afraid
free generous; innocent; open
freestone-coloured sandstone — between
    brown and yellow in colour
French crown French coin; bald head
    caused by syphilis
French crown colour pale yellow like a gold
    coin
fret anger; bar of wood on lute that
    regulates vibrations; corrode; wear
    away; rot
fretten fretted
friar member of religious order of 13th
    century
friend: be friend to make most of
friended be friends with, successful
friends, at in the way of friendship
frieze woollen cloth (cap)
front forelock
fronting opposing
frontlet band worn on head, (fig.) frown
froward refractory, unwilling to obey
fruitful generous

frush batter
fubbed fobbed off
full very
fullam false dice
full-charged fully loaded
fuller one who cleanses wool or cloth
full-gorged fed to full
fume rage
fumitor(y) fumitory, a weed
function operation of faculties; action;
    occupation
Furies avenging deities, daughters of earth
    or night, with serpents twisted in their
    hair and blood dripping from their
    eyes
furnace enclosed place where hot fire
    maintained
furnaces sighs like a furnace
furniture equipment; trappings
furrow-weeds weeds in ploughed fields
Fury goddess of vengeance
fust grow mouldy
fustian nonsense; bombastic; coarse
    cotton
fustilarian comic term, poss. from fustian
    — coarse cloth or fusty-mould growth

gaberdine cloak
gad sharp metal instrument
gage wager; pledge; token
gain-giving misgiving
gait proceeding
Galen Greek physician (AD 129–99) to
    Marcus Aurelius
gall bile; ingredient of ink; anything
    bitter; hurt, harass
gall at scoff at
galled diseased; injured; made sore by
    chafing; reduced
gallant-springing nobly growing
galley sailing ship
Gallia Gaul; Wales
galliard lively dance
galliasses large ships
gallimaufry a silly mixture; the whole lot
Gall(o) glasses Irish soldiers
gallow terrify
gallows gallow-bird, one who deserves
    hanging
gambol skip, frisk about; start
gambold frolic
game hunting; love-play
gamesome sportive, lively
gamester on the game, prostitute;
    athlete; 'smart Alec'
gamut scale of musical notes
Ganymede Jupiter's page
gape long eagerly
Gar variation on God

garboils disturbances

garden, curious-knotted a quaintly laid-out garden of flower or herb beds

Gargantua giant (Rabelais)

garner barn; gather in

Garter Order of the Garter

gaskins loose breeches

gasted frightened

gastness fear, terror

gat begat

gather get information

gauds amusements; trinkets

gauge estimate

gauntlet leather glove reinforced with steel

gauntlet, to throw down the challenge to fight

gave told

gawded made up

gear business matters; nonsense

geck (geek) butt, dupe

gelded castrated, depreciated in value

gelt gelded

gelidus timor occupat artus cold fear fills up the limbs

Gemini (Geminy) Twins

gender offspring; kind; engender

general vulgar

general-gross universally evident

generation offspring; parents; race

generative begotten

genius guardian spirit; soul; own special disposition

gennet SEE jennet

gentle ennoble; yielding; pliant

gentleman usher gentleman who walks before

gentles gentlefolk

George jewel, with figure of Saint George, in insignia of the Order of the Garter

german blood relative

germane related

germen germ, seeds

gest length of stay; deed

ghosted made a ghost of

ghostly spiritual

gib tom-cat

gibbet gallows; hoist with crane

gibbet-maker FOR Jupiter

giber wit, scoffer

gig a whipping-top

giglet wanton

giglot strumpet

gild enrich; cover

gilded made happy (with drink)

gillyvor flower of Dianthus group, a pink

gimmal (gimmers) joints, links

gin snare

ging gang

gird sharp reproof; invest; enclose, encircle; reflect on; mock at

girdle, turn the put up with it

Gis by Jesus

give away give up, abandon

give o'er give up, cease

give out speak about; report

glanders disease of horses, a discharge from nose and swollen jaw

glass hour glass

glassed enclosed in glass

glass-gazing vain

glasses of the eye pupils

glassy reflection in glass

gleek jeer, jest

gleeks scornful remarks

glib geld

glooming gloomy, cloudy

glose SEE gloze

gloss fair appearance

gloss: set a gloss on make something appear right, honest

gloze cover with fair words; flatter; interpret

glozes pretences

glut swallow

go alone without support

go even agree with

go through bargain for

go to come! come! (phrase of derision or incredulity)

goatish lascivious

God buy you God be with you

God 'ild God yield

godden treat as a god; Good day

Gods forbot God forbid

Golgotha field of the skulls, place of the crucifixion

Goliases Goliaths (SEE Goliath)

Goliath strong fighter of the Philistines I Samuel 17: 7 where his spear is likened to a weaver's beam

good: what the good year expletive — what the Devil!

good-den good evening

goodman used as prefix to name

goods, for our for our own good

goose prostitute

gorbellied pot-bellied

Gorboduc legendary British king

Gordian knot fabulous knot, devised by Gordius, undone by Alexander the Great

gorget armour protecting the throat

Gorgon female with snakes for hair who turned all who looked on her to stone

gospelled inbued with the ideas of the Gospel

goss gorse

gossamers filaments floating in air

gossip acts as godparent at christening; old woman; woman who attends a birth

Goths ancient German tribe of east Europe

Gourd a false dice

gout drop

govern arrange

government careful conduct, self control

gown, black mourning gown

grace divine forgiveness; majesty; prayer, answer to prayer; form of address for duke; attendant on Venus; give a good appearance; praise; to honour; gratify; dignified; demeanour

grace, do pay honour

grace to boot heaven help us

graced received favourably

graces qualities

gradation seniority

graff SEE graft

graft grafted, joined to

grafters those from whom the grafts have been made

grain colour deeply, dye

gramercy God reward you (grant mercy)

grammercies many thanks

grand jurors men of substance who could serve on jury

grange country house, usually isolated

grapple hook, clasp

grate vex, annoy

grated begged

gratify reward

gratillity small gratuity

gratulate gratifying

grave engrave

gravel hard

gravel blind partially blind

gravelled at a loss, stranded

gravity sober-mindedness

greasily indecently

Greek meaningless

Greek, foolish buffoon

Greek, merry buffoon

green immature

green sickness anaemia; immaturity

greenly like a callow youth, lacking judgment

greet the time meet the occasion

grew'st remain fixed as if growing

grey-malkin familiar of a witch (poss. a cat)

grief-shot grief-stricken

griffin fabled animal, half lion, half eagle

gripe vulture; fasten on to

grise step; pace; flight of steps

Grissel Griselda, model of wifely obedience in 'The Clerk's Tale' by Chaucer

grize SEE grise

grizzle grey hairs

groat coin worth 4d

gross general aspect

gross in sense clear to see

gross(ly) obviously; substantially; licentiously

groundlings those who stood on the ground floor in the theatre to watch the play

grow to become aware of

grow upon take liberties with

guard braid on uniform or livery

guard, out of lost all resources

guardage guardianship

guardant guard

gud FOR good

gudgeon fresh water fish

guerdon recompense, reward

guidon pennant, standard

guilder Dutch silver coin

guiled beguiling, treacherous

guilts crimes

guinea-hen a 'bird'; prostitute

Guinever King Arthur's queen, Guinevere

guise fashion

gulf gullet

gull dupe; trick

gum(med) glue used for stiffening cloth

gun-stones cannon balls

gurnet a small fish

gust taste; know of; gusto

Guy (Sir) of Warwick, mediaeval hero who slew the giant, Colbrand

gyves shackles

haber-de-pois avoirdupois

habiliment garment

habit dress

hack chop at; (?) seduce

hackney horse kept for hire; prostitute

hag evil fairy, witch

Hagar's offspring Ishmael, a wild man (Genesis)

haggard wild, untrained

hair, against the against the grain

hair, lose sign of syphilis

halberd battle-axe fixed to long pole

halcyon kingfisher, when suspended, turns bill to face wind; breeds on calm days

halcyon days calm days

hal'd called

hale haul, drag

half-achieved half-won

half-caps offhand salutation

half-cheeked bit one where side pieces attaching it to the bridle are broken

half-kirtle part of full kirtle (skirt)

halidom holy relics; salvation

halloo SEE hallow

hallow (*halloo*) make holy; call out with loud voice; hunting call

Hallowmas feast day of All Saints, 1 November

halt limp

halter rope used for hanging

hammered of thought about

hammering fashioning, planning

hand signature

hand: in hand with occupied with

hand, set secretary writing

handfast custom; sign of betrothal

handsaw small saw; one who saws the air, i.e. a bad actor

hangers straps by which rapiers hung from belt

hangmanboy boy fit for hanging; poss. executioner's servant

Hannibal Carthaginian leader

hap good fortune; happens

hapless unfortunate

haply (*happily*) fortunately; by chance; perhaps

happiness, the what luck!

harbinger herald, forerunner

hard poor

hard-favoured ugly

hardiment boldness

hardiment, changing matching valour

hardly harshly

hardly off hard to do

hardocks (plant) burdock

harm misfortunes

harness armour

harped hit on; played on

Harpier FROM Harpy

Harpy fabulous creature with face of woman, body of bird of prey

harrow rake, tear apart; fill with anguish

Harry Henry V (DP)

Harry: four Harry ten shillings = £2

hart stag

hasted hasten

hatch half-door

hatched half-shut

hatches movable planks forming deck

hatchet, pap with a beheading

hatchment escutcheon, tablet with armorial bearings

haud credo (Lat.) I do not believe it

haught haughty

haughty high, noble

hautboy reed instrument

have at him a thrust in fencing

have to't to battle

having, a what one has, property

haviour behaviour

hawk bird of prey, used in hunting; keen sighted person; (?) good actor

hawking clearing the throat

hawthorn-buds dandies

hay thrust through

hay, butter grease it, so horses not eat it

hazard jeopardy; risk; a winning opening in tennis court

head troops, armed force

head, gather collect forces

head lugged led by head

head, make new raise fresh army

head, take rebel against

head, to his to his face

headborough kind of village mayor

headier impetuous

headstall bridle

heal heel

healths drinking toasts

heaps mass

heaps, on in a mass

hearsed in a hearse

heart, put in good encourage

heartiness good heartedness

heat anger; ride swiftly over

heat, i' the immediately

heat-oppressed overheated

hebonon poison ((?) henbane)

Hecate goddess who ruled in heaven (as Cynthia), on earth (as Diana), in the underworld (as Proserpine): she taught witchcraft; one of her dwelling places was where two roads crossed: her approach was heralded by the howling of dogs

hectic fever

Hector Trojan hero, name used to denote valour (DP)

Hecuba wife of Priam, King of Troy (DP)

hedge-pig hedgehog

hedge-priest clergyman of lowest order

hedges creeps along; surrounds

heel: at heel of after that

heels, out at penniless

heft handle; retching

height rank

held out kept up

Helen wife of Menelaus of Troy, renowned for her beauty (DP)

Helicon Greek mountain where the Muses lived

Helicons the Muses

Hellespont Dardanelles

hell-kite bird of prey from hell

helm helmet

helmed directed

hem sewing stitch; enclose; cough

hemlock a weed

hempen hemp-rope

hemp-seed FOR homicide

hent hold; jump over; opportunity

Hermes Mercury, who with his magic pipe charmed asleep Argus

Herod King of Jews. In Mystery plays, a blustering villain

Hesperides fabled garden with golden apples

Hesperus evening star

hest command

hey nonny nonny song refrain, (poss.) ref. to female genitals

Hibocrates FOR Hippocrates

Hic est Sigeia tellus here is the Sigeian land

hic et ubique here and everywhere

hic ibat Simois here ran the river Simois

hic jacet here lies

hic steterat Priami regia celsa senis here would have stood the lofty palace of old King Priam

hide lion skin (particularly that taken from Richard, Coeur de Lion)

hid-fox SEE fox

hie hasten

hiems winter

high fully

high day holiday

high-cross market cross in town

high-engendered heaven born

high-gravel-blind nearly totally blind

high-proof to a great degree

high-sighted seeing from on high

high-stomached proud

hight called

hild held

hilding menial wretch

hind female deer; servant; peasant

hindmost last

hint event, occasion

hip, upon the wrestling term — at a disadvantage

hipped lame in the hip

Hippocrates ancient Greek physician

Hippolyta Queen of Amazons (DP)

Hiren Irene, mistress of Sultan Mahomet II (in lost play by Peele)

history story

hit achieved; agreed with

hit of hit on

hizzing hissing

hob, nob have, have not; hit or miss

hobby-horse Morris dance figure; (fig.) person of loose behaviour, prostitute

hobgoblin imp

hoboy SEE hautboy

hodge-pudding stuffing made of several ingredients

hogshead cask of wine

hold strong hold; bet, wager; withhold; helped

hold in keep silent

hold the credit maintain the good name

hold-door trade trade of bawd, or pimp

hole: find a hole in his coat find a weak spot

Holidam(e) 'Holy dame' (Virgin Mary); holiness

holiday, speaks speaks pleasantly

holla whoa!

Holland fine linen

Holmedon battle field of the Percy and the Douglas families

holp helped

holy: court holy water flattery

Holy-rood day Holy Cross Day (14 Sept.)

home all the way, to the full; find its mark

home, told told a few home truths

homily sermon

honest chaste; generous

honesty integrity, honour

honey-seed FOR homicide

honey-suckle FOR homicidal

honorificabilitudinitatibus supposed to be longest word

honour noble deed

honour, use behave honourably

hood disguise

hood, jealous a jealous woman

hoodman-blind game — blindman's buff

hoodwink blindfold

hook, Welsh a curved billhook

hooted at laughed at, mocked

hoppedance, (hopdance, hoperdidance) evil spirit of dumbness

horn ox-horn used by beggars to announce presence and receive drink; symbol of plenty; symbol of cuckoldry; used instead of glass in window panes, etc.; feeler of snail

horn beasts cuckolds

horn-book a spelling primer, framed in wood covered with a thin layer of transparent horn

horn-mad furious

horsed sit as on a horse

horse-hair used for fiddle bows

hose breeches

hose, French narrow breeches

hose, round breeches puffed out at hips

host lodge

hostler ostler

hot in question argued about heatedly

hot-house bath house, sometimes used as brothel

hour-glass a glass which marks time by running sand

house-keeping hospitality

house-wifery house-keeping

hovel-post post support for a small cottage or shelter

howlet baby owl

hox hamstring

hoy small coasting vessel
hoyday exclamation of surprise
hugger-mugger secretly
hull anchor, lie at
hulling drifting at mercy of waves
humble-bee bumble-bee
humour moisture; forte; liking; whim
humour: run this humour out of breath take joke too far
humours, pass good make best of
'*Hundred Merry Tales*' a popular jest book
Hungarian beggarly (pun on hungry)
hunt counter hunt the wrong way, on wrong tack
hunter's peal horn blowing
hunt's up tune played to wake sportsmen
hurdle a wooden frame
hurly (burly) confusion
hurricano hurricane
husband manage economically
huswife housewife; hussy
hyberbolical exaggerated, extravagant
Hybla area in Sicily famed (in classical period) for honey
Hydra many-headed fabulous creature of Greek mythology
hyen hyena
Hymen(aeus) Hymen, god of marriage
Hyperion sun god
Hyrcan from Hyrcania
Hyrcania region of Caspian Sea
hysterica passio choking in throat

Icarus escaping from Minos with Daedalus, his father, on wings of wax, he flew too near the sun, the wax melted and he fell to his death
Iceland dog a shaggy dog
Ides of March 15th of month
idle empty; unnecessary; foolish
idleness pastime
i'fecks truly
ignis fatuus will o' the wisp
'*ild* reward
Ilion Troy
ill-beseeming unnatural
ill-wresting maligning
Illyria now Yugoslavia
imbare lay bare
imitari (Lat.) copy
immanity inhuman
immask cover
immoment of no importance
imp our repair
impartment something to impart
impasted formed into a paste or crust
impawned pledged, staked
impeach accuse; call in question; imperil
impeachment discredit; hindrance

imperfect not sufficiently explicit
imperseverent stupid
impertinent irrelevant
impetticoat pocket
implorator one who implores
import concern
importance request, importuning
importing important, significant
importunacy asking, begging
importunate urgent
importunity request
impose command
imposition attribution; injunction
impossible incredible
imposthume abscess, discharging matter
imprese crest
impress enforced service
impressure impression, stamp, seal
imputation reputation
in involved
in capite one whose land is held directly from the king; as head, chief
in hac spe vito in this hope, I live
in: to in to bring in
incarnadine make red
incertain uncertain
incessantly immediately
inch, at an very closely
inch-meal inch by inch
inclination disposition
incline to favour
inclining bias towards, favourable disposition
inclips clips in, embraces
include conclude
incontinency lewdness
incontinent immediately; lustful
incontinently forthwith
incony delicious, fine
incorporal incorporeal
incorporate of one body; in league with
incorpsed of one body with
increase produce
incredulous incredible
incursion raid
Ind West Indies
indent bargain with
indented zigzag
indenture legal document; articles of apprenticeship
indentures tripartite triple agreement
index prologue; list of contents
Indian i.e. Red Indian, native of N. America
Indies East Indies
indifferency impartiality
indifferent not showy; neither good nor bad; impartial
indigent needy
indigest shapeless, chaotic

indign shameful
indirection irregular methods
indrenched drenched in
indubitate undoubted
inducement attraction; temptation; lead astray
induction prologue; beginning
indue endow, provide
indurance duress
industriously intentionally
industry assiduity
infamonize FOR disgrace
infamy disgrace
infection FOR affection
infectiously harmfully
infinitive FOR infinite
inform make shapes
informal crazy, mentally disordered
infortunate unfortunate
infuse inspire; imbue
ingener inventor, creator
ingenious conscious; intellectual; witty
ingeniously honestly
ingraft ingrained
ingredience ingredients
ingrossed taken on wholesale
inhearse coffin
inherited realized
inhibition prohibition on acting plays
inhooped confined (of quails — to make them aggressive)
inkhorn horn in which ink kept; (fig.) pedant
inkle kind of linen tape; thread
inland cultured
inly inward
innovation (political) upheaval
inoculate engraft
in's in his
inseparate inseparable
inshelled kept inside shell
inshipped on board
insinewed join in power, allied to
insisture regularity
instalment act of instating to office
instance precedent
instant evidence, proof
instate confer
instinct impulse
instrument weapon
insult on exult over
insultment insult
insulter the winner, one who triumphs
insuppressive insuppressible
integer vitae, scelerisque purus, non eget mauri iaculis, necarcu (Horace) — the upright man, free from crime, does not use the javelins nor the bow of the Moor
integrity true feeling

intellect pun (poss.) = signature
intelligencer secret agent
intelligis ne, Domine do you not understand, master?
intelligo I understand
intend pretend
intendment intention
intenible incapable of retaining
intent intention
intention aim
intentively continuously
interdiction self-condemnation
interessed concerned
interest of share, possession; right to
interjoin join together
interlude brief play
intermission space of time, delay
intermissive intermittent
intermit suspend
interpret supply word
interrogatories questioning
intervallum vacation at law-courts
intestate having died without leaving a will
intestine domestic; internal
intimate suggest, hint at
intoxicates intoxicated, befuddled
intrenchant invulnerable, unable to be cut down
intrince intricate
intrinsicate intricate
invectively with invective, sharply
invention ability to plot, scheme
invest dress
invised (?) invisible; (?) investigated
invitus nubibus in despite of the clouds
invocate invoke
Io daughter of river-god, whom Jupiter raped in the form of a cloud
ipse he himself
ira furor brevis est anger is a brief madness
Iris Roman goddess of the rainbow, a messenger of the gods (DP)
Irish rat could be killed with rhymes
Irish wolves ref. to Irish language likened to howling of wolves
iron weapon
iron-witted dull witted
Ise I shall
ish FOR is
Isis goddess of ancient Egypt
iteration repetition; quotation
iwis for sure, certainly

Jack knave; foolish fellow; serving man; wooden part to which quill attached for plucking virginal string; Jack o' the lantern, will o' the wisp; drinking vessel; small white ball in game of bowls

Jack a'lent small stuffed puppet, set up in Lent for boys to throw stones at

Jack boy, ho boy, news,/The cat is well a catch

Jack dog mongrel

Jack, flouting mocking fellow

Jack guardant any common man on guard

Jack sauce saucy fellow

Jacob Jewish patriarch; form of James (apostle), feast day 11 May

jade exhaust; worn-out horse; contemptuous name for a woman

jakes latrine

Janus two-headed god of old and new year

Japhet eldest son of Noah

jar tick; discord

jar, at a squabbling, disagreeing

Jarmen FOR German

Jason hero who sought and found the Golden Fleece

jaunce jaunt, jog

jay bird of crow family, but with coloured feathers

jealousy suspicion

jennet small Spanish horse

Jephthah Judge of Israel, who sacrificed his daughter

jerkin, buff close-fitting leather jacket

jerks sallies, spurts

Jeronimy, Saint mix-up between St Jerome, and Hieronimo of *The Spanish Tragedy* by Thomas Kyd

jesses straps on a hawk's legs, for use in controlling it

jet jut; encroach; strut

Jew i.e. not Christian

jewel house royal plate and jewels

jewel house, master of in charge of royal plate and jewels

Jezebel wife of King Ahab (SEE 1 Kings 16:31)

jig a quick dance

jigging bouncing

Jill lass; serving girl

Job biblical character, SEE Book of Job

Jockey John, Jack, Jock

John Little John, one of Robin Hood's men

John Drum's entertainment i.e. be beaten as is a drum

joint ring ring made in two halves

joint stool a jointed stool

jointress widow with property settled on her at marriage

jointure estate settled on wife at marriage

jollity (sexual) pleasure

jolt-head stupid fellow

jordan urine receptacle, piss-pot

journal daily

journey-bated worn out by the journey

journeyman hired workman

joust fight in tournament

Jove Jupiter, King of Gods, his sacred tree the oak, hurler of thunderbolts, and seducer of Europa, Leda, Io

jowl hit, strike

joy enjoy

judgment knowledge

Jug poss. nickname for Joan

juggling playing tricks, up to tricks

jump exactly; tally; to hazard

jump at precisely at

jumps fits in with

junkets delicacies, sweetmeats

Juno wife to Jove, to whom peacocks are sacred (DP)

Jupiter SEE Jove

just exact; joust

just-borne justly born

justified acquitted

justle jostle

jut project, lean towards

jutty projection

Juvenal youthful; Roman writer

Juvenalis Roman satiric poet

kam wrong, nonsense

kecksies dried stems of the plant hemlock

keech animal fat used in tallow lights

keel to skim, take scum off a cooking pot

keep fair quarter play fair with, treat honourably

keep time keep control

keepers guardian angels

Keisar Kaiser

ken view; eyeshot; know

Kendal green cloth of green asscoiated with Kendal, Cumbria

kennel gutter, street drain

kerchief cloth

kerchief, wear a sick commonly wore cloth round the head

kern Irish foot soldier

kersey coarse woollen cloth

kettle kettledrum

kibe chilblain; sore area of foot

kickshaw trifling amusements, bits and pieces

kicky-wicky girlfriend

kiln-hole oven opening in kiln

kind nature, natural instinct; type, sort; loving; kin

kind, do his act according to his nature

kind, in this in this respect

kindred of one family; matching

kine cattle

kingdom'd like a kingdom

kirtle short jacket, gown
kitchened to entertain in kitchen
kitchen-trull kitchen maid
kite bird of prey; whore
knacks knick-knacks
knapped break up, nibble at
knee, to to kneel to
knees prayers
knell bell tolled for dead
knife, short cutpurse's tool (SEE short)
knog FOR knock, break, beat
knolled tolled a bell, rung
knot company, group
knot-grass plant, infusion of which believed to stunt growth
know understand; find out

labouring the endeavours of
laboursome laborious
labra(s) lips
lace embellish; cord to fasten dress or bodice
lack-brain idiot
lackey one who goes before or follows as servant
ladder-tackle rigging ladders
lade carry away, ladle out
lading cargo
lady terms effeminate phrases
Laertes' son Ulysses, who persuaded Agamemnon to give Ajax proper burial when he killed himself
lag late; latter part; behind
Lakin Ladykin (Virgin Mary)
lam-damn thrash unmercifully
lame disable, cripple
lamely not scanning properly
Lammastide 1 August
lampass disease in horses in which lining behind front teeth swells
lanched pierced, lanced
languish lingering disease
lanthorn lantern
lap wrap
Lapland sorcerers Lapland notorious for sorcery
lapse delay; take; apprehend
lapsing collapsing
lapwing bird, peewit, which pretends to be injured to draw attention from its nest
lards greases
large, at in detail
largesse gift
lark: take a lark for bunting underestimate
'larum alarm
latch catch (sight of); shut in
latched fastened; smeared
lated belated

latest last, ultimate
late-walking staying out late
lath thin strip of wood; actor's wooden sword
latten compound of copper and calamine, too soft for sword blades
laundry laundress
Laura lady, to whom Petrarch addressed his sonnets
laus deo praise be to God
lave wash
lavolt(a) dance with high leaps
law exclamation, Indeed!
lawn fine linen
lawnd glade
lay (on) belonging to laity; wager
lay for seek to win
lay home attack
lazar leper
lea tilled field
lead lead-covered roofs
leaguer camp
Leah wife to Shylock
leak urinate
lean unto acquiesce in
Leander he swam the Hellespont to visit Hero, his mistress
leapfrog game where children leap over each other
leaping-house brothel
leasing lying
leather-coat russet apple
leave to miss
leaven causes substance to ferment and rot
leavened well prepared
leavy leafy
lecture lesson
Leda mistress of Jupiter, her daughter was Helen of Troy
leed (be-leed) becalmed
leer complexion
lees dregs
leets local courts of justice
leg (fig.) support of body politic
legate Pope's deputy
legatine as Pope's deputy
lege, domine read, sir
legion company of Roman soldiers; possessed by many devils, with a kind of madness (SEE Mark 5–9)
leiger ambassador, messenger
leman sweetheart; mistress; lover
lenders money lenders
lending payment
lenity leniency, mildness
Lenten of Lent, a time of fasting — HENCE meagre, thin
let hindrance
let-alone power of veto

lethargied dulled
lethargy coma, insensibility
Lethe mythical river of forgetfulness
lets hinders
level aim
level at guess at
Leviathan sea monster — the great whale
levies raised army
lewd cheap; worthless; base
lewdly wickedly, lecherously
lewdster lecher
liable subject
libbard leopard/lion
liberal licentious
libertine, a chartered one who is licensed to
  act freely
Lichas attendant on Hercules, SEE Nessus
lictor Roman official who attended
  consuls; officer who attended
  magistrates (cf. beadle)
lie, give him the deceive him; put him
  out; make him capable of lying
lief like as much
lief, as as soon, readily
liege superior lord
lies it is necessary for
lieu, in in the place of
lieutenantry delegating power
life o' th' need necessary for life
lig lie
liggens, by God's oath, (?) by God's
  leggens
light alight; delight; of little value
light, set put little value on
lightness loose behaviour
like please
lily-livered white-faced, cowardly
lily-tinctured whiteness
Limander Leander, youth of Abydos who
  nightly swam the Hellespont to visit
  Hero in Sestus
limbeck still, distilling vessel
limber limp
limb-meal limb from limb
limbo (patrum) place of those who died
  before time of Christianity; border of
  hell; gaol
lime used to make beer/wine dry and
  sparkling; bird lime
Limehouse area in London
lime-kiln burning sensation
limit prescribed time
limn depict, outline, paint
line equator; support; strengthen
line grove line of trees
line their coats padded by backing or
  lining, (fig.) fill their pockets
lined padded
ling fish

linger prolong
link (?)blacking; chain
links torch
linsey-woolsey mixture of flax and wool —
  hence a mish-mash language
linstock a stick for match for firing a gun
lion (fig.) the King
lip kiss
lip, make a mock
liquor dress with oil, or grease
lisp talk with foreign accent
list wish, like; bounds; object; listen to;
  selvage of material
lists enclosed area for tournaments
lither yielding
litigious precarious
little-seeming apparently worthless
livelihood liveliness, appearance of life
liver seat of love, and passions
livers living people
livery dress of household; badge
livery, shadowed dark appearance,
  (?) heraldic term
livery, sue his suits for obtaining lands
loach small freshwater fish
lob hang down; dull person
lobby anteroom
lobby, voiding waiting room
lock lovelock, a curl
lockram cheap fabric
locks of counsel safeguards of secrets
locusts (poss.) sweet juice of the carob
lodestar the Pole Star
lodge beat down (of corn); gamekeeper's
  house
loggats game where thick sticks thrown at
  a stake
loggerhead blockhead
logic, balk chop logic
loll thrust out
lolling tongue hanging out
long-staff quarterstaff
long-winded long-breathed
look to treat carefully
look what whatever
loon stupid fellow
loop hole, gap
looped torn
loose, at his very at the last, critical
  moment
loosely carelessly
lose waste
losel worthless fellow
loss of question lack of argument
lost lost; idle; pointless
lots to blanks thousand to one (lottery)
lousy contemptible
lout lay-about
louted made fool of

Louvre palace of French kings
lower lour
lown lout
lubber clumsy fellow
luce pike, freshwater fish
Lucina Diana, as the goddess of childbirth
lucre gain, bribery
Lucrece Lucretia, Roman matron, model of chastity, who killed herself after being raped by Tarquin (DP)
Lucretia SEE Lucrece
Lud's town London
luffed sailed away
lug drag, pull about
lumpish low-spirited, down in the dumps
lunes moments of madness
Lupercal feast of Lupercus, god of shepherds
lurch loiter with intent, rob
lust-dieted satiated
lustique lusty, sportive
lusty vigorous
lusty, over over-active
Luther leading protagonist of Protestantism
Lutheran follower of Luther
lux tua vita mihi your light is life to me
luxury lust
luxurious lustful
Lycurgus legendary law-giver of Sparta
lym lymmer, species of bloodhound

Mab SEE Queen
mace staff of office
Machiavel Machiavelli, 16th-century political theorist, author of *The Prince*; follower of Machiavelli
machine body
maculation taint
madding insane; making mad
made determined
madrigal part song
maggot-pies magpies
magni dominatur poli, tam lentus audis scelera tam lentus vides ruler of the great skies, are you so slow to hear, so slow to see crimes?
magnifico chief men of Venice
Mahu fiend of stealing
maid virgin; mortal; young fish
maid-pale pale as a maiden
mailed up wrapped up
maim punishment
maimed shortened
main army; gambling stake
make interfere; close
make a push at joke at, scoff at
make it even meet it fully
make one become one

make with have to do
malapert saucy, cheeky
malefaction misdeed
malice wretch; enmity
maliciously viciously
malkin slovenly kitchenmaid
mallecho mischief
Malmsey sweet wine
malthorse dray horse = stupid person
maltworms drinkers of ale
mammering hesitating
mammet doll
mammock pull apart
man, write claim to be a man
manage train a horse; handle, control; carry on; conduct
mandragora mandrake, juice a narcotic
mandrake poisonous plant with forked root, believed to scream when pulled up
manikin puppet
mankind fierce
manned attended
mannerly decent, proper
manners moral behaviour; decency; manual of etiquette
manners, in out of politeness
Manningtree place in Essex, famous for oxen
Mantuan poet, Baptista Spagnolus Mantuanus, d. 1516
manu cita with swift hand
manus hand
marble-constant completely marble
marcantant i.e. mercatante — merchant
March chick forward person (born early in the year)
Marches border-country between England and Wales
marchpane marzipan
margent margin, edge
mark coin worth 13s. 4d. (67p); target; made by those who could not write their own name, in place of a signature
mark prodigious ominous mark, birthmark
markets purchases
marl a kind of clay
marrows marrow in bones
marry indeed!
Mars god of war, husband to Venus
Marshalsea prison in Southwark
mart barter; market
Martlemas feast of St Martin when beef or pork slaughtered for winter use
martlet (bird) house martin
marvel(l) surprise; marvellous
marybuds marigolds
mask (masque) an entertainment or ball where those attending covered their faces with masks

mask, sun-expelling mask to keep sun from face, to prevent sunburn which was thought unbecoming to a lady

masque SEE mask

masquer one who attends, or performs in, a masque

mass usually 'By the mass', exclamation

mastick satirical

match marry; agreement; bargain

match, set a arrange a meeting

mated matched; dismayed; bewildered

material of importance; pertinent

matter something of importance; what happened, true facts; capacity

matter, wants lacking in sense

mattock kind of pickaxe

Maudlin poss. (Mary) Magdalen

maugre despite, in spite of

maund basket with handles

maw mouth; stomach

maypole tall pole for dancing round on Mayday

mazed bewildered

mazzard head

me Hercle by Hercules!

me pompae provexit apex the desire for renown brought me

meacock spiritless

meal flour

mealed floured; sprinkled; coloured

mean limit; tenor; common; cause; small, petty; middle position; method

measure dance; limit

measure a weapon act as umpire or second in duel

meats, broken scraps

mechanic workman

mechanical member of artisan class; low; base

meddle take part

meddler one who has a hand in everything

Medea daughter of King of Colchis, who fled with Jason, and later married King Aegeus of Athens

medice, te ipsum physician heal thyself

medicinable healing

medicine chemical preparation; drug; cure

medlar tree with apple-like fruit, fit for eating when part decayed (colloquial — sex organs); prostitute, loose woman

meed merit; reward; hire; wages

meed, in his in his pay

meet even; suitable

meet, 'tis it's right

meetly sufficient

meinty crowd, mob; household; servant

Meisen area in Germany

mell get involved with

memento mori reminder of death

men of hair in skins, like satyrs

mend amend; complete

Menelaus brother of Agamemnon, husband of Helen of Troy (DP)

Mercury god, son and messenger of Jove

mere absolute; total; only

mered sole

meridian highest point

Merlin wizard or prophet at King Arthur's court

Merops husband to Clymene, King of Ethiopia

mesh'd mixed together; caught, as in a net

mess dish of food; portion of food; group of people served together at table

Messaline poss. Marseilles

metal swordsmen; brave men

metal of India gold

metaphysical supernatural

mete measure

mete at aim at

mete-yard measuring stick

metheglins a sweet spiced drink

methinks I think

metre doggerel

mettle core; substance; disposition

mettle, quick lively disposition

mew shut up, confine (of falcons)

mewling mewing like a cat

micher one who plays truant

miching sneaking

mickle great

microcosm man seen as epitome of universe

Midas king, whose touch turned all to gold

milch moist

milch-kine milking cows

mile-end exercise ground for the London citizen militia

milk-livered cowardly

mill-sixpence sixpence made in stamping mill

millstones grinding stone of wheel

millstones, eyes drop not weep at all

Milo strong Greek athlete

mince make light of

mincing affectation; affected way of walking

mind intention; expression

mind, put in reminded of

minded affected

mineral a drug made from minerals

Minerva goddess of wisdom

mines undermines; passage dug under a hostile fortification

minikin dainty, shrill

minime by no means

minimus the smallest creature

minion hussy; darling; favourite

minister supply, give

minister, murdering agent of murder

ministers agents

minnow tiny fish

Minos SEE Icarus

minstrelsy office of minstrel who provided both music and stories

minute-jack person who changes his mind frequently

minutely every minute

mirable admirable

miracle, doth is miraculous

mire mud

miry muddy

misanthropos a hater of mankind

misconster misconstrue, misjudge

miscreant vile wretch; unbeliever

misdoubt mistrust

misdread fear of evil

miser wretch

misgovernment mismanagement, misconduct

mis(s)graffed wrongly grafted, badly matched

misguide misdirect

misprise mistake

misprision mistake; misunderstanding; wrongful arrest

misprized underrated, despised

misproud arrogant

miss fault; fail to strive for

missive messenger

mistempered put to wrong use

misthought misjudged

mo more

mobled (?) muffled

mocked flattered

modern ordinary, commonplace

modesties self-control

Modo evil spirit of murder

module representation, image

moe more

moiety half; portion

moldwarp mole

mollis aer soft air

mome blockhead

moment consequence

momentany momentary

Monarcho a crazy Italian who haunted Queen Elizabeth's court in the 1580s

Monferrat, Marquis of family who took a leading part in the Crusades, and were great traders in amber

monstered enlarge upon

monsters makes it a monster

monstruosity terrible; unnatural

montant a rising blow

month's mind strong desire

monument sepulchre

monumental as a memento

moody rebellious

moody-mad mad with anger

mooncalf calved by moonlight

moonish changeable

Moorditch draining channel between Bishopsgate and Cripplegate in Moorsfield

Moorfields district outside Moorgate, London, used as assembly ground

mope blunder about

moping sulking; dazed

mopping making grimaces

mor du vinager (lit.) death of vinegar, pseudo-French oath

moraller moralizer

morisco moorish or morris dancer

morris (-dance) country dance

mort Dieu God's death

mort o' the deer hunting call at death of deer

mortal deadly

mortal staring kill with a look

mortality death

mortal-living living as a mortal

mortar piece short piece of firearm with large bore

mortified made insensible; kill; insensitive

mortis'd fixed, locked

mose in the chine last stages of glanders (q.v.)

mote small particle

moth a fluttering idler

mother a choking disease also called 'hysterica passio'

motion impulse; faculties; orbit; request; proposal; puppet show or single puppet

motive organ; instrument; cause; movement

motley fool's (? parti-coloured) dress — HENCE fool

mould mortal

Mount Pelion Titans attempted to reach the gods by piling Mt Ossa on Mt Pelion

mountant lifted up

mountebank quack, charlatan; get by trickery

mounts makes rise

mouse term of affection

mouse-hunt pursuer of women

mousing tearing, mauling

mouth voice of hounds; utter in pompous manner

mouth friends friends in name only

mouth honour insincere honour

mouth, open crying out

mouthed gaping; insincerely spoken

mouths, make make faces

movable piece of furniture

move upset

moved inclined; provoked; urged on

mowing making faces

moy FOR moi

muddy-mettled dull spirited

mulled stupefied

Mulmutius first King of England to be crowned, according to Holinshed

multipotent all powerful

mumbudget silence

mummer dumb-show actor

mummy preparation made from mummies used in medicine or magic; dead flesh

murdering-piece small cannon

mure wall

murmur rumour

murrain plague, sickness affecting cattle

murrion infected with murrain

murther murder

muscadel a sweet wine

muse complain

Muses goddesses who preside over the arts

mushrump mushroom

musit hole for creeping through

musk strong-smelling substance from the musk-deer

musk-cat poss. civet-cat, from which a perfume is obtained

Muskos (?) Muskovites; (?) smelly ones

muskroses species of sweet-smelling rose

muss game where boys scramble for rewards

mussel-shell one who gapes (like a mussel-shell)

mustachio moustache

mustachio purple-hued with red moustaches

mutines mutineers

mutton sheep

mutton, laced- prostitute

Myrmidon name of inn

Myrmidons warrior group of which Achilles was leader

mystery trade, profession; professional skill

Nabuchadnezzar Nebuchadnezzar, King of Babylon, was said to have eaten grass when mad

nag small horse; (fig.) prostitute

nag, Galloway particular breed, small Scottish horses

nail $\frac{1}{16}$ yard of cloth

nailes FOR nails

name authority, reputation

napkin handkerchief

Narcissus youth who fell in love with his own reflection

native origin; natural

natural, a congenital idiot

naturalize make familiar with

naught, be make youself scarce

naughty wicked; worthless

nave navel; central part of wheel

nayward denial

nay-word password

Nazarite Christ, accepted by the Jews as a prophet, but not as the son of God

neaf fist

near-legged knock-kneed

neat tidy; horned cattle

neat's leather hide, from horned cattle, e.g. calf leather, oxhide

neb mouth, beak

neck, on one another's in quick succession

Nedar Helena's father (*A Midsummer Night's Dream*)

need, for a in case of necessity

needer one who is needed

needly of necessity

neele needle

neeze sneeze

Nemean of Nemea in Argolis

Nemean lion killed by Hercules

Neoptolemus son of Achilles

nephews grandchildren

Neptune god of the sea

Nereides river nymphs

Nero Roman emperor who murdered his mother

Nervii warriors of ancient Gaul

nervy sinewy

Nessus centaur (centaurs were considered lustful) who raped Hercules' wife and whose poisoned shirt was sent to Hercules by the hand of Lichas

Nestor King of Pylos, who was present at the siege of Troy, renowned for his eloquence and wisdom (DP)

nether lower

nether-stocks stockings

new-fangled given to love of novelty

Newgate place in London where there was a prison

new-hatched newly come

next nearest

nice trivial; precise; squeamish; discontented; modest

nice-fence skill at fencing

nice-longing capricious, not content with anything

nicely particularly

nicer more trivial

Nicholas, Saint patron saint of scholars

nick reckoning; FOR neck

niggard parsimonious

night-bird nightingale

nightgown kind of dressing gown
nightmare incubus, demon
night-oblation evening prayers
night-rule night activities
nill will not
Nilus River Nile
nine men's morris open air game marked
out in squares
nine worthies nine heroes
ninny, pied jester in parti-coloured dress
Ninus (Ninny) mythical founder of Nineveh
Niobe who cried so over the death of her
children she became a fountain
nit egg of louse
no boot no use, of no avail
Nob, Sir Sir Robert
noble honourable; coin worth 6s. 8d.
(about 33p)
noddle head
noddy simpleton
noises is clamourous
nole head
nonage minority
nonce, for the for the occasion
non-come mad
non-pareil incomparable
non-performance not doing
non-regardance disregard
non-suits reject the request of
nook-shotten with many nooks and corners
Norweyan Norwegian
nose-herbs sweet scented plants
nose, wring- method of resuscitation
not a whit not at all
not all not merely
note fame, worthiness; prescription;
note; list of books
noted seen before
nothing-gift worthlessness
nourish nurse
no-verb non-existent word
novi hominem tanquam te I know the man
as well as I know you
novum dice-game
noyance disturbance
numbers metrical feet
nuncio messenger
nuncle contracted form, 'mine uncle'
nurture manner, education
nut-hook contemptuous term for beadle or
constable
nyas young hawk

O, wooden round (octagonal) wooden
theatre (e.g. the Globe)
oak tree sacred to Jove; door
oathable capable of keeping an oath
Oberon king of the fairy world (DP)
Obidicut fiend of lust

object urge
objection accusation
obligation contract, bond
obliged bound, bonded
obloquy disgrace
obsequiously as a mourner
observance, do perform rites
observancy attentiveness
observation rite
obsque hoc nihil est without this there is
nothing
obstacle obstinate
obstruction stagnation of blood, stillness
occasion usage; need; course of events
occasion, present urgent need
occurrents events
o'conscience (on my conscience) for sure
odd-even between midnight and 1 am
odds, at at loggerheads with
odds: have odds of have better of
Ods-pittikins by God's pity
oeillades 'makes eyes' at someone, ogle
oes circles
of against
off, be raise hat to
off, to be be begotten
off-capped take off cap in respect
offering side the side that makes the
challenge
offert FOR offered
office business; duty; deal officiously with
officed perform duties; having particular
place
officed instruments other faculties
officious busy
old plentiful; long-continued; FOR wold
Olympus home of the gods
omit ignore, neglect
omne bene (Lat.) all is well
oneyers (?) a 'oner'
oneyers, great (oneyres o'yeas) (?) those with
contact with the great; (?) a clerk to
the exchequer; (?) owner; (?) yes-man
open hunting term for bark of hounds on
finding scent
open-arse medlar fruit
operant potent; active
opinion arrogance, conceit; public
opinion; reputation; attitude
opposing displaying
opposities opposing forces
opposition, single private fight
oppugnancy opposition
oracle wise person, soothsayer
orb orbit; circle; fairy ring
orchard usually a garden
order the order of the garter; method
ordinance rank; normal behaviour; that
which is ordained; cannon, artillery

ordinary eating house; meal
ordinate directing
ordnance cannon
orgilous proud
orifex orifice
orison prayer, plea
Orpheus the poet who enchanted the whole of nature with his music
ort small piece; fragment of food
orthography correct spelling and speaking — pedantic
osier willow
ostent show; appearance
othergates otherwise
ouches ornaments, jewels
ounce animal resembling leopard, but with irregular faint spots and a long tail
ouphes elves
ousel blackbird
out outside; fully, quite; not friends; at an end, finished; at a loss
out, be forget lines, be angry
out, had had granted
out of door visible
out of the way beside the point
out, will not will not drop out
out-bragg be more beautiful than
out-craftied out-foxed
outward man outsider, on the outside
outwent went beyond
over-charged overstocked
over-cloyed over-filled
over-count outnumber, cheat
over-experch jump, fly over
over-flourished decorated profusely
over-fraught heavily laden
over-peering look with evil eye
over-posting get over easily
over-raught overtook, cheated
over-scutched well-whipped
over-shot wide of the mark
over-topping over-ambitious
over-weening arrogant
over-wrested over-strained
Ovid (family name — Naso) Latin poet 43 BC to 17 AD. Exiled to live amongst the Goths
owes owns
owy FOR oui
oxslip the great cowslip
oyes oyez! hear ye!
oyster-wench woman who sells oysters

pace set out, direct; obedient movement of trained horse
pace, hold me keep up with me
pack bundle; conspire; be off
packed involved

packing plotting
packhorse drudge
packthread thread for tying up parcels
paction pact
paddle play with; finger
paddock toad
Padua university town of Italy
pageant spectacle, show; orig. platform or cart on which episode of miracle play staged
pageants mimic as in a play
paid settled with, killed
pain effort, work
pained'st most tormented
paint cloth scriptural texts etc. painted on cloth, as alternative to tapestry, for wall hanging
pajock (?) peacock
palabras few words, be brief
palate taste
pale boundary; railing; fence in
palfrey a saddle horse
palisadoes defence stakes
pall fail; wrap up
Pallas goddess Minerva
pallets a poor bed
palliament robe (of candidate for office)
palm emblem of victory
palmer pilgrim, who on return from Holy Land carried a palm
palmy glorious
palpable tangible, may be seen and touched; obvious
palsy paralysis
palter play fast and loose; equivocate
paltry poor, mean
paly pale
pandar (pander) one who procures whores (FROM Pandarus)
Pandarus Cressida's uncle, who brought her and Troilus together (DP)
panged afflicted with pain
Pannonians tribe living on east shores of Adriatic
Pantaloon old fool (Commedia del'Arte)
Pantheon temple at Rome
pantler servant in charge of pantry
pap breast
papers puts down on paper
Paphos town of Venus in Cyprus
Paracelsus 16th-century Swiss physician
paradox joke
paragon surpass; excel; compare; the best
parallels lines
paramour mistress
paraquito parrot
Parca = one of three sisters, the Parcae (Fates, q.v.)
parcel enumerate by item

parcel-bawd part-time procuror
parcelled particular
pard leopard
paring small amount trimmed off
Paris son of King Priam who stole Helen of Troy from her husband, Menelaus (DP)
paritor officer of bishop's court, who issued summonses, often for fornication
park-ward the park district
parle, parley prelude to ending hostilities; conversation
parle, brook allow negotiations
parlous alarming, perilous
parmacity spermaceti, from sperm whale, believed to cure bruising
parrot-teacher chatterer, repeating self as when teaching a bird to talk
part: in part of as portion of
Parthian swift-footed warriors of Parthia
partialize be biased, partial
particularities small affairs
particularly on one individual
particulars individuals
partisan (partizan) long-handled spear, with curved blade
partlet trad. name for hen
parts wealth and position
party-verdict a share in a decision
pash beat; smash; head
pashful FOR bashful
pass fencing thrust; pass over; overlook; go beyond; be borne; die; pass judgment
pass of pate sally of wit
passado a forward thrust in duelling
passage passer by
passages movement of people
passant term of heraldry = walking
passengers wayfarers
passes trespasses
passing very, extremely
passion emotional speech
passionate express with feeling
passioning grieving over
passport written permit for moving across country
passy-measures pavin pavane, stately dance
paste pastry cover
pasterns part of horse's leg between the hoof and the fetlock
pastorals, Whitsun entertainments given at Whitsuntide
pat exactly
patch fool
patchery patching; pretence; roguery
pate head
pated, knotty- blockhead
pated, not- with close-cropped hair

paten dish of silver or gold; plate on which consecrated bread placed in the Eucharist
patrician Roman noblemen, ruling class
pattle FOR battle
pauca verba few words
paucas pallabris pocas palabras — few words
Paul's St Paul's cathedral
paunch stab in the belly
pauser one who delays
pavilioned encamped
pavin SEE passy
pawn pledge
pawned added to; gave in pawn
pax small plate of gold or silver with image of crucifixion on it, which members of the congregation kissed
pays returns, or counters, blow
peaches impeaches
peacock bird, symbol of pride
peak mope about
peaking peeping
pear FOR bear
peascod pea-pod — a lucky gift in wooing
pease peas
peat pet, darling; FOR beat
peck pitch, throw; quarter of a bushel
peculiar particular, one's own
pedant school teacher
pedascule (coined word) 'little pedant'
pedlar (pedler) a vagabond seller of wares
peel'd with a tonsure
peer appear
peerless unequalled
peevish silly, childish
Pegasus winged-horse
peg pin for holding the strings of a musical instrument
Peg-a-Ramsey ballad and popular dance tune
peise weigh
peised poised
pelf possessions
pelican bird fabled to revive its offspring with blood from its own breast
Pelion mountain in Thessaly
pelt hurl, throw
pelting paltry
pen, snow-white goose quill pen
pencil paint brush (used in lady's toilet)
Pendragon father of King Arthur
Penelope Ulysses' wife
pensioner bodyguard
pent imprisoned
Pentecost Whitsun, when the cycle of mystery plays was performed
Penthesilea a queen of the Amazons killed by Achilles
Pepin early Frankish king (d. AD 768)

peppercorn berry of pepper-plant, (fig.) a mere nothing

peppered finished off, made an end of

per stygia, per manes vehor I am born through the Stygian land of the dead — i.e. I am in hell

peradventure perhaps

perchance perhaps; by good fortune, by chance

perdie (perdy) by God

perdition slow ruin, loss

perdu sentry in forlorn position

perdurable everlasting

peregrinate of foreign fashion

peremptory determined; presumptuous

perfect make known

perfected skilled in

perforce by force

perge (Lat.) proceed

periapt amulet, charm

Perigenia beloved by King Theseus

period full-stop

periwig-pated wearing a wig

permafoy par ma fois

pernicious deadly; destructive

perpend attend; consider

Perseus son of Zeus, who rode the winged horse, Pegasus

persever persevere

personate describe; impersonate

perspective optical illusion

persuasion belief, principle

perturbation disturbance

peruse observe

peseech FOR beseech

pestiferous deadly

petar small engine of war

Petrarch Italian poet, who wrote sonnets addressed to Laura

petter FOR better

pew bench seat in church

pew-fellow companion

Phaeton son of Phoebus, the sun god, allowed to drive his father's chariot for one day, but the horses got out of control

phantasime fantastic person

phantasma nightmare

Pharamond legendary king of Franks

Pharaoh Egyptian king, SEE Genesis 4: 1

pheeze (pheazar) settle; drive away; to 'do' someone

Phibbus Phoebus, god of sun

Philemon peasant who entertained Jupiter

Philip and Jacob 1 May, feast of St Philip and St James

Philomel (SEE Tereus) nightingale

Philosopher's stone a stone believed to turn all to gold

Phoebe the moon

Phoebus Roman god of the sun

phoenix mythical bird, which lived in the Arabian desert, died in its own funeral pyre from which a young renewed phoenix rose

Phrygian of Phrygia

physic medicine; tonic

pia mater (colloq.) brain

pick pitch; lure

picked fastidious; foppish

pick-lock tool for picking locks

pickers thieves

pickthanks talebearers

pickt-hatch area of London infamous for its brothels

pie magpie; service book of mediaeval church

piece coin; masterpiece; derogatory term for person

piece out add to, fill out; encourage

pieced mended

piedness mixture of colours

pieze slow down

pig FOR big

pight pitched; determined

pigmies legendary race of dwarfs

pignuts groundnuts

Pigrogromitus invented name for star

pinched afflicted; mocked at; nipped by dog

pinfold pen for strayed cattle

pinnace small fast sailing ship

pioned poss. either dug out or peonied — covered with peonies, or pionies — a type of wild orchis

pioners sappers

pip mark on playing cards

pipe for 'whistle for'

pipe-wine wine piped from barrel

piping shrill

Pippen Pepin, King of France, 8th century

pippin type of apple

pismires ants

piss my tallow urinate fat away

pissing-conduit conduit with small stream

pitch height to which a falcon soars; excellence

pitch and pay pay as you go

pitch balls balls of pitch

pitcher jug with handles

pith strength; vigour

pittie-ward ward = district of a town. Pittie — (?) petit, i.e. the little ward of the Windsor area

piu per dolcera che per forza more by gentleness than by force

pizzle penis, bull's penis dried, was used as whip

plack FOR black
plackett petticoat; slit in petticoat; wearer of petticoat
plague, red plague with red sores
plain complain of
plainer more level
plainsong simple song
plainsong, very simple truth
planched planked
plantage plants
plantain herb, efficient in healing wounds
plash pool
plaster cover, e.g. for wound
plated wearing plate-armour
platform gun platform in fort
Platus god of wealth and gold
plausive plausible; commanding applause
Plautus writer of Latin comedies
play caught — as in 'play a fish'
played home played to a finish
pleached interwoven; folded (of arms)
plebians (plebs) common people of Rome
Pleshey Gloucester's house in Essex
pliant favourable
plighted pleated; sworn
plodded toiled
plood FOR blood
plows FOR blows
pluck up rouse oneself
plue FOR blue
plume-plucked humbled
plummet instrument to measure depth at sea
Pluto King of Underworld
pody FOR body
point puctuation stop; advantageous position; waiting position of falcon from which it attacks; pommel of saddle; direction
point, at ready
point-devise precise, exact
points laces holding up breeches
poise weight, weighty = needing careful assessment
poke pocket
poking-sticks used for stiffening ruffs
Polack native of Poland
pole maypole
pole-axe axe fixed on pole
politic artful, prudent; self-interested
politicians schemers
policy of mind mental prudence
poll head; list of voters
poltroon lazy cowards
pomewater large juicy kind of apple
pomgarnet pomegranate
pompous full of pomp
poniard dagger

Pontic Sea Black Sea
poop wreck (colloq.) female genitals
poor-John dried salted hake
popinjay parrot
poppy opium
porn FOR born
Porpentine Porcupine (name of inn)
porridge potage, soup
porringer small porridge bowl; bowl-shaped cap
port city gate; bearing; style
portage possessions; carriage; porthole
portance bearing; behaviour
portcullis metal grating in door
portly well mannered; dignified; swollen
position hypothesis (i.e. something 'posited'); exposition
possess inform
possessed, well rich
posset hot milk with wine or ale in it; clot, curdle
possibility capability
post messenger; stupid person; at full speed
post horses fast horses
post master man in charge of post horses
post off put off
posted over hurried over
postern small side gate or door
posters travellers
posy inscription on the inside of a ring
pot wooden drinking mug
pot: 'little pot and soon hot' proverb — small men get angry quickly
pot, three-hooped band placed at intervals on wooden drinking mug
potations drink
potatoes sweet potatoes thought to be an aphrodisiac
potch stab at
pothecary apothecary
pottle tankard
pottle-pot large tankard
poulter poulterer
pouncet-box small perforated box for perfumes, cf. pomander
pound, equal a precise pound in weight
pow waw exclamation of contempt
powdering tub vat for salting meat; (colloq.) sweating tub for veneral disease
pox venereal disease
pox: a pox on a curse on
poys FOR boys
prabbles FOR squabbles
practic in practice, practical
practice plot
practisants plotters
practise play a trick

praeclarissimus filius noster Henricus, Rex Angliae et haeres Franciae our most dear son, Henry, King of England and inheritor of France
praemunire a writ against anyone who upheld Papal authority or that of a foreign power in England
praetor Roman judge
pragging FOR bragging
prains FOR brains
praises appraises
prat beat
prater chatterer
prattle chatter, gossip
prave FOR brave
prawls FOR brawls
pray in aid beg the assistance of
preachment sermon
pread FOR bread
precept instruction; lesson; summons
preceptial composed of precepts
precipitation drop, precipice
precise punctilious; clear, untarnished
precisian spiritual adviser
precious used intensively, very, complete
pre-contract pre-marriage contract
precurrer precursor, forerunner
precurse precursor
preeches FOR breeches
prefer advance, rise in position; recommend; proffer
prefigure shape in anticipation
pre-formed original
pregnancy readiness of wit
pregnant obvious, clear; productive; quick, wily
prejudicates prejudges
premised promised
prenominate forenamed
pre-ordinance rule previously established
prerogatifes FOR prerogatives
prescience foreknowledge
prescribe give orders
prescribed limited
presently immediately
presentment presentation
president precedent
press take, by force, into military service
presses clothes press
prest ready
Prester John fabulous emperor of the East
pretence purpose; scheme
pretend intend
prevent anticipate
Priam King of Troy, father of Aeneas (DP)
Priapus god of fertility
prick mark on sundial; bull's eye in target; penis
prick down mark down, list

prick in't pinned to it
prick on urge on, spur on
pricket 2nd-year buck
pricksong written descant to song
pride sexual desire
pride, in on heat
pridge FOR bridge
prig thief
prime original; lecherous
primer more urgent
primero card game
primest most excellent
primy in its prime
principality person of highest quality
principals main beams
princox pert young lad
prings FOR brings
Priscian Latin grammarian
prithee I pray thee
private private communication
prived deprived, bereaved
privilege legal right
privilege, to have privilege to
privily secretly
privity concurrence
privy, made being in the secret of
prizer prize-fighter
prizing regard highly
prizing, not disregarding
probal certain of approval; possible
probation proof; investigation
proceeders one who makes quick progress
process how a thing happens; legal summons
procreants procreators
Procrus Procis (SEE Shafalus)
prodigal the prodigal son (SEE St Luke 15); lavish
prodigies dire events
prodigious abnormal; FOR prodigal
proditor traitor
proface 'may it do you good'
profane blasphemous; outspoken
profess avow
profession skilled knowledge
profession, house of brothel
proffer offer
project conception
prolixious superfluous
prolixity tediousness
Prometheus stole fire from gods to give to humans
promise raise expectations from
promise-crammed crammed with expectation
prompture prompting
prone susceptible, or making others susceptible
proof tested armour; of proven worth; experience

proof, come to turn out well
propension inclination
proper true; one's own; handsome
propertied treated as property
properties stage props; have properties of
property distinctive quality; appropriate
property of blood blood relationship
Propontic Sea of Marmora
proportion metre, cadence; supplies; appointed forces
proportion, first the greatest
proportioned regular
proposing conversing
proppering kind of pear
propriety proper state, normal condition
propugnation defence
prorogue prolong, defer
proscription condemning to death without trial
Proserpina wife of Pluto, god of the Underworld, who returns to the human world each spring
prosperous bringing good results
protest make solemn declaration
Proteus god of the sea, who changed shape at will
provand provender
prove try out, test fidelity of; decide
prove: to prove so turn out to be so
provender provisions
provident prudent
providently providentially
provision foreseeing
provost a gaoler
provulgate make known publicly
prune dried plum; preen, dress up
prunes, stewed favourite dish in brothels — HENCE 'prostitutes'
psalteries stringed instruments
publican Jewish tax gatherer employed by Rome
Pucelle, La Maid (Joan of Arc)
pudder turmoil
pudding mixture of meat and herbs stuffed into animal's stomach or intestine
pudding: yield the crow a pudding dead animal at which crows peck
puddle make muddy
pudency modesty
pueritia little boy
pugging pulling, tugging
puisny unskilled, with ability of novice
puke-stocking stocking of dark grey or blue-black woollen cloth
puling whimpering
pull at take a good drink
pump shoe
pumpion pumpkin
punk harlot

punto thrust with point of sword
punto reverso backhand thrust
pur purr (of cat)
purblind totally or partly blind
purgation purgative; clearing from guilt; legally, proof of innocence
purger one who heals by purging
purl curl
purlieu lands at edge of forest
purloin take, steal
purples, long purple orchis
purse knit up
pursed pocketed
pursuivant junior officer at arms, lower rank than herald
pursy shortwinded, out of condition
purveyer officer sent in advance to make arrangements
push, stand the face up to
pushes against strikes
push-pin child's game
put off dismiss
put on imitate; incite; instigate
put one's finger in eye make oneself cry
put one's finger in fire meddle
put to't show up, expose; mate (of animals)
put up submit to
putter-out traveller who laid bets on his safe return
puttest back repels
puttock kite (bird)
puzzel common whore
Pygmalion artist in love with a female statue he made which the gods brought to life
pyramises FOR pyramids
Pyramus lover of Thisbe (DP)
Pyrrhus Achilles' son
Pythagoras Greek philosopher who believed in the transmigration of souls between animals and men

quail shrink from; overpower; courtesan
quaint elegant, dainty; skilful
qualified mitigated; diluted
qualify assuage; abate; appease
quality rank; calling; particular function; profession
qualm a sudden attack of sickness, faintness
quantity scrap
quarrel at object to
quarry game hunted; heap of slaughtered game
quart, sealed quart measure officially stamped
quarter further addition to coat-of-arms; area

quarter, pass his leave his allotted area
quartered lodged
quartered lodged; belong to military
quat pimple
quatch-buttock fat or flat backside
quean loose woman, hussy
queasy risky
Queen Mab poss. invention of Shakespeare, a fairy 'midwife' to man's imagination
quell murder
quern handmill for grinding corn
questant seeker
quiddities quibbles
quiddits subtle arguments
quietus settling of an account
quill strong feather; poss. instrument with which musicians strike strings of instruments
quillet poss. quidlibet, i.e. verbal trick, quibble
Quinapalus (lit.) 'there on a stick' — an imaginary authority
quince fruit tree
quintain object to be tilted at
quintessence fifth element of which heavenly bodies composed
quiring sing (choir)
quirk quip; extravagance, conceit; caprice
quit release; requite; pay for; remit
quite requite
quittance receipt; discharge from debt
quittance, use of rates of repayment
quiver nimble
quod me alit me extinguit what gives me life, gives me death
quoif cap, hood
quoit a ring for throwing as near as possible to a pin or stake
quondam the former, once
quoniam (FOR *quondam*) that was
quoted noted
quoth 'a says he
quotidian daily; recurrent fever

'*R*' dog's letter, sounds like dog growling
rabbit-sucker baby rabbit
rabblement rabble, crowd of common people
race root; flavour; natural disposition; FOR rase
rack wisp of cloud; torture by stretching
rackets tennis rackets; gunfire noise
raddock bird, the robin, said to cover dead with leaves
rail reproach; be angry
rain cry tears; reign in
raising putting up a rumour

rake cover by raking over
rakes very lean
ramp leap; whore
ramping rampant, rearing
rampired fortified
rancorous bitter
rancours irritants
range roam at large; be ranked
ranger forester
rank foul; overgrown; in season; corrupt; sick
rant speak flamboyantly, bluster
rap make enraptured
rapier sword
rapier, dancing sword worn for ornament
rapt enraptured
rapture (*poss. rupture*) plunder
rarity strangeness
rascal lean inferior deer; rogue
rased erased
rash strike with tusk
rash-levied raised rashly
rate scold
rate, in my in my opinion
ratify confirm; correctly made
ratolorum, i.e. rotulorum SEE custos rotulorum
ratsbane arsenic, used to poison rats
raught reached, lay hold of
ravel become entangled
raven SEE ravin
Ravenspurgh sea-port in Yorkshire
ravin devour eagerly, greedily
raw unskilled
rawly without proper provision
rayed soiled
razes roots (race)
razure erasure
re musical note
reach ability, capacity
readins reading
reak reck, care
re-answer compensate
reaped (fig.) shaved
reared, highest on large scale
reave deprive
rebate abate
rebato stiff collar
rebused abused
receipt prescription
received fashionable
receiving perception
recheat horn call to call hounds off
reck reckon
reckoning esteem
reclusive as a recluse
recognizance token
recognizances acknowledgment of debt
recoil go back in memory

recollected specially composed
recomforted those who have been reassured
recordation remembrance
recountments recounting
recourse continual flow
recover restore
recovery process by which entailed estate
  was transferred
recreant traitor
recreat cowardly
rectorship rule
recure make whole
rede advice
redime te captum quam queas minima redeem
  yourself from captivity at the lowest
  price you can
red-lattice ale houses had lattices painted
  red
redoubted frightening, terrible
redound result in
reek to emit smoke or steam; emanate
  from
reeky (reechy) foul smelling
reels revels
refelled refuted
refer me submit my case to
referred transferred
reflex throw
reft bereft, taken forcibly
region rank
regreet return, exchange, of salutation
regreets, sensible gifts
reguerdon rich reward
rehearse narrate; repeat
reins loins
rejoindure reunion
rejourn adjourn
relation news related
relative relevant
relier overconfident person
relieved supported
relume relight
remain, make stay with
remainder biscuit ship biscuit left over after
  voyage
remediate remedial
remember recall
remembrance memento; recollection
remembrancer one who reminds
remorseful full of compassion
remotion removal; keeping aloof
remove remove oneself, move off; alter;
  separate
remover inconstant person
render declare; surrender; offer
renegado renegade
repair recover; refresh; return
repasture food
repetition report

repined complained
replenish to complete, perfect
replication reverberation, reply
reprehend FOR apprehend
reprobance being damned, reprobation
reproof blame; refutation
reprove disprove
repugn reject
repured purified again
repute believe; evaluate
request, in like equally necessary
requital repayment
reremice bats
reserve preserve
reserved well guarded
resolutes adventurers
resolve convince; inform; melt
resort visiting
respect reputation; regard; favour
respect: in respect of in comparison with
respect upon regard for
respective careful, considerate
respects motives
respice lace a drink
rest in the space of
resty stiff with resting
rest, set up stake everything
rest, set up one's make up one's mind
re-stem retrace
retort throw back, reject; repay
reverb reverberate, echo
reverend aged
reverse back-handed blow
reversion something to be realized in the
  future
reversion, in revert to
revolt turn again
revolt, give the rebel against
revolted disloyal
revolts rebels who have revolted
revolve consider
Rhesus Thracian prince, killed at night by
  Diomede and Ulysses
rhetoric art of speaking
rheum rheumatism; secretion from eyes,
  mouth or nose
rheum, salt running cold
rheum, void spit
rheumy causing rheum
Rhodope Greek courtesan, married king
  of Memphis
Rialto Ponte di Rialto, the bridge and
  money exchange (in Venice)
rib enclose, shut in
ribald-rid filled with licentious persons
riband ribbon
ridge crossbar
ridges roof ridges
rig rig out, prepare

riggish wild, wanton
righteously rightfully
rigol ring, crown
ring, posy of a brief message inscribed inside a ring
ring-carrier go-between, bawd
ring-time time for exchanging rings
Ringwood name of hound
ripe sister older sister
rivage shore
rivality equal partnership
rive burst, split; fire cannon
rivelled wrinkled
riveted trim armour
rivo a drinker's exclamation or toast
road sea road; anchorage; (fig.) harlot
road, make make raids
roan dappled bay horse, mixed colour
roarers violent waves
roast roost
roast, rules the domineers
Robin Hood legendary outlaw
recordation remembrance
roe female deer
rogue roguery; vagabond
roisting rousing
rolls registers of patents, grants, etc.
rolls, master of in charge of these registers
romage upheaval
Roman hand Italic writing
Roman honour stoical dignity and honour
ronyon fat, scabby woman
rood cross on which Christ died
rook cower
ropery roguery
rope-trick tricks deserving a halter; FOR rhetoric
Roscius great Roman actor
rose, red emblem of Lancaster
rose, white emblem of York
rosemary herb of remembrance
roses, cakes of rose petals packed together
roses, provincial rosettes like damask roses (from Provins in N.E. France)
rote, by (recited) by heart
roted spoken by rote
rotundity swollen globe
round blunt, straightforward
roundest rudest
roundel ring dance
roundure roundness
rouse full measure of drink, bumper of
rover rogue, scallywag
rowel point of spur
royal coin (ten shillings)
royalties rights granted by king
roynish scurvy, wretched
rub check, obstacle
rubious ruby-coloured

rude rough, brutal
rudeness violence
rudesby turbulent fellow
rue herb, standing for repentance
ruff starched, pleated neckfrill
ruffianed acted like a ruffian
ruffling bristling; with frills
rug-headed shaggy
ruinate ruin
run to go
runagate fugitive; vagabond; deserter
rush ring made of rush, used in mock marriages
rush-candle rush dipped in tallow fat to make a candle
rushes plants used for covering floors
rushling rustling
russet reddish; grey
ruth pity
rut-time mating time
ruttish in 'rut', as deer in mating season

Saba Queen of Sheba
sack sweet white wine
sack, burnt mulled wine
sackbut bass trumpet
sacring bell rung in Mass
safe provide safe conduct for
saffron used as starch; used to colour pastry
sagittary centaur; name of inn
sail, bear a low act humbly
St Albans area of London
St Anne mother of Virgin Mary
St Bennet St Benedict
St Clare order of Poor Clares founded by St Francis of Assisi and St Clare in 1212
St Colm's Inch Inch Colm in the Firth of Forth
St Denis patron saint of Paris
St Jaques St James of Compostella in Spain
St Lambert his day — 17 September
St Nicholas' clerks highwaymen
St Philip's daughters Acts 19:35
St Valentine saint of lovers. His day, 14 February is when it was believed birds chose their mates
Sala German river
salad days days of inexperience
salamander fabulous lizard that lived in fire
sale, house of brothel
sale-work ready-made goods
Salic law law by which French crown could only be passed on via males
sall FOR shall
sallet salad; headpiece

sallied dirtied, soiled
sally charge of troops, pounce
salt licentious, lecherous
saltiers FOR satyrs
saltpetre used in making of gunpowder
salute: give salute to affect
sa'me FOR save me
Samingo (?) Sir Mingo from song in
   Nash's *Summer's Last Will.* (?) a
   corruption of San Domingo, patron
   saint of drinkers
samphire herb used in pickling
Samson biblical hero of Old Testament
sancta Majestas sacred Majesty
sand-blind not totally blind
sanded sandy colour
sap life
sarcenet thin soft material
satis quod sufficit enough is as good as a
   feast
Saturn Roman god; planet
satyr god of woods, part man, part goat
sauce sting; pay dearly
saucer small pan
saucy insolent; lascivious
savory herb
Savoy Duke of Lancaster's house
sawn seen
sawpit pit over which timber is sawed
saws sayings
say silk cloth
'Sblood expletive — God's blood
scab scurvy fellow
scaffolage stage platform
scald mean, scurvy
scaled weighted; stripped of scales, i.e.
   unmasked
scales balancers, symbol of justice
scaling measuring
scambling scrambling; turbulent;
   disturbed
scamels poss. shellfish
scandalized disgraced
scandalled spoke scandals about
scann'd construed
scant neglect; stint; reduce
scanter limited, sparing
scantle small piece
scantling specimen
scapes escapes
scarecrow figure used to scare away birds
scarf sash worn by soldiers
Scarlet Will Scarlet, one of Robin Hood's
   men
scathe harm; injury
scattered thrown out, random
scattering haphazard, random
scauld scurvy
scene individable unity of place

sceptre rod of kingship
schedule paper with writing on — letter
schools university faculties
scion offshoot
sconce head; fort
sconce, unbarbed uncovered head
score reckoning; chalk up; money owed;
   twenty
score and tally a notched stick to mark
   money transactions, to be split in half,
   one to be kept by the creditor, one by
   the debtor
score, twelve yards, length of archery range
scot and lot final payment, taxes
scotched cut about, hacked
scour clean away
scouring haste, scurry along
screws wrenches apart
scrimers fencers
scrip pouch
scrippage contents of scrip
scrivener public writer of documents
scroyles scoundrels
scrubbed dwarfed or stunted
scruple smallest part
scull shoal of fish
scullion kitchen servant
scurvy paltry, wretched
scuse excuse
scut short tail
scutcheon shield
Scylla a monster who lived in a cave in a
   rock (also named Scylla) in the sea
   between Italy and Sicily, opposite
   Charybdis (q.v.)
Scythian from country of East Europe
se offendendo FOR se defendendo, in self
   defence
sea-coal pit coal
sea-maid mermaid
sea-mark beacon at sea
seal manual seal made by own hand
sealing concluding
seal's up confirmed
seams of water furrows of waves
seamy side side with seams showing, i.e.
   wrong side
sear dry up
season heal; moderate; change into
second supporter
seconds coarse flour
sect cutting
sectary follower of a sect
secure care-free
securing protecting
sedges reeds
seel sew up eyelids (in falconry)
seem to arrange to
seeming mimicry; deception

seizure grasp, clasp
seld seldom
self-bounty innate generosity
self-covered dissembling
self-doing committed by self
self-endeared in love with self
self-explication giving account of self
self-figured planned by one's self
self-mettle his own vigour
self-reproving self-reproach
semblable likeness
semblance image
Semiramis Queen of Assyria, well known for her voluptuous behaviour
semper idem always the same (motto used by Queen Elizabeth)
Seneca writer of Latin tragedies
seniory seniority
Senoys Sienese
sense: to the sense to the quick
senseless-obstinate stupidly obstinate
senses: let senses rule keep one's wits about one
sensible sensitive; made aware of through the senses; capable of perception; capable of feeling
sentences epigrams
septentrion north
sequent one following another; attendant on
sequester confinement
sequestration ending, cessation
sere withered state; trigger mechanism of gun
sere, tickle o' the explode at a touch
serge kind of woollen cloth
serpigo psoriasis, skin disease
servanted bound as a servant
serve in insert, serve up
serviceable dedicated to serve
services, general war
serving, in their by their help
serving man courtier; lover
servitor servant
sessa get off, go away!
set stake, bet; settled, normal; number of games in tennis; setting; seated
set, double twice round
set to restore
setting down lay siege to
several enclosed piece of private property; individual piece of common land
'Sfoot God's foot
shade hide
shadow conceal; hide; shelter; darkening; portrait
shadowed livery dark appearance by which recognized (SEE livery)
Shafalus Cephalus, fable hero married to Procris

shaft kind (part) of arrow
shag shaggy
shake upset
shake a beard treat with contempt
shake your ears sign of displeasure, dislike
shale shell
shambles slaughter houses
shanks shin bones
shape appearance; plan
shaped unto fitted with
shard pottery piece
shard-borne born in dung, or borne aloft by wing-cases
sharded hard shiny wings
shark up pick up
sharp-provided quickly supplied
sheal'd shelled
shearman one who shears cloth
sheep-biter petty thief
sheep's guts material for strings of musical instrument
shelving overhanging
shent rebuked; disgraced
sheriff chief officer of shire or county
sheriff post post marking sheriff's house
sherris-sack sherry
shift confession and absolution; undergarment; trick; resource; change; makeshift; to contrive, manage; to contrive to get; live by wits; escape
shift, make a devise a means
shift, put to cause trouble
ship-tire head-dress like a ship
shive slice
shoal shallows
shoeing-horn shoe-horn, emblem of one subservient to another
shog shove off, move
shop SEE slop
shore sever
shore, to put ashore
short infringe
short knife SEE knife
short-armed not reaching far
shot marksmen; tavern account
shotten herring a herring that has expelled its roe
shough shaggy-haired dog
shoulder-clapper an arresting office
shoulder-shotten dislocated shoulder
shove-groat SEE shovel-board
shove-groat shilling Edward VI's shilling used on the board
shovel-board a game sliding coins across a board
shovel-board, Edward old broad shillings of the reign of Edward VI
shrew me bad luck for me

shrewd bad tempered; sharp
shrewdly very much, very precisely
shrieve sheriff
shrieve's fool insane person in the care of the sheriff (shrieve)
shrift confessional; absolution
shrive forgive; hear confession and give absolution
shrouds sail-ropes
shuffle spirit away
shuttle the weaver's instrument that crosses the weave
Sibyl woman with gift of prophecy
Sibylla the Cumaean Sybil, whom Aeneas consulted before visiting the underworld
si fortuna me tormente, sperato me contente if fortune torments me, hope contents me
sic spectanda fides so is faith to be seen
Sicils Sicily
sickle shekel
sickness, falling epilepsy
siege seat; rank; excrement
sightless unseen
sights eyes
signal token
signet seal (proof of authority or identity)
significants signs
signories (Italian) states
silling FOR shilling
silly simple, helpless
silly-duckling stupidly obsequious
Simois Trojan river
simony trading in ecclesiastical appointments
simpleness purity, simplicity
simples herbs
simple-time herb-time
simplicity stupidity
simulor counterfeiter
sin FOR *chin*
sinew tendon; source of strength; join together firmly
singular expert
singularity oddness, being different
sinister unlucky; unkind; unjust
sink-apace 'cinquepas' — five-step dance
sinking-ripe ready to sink
Sinon Greek who persuaded Trojans to take in the wooden horse
Sir Guy SEE Guy
sirrah name for social inferior, e.g. servant
sir-reverence save your reverence
sister, ripe older sister
sisters three SEE Fates
sit at live at the rate of
sit fas aut nefas be it right or wrong

sithence since
sixpenny strikers men who hold a man up for sixpence
skains-mates knives-companions, i.e. cutthroats
skillet small pot
skill-less ignorant
skimble-skamble nonsense
skinker wine waiter
skipper flighty person
skipping irresponsible
skirr scour, scurry
skirt edge of garment
skirted coat with full skirt
slack lessen; be neglectful; treat indifferently; delay
slander disgrace
slaver be smeared with spit
slaves enslaves
sleave skein
sledded on sledges
sleek-headed smoothly combed
sleevehand wristband
sleeves, down- full-length fitted sleeves
sleeves, side- loose open sleeves
sleided fine-drawn; untwisted; stranded
slice piece of cheese
'Slid by God's (eye) lid
'Slight God's light
slight in sufferance easy going
slighted tossed slightingly, slid unceremoniously
slighty weakly
sling field gun
slip cutting; heir
slip, let let go, release (of hounds)
slipped missed
slips leashes
sliver slice off
slobbery wet and foul
slough skin; cast snake's skin
slovenry slovenly appearance
slubber smear over; spoil; do carelessly
slug-abed lazybones, lie-abed
sluiced channelled; (fig.) seduced
slumbery sleepy
smatter chatter
smit damaged
smock woman's undergarment, (fig.) woman
smoile smile at
smoked smelt out
smooth flatter
smug neat, spruce
Smulkin name of fiend
smutched smudged
snaffle a bridle across the nose
snatch a quick catch or song
snatcher pilferer

snatches quibbles
sneak-up one who sneaks up on people
sneap snub
sneaped pinched with cold
sneaping nipping
sneck up go and be hanged
snipe bird; also contemptuous term = a
 dupe
snipped-taffeta slashed silk
snorting snoring
snuff smouldering candle wick
snuffs quarrels
soaking quick to take in
sob breathing space
sod boiled
sodden worn out by disease
soiled well fed on spring grass
soilure defilement
sold'rest solder together
sol-fa sing
solicit pray for pardon; rouse
solicity soliciting
solidares invented coin
solus alone
Solyman Sultan Solyman fought and won
 battle against the Persians, 1535
somever however
sonance sound
sonties saints
sooth truth; flattery
soothest up flatter, butter up
soothsay foretell
sop bread or cake soaked in wine
sophister a cunning arguer
Sophy Shah of Persia
sore (injunction) strict (order); 4th-year
 buck
sorel 3rd-year buck
sorrow-wreathen tied up by sorrow
sort happen; befit; associate with;
 arrange; suit
sort, in to a degree
sort, may may come about
sortance, hold suit
sorted with in agreement with
sorts classes of society
sot fool
soul seat of true feeling
soul, half a half-wit
souse pounce on
South Sea Pacific Ocean
South, the South wind
sovereign excellent
sovereignty, general universal cures,
 cure-alls
sow-skin pigskin
sowl pull
sowter cobbler
spacious wide-ranging

span distance between thumb and little
 finger
span-counter child's game, like marbles
spanieled follow like a spaniel
spanned measured
sparing forbearing
spavin disease of horses causing lameness
speak show, demonstrate; call to
speak of as kinsman put it kindly
speak within door speak quietly
spear lance
specialities detailed contracts
speculation looking on; seeing with
 understanding
speculations spies
sped done for, dispatched, ruined
speed, go find success
speeding successful
speken speak
spell backward misrepresent
spell-stopped stopped by magic
spend expend, waste
spent used up; exhausted
sphere orb, star
sphery star-like
spicery spices
spices traces
spies eyes
spigot peg in the tap of a wine/beer barrel
spilth spilling
spinners spider
spinster a spinner
spit bar over fire on which meat roasted
'spital hospital
spitting like a spit
splay castrate
spleen source of all strong passions;
 sudden outburst, caprice; malice;
 anger
spleen, full of capricious
spleenful eager
splenetive impetuous
spoil ravage, despoil; booty from battle
spongy drink-sodden
spoon christening spoon
sport flirtation; pleasure, liking;
 gambling or betting; play or
 performance of some kind
spotted stained, sinful
sprack lively
sprag SEE sprack
sprat little fish
sprawl struggle in death
sprays offshoots
springe snake
springhalt twitching in legs of horses
sprighted haunted
sprite spirit of dead; vexation
spruce affected

spur root
spur and stop half-reveal, half-conceal
spurn insult
spurn at reject
squandering random
square just measure; shape, arrange; quarrel; fair, straight; piece of material covering breast
square, keep play fair
squared ruled
squared me let myself be ruled by
squash unripe pea-pod
squinies squints
stablish establish
staff stave, verse; shaft of a lance
staff, set in make oneself at home
stagger in be uncertain
staggers perplexity, bewilderment; cause to stagger; horse disease marked by giddiness
stake down wager
stale make stale (urine); prostitute, cheapen; tool; fool, laughing stock; decoy; out of date, worn out
stalking-horse imitation horse used for stalking
stall keep; shelter; dwell
stamp print image (as on coin); give authority to; seal
stand face, resist; hunter's stance
stand in remain in
stand in act are in full progress
stand for be worth; fight for
standing to it standing firm
stand bed bed with legs
standard standard bearer; standard fruit tree = one that is self-supporting
staniel stannel or wind-hover, type of hawk
staple loop of iron for bolt; fibre of wool
star chamber court of criminal jurisdiction
star, moist moon
star-blasting influence of stars
starings out-staring others
stark utterly, completely
starkly stiffly, absolutely
stars, seven Pleiades
stars, thwarting bad luck
start rouse
start: get start of outstrip
start, on the suddenly shown
starting-hole bolt-hole
startingly in starts
starveling very lean person
starved petty
state chair of state; social position; posture
state-statues statues of statesmen
station position, stance

statist statesman
statuas statues
statute bond
statute-cap apprentice's cap
staunch, hold bind firmly together
stay'd for waited for
stead help, benefit
steadied stood in good stead
stealth stealing away
steeled hard-hearted; strengthened
steep soak in, be absorbed by
stelled fixed; starry
stemming halt; press forward
step pace
steps, tell keep pace
stern steersman
sternage steering; stern
stewed prune prostitute
stews brothel
sticking place point at which slipping back is prevented
stickler-like like an umpire
stiff inflexible
stigmatic one who was branded with a deformity
still continually
stillitory still, press
stillness sobriety
still-piecing re-joining
still-soliciting always begging
still-vexed always perturbed by storms
stilly softly
sting sexual lust
stint stop, cease
stithy smithy, forge
stoccadoes fencing thrust
stock blockhead; stocking; fencing thrust
stock-fish dried cod, beaten before being boiled
stockish brutal, stupid
stocks wooden shackles confining legs
stoic severe or rigorous person
stomach pride; stubborn courage; anger; tolerate
stomach: have stomach for have will to
stomacher covering for protection
stomach-qualmed queasy, feeling sick
stone precious stone; thunderbolt; hail
stone-bow crossbow which could shoot small stones
stones testicles
stool for a witch ducking stool
stoop fly to the lure (of hunting hawks)
stop regulated string of musical instrument; obstruction
stople stop it up
store populate; plenty
story, to to tell about
stoup tankard, jug

stout bold
stover winter food for cattle
straight immediately
straight-pight upright
strain lineage; embrace
strain, make no have little difficulty in
    believing
strait narrow
straited at a loss
Strand London street; sea-shore
strange unusual; unnatural; unfriendly
strangeness aloof, estrangement
stranger any other person, not self
strappado torture where a man's arms are
    strapped behind his back, and he is
    strung up or dropped suddenly,
    dislocating or breaking his limbs
strawy like straw
stray wandering animal
stream current
strength authority, resources
stretch carry out
stride a limit go beyond
strife striving for
stroke blow made with weapon
strond sea-strand
strossers tight breeches
stroyed destroyed
strucken struck
stubble rough cornstalks left after reaping
stuck-in thrust, stab
studied inclined; well-practised
stuff, boiled creatures with venereal disease
stuffed complete
stump of tooth; bawdy expression
stuprum rape
Stygian of the Styx, river of the under-
    world
style title
Styx river of underworld
subornation crime of procuring someone to
    do an evil action
suborned false; bribed to evil
subscribe yield to; sign; acknowledge;
    agree with
subscription allegiance, obedience
substance material wealth
substractors detractors
subtle refined; fastidious; tricky
subvert overthrow
succession, perpetual heirs for ever
sudden unpredictable
suerly FOR surely
sufferance misery, pain endured; patience;
    acceptance of misery; connivance;
    permission; damage
sufficed satisfied
sufficiency sufficiently able, fitness for
    office

suggest suggest; tempt, lead astray;
    prompt to, incite
suit woo, court; attire; request; suitable
    for
suits of pounds request for money
sullens sulks
Sultan Solyman SEE Solyman
summered well-kept (as in summer
    pastures)
summer-seeming short lived, like English
    summer
sumpter pack-horse
sunburnt brown and dried up, not
    favoured by Elizabethans
sun: to get the sun of to get on sunward
    side of enemy, so that sun gets in his
    eyes
superflux superfluity
superscription address
super-serviceable over-officious
superstitious, be idolize
supervise perusal
suppliance diversion
suppliant pleading
supplied satisfied
supplyment supply
supportance support
supposal estimate
supposes suppositions
supposition opinion
supposition, in in doubt, uncertain
sur-addition title of honour in addition to
    name
surance assurance
surcease stop, finish
surety act as surety
surfeit waste time; satiety
surfeit-swelled swollen with over-
    indulgence
surmise speculation
surplice white garment worn (by law in
    Shakespeare's time) by clergymen
sur-reined over-ridden
suspects suspicious of
suspire breathe
sutler provision-seller
suum cuique to each, his own
swabber deckhand
swag-bellied with sagging belly
swain bumpkin; young man
sware swore
swart swarthy
swasher swashbuckler
swashing swaggering
swath swathe, swaddling clothes
swathe grain or grass cut by the sweep of
    a scythe
sway on not to yield
swayed bent down in the back

sways level keeps steady
swear out abjure
sweat sweating sickness, form of plague
sweeting darling
swelling arrogant; developing
sweltered sweated out
swinge beat
swinge-bucklers blusterers
Swithold St Withold (protected one against nightmares)
Switzers Swiss body-guard
swoopstake drawing whole stake at once
swound faint
Sybil of Cumae Apollo granted her as many lives as grains in a handful of sand
Sylla Lucius Cornelius Sulla, dictator, renowned for cruelty
syllable, to the exactly
syllogism logical reasoning
sympathize share by all, match with
synod council of gods; legislative assembly

table palm of hand; written/printed record
tables backgammon; notebook
tabor drum
tabourines drum
tackle rigging
ta(k)'en out copied
taffety made of taffeta, a kind of silk
tag (-rag) rabble
tail (colloq.) penis
taint disparage; spoil
taint, fall into become spoilt
tainted diseased (venereal)
take catch out
take her home make her aware of her situation
take it on take over; rage at
take off lessen, reduce
take up . . . short restrain, put stop to
taken undertaken
taking-off death
takes strike with disease
talent treasure; sum of money worth poss. £100–180
talker one who talks, but does not act
tall lively, spirited; noble, courageous
tall: as tall a man of his hands an active able-bodied man
tallow animal fat or grease used for lighting
tallow catch vehicle for catching fat in
tallow face face of colour of tallow
tally SEE score
'tame (FOR attame) break in to
tang sound loudly
tangle snare
tanlings those tanned by sun

tanta est erga te mentis integritas, regina serenissima so great is our integrity towards you, most gracious Queen
tantaene animis caelestibus irae? is such anger found in holy minds?
Tantalus in Greek myths, punished in hell by having his food and drink always just out of reach
tap tapster
taper candle
taphouse tavern
tapster one who draws ale in an inn and makes up the bill
tardy slow; delay
tardy-apish ape fashions that are outdated
tardiness inadequacy, reticence
targe(t) shield
Tarpeian Rock cliff on Capitoline Hill in Rome. Traitors were thrown down it
Tarquin Roman king who raped Lucrece (DP)
tarre urge on to fight, provoke to fight
tarry wait
Tartar native of Tartary; Tartarus = hell
Tartar's painted bow bow-like outline of top lips
task be given a lesson
tasking challenge
tassel-gentle male falcon
taste try out, test, serve as taster, checking food and drink not poisoned
Taurus Zodiac sign — bull; Asian mountain range
Tavy FOR Davy, David
tawdry-lace necktie
tax censure; criticism
taxed accused
taxation invective
tax home take to task
teem have offspring, breed
teeming-date time for bearing young
teen distress, grief
Telamon father of Ajax (DP)
Tellus the earth
temper mould, fashion; work on; hardness in steel
temperance climate
temporize come to terms, compromise
temporizer time-server, one who compromises
tench fish
tendance care; attendance
tender hold; regard with favour; offer (of marriage); desire; watch over
tender-hefted gentle
tendering caring for
tent bed canopy; make camp; roll of material used to clean and probe wound

tenure content
tercel male of hawk species
Tereus King of Thrace who ravished his sister-in-law Philomele, and cut out her tongue
termagant a tyrant in mediaeval plays
terminations conclusions, ends of sentences
termless indescribable
terras astraea reliquit Astraea, goddess of justice, has left the earth
terrene terrestrial
tertian a fever which recurs every other day
testament will
tester 6d. piece
testerned tip with a tester
testril sixpence
testy angry, irritated
tetchy fretful
tetter scab over; skin eruption
Thane Scottish title, cf. English earl
Theban man of Thebes
theoric theory
Theseus King of Athens, who killed the Minotaur and fought against the Amazons, taking their Queen, Hippolyta as wife (DP)
Thessalian of Thessalia, Thessaly, part of Greece
Thetis sea nymph
thick-eyed dull sighted
thing creature; object; sexual term
think on think twice about
Thirdborough a local constable
Thisbe beloved by Pyramus (DP)
thou-est to address as 'thou' i.e. as to an inferior
thought care; sad contemplation
thoughten, be you did you think of
thought-executing carried out as quickly as thought
Thracian of Thrace
Thracian poet/singer Orpheus, SEE Rhesus
thraldom imprisonment
thrall slave
thrasonical in the bragging manner of Thraso, the soldier in Terence's *Eunuch*
threaden made of thread
three sisters the three Fates (q.v.)
three-man-song song for treble, tenor, bass
three-man beetle heavy rammer for driving in piles
three-pile costly velvet
three-suit servant's annual clothes' allowance
threne threnody, lament
thriftless wasted
thrilling piercing
thronged crushed

thronged up bound up unable to move
throstle thrush
through-fare thoroughfare
thrum tufted end of weavers' threads
thumb: bite thumb at make an insulting gesture
thwart perverse, crooked
Tiber river of Rome
tic'd enticed
tick insect that affects sheep
tickle ticklish, unstable, precarious
tick-tack game, form of backgammon using pegs in holes
tide tidings, news
tide life, tide death come life, come death
tike mongrel dog, cur
tilly-f(v)ally hoity-toity
tilt fight in a tournament
tilt-yard place of tournament or for tilting
time world; society
timely early
time-pleaser time server
Timon ancient misanthrope (DP)
timorous causing fear, terrifying
tinct tincture, colouring
tinder material for kindling fire
tinder box to keep tinder in
tinsel glittering cloth
tipstaves officers of law
tire attire; feed ravenously; head-dress; dress hair
tire-valiant fanciful head-dress
tiring-house dressing room in the theatre
tirrits FOR terrors
'tish FOR it is
tisick cough
tissue cloth of gold or silver
Titan sun god
Titans race of gods
tithe ecclesiastical levy of tenth part
tithe-pig pig given to parson as tithe
tithe-woman tenth woman
tithing district of ten families
tittles trifles
toad poisonous creature believed to have a precious jewel in its head which was an antidote to poison
toasts-and-butter pampered weaklings
toaze tease
todpole tadpole
tods 28 lb (12.7 kg) of wool
tofore heretofore, formerly
toge toga, Roman dress
toil snare
toils put to hard work
token mark, sign (e.g. of plague)
Tom o' Bedlam beggar, lunatic. Hospital of St Mary of Bethlehem (Bedlam) was for the mentally deranged

tomboy strumpet
Tomyris Queen of Scythia, killer of Cyrus
tongs primitive metal percussion
 instrument
tongue give away (a secret)
tongue, keep keep silent
tongues, hath the knows different languages
tool penis
tooth desire, liking
tooth-picker toothpick
top spinning top; go beyond
top gallant highest point of sails on a ship
top: on top of above all others
Topas, Sir SEE DP
topless supreme
topped lopped, pruned
torcher torch bearer
tortive awry
toss carry on point of
tosspot drunkard
touch feeling
touch a vein know a state of mind,
 understand
touch: play the touch act as a touchstone
touch the estimate pay the price estimated
touched guilty
tourney take part in tournaments
tours jousts, tournament
touse tear apart
toward compliant, agreeable; forward,
 precocious; impending
toward, be be happening
Tower Hill district of London where
 scaffold erected
towering circling
town of war garrison town
town-crier man who cries out news and
 notices in a town
toy wanton, dally amorously; nonsense;
 idle fancy
toys, fairy fairy tales
trace range
tractable willing
traduced decried
traffic trade, business; occupation
train device; that which comes behind
traject poss. bridge or ferry
trammel up catch up in net
tranced in a trance
translate change, transform
transmutation change of status
transported carried off
trans-shape transform
trappings hangers-on
trash rubbish; loppings from trees;
 worthless person; weights hung on a
 dog's collar to restrain it — HENCE
 control
travel of regard look around

traverse march on; thrust in fencing
traversed folded
tray-trip dice game
treachers traitors
treble-dated living three times as long
tremor cordis heart palpitation
trenched deep cut, engraved
trencher wooden platter
trencher-friend sponger
trencher-knight one who serves ladies at
 table
trencher-man feeder, eater
trey three in dice
trib FOR trip
tribunal dais
tribunal plebs FOR tribunes of the plebians
tribunes in Rome, the representatives of
 the common people
tributaries those who pay tribute
trick fashion
tricks eleven and twenty long card game
 where one and thirty is a winning
 number
trifled made trifles of
trigon triangle
trigon, fiery particular conjunction of
 three signs of Zodiac, Aries, Leo and
 Sagittarius
trim array; neat; fine; glib
trip interrupt
tripe-visaged face like tripe
triumph revelry, celebration
triumph, led in Roman march of captives
triumphant magnificent
triumviry triumvirate
Troilus Trojan lover of Cressida (DP)
troll sing a round
troll-my-dames a game, rolling balls
 through hoops
troops groups
tropically figuratively
trot old woman
trow, I I assure you
trowest you trust, believe
Troyans (Trojans) boon companions
truant be a truant to
truckle-bed bed on wheels which pushed
 under another bed
trudge run
true penny honest fellow
true-derived honestly obtained
trull prostitute
truncheon baton carried by military
 officers
truncheoners bearers of truncheons
trundle-tail (trindle-tail) with drooping tail
trunk large chest; (fig.) wide, large
trust conclusion
trusters creditors

trustless untrustworthy
try test; a wrestling bout; judge a case
try conclusions test the results
try success see outcome
tubs sweating tub used in cure of
venereal disease; barrel for salting beef
tuck sword, rapier
tucket trumpet, fanfare of trumpets
Tully's orator poss. Cicero's *De Oratore*
tumble roll about; make totter; 'lay'
tun large cask
tun: filling a bottle with a tun (colloq.) having
sexual intercourse
tun-dish funnel
tupping of sheep — copulating
turbond turban
Turk Gregory Turks and Gregory XIII,
known for ferocity
Turk, turn change faith, go to the bad
Turkish tapestry needlework, imitation of
Eastern carpets
turn occasion
turn head stand at bay
turn i' the wheel turn the spit
turn loose leave free to do as like
turn off hangman 'turned off' those he
hanged, by removing ladder under
their feet
turn, serve the just what needed; satisfy
(bawdy)
turncoat renegade
turned forth, the exile
turpitude baseness, depravity
turtle turtle dove, renowned for
constancy
tushes tusks
twiggen-bottle bottle in wicker basket
'twill it will
twilled woven
twind entwine
twine thread
twit sneer at, reproach
Tyburn place of execution in London
Typhon hundred-headed monster
imprisoned beneath Mount Etna

Ud's God's
Ulysses King of Ithaca
umber species of ochre, yellow-brown in
colour
umbrage shadow
unable weak, without power
unaccommodated natural
unadvised unwisely
unaneled without the last rites
unbacked unbroken
unbanded without a hat band
unbated sharp (of rapier, or foil that is not
bated, blunted)

unbent relax strain (e.g. of bow)
unbid unwelcome
unbitted without a bit — uncontrolled
unbolt explain
unbolted unsifted, coarse
unbraced with doublet open, undone
unbraided poss. genuine, unused; poss. for
embroidered
unbreathed unexercised, unemployed
unbreeched not yet in breeches
unchary freely, unguardedly
unclasp reveal
unclew ruin
uncoined genuine
uncomeliness improper behaviour
uncomprehensive unfathomable
unconfirmed immature, inexperienced
uncouple release (hounds)
uncross untroubled
unction ointment, salve
uncurrent worthless, unnatural
underborne trimmed underneath
undercrest support, live up to
undergo accept; undertake; endure
underlings underdogs
underskinker under wine waiter
undertaker one who takes things on
underwrought undermined
uneath scarcely
unexperient inexperienced
unfellowed none like him
unfix unsettle
unfold uncover
unfolded exposed by
unfoldeth give release (e.g. out of pen or
fold)
unfolding lead from a fold
unfortified weak
ungalled unsullied, unspoilt
ungartered without bands holding up
stockings or hose
unhandsome not handsome; unfair in
judgment; inadequate, unfitting
unhatched unused
unheart dishearten
unhousel'd without the sacrament
unhurtful gentle
unicorn mythical animal with a horse's
body and one single horn in its forehead
union large valuable pearl
unjointed incoherent
unjust false
unkindly unnaturally
unlace undo; of animals — carving up; of
purse strings — loosening
unlicensed without assent
unlineal not of family
unmanned uncontrolled
unmannerly rude, inhumanly

unmeet unsuitable
unpaved castrated
unpinked undecorated
unplausive critical
unpolicied plans defeated
unpossessing beggarly
unprevailing unavailing
unproper not one's own
unprovide unsettle, shake one's resolve
unqualitied deprived of qualities, no longer himself
unreclaimed untamed
unrecuring uncurable
unrespective without respect, unthinking; worthless
unreverend irreverent, unseemly
unrolled struck off roll
unrough smooth-cheeked
unscanned unconsidered
unsealed without a legal seal
unseamed opened up
unseminared emasculated
unsevered close-knit, inseparable
unshout take back the shout
unsifted inexperienced
unsisting poss. unresting
unsorted not well chosen
unspeakable too great to be spoken of
unsquared inapt, unsuitable
unstaid immodest; unstable; unrestrained
unswayed ungoverned
untempering unpleasing
untented unstaunched
unthrift spendthrift, over-generous
unthrifty unlucky
untoward unmannerly
untraded infrequently used
untread retrace
untrussing unlacing
untuned discordant; jarring
unwashed hands without delay
unwedgeable not able to be split into wedges
unweighed unconsidered
unwonted unusual
unyoked free, untrammelled
upbraid scold, reproach
up-cast roll up in game of bowls
upon as a result of
uproar, to turn to an uproar
upsho(o)t final outcome
up-spring upstart
urchin hedgehog; goblin
urged put forward, produce arguments
urgently harshly
urinal glass vessel for holding urine
Ursa Major constellation — Great Bear
usance usury
used customary
uses usages

usurp exert evil influence; assume, pretend to be; appropriate
usurp on encroach upon
ut 'doh' of musical scale
utensils furnishings
utter send forth
utterance extremity, to the death
utis fun; (lit.) time between beginning and eighth day of a festival

vagabond an unlicensed traveller
vagram FOR fragrant
vagrom vagrant
vail setting; lower, let fall; do homage; pieces of cloth left after suit cut out
vainly harmlessly
valance of Venice canopy fringes with Venetian embroider
valanced fringed with hangings
validity value
valley-fountain spring in valley
vane weather-vane
vanities fops
vanity wicked character in old morality plays; show
vant van, front
vantbrace armour for forearm
Vapians invented astrology term
variable various, a variety of
varletry mob
varnish outward cover, dress
varnished faces faces with make-up on
vassal abject; slave
vastidity vastness
vasty vast
vaultages vaults
vaulty vaulted
vaunt boast; first skirmishes
vaunt-couriers fore-runners
vaunter boaster
vaward vanguard
vaward of the day early in the day
velure velvet
velvet patch cover for scar, from battle or surgery for syphilis
velvet-guards velvet trimmings and those who wear them
vendible saleable; marriageable
Venetian admittance fashionable in Venice
venew thrust in fencing
veneys bouts
venge revenge, avenge
vengeance damage
vent freedom from restraint, discharge
ventages holes
venter venture
ventricle three ventricles of brain, (1) seat of imagination, (2) seat of reason, (3) seat of memory

Venus Roman goddess of love; married to Mars; son, Cupid; doves are sacred to her; star

verge circle

verger official of church

verily truly

Veronese a ship fitted out at Verona; verrinessa — a cutter

versal universal

Vestal maid, virgin (priestess to Vesta, vowed to chastity)

via forward, off

vial small glass container

vice character in Tudor interludes, who seems to have pared his nails with his dagger; press, with a screw for tightening

videlicet that is to say, namely

video, et gaudeo I see and I rejoice

videsne quis venit? do you see who comes?

vied to do something in competition

vied, out- outbid

view, full of in open view

vild vile

villiago villain

vindicative vengeful

vinewedst most mouldy

viol stringed instrument

viol-de-gamboys base viola or viol de gamba

vir sapit qui pauca loquitur it is a wise man who speaks few words

virginalling playing on virginals

Virginius Roman who killed his daughter to preserve her from slavery and rape

Virgo Zodiac sign

virtue power, authority; heart of

visit afflict

visitation visit

viva voce appearing in person

vizaments FOR avisements (q.v.)

vizard mask

vloutin-stog FOR flouting stock, i.e. laughing stock

vocatur is called

voice, hardest most severe interpretation

volable nimble-witted

volk FOR folk

volley a discharge, i.e. from a gun

voluntary as a volunteer

vor FOR for

votaress woman who has taken vow

vouch maintain; formal promise; testimony

vouched asserted

voucher or double voucher men called to vouch titles to ownership

Vulcan god of fire, who was a blacksmith

Vulcan's badge cuckold's badge

vulgar public; common knowledge

vulgar station position in a crowd

vulgo in common tongue, in the vulgar

vurther FOR further

wad FOR would

wafer-cakes wafer-thin cake

waft beckon

waftage passage

wafting shifting

wafture wave

wag go off; jester; boy

wage risk

waged paid wages

wages measure up to

waggish saucy, pert

wags goes on

wain wagon, cart

wainscot wooden panelling

waist girdle, belt

wake feast of dedication of church

walk a bout form couples for dance

wall, take to the keep to cleaner side of street — i.e. near house wall

wall-eyed with iris of eye discoloured; glaring

wall-newt lizard

Walloon inhabitant of land between the Netherlands and France

waned withered

wanion, with a with a vengeance

wann'd go pale

wan(n)y wan, pale

want lack

wanton play games; loose person; luxuriant growth

wappened exhausted

ward defensive position; prison; lock or bolt on door; minor; particular area of town

warded protected

warded, steel bolt or chains securing prisoner

warden kind of pear

warder staff used to begin or end ceremonial occasions

Ware, bed of famous large Elizabethan bed

war-proof tested in war

warrant justify; swear to; proof; defend

warrant: in warrant for himself on his own responsibility

warranted acknowledged

warrantise warrant, proof

warren park

warrener keeper of a warren

washing slashing

wassail revelry

wassail-candle candle lit at feast

waste spend
wasteful causing to waste away
wat FOR what
watch timepiece; interval of time;
  (military) guard; constables who
  police certain area during the night
watched caught
watchings loss of sleep
water tears
water, in standing between tides, when
  nothing vital happens
water-fly water insect
water-galls rainbow
water-rug type of dog
waters, for all for all humours, fit for
  anything
water-spaniel dog used in duck-hunting
water-work a water-colour painting
wawl wail
way, great largely
wax, a man of a perfect picture of a man
weal welfare
wealsmen men devoted to public good
wear cap with suspicion i.e. hiding cuckold's
  horns
weasand windpipe
weasel wild animal, believed to be very
  quarrelsome
weather, keeps the has precedent over
weather-fends protects from bad weather
web, and the pin cataract of the eye
weed garment; manner of dress; manner
  of expression
ween you do you reckon on
weeping-ripe ready to weep
weet know
welkin sky
well said well done (often refers to action
  not speech
well-advised in one's right mind
well-entered experienced
well-sinewed well prepared
well-willers those who wish you well
wen a skin excrescence, tumour
weraday well-a-day
wether ram
wheak squeak
whelked twisted
whereas in which
whet incite; sharpen
whetstone for sharpening swords, etc.
whey-face face like whey (pale)
whiffler one who goes in front of a
  procession
while passage of time
while, in a breathing in the space of a breath
whiles until
whipping-cheer to be whipped, usually in
  Bridewell Prison

whipster contemptible fellow
whipstock handle of whip
whirligig spinning-top
whistle of speak secretly of
whit, no not a jot
white target centre
whitsters bleachers of linen
whittle small clasp knife
whole solid
whoop shout
whooping cries of delight or astonishment
whore master fornicator
whore of Babylon Church of Rome
whoreson (lit.) son of a whore, gen.
  wretched fellow
wide mistakenly; wide of the mark
wide, go miss (in game of bowls)
wide of indifferent to
wide o' the bow hand wide of the mark
wide-chopped big mouthed
wide-enlarged endowed
wield manage
wight person
wild-mare to play on see-saw
will will (modern); list of bequests left
  by dead person; desire (often sexual);
  sexual appetite; wish; intention
wilful-blame blamed for wilfulness
wimpled muffled, veiled
wince kick
wind (of horse) worm your way (wheel)
wind about beat about the bush, not direct
wind, allow go down wind
wind: have wind of keep watch on
wind, i' the have scent of
windgalls tumours on horse's leg
windring winding/wandering
windy side away from safe side
wing-led in battle order
winnowed separate chaff from grain
winter old
wiry virginal strings
wise fully aware
wishtly intently
wit intelligence; wisdom; understanding;
  quickness of perception
wit snapper one who has a quick answer
  to everything
withal at the same time; with (the rest);
  besides
withering out wearing out
withers part of back rubbed by saddle
without-book without a script
without-door external
wittolly cuckoldy, open to be cuckolded
wolt will you
woman, can woman act like a woman (i.e.
  cry
wondered marvelled

wood mad
woodbine honeysuckle
woodcock bird easy to catch; fool; simpleton
wooden stupid, insensible
wooden thing awkward business
woodman huntsman; woman-chaser, seducer
woollen rough blankets
woolsack sack of wool
woolward wearing wool next to skin
woo't would it
word password
word, at a to be brief
words sets in different light; cajoles
working aim
working-house house of industry
worm snake; believed to cause decay in teeth
wormwood a bitter plant
worship dignity, ease; honour
wort cabbage; unfermented beer
worthied won honours
worthies, nine famous heroes of past
wot know
wrack ruin, wreck
wrangler opponent
wreak vindictive, wreaking vengeance; take notice of
wreathe fold
wrench wind up
wrenching rinsing; pulling into shape
wrest take violently; misinterpret; turn wrong way; key for tuning stringed instrument
wretched poor in both social position, and intellect
wringing pain
writhled wrinkled
wrong insult

wrong-incensed angered by wrong; wrongly angered
wroth anger; misery
wrought carried out; worked upon
wrung rubbed, galled
wry askew
wrying swerving
wry-necked with twisted neck

Xanthippe Socrates' ill-tempered wife

yard measuring tape
yare ready, prompt
yaughan inn keeper
yaw deviate from course
yawn earthquake often when sun or moon is in eclipse
y-clad dressed, adorned
ycleped called
yeast foam
Yedward Edward
yellowing yelling
yellowness jealousy
yellows, the jaundice
yeoman freeholder, common soldier
yerked thrust, stabbed
yesty foaming (as yeast)
yoked joined to (married); burdened with; conquered
yond's yonder is
youngling stripling
younker young man; prodigal; green horn
y-ravished enraptured
y-slacked quietened

zany stage-buffoon, professional fool's stooge
zed most ignored of alphabetical letters
Zodiac signs of Zodiac
Zounds by God's wounds

Genealogical Tree: The Histories

Edward III
1312-77

MORTIMER   LANCASTER

Edward the Black Prince   Lionel   Blanche = John of Gaunt ᵃ =
1330-76   Duke of Clarence   1340-99
                               1338-68

        Richard II ᵃ   Philippa = Edmund Mortimer   . Henry IV ᵃᵇᶜ
        1367-1400   Plantagenet 3rd Earl of March   1367-1413
                                                   1351-81

Roger Mortimer   Sir Edmund Mortimer ᵇ   Elizabeth Mortimer ᵇᶜ   Henry V ᵇᶜᵈ   Thomas ᶜ   John ᶜᵈᵉ
4th Earl of March   1376-c. 1409   =   1387-1422   Duke of Clarence   Duke of Bedford
1374-98   m. Glendower's daughter "Hotspur"   =   c. 1388-1421   1389-1435
                                             1364-1403   Katharine
                                                                     of France = (2) Owen Tudor

Edmund Mortimer ᵉ   Anne Mortimer = Richard ᵈ   Henry VI ᵉᶠᵍ = Margaret   Edmund   =
5th Earl of March   Earl of Cambridge   1421-71   of Anjou ᵉᶠᵍʰ Earl of Richmond
1391-1424   d. 1415   1429-82   d. 1456

                       Richard   = Cicely Neville   Edward
                       3rd Duke of York   (see York)   Prince of Wales
                       1411-60   1453-71

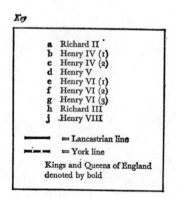

Key

a Richard II
b Henry IV (1)
c Henry IV (2)
d Henry V
e Henry VI (1)
f Henry VI (2)
g Henry VI (3)
h Richard III
j Henry VIII

———— = Lancastrian line
—·—·— = York line

Kings and Queens of England
denoted by bold

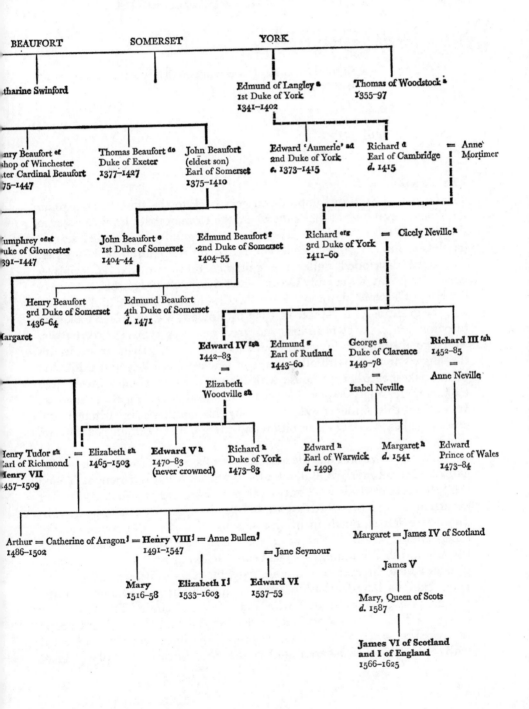

BEAUFORT   SOMERSET   YORK

...tharine Swinford

Edmund of Langley **a**
1st Duke of York
1341–1402

Thomas of Woodstock **a**
1355–97

...nry Beaufort **ef**
...shop of Winchester
...ter Cardinal Beaufort
...75–1447

Thomas Beaufort **de**
Duke of Exeter
1377–1427

John Beaufort
(eldest son)
Earl of Somerset
1375–1410

Edward 'Aumerle' **ad**
2nd Duke of York
c. 1373–1415

Richard **d**
Earl of Cambridge
d. 1415

= Anne
Mortimer

...umphrey **cdef**
...uke of Gloucester
...391–1447

John Beaufort **e**
1st Duke of Somerset
1404–44

Edmund Beaufort **e**
2nd Duke of Somerset
1404–55

Richard **efg**
3rd Duke of York
1411–60

= Cicely Neville **h**

Henry Beaufort
3rd Duke of Somerset
1436–64

Edmund Beaufort
4th Duke of Somerset
d. 1471

...argaret

Edward IV **fgh**
1442–83
=
Elizabeth
Woodville **gh**

Edmund **g**
Earl of Rutland
1443–60

George **gh**
Duke of Clarence
1449–78
=
Isabel Neville

Richard III **fgh**
1452–85
=
Anne Neville

...enry Tudor **gh**
...arl of Richmond
...enry VII
...457–1509

= Elizabeth **gh**
1465–1503

Edward V **h**
1470–83
(never crowned)

Richard **h**
Duke of York
1473–83

Edward **h**
Earl of Warwick
d. 1499

Margaret **h**
d. 1541

Edward
Prince of Wales
1473–84

Arthur = Catherine of Aragon **j**
1486–1502

= Henry VIII **j** = Anne Bullen **j**
1491–1547
= Jane Seymour

Margaret = James IV of Scotland

Mary
1516–58

Elizabeth I **j**
1533–1603

Edward VI
1537–53

James V

Mary, Queen of Scots
d. 1587

James VI of Scotland
and I of England
1566–1625

IV Stratford upon Avon and Shakespeare

Nay, you shall see mine orchard, where in an arbor, we will eat a last year's pipping of my own graffing.

(Henry IV, Part 2)

The Town

The history of Stratford upon Avon goes back to the time when a small settlement developed at the point where the Roman road, from Alcester to the Fosse Way, crossed the River Avon. Originally it included several hamlets around Stratford itself, controlled by the church of Worcester. The town developed under the guidance of the mediaeval guilds — particularly that of the Holy Cross — and the goodwill and beneficence of Sir Hugh Clopton (d. 1496). With the dissolution of the Guild in 1547, and the granting of a charter in 1553 by Edward VI, the town took over the direction of its own affairs, and grew apace as a busy market town, with a good bridge giving north-south access across the river. It was in this thriving community with all its sense of new responsibility and pride that John Shakespeare set up house with his new wife in Henley Street, and took an increasingly responsible part in the local government of the town. It was to this family, well set-up by his mother's inheritance and encouraged by his father's ambition and energy, that William Shakespeare was born.

Today the town still has the atmosphere of a market town, with weekly cattle and street markets. But, over the centuries, what is commonly called the 'Shakespeare Industry' has developed. Whether as a holiday or day excursion centre, Stratford is haunted by the ghost of Shakespeare. His presence is felt as much in inevitable souvenirs as in the conferences of sober-minded scholars. Yet while the town staunchly preserves its own identity in other buildings — Jacobean, Georgian and Victorian, which give an added dimension in a more palpable form to its long history, the place exhibits its relationship with its most famous inhabitant in the various properties associated with him and his family. The Grammar School and the Church are still used as school and church, and access is therefore restricted, but the properties most nearly connected with Shakespeare are cared for by the Shakespeare Birthplace Trust (referred to as the Trust, *see* Birthplace) and are open to visitors. These are:

> Mary Arden's House˝(acquired by the Trust in 1930)
> The Birthplace, Henley Street (acquired by the Trust in 1847)
> Anne Hathaway's Cottage (acquired by the Trust in 1892)
> Hall's Croft (acquired by the Trust in 1949)
> Nash's House (acquired by the Trust in 1876)

Of these, Mary Arden's House is at Wilmcote, about three miles outside Stratford, and Anne Hathaway's Cottage is at Shottery, about a mile outside Stratford; the rest are within the town area.

In 1767 Stratford council decided to rebuild the Town Hall, and, on completion, there was an empty niche on the north wall. Money was not overplentiful and it was suggested that David Garrick, the famous 18th-century interpreter of Shakespearean roles, be asked to provide a statue or bust to fill it, and also a picture linking himself in some way with Shakespeare. In return he would be made an Honorary Burgess (citizen) of the town. The scroll recording this was to be presented in a box made of wood from Shakespeare's own (by tradition) mulberry tree. Garrick was delighted, and, to celebrate the placing of the statue, he organized the first Shakespeare Jubilee in Stratford, in 1769. It was to last for three days. On the first day, guns boomed at regular intervals throughout the day, bells sounded from 6.00 am, and a public breakfast was taken at 9.00 am in the Town Hall. Then those who attended proceeded to the Church where the Oratorio 'Judith', conducted by Dr Arne, was performed, followed, at 2.00 pm, by a procession with choirs singing,

> This is the Day, a Holiday! a Holiday!
> Drive spleen and rancour far away,
> This is the Day, a Holiday! a Holiday!
> Drive Care and Sorrow far away,

and everyone, lord and lady, butcher and baker, artist and critic, joining in. Dinner was taken at 4.00 pm at the Rotunda, built (about where the Royal Shakespeare Theatre is sited today) especially for the purpose. This was followed by a concert, and at night a ball. The second day, early in the morning, it began to rain heavily. The great Pageant of Characters due to take place at 11.00 am had to be cancelled. Garrick's recitation of his 'Ode upon dedicating a Building and erecting a Statue to Shakespeare, at Stratford upon Avon' took place in the Rotunda, however, as arranged, and Garrick, being the actor he was, succeeded brilliantly, from the opening question —

> To what blest genius of the isle
> Shall Gratitude her tribute pay?

to the final answer, asking Fame to proclaim

> The lov'd, rever'd, immortal name!
> Shakespeare! Shakespeare! Shakespeare!

Dinner was taken in the Rotunda, the rain still falling. The great firework display fizzled out, but the costumed ball, for those who succeeded in manœuvring their way over mud and flood, went on until the early hours of the following morning, when the Rotunda itself had become marooned like a sinking ship. Some dancers faced it and 'trudged very deliberately through thick and thin' to get away; others fell in ditches and among some knights errant it was 'very good naturedly agreed . . . to carry the Females through upon their Backs'. The third and last day petered wetly out, though for some that was perhaps not quite the end — *The London Post*, 21 September, in the obituary column:

> John Henry Castle, Esq., at his lodgings at Clopton: his death is attributed to his having laid in damp sheets at Stratford upon Avon, where he went to amuse himself at the so much talked of Jubilee.

Despite the absurd finale, Garrick had gauged a mood well — the activities he planned, where the weather had permitted, had caught on with enthusiasm. And this Jubilee of his had long-lasting results — for example, the formation in 1824 of a Shakespeare Club (which is still in existence).

There came after the Jubilee a growing awareness of a need for some form of permanent theatre in Stratford for the presenting of the plays. The first recorded performance of a Shakespeare play in Stratford is of *Othello* at the Town Hall in 1746. During the late 18th century most of the performances of the plays, or adaptations of them, were put on there. Later, in the next century, barns, either in their natural state or fitted out specially for theatrical events, were hired. However, in the celebrations in April 1827 a corner stone was laid as a foundation for the building of the Shakespeare Theatre, which was completed by the following December and opened with a performance of *As You Like It*.

The new venture was at first quite a success, with Charles Kean appearing during the festivities of 1830. The theatre was refurbished and reopened as the New Royal Shakespearean Rooms in 1844 and refitted again, for the last time, in 1869 as the Theatre Royal. The last performance took place on 30 April 1872, when the property was bought, the theatre pulled down and the site cleared to set out the New Place gardens. Then, in 1874, the Shakespeare Memorial Association was founded by Charles Edward Flower, an affluent local brewer, and he began his campaign for a permanent theatre worthy of the playwright. The first Memorial Theatre was opened in 1879, a somewhat Gothic-looking building, a part of which still remains. The rest was destroyed by fire in 1926, and a new theatre, designed by Miss Elizabeth Scott (the one that now lies alongside the river like a great floodlit liner), was built six years later on the same site.

Today it houses the Royal Shakespeare Company who present a variety of Shakespeare's plays which often then move to London, and often also to other countries (such as America, Australia, Japan), half way across the world. Over the years many of the outstanding actors of the 20th century have played on its boards — Gielgud, Olivier, Burton, Robeson, Redgrave, Edith Evans, Peggy Ashcroft ,and many others.

The other heir to Garrick's Jubilee is the yearly celebration of Shakespeare's birthday in Stratford. This takes place on the Saturday nearest 23 April, Shakespeare's traditional birth day, under the auspices of the Town and the Trust. It includes the unfurling of the flags of many nations and a walk through the streets by the visiting ambassadors and representatives of the various countries attending, to place flowers on Shakespeare's grave in the Church. This was begun in 1892 as a simple celebration by the pupils of the Grammar School, who still join in, leading the procession from the doors of the school itself. It has grown into an international event, in which today, as in Garrick's Jubilee procession, as many local people as celebrities join, each with an appropriate posy or sprig of rosemary, despite any inclemencies of weather.

Mary Arden's House

The Arden family lived in Wilmcote, a hamlet some three miles to the north of Stratford upon Avon. It must have been a large household for both Robert Arden and his wife, Agnes Hill, had been married before, and brought between them some twelve children to the new family. Mary was the youngest of the children of that new family. It was John Jordan, a snapper-up of all considered Shakespearean trifles, who identified the house in Featherbed Lane, now known as Mary Arden's house, as being that of the family. Certainly if this is not precisely the Arden farmhouse, where Shakespeare's mother lived before her marriage, then it must have been very like it, and it is one of the most fascinating of the Trust properties. It is a delightful large 16th-century farmhouse, timber framed, the roof covered with hand-made tiles. It was to Mary that Robert Arden at his death in 1556 left the property called 'Asbyes' and 'the crop apone the grounde sowne and tyllede as hitt is'. The inventory of goods in the house at the time of Robert's death suggests more than mere sufficiency — wealth, rather, and comfort, for it includes eleven painted cloths (strips of material on which were painted biblical or mythological scenes, with suitable texts underneath, such as are mentioned by Shakespeare in both *The Rape of Lucrece* —

> Who fears a sentence or an old man's saw
> Shall by the painted cloth be kept in awe

and *Henry IV, Part 1* — 'slaves as ragged as Lazarus in the painted cloth'), as well as furniture, linen, kitchen ware, farming and agricultural implements, and stock, which included oxen, bullocks, calves and swine, bees and poultry. It seems when John Shakespeare, some time between 1556 and 1558 (when their first daughter was born), took Mary Arden in marriage — and, of course, all her chattels with her — he knew what he was doing. It was, perhaps, in its own way as ambitious a move as his son's in leaving provincial Stratford for that busy metropolis, London.

There has been no change in the basic structure of the buildings. The old dovecote remains, as well as the barns which now house one of the most intriguing collections of old farming implements, side by side with old fire engines, farm carts, gipsy caravans, and the tools of wheelwrights and bricklayers — of the artisans, the Quinces, the Flutes and the Bottoms of subsequent years.

The Birthplace

We know that John Shakespeare, William's father, occupied a house in Henley Street in 1552, for that year he was fined for keeping an unauthorized muckheap in front of his house there (and, one might add, he wasn't the only one to be fined). In 1556 he purchased one house and in 1575 the adjoining two houses at the western end of his house, making extensions also into the garden at the rear. The western section was the living area, the home; the rest, a shop or storehouse, connected with John Shakespeare's trade as a glover and whittawer (a skin and wool dealer). Although there is no conclusive evidence either way, it seems most likely that it would have been here, in John Shakespeare's large house, that his children would have been born, William included (and, tradition has it, in the room above the living room, now known as the birthroom). They would have been taken from there for baptism in the local church and it is in the Henley Street house that they would have grown up.

When William died, the property stayed with members of the family for the next two centuries, firstly belonging to his daughter, Susanna, then to his granddaughter, Elizabeth, and then, until 1806, to a cousin, Thomas Hart. It was then sold to Thomas Court during the early 19th century, the 'shop' part becoming an inn, the Swan (later the Swan and Maidenhead) and the 'home' doubling up as a butcher's shop. When Elizabeth Court, the proprietress of the inn, died, the houses were put up for sale (1847) in London, as the 'most honoured monument of the greatest genius that ever lived'. Committees were formed in Stratford upon Avon and London to raise money, through a national appeal, to buy the house for the nation and so protect it from 'desecration, destruction or removal' (*The Times*). Special performances and concerts were put on, a Shakespeare newspaper was published, and, when the auction took place, after some bidding, the auctioneer accepted the sum of £3,000 from the committee, and the property was bought to be preserved as a national memorial to William Shakespeare.

As a shrine its popularity increases yearly. It was listed on Winter's plan, 1759, and in his second and clearer plan 1768. It was decorated with flags and banners on the occasion of David Garrick's Jubilee Celebrations in 1769. Since then many famous visitors, past and present, have made their way there. The signatures of Sir Walter Scott, Henry Irving and Ellen Terry, amongst others, can be seen inscribed on the glass of the lattice-window of the birthroom. In 1815 Washington Irving made a visit. He was somewhat scathing of both its appearance, 'a small mean looking edifice of wood and plaster', and of the guide, a Mrs Hornby, who, he records, showed him 'the shattered stock of the very matchlock with which Shakespeare shot the deer on his poaching exploits . . . his tobacco . . . the sword with which he played Hamlet. . . .' Certainly some of the 18th- and 19th-century drawings of the building support his statements. The Swan and Maidenhead, for example, at the beginning of the 19th century was refaced with red brick. Only later was the frontage restored to its present half-timbered appearance, as in the manner of the earliest drawings.

The plan to hand the building over to the Government after the auction fell through, and the Stratford upon Avon Birthplace Committee took on the responsibility of restoring and improving the property, demolishing, in 1857, buildings on either side, to lessen the risk of fire, and eventually fitting out the 'shop-inn' part for a museum. Gardens were laid out, which are reputed to contain at least one specimen of each plant mentioned by Shakespeare in his works. In 1891 a trust called the Trustees and Guardians of Shakespeare's Birthplace was brought into being by an Act of Parliament, and its members were given the particular duties of setting up a library, completing the museum, and caring for the Birthplace and other properties connected with the poet and his life that were acquired in Stratford upon Avon and its district.

In the Birthplace today, the 'home' portion has been restored to as near the original conception as possible. Inside, it is set out as a middle-class home, with furniture and household items of the Elizabethan and Jacobean periods, many of them exceedingly beautiful in themselves (the Jacobean bedspread in the birthroom for example), some amusing (the 17th-century baby-minder in the kitchen, looking like something out of the Spanish inquisition). The museum contains not only maps and views of Stratford upon Avon and Warwickshire over the centuries, but deeds and documents concerning the Birthplace itself, and rare books of the period. In its duty towards this property, and others it maintains, the Trust acts with thought, care and diligence, with regard to both the fabric and appearance of the buildings, the interior furnishings, but above all, often one of the most charming aspects of their maintenance, in the informal elegance of their gardens.

The Grammar School

The Grammar School of Stratford upon Avon was originally established by the Guild of the Holy Cross in early mediaeval times for the education of the sons of its members. The Guild was dissolved in 1547, but in 1553, when the town was granted its charter by King Edward VI, it was required to have one schoolteacher. He had a rent-free house and was paid £20 a year. This was a good salary in comparison with other provincial schools, and one which attracted well-qualified teachers to the school. The headquarters of the old Guild became the headquarters of the new borough government. In the Guildhouse, the ground floor was large enough for, and did indeed act as, a temporary theatre for travelling companies of actors, and the first floor became the schoolroom. Although we have no conclusive proof that Shakespeare attended this school, the registers of the time having been destroyed, undoubtedly he attended some kind of formal educational establishment. The earliest precise reference we have is Nicholas Rowe's in 1709, who said that John Shakespeare educated his son 'for some time at a Free-school where 'tis probable he acquired that little Latin that he was master of'. Since his father had a hand in the dealings of the school, and the school is a mere five minutes' walk from the Henley Street home, common sense, if nothing else, makes one conclude that it is more than likely that it was in this school that Shakespeare received his education.

A boy of five or so in Shakespeare's day would have begun his schooling at a 'petty' school. There, with the help of his hornbook (*see* Glossary) he would have first learnt his alphabet, the rudiments of reading, and the Lord's prayer, together with some number work, and been prepared for entry to the next stage of his education — the grammar school. At the Grammar School in Stratford upon Avon Shakespeare may have come under the tuition of Simon Hunt (master there 1571–5), and he certainly would have known the next master, Thomas Jenkins, a scholar from St John's College, Oxford. Perhaps, too, he may have briefly known John Cottom, Jenkins's successor, a Brasenose (Oxford) graduate and a Roman Catholic, whose brother was tortured on the rack and died, a Catholic martyr, in 1582.

Education was a serious business. School began at 6.00 or 7.00 am, continued, with a short break for breakfast, until 11 am, began again after lunch, and, with a short break, continued until 5 pm. Certainly Master William Page's experiences of school (in *The Merry Wives of Windsor*), where he is tested by Sir Hugh Evans (a test which, one hopes, parodies, rather than reflects accurately, the situation), suggests a dryness in what was learnt, paralleled only by the parrot response of the learner. Grammar, learnt from and based on classical authors, ranging from Terence and Plautus to, in the more senior parts of the school, Cicero, Ovid, Virgil and Horace, was all-important. The many echoes of these authorities that haunt Shakespeare's plays, in plot, theme and language, are part of the evidence offered to support the theory that he received such a schooling. Indeed, by 20th-century standards, his 'small Latin' (referred to in Ben Jonson's comment that he had 'small Latin and less Greek') might seem almost formidable, if the Stratford Grammar School followed the normal curriculum for schools of the kind. Greek he would have studied in the last year or so of school, but to no great extent. Had he gone on to a university, he would have been trained there for the rigours of a profession — law, medicine, the church, etc., and presumably would have followed that profession and not become a common player, classed, then, with vagabonds and thieves. This is one time, perhaps, when one must be thankful that the advantages of further education were not, it seems, seized upon.

Today, the school still exists (as King Edward VI Grammar School) and the old buildings are still used — the old schoolhouse, built in 1427, known as the Pedagogue's House, houses the headmaster's office, the Priest's house (or the Old Vicarage) is his home; the lower chamber of the old Guildhall is the senior school library, the upper room (called Big School) is used for teaching, and the council chamber beyond is a junior library. The adjoining chapel, Guild Chapel (founded in 1269 for members of the Guild, and later in the 15th century rebuilt and extended by Sir Hugh Clopton) is the school chapel, used daily for morning prayers. This is in fact a much lived-in and living monument to the past.

Anne Hathaway's Cottage

At Shottery, about a mile west of Stratford upon Avon, is the house, originally called Hewlands, where Anne, daughter of Richard Hathaway, lived. It was the farmhouse home of the Hathaways, built on good stone foundations with timber frame walls, filled in with wattle and daub, and about fifty to ninety acres of land around it. The oldest part dates back to the 15th century, but the bulk of it is 16th and 17th century. The central chimney stack, rebuilt in 1697, has the initials 'IH' on it (in Elizabethan times 'I' could stand for 'J') and part of the far end of the cottage, damaged by fire in 1969, has been well restored.

Inside, the main living room has its original panelling and wide, welcoming hearth, with a bacon cupboard handy at the side, and an old wooden settle, known traditionally as the one shared by William and Anne when courting, although its narrow uprightness seems hardly conducive to wooing or being wooed. Upstairs is the 'Hathaway bed', a dominating fourposter of the late Elizabethan period (Richard Hathaway mentions in his will, 1581, 'two joyned beddes in my parlour'), and many other pieces of furniture that have belonged to the Hathaway family over the years. Possibly, however, one of the greatest attractions of the cottage is its country cottage garden, with box hedges and the 'sweet disorder' of country flowers, leading into an orchard of old fruit trees.

New Place

In July 1597, when he had become well known as an actor and playwright and, presumably, had money to spare for a house with barns and gardens, Shakespeare bought property at the north of Guild Chapel, known as New Place. It stood at the corner of Chapel Street and Chapel Lane, and included a house which had belonged in the late 15th century to that Sir Hugh Clopton who also built the bridge, which is still the main north-south thoroughfare across the River Avon. In 1540 it was, according to John Leland (16th-century antiquary), 'a praty house of brike and timbar', but by the 1560s, it seems that it was becoming decayed and run down. Shakespeare 'repaired and remodelled it to his own mind'. It is believed that it was here that Shakespeare died, for in Winter's map, 1759, the spot is so marked. He left his property to his daughter, Susanna. In July 1643 Queen Henrietta Maria (King Charles I's wife) stayed in Stratford upon Avon for three days, arriving with upwards of 2,000 foot soldiers, 1,000 horse, 100 wagons and a train of artillery. Here she met Prince Rupert at the head of another body of troops, and, tradition has it, the Queen stayed with Susanna in New Place. After that, for a time, the property belonged to Elizabeth, Susanna's daughter, who married Thomas Nash who lived next door. Then it was sold to Sir Edward Walker, Garter King-at-Arms, and through his family it came back into the Clopton family, to be taken down and rebuilt by Sir John Clopton for Hugh Clopton and his wife-to-be, Elizabeth Millward, to live in. There remains now only a sketch made by George Vertue in 1737 which was 'something by memory and the description' of the house as Shakespeare must have known it. The drawing by Winter in 1759, shows the 'Queen Anne' type house built by Sir John Clopton. It was this house which a subsequent, somewhat irascible owner, the Rev. George Gastrell, pulled down. Gastrell was irritated by the constant flow of visitors to see the mulberry tree, traditionally said to have been planted in the garden by Shakespeare, and first chopped down the tree (which resulted in enough Shakespeare mulberry tree souvenirs to have used up a whole forest of mulberry trees!); then, after an argument with the local authorities, three years later he pulled down the house itself.

The remains can now be seen, with beyond, a knott garden (a slightly sunken garden divided by paths into beds [knotts] each having its own intricate pattern of herbs and flowers), and beyond that the great garden, once the orchard and kitchen garden, now lawns and flowerbeds (including an ancient mulberry tree, believed to be a scion of the old stock) freely open to the public.

Nash's House and Hall's Croft

In Stratford upon Avon are two further houses that have connections with Shakespeare and his family — Nash's House and Hall's Croft.

Nash's House adjoins the site of New Place, and was the home of Thomas Nash, the first husband of Shakespeare's grand-daughter, Elizabeth. Downstairs the rooms are furnished with 16th- and 17th-century pieces; upstairs is a museum concerned with the history of Stratford upon Avon from Saxon and Roman times onwards.

Hall's Croft, the home of Susanna and her husband, Dr John Hall, is a large, timber-framed building, the northern part, early 16th century, enlarged in the 17th century, possibly by Dr Hall. Additions made in the 18th and 19th centuries — bay windows, etc. — were removed in 1950, when the house was acquired by the Trust and restored to as near the original of Hall's time as possible. The rooms here are furnished in the style of a middle-class home of the period, and include a dispensary set out with the kinds of medical jars, herbs and instruments that might have been found there in Dr Hall's time. Today some of the rooms are used for exhibitions, lectures, poetry readings, etc., and here the Festival Club (for which short-term membership can be arranged) has its reading rooms, and, in the large downstairs room, under the gaze of David Garrick, the actor, and his wife playing piquet, members can take lunch or tea.

Holy Trinity Church

Shakespeare died on 23 April 1616, and was buried in the chancel of Holy Trinity Church, Stratford upon Avon, on 25 April. On the covering stone to his grave is the famous curse (*see* Shakespeare's Appearance) which prevented his wife and daughter being buried with him, and, over the centuries, protected his grave from desecration. In the past the desecration would have been by the church sexton, who would remove the bones from graves in the chancel to the charnel house, so that the grave space might be used again; today, by those who feel sure an investigation into the grave would solve all the problems of authorship and identity that hover around Shakespeare. The body is said, traditionally, to be buried some seventeen feet down, and the verse was, by tradition, written by Shakespeare himself, so that it seems as if he were determined to protect himself from possible future disturbances. The present gravestone, according to Halliwell-Phillips, replaced a cracked and sunken one in the 18th century.

Some time after his death and before the publication of the First Folio in 1623, a memorial was built to his memory. It is a bust of the playwright himself, set in its own niche, with marble pillars either side. On the cornice above the bust are two cherub figures, one with a spade in one hand, the other resting on his own thigh, the second cherub with an upturned torch in one hand, his other resting on a skull — life and labour, perhaps, as opposed to death and darkness. Between these two figures are Shakespeare's arms, helm and crest. The bust itself wears a plain gown with a Puritan-like collar; a pen is in one hand, paper at the ready under the other; the beard is trim, the moustache curling confidently upward, the face bland and the eyes lacking any kind of speculation. In fact, with its expanse of bald head, it looks like an overfed butcher, a well-paid lawyer, or a satisfied moneylender — anything in fact but the world's outstanding poet and playwright. It has been suggested that the head was taken from a deathmask, which reflected a bloated state at the time of death or just after. The sculptor was Gheerart Janssen, whose shop was near the Globe Theatre in London where so many of Shakespeare's plays were performed. He and his family were presumably reliable sculptors since they were commissioned to make monuments for the well-to-do and the well-known. It seems very probable, therefore, that since some of the Janssen family may well have known Shakespeare himself — they executed a likeness that satisfied not only them, but also those members of Shakespeare's own family who were still living (who may even have commissioned the bust themselves) at the time the bust was set up in the church.

The face was originally painted, but Malone, the 18th-century editor, persuaded the local vicar to have the bust whitewashed over, much to the annoyance of at least one visitor to Stratford:

> Stranger, to whom this monument is shown,
> Invoke the poet's curse upon Malone;
> Whose meddling zeal his barbarous taste betrays,
> And daubs his tombstone as he mars his plays!

Colour was restored in 1861, with rosy cheeks and auburn hair, and a scarlet doublet, colours which have deepened with the years. Beneath the bust are the words:

> Judicio Pylium, genio Socratem, arte Maronem;
> Terra tegit, populus maeret, Olympus habet.

> [With the judgment of Nestor, the genius of Socrates, the art of Virgil,
> The earth covers him, the people mourn him, Olympus claims him.]

> Stay passenger, why goest thou by so fast?
> Read if thou canst, whom envious Death hath plast,
> Within this monument Shakespeare: with whome,
> Quick nature dide: whose name doth deck ye tombe,
> Far more then cost: Sieh [since] all, y^t He hath writt,
> Leaves living art, but page, to serve his witt.
>   Obiit Ano do 1616
>   Aetatis 53 die 23 Ap^r.

It is from this, his memorial bust, that we can place his birth at some time between 24 April 1563 and 23 April 1564, since he died in his fifty-third year. The irony of this deduction, the birth-date from the death, is, perhaps, nicely balanced by the choice of 23 April, St George's Day, as that most likely to have been his birth day.